Applied Business Statistics

Applied Business Statistics

Methods and Excel-based Applications

Fifth edition

TREVOR WEGNER

JUTA

Applied Business Statistics
Methods and Excel-based Applications

First edition 1993
Second edition 2007
Third edition 2012
Fourth edition 2016
Fifth edition 2020

Juta and Company (Pty) Ltd
First floor, Sunclare Building, 21 Dreyer Street, Claremont 7708
PO Box 14373, Lansdowne 7779, Cape Town, South Africa
www.juta.co.za

© 2020 Juta and Company (Pty) Ltd

ISBN 978 1 48513 049 9 (Print)
ISBN 978 1 48513 050 5 (Web PDF)

Project Manager: Seshni Kazadi
Editor: Glenda Younge
Proofreader: Glenda Younge
Typesetter: Lebone Publishing Services
Cover designer: Drag and Drop

Typeset in Photina MT Std 10 pt

The authors and the publisher believe on the strength of due diligence exercised that this work does not contain any material that is the subject of copyright held by another person. In the alternative, they believe that any protected pre-existing material that may be comprised in it has been used with appropriate authority or has been used in circumstances that make such use permissible under the law.

Contents

To
Shirley, Sally, Maryanne, Jessica, Melissa, Amy
and my parents (Sief and Sheila)

Preface

Applied Business Statistics is an introductory and intermediate Statistics text for students of Management. Its business applications approach aims to teach management students how Statistics (also referred to as Data Analytics) is used to provide evidence-driven information to support management decision-making at all management levels and across all disciplines of management practice – be it Marketing, Finance, Human Resources, Production/Logistics, Information Technology or Organisational Behaviour.

This text assumes only a basic level of mathematical ability. It aims to differentiate itself from other business statistics texts in two important ways:

1 by presenting the material in a *non-technical* manner to make it easier for students of management with a limited mathematical background to grasp the subject matter; and
2 by developing an *intuitive understanding* of the techniques by framing them in the context of a management question, giving layperson-type explanations of methods, using illustrative and realistic business examples and focusing on the management interpretations of the statistical findings.

Its overall purpose is to develop a management student's statistical reasoning and statistical decision-making skills in order to give them a competitive advantage in the workplace. Through the many practical worked examples and business-related datasets, which are illustrated using the Excel-based statistical software, a student develops the problem-solving expertise to apply these statistical methods in work-related decision areas.

This fifth edition continues the theme of using Excel-based statistical software as an easy-to-use computational tool to perform statistical analysis. In addition to the use of Excel's Data Analysis module, this fifth edition includes a custom-built statistical software package, **X-Static**, that broadens the scope of statistical analyses available and, very importantly, seeks to guide the interpretation of the statistical findings through the use of easy-to-read visual representations of outputs.

The use of statistical software to generate statistical findings has the advantage of allowing a student:

- to examine more realistic business problems with larger data sets
- to focus more on the statistical interpretation of the statistical findings rather than on the manual computations and
- to transfer this skill of performing statistical analysis more easily to their work environment.

The text emphasises four themes to support *evidence-based* management decision-making:

1 setting the *statistical landscape* in a management context
2 *interpretative decision-making* based on patterns revealed by *exploratory data analyses*
3 *statistical decision-making* guided by the test-based findings of *inferential analyses*
4 *predictive decision-making* using *statistical modelling* evidence.

The thread that links them is the role of data analytics as a management decision-support tool.

In addition, this fifth edition introduces a number of new features. These include:

- The **introduction of emerging and allied trends** in statistical applications in management practice (such as Digital Dashboard Analytics; Big Data/Business Intelligence; Six Sigma in the statistical quality management domain; Artificial Intelligence (AI) and Statistics; and greater use of electronic/digital data-collection methods). These trends emphasise the growing importance of data-driven analytics to support decision-making in management practice.

  Strengthening the Excel-based generation of statistical evidence using a custom-built software product called **X-Static**. While there are many similarities with Excel's Data Analysis, **X-Static** offers some notable additions such as the Chi-square Test of Independence of Association; post hoc analysis with multiple box plot displays in ANOVA; ANOVA with unequal sample sizes; and confidence interval estimation in regression modelling.

- **Enhancing the graphic visualisation** of statistical evidence to promote easier interpretation of statistical findings. These features occur in the **X-Static** software.

- **Revisiting and clarifying certain concepts and methods** to improve their interpretation and comprehension by students.

  These include, *inter alia*, the *concepts* of the *t-statistic*, the *p*-value in hypothesis testing, the matched-pairs test, the 'explained variation' measure in ANOVA and regression, categorical regression coefficients and categorical variable coding.

  Improvements to *methods* include, *inter alia*, rules to determine the number of histogram intervals; the construction of relative frequency distributions and ogives (Chapter 2); deriving the average for grouped data; aligning Excel functions with quartile formulae; the use of Chebyshev's rule to measure spread in non-normal distributions (Chapter 3); and guidelines for the correct formulation of the null and alternative hypotheses.

- **The addition of new *sub-topics*** to existing techniques to enhance their usefulness as decision support tools. These include, in ANOVA (Chapter 9), the introduction of post hoc analysis with visual displays of multiple box plots to identify treatment effects on the response variable; the inclusion of a 'rule of thumb' to test the assumption for equality of variances in ANOVA studies and further clarification of F-limits for equality of variances tests; in Simple Regression (Chapter 12), the inclusion of a confidence interval estimation approach for the response variable, y; deriving R^2 from the ANOVA table (Chapter 12); and, finally, in Multiple Regression (Chapter 13), the inclusion of a new section on Variable Selection Approaches when a large number of regressors are available as estimators of the regression response variable (Stepwise Regression and All Subsets Regression).

This text continues to emphasise the applied nature and relevancy of statistical methods in business practice with each technique being illustrated with practical examples drawn from the South African business environment. These worked examples are solved manually (to show the rationale and mechanics of each technique) and then how statistical software such as Excel's Data Analysis or **X-Static** performs the same task. Clear and meaningful management interpretations are provided for each worked example's statistical findings.

Each chapter is prefaced with a set of learning outcomes and a schematic visual diagram to highlight the chapter's key learning points and to focus the learning process.

The exercises at the end of each chapter focus both on testing a student's understanding of key statistical concepts and on promoting problem-solving skills either manually or through the use of statistical software. Each question requires a student to provide a clear and valid management interpretation of the statistical evidence in the context of the management problem.

Finally, the text is designed to cover the statistics syllabi of diploma and post-graduate diploma (PGDip) courses in management at tertiary institutions and professional institutes. The content is also suitable for a semester course in a degree programme at universities and MBA business schools. In addition, this text can be used as a core reference in quantitative research methodology modules for many MBA and post-graduate programmes which require research dissertations from their students.

In short, this fifth edition aims to further promote the active participation of management students in business decisions that are rooted in evidence-based statistical information by giving them the confidence to use statistical methods meaningfully and to interpret statistical findings in a practical and valid manner.

Trevor Wegner
2020

Setting the Statistical Scene

CHAPTER

1

Statistics in Management

Outcomes

This chapter describes the role of Statistics in management decision-making. It also explains the importance of data in statistical analysis.

After studying this chapter, you should be able to:

- define the term 'management decision support system'
- explain the difference between data and information
- explain the basic terms and concepts of Statistics and provide examples
- recognise the different symbols used to describe statistical concepts
- explain the different components of Statistics
- identify some applications of statistical analysis in business practice
- distinguish between qualitative and quantitative random variables
- explain and illustrate the different types of data
- identify the different sources of data
- discuss the advantages and disadvantages of each form of primary data collection
- explain how to prepare data for statistical analysis
- describe recent trends in data analytics.

1.1 Introduction

Consider these quotes:

'Information is the oil of the 21 century, and analytics is the combustion engine.'
(Peter Sondergaard, Senior VP, Gartner Research)

'The goal (of analytics) is to turn data into information and information into insight.'
(Carly Florina, former CEO, Hewlett Packard)

'If you can measure it, you can manage it.' (Peter Drucker – Management guru)

'Big data is the foundation of all the megatrends that are happening today – from social to mobile to the cloud and gaming.' (Chris Lynch – Vertica Systems)

'Globally, the big data and [data] analytics market is forecast to be worth $40.60 billion by 2023, growing at a Compound Annual Growth Rate (CAGR) of 29.7%.'
(https://www.researchandmarkets.com).

'Numbers have an important story to tell – they rely on you to give them a clear and convincing voice.' (Stephen Few – www.perceptualedge.com)

'Computers speed the process of information handling, but they don't tell us what the information means or how to communicate its meaning to decision makers. These skills are not intuitive; they rely largely on analysis and presentation skills that must be learnt.'
(Stephen Few – www.perceptualedge.com).

These quotes all speak to the importance of data in our evolving technological age as well as the importance of data analytics on how to use the ever-increasing volumes of data wisely and intelligently in management practice. As a result, a course in data analytics (applied business statistics) is, and must be, an integral part of every management programme offered today by academic institutions, business schools and management colleges worldwide.

Management Decision-making

The value of data analytics lies in the term 'management decision support systems'. Decision-making is central to every manager's job. While data analytics drives the decision support process, a key prerequisite for good management decision-making is to **ask the right question**. 'Asking the right question takes as much skill as giving the right answer' (Robert Half – www.roberthalf.com).

Data analytics is initiated when there is a clearly defined **management problem** or a well formulated **management question** that needs to be addressed in an **objective** and **verifiable** manner. For example, a manager must decide which product mix is best to market; which advertising media are most effective; who are the company's high-value customers; what are the causes of high customer churn; whether a consignment of goods is of an acceptable quality; where to locate stores for maximum profitability; what are the reasons for low employee morale; whether females buy more of their product than males; or which portfolio investment exhibits greater volatility in returns.

Each management problem or management question is characterised by one or a number of **critical attributes** (sometimes loosely referred to as key performance indicators) on which data must be collected and analysed to address the management problem/question. These key attributes must be identified and defined as an initial first step in any statistical analysis to effectively and efficiently support management decision-making.

Information

To make sound business decisions, a manager needs high-quality, evidence-based information on the relevant attributes of interest. Information must be timely, accurate, relevant, adequate and easily accessible. However, information to support decision-making is seldom readily available in the format, quality and quantity required by the decision-maker. More often than not, it needs to be generated from data.

Data

What is more readily available – from a variety of sources and of varying quality and quantity – is raw, unprocessed data. Data consists of individual values each of which conveys little useful and usable information to management. Three examples of data are: the purchase value of a single transaction at a supermarket (e.g. R214); the time it takes a worker to assemble a single part (e.g. 7.35 minutes); the brand of cornflakes that a particular consumer prefers (e.g. Bokomo).

Statistics

It is only when a large number of data values are collected, collated, summarised, analysed and presented in easily readable ways that useful and usable information for management decision-making is generated. This is the role of Statistics in management.

Statistics can be defined as the **science of data**. It is a set of mathematically based tools and techniques to transform raw (unprocessed) *data* into a few summary measures that represent useful and usable *information* to support effective *decision-making*. These summary measures are used to *describe profiles* (patterns) *of data, produce estimates, test relationships* between sets of data and *identify trends* in data over time.

Thus Statistics can be seen as an **evidence-based (data-driven) information generator**. It provides an **objective basis** on which a management problem/question can be addressed **with confidence** once the statistical information has been correctly interpreted by the decision-maker.

Figure 1.1 illustrates this transformation process from data to information.

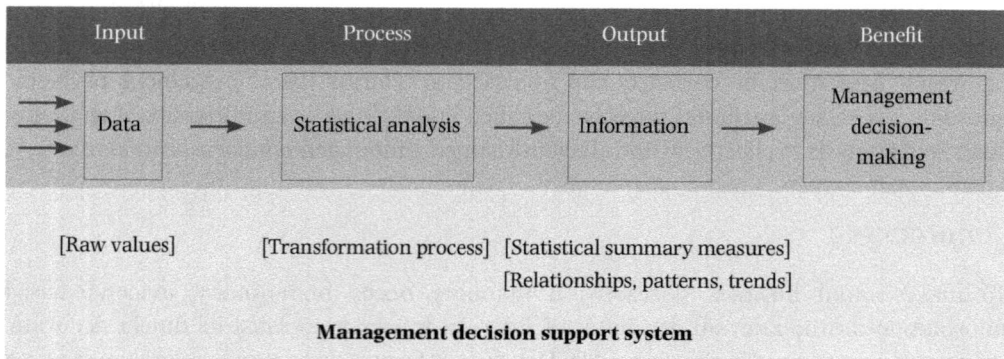

Input	Process	Output	Benefit
Data	Statistical analysis	Information	Management decision-making
[Raw values]	[Transformation process]	[Statistical summary measures] [Relationships, patterns, trends]	

Management decision support system

Figure 1.1 Statistical analysis in management decision-making

Statistical methods can be applied in any management area where data exists (e.g. Human Resources, Marketing, Finance and Operations), in a *decision support role*. Statistics support the decision process by strengthening the quantifiable basis from which a well-informed decision can be made. Quantitative information therefore allows a decision-maker to justify a chosen course of action more easily and with greater confidence.

Business statistics is very often 'common sense' translated into statistical terminology and formulae so that these can be replicated and applied consistently in similar situations elsewhere. A course in Statistics for management students serves to demonstrate this link between the discipline and 'common sense'.

There are further practical reasons why managers in general should develop an appreciation of statistical methods and thinking. They allow a manager to:

- recognise situations where statistics can be applied to enhance a decision process
- perform simple statistical analyses in practice (using Excel, for example) to extract additional information from business data
- interpret, intelligently, management reports expressed in numerical terms
- critically assess the validity of statistical findings before using them in decision-making (A good source for invalid statistical presentations is *How to Lie with Statistics* by Darrell Huff. When examining statistical findings, also bear in mind the adage that you get 'lies, damn lies and then Statistics'.)
- initiate research studies with an understanding of the statistical methods involved
- communicate more easily and more effectively with statistical analysts.

An appreciation of statistical methods can result in new insights into a decision area, reveal opportunities to exploit, and hence promote more informed and effective business decision-making.

This text aims to make a manager an *active participant* rather than a *passive observer* when interacting with statistical findings, reports and analysts. Understanding and using statistical methods *empowers* managers with confidence and *quantitative reasoning skills* that enhance their decision-making capabilities and provide a competitive advantage over colleagues who do not possess them.

1.2 The Language of Statistics

A number of important terms, concepts and symbols are used extensively in Statistics. Understanding them early in the study of Statistics will make it easier to grasp the subject. The most important of the terms and concepts are:

- a random variable and its data
- a sampling unit
- a population and its characteristics, called population parameters
- a sample and its characteristics, called sample statistics.

A **random variable** is any *attribute of interest* on which *data* are collected and analysed.

Data are the *actual values* (numbers) or *outcomes* recorded on a random variable.

Some examples of random variables and their data are:

- the travel distances of delivery vehicles (data: 34 km, 13 km, 21 km)
- the daily occupancy rates of hotels in Cape Town (data: 45%, 72%, 54%)
- the duration of machine downtime (data: 14 min, 25 min, 6 min)
- brand of coffee preferred (data: Nescafé, Ricoffy, Frisco).

A **sampling unit** is the object being measured, counted or observed with respect to the random variable under study.

This could be a consumer, an employee, a household, a company or a product. More than one random variable can be defined for a given sampling unit. For example, an employee could be measured in terms of *age*, *qualification* and *gender*.

A **population** is the collection of *all possible data values* that exist for the random variable under study.

For example:

- for a study on hotel occupancy levels (the random variable) in Cape Town only, *all* hotels in Cape Town would represent the target population
- to research the age, gender and savings levels of banking clients (three random variables being studied), the population would be *all* savings account holders at *all* banks.

A **population parameter** is a measure that describes a characteristic of a population. A *population average* is a parameter, so is a *population proportion*. It is called a parameter if it uses *all the population data values* to compute its value.

A **sample** is a *subset* of data values drawn from a population. Samples are used because it is often not possible to record every data value of the population, mainly because of *cost*, *time* and possibly *item destruction*.

For example:
- a sample of 25 hotels in Cape Town is selected to study hotel occupancy levels
- a sample of 50 savings account holders from each of four national banks is selected to study the profile of their age, gender and savings account balances.

> A **sample statistic** is a measure that describes a characteristic of a sample. The *sample average* and a *sample proportion* are two typical sample statistics.

For example, appropriate sample statistics are:
- the average hotel occupancy level for the sample of 25 hotels surveyed
- the average age of savers, the proportion of savers who are female and the average savings account balances of the total sample of 200 surveyed clients.

Table 1.1 gives further illustrations of these basic statistical terms and concepts.

Table 1.1 Examples of populations and associated samples

Random variable	Population	Sampling unit	Sample
Size of bank overdraft	All current accounts with Absa	An Absa client with a current account	400 randomly selected clients' current accounts
Mode of daily commuter transport to work	All commuters to Cape Town's central business district (CBD)	A commuter to Cape Town's CBD	600 randomly selected commuters to Cape Town's CBD
TV programme preferences	All TV viewers in Gauteng	A TV viewer in Gauteng	2 000 randomly selected TV viewers in Gauteng

Table 1.2 lists the most commonly used statistical terms and symbols to distinguish a sample statistic from a population parameter for a given statistical measure.

Table 1.2 Symbolic notation for sample and population measures

Statistical measure	Sample statistic	Population parameter
Mean	$\bar{x}$	μ
Standard deviation	s	σ
Variance	s^2	σ^2
Size	n	N
Proportion	p	π
Correlation	r	ρ

1.3 Components of Statistics

Statistics consists of three major components: descriptive statistics, inferential statistics and statistical modelling.

Descriptive statistics *condenses sample data into a few summary descriptive measures.*

When large quantities of data have been gathered, there is a need to organise, summarise and extract the essential information contained within this data for communication to management. This is the role of descriptive statistics. These summary measures allow a user to identify profiles, patterns, relationships and trends within the data.

Inferential statistics *generalises sample findings* to the broader *population.*

Descriptive statistics only describes the behaviour of a random variable in a sample. However, management is mainly concerned about the behaviour and characteristics of random variables in the population from which the sample was drawn. They are therefore interested in the 'bigger population picture'. Inferential statistics is that area of statistics that allows managers to understand the population picture of a random variable based on the sample evidence.

Statistical modelling builds models of *relationships* between random variables.

Statistical modelling constructs equations between variables that are related to each other. These equations (called **models**) are then used to *estimate* or *predict* values of one of these variables based on values of related variables. They are extremely useful in forecasting decisions.

Figure 1.2 shows the different components of statistics.

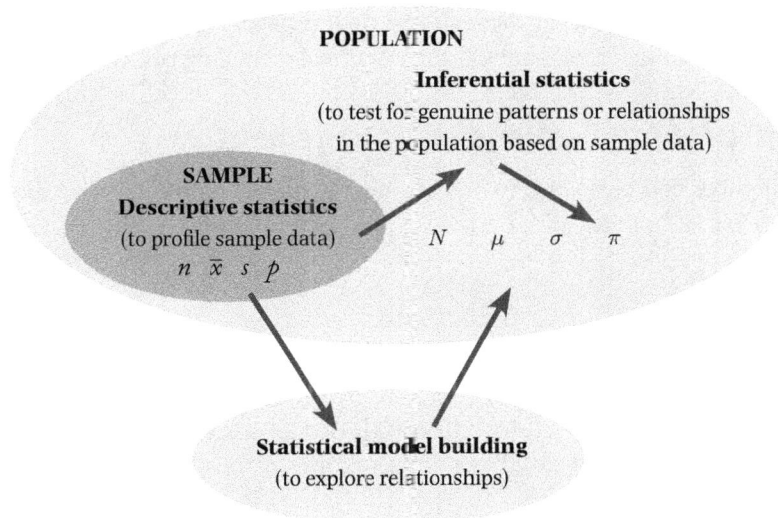

POPULATION

Inferential statistics
(to test for genuine patterns or relationships
in the population based on sample data)

SAMPLE
Descriptive statistics
(to profile sample data)
n $\bar{x}$ s p

N μ σ π

Statistical model building
(to explore relationships)

Figure 1.2 Conceptual overview of the components of statistics

The following scenario illustrates the use of descriptive statistics and inferential statistics in management.

Management Scenario: A Proposed Flexi-hours Working Policy Study

An HR manager plans to introduce a flexi-hours working system to improve employee productivity. She wants to establish the level of support such a system will enjoy amongst the 5 758 employees of the organisation, as well as how support may differ between male and female employees. She randomly samples 218 employees, of whom 96 are female and 122 are male. Each employee is asked to complete a short questionnaire.

Descriptive statistics will summarise the attitudes of the 218 randomly sampled employees towards the proposed flexi-hours work system. An illustrative sample finding could be that 64% of the sampled female employees support the proposal, while support from the sampled male employees is only 57%.

Inferential statistics would be used to generalise the sample findings derived from the 218 respondents to reflect the likely views of the entire company of 5 758 employees. For example, the following two statistical conclusions could be drawn for all employees.

- There is a 95% chance that between 58% and 63% of all employees will support this proposed flexi-hours working system.
- With a 1% margin of error, females are more likely than males to support this proposal.

1.4 Statistics and Computers

Today, with the availability of user-friendly statistical software such as Microsoft Excel, statistical capabilities are within reach of all managers. In addition, there are many other 'off-the-shelf' software packages for business use on laptops and tablets. These include SPSS, SPlus, Minitab, NCSS, Statgraphics, SYSTAT, EViews, UNISTAT and Stata, to name a few. Some work as Excel add-ins such as **X-Static** (which is available with this text) that offers additional statistical features to Excel's Data Analysis add-in. A search of the internet will identify many other statistical packages and list their capabilities. All offer the techniques of descriptive statistics, inferential analysis and statistical modelling covered in this text.

1.5 Statistical Applications in Management

Statistical methods can be applied in any business management area where data exists. A few examples follow for illustrative purposes.

Finance

Stock market analysts use statistical methods to predict share price movements; financial analysts use statistical findings to guide their investment decisions in bonds, cash, equities, property, etc. At a company level, statistics is used to assess the viability of different investment projects, to project cash flows and to analyse patterns of payment by debtors.

Marketing

Marketing research uses statistical methods to sample and analyse a wide range of consumer behaviour and purchasing patterns. Market segmentation studies use statistical techniques to identify viable market segments, and advertising research makes use of statistics to determine media effectiveness.

Human Resources

Statistics is used to analyse human resources issues, such as training effectiveness, patterns of absenteeism and employee turnover, compensation planning and staff planning. Surveys of employee attitudes to employment issues use similar statistical methods to those in market research.

Operations/Logistics

Production managers rely heavily on *statistical quality control methods* to monitor both product and production processes for quality and process improvement through the use of control charts and Six Sigma methodology. In the area of production planning, managers use statistical forecasts of future demand to determine machine and labour utilisation over the planning period.

1.6   Data and Data Quality

An understanding of the nature of data is necessary for two reasons. It enables a user (i) to assess *data quality* and (ii) to select the most appropriate *statistical method* to apply to the data. Both factors affect the validity and reliability of statistical findings.

Data Quality

Data are the *raw material* of statistical analysis. If the quality of data is poor, the quality of information derived from statistical analysis of this data will also be poor. Consequently, user confidence in the statistical findings will be low. A useful acronym to keep in mind is GIGO, which stands for 'garbage in, garbage out'. It is therefore necessary to understand what influences the quality of data needed to produce meaningful and reliable statistical results.

Data quality is influenced by four factors: the *data type*, *data source*, the *method of data collection* and appropriate *data preparation*.

Selection of Statistical Method

The choice of the most appropriate statistical method to use depends firstly on the *management problem* to be addressed and secondly on the *type of data* available. Certain statistical methods are valid for certain data types only. The incorrect choice of statistical method for a given data type can again produce invalid statistical findings.

1.7   Data Types and Measurement Scales

The type of data available for analysis is determined by the nature of its random variable. A random variable is either *qualitative* (categorical) or *quantitative* (numeric) in nature.

> **Qualitative random variables** generate *categorical* (non-numeric) response data. The data is represented by categories only.

The following are examples of qualitative random variables with categories as data:
- The gender of a consumer is either male or female.
- An employee's highest qualification is either a matric, a diploma or a degree.
- A company operates in either the financial, retail, mining or industrial sector.
- A consumer's choice of mobile phone service provider is either Vodacom, MTN, Virgin Mobile, Cell C or 8ta.

Numbers are often assigned to represent the categories (e.g. 1 = male, 2 = female), but they are only codes and have *no numeric properties*. Such categorical data can therefore only be *counted* to determine how many responses belong to each category.

> **Quantitative random variables** generate *numeric* response data. These are real numbers that can be manipulated using arithmetic operations (addition, subtraction, multiplication and division).

The following are examples of quantitative random variables with real numbers as data:
- the age of an employee (e.g. 46 years; 28 years; 32 years)
- machine downtime (e.g. 8 min; 32.4 min; 12.9 min)
- the price of a product in different stores (e.g. R6.75; R7.45; R7.20; R6.99)
- delivery distances travelled by a courier vehicle (e.g. 14.2 km; 20.1 km; 17.8 km).

Numeric data can be further classified as either *discrete* or *continuous*.

> **Discrete data** are *whole number* (or integer) data.

For example, the number of students in a class (e.g. 24; 37; 41; 46), the number of cars sold by a dealer in a month (e.g. 14; 27; 21; 16) and the number of machine breakdowns in a shift (e.g. 4; 0; 6; 2).

> **Continuous data** are any numbers that can occur in an *interval*.

For example, the assembly time for a part can be between 27 minutes and 31 minutes (e.g. assembly time = 28.4 min), a passenger's hand luggage can have a mass between 0.5 kg and 10 kg (e.g. 2.4 kg) and the volume of fuel in a car tank can be between 0 litres and 55 litres (e.g. 42.38 litres).

Measurement Scales

Data can also be classified in terms of its *scale of measurement*. This indicates the 'strength' of the data in terms of how much arithmetic manipulation on the data is possible. There are four types of measurement scales: *nominal*, *ordinal*, *interval* and *ratio*. The scale also determines which statistical methods are appropriate to use on the data to produce valid statistical results.

Nominal data

Nominal data are associated with *categorical* data. If all the categories of a qualitative random variable are of *equal importance*, then this categorical data is termed 'nominal-scaled'.

Examples of nominal-scaled categorical data are:
- gender (1 = male; 2 = female)
- city of residence (1 = Pretoria; 2 = Durban; 3 = Cape Town; 4 = Bloemfontein)
- home language (1 = Xhosa; 2 = Zulu; 3 = English; 4 = Afrikaans; 5 = Sotho)
- mode of commuter transport (1 = car; 2 = train; 3 = bus; 4 = taxi; 5 = bicycle)
- engineering profession (1 = chemical; 2 = electrical; 3 = civil; 4 = mechanical)
- survey question: 'Do you have an Instagram account?' (1 = yes; 2 = no).

Nominal data are the *weakest* form of data to analyse since the codes assigned to the various categories have *no numerical properties*. Nominal data can only be *counted* (or tabulated). This limits the range of statistical methods that can be applied to nominal-scaled data to only a few techniques.

Ordinal data

Ordinal data are also associated with *categorical* data, but have an *implied ranking* between the different categories of the qualitative random variable. Each consecutive category possesses either more or less than the previous category of a given characteristic.

Examples of ordinal-scaled categorical data are:
- size of clothing (1 = small; 2 = medium; 3 = large; 4 = extra large)
- product usage level (1 = light; 2 = moderate; 3 = heavy)
- income category (1 = lower; 2 = middle; 3 = upper)
- company size (1 = micro; 2 = small; 3 = medium; 4 = large)
- response to a survey question: 'Rank your top three TV programmes in order of preference' (1 = first choice; 2 = second choice; 3 = third choice).

Rank (ordinal) data are *stronger* than nominal data because the data possess the numeric property of *order* (but the distances between the ranks are *not equal*). It is therefore still numerically weak data, but it can be analysed by more statistical methods (i.e. from the field of non-parametric statistics) than nominal data.

Interval data

Interval data are associated with *numeric* data and quantitative random variables. It is generated mainly from rating scales, which are used in survey questionnaires to measure respondents' attitudes, motivations, preferences and perceptions.

Examples of rating scale responses are shown in Table 1.3. Statements 1, 2 and 3 are illustrations of *semantic differential rating scales* that use bipolar adjectives (e.g. very slow to extremely fast service), while statement 4 illustrates a *Likert rating scale* that uses a scale that ranges from strongly disagree to strongly agree with respect to a statement or an opinion.

Table 1.3 Examples of interval-scaled quantitative random variables

1. How would you rate your chances of promotion after the next performance appraisal?				
Very poor	Poor	Unsure	Good	Very good
1	2	3	4	5
2. How satisfied are you with your current job description?				
Very dissatisfied	Dissatisfied	Satisfied	Very satisfied	
1	2	3	4	
3. What is your opinion of the latest *Idols* TV series?				
Very boring	Dull	OK	Exciting	Fantastic
1	2	3	4	5
4. The performance appraisal system is biased in favour of technically oriented employees.				
Strongly disagree	Disagree	Unsure	Agree	Strongly agree
1	2	3	4	5

Interval data possess the two properties of *rank-order* (same as ordinal data) and *distance* in terms of 'how much more or how much less' an object possesses of a given characteristic. However, it has *no zero point*. Therefore it is not meaningful to compare the ratio of interval-scaled values with one another. For example, it is not valid to conclude that a rating of 4 is twice as important as a rating of 2, or that a rating of 1 is only one-third as important as a rating of 3.

Interval data (rating scales) possess sufficient numeric properties to be treated as numeric data for the purpose of statistical analysis. A much wider range of statistical techniques can therefore be applied to interval data compared with nominal and ordinal data.

Ratio data

Ratio data consists of all *real numbers* associated with quantitative random variables. Examples of ratio-scaled data are: employee ages (years), customer income (R), distance travelled (km), door height (cm), product mass (g), volume of liquid in a container (ml), machine speed (rpm), tyre pressure (psi), product prices (R), length of service (months) and number of shopping trips per month (0; 1; 2; 3; etc.).

Ratio data have all the properties of numbers (*order*, *distance* and an *absolute origin of zero*) that allow such data to be manipulated using all arithmetic operations (addition, subtraction, multiplication and division). The zero origin property means that ratios can be computed (5 is half of 10, 4 is one-quarter of 16, 36 is twice as great as 18, for example).

Ratio data are the *strongest* data for statistical analysis. Compared to the other data types (nominal, ordinal and interval), the most amount of statistical information can be extracted from it. Also, more statistical methods can be applied to ratio data than to any other data type.

Figure 1.3 diagrammatically summarises the classification of data.

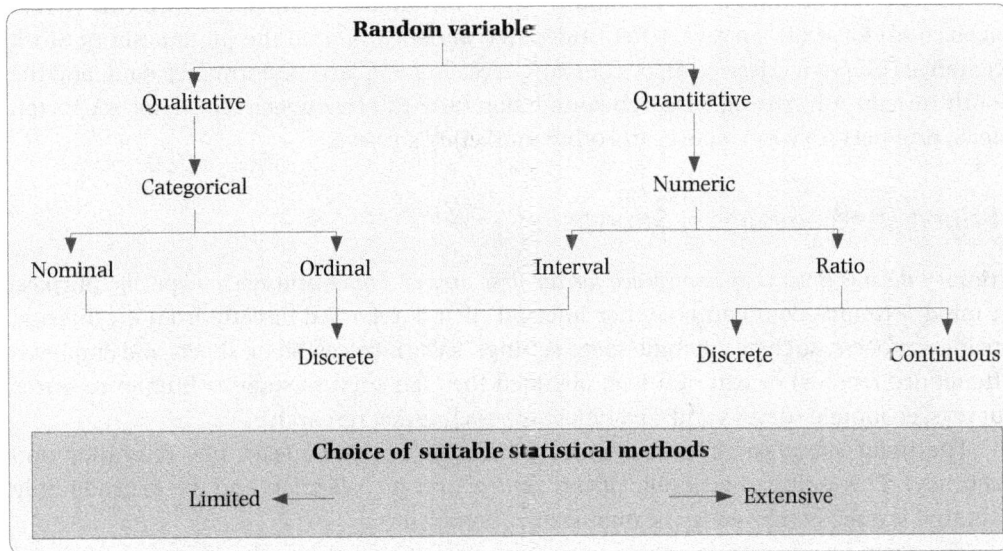

Figure 1.3 Classification of data types and influence on statistical analyses

1.8 Data Sources

Data for statistical analysis is available from many different sources. A manager must decide how reliable and accurate a set of data from a given source is before basing decisions on findings derived from it. Unreliable data results in invalid findings.

Data sources are typically classified as (i) internal or external; and (ii) primary or secondary.

Internal and External Sources

In a business context, **internal data** is sourced from *within a company*. It is data that is generated during the normal course of business activities. As such, it is relatively inexpensive to gather, readily available from company databases and potentially of good quality (since it is recorded using internal business systems). Examples of internal data sources are:

- sales vouchers, credit notes, accounts receivable, accounts payable and asset registers for *financial data*
- production cost records, stock sheets and downtime records for *production data*
- time sheets, wages and salaries schedules and absenteeism records for *human resource data*
- product sales records and advertising expenditure budgets for *marketing data*.

External data sources exist *outside an organisation*. They are mainly business associations, government agencies, universities and various research institutions. The cost and reliability of external data is dependent on the source. A wide selection of *external databases* exist and, in many cases, can be accessed via the internet, either free of charge or for a fee. A few examples relevant to managers are: Statistics South Africa (Stats SA) (www.statssa.gov. za) for macro-economic data, the South African Chamber of Business (SACOB) (www. sacob.co.za) for trade surveys, I-Net Bridge (www.inet.co.za) and the Johannesburg Stock Exchange (JSE) (www.jse.co.za) for company-level financial and performance data, and the South African Advertising Research Foundation (SAARF) (www.saarf.co.za) for AMPS (all media products surveys) reports and other marketing surveys.

Primary and Secondary Sources

Primary data is data that is *recorded for the first time at source* and with a specific purpose in mind. Primary data can be either internal (if it is recorded directly from an internal business process, such as machine speed settings, sales invoices, stock sheets and employee attendance records) or external (e.g. obtained through surveys such as human resource surveys, economic surveys and consumer surveys [market research]).

The main *advantage* of primary-sourced data is its *high quality* (i.e. relevancy and accuracy). This is due to generally *greater control* over its collection and the focus on only data that is directly *relevant* to the management problem.

The main *disadvantage* of primary-sourced data is that it can be *time consuming* and *expensive* to collect, particularly if sourced using surveys. Internal company databases, however, are relatively quick and cheap to access for primary data.

Secondary data is data that *already exists* in a processed format. It was previously collected and processed by others for a purpose other than the problem at hand. It can be internally sourced (e.g. a monthly stock report or a quarterly absenteeism report) or externally sourced (e.g. economic time series on trade, exports, employment statistics from Stats SA or advertising expenditure trends in South Africa or by sector from SAARF).

Secondary data has two main *advantages*. First, its access time is relatively short (especially if the data is accessible through the internet), and second it is generally less expensive to acquire than primary data.

Its main *disadvantages* are that the data may not be problem specific (i.e. problem of its relevancy), it may be out of date (i.e. not current), it may be difficult to assess data accuracy, it may not be possible to manipulate the data further (i.e. it may not be at the right level of aggregation), and combining various secondary sources of data could lead to data distortion and introduce bias.

Despite such shortcomings, an analyst should always consider relevant secondary database sources before resorting to primary data collection.

1.9 Data Collection Methods

The method(s) used to collect data can *introduce bias* into the data and also affect *data accuracy*. The main methods of data collection are observation, surveys and experimentation.

Observation

Primary data can be collected by *observing* a respondent or a process in action. Examples include vehicle traffic surveys, pedestrian-flow surveys, in-store consumer behaviour studies, employee work practices studies and quality control inspections. The data can be recorded either manually or electronically. Electronic data collection, through the use of sensors, is becoming increasingly more common-place as a data recording method. Such data is more reliable, more consistent and therefore more accurate (giving better quality data) than manual data-recording methods that rely on the human factor.

The *advantage* of the observation approach is that the respondent is unaware of being observed and therefore behaves more naturally or spontaneously. This reduces the likelihood of gathering *biased* data.

The *disadvantage* of this approach is the *passive* form of data collection. There is no opportunity to probe for reasons or to further investigate underlying causes, behaviour and motivating factors.

Surveys

Survey methods gather *primary data* through the *direct questioning* of respondents using questionnaires to structure and record the data collection. Surveys are the most common form of data collection in consumer marketing and socio-economic research. Surveys capture mainly *attitudinal-type* data (i.e. opinions, awareness, knowledge, preferences, perception, intentions and motivations). Surveys are conducted either through personal interviews, telephone surveys or e-surveys (replacing postal surveys).

A *personal interview* is a face-to-face contact with a respondent during which a questionnaire is completed.

This approach offers a number of *advantages*:
- a higher response rate is generally achieved
- it allows probing for reasons
- the data is current and generally more accurate
- it allows questioning of a technical nature
- non-verbal responses (body language and facial expressions) can be observed and noted
- more questions can generally be asked
- the use of aided-recall questions and other visual prompts is possible.

On the *negative* side, personal interviews are *time consuming* and *expensive* to conduct because of the need for trained interviewers and the time needed to find and interview respondents. These cost and time constraints generally result in fewer interviews being conducted.

Telephone interviews are used extensively in *snap (straw) opinion polls*, but they can also be used for lengthier, more rigorous surveys.

A telephone interview has the following *advantages*:
- It keeps the data current by allowing quicker contact with geographically dispersed (and often highly mobile) respondents (using mobile phone contacts).
- Call-backs can be made if the respondent is not available right away.
- The cost is relatively low.
- People are more willing to talk on the telephone, from the security of their home.
- Interviewer probing is possible.
- Questions can be clarified by the interviewer.

- The use of aided-recall questions is possible.
- A larger sample of respondents can be reached in a relatively short time.

Disadvantages include:
- the loss of respondent anonymity
- the inability of the interviewer to observe non-verbal (body language) responses
- the need for trained interviewers, which increases costs
- the likelihood of interviewer bias
- the possibility of a prematurely terminated interview (and therefore loss of data) if the respondent puts down the telephone
- the possibility that sampling bias can be introduced into the results if a significant percentage of the target population does not have access to a telephone (i.e. landline or mobile phone).

An *e-survey* approach uses the technology of e-mails, the internet and mobile phones (e.g. SMS) to conduct surveys and gather respondent data. E-surveys have largely replaced postal surveys. With e-surveys, the questionnaire answers are stored directly into a database that is linked to statistical software which generates and reports statistical findings in summary report format. Typical software online survey tools that are used to design customised questionnaires and generate statistical results include SurveyMonkey, SoGoSurvey, Google Forms, Zoho Survey and SurveyGizmo. They are most suitable when the target population from which *primary data* is required is *geographically dispersed* and it is not practical to conduct personal interviews.

E-surveys are becoming *increasingly popular* for the reasons listed below:
- An e-survey *automates* the process of *collating data*, thus eliminating data-capturing errors.
- E-surveys are significantly *cheaper and faster* than personal or postal interviews.
- It is possible to reach local, national and international target populations.
- The data is *current* and more likely to be *accurate* (leading to high data quality).

They also offer the following *advantages* over personal interviews:
- Interviewer bias is eliminated as there is no direct questioning by an interviewer.
- Respondents have more time to consider their responses.
- The anonymity of each respondent is assured, generally resulting in more honest responses (respondents are more willing to answer personal and sensitive questions).

The primary *drawback* of e-surveys is twofold at present:
- There is a lack of comprehensive sampling frames (e.g. e-mail address lists) targeting specific user groups.
- Not all potential target groups have access to e-mail, the internet or mobile phone facilities, thus introducing possible sampling bias.

E-surveys also have similar drawbacks to the traditional postal survey approach, including that:

- They lack personal communication between the researcher and the respondent, which leads to less control over the data collection procedure.
- They have varied, but relatively low response rates (target population dependent) but can typically range from 5% to 20%.
- The respondent cannot clarify questions.
- Of necessity, survey questionnaires must be shorter and simpler to complete, hence less data on the management issues is gathered.
- The opportunity to probe or investigate further is limited.
- There is no control over who actually answers the questionnaire, which increases the chances of bias.

The advantages and disadvantages listed above apply to any *self-administered* questionnaire such as those handed out randomly in shopping malls, car parks, shops or wherever the target population can be most readily reached. The respondent is requested to complete the questionnaire and to return it by mail or to hand it in at a specified venue.

All surveys rely on a **questionnaire** to structure and record the data collection. Its *design* is critical to the success of a study. The choice of questions as well as their structure, wording and sequencing in the questionnaire can affect the relevancy, bias and accuracy of the collected data. This all has an influence on data quality. Guidelines on questionnaire design can be found in marketing research texts and quantitative research methodology texts.

Experimentation

Primary data can also be obtained by *conducting experiments*. This means that the analyst *manipulates certain variables under controlled conditions*. Data on the primary variable under study can then be monitored and recorded, while a conscious effort is made to control the effects of a number of influencing factors. Statistical methods called **experimental design models** are used to analyse experimental data.

Examples include:

- price manipulation of products to monitor demand elasticity
- testing advertising effectiveness by changing the frequency and choice of advertising media
- altering machine settings in a supervised manner to examine the effects on product quality.

The main *advantage* of data gathered through experimentation is its *high quality*. The data is likely to be accurate and 'noise free' and the statistical findings produced from such data are generally more reliable and valid than results based on data from surveys.

Experimentation has two main *disadvantages*: it is a costly and time-consuming data collection process, and it may be impossible to control certain extraneous factors, which can confound the results (i.e. assign causal influences to incorrect contributory factors).

1.10 Data Preparation

Data is the lifeblood of statistical analysis. It must therefore be *relevant*, '*clean*' and in the *correct format* for statistical analysis.

Data Relevancy

The random variables and the data selected for analysis must be *problem specific*. The right choice of variables must be made to ensure that the statistical analysis addresses the business problem under investigation.

Data Cleaning

Data, when initially captured, is often 'dirty'. Data must be checked for typographic errors, out-of-range values and outliers. When dirty data is used in statistical analysis, the results will produce poor-quality information for management decision-making.

Data Enrichment

Data can often be made *more relevant* to the management problem by transforming it into more meaningful measures. This is known as data enrichment. For example, the variables 'turnover' and 'store size' can be combined to create a new variable – 'turnover per square metre' – that is more relevant to analyse and compare stores' performances.

1.11 Recent Trends in Data Analytics

A number of new trends in data analytics can be observed in practice. Amongst the most noticeable of these are the following: the use of online surveys (to gather survey-based data rapidly from widely dispersed respondent groups) (see Section 1.9); the increasing use of electronic sensors to gather observational data (see Section 1.9); the development of digital dashboard indicators to reflect the health of an organisation or process at a glance; Big Data and Business Intelligence (BI) (the analysis of very large data sets gathered from online real-time systems) and Artificial Intelligence (AI). A brief overview of each of the latter three trends is given below.

Digital Dashboard Analytics

A data dashboard is a visual information management tool. It displays, mostly in a single screenshot, summary values of key performance metrics to monitor and track the 'health-status' – at a glance – of a company's performance, or of individual departments or of specific processes either on a continuous real-time basis or at regular intervals. The display uses visualisation tools such as line and trend graphs, summary tables and charts (bar charts, pie charts). Dashboards are linked to back-end databases where the data is often captured in real-time and processed into the summary values for display on the dashboard.

Figure 1.4 illustrates a data dashboard of HR Employee Activities.

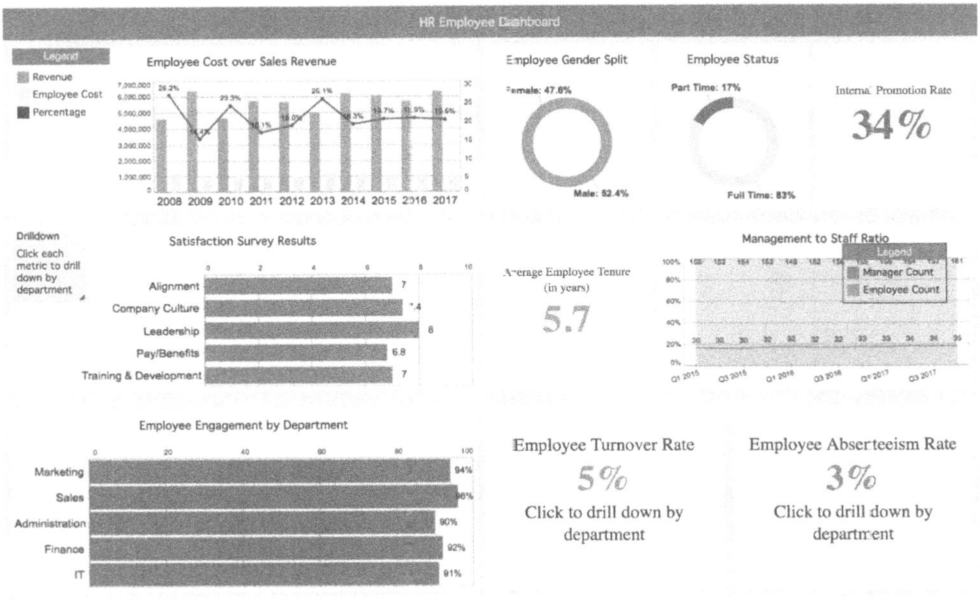

Figure 1.4 A data dashboard of HR Employee Activities

Source: ClearPoint Strategy (https://www.clearpointstrategy.com)

Big Data and Business Intelligence (BI)

Big data is nothing more than very large volumes ('mountains') of data available for statistical analysis. These 'mountains' of data are collected using online real-time systems such as financial systems (credit card transactions, banking transactions, share trading), telecommunication systems (mobile phone calls, SMS, e-mails), social media (Facebook, Google Search, Twitter, etc.), online shopping (Amazon, Takealot, Uber, etc.), automated processes (product quality control), aircraft and motor vehicle performance monitoring (e.g. Formula 1 racing cars) and many more online real-time systems.

The quantitative tools and techniques in 'big data' analyses are data mining, text mining and predictive analytics. They are collectively referred to as business intelligence (BI). The purpose of these advanced statistical software tools (e.g. Oracle, Cognos, SAS, SAP, etc.) is to extract value (in the form of profiles, patterns, trends and relationships) that is imbedded in these very large databases. This allows managers and other relevant decision-makers to gain useful strategic insights into potentially new marketing opportunities, improve customer experiences and streamline company performance with the ultimate goal of growing company revenue.

Artificial Intelligence (AI) – Machine Learning Algorithms

Artificial intelligence is the term applied to machines that attempt to mirror 'cognitive human behaviour' in terms of problem-solving and decision-making. It is aligned to Statistics in that it is heavily data-driven and draws on many statistical concepts and principles to guide the development and evaluation of the AI learning algorithms. Statistical concepts such as population definition, sampling methods, data collection methods, probability and statistical principles, such as experimental designs, randomisation and modelling approaches, are imbedded in these machine-learning algorithms. Many of the AI applications are in their infancy but include self-drive vehicles, speech and facial recognition and automated medical diagnoses. These human–machine learning algorithms (AI) can be referred to as **Intelligent Decision Support Systems (IDSS)** as they provide end-users with the capability of *intelligent* assistance to often complex problems that can significantly improve the quality of decision-making.

1.12 Summary

This chapter has emphasised the importance of statistics as a support tool in management decision-making. Managers need to be familiar with the language of statistics if they are to understand reports that contain statistical findings and if they are to interact effectively with statistical analysts.

Common terms, notation and concepts in statistical analysis were introduced and the major components of the field of Statistics (i.e. descriptive statistics, inferential statistics and statistical modelling) were identified and described. The inclusion of a few illustrative applications of the use of statistics in management and economics were given to highlight how important it is for managers to have a basic understanding of applied business statistics.

This chapter also examined data as the raw material of statistics. An understanding of data is useful to assess its quality and hence the validity of the statistical findings on which it is based. *Data quality* is influenced by four important factors: data type, data source, method(s) used to gather the data and the process of data preparation. Data can be classified by type. The manner in which each data type influences the choice of an appropriate statistical method will be addressed more fully in later chapters. As shown in this chapter, data sources, data-gathering methods and data-preparation issues all have an influence on the quality of data, and hence the accuracy, reliability and validity of statistical findings.

Finally, three significant new trends in the evolution of the field of statistics were identified, namely digital dashboard analytics, 'big data' that is encompassed in the term 'business intelligence' and artificial intelligence (machine learning algorithms).

Exercises

1   Explain the value of business statistics in management.
2   What is the difference between descriptive statistics and inferential statistics?
3   Explain the role of statistical modelling in business practice.
4   Name three factors that influence data quality.
5   Why is it important to know whether the data type is categorical or numerical in terms of the choice of statistical analysis?
6   When preparing data for statistical analysis, what three properties must be considered in order to produce useful and usable information for managers from the statistical findings?
7   A survey of a random sample of 68 human resource (HR) managers asked them to identify the performance appraisal system their company used. The options were:
       1 = a trait method
       2 = a behavioural method
       3 = a results method.
The survey found that only 15% used the trait method, 39% used the behavioural method and 46% used the results method. The study aims to describe the profile of performance appraisal systems used by all JSE companies.
   (a)   Define the random variable of interest.
   (b)   What is the population of interest?
   (c)   What is the sample?
   (d)   What is the sampling unit in this scenario?
   (e)   Is the '46% who use the results method' a parameter or a statistic?
   (f)   Why is it important that the sample of 68 HR managers be randomly selected?
8   *Fair Lady* magazine believes that it has a 38% share of the national female readership market of women's magazines. When 2 000 readers of women's magazines were randomly selected and interviewed, 700 stated that they read *Fair Lady* regularly. Does the sample evidence support their claim?
   (a)   What is the random variable of interest?
   (b)   What is the population of interest?
   (c)   What is the sample?
   (d)   What is the sampling unit in this scenario?
   (e)   What percentage of readers interviewed read *Fair Lady* regularly? Is this a statistic or a parameter? Explain.
   (f)   Does the problem scenario require inferential statistics or only descriptive statistics to answer the question? Explain.
9   The marketing director of a company selling security alarms wants to determine the effectiveness of their recent advertising strategy. Over the past six months they had varied both the number of ads placed per week and the advertising media (press, pamphlets, magazines) used each week. Weekly sales volume data were recorded, as well as the number of ads placed per week and the advertising media used each week.
   (a)   How many random variables are there in this study? Name them.
   (b)   Which random variable is being predicted?
   (c)   Which random variables are assumed to be related to the variable being predicted?
   (d)   Which area of statistical analysis is suggested by this management scenario?

10 For each of the following scenarios, identify, with reasons, whether it is adequate to use only descriptive statistical methods to address the problem situation or whether inferential statistical methods are also needed.

Scenario 1
South Coast Estate Agency wants to determine the average selling price per square metre and size of accommodation of all residential properties in Margate, KwaZulu-Natal. The data from the 25 residential properties sold by their agents, out of the 230 total sales in the area last year, was gathered from deeds of sale documents.

Scenario 2
The owner of the Numbi Restaurant asked a sample of 18 patrons who ate at the restaurant on a particular Saturday evening to complete a short questionnaire to determine their perception of the quality of service and food received that evening.

Scenario 3
The organisers of the Design for Living exhibition held annually at the Good Hope Centre, Cape Town - conducted a survey during the latest exhibition by randomly selecting 544 visitors as they left the exhibition hall. The survey's objective was to give the organisers some insight into what the sample of visitors found worthwhile about the exhibition and what innovations, if any, they would like to see at future exhibitions.

Scenario 4
An environmental awareness NGO conducted a study in Nelspruit into consumers' attitudes towards 'green' (i.e. environmentally friendly) household products. A randomly selected sample of 196 shoppers was interviewed on their attitudes towards purchasing 'green' household products. The objective was to estimate the likely percentage of Nelspruit households who would buy 'green' household products.

Scenario 5
Metrorail, the train commuter service in Cape Town, has been working on improving service to its commuters. A random sample of 875 commuters was interviewed recently on trains over a period of a week and asked their opinion on issues of personal safety on trains, comfort, cleanliness, convenience and punctuality. The results of the sample are to be used to measure the improvement in service.

Scenario 6
Metrorail also recently conducted a campaign to attract road (bus, taxi and car) commuters to using their rail service. Metrorail's management commissioned a survey one month after the campaign ended to find out the success of their campaign. The brief of the researchers was to estimate the percentage of road commuters that converted to train commuting as a result of the campaign.

Scenario 7
The Star newspaper in Gauteng conducted a survey amongst a random cross-section of its subscriber readers to identify the popularity of the various sections of the newspaper amongst all its readers.

11   For each of the following random variables, state the data type of each random variable (categorical or numeric), the measurement scale (nominal, ordinal, interval or ratio scaled) and whether it is discrete or continuous. Also give two illustrative data values for each of these random variables:

(a)   ages of athletes in a marathon

(b)   floor area of Foschini stores

(c)   highest qualification of employees in an organisation

(d)   marital status of employees

(e)   different types of aircraft used by SAA for domestic flights

(f)   types of child abuse (physical, sexual, emotional or verbal)

(g)   performance appraisal rating scores assigned to employees

(h)   ranked preferences of employees to three different pay schemes

(i)   consumer responses to each of the following statements:

   (i)   Rank your preference of the fruit juices that you have just tasted.
      Orange [1]   Guava [2]   Apple [3]   Grape [4]

   (ii)   Do you enjoy your job?
      [Yes]   [No]

   (iii)   Which mode of transport do you mostly use to commute to work?
      Car [1]   Bus [2]   Train [3]   Taxi [4]   Motorcycle [5]   Bicycle [6]

   (iv)   'Returns on JSE equities are no better than those on unit trusts.'
      Rate your response to this statement using the Likert rating scale:
      Strongly disagree [1] Disagree [2] Unsure [3] Agree [4] Strongly agree [5]

(j)   masses (in kg) of bags of potatoes

(k)   brand of coffee you prefer

(l)   time taken (in minutes) to travel to work

(m)   grades used to classify red meat (prime, super, first grade and standard)

(n)   monthly premiums payable on life assurance policies

(o)   number of patrons in a cinema

(p)   number of outlets owned by a chain store

(q)   flying time of an Airbus A-300 between Johannesburg and Dakar

(r)   responses to the following question:
   How would you rate the service level of your bank?
   Use the following semantic differential rating scale:
   Extremely poor [1]   Very poor [2]   Poor [3]   Unsure [4]   Good [5]
   Very good [6]   Excellent [7]

(s)   number of copies of the *Cape Times* sold daily by a café in Paarl

(t)   different sectors of investments in unit trusts.

12 Refer to the financial analysis schedule below:

Financial analysis study

(1) Economic sector

Mining ☐	Manufacturing ☐
Retail ☐	Insurance ☐
Financial ☐	Computers ☐

Other (specify) ....

(2) Head office region:

Gauteng ☐	Western Cape ☐
Free State ☐	Eastern Cape ☐
Limpopo ☐	KwaZulu-Natal ☐

Other (specify) ....

(3) Company size (in terms of number of employees) ⬜

(4) Turnover (rand per annum):

<1 million ☐	1–<5 million ☐
5–<10 million ☐	10–<20 million ☐
20–<50 million ☐	More than 50 million ☐

(5) Share price (in cents) as at 31 December 2015 ⬜

(6) Earnings per share (in cents) for 2015 tax year ⬜

(7) Dividends per share (in cents) for 2015 tax year ⬜

(8) Number of shareholders as at 31 December 2015 ⬜

(9) Return on investment for 2015 tax year ⬜ %

(10) Inflation index for your economic sector ⬜ %

(11) Year company was established ⬜

The data captured in this schedule are extracted from financial reports of JSE-listed companies and are used to compile a database on the financial status of JSE-listed companies.

(a) How many random variables are being studied in the questionnaire?

(b) For each question, identify:

    (i)   the name of the random variable being measured

    (ii)   the data type (categorical or numeric)

    (iii)   the measurement scale (nominal, ordinal, interval or ratio)

    (iv)   whether the data are discrete or continuous.

(c) Give an illustrative data value for each random variable in the study.

13   Refer to the Voyager service quality questionnaire below. (Voyager is an SAA customer loyalty programme.)

(a)   How many random variables are being studied in the questionnaire?

(b)   For each question, identify:

   (i)   the name of the random variable being measured

   (ii)   the data type (categorical or numeric)

   (iii)   the measurement scale (nominal, ordinal, interval or ratio)

   (iv)   whether the data is discrete or continuous.

(c)   Give an illustrative data value for each random variable in the study.

Voyager service quality questionnaire

Section A: *Demographics*

(1)   Gender
Male   ☐   Female   ☐

(2)   Home language
English   ☐   Afrikaans   ☐   Xhosa   ☐   Other   ☐

(3)   Which of the following best describes your position in your company?
Junior manager   ☐   Middle manager   ☐   Senior manager   ☐
Director   ☐

(4)   When did you join Voyager?
Pre-2010   ☐   2011   ☐   2012   ☐   2013   ☐   2014   ☐

(5)   What is your Voyager membership status?
Blue   ☐   Silver   ☐   Gold   ☐   Platinum   ☐

Section B: *Voyager usage level*

(6)   Have you ever claimed Voyager Awards?
Yes   ☐   No   ☐

(7)   (*a*)   Did you encounter any problems in claiming Voyager Awards?
Yes   ☐   No   ☐
(*b*)   If 'yes', what kinds of problems did you encounter?
....
....
....

(8)   How often have you used services by a Voyager Partner in the following categories?

	Never	Rarely	Sometimes	Often	Always
Airlines	1	2	3	4	5
Car rentals	1	2	3	4	5
Hotels and resorts	1	2	3	4	5
Financial services	1	2	3	4	5
Telecommunications	1	2	3	4	5

Section C: *Voyager service quality perceptions*

(9) The following statements relate to your feelings about Voyager services. For each statement, indicate your level of support by circling the appropriate number.

	Strongly disagree	*Disagree*	*Neutral*	*Agree*	*Strongly agree*
I receive my statements regularly	1	2	3	4	5
The Voyager Guide is user friendly	1	2	3	4	5
Voyager centres are conveniently situated	1	2	3	4	5
Voyager staff have good communication skills	1	2	3	4	5
My queries are always dealt with effectively	1	2	3	4	5
Voyager staff are knowledgeable about their product	1	2	3	4	5

(10) Rank the following four Voyager facilities from most useful (assign rank = 1) to least useful (assign rank = 4).

Rank

The Voyager Guide

Voyager partnership plan

Voyager in-flight services

Voyager holiday specials

Thank you for completing this questionnaire.

14   What essential differences in data types would be noticed between the data gathered for the financial analysis study (question 12) and the Voyager service quality study (question 13)?

Exploratory Data Analysis

Summarising Data: Summary Tables and Graphs

Outcomes

Managers can easily understand sample data when it is summarised into an appropriate table and then displayed graphically. This chapter explains how to summarise data into table format and then how to display the results in an appropriate graph or chart.

After studying this chapter, you should be able to:

- summarise *categorical* data into a frequency table and a cross-tabulation table
- interpret the findings from a categorical frequency table and a cross-tabulation table
- construct and interpret appropriate bar and pie charts
- summarise *numeric* data into a frequency distribution and a cumulative frequency distribution
- construct and interpret a histogram and an ogive
- construct and interpret a scatter plot of two numeric measures
- display *time series* data as line graphs and interpret trends
- segment numeric data into categories
- interpret how numeric measures differ by categories
- use Excel and X-Static to produce summary tables and charts.

2.1 Introduction

Managers can only benefit from statistical findings if the information can easily be interpreted and effectively communicated to them. Summary tables and graphs are commonly used to convey descriptive statistical results. A table or a graph can convey information much more quickly and vividly than a written report. For graphs in particular, there is much truth in the adage 'a picture is worth a thousand words'. In practice, an analyst should always consider using summary tables and graphical displays ahead of written texts, in order to convey statistical information to managers.

Summary tables and graphs can be used to summarise (or profile) a single random variable (e.g. most-preferred TV channel by viewers or pattern of delivery times) or to examine the relationship between two random variables (e.g. between gender and news-paper readership). The choice of a summary table and graphic technique depends on the data type being analysed (i.e. categorical or numeric).

The sample dataset in Table 2.1 of the shopping habits of 30 grocery shoppers will be used to illustrate the different summary tables and graphs.

(See Excel file C2.1 – *grocery shoppers.*)

Table 2.1 Sample data set of grocery shoppers

2.2 Summarising Categorical Data

Single Categorical Variable

Categorical Frequency Table

A **categorical frequency table** summarises data for a *single categorical variable*. It shows how many times each category appears in a sample of data and measures the relative importance of the different categories.

Follow these steps to construct a categorical frequency table:
- List all the categories of the variable (in the first column).
- Count and record (in the second column) the number of occurrences of each category.
- Convert the counts per category (in the third column) into *percentages* of the total sample size. This produces a **percentage categorical frequency table**.

It is always a good idea to express the counts as percentages because this makes them easy to understand and interpret. In addition, it makes the comparisons between samples of different sizes easier to explain.

A categorical frequency table can be displayed *graphically* either as a **bar chart** or a **pie chart**.

Bar Chart

To construct a bar chart, draw a horizontal axis (*x*-axis) to represent the categories and a vertical axis (*y*-axis) scaled to show either the frequency counts or the percentages of each category. Then construct vertical bars for each category to the height of its frequency count (or percentage) on the *y*-axis.

Note that the sum of the frequency counts (or %) across the bars must equal the sample size (or 100%). The bars must be of equal width to avoid distorting a category's importance. However, neither the order of the categories on the *x*-axis, nor the widths of the bars matter. It is only the bar heights that convey the information of category importance.

Pie Chart

To construct a pie chart, divide a circle into category segments. The size of each segment must be proportional to the count (or percentage) of its category. The sum of the segment counts (or percentages) must equal the sample size (or 100%).

Example 2.1 Grocery Shoppers Survey

A market research company conducted a survey amongst grocery shoppers to identify their demographic profile and shopping patterns. A random sample of 30 grocery shoppers was asked to complete a questionnaire that identified:
- at which grocery store they most preferred to shop
- the number of visits to the grocery store in the last month

- the amount spent last month on grocery purchases
- their age, gender and family size.

The response data to each question is recorded in Table 2.1. Each column shows the 30 responses to each question and each row shows the responses of a single grocery shopper to all six questions.

Refer to the 'store preference' variable in Table 2.1.
1 Construct a percentage frequency table to summarise the store preferences of the sample of 30 grocery shoppers.
2 Show the findings graphically as a bar chart and as a pie chart.

Management Questions

1 Which grocery store is most preferred by shoppers?
2 What percentage of shoppers prefer this store?
3 What percentage of shoppers prefer to shop at Spar grocery stores?

Solution

1 For the categorical variable 'store preference' there are three categories of grocery stores that shoppers use: 1 = Checkers; 2 = Pick n Pay; 3 = Spar.

To construct the percentage frequency table, first count the number of shoppers that prefer each store – there are 10 ones (Checkers), 17 twos (Pick n Pay) and 3 threes (Spar). Then convert the counts into percentages by dividing the count per store by 30 (the sample size) and multiplying the result by 100 (i.e. Checkers = $\frac{10}{30} \times 100 = 33.3\%$; Pick n Pay = $\frac{17}{30} \times 100 = 56.7\%$; Spar = $\frac{3}{30} \times 100 = 10\%$).

The percentage frequency table of grocery store preferences is shown in Table 2.2.

Table 2.2 Percentage frequency table for grocery store preference of shoppers

Preferred store	Count	Percentage
1 = Checkers	10	33.3%
2 = Pick n Pay	17	56.7%
3 = Spar	3	10.0%
Total	30	100%

2 The frequency table can be displayed *graphically*, either as a *bar chart* or a *pie chart*. The relative importance of each category of the frequency table is represented by a bar in a bar chart (see Figure 2.1) or by a segment of a circle in a pie chart (see Figure 2.2).

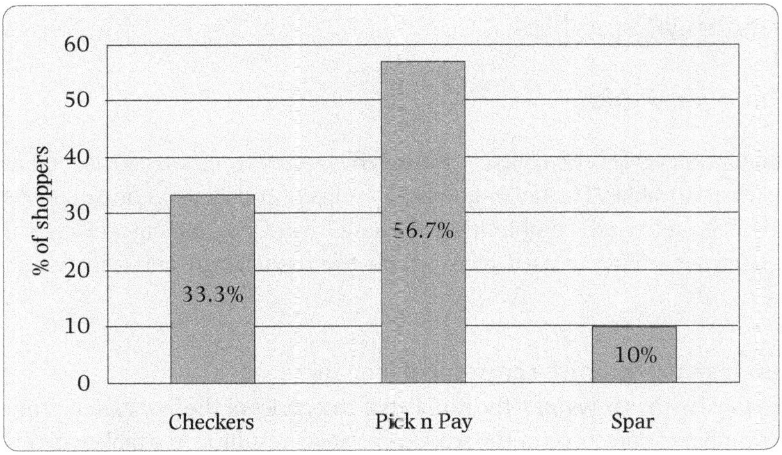

Figure 2.1 Bar chart of grocery shoppers' store preferences

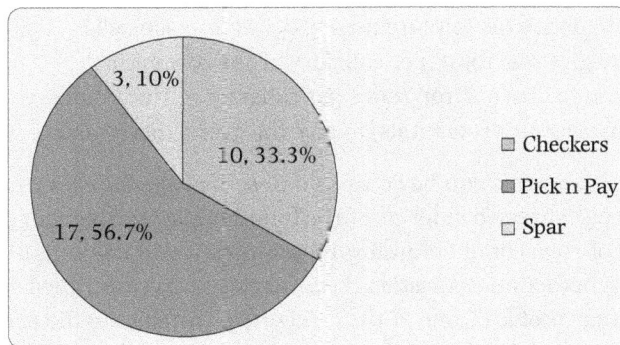

Figure 2.2 Pie chart of grocery shoppers' store preferences

Management Interpretation

1 The grocery store most preferred by shoppers is Pick n Pay.
2 More than half of the sampled shoppers (56.7%) prefer to shop at Pick n Pay for their groceries.
3 Only 10% of the sampled shoppers prefer to do their grocery shopping at Spar.

Charts and graphs must always be clearly and adequately labelled with headings, axis titles and legends to make them easy to read and to avoid any misrepresentation of information. The data source must, where possible, also be identified to allow a user to assess the credibility and validity of the summarised findings.

Bar charts and pie charts display the same information graphically. In a *bar chart*, the importance of a category is shown by the *height of a bar*, while in a *pie chart* this importance is shown by the *size of each segment* (or slice). The *differences between the categories* are clearer in a *bar chart*, while a *pie chart* conveys more of a sense of the *whole*. A limitation of both the bar chart and the pie chart is that each displays the summarised information on only one variable at a time.

Two Categorical Variables

Cross-tabulation Table

A **cross-tabulation table** (also called a **contingency table**) summarises the *joint responses* of two categorical variables. The table shows the number (and/or percentage) of observations that jointly belong to each combination of categories of the two categorical variables.

This summary table is used to examine the **association** between two categorical measures.

Follow these steps to construct a cross-tabulation table:
- Prepare a table with m rows (m = the number of categories of the first variable) and n columns (n = the number of categories of the second variable), resulting in a table with ($m \times n$) cells.
- Assign each pair of data values from the two variables to an appropriate category–combination cell in the table by placing a tick in the relevant cell.
- When each pair of data values has been assigned to a cell in the table, count the number of ticks per cell to derive the joint frequency count for each cell.
- Sum each row to give row totals per category of the row variable.
- Sum each column to give column totals per category of the column variable.
- Sum the column totals (or row totals) to give the grand total (sample size).

These joint frequency counts can be converted to *percentages* for easier interpretation. The percentages could be expressed in terms of the total sample size (percent of total), or of row subtotals (percent of rows) or of column subtotals (percent of columns).

To determine whether an *association exists* between two categorical variables, compare the overall percentage profile of one of the categorical variables to the percentage profile of this same variable for each level of the second categorical variable. If the overall percentage profile is the same (or very similar) to each level's percentage profile, then there is no association. If at least one level's percentage profile differs significantly from the overall percentage profile, then an association exists.

The cross-tabulation table can be displayed *graphically* either as a **stacked bar chart** (also called a component bar chart) or a **multiple bar chart**. An inspection of the charts can also reveal evidence of an association of not. The more similar the chart profiles are (based on either row percentage-wise or column percentage-wise computations), the less likely there is an association and vice versa.

Stacked Bar Chart

Follow these steps to construct a stacked bar chart:
- Choose, say, the row variable, and plot the frequency of each category of this variable as a simple bar chart.
- Split the height of each bar in proportion to the frequency count of the categories of the column variable.

This produces a simple bar chart of the row variable with each bar split proportionately into the categories of the column variable. The categories of column variable are 'stacked' on top of each other within each category bar of the row variable.

Note: The stacked bar chart can also be constructed by choosing the column variable first and then splitting the bars of the column variable into the category frequencies of the row variable.

Multiple Bar Chart

Follow these steps to construct a multiple bar chart:
- For each category of, say, the row variable, plot a simple bar chart constructed from the corresponding frequencies of the categories of the column variable.
- Display these categorised simple bar charts next to each other on the same axes.

The multiple bar chart is similar to a stacked bar chart, except that the stacked bars are displayed next to rather than on top of each other.

The two charts convey *exactly the same information* on the association between the two variables. They differ only in how they emphasise the *relative importance* of the categories of the two variables.

Example 2.2 Grocery Shoppers Survey – Store Preferences by Gender

Refer to the 'store preference' variable and the 'gender' variable in Table 2.1.
1   Construct a cross-tabulation table of frequency counts between 'store preference' (as the row variable) and 'gender' (as the column variable) of shoppers surveyed.
2   Display the cross-tabulation as a stacked bar chart and as a multiple bar chart.
3   Construct a percentage cross-tabulation table to show the percentage split of gender for each grocery store.

Management Questions

1   How many shoppers are male and prefer to shop at Checkers?
2   What percentage of all grocery shoppers are females who prefer Pick n Pay?
3   What percentage of all Checkers' shoppers are female?
4   Of all male shoppers, what percentage prefer to shop at Spar for their groceries?
5   Is there an association between gender and store preference (i.e. does store preference differ significantly between male and female shoppers)?

Solution

1   The row categorical variable is 'store preference': 1 = Checkers; 2 = Pick n Pay; 3 = Spar. The column categorical variable is 'gender': 1 = female; 2 = male.

Table 2.3 Cross-tabulation table – grocery store preferences by gender

Store	Gender		Total
	1 = Female	2 = Male	
1 = Checkers	7	3	10
2 = Pick n Pay	10	7	17
3 = Spar	2	1	3
Total	19	11	30

To produce the cross-tabulation table, count how many females prefer to shop at each store (Checkers, Pick n Pay and Spar) and then count how many males prefer to shop at each store (Checkers, Pick n Pay and Spar). These *joint frequency counts* are shown in Table 2.3. The cross-tabulation table can also be completed using percentages (row percentages, column percentages or as percentages of the total sample).

2   Figure 2.3 and Figure 2.4 show the stacked bar chart and multiple bar chart respectively for the cross-tabulation table of joint frequency counts in Table 2.3.

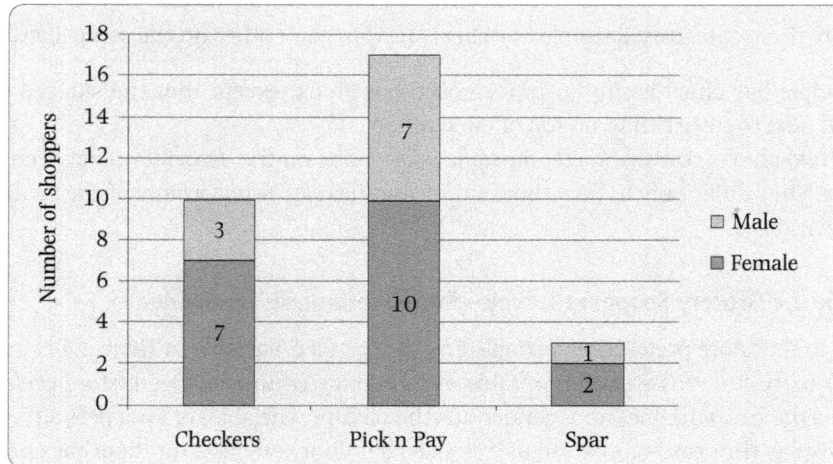

Figure 2.3 Stacked bar chart – grocery store preferences by gender

The stacked bar chart highlights overall store preference, with each store split by gender.

Pick n Pay is the most preferred shop (17 shoppers out of 30 prefer Pick n Pay), followed by Checkers (10 out of 30) and only 3 prefer to shop at Spar. In addition, of the 17 shoppers who prefer Pick n Pay, 10 are female and 7 are male; of the 10 shoppers who prefer Checkers, 7 are female and 3 are male; and of the 3 shoppers who prefer Spar, 2 are female and only 1 is male.

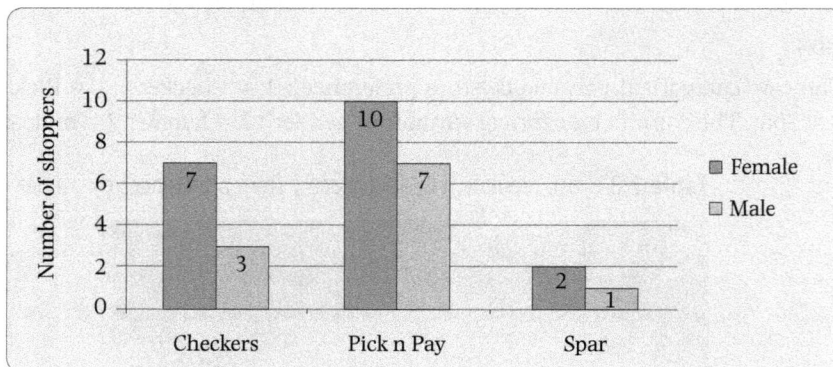

Figure 2.4 Multiple bar chart – grocery store preferences by gender

The multiple bar chart places more emphasis on the gender differences between stores.

3   Table 2.4 shows, for each store separately, the percentage split by gender (row percentages), while Table 2.5 shows, for each gender separately, the percentage breakdown by the grocery store preferred (column percentages).

Table 2.4 Row percentage cross-tabulation table (store preferences by gender)

Store	Gender		Total
	1 = Female	2 = Male	
1 = Checkers	70%	30%	100%
2 = Pick n Pay	59%	41%	100%
3 = Spar	67%	33%	100%
Total	63%	37%	100%

From Table 2.4, of those shoppers who prefer Checkers, 70% are female and 30% are male. Similarly, of those who prefer Pick n Pay, 59% are female and 41% are male. Finally, 67% of customers who prefer to shop at Spar are female, while 33% are male. Overall, 63% of grocery shoppers are female, while only 37% are male.

Table 2.5 Column percentage cross-tabulation table (store preferences by gender)

Store	Gender		Total
	1 = Female	2 = Male	
1 = Checkers	37%	27%	33%
2 = Pick n Pay	53%	64%	57%
3 = Spar	11%	9%	10%
Total	100%	100%	100%

From Table 2.5, of all female shoppers, 37% prefer Checkers, 53% prefer Pick n Pay and 11% prefer to shop for groceries at Spar. For males, 27% prefer Checkers, 64% prefer Pick n Pay and the balance (9%) prefer to shop at Spar for their groceries. Overall, 33% of all shoppers prefer Checkers, 57% prefer Pick n Pay and only 10% prefer Spar for grocery shopping.

Management Interpretation

1   Of the 30 shoppers surveyed, there are only three males who prefer to shop at Checkers.
2   33.3% (10 out of 30) of all shoppers surveyed are females who prefer to shop at Pick n Pay.
3   70% (7 out of 10) of all Checkers shoppers are female. (Refer to the row percentages in Table 2.4.)
4   Only 9% (1 out of 11) of all males prefer to shop at Spar. (Refer to the column percentages in Table 2.5.)
5   Since the percentage breakdown between male and female shoppers across the three grocery stores is reasonably similar to the overall gender profile regardless of store preference (i.e. 63% female and 37% male), it can be concluded that gender and store preference are not statistically associated.

2.3 Summarising Numeric Data

Numeric data can also be summarised in table format and displayed graphically. The table is known as a numeric frequency distribution and the graph of this table is called a histogram.

From Table 2.1, the numeric variable 'age of shoppers', will be used to illustrate the construction of a numeric frequency distribution and its histogram.

Single Numeric Variable

Numeric Frequency Distribution

A **numeric frequency distribution** summarises numeric data into intervals of *equal width*. Each interval shows how many numbers (data values) fall within the interval.

Follow these steps to construct a numeric frequency distribution:
- Determine the *data range*.

$$\text{Range} = \text{Maximum data value} - \text{Minimum data value} \qquad \text{2.1}$$

For the age of grocery shoppers, the age data range is $69 - 23 = 46$ years.
- Choose the *number of intervals* (k). While there is no strict formula to find k, each one of the following rules can be used as a guide based on sample size (n): Sturges' rule ($k = 1 + 2.322*\log_{10}(n)$); Rice's rule ($k = 2 \times \sqrt[3]{n}$) and the Square-root rule ($k = \sqrt{n}$). **X-Static uses Rice's rule.** As a general rule, choose between 5 and 10 intervals, depending on the sample size: the smaller the sample size, the fewer the number of intervals, and vice versa. For $n = 30$ shoppers, choose five intervals.
- Determine the *interval width*.

$$\text{Interval width} = \frac{\text{Data range}}{\text{Number of intervals}} \qquad \text{2.2}$$

Use this as a guide to determine a 'neat' interval width. For the 'age' variable, the approximate interval width is $\frac{46}{5} = 9.2$ years. Hence choose an interval width of 10 years.
- Set up the *interval limits*. The lower limit for the first interval should be a value smaller than or equal to the minimum data value and should be a number that is easy to use. Since the youngest shopper is 23 years old, choose the lower limit of the first interval to be 20.

The *lower limits* for successive intervals are found by adding the interval width to each preceding lower limit. The *upper limits* are chosen to avoid overlaps between adjacent interval limits.

Lower limit	Upper limit
20	< 30 (or 29)
30	< 40 (or 39)
40	< 50 (or 49)
50	< 60 (or 59)
60	< 70 (or 69)

The format of <30 (less than 30) should be used if the source data is continuous, while an upper limit such as 29 can be used if the data values are discrete.

- *Tabulate* the data values. Assign each data value to one, and only one, interval. A *count* of the data values assigned to each interval produces the *summary table*, called the **numeric frequency distribution**.

When *constructing* a numeric frequency distribution, ensure that:
- the interval widths are equal in size
- the interval limits do not overlap (i.e. intervals must be *mutually exclusive*)
- each data value is assigned to only one interval
- the intervals are fully *inclusive* (i.e. cover the data range)
- the sum of the frequency counts must equal the sample size, *n*, or that the percentage frequencies sum to 100%.

The frequency counts can be converted to *percentages* (or *proportions*) by dividing each frequency count by the sample size. The resultant summary table is called a **percentage (or relative) frequency distribution**. It shows the percentage (or proportion) of data values within each interval.

Histogram

A **histogram** is a graphic display of a numeric frequency distribution.

Follow these steps to construct a histogram:
- Arrange the intervals consecutively on the *x*-axis from the lowest interval to the highest. There must be no gaps between adjacent interval limits.
- Plot the height of each bar (on the *y*-axis) over its corresponding interval, to show either the frequency count or percentage frequency of each interval. The area of a bar (width × height) measures the density of values in each interval.

Example 2.3 Grocery Shoppers Survey – Profiling the Ages of Shoppers

Refer to the 'age of shoppers' variable in Table 2.1.
1. Construct a numeric frequency distribution for the age profile of grocery shoppers.
2. Compute the percentage frequency distribution of shoppers' ages.
3. Construct a histogram of the numeric frequency distribution of shoppers' ages.

Management Questions

1. How many shoppers are between 20 and 29 years of age?
2. What is the most frequent age interval of shoppers surveyed?
3. What percentage of shoppers belong to the most frequent age interval?
4. What percentage of shoppers surveyed are 60 years or older?
5. What is the maximum age for the youngest 20% of shoppers surveyed?

Solution

1 and 2
The numeric and percentage frequency distributions for the ages of grocery shoppers are shown in Table 2.6, and are based on the steps shown above.

Table 2.6 Numeric (and percentage) frequency distribution – age of shoppers

Age (years)	Tally	Count	Percentage	Relative
20 – 29	|||||		6	20%	0.2
30 – 39	||||| ||||	9	30%	0.3
40 – 49	||||| |||	8	27%	0.27
50 – 59	||||	4	13%	0.13
60 – 69	|||	3	10%	0.1
Total		30	100%	1

3   Figure 2.5 shows the histogram of the numeric frequency distribution for shoppers'
     ages.

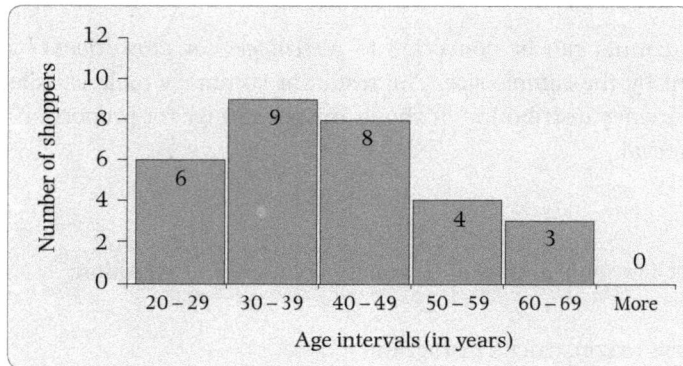

Figure 2.5 Histogram – age of shoppers

Management Interpretation

1   There are six shoppers between the ages of 20 and 29 years.
2   The most frequent age interval is between 30 and 39 years.
3   30% of shoppers surveyed are between 30 and 39 years of age.
4   10% of shoppers surveyed are 60 years or older
5   The youngest 20% of shoppers are no older than 29 years.

If the numeric data are *discrete values* in a limited range (5-point rating scales, number of
children in a family, number of customers in a bank queue, for example), then the *individual
discrete values* of the random variable can be used as the 'intervals' in the construction of a
numeric frequency distribution and a histogram. This is illustrated in Example 2.4 below.

Example 2.4 Grocery Shoppers Survey – Profiling the Family Size of Shoppers

Refer to the random variable 'family size' in the database in Table 2.1. Construct a
numeric and percentage frequency distribution and histogram of the family size of
grocery shoppers surveyed.

Management Questions

1   Which is the most common family size?
2   How many shoppers have a family size of three?
3   What percentage of shoppers have a family size of either three or four?

Solution

Family size is a discrete random variable. The family sizes range from 1 to 5 (see data in Table 2.1). Each family size can be treated as a separate interval. To tally the family sizes, count how many shoppers have a family size of one, two, three, four and of five.

Table 2.7 and Figure 2.6 show the numeric and percentage frequency table and histogram for the discrete numeric data of family size of grocery shoppers.

Table 2.7 Numeric (and percentage) frequency distribution – family size of shoppers

Family size	Tally	Count	Percentage
1	IIII	4	13.3%
2	IIIII IIIII I	11	36.7%
3	IIIII III	8	26.7%
4	IIIII	5	16.7%
5	II	2	6.6%
Total		30	100%

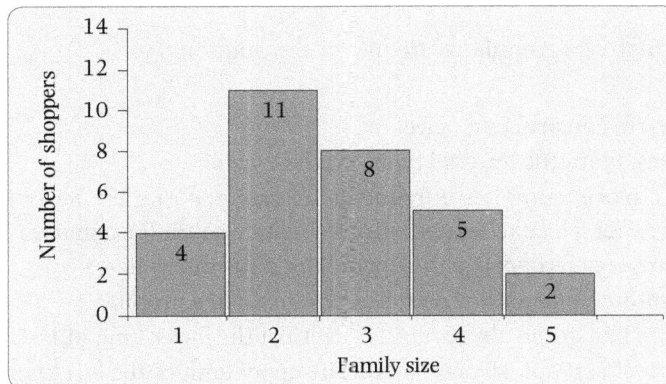

Figure 2.6 Histogram – family size of shoppers

Management Interpretation

1. The most common family size of grocery shoppers is two.
2. There are eight shoppers that have a family size of three.
3. 43.4% (26.7% + 16.7%) of shoppers surveyed have a family size of either three or four.

Cumulative Frequency Distribution

Data for a single numeric variable can also be summarised into a **cumulative frequency distribution**.

A **cumulative frequency distribution** is a summary table of *cumulative frequency counts* which is used to answer questions of a '*more than*' or '*less than*' nature.

Follow these steps to construct a *less than* cumulative frequency distribution from a numeric frequency distribution:

- For each interval, starting with the *lowest interval*, ask the question: 'How many data values are *below* this interval's *upper limit?*'
- The answer is: the sum of all frequency counts (or percentages, or proportions) that lie below this current interval's *upper limit.*
- This is repeated until the last interval is reached.
- A shortcut method to find each successive *less than* cumulative frequency count (or percentage, or proportion) is to add each interval's frequency count to the cumulative frequency immediately preceding it.
- The last interval's cumulative frequency count must always equal the sample size, *n*, (or 100% or 1).

To find the *more than* cumulative frequency distribution, start from the *highest* interval's *lower limit* by asking the question: 'How may data values are above this interval's *lower limit?*' Then work back to the first interval by adding each successive interval's frequency to the preceding cumulative frequency.

Ogive

An **ogive** is a graph of a cumulative frequency distribution.

Follow these steps to construct an ogive:
- On a set of axes, mark the interval limits on the *x*-axis.
- On the *y*-axis, plot a cumulative frequency of *zero* opposite the *lower limit* of the first interval. Thereafter, plot each cumulative frequency count (or cumulative percentage or cumulative proportion) opposite the upper limit of its interval.
- Join these cumulative frequency points to produce a line graph.
- The cumulative line graph always starts at zero at the lower limit of the first interval.
- The cumulative line graph always ends at the upper limit of the last interval.

This ogive graph can now be used to read off cumulative answers to questions of the following type:
- How many (or what percentage) of observations lie below (or above) this value?
- What data value separates the data set at a given cumulative frequency (or cumulative percentage)?

Note: The ogive graph can provide answers for both *less than* and *more than* type of questions from the same graph.

Example 2.5 Grocery Shoppers Survey – Analysis of Grocery Spend

Refer to the numeric variable 'spend' (amount spent on groceries last month) in Table 2.1.

1   Compute the numeric frequency distribution and percentage frequency distribution for the amount spent on groceries last month by grocery shoppers.

2   Compute the cumulative frequency distribution and its graph, the ogive, for the amount spent on groceries last month.

Management Questions

1   What percentage of shoppers spent less than R1 200 last month?
2   What percentage of shoppers spent R1 600 or more last month?
3   What percentage of shoppers spent between R800 and R1 600 last month?
4   What was the maximum amount spent last month by the 20% of shoppers who spent the least on groceries? Approximate your answer.
5   What is the approximate minimum amount spent on groceries last month by the top-spending 50% of shoppers?

Solution

1   The numeric frequency distribution for amount spent is computed using the construction steps outlined earlier.

The range is R2 136 − R456 = R1 680. Choosing five intervals, the interval width can be set to a 'neat' width of R400 (based on $\frac{R1\ 680}{5}$ = R336). The lower limit of the first interval is set at a 'neat' limit of R400, since the minimum amount spent is R456. The numeric and percentage frequency distributions are both shown in Table 2.8.

Table 2.8 Numeric (and percentage) frequency distributions – grocery spend

Grocery spend (R)	Count	Percentage
400 −< 800	7	23.3%
800 −< 1 200	14	46.7%
1 200 −< 1 600	5	16.7%
1 600 −< 2 000	3	10.0%
2 000 −< 2 400	1	3.3%
Total	30	100%

2   The cumulative frequency distribution (ogive) for amount spent on groceries last month is computed using the construction guidelines outlined above for the ogive.

Based on the numeric frequency distribution in Table 2.8, with R400 being the minimum grocery spend, the following cumulative counts are derived:
- 7 shoppers spent up to R800
- 21 (= 7 + 14) shoppers spent up to R1 200
- 26 (= 21 + 5) shoppers spent up to R1 600
- 29 (= 26 + 3) shoppers spent up to R2 000
- all 30 shoppers (= 29 + 1) spent no more than R2 400 on groceries last month.

The cumulative frequency distributions for both the frequency counts and percentages are shown in Table 2.9.

Table 2.9 Cumulative frequency distributions (count and percentage) – grocery spend

Numeric frequency distribution			Cumulative distribution	
Grocery spend (R)	Count	Percentage	Count	Percentage
400 –< 800	7	23.3%	7	23.3%
800 –< 1 200	14	46.7%	21	70.0%
1 200 –< 1 600	5	16.7%	26	86.7%
1 600 –< 2 000	3	10.0%	29	96.7%
2 000 –< 2 400	1	3.3%	30	100.0%
Total	30	100%		

Figure 2.7 shows the percentage ogive graph. Note that the % cumulative frequency is 0% at R400 (the lower limit of the first interval) and 100% at the upper limit of R2 400 for the last interval. This means that no shopper spent less than R400 or more than R2 400 last month on groceries.

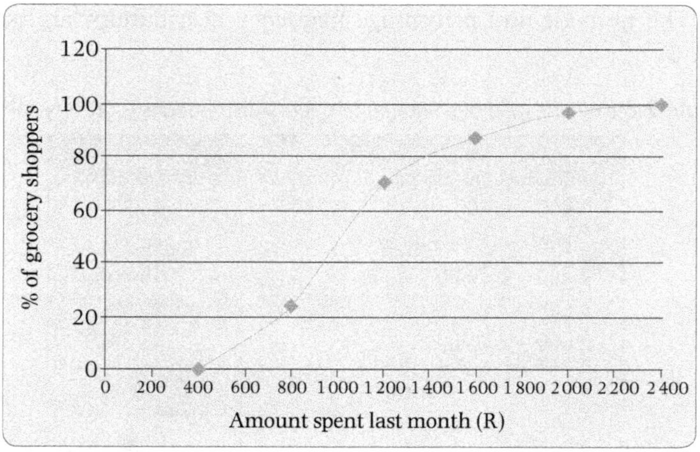

Figure 2.7 Ogive (%) – grocery spend

Management Interpretation

1 70% of shoppers spent less than R1 200 on groceries last month.
2 13.3% (100% − 86.7%) of shoppers spent R1 600 or more on groceries last month.
3 63.4% (86.7% − 23.3% or 46.7% + 16.7%) of shoppers spent between R800 and R1 600 on groceries last month.
4 The bottom 20% of shoppers spent no more than R770 (approximately) on groceries last month. (Using the percentage ogive, this answer is found by projecting 20% from the y-axis to the ogive and reading off the amount spent on the x-axis.)
5 From the y-axis value at 50%, the minimum amount spent on groceries by the top-spending 50% of shoppers is (approximately) R1 000.

Note: The ogive is a *less than* cumulative frequency graph, but it can also be used to answer questions of a *more than* nature (by subtracting the less than cumulative percentage from 100%, or the cumulative count from *n*, the sample size).

Box Plot

A **box plot** visually displays the *profile of a numeric variable* by showing its *minimum* and *maximum* values and various intermediate descriptive values (such as *quartiles* and *medians*).

The box plot is covered in Chapter 3, as it is constructed from descriptive statistical measures for numeric variables that will only be derived in that chapter.

Two Numeric Variables

The **relationship** between two numeric random variables can be examined graphically by plotting their values on a set of axes.

The graphs that are useful to display the relationship between two numeric random variables are: a **scatter plot**, a **trendline graph** and a **Lorenz curve**. Each graph addresses a different type of management question.

Scatter Plot

A **scatter plot** displays the data points of *two numeric variables* on an *x–y* graph.

A visual inspection of a scatter plot will show the nature of a relationship between the two variables in terms of its *strength* (the closeness of the points), its *shape* (linear or curved), its *direction* (direct or inverse) and any *outliers* (extreme data values).

For example, a plot of advertising expenditure (on the *x*-axis) against sales (on the *y*-axis) could show what relationship, if any, exists between advertising expenditure and sales. Another example is to examine what influence training hours (on the *x*-axis) could have on worker output (on the *y*-axis).

Follow these steps to construct a scatter plot:
- Label the horizontal axis (*x*-axis) with the name of the influencing variable (called the **independent variable**, *x*).
- Label the vertical axis (*y*-axis) with the name of the variable being influenced (called the **dependent variable**, *y*).
- Plot each pair of data values (*x*; *y*) from the two numeric variables as coordinates on an *x–y* graph.

Example 2.6 Grocery Shoppers Survey – Amount Spent by Number of Store Visits

Refer to the dataset in Table 2.1.

Construct a scatter plot for the amount spent on groceries and the number of visits to the grocery store per shopper by the sample of 30 shoppers surveyed.

Management Questions

By inspection of the scatter plot, describe the nature of the relationship between the number of visits and amount spent.

Solution

To construct the scatter plot, we need to define the x and y variables. Since the number of visits is assumed to influence the amount spent on groceries in a month, let x = number of visits and y = amount spent.

On a set of axes, plot each pair of data values for each shopper. For example, for shopper 1, plot x = 3 visits against y = R946; for shopper 2, plot x = 5 visits against y = R1 842.

The results of the scatter plot are shown in Figure 2.8.

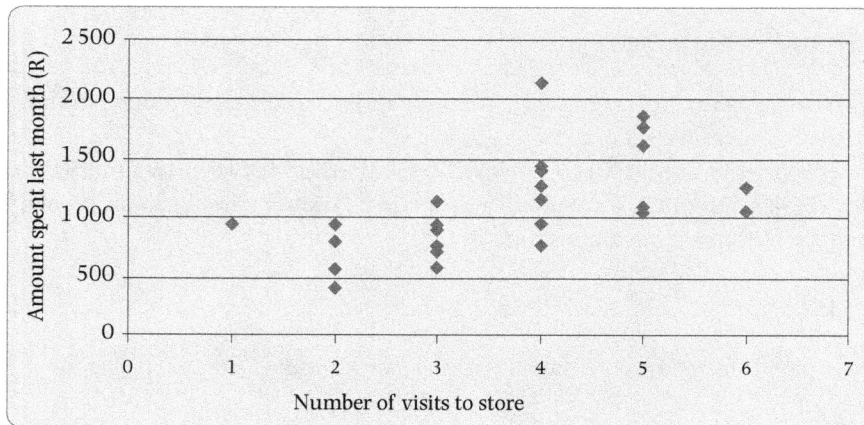

Figure 2.8 Scatter plot – monthly amount spent on groceries against number of visits

Management Interpretation

There is a moderate, positive linear relationship between the number of visits to a grocery store in a month and the total amount spent on groceries last month per shopper. The more frequent the visits, the larger the grocery bill for the month. There is only one possible outlier – shopper 13, who spent R2 136 over four visits.

Note: Both the *strength* and the *direction* of the relationship that is observed in a scatter plot can be measured by a **correlation coefficient** $(-1 \leq r \leq +1)$ using the Excel function **CORREL(array1, array2)**. This statistic is covered in detail in Chapter 12 (section 12.3).

Trendline Graph

A **trendline graph** plots the values of a *numeric random variable* over *time*.

Such data are called **time series data**. The x-variable is *time* and the y-variable is a *numeric measure* of interest to a manager (such as turnover, unit cost of production, absenteeism or share prices).

Follow these steps to construct a trendline graph:

- The horizontal axis (x-axis) represents the consecutive time periods.
- The values of the numeric random variable are plotted on the vertical (y-axis) opposite their time period.
- The consecutive points are joined to form a trendline.

Trendline graphs are commonly used to *identify and track trends* in time series data.

Example 2.7 Factory Absenteeism Levels Study

Refer to the time series data in Table 2.10 on weekly absenteeism levels at a car manufacturing plant.
(See Excel file C2.2 – *factory absenteeism*.)

Table 2.10 Data on employee-days absent for a car manufacturing plant

Week	1	2	3	4	5	6	7	8	9	10	11	12	13	14	15	16
Absent	54	58	94	70	61	61	78	56	49	55	95	85	60	64	99	80
Week	17	18	19	20	21	22	23	24	25	26	27	28	29	30	31	32
Absent	62	78	88	73	65	84	92	70	59	65	105	84	80	90	112	94

Produce a trendline plot of the weekly absenteeism levels (number of employee-days absent) for this car manufacturing plant over a period of 32 weeks.

Management Question

By an inspection of the trendline graph, describe the trend in weekly absenteeism levels within this car manufacturing plant over the past 32 weeks.

Solution

To plot the trendline, plot the weeks (x = 1, 2, 3, ..., 32) on the x-axis. For each week, plot the corresponding employee-days absent on the y-axis. After plotting all 32 y-values, join the points to produce the trendline graph as shown in Figure 2.9.

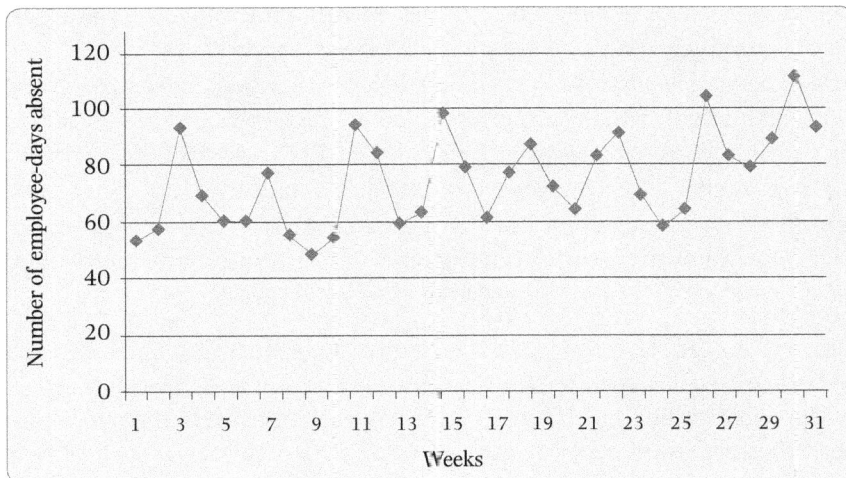

Figure 2.9 Trendline graph for weekly absenteeism levels – car manufacturing plant

Management Interpretation

Over the past 32 weeks there has been a modest increase in absenteeism, with an upturn occurring in more recent weeks. A distinct 'monthly' pattern exists, with absenteeism in each month generally low in weeks one and two, peaking in week three and declining moderately in week four.

Lorenz Curve

A **Lorenz curve** plots the *cumulative frequency distributions* (ogives) of *two numeric random variables* against each other. Its purpose is to show the *degree of inequality* between the values of the two variables.

For example, the Lorenz curve can be used to show the relationship between:
- the value of inventories against the volume of inventories held by an organisation
- the spread of the total salary bill amongst the number of employees in a company
- the concentration of total assets amongst the number of companies in an industry
- the spread of the taxation burden amongst the total number of taxpayers.

A Lorenz curve shows what percentage of one numeric measure (such as inventory value, total salaries, total assets or total taxation) is accounted for by given percentages of the other numeric measure (such as volume of inventory, number of employees, number of companies or number of taxpayers). The degree of concentration or distortion can be clearly illustrated by a Lorenz curve. It is commonly used as a measure of social/economic inequality. It was originally developed by M Lorenz (1905) to represent the distribution of income amongst households.

Follow these steps to construct a Lorenz curve:
- Identify intervals (similar to a histogram) for the y-variable, for which the distribution across a population is being examined (e.g. salaries across employees).
- Calculate the *total value* of the y-variable per interval (total value of salaries paid to all employees earning less than R1 000 per month; total value of salaries paid to all employees earning between R1 001 and R2 000 per month; etc.).
- Calculate the *total number* of objects (e.g. employees, households or taxpayers) that fall within each interval of the y-variable (number of employees earning less than R1 000 per month; number of employees earning between R1 001 and R2 000 per month; etc.).
- Derive the cumulative frequency percentages for each of the two distributions above.
- Scale each axis (x and y) from 0% to 100%.
- For each interval of the y-variable, plot each pair of cumulative frequency percentages on the axes and join the coordinates (similar to a scatter plot).

If the distributions are similar or equal, the Lorenz curve will result in a 45° line from the origin of both axes (called the line of uniformity or the line of equal distribution). The more unequal the two distributions, the more bent (concave or convex) the curve becomes. A Lorenz curve always starts at coordinate (0%; 0%) and ends at coordinate (100%; 100%).

Example 2.8 Savings Balances versus Number of Savers Study

A bank wished to analyse the value of savings account balances against the number of savings accounts of a sample of 64 bank clients.

The two numeric frequency distributions and their respective percentage ogives (for the value of savings balances and number of savings accounts) are given in Table 2.11.

Table 2.11 Percentage cumulative frequency distributions of savings balances across savers

Savings balances (R)	Frequency distributions		Percentage ogives	
	Number of savers	Total savings (R)	Percentage of savers	Percentage of total savings
Below 0	0	0	0	0
0 −< 500	12	4 089	19	4
500 −< 1 000	18	14 022	47	18
1 000 −< 3 000	25	35 750	86	53
3 000 −< 5 000	6	24 600	95	78
5 000 −< 10 000	3	22 542	100	100
Total	64	101 003		

Calculate the Lorenz curve of savings account balances against the number of savings accounts (savers).

Management Question

Are there equal proportions of savers across all levels of saving accounts balances? Comment by inspecting the pattern of the Lorenz curve.

Solution

Figure 2.10 shows the Lorenz plot of the percentage of savers ogive against the percentage of savings balances ogive.

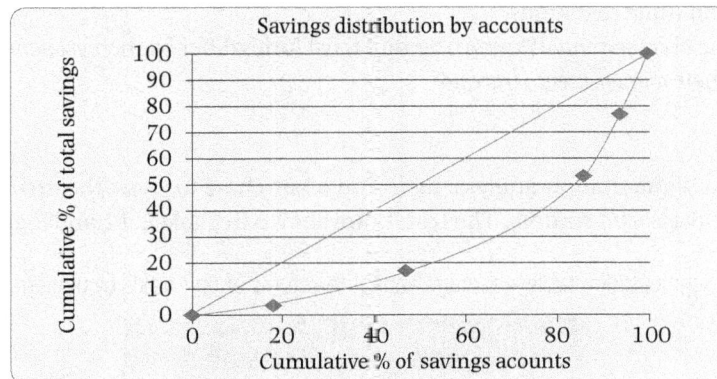

Figure 2.10 Lorenz curve of distribution of savings balances across savers

Management Interpretation

The diagonal (45°) line shows an equal distribution of total savings across all savers (e.g. 60% of savings account clients hold 60% of the total value of savings).

In this example, an unequal distribution is evident. For example, almost half (47%) of all savers hold only 18% of total savings. At the top end of the Lorenz curve, it can be seen that the biggest 5% of savings accounts represent 22% of total savings. Overall, this bank has a large number of small savers, and a few large savers.

A Single Numeric Variable and One (or More) Categorical Variables

Segmentation Analysis – Splitting a Numeric Variable into Categories

In segmentation analysis, the descriptive measure (i.e. mean, standard deviation) of a single numeric variable is split into the categories of one or more categorical variables. Its *purpose* is to *identify a possible relationship* between the numeric variable and the categorical variable(s).

For **example**, the ages of MBA students can be split by the categorical variable *gender* to determine whether the *average age* of male and female MBA students is the same or different.

Segmentation analysis is shown in a *cross-tabulation table* (or a two-way pivot table) where the rows and columns of the table represent the categorical variables and values inside the table show the descriptive statistic (e.g. mean) of the *numeric* variable.

Example 2.9 Unit Trusts – Annual % Return

Seventy-two (72) unit trust funds were surveyed and their *annual % return* for last year was measured. In addition, the *economic focus* (i.e. industrial, financial, property) of each unit trust and its *management strategy* (active management; passive [index-tracking] management) was recorded.
(See Excel file C2.4 – *unit trust returns*.)

Management Questions

1   Does the *management strategy* (active or passive) influence the *average annual % return* on unit trust funds?
2   Does the *average annual % return* on unit trust funds differ by their *economic focus* and/ or by their *management strategy?*

Solution 1

Construct a segmentation analysis table and a **bar chart** to show the *average annual % return* by *management strategy*. The results are shown in Table 2.12 and Figure 2.11.

Table 2.12 Segmentation table – average annual % returns of unit trusts by management strategy

Management strategy	% Return
Active	7.07
Passive	6.61
Total	6.84

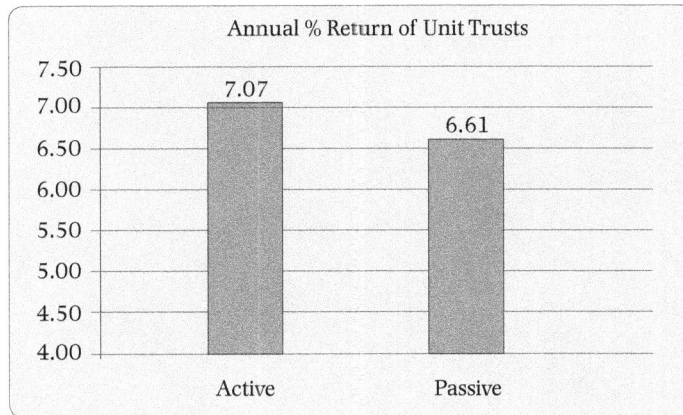

Figure 2.11 Bar chart – annual % return of unit trusts by management strategy

Note: The graph of a segmentation table is either a simple bar chart (if the numeric variable is segmented by only one categorical variables) or a *multiple* (or stacked) *bar chart* (if the numeric variable is split into the different categories of two categorical variables).

Management Interpretation

1 The *overall average annual % return* of the sampled unit trust funds is 6.84%.
2 The *average annual % return* of the actively managed funds is 7.07% p.a. while that of the index-tracking (passive) funds is 6.61% p.a. By inspection, actively managed funds perform marginally better, on average, than index-tracking funds.

Solution 2

Construct a **two-way pivot** (cross-tabulation) table and **multiple bar chart** to show the *average annual % return* by *economic focus* and *management strategy* collectively. The results are shown in Table 2.13 (two-way pivot table) and Figure 2.12 (the multiple bar chart).

Table 2.13 Table of average *annual % return by economic focus and management strategy*

Strategy	Economic focus			
	Industrial	Financial	Property	Total
Active	5.31	8.85	7.05	7.07
Passive	6.83	5.18	7.83	6.61
Total	6.07	7.02	7.44	6.84

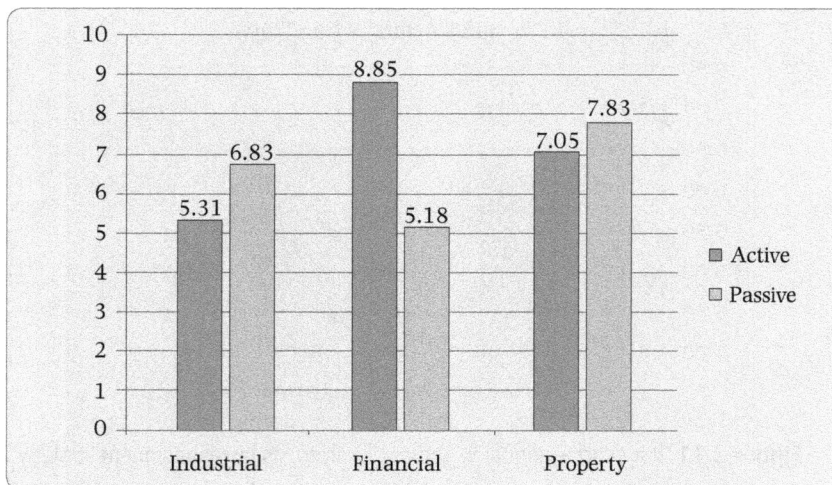

Figure 2.12 Multiple bar chart – % returns by economic focus and strategy

Management Interpretation

By inspection, it appears that the average *annual % returns* of unit trust funds varies significantly across economic sectors and by *management strategy*. Thus there is a likely statistical association (or influence) between the two categorical variables (*economic focus* and *management strategy*) and the numeric response measure (*annual % returns*). The nature of the relationship is as follows:

- The best-performing unit trusts are the actively managed financial funds (8.85% p.a.) while the passively managed financial funds are the worst performing funds (5.18% p.a.).
- The property-focused unit trust funds (7.44% p.a.), regardless of management strategy, outperformed the financial- and industrial-focused funds. The industrial-focused funds underperformed by almost 1.5% p.a. relative to the property-focused funds, on average.
- Actively managed funds have outperform index-tracking funds by almost 0.5% p.a. on average.

Other numeric descriptive statistical measures (such as minimum, maximum, medians, quartiles, standard deviation, sub-sample sizes, etc.) can also be included in a segmentation table to give further insight into any relationship. In **segmentation table analysis**, the '**mean**' of a numeric variable is usually an indication of the '**magnitude**' of a problem, while the '**count**' of a categorical variable is an indication of the '**frequency**' of occurrences.

2.4 The Pareto Curve

A useful application of the bar chart – especially in quality control studies – is called a **Pareto curve**. A Pareto curve is a combination of a *sorted bar chart* and a cumulative categorical frequency table. In a sorted bar chart the categories on the *x*-axis are placed in *decreasing order of frequency* (or importance).

As a tool in quality management, its purpose is to graphically identify and separate the '*critical few*' problems from the '*trivial many*' problems (the 80/20 rule). For example, what are the top three causes of machine failure out of a possible 25 causes – and what percentage of failures do they represent? This allows a manager to focus on the few critical issues and address these issues ahead of the remaining many trivial issues.

Follow these steps to construct a Pareto curve:
- Construct a *categorical frequency table* for the categorical random variable.
- Rearrange the categories in *decreasing order* of frequency counts (or percentages).
- Calculate the *cumulative frequency counts* (or cumulative percentages) starting from the highest frequency category to the lowest frequency category.
- Plot both the *bar chart* (using the left *y*-axis for the frequency counts or percentages) and the *percentage cumulative frequency polygon* (using the right *y*-axis) on the same *x–y* axes.

Example 2.10 Customer Complaints Study

A customer service manager has analysed 300 customer complaints received over the past year into eight categories, as shown in the categorical frequency table in Table 2.14. (See Excel file C2.3 – *customer complaints*.)

Table 2.14 Categorical frequency table of customer complaints

Code	Description	Count
1	Poor product knowledge	26
2	Product options limited	47
3	Internet site frequently down	12
4	Slow response times	66
5	Unfriendly staff	15
6	Non-reply to queries	22
7	Cost of service is excessive	82
8	Payment options limited	30
Total		**300**

Use the table to construct a Pareto curve.

Management Questions

1. From the Pareto curve, identify the top three customer complaints.
2. What percentage of all complaints received do these top three complaints represent?
3. What is the least important complaint and what percentage of customers complained about this issue?

Solution

The categorical variable is 'customer complaints', which is grouped into eight categories. Table 2.15 shows the summary table for the calculation of the Pareto curve where the categories have been sorted by frequency count.

Table 2.15 Pareto curve – cumulative % table of sorted customer complaints

Code	Description	Count	Cumulative count	Cumulative percent
7	Cost of service is excessive	82	82	27%
4	Slow response times	66	148	49%
2	Product options limited	47	195	65%
8	Payment options limited	30	225	75%
1	Poor product knowledge	26	251	84%
6	Non-reply to queries	22	273	91%
5	Unfriendly staff	15	288	96%
3	Internet site frequently down	12	300	100%
	Total	300		

Figure 2.13 shows the sorted bar chart of customer complaints with frequency counts on the left y-axis and cumulative frequency percentages on the right y-axis.

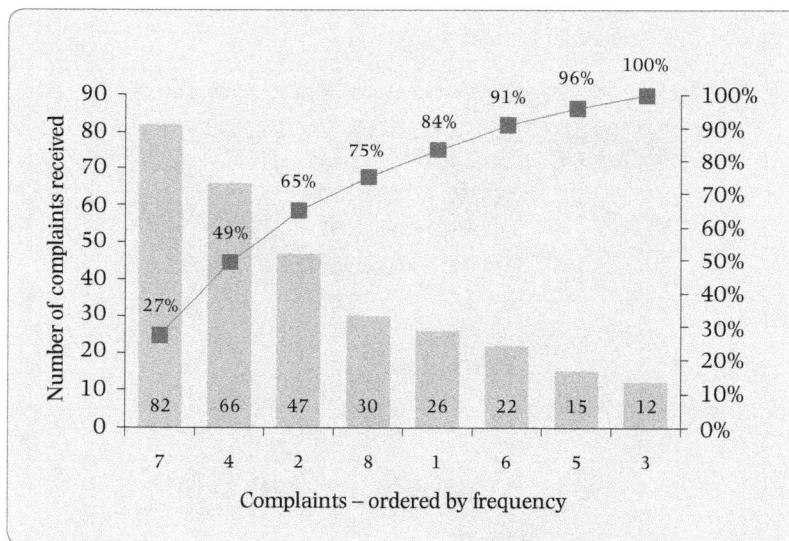

Figure 2.13 Pareto curve – customer complaints study

Management Interpretation

1   The top three customer complaints are 7: Cost of service is excessive, 4: Slow response times, and 2: Product options limited (identified by the left three bars.)
2   These top three complaints represent 65% of all complaints received over the past year (read off the cumulative percentage curve on the right y-axis).
3   The least important complaint is 3: Internet site frequently down, representing only 4% of all complaints received over the past year.

2.5 Using **Excel** (2016) and X-Static for Summary Tables and Charts

Pivot Tables

The **PivotTable** option within the **Insert** tab can be used to construct both *categorical frequency tables* (called a one-way pivot table in Excel) and *cross-tabulation tables* (called a two-way pivot table in Excel). The **Chart** option is used to display these tables graphically.

Follow these steps to create a one-way pivot table (in Excel 2016):
- Highlight the data range of the categorical variable(s) to be summarised.
- From the menu bar in Excel, select **Insert**, then select the **PivotTable** icon.
- In the **Create PivotTable** input screen, check that the correct data range is selected.
- From the **PivotTable Field List** box, drag the categorical variable to the **Row Labels** box (or the **Column Labels** box) and then again drag it to the **Σ Values** box. The one-way pivot table is constructed as the variable is dragged to each box in turn.
- Check that the **Σ Values** box displays **Count of <variable name>**. If not, click the down arrow in the **Σ Values** box and select **Count** from the **Value Field Settings** dialog box.

Figure 2.14 shows the construction of the categorical frequency table (one-way pivot table) for the store 'preference variable' using the **PivotTable Field List** dialog box.

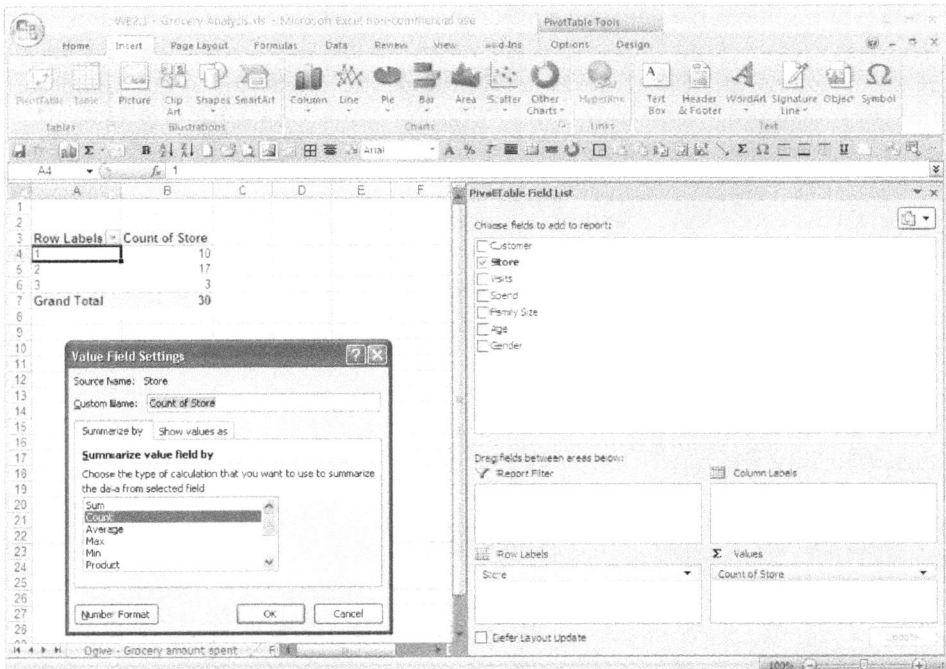

Figure 2.14 PivotTable Field List dialog box – construction of store preference frequency table

To construct a cross-tabulation table (or two-way pivot table), follow the same steps as for a one-way pivot table, but drag one of the categorical variables to the **Row Labels** box and the other categorical variable to the **Column Labels** box. Then drag either of these two variables to the **Σ Values** box, and again check that the **Count** operation is displayed.

To illustrate, to construct a cross-tabulation table between store preference and gender, drag the 'store preference' variable to the **Row Labels** box, the 'gender' variable to the **Column Labels** box and the 'gender' variable again to the **Σ Values** box, ensuring the **count** operation is shown in this box. This will produce a cross-tabulation table identical to Table 2.3 with 'store preference' as the row variable and 'gender' as the column variable.

Bar Charts and Pie Charts

To construct a chart from a pivot table (pie chart, column bar chart, stacked bar chart or multiple bar chart), place the cursor in the pivot table area and select the **Insert** tab and the **Chart** option from the menu bar. Then select the chart type (**Column, Pie** or **Bar**) to display the pivot table graphically. The charts that are produced are the same as those shown in Figure 2.1 (**Column Bar Chart**), Figure 2.2 (**Pie Chart**), Figure 2.3 (**Stacked Column Bar Chart**) and Figure 2.4 (**Clustered Column Bar Chart**).

Scatter Plots and Line Graphs

For numeric data, the scatter plot and the trendline graphs can be generated by highlighting the data range of the numeric variables to be displayed and selecting the **Chart** option within the **Insert** tab in the menu bar. The **Scatter** chart type will produce the scatter plot for two numeric variables (see Figure 2.8), while the Excel function **CORREL (array 1, array 2)** will compute the correlation coefficient between two numeric variables. To display a trendline graph for a time series set of data (see Figure 2.9), select the **Line** chart type option.

The Lorenz curve can be constructed using the **Scatter** chart type and selecting the option **Scatter with Smooth Lines and Markers**. The input data would comprise the cumulative percentage ogives for the two numeric random variables being compared.

The Data Analysis Add-In

Excel offers a data analysis add-in that extends the range of statistical analyses that can be performed to include more advanced statistical techniques. To add this module, follow this sequence in Excel (2016): click the **Office** button, select **Excel Options** and then **Add-Ins**. At the **Manage** option, select **Excel Add-ins > Go** and, in the **Add-Ins** dialog box, tick **Analysis ToolPak** and click **OK**.

To use any of the statistical tools within the data analysis add-in, select the **Data** tab and then the **Data Analysis** option in the **Analysis** section of the menu bar.

Figure 2.15 and Figure 2.16 show all 19 statistical techniques available in **Data Analysis**.

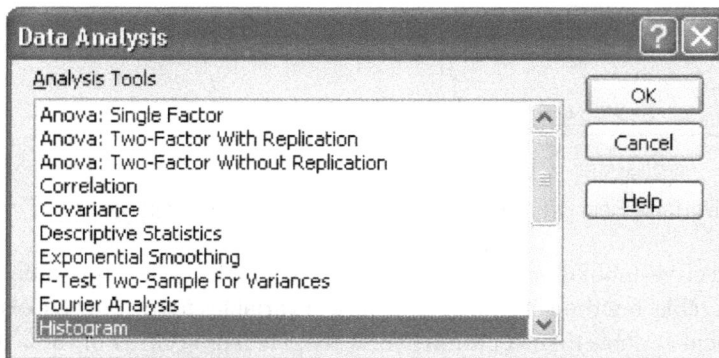

Figure 2.15 Excel's **Data Analysis** dialog box (first 10 techniques)

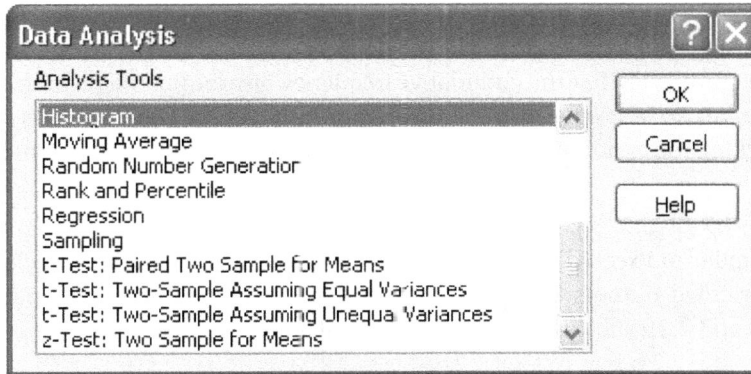

Figure 2.16 Excel's **Data Analysis** dialog box (remaining nine techniques)

Numeric Frequency Distribution and Histogram

The **Histogram** option within **Data Analysis** is used to create numeric frequency distributions, histograms, ogives (both count and percentages) and the Pareto curve.

To apply the histogram option, first create a data range consisting of a label heading and the upper limits of each interval in column format. Excel calls this data range of interval upper limits a **Bin Range**. In Example 2.3 (shoppers' age profile), the bin range was defined by the upper limits of 29, 39, 49, 59 and 69 years. Then complete the data input preparation dialog box for the histogram, shown in Figure 2.17.

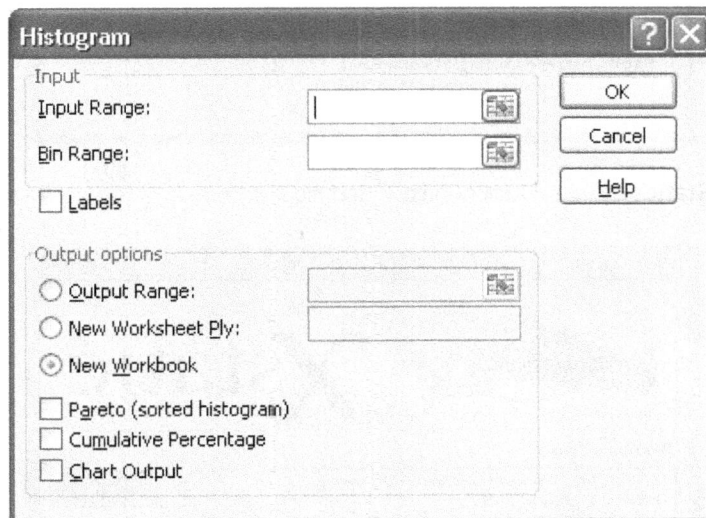

Figure 2.17 Histogram data input preparation dialog box

To produce a numeric frequency distribution and histogram, complete the following inputs:

- The **Input Range** defines the dataset (include the variable name).
- The **Bin Range** defines the data range of the inclusive upper limits of each interval.
- Tick the **Labels** box (to indicate that the variable names have been included in each of the **Input Range** and **Bin Range**).
- Tick the **Chart Output** box to display the histogram in the output.

59

The output is similar to that shown in Table 2.6 (numeric frequency distribution) and Figure 2.5 (histogram) for the age profile of shoppers.

Note in Figure 2.17 that the cumulative frequency distribution (percentage ogive) and the Pareto curve can be produced in the **Histogram** option of the **Data Analysis** add-in. This is done by ticking the option **Pareto (sorted histogram)** and **Cumulative Percentage**.

Using X-Static

X-Static is similar to Excel's Data Analysis add-in, but provides additional techniques and more user-oriented outputs with visual graphics to assist management interpretation. Figures 2.18 and 2.19 show the range of analytical tools available.

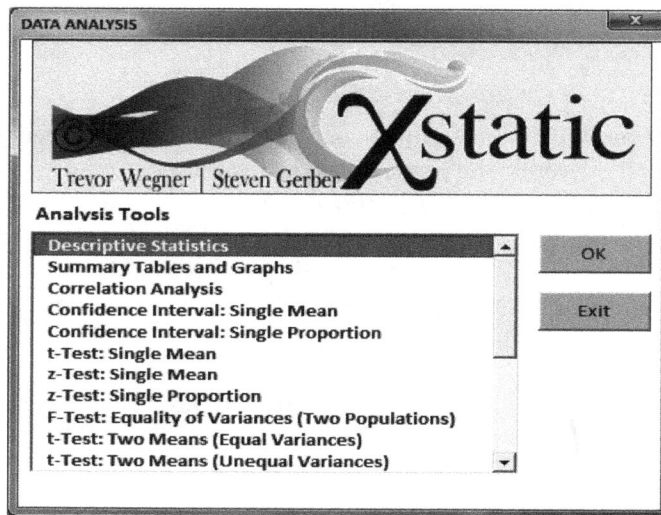

Figure 2.18 X-Static's Analytical Toolbox (first 11 techniques)

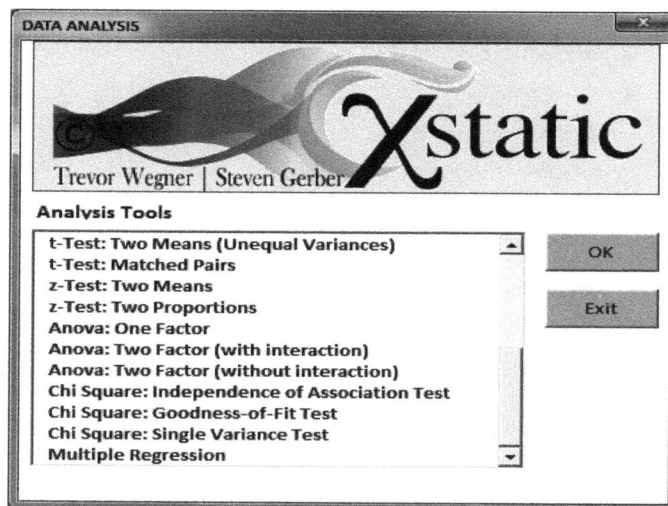

Figure 2.19 X-Static's Analytical Toolbox (remaining 10 techniques)

The **Summary Tables and Graphs** option in **X-Static** generates frequency distributions and cumulative frequency distributions as well as the graphic displays of histograms, ogives and box plots.

Note: When constructing a histogram using Excel's **Data Analysis** add-in, the **Bin Range** upper limits are *inclusive* (e.g. ≤40) meaning that data values that equal the upper limits are included in that interval. In **X-Static**, on the other hand, the upper limits are *exclusive* (e.g. <40) meaning that data values at these limits actually fall into the next interval.

2.6 Summary

This chapter identified a number of approaches to summarise statistical data and present the results graphically for easier interpretation by managers.

- The *categorical frequency table* summarises and profiles a single categorical random variable. When two categorical variables are examined simultaneously for a possible association, a *cross-tabulation table* summarises their joint frequencies.
- *Charts*, such as the pie chart, the simple bar chart, the stacked (or component) bar chart and the multiple (clustered) bar chart, are all used to pictorially display *categorical* data from *qualitative* random variables. The Pareto curve was introduced as a sorted bar chart to highlight the role of bar charts, mainly in the field of quality management.
- *Numeric* random variables are summarised into numeric frequency distributions, which are most often displayed graphically in the form of a histogram.
- *Ogives*, which are graphs of cumulative frequency distributions, are useful to address *more than* or *less than* management questions.
- Other graphical forms are the *line graph* (which is used to display time series data), the *Lorenz curve* (used to explore inequality issues) and the *box plot* (to be covered in Chapter 3).
- When the relationship between *two numeric random variables* is being explored, a *scatter plot* is appropriate to examine the nature of the numeric relationship.
- The relationship between a numeric variable and one or more categorical variables is explored through the use of pivot tables. In a pivot table, the descriptive measures of a numeric variable (e.g. its mean, its standard deviation) are split into sub-categories to identify possible differences (influences) due to the categorical variable(s).

This chapter also introduced Excel (2016) and **X-Static** to create summary tables (pivot tables and frequency distributions) and display them graphically using the various chart options. In conclusion, graphical representations should always be considered when statistical findings are to be presented to management. A graphical representation promotes more rapid assimilation of the information to be conveyed than written reports and tables.

Exercises

All computational exercises can be performed either manually or by using Excel.

1   Complete the sentence: 'A picture is worth a ....'.

2   What is the name given to the *chart* that displays:
    (a)   the summarised data of a single categorical variable?
    (b)   the summarised data of two categorical variables simultaneously?
    (c)   the summarised data of a single numeric variable?
    (d)   the relationship between two numeric variables?

3   What is the name given to the *table* that summarises the data of two categorical variables?

4   Explain at least three differences between a bar chart and a histogram.

5   What is the name of the chart that is used to display time series data?

6   X2.6 – magazines
    (a)   Construct a pie chart showing the percentage of 500 young female readers surveyed who most prefer each of the following magazines:

Magazine	Count
True Love	95
Seventeen	146
Heat	118
Drum	55
You	86

    (b)   Interpret the findings of the pie chart.

7   (a)   Construct a percentage bar chart from the frequency table given in question 6.
    (b)   What percentage of young female readers surveyed most prefer *Heat*?

8   X2.8 – job grades
    The job grades (A, B, C or D) of 40 clerical employees are as follows:

B	A	A	D	B	D	B	A	D	C
D	A	B	B	C	A	D	C	A	B
B	A	B	C	A	A	C	B	D	D
A	A	B	B	A	D	A	C	A	D

    (a)   Construct a categorical frequency table of these job grades.
    (b)   Show the frequency table in percentage terms.
    (c)   What percentage of employees are in job grade D?
    (d)   Show the percentage frequency table as a pie chart and as a bar chart.

9   X2.9 – office rentals
    The monthly rental per square metre for office space in 30 buildings in Durban central (in rand) are shown in the following table.

		Rental (R)			
189	156	250	265	376	300
350	315	290	285	225	242
324	280	212	310	395	360
285	225	230	255	185	193
325	248	340	250	285	300

(a) Construct a numerical frequency distribution of office rentals by using the classes: $150-\leq 200$; $201-\leq 250$; $251-\leq 300$; $301-\leq 350$; $351-\leq 400$.

(b) Compute the percentage frequencies and cumulative percentage frequencies for office rentals.

(c) From the frequency distribution, answer the following questions:

 (i) What percentage of office space costs less than or equal to $R200/m^2$?

 (ii) What percentage of office space costs at most $R300/m^2$?

 (iii) What percentage of office space costs more than $R350/m^2$?

 (iv) If a legal company that is looking to rent office space is prepared to pay between $R300/m^2$ and $R400/m^2$, how many buildings can they consider?

10 X2.10 – storage dams

The capacities (in millions of litres) of each of the four major storage dams that supply the water requirements of Cape Town are shown in the table below.

Storage dam	Capacity (Mℓ)
Wemmershoek	158 644
Steenbras	95 284
Voëlvlei	244 122
Theewaterskloof	440 255

(a) Construct a pie chart showing the percentage of water supplied by each storage dam. (Use Excel's **Pie** option in the Insert > Chart tab.)

(b) What percentage of Cape Town's water supply is provided by:

 (i) the Voëlvlei dam?

 (ii) Wemmershoek and Steenbras dams together?

11 X2.11 – taste test

A sample of 250 regular fruit juice drinkers were given a blind taste test of five different fruit juice brands labelled A, B, C, D and E. Each person was asked to indicate which fruit juice (by the alphabetic label) they most preferred. The results are given below.

Blind label	Brand	Number
A	Liqui-Fruit	45
B	Fruiti Drink	26
C	Yum Yum	64
D	Fruit Quencher	38
E	Go Fruit	77

(a)   Construct a percentage frequency table and then show the results graphically both as a percentage bar chart and as a percentage pie chart. (Use Excel's **Pie** and **Column (Bar)** chart options in the **Insert > Chart** tab).

(b)   What percentage of the sample prefer Liqui-Fruit?

(c)   What percentage of the sample prefer either Yum Yum or Go Fruit?

12   X2.12 – annual car sales

The following table shows the number of passenger cars sold by each manufacturer last year.

Manufacturer	Annual sales
Toyota	96 959
Nissan	63 172
Volkswagen	88 028
Delta	62 796
Ford	74 155
MBSA	37 268
BMW	51 724
MMI	25 354

For (a) and (b), use Excel's **Column (Bar)** and **Pie** chart options in the **Insert > Chart** tab.

(a)   Construct a bar chart to show the number of passenger cars sold by each manufacturer.

(b)   Construct a percentage pie chart to show the market share of the passenger car market held by each of the car manufacturers last year.

(c)   What percentage of the total passenger car market is held by the top three car manufacturers?

13   X2.13 – half-yearly car sales

The following table shows the number of passenger cars sold by each manufacturer in each half-year (first and second half) of last year.

Manufacturer	First half	Second half	Annual sales
Toyota	42 661	54 298	96 959
Nissan	35 376	27 796	63 172
Volkswagen	45 774	42 254	88 028
Delta	26 751	36 045	62 796
Ford	32 628	41 527	74 155
MBSA	19 975	17 293	37 268
BMW	24 206	27518	51 724
MMI	14 307	11 047	25 354

(a)   Construct a multiple bar chart showing the number of new car sales by manufacturer between the first and the second half of last year. (Use Excel's **Column (Bar)** chart option in the **Insert > Chart** tab.)

(b)   By inspection of the multiple bar chart, identify which car manufacturers performed better in terms of new car sales in the first half of the year compared to the second half of the year.

(c) Also by inspection of the multiple bar chart, identify which car manufacturer showed the largest percentage change (up or down) in sales from the first half to the second half of the year.

14 X2.14 – television brands

A survey of a random sample of 125 households recorded the brand of televisions owned.

(a) Construct a categorical percentage frequency table of TV brands owned. (Use Excel's **PivotTable** option in the **Insert > Table** tab.)

(b) Show the findings from (a) graphically as a percentage bar chart.

(c) Which brand of TV is least popular amongst households?

(d) What percentage of households own the most popular TV brand?

15 X2.15 – estate agents

The Estate Agency Affairs Board analysed the number of residential properties sold by each estate agent in the second half of last year in East London. A random sample of 48 estate agents was selected and the number of houses each sold during this period was recorded. The data is as follows:

5	4	8	4	6	8	8	3	5	6	4	4
7	4	5	4	4	3	3	7	5	3	7	3
6	3	5	3	5	4	4	7	6	3	3	4
3	4	6	4	7	4	3	6	3	4	4	6

(a) Construct a frequency count table to show the sales performance of the sample of East London estate agents.
Note: Since the numeric data is discrete and in a limited data range, it is possible to use Excel's **PivotTable** option in the **Insert > Table** tab.

(b) Construct a histogram of the frequency count distribution.

(c) What is the most frequent number of residential properties sold by an estate agent in the second half of last year in East London?

(d) Repeat (a) and (b) using the Excel's **Histogram** option in **Data Analysis (Data > Data Analysis > Histogram)**. Set a bin range to each discrete value of 3; 4; 5; 6; 7 and 8.

16 X2.16 – fast foods

Keen competition exists amongst fast-food outlets for the food spend of consumers. A recent survey established consumers' preferences for various fast-food outlets and type of fast foods (chicken, pizzas, beef burgers and fish).

Fast food outlet	Count
KFC (chicken)	56
St Elmo's (pizza)	58
Steers (beef burgers)	45
Nandos (chicken)	64
Ocean Basket (fish)	24
Butler's (pizza)	78

For (a) and (b), use Excel's **Column (Bar)** and **Pie chart** options in the **Insert > Chart** tab.

(a) Construct a percentage bar chart to show customers' preferences for different fast-food outlets.

(b) Construct a pie chart to show the percentage of customers who prefer each food type (i.e. chicken, pizza, beef burger and fish).

(c) Write a short summary on the findings of (a) and (b).

17 X2.17 - airlines

A travel agency surveyed 70 passengers to identify which airline (SAA, kulula.com or Comair) they prefer to use for domestic travel. The passenger's type of travel, namely business or tourist, was also recorded.

(a) Construct a cross-tabulation (two-way pivot) table between the choice of airline and type of travel. (Use Excel's **PivotTable** option in the **Insert > Table** tab.)

(b) Show the pivot table as a percentage of each passenger type per airline.

(c) Display the percentage cross-tabulation (two-way pivot) table as a multiple bar chart.

(d) What percentage of passengers prefer to fly with SAA?

(e) Which airline is most preferred by tourists?

(f) Can it be stated that most business travellers prefer to fly with kulula.com?

18 X2.18 – car occupants

A traffic survey was conducted in central Cape Town recently to establish the number of occupants per car commuting into the CBD between 8.00 a.m. and 9.00 a.m. daily from the northern suburbs. Sixty cars were randomly selected at an entry point into the CBD and the number of occupants was noted. The following data was recorded:

1	1	1	5	3	2	1	2	1	1	2	2
3	2	2	5	3	1	3	2	5	2	1	3
2	4	3	2	3	5	1	1	4	1	2	2
1	4	1	1	1	1	2	4	3	1	1	2
5	1	1	1	3	1	2	3	5	4	1	5

(a) Define the random variable and the data type.

(b) Use Excel's **Data > Data Analysis > Histogram** option to prepare:

(i) a numeric percentage frequency distribution (*Hint*: Use the discrete values as bins.)

(ii) a histogram of occupants per car

(iii) a less-than cumulative frequency distribution and ogive of car occupants.

(c) From the results, determine:

(i) what percentage of motorists travel alone

(ii) what percentage of vehicles have at least three occupants

(iii) what percentage of vehicles have no more than two occupants.

19 X2.19 – courier trips

The distance travelled (in km) by a courier service motorcycle on 50 trips was recorded by the driver.

24	30	20	6	28	23	17	16	21	20
18	19	22	26	31	21	13	15	20	9
18	20	34	29	24	23	25	17	35	29
19	10	17	11	14	·15	27	18	8	22
13	28	26	18	16	27	22	25	14	24

(a) Define the random variable and the data type.
(b) Use Excel's **Data > Data Analysis > Histogram** option to prepare:
   (i) a numeric frequency distribution (use bin ranges: 10, 15, 20, 25, 30 and 35)
   (ii) a percentage frequency distribution
   (iii) a histogram of the distances travelled by the courier per trip.
(c) From the results, determine:
   (i) the percentage of deliveries that were between 25 km and 30 km
   (ii) the percentage of deliveries within a 25 km radius
   (iii) the percentage of deliveries beyond a 20 km radius
   (iv) below which distance 52% of the deliveries were made
   (v) above which distance the longest 24% of the deliveries were made.
(d) If the company has a policy that no more than 10% of all deliveries should be more than 30 km from their depot, are they adhering to this policy? Justify your answer.

20 X2.20 – fuel bills

The monthly expenditures (in rand) on fuel by 50 randomly sampled motorists in Tshwane are given below.

289	312	400	368	514	415	550	348	774	528
450	330	278	394	662	380	295	560	360	736
515	365	460	433	602	425	265	450	545	414
385	485	293	646	448	350	495	792	456	385
256	680	696	486	356	390	285	400	408	544

(a) Define the random variable and the data type.
(b) Use Excel's **Data > Data Analysis > Histogram** option to prepare:
   (i) a numeric frequency distribution with bin ranges 300, 400, 500, 600, 700 and 800
   (ii) a percentage frequency distribution
   (iii) a histogram of monthly fuel bills.
(c) What percentage of Tshwane motorists spend between R 500 and R 600 (inclusive) per month on fuel?
(d) Construct the less-than cumulative percentage distribution for fuel bills and show it graphically as an ogive.
(e) From the cumulative graph, approximate the percentage of Tshwane motorists that spend less than R 550 on fuel per month.
(f) From the graph, find the percentage of Tshwane motorists that spend more than R 500 on fuel per month.

21 X2.21 – car sales

The sales records of an Opel car dealer in Durban show the quarterly sales of the Opel Corsa light passenger vehicle for the past six years. Refer to the Excel file X2.21.

(a) Use Excel's **Line** chart option in the **Insert > Chart** tab to construct a line graph showing the pattern of quarterly sales of the Corsa vehicle by the dealer.
(b) If you were the dealer, would you renew your dealership of the Opel Corsa range next year based on past sales performance? Comment.

22   X2.22 – market shares

The following table shows the market shares for each of two makes of motor vehicles for the past 10 years.

Year	Volkswagen	Toyota
1	13.4	9.9
2	11.6	9.6
3	9.8	11.2
4	14.4	12.0
5	17.4	11.6
6	18.8	13.1
7	21.3	11.7
8	19.4	14.2
9	19.6	16.0
10	19.2	16.9

(a)   Produce a trendline graph showing the trend in market share (%) for Volkswagen and Toyota motor vehicle sales over the past ten years. (Use Excel's **Line** chart option in the **Insert > Chart** tab.)

(b)   Describe the trend in market shares for each car manufacturer over the past 10 years.

(c)   If you were to be offered a five-year dealership of one of these motor vehicle makes, which one would you choose? Why?

23   X2.23 – defects

The production manager of a crockery (cups, saucers, plates and bowls) manufacturer recorded the inspection time (in minutes) by the quality controller on each of 30 consignments consisting of 500 items each, and noted the number of defective items found in each consignment. Refer to the Excel file X2.23.

(a)   Produce a scatter plot for the inspection time (x) and the number of defects found (y). (Use Excel's **Scatter plot** (with only markers) option in the **Insert > Chart** tab.)

(b)   By inspection of the scatter plot, does there appear to be a relationship between the amount of time spent on inspection of a consignment and the number of defective items founds in the batch? Briefly explain your answer.

24   X2.24 – leverage

A financial analyst surveyed 30 JSE-listed companies and recorded the leverage ratio (percentage of capital financed by debt) and their percentage growth in net profits over the past year. The analyst wants to know if leverage influences profit growth. Refer to the Excel file X2.24.

(a)   Produce a scatter plot between the leverage ratio (x) and the profit growth (y) of the JSE-listed companies. (Use the **Scatter plot** [with only markers] option in the **Insert > Chart** tab. Also set the minimum scale on the x-axis to 30.)

(b)   Can the analyst conclude that the degree of leverage influences a company's growth in net profits (as a percentage)? In what way? Explain briefly.

For the following exercises, use Excel's **PivotTable** option to perform the analysis.

25   X2.25 – ROI%

An investment analyst studies the ROI% of listed companies to structure investment portfolios for clients. She is considering an investment portfolio comprising *mining* and *service sector* companies. The ROI% of a random sample of listed companies from each sector is recorded (and shown in the Excel file).

    (a)   Construct a one-way breakdown table of sample means and standard deviations per sector.

    (b)   Interpret and compare the profile of ROI% across the two sectors. Which sector, if any, produces higher average ROI%? Also which sector, if any, has greater *volatility* in ROI%? Do any of the observed sample differences appear to be statistically significant or due purely to sampling error? Comment.

26   X2.26 – product location

A supermarket retailer wants to determine whether product location within a store has any effect on the sale of a mineral water product. Both the aisle location (front-of-store, middle-of-store, back-of-store) and shelf location (top shelf, middle shelf) were considered. A random sample of 30 stores of equal sales potential for this product were selected with each of five stores randomly assigned to one of the six combinations of aisle location and shelf location. Refer to the Excel dataset for the *sales volumes* recorded (in thousands of rand) of the product in each store over the trial period of eight weeks.

    (a)   Construct a two-way breakdown table of sample means and standard deviations per combination of aisle location and shelf location.

    (b)   Interpret and compare the profile of *sales volumes* across the different combinations. Consider whether mean *sales volumes* differ significantly depending on aisle location? Shelf location? Or a combination of aisle location and shelf combination. Is the *variation* in *sales volumes* consistent across the different location combinations?

        Do any of the observed sample differences appear to be statistically significant or due purely to sampling error? Comment.

    (c)   What recommendation would you make to the supermarket retailer to display the mineral water product to achieve maximum *sales volumes*?

27   X2.27 – property portfolio

A property investment company that derives its revenue from the rental of properties it owns conducts an *annual financial performance review* of its property portfolio. For each of the 324 properties in the portfolio, the annual *net profit %* based on rental income minus operating expenses (maintenance, rates, utilities, etc.) is determined. Each property is also classified by: type of *business usage* ((1) commercial [i.e. offices], (2) industrial or (3) retail) and its *regional location* ((1) region A and (2) region B). Refer to the Excel file for the sample data set.

At the review committee meeting next week, the management have asked you to present a summary report that *profiles the financial performance* of properties in the portfolio. The report should focus on three areas in particular:

- *under-performing properties*:
  Company policy is to dispose of (i.e. sell off) under-performing properties. An under-performing property is defined as one that has a *net profit* % p.a. of 5% or less;
- the identification of property segments of high volatility *in returns* in the portfolio; and
- the identification of *potential growth segments* within the portfolio (for possible future acquisition by the company based on higher average returns with relatively low volatility of returns).

Conduct the following statistical analyses based on the sample data:

(a) For the *net profit* % variable, construct a numerical frequency distribution, a cumulative % frequency distribution, and a histogram.
(Use interval widths of 2.5% starting at a lower limit of −5%.)

(b) Construct a cross-tabulation table (two-way pivot table) of the *count* of properties classified by *regional location* and type of *business usage*. Also, for each *regional location*, show the percentage of properties by type of *business usage*.

(c) Construct a two-way breakdown table of *net profit* % p.a. by *business usage* and *regional location* (showing the *average, standard deviation, minimum* and *maximum net profit* %) of properties within each segment.

Answer the following questions:

(d) Describe the *profile of properties* in the company's property portfolio.

(e) Describe the performance of the company's property portfolio by examining the profile of *net profit* % across the different segments. In particular, focus on the *three areas of interest* for the review meeting.

(f) Propose suitable courses of action for management in order to maximise the financial performance of their property portfolio in the short-to-medium term.

Describing Data: Numeric Descriptive Statistics

Outcomes

Summary tables (pivot tables) and graphs provide a broad overview of the profile of random variables. However, more specific numeric measures are required. These are provided by a set of numeric measures called *descriptive statistics*. These statistics identify the *location*, *spread* and *shape* of the data. In this chapter they will be explained and the conditions under which each would be appropriate to describe sample data will also be reviewed.

After studying this chapter, you should be able to:

- describe the various central and non-central location measures
- calculate and interpret each of these location measures
- describe the appropriate central location measure for different data types
- describe the various measures of spread (or dispersion)
- calculate and interpret each measure of dispersion
- describe the concept of skewness
- calculate and interpret the coefficient of skewness
- explain how to identify and treat outliers
- calculate the five-number summary table and construct its box plot
- explain how outliers influence the choice of valid descriptive statistical measures
- use Excel and X-Static to produce numeric descriptive statistics.

3.1 Introduction

Summary tables and graphs, as seen in Chapter 2, are useful to communicate *broad overviews* of the profiles of random variables. However, managers also need specific *numerical measures* (called statistics) to convey more precise information about the behaviour of random variables. This is the purpose of numeric descriptive statistics.

Three characteristics are commonly used to describe the data profile of a random variable. These are:

1   measures of location (both central and non-central)
2   measures of spread (or dispersion)
3   a measure of shape (skewness).

Location refers to where the data values are *concentrated*. Central location is a representative 'middle' value of concentration of the data, while non-central location measures identify relevant 'off-centre' reference points in the data set (such as quartiles). **Dispersion** refers to the extent to which the data values are *spread* about the central location value. Finally, **skewness** identifies the shape (or degree of *symmetry*) of the data values about the central location measure.

To illustrate, an electronic goods company has recorded the daily sales (in rand) over a 12-month trading period. The average daily sales is a measure of central location, while the extent to which daily sales vary around the average daily sales would be a measure of dispersion. Finally, a measure of skewness would identify whether any very large or very small daily sales values relative to the average daily sales have occurred over this period.

3.2 Central Location Measures

A **central location statistic** is a single number that gives a sense of the 'centrality' of data values in a sample.

Managers and management reports often make statements containing phrases such as:

● the average salary per job grade
● the most popular healthcare plan
● the average quantity of milk purchased by a household of four persons
● half of our employees spend less than R178 per month commuting to work
● the mean age of our employees.

These statements all refer to a *typical* or *central data value* used to represent where the majority of data values lie. They are called central location statistics.

Three commonly used central location statistics are:

1   the arithmetic mean (also called the average)
2   the median (also called the second quartile, the middle quartile or the 50th percentile)
3   the mode (or modal value).

All three measures (mean, median and mode) can be used for numeric data, while only the mode is valid for categorical data.

Arithmetic Mean (Average)

The **arithmetic mean** (or average), $\bar{x}$, lies at the *centre* of a set of numeric data values.

It is found by adding up all the data values and then dividing the total by the sample size as shown in the following formula:

$$\bar{x} = \frac{\text{Sum of all the observations}}{\text{Number of observations}} = \frac{\Sigma x_i}{n} \qquad \qquad 3.1$$

Where: $\bar{x}$ = the sample arithmetic mean (average)
n = the number of data values in the sample
x_i = the value of the ith data value of random variable x
Σx_i = the sum of the n data values, i.e. $x_1 + x_2 + x_3 + x_4 + ... + x_n$

Example 3.1 Financial Advisors' Training Study

The number of seminar training days attended last year by 20 financial advisors is shown in Table 3.1. What is the average number of training days attended by these financial advisors?
(See Excel file C3.1 – *financial training*.)

Table 3.1 Financial advisors' training days ($n = 20$)

16	20	13	19	24	22	18	18	15	20
21	21	18	20	18	20	15	20	18	20

Solution

To find the average, sum the number of days for all 20 financial advisors ($\Sigma x_i = 376$) and divide this total by the number of financial advisors ($n = 20$).

$$\bar{x} = \frac{376}{20} = 18.8 \text{ days}$$

On average, each financial advisor attended 18.8 days of seminar training last year.

Arithmetic Mean for Grouped Numeric Data

When numeric data is grouped into intervals and shown in a numeric frequency distribution, the arithmetic mean can be approximated as follows:
- find the midpoint of each interval to represent all the x values in each interval (x_i) (i.e. sum the upper and lower limit values of each interval and divide the sum by 2).
- multiply each interval's midpoint x_i value by the frequency count f_i for each interval (i.e. $x_i f_i$). Each product represents the approximate sum of the x-values in each interval.
- Sum the $x_i f_i$ values over all intervals (i.e. $\Sigma x_i f_i$). This approximates the total sum of all the data values in the sample data set.
- Finally, divide the total sum (i.e. $\Sigma x_i f_i$) by the sample size, n. This gives an approximate arithmetic mean for grouped data.

$$\bar{x} \text{ (for grouped data)} = \frac{\Sigma x_i f_i}{n} \qquad \qquad 3.2$$

Example 3.2 Delivery Truck Fuel Consumption Study

The fuel consumption of 20 delivery trucks (measured in kilometres travelled per litre of fuel) is summarised in Table 3.2.
(See Excel file C3.2 – *fuel consumption*.)

Table 3.2 Delivery trucks' fuel consumption (in km/litre) ($n = 20$ trucks)

Interval	Midpoint x_i	Frequency f_i	$x_i f_i$
6–< 9	7.5	4	30
9–< 12	10.5	9	94.5
12–< 15	13.5	5	67.5
15–< 18	16.5	2	33
		$n = 20$	225

$$\bar{x} = \frac{225}{20} = 11.25 \text{ km/litre}$$

Note: The formula for the arithmetic mean for grouped data is the same as the formula used to compute a weighted arithmetic mean (see the section on *Other Measures of Central Location*).

The arithmetic mean has the following two *advantages*:
1   It uses all the data values in its calculation.
2   It is an unbiased statistic (meaning that, on average, it represents the true mean).

These two properties make it the most widely used measure of central location.

The arithmetic mean, however, has two *drawbacks*:
1   It is not appropriate for categorical (i.e. nominal or ordinal-scaled) data.
    For example, it is not meaningful to refer to the 'average' colour of cars or 'average' preferred brand or 'average' gender. The arithmetic mean can only be applied to numeric (i.e. interval and ratio-scaled) data.
2   It is distorted by **outliers**. An outlier is an extreme value in a data set.
    For example, the mean of 3, 4, 6 and 7 is 5. However, the mean of 3, 4, 6 and 39 is 13, which is not representative of the majority of the data values.

These two drawbacks require that other measures of central location be considered. Two alternative central location measures are the median and the mode.

Median

The **median** (M$_e$) is the *middle number* of an ordered set of data. It divides an ordered set of data values into two equal halves (i.e. 50% of the data values lie below the median and 50% lie above it).

Follow these steps to calculate the median for ungrouped (raw) numeric data:
- Arrange the *n* data values in ascending order.
- Find the median by first identifying the middle position in the data set as follows:
  - If *n* is odd, the median value lies in the $\left(\frac{n+1}{2}\right)^{th}$ position in the data set.
  - If *n* is even, the median value is found by identifying the $\left(\frac{n}{2}\right)^{th}$ position and then averaging the data value in this position with the next consecutive data value.

Example 3.3(a) Monthly Car Sales (*n* = 9 months)

Find the median number of cars sold per month by a dealer over the past nine months based on the following monthly sales figures:

27	38	12	34	42	40	24	40	23

Solution

Order the data set:

12	23	24	27	34	38	40	40	42

Since *n* = 9 (i.e. *n* is odd), the median position is $\frac{9+1}{2}$ = 5th position. The median value therefore lies in the 5th data position. Thus the median monthly car sales is 34 cars. This means that there were four months when car sales were below 34 cars per month and four months when car sales were above 34 cars per month (not necessarily consecutive months).

Example 3.3(b) Monthly Car Sales (*n* = 10 months)

Find the median number of cars sold per month by a dealer over the past ten months based on the following monthly sales figures:

27	38	12	34	42	40	24	40	23	18

Solution

Order the data set:

12	18	23	24	**27**	34	38	40	40	42

Since *n* = 10 (i.e. *n* is even), the data value in the $\left(\frac{10}{2}\right)^{th}$ = 5th position is 27.

Average the 5th and 6th position values (i.e. $\frac{27 + 34}{2} = 30.5$) to give the median value. Thus the median monthly car sales is 30.5 cars. This means that there were five months when car sales were below 30.5 cars per month and five months when car sales were above 30.5 cars per month.

Median for Grouped Numeric Data

Use these methods when the data is already summarised into a numeric frequency distribution (or ogive).

- *Graphical approach*
  Using the '*less than*' ogive graph, the median value is found by reading off the data value on the *x*-axis that is associated with the 50% cumulative frequency located on the *y*-axis.
- *Arithmetic approach*
  - Based on the sample size, *n*, calculate $\frac{n}{2}$ to find the median position.
  - Using the cumulative frequency counts of the '*less than*' ogive summary table, find the median interval (i.e. the interval that contains the median position [the $(\frac{n}{2})^{th}$ data value]).
  - The median value can be approximated using the midpoint of the median interval, or calculated using the following formula to give a more representative median value:

$$M_e = O_{me} + \frac{c\left[\frac{n}{2} - f(<)\right]}{f_{me}}$$

3.3

Where: O_{me} = lower limit of the median interval
  c = class width
  n = sample size (number of observations)
  f_{me} = frequency count of the median interval
  $f(<)$ = cumulative frequency count of all intervals before the median interval

The formula takes into account 'how far' into the median interval the median value lies.

Example 3.4 Courier Delivery Times Study

A courier company recorded 30 delivery times (in minutes) to deliver parcels to their clients from its depot. The data are summarised in the numeric frequency – and cumulative frequency – distributions as shown in Table 3.3.

Table 3.3 Numeric frequency and cumulative frequency distributions for courier delivery times (minutes)

Time	Frequency	Cumulative
10–< 20	3	3
20–< 30	5	8
30–< 40	9	**17**
40–< 50	7	24
50–< 60	6	30
Total	**30**	

Find the median delivery time of parcels to clients by this courier company.

Solution

Since $n = 30$, the median delivery time will be in the $(\frac{30}{2})^{th} = 15^{th}$ ordered data position. Using the cumulative counts in Table 3.3, the 15th data value falls in the $30-< 40$ minutes interval. This identifies the median interval. An approximate median delivery time for parcels is therefore 35 minutes (the interval midpoint). However, a more representative median value can be found by using Formula 3.3, where:

O_{me} = 30 minutes
c = 10 minutes
f_{me} = 9 deliveries
$f(<)$ = 8 deliveries

$$M_e = 30 + 10\frac{(\frac{30}{2} - 8)}{9} = 30 + 7.78 = 37.78 \text{ minutes}$$

Thus the median parcel delivery time is 37.78 minutes. This means that half the deliveries occurred within 37.78 minutes while the other half took longer than 37.78 minutes.

The median has one major *advantage* over the mean – it is not affected by outliers. It is therefore a more representative measure of central location than the mean when significant outliers occur in a set of data.

The median has *two drawbacks*. *Firstly* it cannot be calculated for categorical data. It makes no sense, for example, to refer to the 'middle' economic sector. Thus the median, like the mean, can also only be applied to numeric data. *Secondly*, the median is more affected by sampling fluctuations than the mean as it uses only the middle data values (and not all the data values) and is therefore less stable than the mean.

Mode

The **mode** (M_o) is defined as the *most frequently occurring value* in a set data. It can be calculated both for categorical data and numeric data.

The following are illustrative statements that refer to the mode as the central location measure:
- Colgate is the brand of toothpaste most preferred by households.
- The most common family size is four.
- The supermarket frequented most often in Kimberley is Checkers.
- The majority of machine breakdowns last between 25 and 30 minutes.

Follow these steps to calculate the mode:
- For small samples of ungrouped data, rank the data from lowest to highest, and identify, by inspection, the data value that occurs most frequently.
- For large samples of discrete or categorical (nominal and ordinal-scaled) data:
  - construct a categorical frequency table (see Chapter 2)
  - identify the modal value or modal category that occurs most frequently.

- For large samples of continuous, numeric (ratio-scaled) data:
  - calculate a numeric frequency distribution (see Chapter 2)
  - identify the modal interval as the interval with the highest frequency count
  - use either the midpoint of the modal interval as an approximate modal value or apply the following formula to calculate a more representative modal value.

$$M_o = O_{mo} + \frac{c(f_m - f_{m-1})}{2f_m - f_{m-1} - f_{m+1}}$$ 3.4

Where: O_{mo} = lower limit of the modal interval
  c = width of the modal interval
  f_m = frequency of the modal interval
  f_{m-1} = frequency of the interval preceding the modal interval
  f_{m+1} = frequency of the interval following the modal interval

The modal formula weights ('pulls') the modal value from the midpoint position towards the adjacent interval with the higher frequency count. If the interval to the left of the modal interval has a higher frequency count than the interval to the right of the modal interval, then the modal value is pulled down below the midpoint value, and vice versa.

Example 3.5 Courier Delivery Times Study

Refer to Example 3.4 for the problem description and Table 3.4 for the sample data of 30 delivery times that have been summarised into a numeric frequency distribution.

Find the modal delivery time of parcels to clients from the courier service's depot (i.e. what is the most common courier delivery time?)

Table 3.4 Numeric frequency distribution of courier delivery times (minutes)

Time intervals	Frequency count
10 –< 20	3
20 –< 30	5
30 –< 40	9
40 –< 50	7
50 –< 60	6
Total	30

Solution

From the numeric frequency distribution, the modal interval (interval with the highest frequency) is 30 –< 40 minutes. The midpoint of 35 minutes can be used as the approximate modal courier delivery time.

To calculate a more representative modal value, apply the modal Formula 3.4 with:

O_{mo} = 30 minutes
c = 10 minutes
f_m = 9 deliveries
f_{m-1} = 5 deliveries
f_{m-1} = 7 deliveries

$$M_o = 30 + \frac{10(9-5)}{(2(9)-5-7)} = 30 + 6.67 = 36.67 \text{ minutes}$$

Thus the most common courier delivery time from depot to customers is 36.67 minutes.

The mode has several *advantages:*
- It is a valid measure of central location for *all data types* (i.e. categorical and numeric). If the data type is categorical, the mode defines the most frequently occurring category. If the data type is numeric, the mode is the most frequently occurring data value (or the midpoint value of a modal interval, if the numeric data has been grouped into intervals).
- The mode is not influenced by outliers, as it represents the most frequently occurring data value (or response category).

The mode also has one main *disadvantage:*
- It is a representative measure of central location only if the histogram of the numeric random variable is unimodal (i.e. has one peak only). If the shape is bi-modal, there is more than one peak, meaning that two possible modes exist, in which case there is no single representative mode.

Which Central Location Measure is Best?

A central location measure must be *representative* of its data values. The choice depends mainly on (i) the data type of the random variable being analysed and (ii) whether outliers are present or not in the data set.

Data Type

If the data type is *categorical* (nominal or ordinal scaled), then the *mode* is the only valid and representative measure of central location. All three measures (mean, median and mode) can, however, be used for *numeric* (interval or ratio-scaled) data.

Outliers

Outliers distort the mean but do not affect the median or the mode. Thus, if outliers are detected in a set of data, then the *median* (or mode) should be chosen. In such cases, the median is preferred to the mode as it can be used in further analysis. However, if there are good reasons to remove the outlier(s) from the data set (because they are errors or atypical data values), the mean can again be used as the best central location measure.

Other Measures of Central Location

Two other useful, but less common, measures of central location are the geometric mean and the weighted arithmetic mean.

Geometric Mean

> The **geometric mean** is used to find the average of *percentage change data*, such as indexes, growth rates or rates of change.

When each data value is calculated from a different base, the appropriate measure of central location is the geometric mean.

For example, if a company's share price is R25 at the end of Week 1, R30 at the end of Week 2 and R33 at the end of Week 3, then the weekly *percentage changes* are 20% from Week 1 to Week 2, and 10% from Week 2 to Week 3. The average weekly percentage change in the share price can be found using the geometric mean.

Follow these steps to calculate the geometric mean:
- Multiply all n observations (which are percentage changes).
- Take the nth root of the product.

The formula for the geometric mean (GM) is as follows:

$$GM = \sqrt[n]{x_1 x_2 x_3 \ldots x_n}$$

3.5

The percentage changes must be expressed as decimal values. For example, a 7% increase must be written as 1.07 and a 4% decrease must be written as 0.96.

Example 3.6 Electricity Tariff Study

The electricity tariff has increased by 12%, 8% and 16% per annum over a three-year period. Find the average annual percentage increase in the electricity tariff.

Solution

Geometric mean $= \sqrt[3]{1.12 \times 1.08 \times 1.16}$

$\qquad\qquad\quad = 1.1195$

Electricity tariffs have increased by an average of 11.95 % annually over the past three years.

Weighted Arithmetic Mean

> The **weighted arithmetic mean** (or weighted average) is used when *different weights* are given to each data value to arrive at an average value.

The arithmetic mean assumes that each data value is equally weighted (i.e. a weight of $\frac{1}{n}$ in a sample of n observations). However, if the importance (weight) of each data value is different, the weighted arithmetic mean should be used.

Follow these steps to calculate the weighted arithmetic mean (based on a numeric frequency distribution):

- Each observation, x_i, is first multiplied by its frequency count, f_i (weighting).
- These weighted observations are then summed.
- This sum is then divided by the sum of the weights.

In formula terms, the weighted arithmetic mean is given as follows:

$$\text{Weighted } \bar{x} = \frac{\Sigma f_i x_i}{\Sigma f_i}$$

3.6

Note: The weighted average formula (3.6) is the same as the arithmetic mean for grouped data formula (3.2).

Example 3.7 Training Consultant's Earnings Study

A training consultant is paid R550 per hour for one eight-hour training programme, R420 per hour for a second training programme of six hours and R800 for a two-hour seminar. What are the training consultant's average earnings per hour for the three programmes?

Solution

Since the duration of each programme differs (i.e. 8, 6 and 2 hours respectively), the three hourly rates (R550, R420 and R800 respectively) cannot simply be averaged. The weighted arithmetic mean must be applied.

$$\text{Weighted arithmetic mean} = \frac{550(8) + 420(6) + 800(2)}{16} = \frac{8\ 520}{16} = R532.50$$

The consultant is paid an average hourly rate of R532.50 across all three training programmes.

3.3 Non-central Location Measures

Quartiles

Quartiles are non-central measures that divide an ordered data set into quarters (i.e. four equal parts).

The *lower quartile*, Q_1, is that data value that separates the lower (bottom) 25% of (ordered) data values from the top 75% of ordered data values.

The *middle quartile*, Q_2, is the median. It divides an ordered data set into two equal halves.

The *upper quartile*, Q_3, is that data value that separates the top (upper) 25% of (ordered) data values from the bottom 75% of ordered data values.

Figure 3.1 graphically illustrates the position of each quartile in an ordered data set.

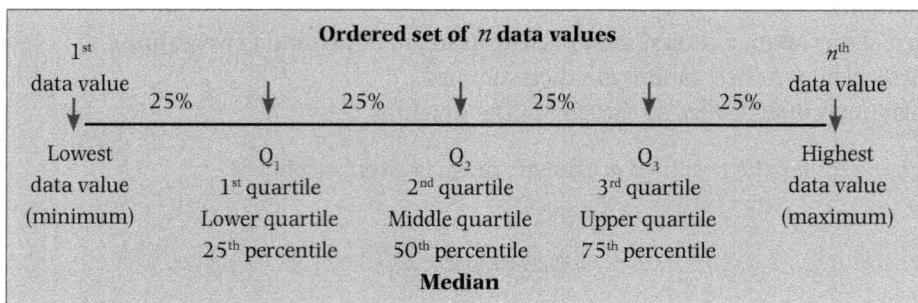

Figure 3.1 Graphical illustration of quartiles

The following illustrates the use of quartiles in human resource management, where they are used to describe salary scales. For a given job grade, the salary scale per month, for example, could be as follows:

Lower limit	R8 250	The minimum salary paid for the job grade is R8 250 per month.
Lower quartile	R9 600	The lowest paid 25% of employees receive no more than R9 600 per month.
Median	R11 000	50% of employees are paid R11 000 or less per month.
Upper quartile	R12 650	The highest paid 25% of employees receive more than R12 650 per month.
Upper limit	R14 150	The maximum salary paid for the job grade is R14 150 per month.

Note: A quartile value is an *inclusive* upper limit when interpreting a quartile.

Quartiles are calculated in a similar way to the median. The only difference lies in the identification of the quartile position and, consequently, in the choice of the quartile interval.

Follow these steps to calculate quartiles (lower, middle and upper) for *ungrouped (raw) data:*
- Sort the data in ascending order.
- Each quartile position is determined as follows (regardless of whether n is even or odd):
  - For Q_1 use $\frac{n+1}{4}$ or $0.25\,(n+1)$.
  - For Q_2 use $\frac{n+1}{2}$ or $0.5\,(n+1)$ (same as used in the median calculation).
  - For Q_3 use $\frac{3 \times (n+1)}{4}$ or $0.75\,(n+1)$.
- Count to the quartile position (rounded down to the nearest integer) to find the (approximate) quartile value. If the quartile position in not an integer, a more exact quartile value is found by multiplying the fraction part of the quartile position with the difference between the approximate quartile value and its consecutive value, and adding this result to the approximate quartile value.

In formula terms:

Quartile value = approximate quartile value + fraction part of quartile position × (consecutive value after quartile position − approximate quartile value)   3.7

Example 3.8 Household Electricity Consumption Study

The daily electricity consumption in kilowatt hours (kWh) by a sample of 20 households in Rustenburg is recorded in Table 3.5.
(See Excel file C3.3 – *electricity consumption.*)

Table 3.5 Daily household electricity consumption (kWh)

58	50	33	51	38	43	60	55	46	43
51	47	40	37	43	48	61	55	44	35

1   Find the lower quartile value of daily household electricity consumption.
2   Find the upper quartile value of daily household electricity consumption.

Solution

1   The sorted daily electricity consumption values (in ascending order) are shown in Table 3.6.

Table 3.6 Sorted daily household electricity consumption (kWh)

Position	1	2	3	4	5	6	7	8	9	10	11	12	13	14	15	16	17	18	19	20
Data	33	35	37	38	40	43	43	43	44	46	47	48	50	51	51	55	55	58	60	61

For $n = 20$ households, the Q_1 position is $\frac{20+1}{4} = 5.25$. This means that the lower quartile, Q_1, is found in the 5.25^{th} position within the ordered dataset. The data value in the 5th position is 40 kWh. This is the approximate Q_1 value. A more representative Q_1 value is found from Formula 3.7 as follows:

–   The fractional part of the lower quartile position is 0.25 (i.e. $5.25^{th} - 5^{th}$ positions).

–   The next data value after the approximate Q_1 value is 43 (the data value in the 6th position).

–   Add $0.25 \times (43 - 40) = 0.75$ to the approximate Q_1, giving $40 + 0.75 = 40.75$ kWh.

Thus, the lower quartile daily electricity consumption value is 40.75 kWh.
This means that 25% of Rustenburg households use no more than 40.75 kWh of electricity daily.

2   For $n = 20$ households, the Q_3 position is $\frac{3(20+1)}{4} = 15.75$. Thus Q_3 is found in the 15.75^{th} position within the ordered dataset. The data value in the 15th position is 51 kWh. This is the approximate Q_3 value. Using Formula 3.7, a more representative Q_3 value may be found.

–   The fractional part of the upper quartile position is 0.75 (i.e. $15.75^{th} - 15^{th}$ positions).

–   The next data value after the approximate Q_3 is 55 (the data value in the 16th position).

–   Add $0.75 \times (55 - 51) = 3$ to the approximate Q_3, giving $51 + 3 = 54$ kWh.

Thus, the upper quartile daily electricity consumption value is 54 kWh. This means that 25% of Rustenburg households use more than 54 kWh of electricity daily.

Use the following steps to calculate quartiles for *grouped data* from a numeric frequency distribution:

- A formula similar to the median formula is used to find both the lower and upper quartiles.
- The formula is modified to identify either the lower or the upper quartile position, which is then used to find the lower or upper quartile interval. All other terms are identical to those of the median formula.
- *Lower quartile* (Q_1): The lower quartile is found in the $(\frac{n}{4})^{th}$ position using the following formula:

$$Q_1 = O_{Q1} + \frac{c\left[\frac{n}{4} - f(<)\right]}{f_{Q1}}$$

3.8

Where: O_{Q1} = the lower limit of the Q_1 interval
n = sample size
$f(<)$ = the cumulative frequency of the interval before the Q_1 interval
c = interval width
f_{Q1} = the frequency of the Q_1 interval

- *Upper quartile* (Q_3): The upper quartile is found in the $(\frac{3n}{4})^{th}$ position using the following formula:

$$Q_3 = O_{Q3} + \frac{c\left[\frac{3n}{4} - f(<)\right]}{f_{Q3}}$$

3.9

Where: O_{Q3} = the lower limit of the Q_3 interval
n = sample size
$f(<)$ = the cumulative frequency of the interval before the Q_3 interval
c = interval width
f_{Q3} = the frequency of the Q_3 interval

Example 3.9 Courier Delivery Times Study

Refer to Example 3.4 for the problem description and the numeric frequency and cumulative frequency distribution as shown in Table 3.3 (and repeated in Table 3.7).

Table 3.7 Numeric frequency distribution and ogive for courier delivery times (minutes)

Time	Frequency	Cumulative
10–< 20	3	3
20–< 30	5	8
30–< 40	9	17
40–< 50	7	24
50–< 60	6	30
Total	30	

1   Find the lower quartile delivery time of parcels to clients.
2   Find the upper quartile delivery time of parcels to clients.

Solution

1   Using the data from Table 3.7 with $n = 30$, the following measures are defined:
    – the Q_1 position is $\frac{30}{4} = 7.5^{th}$ position
    – the Q_1 interval is therefore $20-< 30$ minutes (the 7.5^{th} value lies in this interval)
    – the lower limit of the Q_1 interval $O_{G1} = 20$ minutes
    – the interval width is $c = 10$ minutes
    – the frequency of the Q_1 interval is $f_{Q1} = 5$ deliveries
    – the cumulative frequency count up to the Q_1 interval is $f(<) = 3$ deliveries.

    Then, using the lower quartile formula, the Q_1 delivery time is
    $$\frac{20 + 10(7.5 - 3)}{5} = 29 \text{ minutes.}$$
    Thus 25% of parcels will be delivered to their clients within 29 minutes.

2   Using the data from Table 3.7 with $n = 30$, the following measures are defined:
    – the Q_3 position is $\frac{3(30)}{4} = 22.5^{th}$ position
    – the Q_3 interval is therefore $40-< 50$ minutes (the 22.5^{th} value lies in this interval)
    – the lower limit of the Q_3 interval $O_{Q3} = 40$ minutes
    – the interval width is $c = 10$ minutes
    – the frequency of the Q_3 interval is $f_{Q3} = 7$ deliveries
    – the cumulative frequency count up to the Q_3 interval is $f(<) = 17$ deliveries

    Then, using the upper quartile formula, the Q_3 delivery time is
    $$\frac{40 + 10(22.5 - 17)}{7} = 47.9 \text{ minutes.}$$

    Thus, 25% of parcel deliveries will take longer than 47.9 minutes to be delivered to their clients.

Percentiles

Percentiles are similar to quartiles. The lower quartile is the 25th percentile and the upper quartile is the 75th percentile. This idea can be extended to find the data value below which *any percentage* of data values can fall. For example, the 30th percentile is that data value below which 30% of all data values will lie and the 80th percentile represents the data value above which the top 20% of data values will lie.

Percentiles are calculated in the same way as quartiles. First find the *percentile position*, then identify the *percentile value* in that position.

To illustrate, for any sample size, n:
- to find the 40th percentile, the 40th percentile position is $0.40(n + 1)$
- to find the 84th percentile, the 84th percentile position is $0.84(n + 1)$.

Once the percentile position is found, apply the same rules as for quartiles to find the appropriate percentile value.

3.4 Measures of Dispersion

Dispersion (or spread) refers to the extent to which the data values of a numeric random variable are scattered about their central location value.

Figure 3.2 shows the ages of people representing three separate populations (A: ages of MBA students, B: ages of mineworkers, and C: ages of spectators at a sports event). Each population has the same mean age (32 years, for example) but different measures of dispersion (e.g. graph A spread = 3 years, graph B spread = 5.2 years, and graph C spread = 9.4 years).

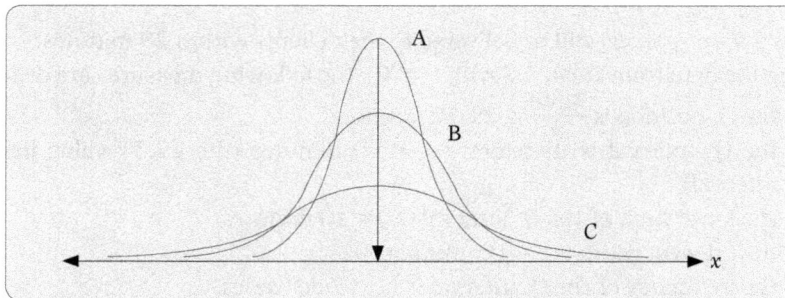

Figure 3.2 Varying spreads for three groups with the same central location

The degree of dispersion in a set of data influences the *confidence* that a user can have in the *reliability* of the central location measures. Widely dispersed data values about their central location indicate low reliability and less confidence in the central location as a representative measure. Conversely, a high concentration of data values about their central location indicates high reliability and greater confidence in the representativeness of the central location value.

The measures that are commonly used to describe data dispersion are:
- range
- interquartile range
- variance
- standard deviation
- coefficient of variation.

Range

The **range** is the difference between the highest and lowest data values.

$$Range = Maximum\ value - Minimum\ value$$
$$R = x_{max} - x_{min}$$

3.10

Example 3.10 Household Electricity Consumption Study

Refer to Example 3.8 and the data set of electricity consumption per household (Table 3.5). Find the *range* of the electricity consumption across households in Rustenburg.

Solution

Given x_{max} = 61 kWh and x_{min} = 33 kWh

Range, R = 61 – 33 = 28 kWh

Household electricity consumption ranged from 33 kWh to 61 kWh. There is a spread of 28 kWh between the household using the least amount of electricity and the household using the most amount of electricity.

The range, however, is an *unstable, volatile* and *unreliable* measure of spread because it is easily distorted by outliers. In addition, it can vary greatly between samples taken from the same population. Its other drawback is that it provides no information about the *clustering* of data values between the minimum and maximum data values, as it uses only these two extreme data values to calculate it.

However, it is always a useful first indication of the spread of data in a data set. It must be used with care and always examined along with other measures of dispersion.

Interquartile Range (IQR)

The **interquartile range** is the difference between the upper quartile and the lower quartile.

$$IQR = Q_3 - Q_1$$
\hfill 3.11

It measures the range of the middle 50% of data values and is a more stable measure of spread than the range.

Example 3.11 Household Electricity Consumption Study

Refer to Example 3.8 and the data set of electricity consumption per household (Table 3.5). Find the *interquartile range* of household electricity consumption in Rustenburg.

Solution

Given the lower quartile (Q_1) = 40 75 kWh and the upper quartile (Q_3) = 54 kWh

Interquartile Range (IQR) = 54 kWh – 40.75 kWh = 13.25 kWh.

The range (or spread) of daily electricity consumption for the middle 50% of Rustenburg households is 13.25 kWh.

Variance

The **variance** is a measure of *average squared deviation* from the central value.

It is the most widely used and reliable measure of dispersion, as it uses every data value in a sample in its calculation.

Follow these steps to calculate a sample variance:
- Calculate the sample mean, $\bar{x}$.
- Calculate the deviation of each data value from the mean, $(x_i - \bar{x})$.
- Square these deviations (to avoid positive and negative deviations cancelling each other when they are summed), $(x_i - \bar{x})^2$.
- Sum these squared deviations, $\Sigma(x_i - \bar{x})^2$.
- Finally, average the squared deviations by dividing by $(n - 1)$.

In formula terms:

$$\text{Variance} = \frac{\text{Sum of squared deviations}}{\text{Sample size} - 1}$$

$$s^2 = \frac{\Sigma(x_i - \bar{x})^2}{n - 1}$$

3.12

To make it easier to calculate the variance manually, the following formula can be used:

$$s^2 = \frac{\Sigma x_i^2 - n\bar{x}^2}{n - 1}$$

3.13

Note: Division by the sample size, n, would be logical, but the variance statistic would then be a biased measure of dispersion. It is unbiased (desirable) when division is by $(n - 1)$. For large samples ($n > 40$), this distinction becomes less important.

The symbol s^2 is used to define the variance for sample data, while the symbol σ^2 (sigma) is used to define the variance of population data. To calculate the population variance, σ^2, the numerator of Formula 3.12 above is divided by N, the population size.

Example 3.12 Household Electricity Consumption Study

Refer to Example 3.8 and the data set of electricity consumption per household (Table 3.5).

Find the *variance* of the electricity consumption across the sample of households in Rustenburg.

Solution
- Sample mean $= \frac{938}{20} = 46.9$ kWh.
- Calculate the squared deviation of each data value from the sample mean and sum them.
  $(58 - 46.9)^2 + (50 - 46.9)^2 + (33 - 46.9)^2 + (51 - 46.9)^2 + \dots + (35 - 46.9)^2$
  $= 1\,283.8$

- Average the sum of these squared deviations by dividing by $(n - 1) = 19$.

$$s^2 = \frac{1\,283.8}{20-1} = 67.57$$

The variance of household electricity consumption is 67.57 $(kWh)^2$.

Since the variance measure is expressed in squared units, its meaning in a practical sense is obscure. To provide meaning, the dispersion measure should be expressed in the original unit of measure of the random variable. This is the purpose of the standard deviation.

Standard Deviation

The **standard deviation** is the square root of the variance.

$$s = \sqrt{\text{variance}}$$
$$= \sqrt{s^2}$$

In formula terms:

$$s = \sqrt{\frac{\sum(x_i - \bar{x})^2}{n-1}}$$

3.14

The standard deviation expresses dispersion in the original unit of measure of the random variable. The symbol s is used to define the *sample* standard deviation, and σ is the *population* standard deviation symbol.

Example 3.13 Household Electricity Consumption Study

Refer to the sample data set of household electricity consumption (Table 3.5) in Example 3.8.

Find the *standard deviation* of the electricity consumption for the sample of households in Rustenburg.

Solution
From Example 3.12, the sample variance, $s^2 = 67.57$ $(kWh)^2$.
Then the sample standard deviation, $s = \sqrt{67.57} = 8.22$ kWh.
The standard deviation of household electricity consumption in Rustenburg is 8.22 kWh.

The following interpretation can be applied to the standard deviation, if the histogram of a numeric random variable is bell-shaped about its mean (called the **Empirical Rule**):
- 68.3% of all data values will lie within one standard deviation of the mean, i.e. between the lower limit of $(\bar{x} - s)$ and the upper limit of $(\bar{x} + s)$.
- 95.5% of all data values will lie within two standard deviations of the mean, i.e. between the lower limit of $(\bar{x} - 2s)$ and the upper limit of $(\bar{x} + 2s)$.
- 99.7% (almost all) of the data values will lie within three standard deviations of the mean, i.e. between the lower limit of $(\bar{x} - 3s)$ and the upper limit of $(\bar{x} + 3s)$.

Figure 3.3 shows the areas under a bell-shaped (normal) distribution associated with one, two and three standard deviations about the mean.

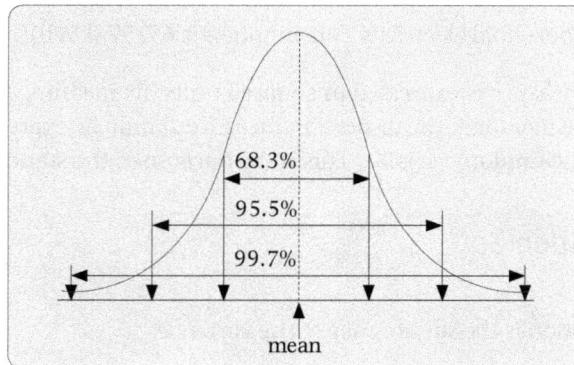

Figure 3.3 Percentage (%) of data values within one, two and three standard deviations of the mean

In Example 3.13, $s = 8.22$ kWh can be interpreted in the following way:

Given $\bar{x} = 46.9$ kWh and $s = 8.22$ kWh, and assuming a bell-shaped pattern of data values about the mean, then:

- 68.3% of households use between 38.68 and 55.12 kWh of electricity per day.
- 95.5% of households use between 30.46 and 63.34 kWh of electricity per day.
- Almost all households (99.7%) use between 22.24 and 71.56 kWh of electricity per day.

> *Note:* The closer all the data values are to the mean, the smaller the standard deviation becomes, resulting in a narrower, more peaked, bell-shaped histogram. Conversely, the more widespread the data values around the mean, the larger the standard deviation becomes resulting in a wider and flatter bell-shaped histogram.

The standard deviation, s, (and the variance, s^2) is a *relatively stable* measure of dispersion across different samples drawn from the same population. It is therefore a very powerful statistic that is used extensively in further statistical analysis. However, its main drawback, like the mean, is that it is distorted by *outliers*.

The Empirical Rule that is used to interpret standard deviations only applies to bell-shaped distributions. A rule that can be used to explain the spread of data in *any-shaped* distribution is called **Chebyshev's Theorem**, which is interpreted as follows:

- *at least* $\frac{3}{4}$ (75%) of all data lies within two standard deviations of the mean;
- *at least* $\frac{8}{9}$ (88.9%) of all data lies within three standard deviations of the mean;
- *at least* $\frac{15}{16}$ (93.75%) of all data lies within four standard deviations of the mean.

In general, *at least* $(1 - \frac{1}{k^2})$ $(k > 1)$ of all data lies within k standard deviations of the mean.

Coefficient of Variation

The **coefficient of variation** (CV) is a measure of *relative variability*.

It is calculated as follows:

$$\text{Coefficient of variation (CV)} = \frac{\text{Standard deviation}}{\text{Mean}} \%$$
$$= \frac{s}{\bar{x}} \%$$

3.15

The coefficient of variation expresses a random variable's variability in percentage terms. Therefore it is possible, through the coefficient of variation, to compare the variability of data across different samples, especially if the random variables are recorded in different units of measurement (such as cm, kg and minutes).

A coefficient of variation is always interpreted as a *percentage*. The *smaller* the CV, the *more concentrated* the data values are about their mean; conversely, a *large* CV implies that the data values are more *widely dispersed* about their mean value. The lower limit of a CV is zero, but there is no upper limit.

For Example 3.8 (household electricity consumption study) with $\bar{x} = 46.9$ kWh and $s = 8.22$ kWh:

$$\text{CV} = \frac{3.22}{46.9} \times 100 = 17.53\%$$

The relatively low CV (17.53%) indicates that the daily electricity consumptions across households is reasonably similar (i.e. the data values are relatively close to the mean).

Example 3.14 Airline Passengers – Mass and Height Study

For a random sample of 30 airline passengers, each person's mass and height was recorded and summarised in Table 3.8.

1   Calculate the *coefficient of variation* for each measure to compare the relative variability between passenger masses and passenger heights.
2   Which variable shows greater relative variability?

Table 3.8 Descriptive statistics and CV for passenger masses and heights

	Passenger mass	Passenger height
Average	78 kg	166 cm
Standard deviation	16.4 kg	20.1 cm
Coefficient of variation (CV)	21.03%	12.11%

Solution

1. For passenger masses: $\qquad CV = \frac{16.4}{78} \times 100 = 21.03\%$

   For passenger heights: $\qquad CV = \frac{20.1}{166} \times 100 = 12.11\%$

2. Since the CV of masses (21.03%) is greater than the CV of heights (12.11%), passengers' masses show greater variability than their heights about their respective averages.

3.5 Measure of Skewness

Skewness describes the *shape* of a unimodal histogram for numeric data.

Three common shapes of a unimodal histogram can generally be observed:
1. symmetrical shapes
2. positively skewed shapes (skewed to the right)
3. negatively skewed shapes (skewed to the left).

It is important to know the shape of the histogram because it affects the choice of central location and dispersion measures to describe the data, and may distort statistical findings generated from inferential techniques (see chapters 7 to 12).

Symmetrical Distribution

A histogram is symmetrical if it has a *single central peak* and *mirror image slopes* on either side of the centre position as shown in Figure 3.4. It is also called a bell-shaped curve or a normal distribution.

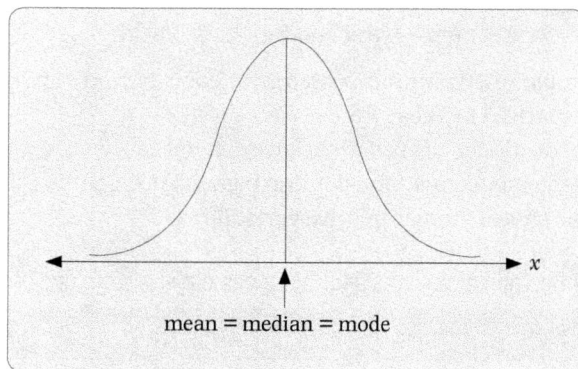

Figure 3.4 Symmetrical histogram

For example, the random variable 'volume of juice in one-litre cartons' is likely to produce a symmetrical histogram around a mean fill of one litre.

If a distribution is symmetrical, all three central location measures (mean, median and mode) will be *equal* and therefore any one of them could be chosen to represent the central location measure for the sample data.

Positively Skewed Distribution

A histogram is positively skewed (or skewed to the right) when there are a few extremely *large* data values (outliers) relative to the other data values in the sample. A positively skewed distribution will have a 'long' tail to the *right*, as shown in Figure 3.5.

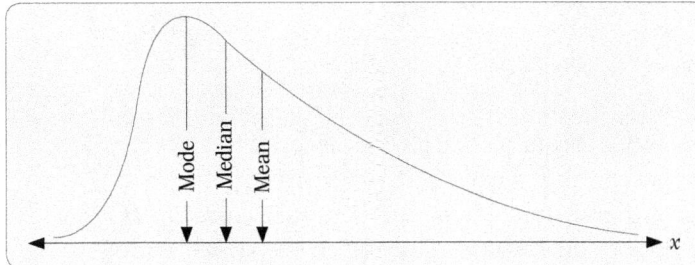

Figure 3.5 Positively skewed histogram

For example, the duration of stay of foreign visitors to Cape Town may well exhibit positive skewness, since the majority of visitors are likely to spend no more than a few days, with a small number spending a few weeks or even months in Cape Town.

The mean is most influenced ('inflated and distorted') by the few extremely large data values and hence will lie furthest to the *right* of the mode and the median. The median is therefore preferred as the representative measure of central location in right-skewed distributions.

Negatively Skewed Distribution

A histogram is negatively skewed (or skewed to the left) when there are a few extremely *small* data values (outliers) relative to the other data values in the sample. A negatively skewed distribution will have a 'long' tail to the *left*, as shown in Figure 3.6.

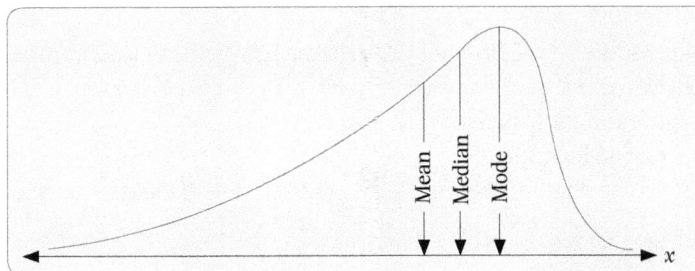

Figure 3.6 Negatively skewed histogram

For example, the lead time (in days) of selling houses may well exhibit negative skewness. Only a few houses are likely to be sold within a few days of being marketed, while the majority are usually sold after lengthy periods of time (even a few months).

The mean, again, will be most influenced ('deflated and distorted') by the few extremely small data values and hence will lie furthest to the *left* of the mode and the median. The median is therefore preferred as the representative measure of central location in left-skewed distributions.

Pearson's Coefficient of Skewness

Pearson's coefficient of skewness (Sk_p) measures skewness in a sample of numeric data.

It is calculated using the following formula:

$$Sk_p = \frac{n\Sigma(x_t - \bar{x})^3}{(n-1)(n-2)s^3}$$
3.16

The skewness coefficient is interpreted as follows:
- If $Sk_p = 0$, the histogram is *symmetrical*. Hence $\bar{x} = M_e = M_o$.
- If $Sk_p > 0$, the histogram is *positively skewed*. In such cases, $\bar{x} > M_e$.
- If $Sk_p < 0$, the histogram is *negatively skewed*. In such cases, $\bar{x} < M_e$.

There is no lower or upper limit for Pearson's skewness coefficient. The further the skewness coefficient deviates from zero (in either a negative or a positive direction), the more skewed the distribution. As a rule of thumb, a skewness coefficient below −0.5 or above +0.5 indicates excessive skewness caused by a few very extreme outliers in the data.

For example, if $Sk_p = 0.28$, the histogram is only moderately skewed to the right. If $Sk_p = -1.83$, there is excessive negative skewness caused by one or a few very small data values.

A useful *approximation formula* for skewness is based on the difference between the mean and the median. The greater the difference between these two measures, the greater the skewness in the sample data. The following formula can be used as a guide:

$$\frac{3(\text{Mean} - \text{Median})}{\text{Standard deviation}}$$
3.17

This approximation formula is interpreted in the same way as Pearson's skewness coefficient.

Example 3.15 Household Electricity Consumption Study

Refer to the sample data set of household electricity consumption (Table 3.5) in Example 3.8.
1 Calculate the *coefficient of skewness* of daily household electricity usage using:
  (a) the approximation skewness formula
  (b) the accurate formula.
2 Comment on the degree of symmetry or skewness in electricity usage.

Solution

1 (a) Given $\bar{x} = 46.9$ kWh, median $= 46.5$ kWh and $s = 8.22$ kWh, using the approximation skewness Formula 3.17:
$$Sk_p = \frac{3(46.9 - 46.5)}{8.22}$$
$$= 0.146$$
   (b) Given $\bar{x} = 46.9$ kWh, $s = 8.22$ kWh and $n = 20$, first calculate $\Sigma(x - \bar{x})^3$:
$$(58 - 46.9)^3 + (50 - 46.9)^3 + ... + (35 - 46.9)^3 = 1\,073.16$$
Then $Sk_p = \frac{20(1\,073.16)}{(19)(18)(8.22)^3} = 0.113$ ... (using Formula 3.16)

2   Since both skewness coefficients are small positive values, there is very slight positive skewness in the histogram of household electricity usage (in kWh). Since these values are close to zero, it can be concluded that the histogram of daily household electricity usage is approximately symmetrical (normal) about the mean of 46.9 kWh. No excessive outliers occur in the sample data.

Outliers

An outlier is an *extreme value* relative to the majority of values in a dataset. For example, $x = 2$ cars is an outlier in a dataset {$x = 16, 12, 2, 15, 13, 11$ and 17 cars} of monthly car sales. Similarly, $x = 1\,922$ kWh is an outlier in a dataset {$x = 326, 412, 1\,922, 296, 314, 384$ and 370 kWh} for the variable $x =$ monthly household electricity usage.

Identifying Outliers

Two methods can be used to identify outliers in a set of data:

1. The z-score approach
A z-score is a *standardised unit of measure* of a data value. It is found by subtracting the data value (x) from its mean (μ) and dividing the difference by its standard deviation (σ).

i.e.
$$z = \frac{(x - \mu)}{\sigma} \qquad \text{or} \qquad z = \frac{(x - \bar{x})}{s}$$
3.18

The z-scores for any numeric variable have a mean of zero (0) and a standard deviation of one (1).

For example, if the ages of all employees in a business is normally distributed with a mean (μ) of 40 years and a standard deviation (σ) of 4 years, then the z-scores for employees with the following ages $x = (30, 35, 38, 40, 44$ and 49 years) is $z = (-2.5, -1.25, -0.5, 0, +1$ and $+2.25)$ respectively.

Each z-score is a measure of how far (i.e. how many standard deviations of $\sigma = 4$ years) the employee's age deviates from the mean age of all employees ($\mu = 40$ years). Note that the 38-year-old employee (with a z-score $= -0.5$) is only half a standard deviation (2 years) younger than the mean of 40 years; while the 49-year-old employee (with a z-score $= +2.25$) is 2.25 standard deviations (9 years) older than the mean age of 40 years.

An *outlier* is identified when a data value (x) has a z-score either **below −3** or **above +3**. This rule of thumb is derived from the property that values (x) of a normally distributed random variable lie within the limits of 3 standard deviations from its mean (i.e. $-3 \leq$ z-score $\leq +3$) (i.e. the Empirical Rule). Thus x-values with z-scores beyond these limits of ±3 standard deviations represents outlier values. Refer to **section 3.4** for the interpretation of a standard deviation.

2. The quartiles approach
An outlier (or extreme value) is any data value of a numeric variable that lies either

(a)
$$\text{below a lower limit of } Q_1 - 1.5 * (Q_3 - Q_1)$$
3.19(a)

or

(b)
$$\text{above an upper limit of } Q_3 + 1.5 * (Q_3 - Q_1)$$
3.19(b)

These lower and upper limits correspond approximately to the z-score limits of −3 and +3 standard deviations from the mean of the numeric variable.

Treatment of Outliers

In descriptive statistics, outliers are highlighted in graphs such as histograms, box plots or scatter plots. They should then be identified (using one of the above methods) and removed from the dataset to avoid distorting the numeric descriptive measures such as the mean and standard deviation. Their values – and any related information – must be noted and reported separately for further investigation to identify their cause (i.e. why they occurred – either to prevent future occurrences if an outlier is an undesirable event (e.g. a machine with a very long downtime due to the non-availability of a faulty component) or to derive value from them if an outlier is a beneficial event (e.g. a customer with a very high average spend per purchase).

Outliers must *not be included* in a dataset used for inferential statistics or they will distort (bias) the inferential findings that are intended to describe the broader population picture in a true and unbiased way.

3.6 The Box Plot

A complete profile of a numeric random variable can be summarised in terms of five descriptive statistical measures known as the **five-number summary table**, as shown in Table 3.9 and displayed graphically as a **box plot**.

Table 3.9 The five-number summary table for a numerical variable

1	Minimum data value	x_{min}
2	Lower quartile	Q_1
3	Median	M_e or Q_2
4	Upper quartile	Q_3
5	Maximum data value	x_{max}

The box plot shows – in one easy-to-read graph – the range of the data (between the minimum and the maximum data values) and the spread of data values between the quartiles and median. It also highlights the degree of skewness in the data.

Follow these steps to construct a box plot:
- On a horizontal number line, construct a box between the Q_1 and Q_3 numeric positions.
- Mark the median inside the box at its numeric value position on the number line.
- Draw a horizontal line from the minimum value position to the Q_1 position. This is called the lower whisker.
- Draw another horizontal line from the Q_3 position to the maximum value position. This is called the upper whisker.

Example 3.16 Household Electricity Consumption Study

Refer to the sample data set of household electricity consumption (Table 3.5) in Example 3.8.

Construct a *five-number summary table* of daily household electricity consumption and display the results in a *box plot*.

Solution

Based on the data in Table 3.5, the five-number summary table values are:

Minimum = 33 kWh
Q_1 = 40.75 kWh
Median = 46.5 kWh
Q_3 = 54 kWh
Maximum = 61 kWh

The box plot of these central and non-central location values is shown in Figure 3.7.

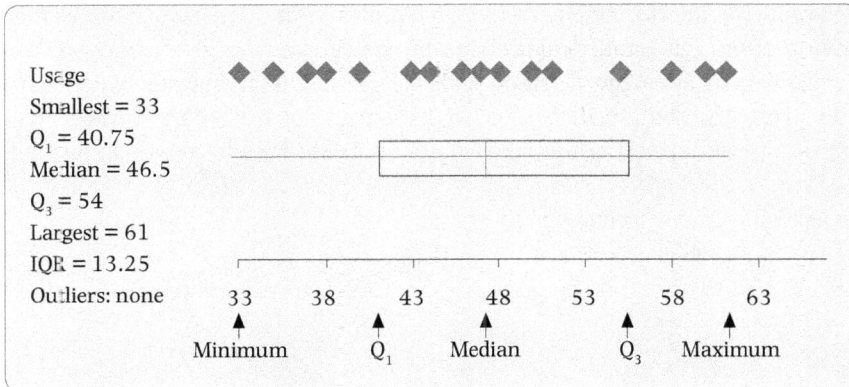

Figure 3.7 Box plot of household electricity consumption (kWh)

The box plot shows very slight positive skewness (there is a marginally wider spread of values from the median to Q_3 than from Q_1 to the median). For practical purposes, the spread of household electricity consumption value appears almost symmetrical about the median usage.

Follow these steps to observe skewness in a box plot:

- If a box plot is *symmetrical* about the median (i.e. the quartiles, minimum and maximum values are equidistant from the median in both directions), *no skewness* exists.
- If the lower whisker and the box is 'stretched' at the *lower end* of the box plot, the histogram is *negatively skewed* with a few extremely small values causing the skewness.
- If the upper whisker and the box is 'stretched' at the *upper end* of the box plot, the histogram is *positively skewed* with a few extremely large values causing the skewness.
- In a box plot, if outlier(s) exist, then:
  - draw the lower and upper 'whiskers' to end at the limits computed from Formula 3.19
  - show the outliers as separate (red) data points beyond the 'whiskers'.

In Example 3.8 (household electricity consumption), an outlier would be any daily household electricity consumption that is either:

(a) below 20.875 kWh (i.e. $40.75 - (1.5 \times (54 - 40.75))$)   See Formula 3.19(a)

    or

(b) above 73.875 kWh (i.e. $54 + (1.5 \times (54 - 40.75))$)   See Formula 3.19(b)

Since no data values in Table 3.5 lie below the lower limit of 20.875 kWh (minimum = 33 kWh) or above the upper limit of 73.875 kWh (maximum = 61 kWh), there are no outliers in this data set.

3.7 Bi-modal Distributions

A **bi-modal** (or **multi-modal**) distribution is a histogram with two (or more) peaks.

If a *bi-modal* (or multi-modal) pattern (distribution) in a histogram is observed, it generally means that the data values of the variable are *not homogeneous*. Therefore it is necessary to segment the total sample into separate homogeneous sub-samples based on an *identified external influencing factor* (e.g. gender; shift; supplier; brand used) before proceeding with further descriptive and inferential analysis of the data. Thereafter, identical, but separate, statistical analysis is performed on each sub-sample of data. This will result in more valid, relevant and meaningful statistical findings. Statistical analysis of a heterogeneous sample of data will result in misleading/distorted statistical findings for management decision-making.

To **illustrate**, the combined *distribution* (histogram) of the *cooling time* (in minutes) of a solvent produced during both day and night shifts shows a bi-modal pattern as seen in Figure 3.8.

(See Excel file C3.4 – *cooling times*.)

Figure 3.8 Bi-modal histogram – cooling time of a solvent (combined day and night)

When the total sample data is *segmented* into two separate sub-samples by *shift* (day versus night), the resultant histograms per sub-sample are each normally distributed as shown in Figure 3.9.

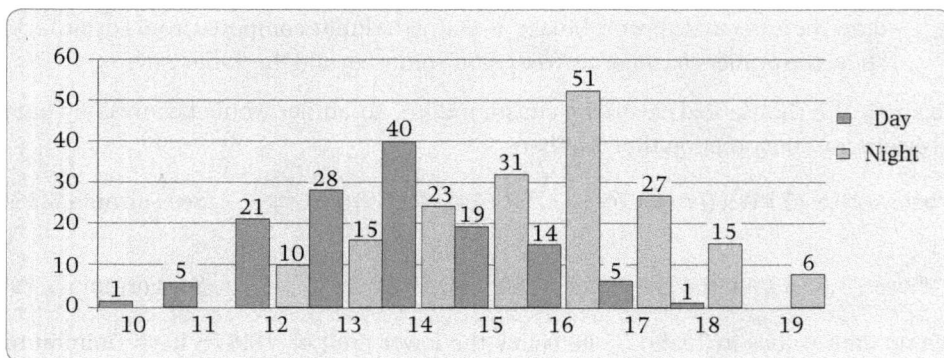

Figure 3.9 Segmented histograms – cooling times of a solvent (day vs night)

Refer to **segmentation table analysis** in Chapter 2.3 to further analyse a numeric variable (e.g. *solvent cooling time*) in terms of means and standard deviations between the sub-samples generated from a categorical variable (e.g. *shift* [day and night]) to explore possible relationships between these two variables.

3.8 Choosing Valid Descriptive Statistics Measures

The choice of valid statistical measures to describe the profile for any random variable is determined by its *data type*, and by the *shape* of its histogram (for numeric variables only).

For *categorical type* data (such as gender, dwelling type, job, sector, 'Are you employed? [Yes/No]') the only valid descriptive statistical measures are the categorical frequency table (count and percentage); the bar and pie charts; and the modal category. Measures of dispersion and skewness do not exist for categorical data as they have no meaning.

For *numeric type* data, the appropriate descriptive statistical measures that can be used are:
- a numeric frequency distribution (counts and percentages) and cumulative frequency distribution (ogives)
- the histogram and frequency polygons
- all central location measures: mean, median and mode (including geometric mean and weighted arithmetic mean)
- the non-central location measures of quartiles and percentiles
- all measures of dispersion: range, variance, standard deviation, coefficient of variation
- a measure of skewness (Pearson's coefficient of skewness)
- a graph of descriptive statistics measures: the box plot.

If the shape of the histogram for a numeric random variable is symmetrical (bell-shaped) then all three measures of central location (mean, median and mode) can be used to represent the central location of the data values. It is always recommended that the mean be quoted when reporting statistical findings in such instances.

If, however, the histogram is significantly skewed (either negatively or positively), the mean is not a representative measure of central location. Then one of two courses of action is recommended:
- Option 1: Select the median to represent the measure of central location.
- Option 2: Remove the outlier(s) from the data set and recalculate the mean. The revised mean can now be used to represent central location as it is no longer distorted by the (excluded) extreme data values. The outliers must, however, be reported in any findings as well as investigated to identify underlying causes, either for remedial action or exploiting opportunities.

3.9 Using Excel (2016) and X-Static to Compute Descriptive Statistics

Excel functions, the **Data Analysis** add-in, and **X-Static** can be used to compute all the descriptive statistical measures of location, non-central location, spread and shape.

Function Keys

The following function keys can be used:

- Central location measures
  - arithmetic mean   **=AVERAGE(data range)**
  - median   **=MEDIAN(data range)**
  - mode   **=MODE(data range)**
  - geometric mean   **=GEOMEAN(percentage change data)**

> *Note:* For the geometric mean, all percentage change data must be inputted as a decimal, (e.g. a 12% increase is inputted as 1.12; while a 8% decrease is inputted as 0.92). For example **=GEOMEAN(1.12,1.08,1.16)** = 1.1195 (i.e. an 11.95% average increase).

- Non-central location measures
  - minimum data value   **=MIN(data range)**
  - lower quartile   **=QUARTILE.EXC(data range,quart)** (quart = 1 refers to Q_1)
  - upper quartile   **=QUARTILE.EXC(data range,quart)** (quart = 3 refers to Q_3)
  - maximum data value   **=MAX(data range)**
  - percentiles   **=PERCENTILE.EXC(data range,percent (as a decimal))**

  The **QUARTILE** function can be used to compute all the values of the five-number summary table (i.e. min, Q_1, median, Q_3, max) by assigning different numeric codes to the 'quart' term in the function as follows: 0 = minimum data value; 1 = Q_1; 2 = median; 3 = Q_3; and 4 = maximum data value.

- Dispersion
  - variance   **=VAR.S(data range)**
  - standard deviation   **=STDEV.S(data range)**
- Shape
  - skewness   **=SKEW(data range)**

Data Analysis Add-in

The **Descriptive Statistics** option in the **Data Analysis** add-in (see Figure 3.10) will compute all the above descriptive measures, except the quartiles.

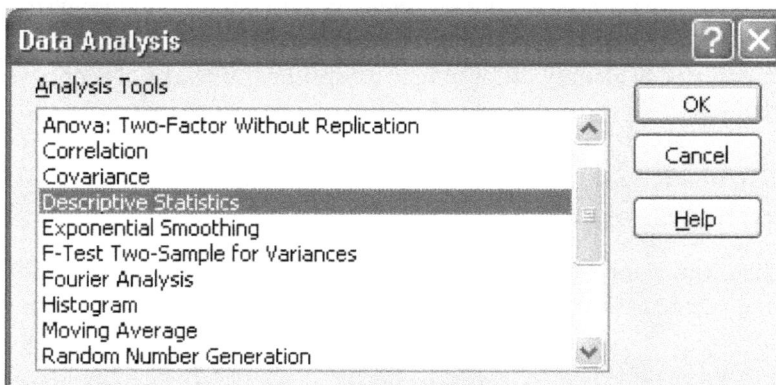

Figure 3.10 The descriptive statistics option in **Data Analysis** add-in

Example 3.17 Household Electricity Consumption Study

Refer to the data in Table 3.5.

Compute the *descriptive statistical measures* for daily household electricity consumption.

Solution

The output showing all the descriptive statistics measures for daily household electricity consumption is shown in Table 3.10.

Table **3.10** Descriptive statistics measures for daily household electricity consumption

Electricity usage (kWh)	
Mean	46.9
Standard error	1.838
Median	46.5
Mode	43
Standard deviation	8.22
Sample variance	67.57
Kurtosis	−0.854
Skewness	0.113
Range	28
Minimum	33
Maximum	61
Sum	938
Count	20

Excel does not offer an option to construct a box plot. Such options are, however, available in many other statistical software packages such as SPSS, Minitab and X-Static.

X-Static

Figure 3.11 shows the full selection of descriptive statistical measures available in **X-Static**. If all descriptive measures are required, the 'All' tickbox can be selected only, otherwise specific descriptive measures can be selected individually.

Refer to **Appendix 2** for a *flowchart summary of Descriptive Statistics tools*. It shows the appropriate statistical methods for different data types of variables. It summarises the statistical methods for a single categorical variable; for two categorical variables together; for a single numeric variable; for two numeric variables together; and finally, for a single numeric variable segmented by one or more categorical variables.

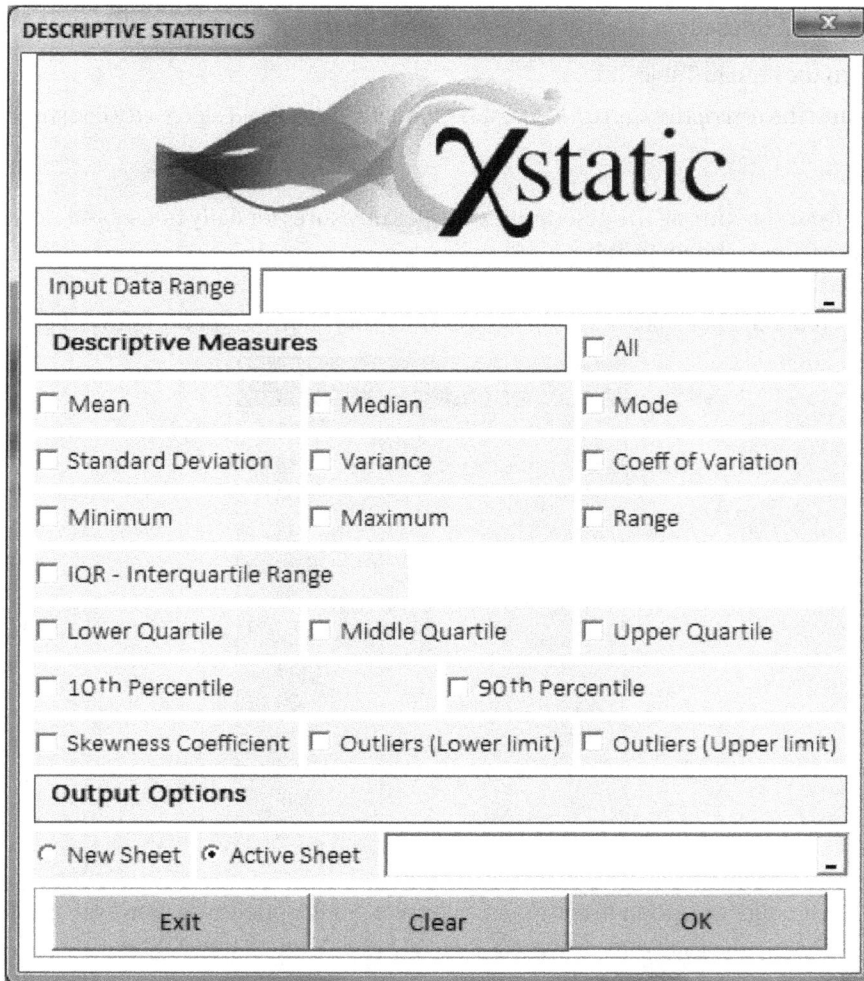

Figure 3.11 The Descriptive Statistics measures available in X-Static.

3.10 Summary

This chapter covered all the numeric descriptive statistical measures that can be used to profile sample data. These measures expressed the location, spread and shape of the sample data in numeric terms. Each measure was defined and calculated, and the conditions under which each would be appropriate to use were identified. The influence of data type and the presence of outliers are identified as the primary criteria determining the choice of a suitable numeric descriptive measure to describe sample data. A method for identifying outliers was described.

For qualitative random variables represented by categorical data, only the mode is appropriate to describe the profile of its sample data. Measures of spread and skewness are not relevant for categorical data. All numeric descriptive measures are appropriate to describe the profile of quantitative random variables.

All descriptive measures can be computed in Excel by using the appropriate function keys or the **Descriptive Statistics** module of either the Data Analysis add-in or X-Static. Boxplots can be produced using Excel (2016) onwards and using **X-Static's Summary Tables and Graphs** module.

These descriptive measures – particularly the mean, standard deviation (variance) and concept of symmetry – are important for the area of inferential analysis and statistical modelling, which will be covered in chapters 7 to 13.

The chapter ended with an overview of all the exploratory data techniques that are relevant to either a categorical or a numeric random variable. This identifies valid statistical techniques for each type of random variable (i.e. qualitative and quantitative). A summary flowchart of descriptive statistical tools is given in Appendix 2.

Exercises

This symbol denotes data available online

1   Identify the central location measure (mean, median, mode) referred to in each statement.
    (a)   Half of our employees have more than 10 years' work experience.
    (b)   The most popular city amongst foreign tourists is Cape Town.
    (c)   The average time taken to complete a task is 18 minutes.

2   Which non-central location measure (lower or upper quartile) is described in the following statement?

    'In terms of work experience, 25% of our employees each have more than 15 years of experience.'

3   For which of the following statements would the arithmetic mean be inappropriate as a measure of central location? (Give a reason.) State which measure of central location would be more appropriate, if necessary.
    (a)   the ages of children at a playschool
    (b)   the number of cars using a parking garage daily
    (c)   the brand of cereal preferred by consumers
    (d)   the value of transactions in a clothing store
    (e)   the weight of hand luggage carried by airline passengers
    (f)   your choice of daily newspaper available in your city
    (g)   the responses by citizens on a five-point rating scale to the statement:
          'South Africa should be divided into two time zones.'

4   Which statements below are true and which are false? Give a reason for your answer. If the median mass of five parcels for delivery by a courier service is 6.5 kg and one further 7 kg parcel is added to the consignment, then:
    (a)   the new median mass will be about 6.6 kg
    (b)   the median will increase
    (c)   it is impossible for the new median mass to be less than it was
    (d)   it is impossible for the new median mass to stay exactly at 6.5 kg
    (e)   the median may increase, but that depends on the actual masses of all five parcels.

5   The following measures of central location were calculated for the number of people per household in Mossel Bay: mode = 2 people; mean = 4.1 people; median = 3 people.

    If there are 9 245 households in the municipal district of Mossel Bay, which of the following methods is appropriate to calculate the likely total number of persons living in Mossel Bay?
    (a)   Multiply the number of households by 2.
    (b)   Multiply the number of households by 4.1.
    (c)   Multiply the number of households by 3.

6   X3.6 – unit trusts
    The percentage returns last year for seven general equity unit trusts were 9.2; 8.4; 10.2; 9.6; 8.9; 10.5 and 8.3. Calculate the mean and standard deviation of percentage returns.

The following calculations can be performed either manually, using a calculator, or using Excel.

7   X3.7 – luggage weights

The mass (in kg) of the hand luggage of seven air passengers was as follows:

11	12	8	10	13	11	9

(a)   Find the average and standard deviation of the hand luggage masses.
(b)   Interpret the meaning of each descriptive statistic in (a).
(c)   Find the coefficient of variation of the hand luggage masses.
(d)   Is there high relatively variability in the mass of hand luggage between passengers? Explain briefly.

8   X3.8 – bicycle sales

The number of bicycles sold monthly by a bicycle dealer was:

25	18	30	18	20	19	30	16	36	24

(a)   Find the mean and median number of bicycles sold monthly. Interpret each descriptive statistics measure.
(b)   Find the range, variance and standard deviation of the number of bicycles sold monthly. Interpret the range and standard deviation measures.
(c)   Calculate the lower and upper quartiles of monthly bicycle sales. Interpret.
(d)   Use the approximate skewness formula to estimate the degree of symmetry in the distribution of monthly bicycle sales. Interpret its meaning.
(e)   Construct a box plot of monthly bicycle sales. Interpret the plot.
(f)   If the dealer uses the formula 'mean plus one standard deviation' to decide on the opening stock level of bicycles at the beginning of next month, will he run out of stock during the month if he receives orders for 30 bicycles next month? Assume no extra bicycles can be ordered.

9   X3.9 – setting times

The setting time for ceramic tile glue is an important quality feature of the product. A manufacturer of ceramic tile glue tested a sample of nine batches from a large consignment and recorded the setting times (in minutes) of each batch:

27	22	31	18	20	25	21	28	24

(a)   Find the mean and standard deviation of setting times of the ceramic tile glue.
(b)   How consistent are the setting times across the different batches? Compute the coefficient of variation as a consistency index measure.
(c)   If the consistency index must be less than 10% for the consignment to be passed by the quality controller, will this consignment be approved for dispatch? Explain your answer.

10   X3.10 – wage increases

A labour consultant analysed the agreed percentage wage increases in 16 wage negotiations conducted between labour unions and employers. They were:

5.6	7.3	4.8	6.3	8.4	3.4	7.2	5.8
8.8	6.2	7.2	5.8	7.6	7.4	5.3	5.8

(a) Find the mean and median negotiated percentage wage increases.

(b) Find the variance and standard deviation of the percentage wage increases.

(c) Compute two standard deviation limits about the mean. Interpret these.

(d) How consistent are the percentage wage increases agreements? Compute the coefficient of variation as a consistency index measure.

11 Two groups of bank trainees each wrote a banking exam with the following percentage results:

	Mean	Variance	Sample size
Group 1	76	110	34
Group 2	64	88	26

(a) Compute the coefficient of variation of exam scores for each trainee group.

(b) Which group showed greater consistency in exam score performance? Why?

12 X3.12 – meal values

A restaurant owner randomly selected and recorded the value of meals enjoyed by 20 diners on a given day. The values of meals (in rand) were:

44	65	80	72	90	58	44	47	48	35
65	56	36	69	48	62	51	55	50	44

(a) Define the random variable and its data type.

(b) Compute the mean and standard deviation of the value of meals at the restaurant.

(c) What is the median value of a meal at the restaurant? Interpret its meaning.

(d) What meal value occurs most frequently?

(e) Which central location measure would you choose? Why?

13 X3.13 – days absent

The human resources department of a company recorded the number of days absent of 23 employees in the technical department over the past nine months:

5	4	8	17	10	9	30	5	6	15	10	9
2	16	15	18	4	12	6	6	15	10	5	

(a) Find the mean, median and modal number of days absent over this nine-month period.
Interpret each central location measure.

(b) Compute the first quartile and the third quartile of the number of days absent. Interpret these quartile values for the human resources manager.

(c) The company's policy is to keep its absenteeism level to within an average of one day per employee per month. Based on the findings in (a), is the company successful in managing its absenteeism level? Explain.

14 X3.14 – bad debts

The Gauteng chamber of business conducted a survey amongst 17 furniture retailers to identify the percentage of bad debts in each company's debtors' book. The bad debts percentages are as follows:

2.2	4.7	6.3	5.8	5.7	7.2	2.6	2.4	6.1	6.8
2.2	5.7	3.4	6.6	1.8	4.4	5.4			

(a)   Find the average and standard deviation of the percentage of bad debts amongst the 17 furniture retailers surveyed.

(b)   Find the median percentage of bad debts amongst the 17 furniture retailers surveyed.

(c)   Interpret the findings from (a) and (b).

(d)   Is there a modal percentage of bad debts? If so, identify it and comment on its usefulness.

(e)   Calculate the skewness coefficient for percentage of bad debts. Is the data skewed?

(f)   Compute the first quartile and the third quartile of the percentage of bad debts amongst the furniture retailers surveyed. Interpret these quartile values.

(g)   The chamber of business monitors bad debt levels and will advise an industry to take corrective action if the percentage of bad debts, on average, exceeds 5%. Should the chamber of business send out an advisory note to all furniture retailers based on these sample findings? Justify your answer.

15   X3.15 – fish shop

A fish shop owner recorded the daily turnover of his outlet for 300 trading days as shown in the frequency table.

Daily turnover	Number of days
500 –< 750	15
750 –< 1 000	23
1 000 –< 1 250	55
1 250 –< 1 500	92
1 500 –< 1 750	65
1 750 –< 2 000	50

(a)   Compute and interpret the (approximate) average daily turnover of the fish shop.

(b)   Find the median daily turnover of the fish shop. Interpret its meaning.

(c)   What is the modal daily turnover of the fish shop?

(d)   Find the maximum daily turnover associated with the slowest 25% of trading days.

(e)   What daily turnover separates the busiest 25% of trading days from the rest?

16   X3.16 – grocery spend

An economist conducted a study to identify the percentage of family income allocated to the purchase of groceries. She surveyed a random sample of 50 families and compiled the following numeric frequency distribution:

Percent of income	Number of families
10–under 20%	6
20–under 30%	14
30–under 40%	16
40–under 50%	10
50–under 60%	4

(a)   Compute and interpret the (approximate) mean percentage of family income allocated to grocery purchase.
(b)   What is the maximum percentage of income that is allocated to grocery purchase by:
   (i)   the lower 50% of families?
   (ii)   the lower 25% of families?
(c)   25% of families spend more than a specific percentage of their income on groceries. What is that percentage of income value?

17   X3.17 – equity portfolio
Find the average price paid per share in an equity portfolio consisting of:
40 shares bought for R15 each; 10 shares bought for R20 each; 5 shares bought for R40 each; and 50 shares bought for R10 each. Use the weighted average formula.

18   X3.18 – car sales
Value Cars, a pre-owned car dealership with branches throughout Gauteng, last month sold 5 cars at R25 000 each; 12 cars at R34 000 each; and 3 cars at R55 000 each. What was the average price per car sold by Value Cars last month? Use the weighted average formula.

19   X3.19 – rental increases
Office rental agreements contain escalation clauses. For a particular office complex in the Nelspruit CBD, the escalation rates based on the previous year's rental over four years were 16%, 14%, 10% and 8% respectively.
Use the geometric mean to find the average annual escalation rate in office rentals for this office complex over the four-year period.

20   X3.20 – sugar increases
The price of a kilogram of sugar increased by 5%, 12%, 6%, 4%, 9% and 3% over the past six years.
(a)   Find the average annual percentage increase in the price of sugar (per kg) using the geometric mean.
(b)   Why is the geometric mean more suitable than the arithmetic mean?

21   X3.21 – water usage
Thirty households in a Paarl suburb were surveyed to identify their average water usage per month (in kilolitres, kl). The usage per household was:

10	18	30	13	42	14	9	15	19	20
25	15	24	12	15	16	22	22	8	33
50	26	16	32	25	26	16	26	25	12

Use Excel's **Data > Data Analysis > Descriptive Statistics** option and, where necessary, the function key **QUARTILE.EXC** to answer the following questions:
(a)   Find the mean, median and modal water usage across the 30 households.
(b)   Find the variance and standard deviation of water usage per household.
(c)   Find the first and the third quartile of water usage amongst the 30 households.
(d)   Interpret the findings from (a) to (c) for the municipal officer who conducted this survey.
(e)   If there are 750 households in the Paarl suburb, what is the most likely total water usage (in kl) amongst all these households:
   (i)   in a month?
   (ii)   in a year?

22   X3.22 – veal dishes

The price of a veal cordon bleu meal (in rand) was taken from the menus of 28 Durban restaurants in a survey conducted by *Lifestyle* magazine into the cost of 'dining out'. The prices are:

| 48 | 66 | 60 | 90 | 58 | 58 | 53 | 63 | 64 | 55 | 64 | 58 | 54 | 72 |
| 56 | 80 | 55 | 62 | 75 | 48 | 55 | 45 | 48 | 72 | 52 | 68 | 56 | 70 |

Use Excel's **Data > Data Analysis > Descriptive Statistics** option and, where necessary, the function keys **QUARTILE.EXC** and **PERCENTILE.EXC**, to answer the following questions:

(a)   Define the random variable and its data type.

(b)   Find the mean and median price of a veal cordon bleu meal. Interpret each measure.

(c)   Can you identify a modal price? Give its value and discuss its usefulness.

(d)   Identify the value of the standard deviation of the price of veal cordon bleu.

(e)   Compute the skewness coefficient. Does the data appear to be skewed? If so, why?

(f)   Which central location measure would you choose to report in the article on 'dining out'? Why?

(g)   What is the least price that a patron to one of these restaurants would pay if they dined out at any one of the most expensive 25% of restaurants?

(h)   The least expensive 25% of restaurants do not charge above what price for the veal cordon bleu meal?

(i)   What is the least price to be paid for the most expensive 10% of veal cordon bleu meals?

23   X3.23 – fuel bills

The monthly fuel bills of a random sample of 75 Paarl motorists who commute to work daily by car were recorded in a recent survey.

(a)   Use the **Descriptive Statistics module** in either **Data Analysis** or **X-Static** to find the mean, median, variance standard deviation and skewness coefficient of the monthly fuel bill of the sample of car commuters.

(b)   Interpret the meaning of each descriptive statistic in (a).

(c)   Is the data skewed? If so, in what direction? What would be the cause of skewness?

(d)   Find the coefficient of variation for monthly fuel bills. Is the relative variability between the sampled motorists' monthly fuel bills low?

(e)   Use the Excel function key **QUARTILE.EXC** to find the lower and upper quartiles of monthly fuel bills of motorists. Interpret each quartile.

(f)   Compile the five-number summary table for monthly fuel bills.

(g)   Construct a box plot of monthly fuel bills.

(h)   Describe the profile of the monthly fuel bills of Paarl motorists who use their cars to commute daily to work and back.

(i)   Assume that the cost of fuel is R10 per litre and that there are 25 000 motorists who commute to work daily in Paarl by car. Estimate the most likely total amount of fuel used (in litres) by all car commuters in Paarl in a month.

24 X3.24 – service periods

The Association of Professional Engineers recently surveyed a sample of 100 of its members to identify their years of experience.

(a) Use the **Descriptive Statistics module** in either **Data Analysis** or **X-Static** to find the mean, median, standard deviation and skewness measure of the years of experience for the sample of professional engineers.

(b) Interpret the meaning of each descriptive statistical measure in (a).

(c) Use either the **Histogram option** in **Data Analysis** or the **Summary Tables and Graphs module** in **X-Static** to compute a frequency distribution and a histogram of the years of experience for the sample data. (*Hint*: Use the bin range given in the database.)

(d) Compute an interval for the years of experience of professional engineers that covers one standard deviation either side of the sample mean.
What percentage of the sampled professional engineers does this represent?

(e) The Association of Professional Engineers would like to see a mix of 'experience' and 'new blood' amongst its members. Ideally they would like to have at least 20% of their members with less than three years of experience (i.e. 'new blood' members) and at least 20% of their members with more than 12 years of service (i.e. 'experienced' members). Based on the histogram and frequency distribution in (c), is this desired mix of experience being achieved? Comment.

25 X3.25 – dividend yields

A survey of 44 JSE-listed companies recorded their dividend yields (as a percentage) for last year as shown in the following table:

5.3	4.8	3.1	4.1	6.1	4.1	3.2	4.6	7.6	1.6
4.6	1.9	4.8	2.9	1.5	5.1	2.8	3.6	3.3	5.5
2.8	4.2	3.6	3.1	5.9	2.9	3.6	4.1	4.9	2.7
3.7	7.1	6.2	2.8	5.1	3.8	3.4	3.9	5.8	6.3
6.8	4.3	5.1	5.4						

(a) Define the random variable and its data type.

(b) Use the **Descriptive Statistics module** in either **Data Analysis** or **X-Static** to find the mean, median, mode, standard deviation and skewness measure of the dividend yields of the JSE-listed companies.

(c) Interpret the meaning of each descriptive statistical measure in (b).

(d) Which central location measure would you use to report on the dividend yields of companies? Why?

(e) Use either the **Histogram option** in **Data Analysis** or the **Summary Tables and Graphs module** in **X-Static** to compute a numeric frequency distribution and a histogram of the dividend yields of the sampled JSE companies. (*Hint*: Use the bin range given in the database.)

(f) Use Excel's function key operations (**MIN, MAX, MEDIAN** and **QUARTILE.EXC**) to compute the five-number summary table.

(g) Construct a box plot of the dividend yields of the JSE-listed companies and interpret the profile of the dividend yields declared by JSE companies last year.

(h) What was the minimum dividend yield declared by the top 10% of JSE companies? (*Hint:* Use the **PERCENTILE.EXC** function key.)

(i) What percentage of JSE companies did not declare more than a 3.5% dividend yield last year? (*Hint:* Compute the cumulative frequency distribution to find the cumulative percentages.)

26 X3.26 – rosebuds

A commercial flower grower in Eazyview sells fresh-cut rosebuds to retailers in Johannesburg. The unit price per rosebud (in cents) varies according to supply and demand. The grower has recorded the unit selling price for 100 transactions over the past two months.

(a) Define the random variable and data type.

(b) Use the **Descriptive Statistics module** in either **Data Analysis** or **X-Static** to find the mean, standard deviation, median and skewness coefficient descriptive measures of the unit selling price of rosebuds.

(c) Compute and interpret the coefficient of variation of the unit selling price of rosebuds.

(d) Use Excel's function key **QUARTILE.EXC** to compute the upper and lower quartiles of the unit selling price of rosebuds.

(e) What the highest unit selling price for the cheapest 25% of transactions?

(f) What was the minimum unit selling price received for the highest priced 25% of transactions?

(g) What was the lowest unit selling price received for the highest-valued 10% of transactions?

(h) What was the highest unit selling price received for the lowest-valued 10% of transactions? (*Hint:* For (g) and (h) use the Excel function key **PERCENTILE.EXC.**)

(i) Construct the five-number summary table and draw a box plot. Interpret the profile of the unit selling price of rosebuds for the flower grower.

Mini Case Studies

27 X3.27 – savings balances   Savings Profiles of Bank Clients

Savings data for a sample of 175 clients has been extracted from a bank's client database. For each client, their *gender* (1 = female, 2 = male); *marital status* (1 = married, 2 = single) and month-end *savings balance* (in R10s) was recorded. The table below shows the first 10 records only for the sample data of 175 records.

Sample Data – Client Profiles (only the first 10 records are shown)

Client	Gender	Marital	Savings (R10s)
1	2	1	187
2	2	1	254
3	2	1	532
4	2	1	312
5	2	1	546
6	1	1	483
7	2	2	356
8	1	1	1 312
9	2	2	252
10	2	1	226

(a) You are required to perform the following analysis (using Excel (2016) or **X-Static**).

(i) A numeric frequency distribution and histogram of month-end savings balances (use intervals 0 – 200, 201 – 400, 401 – 600, 601 – 800, 801 – 1 000, > 1 000)

(ii) The descriptive statistics for month-end savings balances (use **Descriptive Statistics**). Also compute the lower quartile and upper quartile month-end savings balances. Use **QUARTILE.EXC**.

(iii) A cross-tabulation table of gender and marital status showing frequency counts.

(iv) A segmentation (two-way pivot) table showing the average month-end savings balances split by gender and marital status.

(b) Answer the following management questions.

(i) Name each of the random variables in this study. For each, state whether it is a *categorical* or a *numeric* random variable and define its *data measurement scale* (nominal, ordinal, interval, ratio).

(ii) Based on the summary profiles produces in a(i – iv) above, provide a *brief report* to the bank's management on the *saving behaviour* of these sampled clients.

(iii) If management wish to attract further clients and increase savings levels through a marketing campaign, are there any groupings potential clients that the bank could target based on the evidence available in the summary profiles? Justify your answer.

28   X3.28 – medical claims   **Medical Scheme Claims Pattern Study**

An analyst was requested to examine the claims pattern of members of
a particular medical scheme. She randomly sampled 150 scheme members and
recorded the following variables for each member:

- their *marital status* (1 = married, 2 = single)
- their *age* group (age bands of (1 = (26 – 35), 2 = (36 – 45), 3 = (46 – 55))
- their *claims ratio* (member's total claims for last year/total contributions for last year).

The *claims ratio* is an indicator of cross-subsidisation of members.
The data (only the first 10 of 150 records) is shown in the table below.

Sample Data – Members Profiles (only first 10 records shown)

Member	Marital	Age	Ratio
1	2	2	0.278
2	1	3	1.685
3	2	2	0.548
4	2	1	1.647
5	2	1	1.022
6	1	2	1.988
7	1	3	0.111
8	1	3	2.248
9	2	3	1.145
10	2	2	0.297

(a)   You are required to perform the following analysis (using Excel [2016] or **X-Static**).

(i)   a numeric frequency distribution and a histogram of claims ratios (use intervals $0 - <0.25, 0.25 - <0.50, 0.50 - <0.75$, etc. until $2.50 - <2.75$).

(ii)   The descriptive statistics for claims ratios (use **Descriptive Statistics**). Also compute the lower quartile and upper quartile. Use **QUARTILE.EXC**.

(iii) A cross-tabulation table of marital status and age groups showing frequency counts.

(iv)   A segmentation (two-way pivot) table of the claims ratios showing the average, standard deviation, minimum and maximum data values of claims ratios split by marital status and age groups.

(b)   Answer the following management questions.

(i)   Identify each of the variables in this study. For each, state whether it is a *qualitative* or *quantitative* variable and define its *data measurement scale* (nominal, ordinal, interval, ratio).

(ii)   Based on the summary profiles derived in a(i – iv) above, provide a *brief report* to the medical scheme management about the *claims ratio pattern* of its members.

(iii) Is there any cause for concern for the *financial viability* of this medical scheme? Provide any evidence based on the findings above to support your comments.

The Foundation of Statistical Inference: Probability and Sampling

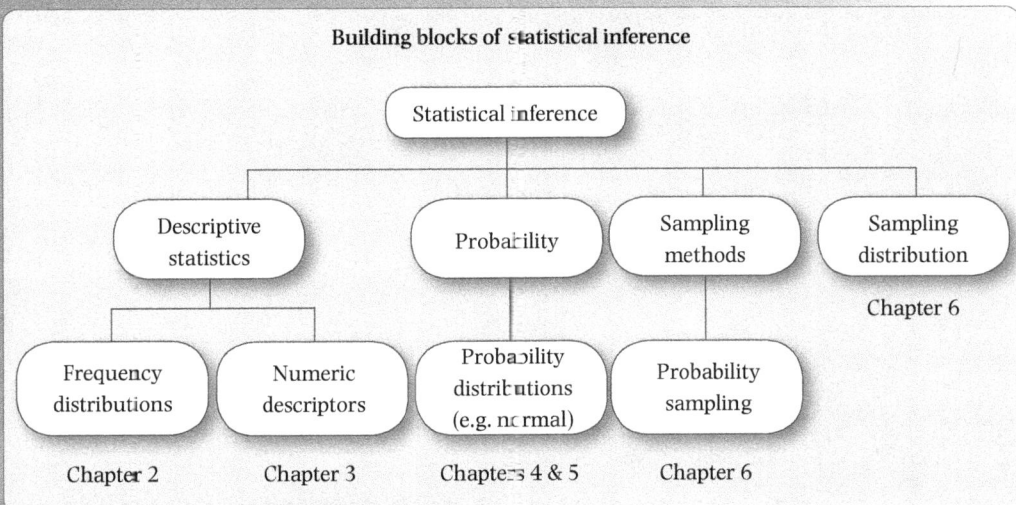

Building blocks of statistical inference

Statistical inference

Descriptive statistics

Probability

Sampling methods

Sampling distribution

Chapter 6

Frequency distributions

Numeric descriptors

Probability distributions (e.g. normal)

Probability sampling

Chapter 2   Chapter 3   Chapters 4 & 5   Chapter 6

Basic Probability Concepts

Outcomes

To generalise sample findings to estimate population parameters, the reliability, precision and level of certainty of such estimates must be determined. This is done through probability theory. Probability theory describes ways in which uncertainty can be quantified and measured. The chapter provides a brief overview of the basic concepts of probability to help a manager to understand and use probabilities in decision-making.

After studying this chapter, you should be able to

- understand the importance of probability in statistical analysis
- define the different types of probability
- describe the properties and concepts of probabilities
- apply the rules of probability to empirical data
- construct and interpret probabilities from joint probability tables
- apply Bayes' theorem to revise prior probabilities
- understand the use of counting rules (permutations and combinations).

4.1 Introduction

Many business decisions are made under conditions of uncertainty. Probability theory provides the foundation for quantifying and measuring uncertainty. It is used to estimate the reliability in making inferences from samples to populations, as well as to quantify the uncertainty of future events. It is therefore necessary to understand the basic concepts and laws of probability to be able to manage uncertainty.

A **probability** is the chance, or likelihood, that a particular event will occur.

These are examples of events representing typical probability-type questions:
- What is the likelihood that a task will be completed within 45 minutes?
- How likely is it that a product will fail within its guarantee period?
- What is the chance of a telesales consultant making a sale on a call?

4.2 Types of Probability

Probabilities are broadly of two types: subjective or objective.

Where the probability of an event occurring is based on an educated guess, expert opinion or just plain intuition, it is referred to as a **subjective probability**. Subjective probabilities cannot be statistically verified and are not used extensively in statistical analysis.

Alternatively, when the probability of an event occurring can be verified statistically through surveys or empirical observations, it is referred to as an **objective probability**. This type of probability is used extensively in statistical analysis.

Mathematically, a probability is defined as the ratio of two numbers:

$$P(A) = \frac{r}{n}$$ 4.1

Where: A = event of a specific type (or with specific properties)
 r = number of outcomes of event A
 n = total number of all possible outcomes (called the **sample space**)
 P(A) = probability of event A occurring

Example 4.1 Motor Vehicle Loyalty Study

Assume that 355 Ford car owners ($n = 355$) were randomly selected and asked the following question: 'When you buy your next car, will you buy another Ford product?' (event A).

The outcome is either 'Yes' or 'No'. Assume that 76 respondents answered 'Yes' ($r = 76$). Then $P(A) = \frac{76}{355} = 0.214$.

There is a 21.4% chance that a current Ford owner will remain loyal to the Ford brand name and purchase another Ford on his or her next car purchase. Alternatively stated, one in five Ford car owners is brand loyal.

Deriving Objective Probabilities

There are three ways in which objective probabilities can be derived:

1   *a priori* (when the outcomes are known in advance, such as tossing a coin, selecting playing cards or rolling dice)
2   *empirically* (when the values of *r* and *n* are not known in advance but can be observed and derived empirically through data collection (i.e. using surveys))
3   *mathematically* (through the use of theoretical *probability distribution functions*, which are mathematical formulae that are used to calculate probabilities for certain event types).

This chapter focuses on calculating and interpreting empirically derived objective probabilities, while Chapter 5 shows how objective probabilities can be derived from theoretical distributions.

4.3   Properties of a Probability

There are five basic properties that apply to every probability:

1   A probability value lies only between 0 and 1 inclusive (i.e. $0 \leq P(A) \leq 1$).
2   If an event A *cannot occur* (i.e. an impossible event), then $P(A) = 0$.
3   If an event A is *certain to occur* (i.e. a certain event), then $P(A) = 1$.
4   The sum of the probabilities of all possible events (i.e. the *collectively exhaustive* set of events) equals one, i.e. $P(A_1) + P(A_2) + P(A_3) + ... + P(A_k) = 1$, for k possible events.

   For example, if cash, cheque, debit card or credit card (i.e. $k = 4$) are the only possible payment methods (events) for groceries, then for a randomly selected grocery purchase, the probability that a customer pays by either cash, cheque, debit card or credit card is: $P(A_1 = \text{cash}) + P(A_2 = \text{cheque}) + P(A_3 = \text{debit card}) + P(A_4 = \text{credit card}) = 1$.

5   *Complementary probability:* If $P(A)$ is the probability of event A occurring, then the probability of event A not occurring is defined as $P(\overline{A}) = 1 - P(A)$.

   For example, if there is a 7% chance that a part is defective, then $P(\text{a defective part}) = 0.07$ and $P(not \text{ a defective part}) = 1 - 0.07 = 0.93$.

The following example illustrates how managers can quantify uncertain events and use them as a basis for decision-making.

Example 4.2 Petrol Brand Preference Study

Table 4.1 shows the percentage frequency table for the petrol brand most preferred by 50 motorists who live in George.
(See Excel file C4.1 – *petrol brands*.)

Table 4.1 Petrol brand preference – frequency counts and percentages

Petrol brand	Count	Percentage
BP	13	26%
Caltex	9	18%
Engen	6	12%
Shell	22	44%
Total	50	100%

(a) What is the likelihood that a randomly selected motorist prefers Engen?
(b) What is the chance that a randomly selected motorist does not prefer Shell?
(c) What is the probability of finding a motorist who prefers either the BP, Caltex, Engen or Shell brand of petrol?

Solution

(a) Let A = event (motorist who prefers Engen petrol).

Then $P(A) = \frac{6}{50} = 0.12$.

Thus there is only a 12% chance of finding a motorist who prefers Engen.

(b) Let A = event (motorist who prefers Shell petrol).

Let $\overline{A}$ = event (motorist who does not prefer Shell petrol).

Since $P(A) = \frac{22}{50} = 0.44$, then $P(\overline{A}) = 1 - P(A) = 1 - 0.44 = 0.56$.

Thus there is a 56% chance of finding a motorist who does not prefer Shell petrol. This means that more than half the motorists surveyed (56%) prefer another brand of petrol.

(c) Let A_1 = event (motorist who prefers the BP brand of petrol).

Let A_2 = event (motorist who prefers the Caltex brand of petrol).

Let A_3 = event (motorist who prefers the Engen brand of petrol).

Let A_4 = event (motorist who prefers the Shell brand of petrol).

These four events represent the *collectively exhaustive* set of events for the variable 'petrol brand preferred'. It is called the sample space.

Then $P(A_1) + P(A_2) + P(A_3) + P(A_4) = \frac{13}{50} + \frac{9}{50} + \frac{6}{50} + \frac{22}{50} = 1$.

Thus there is complete certainty that a randomly chosen motorist will prefer one of these four petrol brands.

4.4 Basic Probability Concepts

The following concepts are relevant when calculating probabilities associated with two or more events occurring:

- the *intersection* of events
- the *union* of events
- *mutually exclusive* events
- *collectively exhaustive* events
- *statistically* independent events.

These basic probability concepts will be illustrated using the following example:

Example 4.3 JSE Companies – Sector and Size Study

One hundred and seventy (170) companies from the JSE were randomly selected and classified by sector and size. Table 4.2 shows the **cross-tabulation table** of joint frequencies for the two categorical random variables 'sector' and 'company size'. (See Excel file C4.2 – *jse companies*.)

Table 4.2 Cross-tabulation table – JSE companies by sector and size

Sector	Company size			Row total
	Small	Medium	Large	
Mining	3	8	30	41
Financial	9	21	42	72
Service	10	6	8	24
Retail	14	13	6	33
Column total	36	43	86	170

These frequency counts are used to derive **empirical probabilities**, since the data was gathered from a survey and organised into a summary table.

Concept 1: Intersection of Two Events (A ∩ B)

The **intersection** of two events A and B is the set of all outcomes that belong to both A and B *simultaneously*. It is written as A ∩ B (i.e. A and B), and the keyword is **'and'**.

Figure 4.1 shows the intersection of events graphically, using a Venn diagram. The intersection of two simple events in a Venn diagram is called a **joint event**.

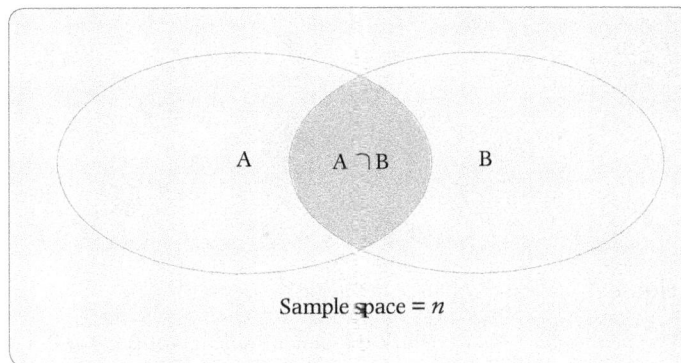

Figure 4.1 Venn diagram of the intersection of two events (A ∩ B)

(a) What is the probability that a randomly selected JSE company will be small and operate in the service sector?

Solution

(a) Let A = event (small company).

Let B = event (service sector company).

Then (A ∩ B) is the set of all small *and* service sector companies.

From Table 4.2, there are 10 companies that are both small *and* operate in the service sector, out of 170 JSE companies surveyed. This is shown graphically in the Venn diagram in Figure 4.2.

Thus $P(A \cap B) = P(\text{small} \cap \text{service}) = \frac{10}{170} = 0.0588$.

There is only a 5.9% chance of selecting a small service sector JSE company.

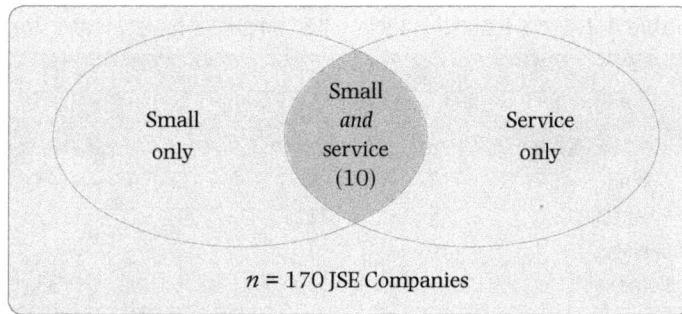

Figure 4.2 Venn diagram of small and service JSE companies (intersection)

Concept 2: Union of Two Events (A ∪ B)

> The **union** of two events A and B is the set of all outcomes that belong to *either* event A or B or both. It is written as A ∪ B (i.e. either A *or* B or both) and the key word is '**or**'.

Figure 4.3 shows the union of events graphically using a Venn diagram.

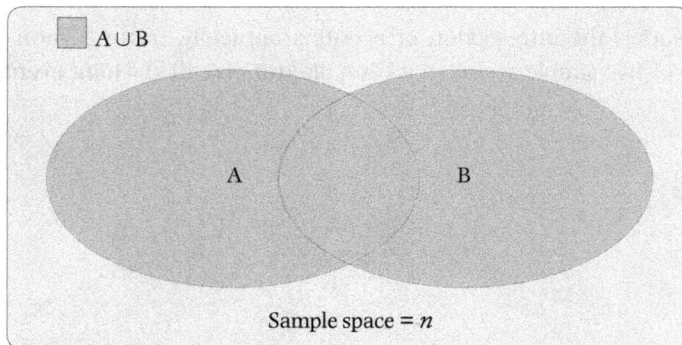

Figure 4.3 Venn diagram of the union of events (A ∪ B)

(b) What is the probability that a randomly selected JSE company will be *either* a small company *or* a service sector company, *or both?*

Solution

(b) Let A = event (small company).

Let B = event (service company).

Then (A ∪ B) is the set of all small *or* service *or both* (small and service) companies. As seen in Table 4.2, there are 36 small companies (includes 10 service companies), 24 service companies (includes 10 small companies) and 10 small and service companies. Therefore, there are 50 separate companies (36 + 24 − 10) that are *either* small *or* service, *or both*. Note that the intersection (joint) event is subtracted once to avoid double counting. This is shown in the Venn diagram in Figure 4.4 below.

Thus $P(A \cup B) = P(\text{small} \cup \text{service}) = \frac{36 + 24 - 10}{170} = \frac{50}{170} = 0.294$.

There is a 29.4% chance of selecting *either* a small *or* a service JSE company, *or both*.

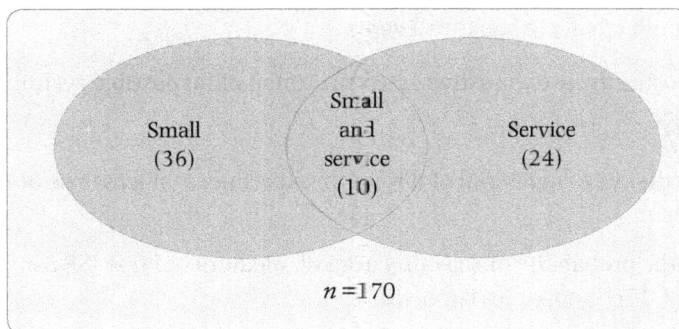

Figure 4.4 Venn diagram of small or service JSE companies (union)

Concept 3 Mutually Exclusive Events

Events are **mutually exclusive** if they *cannot occur together* on a single trial of a random experiment (i.e. not at the same point in time).

Figure 4.5 graphically shows events that are mutually exclusive (i.e. there is *no intersection*) using a Venn diagram.

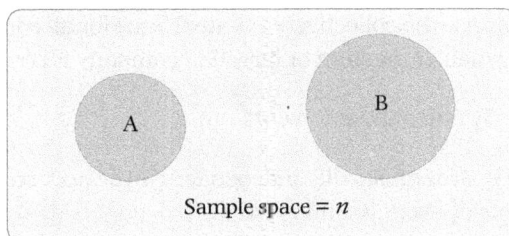

Figure 4.5 Venn diagram of mutually exclusive events, $A \cap B = 0$

(c) What is the probability of a randomly selected JSE company being both a small and a medium-sized company?

Solution

(c) Let A = event (small company).

Let B = event (medium company).

Events A and B are *mutually exclusive*, since a randomly selected company *cannot* be both small and medium at the same time.

Thus $P(A \cap B) = P(\text{small} \cap \text{medium}) = 0$ (i.e. the joint event is null).

There is *no chance* of selecting a small- and medium-sized JSE company simultaneously. It is therefore an *impossible event*.

Events are *non-mutually exclusive* if they *can occur together* on a single trial of a random experiment (i.e. at the same point in time). Figure 4.1 graphically shows events that are non-mutually exclusive (i.e. there is an intersection). Example (a) above illustrates probability calculations for events that are not mutually exclusive.

Concept 4: Collectively Exhaustive Events

> Events are **collectively exhaustive** when the union of all possible events is equal to the sample space.

This means, that in a single trial of a random experiment, at least one of these events is certain to occur.

(d) What is the probability of selecting a small, medium or large JSE company from the sample of 170 companies surveyed?

Solution

(d) Let A = event (small company).
   Let B = event (medium company).
   Let C = event (large company).
   Since $(A \cup B \cup C)$ = (the sample space of all JSE companies)
   then $P(A \cup B \cup C) = P(\text{small}) + P(\text{medium}) + P(\text{large})$
$$= \frac{36}{170} + \frac{48}{170} + \frac{86}{170}$$
$$= 0.212 + 0.282 + 0.506 = 1$$

Since the events comprise the collectively exhaustive set for all company sizes, the event of selecting either a small or medium or large JSE company is *certain to occur*.

Concept 5: Statistically Independent Events

> Two events, A and B, are **statistically independent** if the occurrence of event A has *no effect* on the outcome of event B, and *vice versa*.

For example, if the proportion of male clients of Nedbank who use internet banking is the same as the proportion of Nedbank's female clients who use internet banking, then 'gender' and 'preference for internet banking' at Nedbank are statistically independent events.
A test for statistical independence will be given in section 4.6.

A word of caution

The terms 'statistically independent' events and 'mutually exclusive' events are often confused. They are two very different concepts. The distinction between them is as follows:
● When two events are mutually exclusive, they cannot occur together.
● When two events are statistically independent, they can occur together, but they do not have an influence on each other.

4.5 Calculating Objective Probabilities

Objective probabilities can be classified into three types: marginal probability, joint probability and conditional probability.

Marginal Probability P(A)

A **marginal probability** is the probability of a *single event* A occurring only.

A single event refers to the outcomes of only one random variable. Since a frequency table describes the outcomes of only one random variable, it is used to calculate marginal probabilities.

For example, the probabilities calculated in Example 4.2 (petrol brand preference study) are illustrations of marginal probabilities because they relate to the outcomes of the single random variable (petrol brand preference) only.

Example 4.4 JSE Companies – Sector and Company Size Study

Refer to Table 4.3, which illustrates the calculation of the different probability types.

Table 4.3 Cross-tabulation table – JSE companies by sector and size

Sector	Company size			Row total
	Small	Medium	Large	
Mining	3	8	30	41
Financial	9	21	42	72
Service	10	6	8	24
Retail	14	13	6	33
Column total	36	48	86	170

(a) What is the probability that a randomly selected JSE company is large?
(b) What is the chance that a JSE-listed mining company is randomly selected?

Solution

(a) The 'Column total' row in Table 4.3 describes the outcomes for the random variable 'company size' only and is therefore used to find marginal probabilities for the variable 'company size'.

Let A = event (large company)

From Table 4.3, there are 86 large companies in the sample of 170 companies. Thus $P(A) = \frac{86}{170} = 0.506$ (50.6%).

There is a 50.6% chance that a randomly selected JSE company will be large.

(b) The 'Row total' column in Table 4.3 describes the outcomes for the random variable 'sector' only and is therefore be used to find marginal probabilities for the variable 'sector'.

Let B = event (mining company).

From Table 4.3, there are 41 mining companies in the sample of 170 companies. Thus $P(B) = \frac{41}{170} = 0.241$ (24.1%).

There is a 24.1% chance that a mining company will be randomly selected.

Joint Probability P(A ∩ B)

A **joint probability** is the probability that *both* event A and event B will occur simultaneously on a single trial of a random experiment.

A **joint event** refers to the outcomes of *two or more* random variables occurring together as illustrated in Figure 4.1. It is the same as the intersection of two events in a Venn diagram (see Concept 1 above).

Since a cross-tabulation table shows the outcomes of two random variables simultaneously, it is used to find joint probabilities.

Example 4.4 contd.

(c) What is the probability that a randomly selected JSE company is a medium-sized financial company?

Solution

(c) Let A = event (medium-sized company).
    Let B = event (financial company).

From Table 4.3, there are 21 medium-sized financial companies in the study. Thus $P(A \cap B) = \frac{21}{170} = 0.124$ (12.4%).

There is a 12.4% chance of randomly selecting a medium-sized financial company.

Conditional Probability P(A|B)

A **conditional probability** is the probability of event A occurring, given that event B has already occurred. It is written as P(A|B).

In formula terms, a conditional probability is defined as follows:

$$P(A|B) = \frac{P(A \cap B)}{P(B)}$$

    4.2

The essential feature of the conditional probability is that the *sample space is reduced* to the set of outcomes associated with the *given* prior event B only. The prior information (i.e. event B) can change the likelihood of event A occurring.

Example 4.4 contd.

(d) What is the probability that a randomly selected company is a retail company, *given* that it is known (in advance) to be a medium-sized company?

Solution

Let A = event (retail company).
Let B = event (medium-sized company).
Then P(A|B) = P(retail company | medium-sized company).

The sample space is reduced to the subset of 48 medium-sized companies only (as shown in Table 4.4). Within this sub-sample of 48 medium-sized companies, there are 13 retail companies.

Table 4.4 Cross-tabulation table – JSE companies by sector and size

Sector	Company size			Row total
	Small	Medium	Large	
Mining	3	3	30	41
Financial	9	21	42	72
Service	10	5	8	24
Retail	14	13	6	33
Column total	36	48	86	170

Thus $P(A|B) = P(\text{retail}|\text{medium}) = \frac{13}{48} = 0.271$ (27.1%).

This same result can be found by applying Formula 4.2 as follows:

- $P(B) = P(\text{medium-sized}) = \frac{48}{170} = 0.2824$ (marginal probability).
- $P(A \cap B) = P(\text{retail} \cap \text{medium-sized}) = \frac{13}{170} = 0.0765$ (joint probability).
- Then $P(A|B) = \frac{\frac{13}{170}}{\frac{48}{170}} = \frac{13}{48} = 0.271$ (conditional probability).

There is a 27.1% chance that a randomly selected JSE company will be a retail company, *given* that it is known (in advance) to be a medium-sized company.

4.6 Probability Rules

Probability rules have been developed to calculate probabilities of compound or multiple events occurring simultaneously. There are two basic probability rules:

1. The **addition rule**
   - for non-mutually exclusive events, and
   - for mutually exclusive events.

   The addition rule relates to the *union* of events. It is used to find the probability of *either* event A *or* event B, *or both* events occurring simultaneously in a single trial of a random experiment.

2. The **multiplication rule**
   - for statistically dependent events, and
   - for statistically independent events.

   The multiplication rule relates to the *intersection* of events. It is used to find the probability of event A *and* event B occurring together in a single trial of a random experiment.

Refer to Table 4.5, which illustrates the application of these probability rules.

Addition Rule for Non-Mutually Exclusive Events

If two events are *not* mutually exclusive, they *can occur together* in a single trial of a random experiment. Then the probability of *either* event A or event B or *both* occurring in a single trial of a random experiment is defined as:

$$P(A \cup B) = P(A) + P(B) - P(A \cap B) \qquad \qquad 4.3$$

In Venn diagram terms, the union of two non-mutually exclusive events is the *combined outcomes* of the two overlapping events A and B – as described in Concept 2 and shown graphically in figures 4.3 and 4.4.

Example 4.5 JSE Companies – Sector and Size Study

Table 4.5 Cross-tabulation table – JSE companies by sector and size

Sector	Company size			Row total
	Small	Medium	Large	
Mining	3	8	30	41
Financial	9	21	42	72
Service	10	6	8	24
Retail	14	13	6	33
Column total	36	48	86	170

(a) What is the probability that a randomly selected JSE-listed company is *either* a large company *or* a financial company, *or both?*

Solution

(a) Let A = event (large company).

Let B = event (financial company).

Events A and B *are not mutually exclusive* as they can occur simultaneously (i.e. a company can be *both* large and financial).

From Table 4.5, the following marginal and joint probabilities can be derived:

$$P(A) = P(\text{large}) = \frac{86}{170} = 0.5059$$
$$P(B) = P(\text{financial}) = \frac{72}{170} = 0.4235$$
$$P(A \cap B) = P(\text{large and financial}) = \frac{42}{170} = 0.2471$$

Then $P(A \cup B) = P$ (*either* large *or* financial or *both*)

$$= P(\text{large}) + P(\text{financial}) - P(\text{large and financial})$$
$$= 0.5059 + 0.4235 - 0.2471$$
$$= 0.682\ (68.2\%)$$

There is a 68.2% chance that a randomly selected JSE-listed company will be *either* a large company *or* a financial company, *or both* (i.e. a large financial company).

Addition Rule for Mutually Exclusive Events

If two events are mutually exclusive, they *cannot occur together* in a single trial of a random experiment. Then the probability of *either* event A *or* event B (but *not both*) occurring in a single trial of a random experiment is defined as:

$$P(A \cup B) = P(A) + P(B) \qquad\qquad 4.4$$

i.e. it is the sum of only the two marginal probabilities of events A and B.

In Venn diagram terms, the union of two non-mutually exclusive events is the *sum of the outcomes* of each of the two (non-overlapping) events A and B *separately* – as described in Concept 3 and shown graphically in Figure 4.5.

For mutually exclusive events, there is *no intersectional* event. Thus $P(A \cap B) = 0$.

Example 4.5 contd.

(b) What is the probability that a randomly selected JSE-listed company is either a mining company or a service company?

Solution

Let A = event (mining company).

Let B = event (service company).

Events A and B are mutually exclusive as they cannot occur simultaneously (a company cannot be both a mining company and a service company), so $P(A \cap B) = 0$.

From Table 4.5, the following marginal probabilities can be derived:

$$P(A) = P(\text{mining}) = \frac{41}{170} = 0.241 \ (24.1\%)$$

$$P(B) = P(\text{service}) = \frac{24}{170} = 0.141 \ (14.1\%)$$

$$P(A \cap B) = 0$$

Then $P(A \cup B)$ = P(either mining or service)

$$= P(\text{mining}) + P(\text{service})$$

$$= 0.241 + 0.141$$

$$= 0.382 \ (38.2\%)$$

There is a 38.2% chance that a randomly selected JSE-listed company will be either a mining company or a service company, but not both.

Multiplication Rule for Statistically Dependent Events

The multiplication rule is used to find the *joint probability* of events A and B occurring together in a single trial of random experiment (i.e. the *intersection* of the two events). This rule assumes that the two events A and B are associated (i.e. they are dependent events).

The multiplication rule for dependent events is found by rearranging the conditional probability formula (Formula 4.2), resulting in:

$$P(A \cap B) = P(A \mid B) \times P(B) \qquad\qquad 4.5$$

Where $P(A \cap B)$ = joint probability of A and B
   $P(A \mid B)$ = conditional probability of A given B
   $P(B)$ = marginal probability of B only

Example 4.5 contd.

(c) What is the probability of selecting a small retail company from the JSE-listed sample of companies?

Solution

Let A = event (small company).

Let B = event (retail company).

Intuitively, from Table 4.5, $P(A \cap B) = P(\text{small and retail}) = \frac{14}{170} = 0.082$ (8.2%).

Alternatively, this probability can be calculated from the multiplication rule Formula 4.5.

$$P(B) = P(\text{retail}) = \frac{33}{170} = 0.1942$$
$$P(A|B) = P(\text{small}|\text{retail}) = \frac{14}{33} = 0.4242$$

Then
$$\begin{aligned} P(A \cap B) &= P(A|B) \times P(B) \\ &= P(\text{small}|\text{retail}) \times P(\text{retail}) \\ &= 0.4242 \times 0.1942 \\ &= 0.082 \ (8.2\%) \end{aligned}$$

There is only an 8.2% chance that a randomly selected JSE-listed company will be a small retail company.

Multiplication Rule for Statistically Independent Events

If two events A and B are statistically independent (i.e. there is no association between the two events) then the multiplication rule reduces to the product of the two marginal probabilities only.

$$P(A \cap B) = P(A) \times P(B) \tag{4.6}$$

Where: $P(A \cap B)$ = joint probability of A and B

$P(A)$ = marginal probability of A only

$P(B)$ = marginal probability of B only

The following test can be applied to establish if two events are statistically independent. Two events are statistically independent if the following relationship is true:

$$P(A|B) = P(A) \tag{4.7}$$

This means that if the *marginal probability* of event A *equals* the *conditional probability* of event A *given* that event B has occurred, then the two events A and B are statistically independent. This implies that the prior occurrence of event B in *no way influences* the outcome of event A.

Example 4.5 contd.

(d) Is company size statistically independent of sector in the JSE-listed sample of companies?

Solution

To test for statistical independence, select one outcome from each event A and B and apply the decision rule in Formula 4.7 above.

Let A = event (medium-sized company).

Let B = event (mining company).

Then
$$P(A) = P(\text{medium-sized company}) = \frac{48}{170} = 0.2824 \ (28.24\%)$$
$$P(A|B) = P(\text{medium-sized company}|\text{mining}) = \frac{8}{41} = 0.1951 \ (19.51\%)$$

Since the two probabilities are not equal (i.e. $P(A|B) \neq P(A)$), the empirical evidence indicates that company size and sector are statistically dependent (i.e. they are related).

4.7 Probability Trees

A **probability tree** is a graphical way to apply probability rules where there are *multiple events* that *occur in sequence* and these events can be represented by branches (similar to a tree).

Example 4.6 Product Failure Study

A product consists of two components. The product fails when either or both components fail. There is a 5% chance that component 1 will fail and a 10% chance that component 2 will fail. The components can fail independently of each other.
   (See Excel file C4.3 – *product failure*.)

What is the probability that the product will fail (i.e. that either or both components will fail together)?

Solution

This problem can be represented in a probability tree as shown in Figure 4.6.

The first two branches represent the two outcomes of component 1 (i.e. F_1 = component 1 fails and S_1 = component 1 does not fail). The second set of branches represents the two outcomes of component 2 (i.e. F_2 = component 2 fails and S_2 = component 2 does not fail).

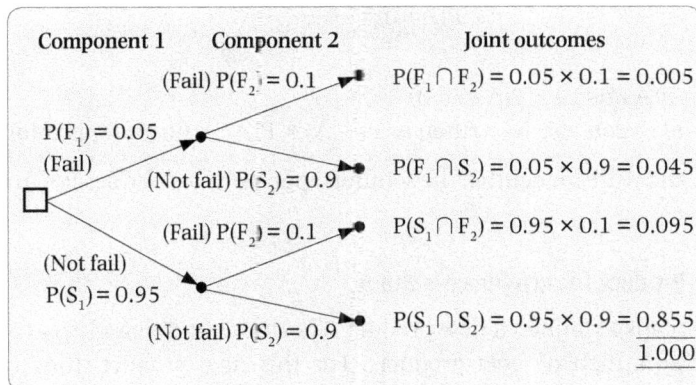

Component 1	Component 2	Joint outcomes
	(Fail) $P(F_2) = 0.1$	$P(F_1 \cap F_2) = 0.05 \times 0.1 = 0.005$
$P(F_1) = 0.05$ (Fail)		
	(Not fail) $P(S_2) = 0.9$	$P(F_1 \cap S_2) = 0.05 \times 0.9 = 0.045$
	(Fail) $P(F_2) = 0.1$	$P(S_1 \cap F_2) = 0.95 \times 0.1 = 0.095$
(Not fail) $P(S_1) = 0.95$		
	(Not fail) $P(S_2) = 0.9$	$P(S_1 \cap S_2) = 0.95 \times 0.9 = \underline{0.855}$
		$\overline{1.000}$

Figure 4.6 Probability tree for product failure study

The *end of each branch* represents the *joint event* of outcomes for both components together. For example, the top branch represents component 1 failing and component 2 failing. Therefore the joint probability of both components failing is found by multiplying their marginal probabilities (i.e. applying Formula 4.6 – the multiplication rule for statistically independent events). The application of Formula 4.6 is repeated for each branch of the tree.

Since the *product will fail* when *either* component 1 fails (and not component 2) *or* component 2 fails (and not component 1) *or both* components together (component 1 and component 2) fail.

Thus $P(\text{product fails}) = P(F_1 \cap S_2) + P(S_1 \cap F_2) + P(F_1 \cap F_2)$.

These joint probabilities can be read off the end of each appropriate branch in the probability tree.

$$P(\text{product fails}) = 0.045 + 0.095 + 0.005$$
$$= 0.145$$

Thus there is a 14.5% chance that this product will fail.

Note: If the two events A and B occur in a sequence and are not statistically independent of each other, then the second set of branches will represent the conditional probability of B given that event A has occurred. Then the joint probabilities at the end of each branch will be found by applying Formula 4.5 – the multiplication rule for statistically dependent events.

4.8 Bayes' Theorem

Often the outcome of one event A can be influenced by information obtained from a related event, B. **Bayes' theorem** shows how to *revise* the *initial probability* of event A occurring (i.e. **P(A)**) into a *updated probability* of event A occurring in the light of the new information available from a related event B (i.e. **P(A|B)**).

The formula to compute the *updated probability* for event A (called the **posterior probability**) from the *initial probability* of event A (called the **prior probability**) in the light of new information from event B was developed by Thomas Bayes (circa 1750). It is based on the conditional probability.

$$P(A \mid B) = \frac{P(A \text{ and } B)}{P(B)}$$

4.8

Where: $P(B) = P(A \text{ and } B) + P(\overline{A} \text{ and } B)$

And: $P(A \text{ and } B)$ can also be written as $P(B \mid A) \times P(A)$ – the multiplication rule

Since events A and B are sequential, the solution approach can also be shown in a probability tree.

Example 4.7 Product Launch Success Study

A company plans to launch a new product. They have traditionally had a 40% success rate with the launch of new products. For this new product, they commissioned market research to test the acceptance of product A in the market place. Market research is known to predict a positive test market result for 80% of successfully launched products; and a positive test market result for 30% of failed product launches.
(See Excel file C4.4 – *product launch*.)

Assume a market test result comes back positive, what is the probability that the product will be successfully launched?

Solution

Let   S = the product launch is a success   Y = Market research is positive (predicts product success)

F = the product launch is a failure   N = Market research is negative (predicts product failure)

From the management scenario, the following probabilities can be derived:

S is the prior event – 'product success'.   P(S) = 0.4 (prior probability) and P(F) = 0.6

New information from market research results in the following revised probabilities:

P(Y|S) = 0.8   and   P(Y|F) = 0.3

Required to find P(S|Y) – the posterior probability

i.e. the probability of a successful launch (S) given that the market research findings are positive (Y) for a successful launch.

P(S|Y) = P(S and Y) / P(Y)   (Bayes' Theorem)

Now: P(S and Y) = P(Y|S) × P(S) = 0.8 × 0.4 = 0.32   (multiplication rule)

            P(F and Y) = P(Y|F) × P(F) = 0.3 × 0.6 = 0.18   (multiplication rule)

and   P(Y) = P(S and Y) + P(F and Y) = 0.32 + 0.18 = 0.50

Then   P(S|Y) = 0.32 |0.50 = 0.64

These probabilities can be computed and displayed in a probability tree as follows:

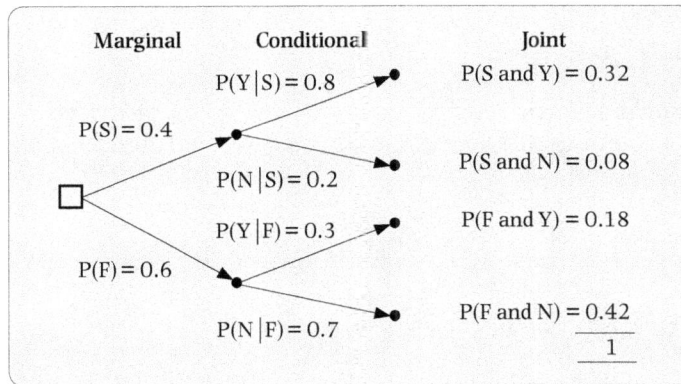

Figure 4.7 Probability tree of product launch based on market research information

Interpretation

There is a 64% chance that the product will be successfully launched given that it has a positive market research report.

4.9 Counting Rules – Permutations and Combinations

Probability calculations involve *counting* the number of event outcomes (*r*) and the total number of possible outcomes (*n*) and expressing these as a ratio. Often the values for *r* and *n* cannot be counted because of the large number of possible outcomes involved. Counting rules assist in finding values for *r* and *n*.

There are three basic counting rules: the multiplication rule, the permutations rule and the combinations rule.

The Multiplication Rule of Counting

For a Single Event

The *total number of different ways* (**permutations**) in which *n* objects (i.e. the full sample space) can be arranged (ordered) is given by *n*! (read as 'n factorial').

$$n! = n \text{ factorial} = n \times (n-1) \times (n-2) \times (n-3) \times \dots \times 3 \times 2 \times 1 \qquad 4.9$$

Note: $0! = 1$

Example 4.8 Swimming Lane Allocation Study

In a six-lane swimming pool, how many unique arrangements (permutations) of six swimmers can be considered?

Solution

The single event is the order of swimmers in lanes.

The number of different (unique) orderings of the six swimmers in the six lanes is given by:

$6! = 6 \times 5 \times 4 \times 3 \times 2 \times 1 = 720$ different swimming arrangements (permutations)

For Combined Events

If a particular random process has n_1 possible outcomes for event 1, n_2 possible outcomes for event 2, ..., n_j possible outcomes for the jth event, then the total number of possible outcomes for the j events collectively is:

$$n_1 \times n_2 \times n_3 \times \dots \times n_j \qquad 4.10$$

Example 4.9 Restaurant Menu Selection Study

A restaurant menu has a choice of four starters, 10 main courses and six desserts. What is the total number of possible unique meals that can be ordered from this restaurant?

Solution

There are three events: starter ($n_1 = 4$), main course ($n_2 = 10$) and dessert ($n_3 = 6$).
The total number of possible (unique) permutations of meals (each consisting of a starter, a main and a dessert) that can be ordered is:

$4 \times 10 \times 6 = 240$ different possible meal permutations

When only a subset of objects (r) are drawn from a larger set of objects (n), then the number of ways in which these r objects can be selected from n objects can be found by using either the permutations rule or the combinations rule, depending on whether the order of the selection is important or not.

Permutations Rule

A **permutation** is the number of distinct ways of selecting (or arranging) a subset of r objects drawn from a larger group of n objects, where the *order of selection of objects is important.*

Each possible arrangement of the subset of r objects is called a permutation. The number of distinct ways (permutations) of arranging r objects selected from n objects, where *order is important*, is given by:

$$_nP_r = \frac{n!}{(n-r)!}$$

4.11

Where: r = number of objects selected at a time
         n = total number of objects from which to select

Example 4.10 Worker Assignment Study

A factory has three machines and eight possible machine operators.
(a) How many distinct assignments (orderings) of machine operators to machines are possible?
(b) What is the probability of one particular ordering of machine operators to the three machines?

Solution

(a) Given $n = 8$ machine operators and $r = 3$ machines.

Then $_8P_3 = \frac{8!}{(8-3)!} = \frac{8!}{5!}$

$$= \frac{8 \times 7 \times 6 \times 5 \times 4 \times 3 \times 2 \times 1}{5 \times 4 \times 3 \times 2 \times 1}$$

$$= 336 \text{ permutations}$$

There are 336 distinct assignments of 8 workers to 3 machines.

(b) The probability of selecting a particular grouping of three machine operators is:

P(particular order of 3 machine operators) $= \frac{1}{336}$
$$= 0.00297 \,(0.297\%)$$

Any particular ordering (where order of assignment to the three machines is important) has only a very small probability (only 0.297% chance) of being selected.

Combinations Rule

A **combination** is the number of distinct ways of selecting (or arranging) a subset of r objects drawn from a larger group of n objects where the *order of selection of objects is not important*.

Each separate grouping of the subset of r objects is called a combination.
The number of ways of selecting r objects from n objects, not considering order of selection, is given by:

$$_nC_r = \frac{n!}{r!(n-r)!}$$

4.12

Where: r = number of objects selected at a time
         n = total number of objects from which to select

Example 4.11 Fruit Juice Shelf Display Study

A company produces fruit juice in 10 different flavours. A local supermarket sells the product, but has only sufficient shelf space to display three of the company's 10 fruit juice flavours at a time.

(a) How many possible groupings (combinations) of three flavours can the fruit juice company display on the local supermarket shelf?

(b) What is the probability that a particular combination of three fruit juice flavours will be selected by the juice company for display?

Solution

(a) The *order* in which the three fruit juices flavours are chosen for display is *not important*, hence apply the combination Formula 4.12.

Given $n = 10$ fruit flavours, and $r = 3$ flavours for display.

Then $_{10}C_3 = \dfrac{10!}{3!(10-3)!} = \dfrac{10!}{3!\,7!}$

$$= \frac{10 \times 9 \times 8 \times 7 \times 6 \times 5 \times 4 \times 3 \times 2 \times 1}{(3 \times 2 \times 1)(7 \times 6 \times 5 \times 4 \times 3 \times 2 \times 1)}$$

$$= 120 \text{ combinations}$$

There are 120 different displays of three fruit juice flavours at a time that can be selected from a possible 10 flavours, without regard to order.

(b) The probability of selecting a particular combination of three fruit juice flavours out of a possible 10 flavours is:

P(any one combination of 3 flavours out of 10 flavours) $= \dfrac{1}{120}$

$$= 0.0083$$

There is only a 0.83% chance that a particular combination of three fruit juice flavours will be selected.

4.10 Summary

This chapter introduced the concept of probabilities as the foundation for inferential statistics, which is covered in later chapters. The term 'probability' is a measure of the uncertainty associated with the outcome of a specific event, and the properties of probabilities were defined. Also examined were the concepts of probabilities, such as the union and intersection of events, mutually exclusive events, collectively exhaustive sets of events and statistically independent events. These concepts describe the nature of events for which probabilities are calculated.

The basic probability types, namely marginal, joint and conditional, were calculated from cross-tabulation tables. Probability calculations for multiple events were also derived using the addition rule and the multiplication rule. Probabilities associated with sequential events are shown in a probability tree and Bayes' theorem to revise probabilities in the light of new information is introduced. Finally, the counting rules for permutations and combinations were introduced as a way of finding the number of outcomes associated with specific events.

The next chapter will calculate probabilities for random variables that follow certain defined theoretical patterns, called probability distributions.

Exercises

This symbol denotes data available online

1   If an event has a probability equal to 0.2, what does this mean?
2   What term is used to describe two events that cannot occur simultaneously in a single trial of a random experiment?
3   What is meant when two terms are said to be 'statistically independent'?
4   If $P(A) = 0.26$, $P(B) = 0.35$ and $P(A \text{ and } B) = 0.14$, what is the value of $P(A \text{ or } B)$?
5   If $P(X) = 0.54$, $P(Y) = 0.36$ and $P(X \text{ and } Y) = 0.27$, what is the value of $P(X|Y)$? Is it the same as $P(Y|X)$?

6   X4.6 – economic sectors
      In a survey of companies, it was found that 45 were in the mining sector, 72 were in the financial sector, 32 were in the IT sector and 101 were in the production sector.
      (a)   Show the data as a percentage frequency table.
      (b)   What is the probability that a randomly selected company is in the financial sector?
      (c)   If a company is selected at random, what is the probability that this company is *not* in the production sector?
      (d)   What is the likelihood that a randomly selected company is *either* a mining company *or* an IT company?
      (e)   Name the probability types or rules used in questions (b), (c) and (d).

7   X4.7 – apple grades
      An apple cooperative in Elgin, Western Cape, receives and groups apples into A, B, C and D grades for packaging and export. In a batch of 1 500 apples, 795 were found to be grade A, 410 were grade B, 106 were grade C and the rest grade D.
      (a)   Construct a percentage frequency distribution of apple grades.
      (b)   What is the probability that a randomly selected apple from the batch will belong to grade A?
      (c)   If an apple is selected at random from the batch, what is the likelihood that it is *either* of grade B *or* D?
      (d)   Grade C and D apples are not exported. What is the probability that a randomly selected apple is export quality?
      (e)   Name the probability types or rules used in questions (b), (c) and (d).

8   X4.8 – employment sectors
      Statistics South Africa reported the number of people employed by sector in a given year as follows (in thousands): 6 678 in the formal business sector (excluding agriculture); 1 492 in the commercial agricultural sector; 653 in subsistence agriculture; 2 865 in the informal business sector; and 914 in the domestic service sector.
      (a)   Construct a percentage frequency distribution of employment by sector.
      (b)   What is the probability that a randomly selected employed person works in the domestic service sector?
      (c)   If an employed person is selected at random from the workforce, what is the likelihood that the person earns a living through agriculture?
      (d)   If a person is known to work in the business sector (both formal and informal), what is the likelihood that the person is an informal trader?
      (e)   Name the probability types or rules used in questions (b), (c) and (d).

9   X4.9 – qualification levels

The human resources department of an insurance company analysed the qualifications profile of their 129 managers in terms of their highest qualification achieved. The findings are shown in the cross-tabulation (two-way pivot) table.

Qualification	Managerial level		
	Section head	Dept head	Division head
Matric	28	14	?
Diploma	20	24	6
Degree	?	10	14
Total	53	?	28

(a)   Define the two random variables, their measurement scale and data type.

(b)   Complete the above cross-tabulation table (joint frequency table).

(c)   What is the probability that a manager selected at random:

(i)   has only a matric?

(ii)   is a section head and has a degree?

(iii)   is a department head given that the manager has a diploma?

(iv)   is a division head?

(v)   is either a division head or a section head?

(vi)   has either a matric, or a diploma, or a degree?

(vii)   has a degree given that the person is a department head?

(viii) is either a division head or has a diploma or both?

(d)   For each probability calculated in (c) state:

(i)   the type of probability (i.e. marginal, joint or conditional)

(ii)   which probability rule, if any, was applied (i.e. addition rule or multiplication rule).

(e)   Are the events in (c)(v) and (vi) mutually exclusive?

10   X4.10 – bonus options

A company offered each of its employees a choice of three performance bonus options: a cash bonus option, a profit-sharing option and a shares option. The number of employees who selected each bonus option together with their work function (administration or production) is shown in the following cross-tabulation (two-way pivot) table.

	Cash bonus	Profit-sharing	Shares option
Admin	28	44	68
Production	56	75	29

(a)   What is the probability that an employee selected the cash bonus option?

(b)   If income tax must only be paid on the cash bonus or the profit-sharing option, what is the probability that an employee selected a tax-free bonus option?

(c) What is the likelihood that an employee works in production and chose the cash bonus option?

(d) If an employee is in administration, what is the likelihood that the employee chose the shares option?

(e) If a cash bonus option was chosen, what is the probability that it was chosen by a production worker?

(f) If event A = shares option and event B = an administration employee, test whether the choice of performance bonus option is statistically independent of the work function of the employee.

(g) State the probability type (marginal, joint or conditional) or probability rule that applied in each of (a) to (e).

11 X4.11 – age profile

The following table shows the 300 employees of a glass manufacturing company, cross-classified on the basis of age and department:

Age	Department			Total
	Production	Sales	Administration	
< 30	60	25	18	103
30–50	70	29	25	124
> 50	30	8	35	73
Total	160	62	78	300

(a) An employee is selected at random from this company. Calculate the probability that the employee is:
  (i) under 30 years of age
  (ii) a production worker
  (iii) a sales person and between 30 and 50 years of age
  (iv) over 50, given that he or she is in administration
  (v) a production worker or under 30 years, or both.

(b) Are the two events 'age' and 'department' mutually exclusive? Justify your answer.

(c) Are age and department statistically independent? Justify your answer.

(d) State the probability type and probability rule, if appropriate, used in each of (a)(i)–(v).

12 X4.12 – digital cameras

Consider the following cross-tabulation table of brand preference for digital cameras and their primary usage (professional or personal):

Usage	Digital camera brand preference			Total
	Canon	Nikon	Pentax	
Professional	48	15	27	90
Personal	30	95	65	190
Total	78	110	92	280

(a) What is the probability of randomly selecting a professional user?
(b) What is the probability of selecting a user who prefers the Nikon brand?
(c) Find the probability that a user prefers the Pentax brand *given* that their usage is primarily personal.
(d) Is brand preference statistically independent of primary usage? Justify your answer with a statistical illustration and explain the meaning of your finding.
(e) What is the likelihood that a randomly selected user prefers the Canon brand and is a professional user?
(f) Find the probability of randomly selecting either a professional user or a user who prefers the Nikon brand of digital camera or both.
(g) Are the two events primary usage and brand preference mutually exclusive? Justify your answer statistically.

13 An electronic device consists of two components, A and B. The probability that component A will fail within the guarantee period is 0.20. There is also a 15% chance that component B will fail within the guarantee period. Assume the components operate entirely independently of each other.
(a) Draw a probability tree to show all the outcomes and their probabilities for the components (events) A and B.
(b) What is the probability that both components will fail within the guarantee period?
(c) If either or both components fail within the guarantee period, the company will replace the electronic device free of charge. What is the probability that the electronic device will *not* need to be replaced during the guarantee period?

14 Personal Financial Advisors (PFA) are required by law to write a professional exam. PFAs can choose to attend a workshop to prepare for the exam. 30% attended a preparatory workshop and, of these advisors, 80% of them passed the professional exam. Of those that did not attend a preparatory workshop, only 60% passed the professional exam.
(a) Draw a probability tree to show all the outcomes and their probabilities for the two events, workshop (attend/not attend) and exam result (pass/fail)). Let the first branch be the event {workshop} and the second branch be the event {exam result}.
(b) Use the probability tree to find the following probabilities:
(i) What is the probability of a PFA passing the exam *and* having attended a workshop?
(ii) What is the probability of a PFA passing the exam (regardless of whether they attended a workshop or not)?

15 Find the value of:
(i) $6!$
(ii) $3! \, 5!$
(iii) $4! \, 2! \, 3!$
(iv) $_7C_4$
(v) $_9C_6$
(vi) $_8P_3$
(vii) $_5P_2$
(viii)$_7C_7$
(ix) $_7P_4$

Explain the meaning of each of these calculations in terms of a practical scenario.

16 A company has 12 products in its product range. It wishes to advertise in the local newspaper but, due to space constraints, it is allowed to display only seven of its products at one time. How many different ways can this company compose a display of seven products out of its range of 12 products to insert into the local newspaper?

17   There are five levels of shelving in a supermarket. If three brands of soup must each be placed on a separate shelf, how many different ways can a packer arrange the soup brands?

18   For a balanced investment portfolio consisting of four equities, an investor must select only one equity from each of nine economic sectors (labelled 1 to 9).
      (a)   How many different portfolios consisting of four equities can be selected?
      (b)   What is the probability that the portfolio will consist of one equity each from economic sectors 3, 5, 7 and 8?

19   What is the probability that each of five identical screws that are removed from the back cover of a stove will be replaced in exactly the same holes from which they were removed?

20   A selection of 10 tourist attractions is available in Cape Town.
      (a)   How many separate selections are there of three attractions, not considering the order in which the three attractions are visited?
      (b)   What is the probability of selecting a particular day tour package of three attractions, regardless of the order in which they are visited?

21   A planning committee for a major development project, such as a shopping mall, must consist of two architects and four engineers. There are four architects and seven engineers available from which to choose.
      (a)   How many different combinations of committee members can be formed?
      (b)   If the committee must also include an environmental lawyer, of which there are two available, how many different committee compositions are now possible?

22   A project manager would like to estimate the probability of completing a project *on time* when a major '*scope change*' has occurred. (Note: a 'scope change' is a change to a project's brief). From historical records of similar projects, 70% of projects were completed on time. Also, the records showed that of the projects that were completed 'on time', 40% of them had a major *scope change*, while of the projects that were not completed *on time*, 80% of them had a major *scope change*.
      Find the probability of completing a project on time given that a major scope change had occurred.

23   A sports psychologist conducted a study into the sporting habits of married couples. In a survey amongst 300 married couples under 30 years of age, the psychologist established the following facts: 60% of the married men participated in sport. Of these married couples, 40% of the wives also participated in sport. Of the married couples where the husband did not participate in sport, 30% of the wives participated in sport.
      The sports psychologist wished to determine the probability that the husband participates in sport when it is known that the wife participates in sport?

24   Airline A operates 60% of all scheduled flights from Lanseria airport near Johannesburg while Airline B operates the balance of 40% of scheduled flights from this airport. Their on-time departure rates are 80% for airline A (i.e. 80% of airline A's scheduled flights leave on time) and 65% for airline B.
      A flight has just *left on time*. What is the probability that this flight was an airline A flight given its departure status?

25 Research has shown that 60% of new business ventures (NBV) are *started by graduates*, while the remaining 40% are *started by non-graduates*. Also, 80% of new business ventures started by graduates are *successful*, while only 65% of those started by non-graduates are successful. A successful new business venture is defined as a business that survives beyond 3 years.

   Given that a NBV has *failed*, what is the probability that it was *started by a graduate?*

26 A commercial airline (e.g. KLM) has noticed that 40% of its customers buy their tickets *online* (i.e. purchase an e-ticket on the internet) while the remaining 60% of their customers still use travel agencies. They have also established that 80% of e-ticket customers travel for *business* reasons, while only 45% of their non-e-ticket customers are business travellers.

   Given that a randomly chosen customer is known to travel for *business* reasons, what is the probability that his/her ticket was bought *online?*

Probability Distributions

Outcomes

Probabilities can also be derived using mathematical functions known as probability distributions. Probability distributions quantify the uncertain behaviour of many random variables in business practice. This chapter will introduce a few important probability distributions that occur most often in management situations. Probability distributions can describe patterns of outcomes for discrete as well as continuous events.

After studying this chapter, you should be able to:

- understand the concept of a probability distribution
- describe three common probability distributions used in management practice
- identify applications of each probability distribution in management
- calculate and interpret probabilities for each of these distributions.

5.1 Introduction

A **probability distribution** is a list of all the possible outcomes of a random variable and their associated probabilities of occurrence.

Chapter 4 showed that probabilities can be derived *empirically* through data collection and the construction of frequency distributions. The frequencies associated with each outcome of the random variable under study are then used to calculate the probabilities of specific events occurring. A probability distribution is therefore similar to a frequency distribution. In contrast, this chapter will show how to use *mathematical functions* to find probabilities.

There are numerous problem situations in practice where the outcomes of a specific random variable follow *known probability patterns*. If the behaviour of a random variable under study can be matched to one of these known probability patterns, then probabilities for outcomes associated with the random variable can be found directly by applying an appropriate theoretical probability distribution function. This avoids the need for empirical data capture and summary analysis to derive these probabilities.

5.2 Types of Probability Distribution

Probability distribution functions can be classified as *discrete* or *continuous*. Therefore the choice of a particular probability distribution function in practice depends on the data type of the random variable (i.e. discrete or continuous) under study.

This chapter will describe two discrete probability distribution functions (called the binomial and the Poisson distributions) and one continuous probability function (called the normal distribution).

5.3 Discrete Probability Distributions

Discrete probability distributions assume that the outcomes of a random variable under study can take on *only specific* (usually *integer*) values.

Examples include the following:
- A maths class can have 1, 2, 3, 4, 5 (or any integer) number of students.
- A bookshop has 0, 1, 2, 3 (or any integer) number of copies of a title in stock.
- A machine can produce 0, 1, 2, 3, 4 (or any integer) defective items in a shift.
- A company can have 0, 1, 2, 3 (or any integer) employees absent on a day.

In discrete probability distributions, a non-zero probability exists for each possible outcome of the random variable (within the sample space). The probability is zero for values of the random variable that are not in the sample space.

Two common discrete probability distribution functions are the *binomial probability distribution* and the *Poisson probability distribution*.

For a discrete random variable to follow either a binomial or a Poisson process, it must possess a number of specific characteristics. These features will be identified for each of these probability distribution functions in the following sections.

5.4 Binomial Probability Distribution

A discrete random variable follows the **binomial distribution** if it satisfies the following four conditions:

1   The random variable is observed n number of times (this is equivalent to drawing a sample of n objects and observing the random variable in each one).

2   There are *only two*, mutually exclusive and collectively exhaustive, *outcomes* associated with the random variable on each object in the sample. These two outcomes are labelled *success* and *failure* (e.g. a product is defective or not defective; an employee is absent or not absent from work; a consumer prefers brand A or not brand A).

3   Each outcome has an associated probability.
    –   The probability for the *success* outcome is denoted by p.
    –   The probability for the *failure* outcome is denoted by $1 - p$.

4   The objects are assumed to be *independent* of each other, meaning that p remains constant for each sampled object (i.e. the outcome on any object is not influenced by the outcome on any other object). This means that p is the same (constant) for each of the n objects.

If these four conditions are satisfied, then the following *binomial question* can be addressed.

The Binomial Question

'What is the probability that x successes will occur in a randomly drawn sample of n objects?'

This probability can be calculated using the **binomial probability distribution** formula:

$$P(x) = {}_nC_x \, p^x (1 - p)^{n-x} \qquad \text{for } x = 0, 1, 2, 3, ..., n \qquad\qquad 5.1$$

Where: n = the sample size, i.e. the number of independent trials (observations)
x = the number of *success* outcomes in the n independently drawn objects
p = probability of a *success* outcome on a single independent object
$(1 - p)$ = probability of a *failure* outcome on a single independent object

The x values represent the *number* of the *success* outcomes that can be observed in a sample of n objects. It is called the *domain*. Since the number of success outcomes cannot exceed the number of trials, the domain for the binomial probability distribution is limited to all the integer values (including zero) up to the sample size, n.

The rationale of the *binomial process* is illustrated by the following problem:

Example 5.1 Car Hire Request Study

The Zeplin car hire company has a fleet of rental cars that includes the make Opel. Experience has shown that one in four clients requests to hire an Opel.

If five reservations are randomly selected from today's bookings, what is the probability (or likelihood) that two clients will have requested an Opel?

Solution

The random variable (i.e. the number of hire requests for an Opel) is discrete, since 0, 1, 2, 3, 4, etc. Opels can be requested for hire on a given day. For this discrete random variable to follow the binomial process, it must satisfy the four conditions defined above.

Condition 1 is satisfied, since the random variable is observed five times (i.e. a sample of five hiring requests was studied). Hence $n = 5$. Each of the five reservation requests is a single trial (or object) in the study of car hire request patterns.

Condition 2 is satisfied, since there are only two possible outcomes on each client request:
- A client requests the hire of an Opel (*success* outcome).
- A client requests the hire of another make of car, i.e. not an Opel (*failure* outcome).

Condition 3 is satisfied, since the probability of the *success* outcome is constant and is derived from the statement that 'experience has shown that one in four clients request to hire an Opel'.

Thus p (= probability of a client requesting to hire an Opel) = 0.25
   $(1 - p)$ (= probability of a client requesting another make of car) = 0.75

Condition 4 is satisfied, since the trials are independent. Each client's car preference request is independent of every other client's car preference request. This implies that p will not change from one client request to another.

Since all the conditions for the binomial process have been satisfied, the binomial question can be addressed: 'What is the probability that two out of five clients will request to hire an Opel?'

Find: $P(x = 2)$ when $n = 5$ and $p = 0.25$.
Then: $P(x = 2) = {}_5C_2(0.25)^2 (1 - 0.25)^{5-2} = (10)(0.0625)(0.4219) = 0.264$

Thus there is a 26.4% chance that two out of five randomly selected clients will request an Opel.

How to Select p

The *success* outcome is always associated with the probability, p. The outcome that must be labelled as the *success* outcome is identified from the binomial question.

To illustrate, in Example 5.1, the binomial question relates to a client requesting the hire of an Opel, thus the *success* outcome is 'receiving a *hire request for an Opel*'. The *failure* outcome is 'receiving a *hire request* for *another make of car*'.

Example 5.2 Life Assurance Policy Surrender Study

Global Insurance has found that 20% (one in five) of all insurance policies are surrendered (cashed in) before their maturity date. Assume that 10 policies are randomly selected from the company's policy database.
(a) What is the probability that four of these 10 insurance policies will have been surrendered before their maturity date?
(b) What is the probability that *no more than* three of these 10 insurance policies will have been surrendered before their maturity date?
(c) What is the probability that at *least* two out of the 10 randomly selected policies will be surrendered before their maturity date?

Solution

(a) The random variable 'number of policies surrendered' is discrete, since there can be 0, 1, 2, 3, ..., 9, 10 surrendered policies in the randomly selected sample of 10 policies. This random variable 'fits' the binomial probability distribution for the following reasons:

- The random variable is observed 10 times (10 policies were randomly sampled). Each policy is an observation of the random variable (i.e. policy surrender status). Hence $n = 10$.
- There are only two possible outcomes for each policy, namely:
  – a policy is *surrendered* before maturity (the *success* outcome)
  – a policy is *not surrendered* before maturity (the *failure* outcome).
- A probability can be assigned to each outcome for a policy, namely:
  – p (= probability of a policy being surrendered) = 0.20
  – $(1 - p)$ (= probability of a policy not being surrendered) = 0.80
  Note that the success outcome refers to surrendering a policy since the binomial question seeks probabilities for surrendered policies.
- The trials are independent. Each policy's status (surrendered or not) is independent of every other policy's status. Thus $p = 0.20$ is constant for each policy.

Since all the conditions for the binomial process have been satisfied, the binomial question can be addressed: 'What is the probability that four of these 10 insurance policies will have been surrendered before maturity date?'

Find: $P(x = 4)$ when $n = 10$ and $p = 0.2$.

Then: $P(x = 4) = {}_{10}C_4(0.20)^4(1 - 0.20)^{10-4} = (210)(0.0016)(0.2621) = 0.088$

Thus there is an 8.8% chance that four out of 10 randomly selected policies will have been surrendered before maturity.

(b) The binomial approach still applies. In terms of the binomial question, '*no more than 3*' implies that either 0 or 1 or 2 or 3 of the sampled policies will be surrendered before maturity.

Thus find $P(x \leq 3)$. (This is a cumulative probability.)

Using the addition rule of probability for mutually exclusive events, the cumulative probability is:

$P(x \leq 3) = P(x = 0) + P(x = 1) + P(x = 2) + P(x = 3)$

The three binomial probabilities must now be calculated separately and summed:

$P(x = 0) = {}_{10}C_0 (0.20)^0(1 - 0.20)^{10-0} = 0.107$
$P(x = 1) = {}_{10}C_1 (0.20)^1(1 - 0.20)^{10-1} = 0.269$
$P(x = 2) = {}_{10}C_2 (0.20)^2(1 - 0.20)^{10-2} = 0.302$
$P(x = 3) = {}_{10}C_3 (0.20)^3(1 - 0.20)^{10-3} = 0.201$
Then $P(x \leq 3) = 0.107 + 0.269 + 0.302 + 0.201 = 0.879$

There is an 87.9% chance that *no more than three* out of the 10 policies randomly selected will be surrendered before their maturity date.

(c) This question translates into finding the cumulative probability of $P(x \geq 2)$
i.e. $P(x \geq 2) = P(x = 2) + P(x = 3) + P(x = 4) + ... + P(x = 10)$.

This requires that nine binomial calculations be performed. However, to avoid onerous calculations, the complementary law of probability can be used, as follows:

$$P(x \geq 2) = 1 - P(x \leq 1)$$
$$= 1 - [P(x = 0) + P(x = 1)]$$
$$= 1 - [0.107 + 0.269] \text{ (from (b) above)} = 1 - 0.376 = 0.624$$

Thus there is a 62.4% chance that at least 2 out of the 10 randomly selected policies will be surrendered before their maturity date.

Useful Pointers on Calculating Probabilities

- Key words such as *at least, no more than, at most, no less than, smaller than, larger than, greater than, no greater than* always imply cumulative probabilities (i.e. the summing of individual marginal probabilities.
- The *complementary* rule should be considered whenever practical to reduce the number of probability calculations.

Descriptive Statistical Measures of the Binomial Distribution

A measure of central location and a measure of dispersion can be calculated for any random variable that follows a binomial distribution using the following formulae:

$$\text{Mean: } \mu = np$$
$$\text{Standard deviation: } \sigma = \sqrt{np\,(1-p)}$$

5.2

For Example 5.2 (insurance policy surrender study), where $p = 0.20$ and $n = 10$:
- the mean (average) number of surrendered policies is $(10)(0.2) = 2$ policies, on average, out of 10 policies.
- the standard deviation would be $\sqrt{(10)(0.2)(0.8)} = 1.27$ policies.

Section 5.9 shows how to use Excel to compute binomial probabilities.

5.5 Poisson Probability Distribution

A Poisson process is also a discrete process.

A **Poisson process** measures the *number of occurrences* of a particular outcome of a discrete random variable in a *predetermined time, space or volume interval* for which an *average number of occurrences* of the outcome is known or can be determined.

These are examples of a Poisson process:
- the number of breakdowns of a machine in an eight-hour shift
- the number of cars arriving at a parking garage in a one-hour time interval
- the number of sales made by a telesales person in a week
- the number of problems identified at the end of a construction project
- the number of particles of chorine in one litre of pool water
- the number of typing errors on a page of a newspaper.

In each case, the number of occurrences of a given outcome of the random variable, x, can take on any integer value from 0, 1, 2, 3, ... up to infinity (in theory).

The Poisson Question

'What is the probability of x occurrences of a given outcome being observed in a predetermined time, space or volume interval?'

The Poisson question can be answered by applying the **Poisson probability distribution** formula:

$$P(x) = \frac{e^{-\lambda}\lambda^x}{x!} \qquad \text{for } x = 0, 1, 2, 3 \ldots \qquad\qquad 5.3$$

Where: λ = the mean number of occurrences of a given outcome of the random variable for a predetermined time, space or volume interval

e = a mathematical constant, approximately equal to 2.71828

x = number of occurrences of a given outcome for which a probability is required (x is the domain, which can be any discrete value from 0 to infinity)

Example 5.3 Web-based Marketing Study

A web-based travel agency uses its website to market its travel products (holiday packages). The agency receives an average of five web-based enquiries per day for its different travel products.

(a) What is the probability that, on a given day, the agency will receive only three web-based enquiries for its travel products?

(b) What is the probability that, on a given day, the travel agency will receive *at most* two web-based enquiries for travel packages?

(c) What is the probability that the travel agency will receive *more than four* web-based enquiries for travel packages on a given day?

(d) What is the probability that the travel agency will receive *more than four* web-based enquiries for travel packages in any *two-day* period?

Solution

(a) The random variable x = number of web-based enquiries received per day 'fits' the Poisson process for the following reasons:

- The random variable is discrete. The agency can receive {0, 1, 2, 3, 4, ...} web-based enquiries per day. Any number of enquiries can be received per day.
- The random variable is observed in a predetermined time interval (i.e. one day).
- The average number of web-based enquiries per day, a, is known. Here $\lambda = 5$.

Find $P(x = 3)$ when λ (average number of web-based enquiries per day) = 5.

$$P(x = 3) = \frac{e^{-5} \cdot 5^3}{3!}$$

$$= 0.006738 \times 20.833 = 0.1404$$

Thus there is only a 14.04% chance that the travel agency will receive only three web-based enquiries on a given day when the average number of web-based enquiries per day is five.

(b) In terms of the Poisson question, '*at most* two web-based enquiries' implies either 0 or 1 or 2 enquiries on a given day.

These possible outcomes (0, 1, 2) are mutually exclusive, and the combined probability can be found using the addition rule of probability for mutually exclusive events. Thus:

$P(x \le 2) = P(x = 0) + P(x = 1) + P(x = 2)$

Each probability is calculated separately using Formula 5.3.

$P(x = 0$ web-based enquiries):

$$P(x = 0) = \frac{e^{-5}5^0}{0!} = 0.006738(1) = 0.00674 \qquad \text{(Recall } 0! = 1.\text{)}$$

$P(x = 1$ web-based enquiry):

$$P(x = 1) = \frac{e^{-5}5^1}{1!} = 0.006738(5) = 0.0337$$

$P(x = 2$ web-based enquiries):

$$P(x = 2) = \frac{e^{-5}5^2}{2!} = 0.006738(12.5) = 0.0842$$

Then $P(x \le 2) = 0.00674 + 0.0337 + 0.0842 = 0.12464$.

Thus there is only a 12.5% chance that at most two web-based enquiries for travel packages will be received by this travel agency on a given day, when the average number of web-based enquiries received per day is five.

(c) The Poisson question requires us to find $P(x > 4)$ when $\lambda = 5$.
Since x is a discrete random variable, the first integer value of x above four is $x = 5$. Hence the problem becomes one of finding:

$$P(x \ge 5) = P(x = 5) + P(x = 6) + P(x = 7) + \dots$$

To solve this problem, the complementary rule of probability must be used. The complement of $x \ge 5$ is all $x \le 4$. Thus:

$$P(x \ge 5) = 1 - P(x \le 4)$$
$$= 1 - [P(x = 0) + P(x = 1) + P(x = 2) + P(x = 3) + P(x = 4)]$$
$$= 1 - [0.0067 + 0.0337 + 0.0842 + 0.1404 + 0.1755] \qquad \text{(Formula 5.3)}$$
$$= 1 - 0.4405 = 0.5595$$

Thus there is a 55.95% chance that the travel agency will receive more than four web-based enquiries for their travel packages on a given day, when the average number of web-based enquiries received per day is five.

(d) Notice that the time interval over which the web-based enquiries are received has changed from one day to *two days*. Thus $\lambda = 5$ per day, on average, must be adjusted to $\lambda = 10$ per *two days*, before the Poisson formula can be applied.

Then find $P(x > 4)$ where $\lambda = 10$.

$$P(x > 4) = P(x \ge 5) = [P(x = 5) + P(x = 6) + P(x = 7) + \dots + P(x = \infty)]$$

This can be solved using the complementary rule as follows:

$$P(x > 4) = 1 - P(x \leq 4)$$

$$= 1 - [P(x = 0) + P(x = 1) + P(x = 2) + P(x = 3) + P(x = 4)]$$

Each Poisson probability is calculated separately using Formula 5.3 with $\lambda = 10$.

$$P(x > 4) = 1 - [0.0000454 + 0.000454 + 0.00227 + 0.00757 + 0.01892]$$

$$= 1 - 0.02925 = 0.97075$$

Thus there is a 97.1% chance that the travel agency will receive *more than* four web-based enquiries for their travel packages in any *two-day period* when the average number of web-based enquiries received is 10 per two-day period.

A Word of Caution

Always check that the interval for the average rate of occurrence is the same as the predetermined time, space or volume interval of the Poisson question. If not, always adjust the average rate to coincide with the predetermined interval in the question.

Descriptive Statistical Measures of the Poisson Distribution

A measure of central location and a measure of dispersion can be calculated for any random variable that follows a Poisson process using the following formulae:

$$\text{Mean: } \mu = \lambda$$
$$\text{Standard deviation: } \sigma = \sqrt{\lambda}$$

5.4

Section 5.9 shows how to use Excel to compute Poisson probabilities.

5.6 Continuous Probability Distributions

A *continuous* random variable can take on *any value* (as opposed to only discrete values) in an *interval*.

Examples include:
- the *length of time* to complete a task
- the *mass* of a passenger's hand luggage
- the daily *distance travelled* by a delivery vehicle
- the *volume* (in litres) of fuel in a tank.

Because there are an infinite number of possible outcomes associated with a continuous random variable, continuous probability distributions are represented by curves for which the *area under the curve* between two x-limits represents the *probability* that x lies within these limits (or *interval*).

The most widely used continuous probability distribution in practice is the normal distribution because a large majority of continuous random variables have outcomes that follow a normal pattern.

5.7 Normal Probability Distribution

The **normal probability distribution** has the following properties:
- The curve is bell-shaped.
- It is symmetrical about a central mean value, μ.
- The tails of the curve never touch the x-axis, meaning that there is always a non-zero probability associated with every value in the problem domain (i.e. asymptotic).
- The distribution is always described by two parameters: a mean (μ) and a standard deviation (σ).
- The total area under the curve will always equal one, since it represents the total sample space. Because of symmetry, the area under the curve below μ is 0.5, and above μ is also 0.5.
- The probability associated with a particular interval of x-values is defined by the area under the normal distribution curve between the limits of x_1 and x_2.

Figure 5.1 illustrates the shape of the normal probability distribution and highlights the area under the curve between the x-limits of x_1 and x_2. This area represents the probability that x lies between the limits of x_1 and x_2 for a normally distributed random variable with a mean of μ and a standard deviation of σ.

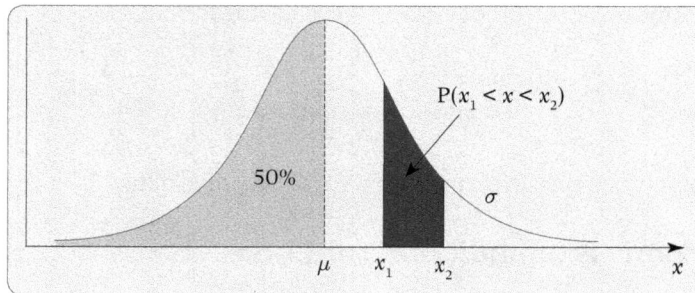

Figure 5.1 The normal probability distribution showing $P(x_1 < x < x_2)$

Finding Probabilities Using the Normal Distribution

To find the probability that x lies between x_1 and x_2, it is necessary to find the area under the bell-shaped curve between these x-limits. This is done by converting the x-limits into limits that correspond to another normal distribution called the **standard normal distribution** (or z-**distribution** as it is commonly called) for which areas have already been worked out. These areas are given in a statistical table (see Table 1 in Appendix 1).

5.8 Standard Normal (z) Probability Distribution

The **standard normal distribution**, with random variable z, has the following properties:

$$\text{Mean: } \mu_z = 0$$
$$\text{Standard deviation: } \sigma_z = 1$$

5.5

Probabilities (areas) based on the standard normal distribution can be read from standard normal tables. The **z-table** (Table 1 in Appendix 1) gives the probability that z lies between its mean ($\mu_z = 0$) and a given upper z-limit, say $z = k$ (i.e. $P(0 < z < k)$) as shown in Figure 5.2.

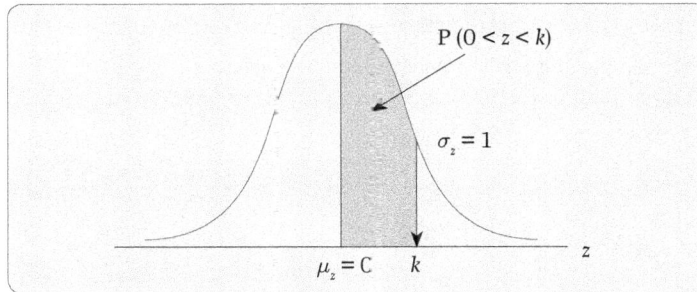

Figure 5.2 Standard normal distribution showing $P(0 < z < k)$

When reading values (areas) off the z-table, it should be noted that:
- the z-limit (to one decimal place) is listed down the left column, and the second decimal position of z is shown across the top row
- the value read off at the *intersection* of the z-limit (to two decimal places) is the *area under the standard normal curve* (i.e. probability) between $0 < z < k$.

The following examples illustrate the use of the standard normal (z) table to find probabilities (areas) for different ranges of z-limits.

Example 5.4 Using the z-table to Find Normal Probabilities

Refer to the z-table (Table 1 in Appendix 1).

Determine:
(a) $P(0 < z < 1.46)$
(b) $P(-2.3 < z < 0)$
(c) $P(z > 1.82)$
(d) $P(-2.1 < z < 1.32)$
(e) $P(1.24 < z < 2.075)$

Solution

(a) Refer to Figure 5.3, which shows the required area.

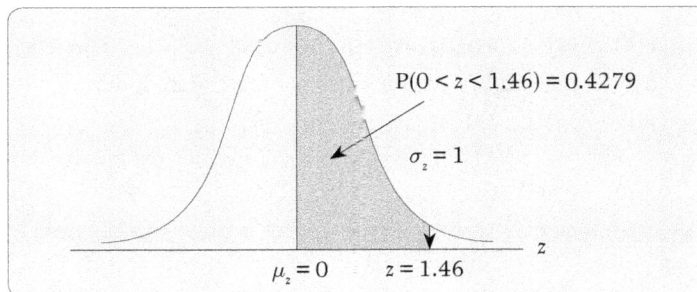

Figure 5.3 Standard normal area between $z = 0$ and $z = 1.46$

From the z-table, identify $z = 1.4$ down the left column of z. Then read across the columns at the $z = 1.4$ row until $z = 0.06$. The area found at this intersection is 0.4279.

So $P(0 < z < 1.46) = 0.4279$

Thus there is a 42.79% chance that a z-value will lie between $z = 0$ and $z = 1.46$.

(b) Refer to Figure 5.4, which shows the required area.

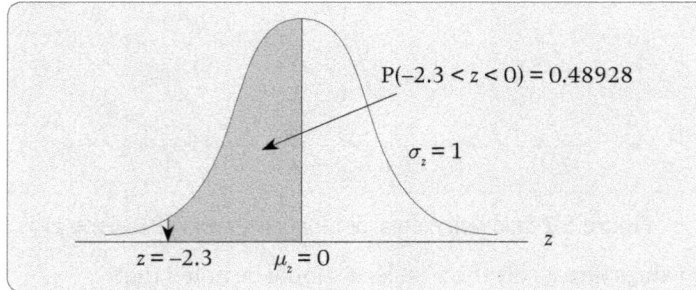

Figure 5.4 Standard normal area between $z = -2.3$ and $z = 0$

Because of symmetry, this area (probability) is equivalent to finding the area $P(0 < z < 2.3)$ on the positive z side. Reading from the z-table (left column), at $z = 2.3$, this area equals 0.48928.

So $P(-2.3 < z < 0) = 0.48928$

Thus there is a 48.93% chance that a z-value will lie between $z = -2.3$ and $z = 0$.

(c) Refer to Figure 5.5, which shows the required area.

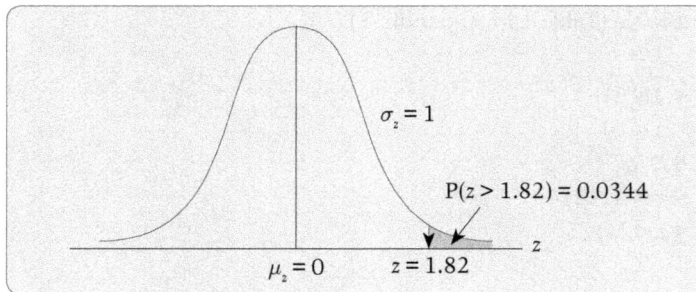

Figure 5.5 Standard normal area above $z = 1.82$

The z-table only gives areas between the midpoint ($z = 0$) and an upper z-limit, k (i.e. between $0 < z < k$). The area above k is found by subtracting the area between ($0 < z < k$) from 0.5, which is the total area above the midpoint of $z = 0$.

From the z-table, $P(0 < z < 1.82) = 0.4656$.
Then $P(z > 1.82) = 0.5000 - 0.4656$ (Complementary probability rule.)
$\qquad\qquad = 0.0344$

Thus there is only a 3.44% chance that a z-value will lie above $z = 1.82$.

(d) Refer to Figure 5.6, which shows the required area.

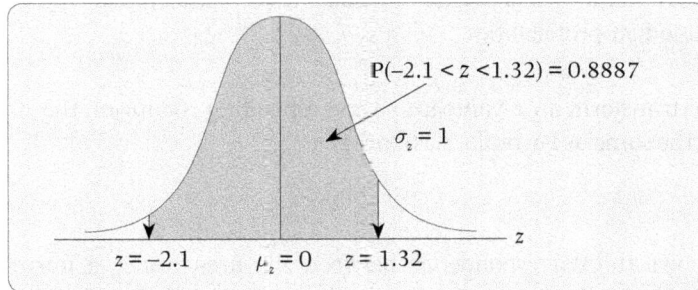

Figure 5.6 Standard normal area between $z = -2.1$ and $z = 1.32$

$P(-2.1 < z < 1.32)$ is equal to the sum of two mutually exclusive areas, each of which can be looked up separately in the z-table.

Thus $P(-2.1 < z < 1.32) = P(-2.1 < z < 0) + P(0 < z < 1.32)$

From the z-table $\quad$ $P(-2.1 < z < 0) = 0.4821$ (Using symmetry.)

and $\quad\quad\quad\quad\quad$ $P(0 < z < 1.32) = 0.4066$

Then $P(-2.1 < z < 1.32) = 0.4821 + 0.4066 = 0.8887$

Thus there is an 88.87% chance that a z-value will lie between $z = -2.1$ and $z = 1.32$.

(e) Refer to Figure 5.7, which shows the required area.

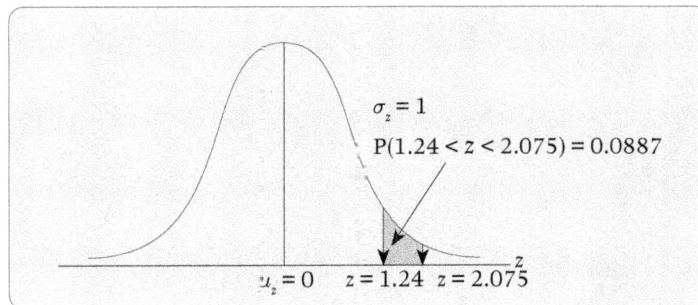

Figure 5.7 Standard normal area between $z = 1.24$ and $z = 2.075$

Again, split the required area into two parts, $P(0 < z < 1.24)$ and $P(0 < z < 2.075)$. The difference between these two areas isolates the required probability.

From the z-table $\quad$ $P(0 < z < 2.075) = 0.4812$ $\quad\quad$ (*Note*: 2.075 is rounded to 2.08.)

$\quad\quad\quad\quad\quad\quad\quad$ $P(0 < z < 1.24) = 0.3925$

Then $P(1.24 < z < 2.075) = 0.4812 - 0.3925 = 0.0887$

Thus there is only an 8.87% chance that a z-value lies between $z = 1.24$ and $z = 2.075$.

Finding Probabilities for x-limits using the z-distribution

Many numeric random variables x (such as electricity consumption (kWh), delivery time (minutes) and product mass (g)) follow a normal probability distribution, each with their own mean (μ) and standard deviation (σ) values in different units of measure.

> To use the standard normal (z) table to find probabilities associated with outcomes of these numeric random variables, each x-value must be converted into a z-value, which is then used to read off probabilities.

The formula to transform an x-value into a corresponding z-value on the standard normal distribution is the same as Formula 3.16 (p 94). i.e.:

$$z = \frac{x - \mu}{\sigma}$$

5.6

Figure 5.8 shows the correspondence between the area under a normal distribution between $x = 14$ and $x = 20$ with a mean $(\mu) = 20$ and a standard deviation $(\sigma) = 4$ and the *standardised* (z) normal probability distribution. The equivalent z-values for the given x-values are found by using the above z transformation formula.

For $x = 14$, the equivalent z-value is: $z = \frac{14 - 20}{4} = -1.5$

Similarly, for $x = 20$, the equivalent z-value is: $z = \frac{20 - 20}{4} = 0$

Thus finding $P(14 < x < 20)$ is equivalent to finding $P(-1.5 < z < 0)$.

Using the z-table, $P(-1.5 < z < 0) = 0.4332$.

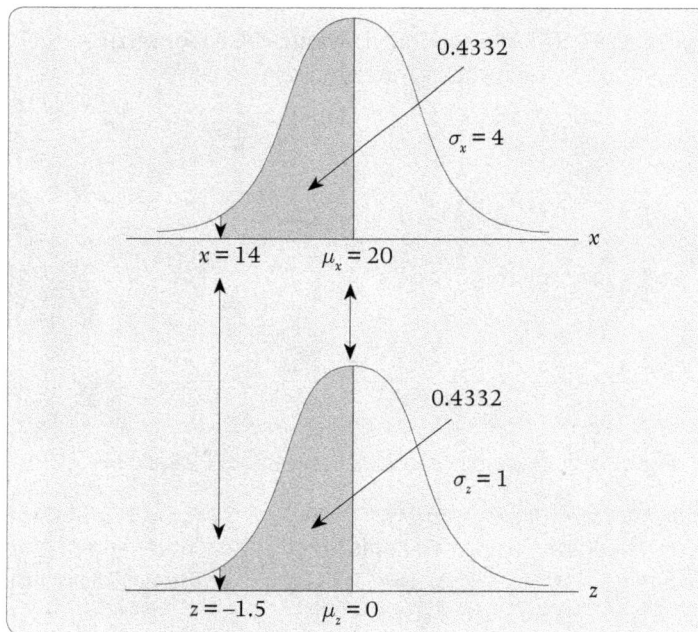

Figure 5.8 Equivalence between x- and z-values under a normal distribution

The Meaning of the z-value

A z-value measures how far (in standard deviation terms) an x-value lies from its mean, μ. In the above illustration, for $x = 14$ with $\mu = 20$ and $\sigma = 4$, the corresponding $z = -1.5$ implies that the value of $x = 14$ lies 1.5 standard deviations *below* (due to negative sign) the mean of 20. Similarly, for $x = 20$ with $\mu = 20$ and $\sigma = 4$, the corresponding $z = 0$ implies that the value of $x = 20$ lies at its mean of 20 (i.e. zero deviation from its mean).

Example 5.5 Courier Service Delivery Time Study

A courier service company has found that their delivery time of parcels to clients is normally distributed with a mean of 45 minutes ($\mu = 45$) and a standard deviation of eight minutes ($\sigma = 8$).

What is the probability that a randomly selected parcel:
(a) will take between 45 and 51 minutes to deliver to the client?
(b) will take less than 48 minutes to deliver?

Solution

(a) Find $P(45 < x < 51)$

   Step 1: Always sketch a normal probability distribution and indicate the area (probability) to be found, as shown in Figure 5.9.

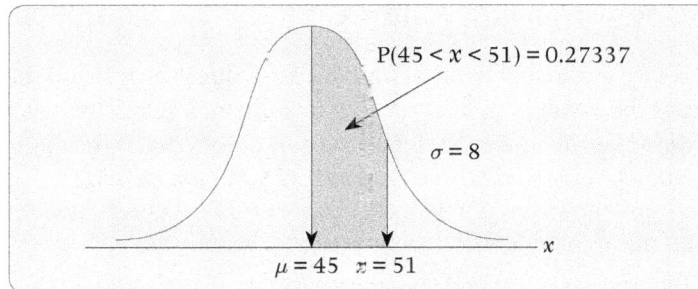

Figure 5.9 Area under normal curve between $x = 45$ and $x = 51$

   Step 2: Transform the x-limits into corresponding z-limits using Formula 5.6.
   In this example, $x = 45$ corresponds to $z = \frac{45 - 45}{8} = 0$
   and $x = 51$ corresponds to $z = \frac{51 - 45}{8} = 0.75$.
   Thus $P(45 < x < 51)$ is equivalent to finding $P(0 < z < 0.75)$.

   Step 3: Calculate the required probability of $P(0 < z < 0.75)$ using the z-table.
   The area between $(0 < z < 0.75)$ is equal to 0.2734.
   Then $P(45 < x < 51) = 0.2734$.

   Thus there is a 27.34% chance that a randomly selected parcel will take between 45 minutes and 51 minutes to deliver to the client.

(b) Find $P(x < 48)$

   Step 1: Sketch a normal probability distribution and indicate the area (probability) to be found, as shown in Figure 5.10.

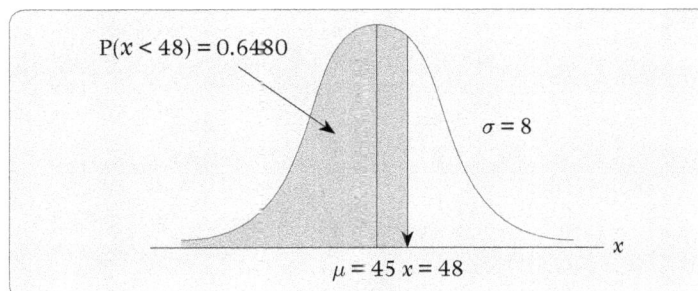

Figure 5.10 Area under normal curve below $x = 48$

Step 2: Transform the x-limits into corresponding z-limits using Formula 5.6.
In this example, $x = 48$ corresponds to $z = \frac{48 - 45}{8} = 0.375$.
Thus $P(x < 48)$ is equivalent to finding $P(z < 0.375)$.

Step 3: Calculate the required probability $P(z < 0.375)$ using the z-table.
$P(z < 0.375)$ is found by splitting the area into $P(z < 0)$ and $P(0 < z < 0.375)$, since the z-table only calculates the area above $z = 0$.
The area between $(0 < z < 0.375)$ is equal to 0.1480 (use $z = 0.38$) while the area below $z = 0$ is equal to 0.5 (the lower half of the normal curve).
Then $P(x < 48) = P(z < 0.375) = 0.5 + 0.1480 = 0.6480$

Thus there is a 64.8% chance that a randomly selected parcel will be delivered to the client within 48 minutes.

Find x-limits for Given Probabilities of a Normal Distribution

Often the probability associated with an unknown x-value is given, and the management question is to find the x-value. To illustrate, assume the marketing manager of a national clothing store would like to answer the following question: 'What is the minimum purchase value of transactions, x, for the highest-spending 15% of customers?'

A three-step approach is used to identify the required x-value. It involves reversing the procedure to find the area under the normal curve for given z-limits.

Step 1: Sketch the normal curve and show the position of the x-value that corresponds to the given probability (i.e. area under the normal curve).

Step 2: Use the z-table to identify the z-value that corresponds to the area under the normal curve, as shown in Step 1. This z-value is found by locating the required area in the z-table and then reading off the z-value that is associated with this known area.

Step 3: Use the z transformation to convert the z-value into its corresponding x-value.

Example 5.6 Find z-values Corresponding to Given Areas (Probabilities)

(a) Find k such that $P(0 < z < k) = 0.3461$.
(b) Find k such that $P(k < z < 0) = 0.1628$.
(c) Find k such that $P(z > k) = 0.8051$.

Solution

(a) This probability (area) is shown in Figure 5.11.

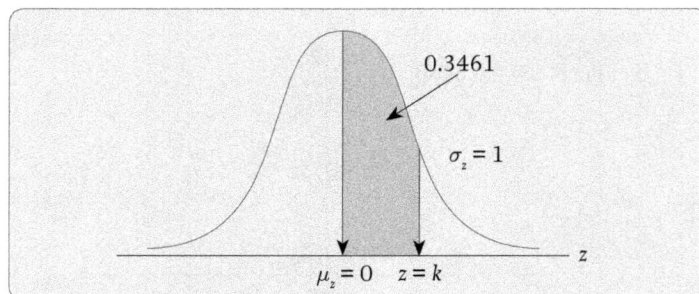

Figure 5.11 z-distribution showing $P(0 < z < k) = 0.3461$

To find k such that $P(0 < z < k) = 0.3461$, the body of the z-table is scanned for the area (probability) 0.3461 (or its closest value). Then the $z = k$ value corresponding to this area is read off.

Thus $k = 1.02$, since $P(0 < z < 1.02) = 0.3461$.

This means that 34.61% of all z-values lie between $z = 0$ and $z = 1.02$.

(b) Refer to Figure 5.12, which shows the appropriate area (probability).

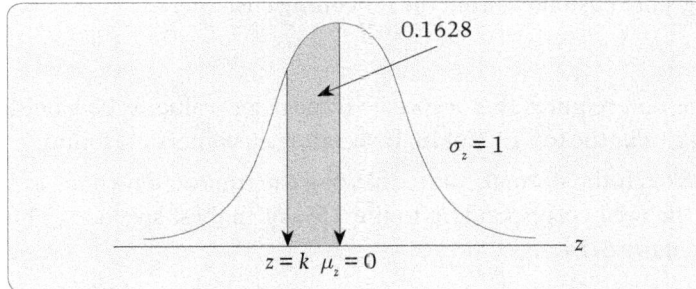

Figure 5.12 z-distribution showing $P(k < z < 0) = 0.1628$

From the expression $(k < z < 0)$, k will be a *negative* value. Scan the z-table for an area of 0.1628. This corresponds to a z-value of 0.42. Since k is negative, $k = -0.42$.

Thus $k = -0.42$ satisfies $P(-0.42 < z < 0) = 0.1628$.

This means that 16.28% of all z-values lie between $z = -0.42$ and $z = 0$.

(c) Refer to Figure 5.13, which shows the appropriate area (probability).

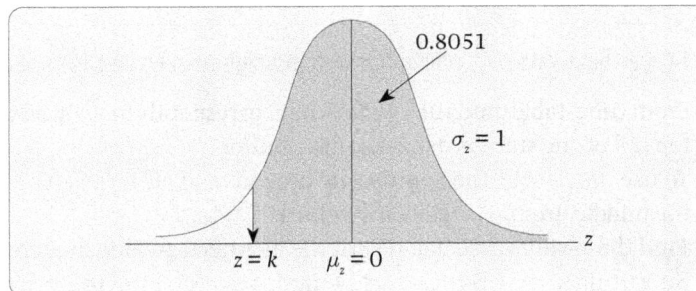

Figure 5.13 z-distribution showing $P(z > k) = 0.8051$

For the area above k to be 0.8051, which is greater than 0.5, k must lie below $z = 0$ (the mean value of the z-distribution). Thus k will again have a negative sign.

Also, the area that must be found in the z-table is not 0.8051, but 0.3051 (i.e. $0.8051 - 0.5000$), as the z-table shows areas for only half the z-distribution (i.e. between $z = 0$ and an upper limit $z = k$).

The area of 0.3051 corresponds to a z-value of 0.86.

Since k is negative, $k = -0.86$.

Then $P(z > -0.86) = 0.8051$.

This means that 80.51% of all z-values lie above $z = -0.86$.

The method of finding z-values that are associated with given probabilities can be extended to find corresponding x-values associated with given probabilities (i.e. Step 3 above). This will be illustrated in the following example.

Example 5.7 Clothing Transactions Purchase Value Study

Assume that the purchase value of transactions, x, at a national clothing store such as Edgars, is normally distributed with a mean of R244 and a standard deviation of R68.

(a) What is the minimum purchase value of transactions for the highest-spending 15% of clothing store customers?

(b) What purchase value of transactions separates the lowest-spending 20% of clothing store customers from the remaining customers?

Solution

(a) This question requires that a specific transaction value, x, be identified such that *above this value* the top 15% of high-spending customers are found.

   Step 1: Sketch the normal curve, showing the transaction value, x, that identifies the area corresponding to the 15% of highest spenders. This is shown in Figure 5.14.

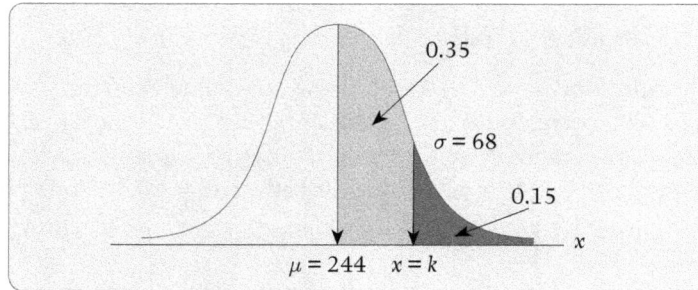

Figure 5.14 Purchase value of clothing transactions: highest-spending 15% of customers

   Step 2: From the z-table, find the z-value that corresponds to an area of 0.15 in the top tail of the standard normal distribution.

   To use the z-table, the appropriate area to read off is $0.5 - 0.15 = 0.35$ (i.e. the middle area). The closest z-value is 1.04.

   Step 3: Find the x-value associated with the identified z-value in Step 2.

   Substitute $z = 1.04$, $\mu = 244$ and $\sigma = 68$ into the z transformation Formula 5.6, and solve for x.

$$z = \frac{x - \mu}{\sigma} \text{ (Solve for } x: x = \mu + z\sigma)$$
$$1.04 = \frac{x - 244}{68}$$
$$x = 244 + (1.04 \times 68) = 244 + 70.72 = R314.72$$

Thus the highest-spending 15% of clothing store customers spend *at least* R314.72 per transaction.

(b) This question requires that a specific transaction value, x, be identified such that the area *below this value* is 20%, which represents the lowest spending 20% of clothing store customers.

   Step 1: Sketch the normal curve, showing the transaction value, x, that identifies the area corresponding to the 20% of lowest spenders. This is shown in Figure 5.15.

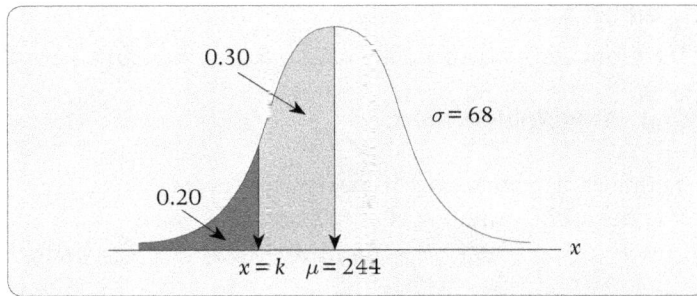

Figure 5.15 Purchase value of clothing transactions – lowest-spending 20% of customers

Step 2: From the z-table, find the z-value that corresponds to an area of 0.20 in the bottom tail of the standard normal distribution.

To use the z-table, the area that must be found is $0.5 - 0.20 = 0.30$ (i.e. the middle area).

The closest z-value read off the z-table is 0.84. However, since the required z-value is below its mean, the z-value will be negative. Hence $z = -0.84$.

Step 3: Find the x-value associated with the identified z-value in Step 2. Substitute $z = -0.84$ $\mu = 244$ and $\sigma = 68$ into the z transformation Formula 5.6 and solve for x.

$-0.84 = \frac{x - 244}{68}$

$x = 244 + (-0.84 \times 68) = 244 - 57.12 = R186.88$

Thus the lowest-spending 20% of clothing store customers spend *at most* R186.88 per transaction.

5.9 Using Excel (2016) to Compute Probabilities

Binomial Distribution

The **BINOM.DIST** function in Excel computes both marginal and cumulative binomial probabilities.

=BINOM.DIST(number_s,trials,probability_s,cumulative)

Where: number_s = x (the number of *success* outcomes)

trials = n (sample size)

probability_s = p (the probability of observing the *success* outcome on a single trial)

cumulative = {*true or false*} (*true* = compute the cumulative probability up to and including x; *false* = compute only the marginal probability of x)

- For Example 5.1, $P(x = 2)$ is a marginal probability, hence set cumulative = *false*. Thus to find $P(x = 2)$, type =**BINOM.DIST(2,5,0.25,false)** to give 0.264.
- For Example 5.2(b), $P(x \leq 3)$ is a cumulative probability, hence set cumulative = *true*. Thus to find $P(x \leq 3)$, type =**BINOM.DIST(3,10,0.20,true)** to give 0.879.
- For Example 5.2(c), to find $P(x \geq 2) = 1 - P(x \leq 1)$ apply both the complementary rule of probability and the cumulative function (i.e. set cumulative = *true*). Thus to find $P(x \geq 2)$, type =**1-BINOM.DIST(1,10,0.20,true)** to give 0.624.

Poisson Distribution

The **POISSON.DIST** function computes both marginal and cumulative Poisson probabilities.

=POISSON.DIST(x,mean,cumulative)

Where: x = the number of occurrences of the observed event

mean = a (the average number of occurrences)

cumulative = {*true or false*} (*true* = cumulative probability; *false* = marginal probability)

- For Example 5.3(a), P(x = 3) is a marginal probability, hence set cumulative = *false*. Thus to find P(x = 3), type =**POISSON.DIST(3,5,false)** to give 0.1404.
- For Example 5.3(b), P($x \leq 2$) is a cumulative probability, hence set cumulative = *true*. Thus to find P($x \leq 2$), type =**POISSON.DIST(2,5,true)** to give 0.12464.
- For Example 5.3(c), P($x \geq 5$) = 1 − P($x \leq 4$). Apply both the complementary rule of probability and the cumulative function (i.e. set cumulative = *true*). Thus to find P($x \geq 5$), type =1-**POISSON.DIST(4,5,true)** to give 0.5595.

Standard Normal Distribution (z) – Finding Probabilities for z-values

The **NORM.S.DIST** function computes cumulative normal probabilities for z-values.

=NORM.S.DIST(z,cumulative)

Where: z = specified z-limit

cumulative = true

This function computes the cumulative probability from ($-\infty$ to the z-limit).

- For Example 5.4(a), P($0 < z < 1.46$) = P($z < 1.46$) − P($z < 0$) (where P($z < 0$) = 0.5). Thus to find P($0 < z < 1.46$), type =**NORM.S.DIST(1.46,true)**–**NORM.S.DIST(0,true)** to give 0.4279.
- For Example 5.4(b), P($-2.3 < z < 0$) = P($z < 0$) − P($z < -2.3$). Thus to find P($-2.3 < z < 0$), type =**NORM.S.DIST(0,true)**–**NORM.S.DIST(–2.3,true)** to give 0.48928.
- For Example 5.4(c), P($z > 1.82$) is the complement of the cumulative probability from $-\infty$ up to $z = 1.82$. Thus to find P($z > 1.82$), type =1–**NORM.S.DIST(1.82,true)** to give 0.0344.
- For Example 5.4(d), P($-2.1 < z < 1.32$) can be found by subtracting the two cumulative probabilities P($-\infty < z < 1.32$) and P($-\infty < z < -2.1$). Thus to find P($-2.1 < z < 1.32$), type =**NORM.S.DIST(1.32,true)**–**NORM.S.DIST(–2.1, true)** to give 0.8887.

Normal Distribution – Finding Probabilities for x-values

The **NORM.DIST** function computes cumulative normal probabilities for x-values.

> **=NORM.DIST(x,mean,standard_dev,cumulative)**

The values x, mean (μ), and standard_dev (σ) are specified in the management problem. Cumulative = *true* specifies that *cumulative normal* probabilities are computed.

   This function computes normal probabilities directly for an x random variable with a given mean, μ, and standard deviation, σ, without first having to convert to a z-value.

- For Example 5.5(a), $P(45 < x < 51)$ can be found by subtracting the two cumulative probabilities $P(-\infty < x < 51)$ and $P(-\infty < x < 45)$.
  To find $P(45 < x < 51)$, type **=NORM.DIST(51,45,8,true)–NORM.DIST(45,45,8,true)** to give 0.2734.
- For Example 5.5(b), $P(x < 48)$ is found by typing **=NORM.DIST(48,45,8,true)** to give 0.64617.

Standard Normal Distribution – Finding z-limits

The **NORM.S.INV** (i.e. standard normal inverse) function finds the z-limit associated with the *cumulative probability* up to z.

> **=NORM.S.INV(cumulative probability)**

- For Example 5.6(a), to find k such that $P(0 < z < k) = 0.3461$, the cumulative area up to k must be used in the Excel function. The cumulative area is $0.5 + 0.3461 = 0.8461$.
  Thus type **=NORM.S.INV(0.8461)** to give 1.01985. Thus $k = 1.02$.
- For Example 5.6(b), to find k such that $P(z > k) = 0.8051$, the cumulative area of the *complement* up to k must be used in the Excel function. The cumulative area up to k is $1.0 - 0.8051 = 0.1949$.
  Thus type **=NORM.S.INV(0.1949)** to give −0.85998. Thus $k = -0.86$.

Normal distribution – Finding x-limits

The **NORM.INV** (i.e. normal inverse) function finds the x-limit associated with a normal probability distribution with a specified mean μ and standard deviation σ.

> **=NORM.INV(cumulative probability, mean, standard_dev)**

This function identifies the x-value directly (for a given mean, μ, and standard deviation, σ) without first having to identify a z-value and then convert it back to an x-value.
- For Example 5.7(b), to find k such that the cumulative area up to k is 0.20, type **=NORM.INV(0.20,244,68)** to give 186.7698. Thus $k = 186.8$ (rounded).

Generating Normally Distributed Random Values

This Excel function can also be used to generate hypothetical data values for a random variable that is normally distributed.

For example, if 'machine breakdown time' is normally distributed with a mean 36 minutes and a standard deviation of 4 minutes, then any number of 'machine breakdown times' data values can be simulated as follows: =**NORM.INV(RAND(),36,4)** where **RAND()** is an Excel function that generates a random number between 0 and 1.

5.10 Summary

This chapter covered three theoretical probability distributions. The binomial and the Poisson probability distributions are used to find probabilities for discrete numeric random variables, while the normal probability distribution calculates probabilities for continuous numeric random variables.

Each probability distribution's specific properties are described and it was emphasised that these must be matched to a problem situation before the distribution can be validly applied to find probabilities.

The standard normal (z) probability distribution was introduced as a way of calculating probabilities for any normally distributed random variable x. The z-table was used to find the required normal probabilities. The standard normal (z) probability distribution was also used to find values of an x random variable associated with given probabilities.

Excel's functions can also be used to compute binomial (**BINOM.DIST**), Poisson (**POISSON.DIST**) and normal (**NORM.S.DIST; NORM.DIST**) probabilities, while the inverse normal distribution functions (**NORM.S.INV** and **NORM.INV**) can be used to find values of z and x for normally distributed random variables.

These probability distributions, and in particular the z-distribution, will be used extensively in inferential statistics when the topics of confidence intervals and hypothesis testing are discussed.

Exercises

1   Name two commonly used discrete probability distributions.

2   Indicate whether each of the following random variables is discrete or continuous:
    (a)   the mass of cans coming off a production line
    (b)   the number of employees in a company
    (c)   the number of households in Gauteng that have solar heating panels
    (d)   the distance travelled daily by a courier service truck.

3   (a)   Use the binomial formula to find each of the following probabilities:
          (i) $n = 7, p = 0.2$ and $x = 3$
          (ii) $n = 10, p = 0.2$ and $x = 4$
          (iii) $n = 12, p = 0.3$ and $x \leq 4$
          (iv) $n = 10, p = 0.05$ and $x = 2$ or 3
          (v) $n = 8, p = 0.25$ and $x \geq 3$
    (b)   Use the Excel function **BINOM.DIST** to find the binomial probabilities in (a).

4   Once a week a merchandiser replenishes the stocks of a particular product brand in six stores for which she is responsible. Experience has shown that there is a one-in-five chance that a given store will run out of stock before the merchandiser's weekly visit.
    (a)   Which probability distribution is appropriate in this problem? Why?
    (b)   What is the probability that, on a given weekly round, the merchandiser will find exactly one store out of stock?
    (c)   What is the probability that, at most, two stores will be out of stock?
    (d)   What is the probability that no stores will be out of stock?
    (e)   What is the mean number of stores out of stock each week?

    Note: Calculate the probabilities in (b)–(d) using the binomial formula and then the Excel function **BINOM.DIST**.

5   A telemarketing company that sells homeowner insurance has found that 15% of all calls made to households lead to a sale of a homeowner insurance policy. Assume that each call is independent of all other calls.
    (a)   Find the probability that no sales result from 12 calls.
    (b)   What is the likelihood that fewer than three homeowner policies are sold in 15 calls?

    Note: Calculate the probabilities in (a) and (b) using the binomial formula and then the Excel function **BINOM.DIST**.

6   A marketing manager makes the statement that the long-run probability that a customer would prefer the deluxe model to the standard model of a product is 30%.
    (a)   What is the probability that exactly three in a random sample of 10 customers will prefer the deluxe model?
    (b)   What is the probability that more than two in a random sample of 10 customers will prefer the standard model?

    Note: Calculate the probabilities in (a) and (b) using the binomial formula and then the Excel function **BINOM.DIST**.

7   A Tata truck dealer has established that 5% of new Tata trucks sold are returned for defective assembly repairs within their 12-month warranty period. Assume that the dealer has recently sold eight new Tata trucks.

(a) What is the probability that only one of the eight Tata trucks will be returned for defective assembly repairs within its 12-month warranty period?

(b) What is the probability that at most two of the eight Tata trucks will be returned for defective assembly repairs within their 12-month warranty period?

(c) What is the probability that all eight Tata trucks sold are fault free and will not need repairs due to defective assembly within their 12-month warranty period?

(d) If the Tata truck dealer sells 64 new trucks per year, what is the average number of trucks sold that will need assembly defective repairs under their 12-month warranty agreement?

Note: Calculate the probabilities in (a)–(c) using the binomial formula and then the Excel function **BINOM.DIST**.

8   Micropal SA is a research organisation that monitors unit trust performances in South Africa. It has found that there is a four-in-five chance that a general equity unit trust fund will *perform better* than the overall JSE share index over any one-year period. If six general equity unit trust funds are randomly selected from all general equity unit trust funds, what is the probability that:

(a) all of these general equity unit trust funds performed better than the overall JSE share index over the past year?

(b) only two or three of these general equity unit trust funds performed better than the overall JSE share index over the past year?

(c) at most two *performed worse* than the overall JSE share index over the past year?

Note: Calculate the probabilities in (a)–(c) using the binomial formula and then the Excel function **BINOM.DIST**.

9   Markinor, which is a market research company, has found from experience that one-in-five people are willing to participate in focus group interviews. The company has been commissioned to conduct a focus group interview on the consumption patterns of bread for a bakery client.

(a) If 12 people are approached, what is the probability that only two are willing to participate in the focus group interview?

(b) Five people are required for the focus group interview. What is the probability that Markinor will find sufficient consumers to participate in the focus group interview session if it randomly approached 12 people?

(c) What is the probability that Markinor will recruit more than the required five consumers for the focus group interview session if it randomly approached 12 people?

Note: Calculate all the probabilities using the binomial formula and then the Excel function **BINOM.DIST**.

10   A market research study into the reading habits of magazine readers found that 10% of the general population of magazine readers are 'heavy readers' (i.e. read more than six different magazines per week). They also found that 35% of pensioners who read magazines are 'heavy' readers of magazines.

(a) Find the probability of there being fewer than two 'heavy readers' of magazines in any 10 randomly selected sample from the following groups:

–   the general population of magazine readers
–   the pensioner sub-population of magazine readers.

(b)   If a random sample of 280 pensioners who read magazines were interviewed, how many of them are *not likely* to be 'heavy readers' of magazines?

11   A telephone helpline receives calls that can be described by the Poisson process. The average rate at which calls come in is three calls per minute.

(a)   Find the probability that the helpline will receive exactly five calls in a given minute.

(b)   What is the likelihood that the helpline will receive four or more calls in a given minute?

(c)   What chance is there that no calls will be received in a given minute?

Note: Calculate the probabilities in (a)–(c) using the Poisson formula and then the Excel function **POISSON.DIST.**

12   A motor spares dealer sells, on average, four car batteries per week.

(a)   What is the probability that the dealer will sell no more than two batteries in a given week?

(b)   If the dealer has three batteries in stock at the beginning of a given week, what is the probability that the dealer will run out of stock in that week?

Note: Calculate all the probabilities using the Poisson formula and then the Excel function **POISSON.DIST.**

13   A company that supplies ready-mix concrete receives, on average, six orders per day.

(a)   What is the probability that, on a given day:

(i)   only one order will be received?

(ii)   no more than three orders will be received?

(iii)   at least three orders will be received?

(b)   What is the probability that, on a given *half-day*, only one order will be received? (*Hint:* Refer to the 'word of caution' in section 5.4.)

(c)   What is the mean and standard deviation of orders received per day?

14   The number of tubes of toothpaste purchased by a typical family is a random variable having a Poisson distribution with an average of 1.8 tubes per month.

(a)   What is the probability that a typical family will purchase at least three tubes of toothpaste in any given month?

(b)   What is the likelihood that a typical family will purchase less than four tubes of toothpaste in any given month?

Note: Calculate all the probabilities using the Poisson formula and then the Excel function **POISSON.DIST.**

15   A short-term insurance company receives seven motor vehicle claims, on average, per day. Assume that the daily claims rate follows a Poisson process.

(a)   What is the probability that on a given day no more than five motor vehicle claims will be received?

(b)   How likely is it that either six or nine motor vehicle claims will be received on a given day?

(c)   What is the chance that more than 20 motor vehicle claims will be received by the company over any *two-day* period? (*Hint:* Refer to the 'word of caution' in section 5.4.)

Note: Calculate all the probabilities using the Poisson formula and then the Excel function **POISSON.DIST.**

16 (a) Find the following probabilities using the standard normal z-tables.
Give a sketch with the appropriate area shaded in.
   (i) $P(0 < z < 1.83)$
   (ii) $P(z > -0.48)$
   (iii) $P(-2.25 < z < 0)$
   (iv) $P(1.22 < z)$
   (v) $P(-2.08 < z < 0.63)$
   (vi) $P(z < -0.68)$
   (vii) $P(0.33 < z < 1.5)$

(b) Find the probabilities in (a) using the Excel function **NORM.S.DIST**.

17 (a) Find the missing values for the following probabilities for the standard normal z-distribution using the z-tables:
   (i) $P(z < ?) = 0.9147$
   (ii) $P(z > ?) = 0.5319$
   (iii) $P(0 < z < ?) = 0.4015$
   (iv) $P(? < z < 0) = 0.4803$
   (v) $P(? < z) = 0.0985$
   (vi) $P(z < ?) = 0.2517$
   (vii) $P(? < z) = 0.6331$

(b) Find the values in (a) using the Excel function **NORM.S.INV**.

18 (a) Given that x (= flight times between cities A and B) follows a normal distribution with a mean (μ) of 64 minutes and a standard deviation (σ) of 2.5 minutes, use the standard normal z-table to find:
   (i) $P(x < 62)$
   (ii) $P(x > 67.4)$
   (iii) $P(59.6 < x < 62.8)$
   (iv) $P(x > ?) = 0.1026$
   (v) $P(x > ?) = 0.9772$
   (vi) $P(60.2 < x < ?) = 0.6652$

(b) Interpret the meaning of each probability in (a).

(c) Use the Excel functions **NORM.DIST** and **NORM.INV** to solve for the values in (a).

19 The manager of a local gym has determined that the length of time patrons spend at the gym is a normally distributed variable with a mean of 80 minutes and a standard deviation of 20 minutes.

(a) What proportion of patrons spend more than two hours at the gym?

(b) What proportion of patrons spend less than one hour at the gym?

(c) What is the least amount of time spent by 60% of patrons at the gym?

Note: Calculate the results for (a)–(c) using the z-table and then the appropriate Excel function (i.e. **NORM.DIST** or **NORM.INV**).

20 The lifetime of a certain type of automatic washing machine is normally distributed with mean and standard deviation equal to 3.1 and 1.1 years, respectively.

(a) If this type of washing machine is guaranteed for one year, what percentage of original sales will require replacement if they fail within the guarantee period?

(b) What percentage of these washing machines is likely to be operating after 4 years? After 5.5 years?

(c)   If the manufacturer of these washing machines wants to ensure that no more than 5% of these washers will be replaced within a guarantee period, what new guarantee period should they choose?

Note: Calculate the results for (a)–(c) using the z-table and then the appropriate Excel function (i.e. **NORM.DIST** or **NORM.INV**).

21   A recent survey by a local municipality established that daily water usage by its households is normally distributed with a mean of 220 litres and a standard deviation of 45 litres.

    (a)   Use standard normal z-tables to answer the following questions:

        (i)   What percentage of households is likely to use more than 300 litres of water per day?

        (ii)   What is the probability of finding a household that uses less than 100 litres of water per day?

        (iii)   What is the most amount of water used per day by the lowest-consuming 15% of households?

        (iv)   The municipality plans to implement a differential tariff policy to charge households that use more than a certain volume of water per day a higher rate per litre. If the municipality wants no more than 20% of households to pay this higher rate per litre, how much water per day must a household use before they will pay the higher rate per litre?

    (b)   Use the Excel function **NORM.DIST** to solve (a)(i) and (ii).

    (c)   Use the Excel function **NORM.INV** to solve (a)(iii) and (iv).

22   A study was recently conducted on the reaction time of long-distance truck drivers (after two hours of non-stop driving). Assume reaction times (after two hours of non-stop driving) are known to be normally distributed, with a mean of 1.4 seconds and a variance of 0.0625 seconds. Reaction times would be recorded (in seconds between the presentation of a stimulus and braking) by subjecting a truck driver to a simulated environment.

    (a)   What is the probability that a particular truck driver who has been driving for two hours non-stop has a reaction time of:

        (i)   more than two seconds?

        (ii)   between 1.2 and 1.4 seconds?

        (iii)   less than 0.9 seconds?

        (iv)   between 0.5 and one second?

    (b)   If a random sample of 120 truck drivers is drawn on the Golden Highway Plaza (N1, near Johannesburg), what percentage are likely to have a reaction time slower than 1.8 seconds? How many truck drivers does this represent?

    (c)   The National Transport Department is implementing a policy that requires truck drivers to undergo further training if their reaction time is slower than 1.7 seconds. How many drivers out of a random sample of 360 are likely to need further training?

Note: Use the z-tables and then the Excel function **NORM.DIST** to answer the questions.

23   A machine filling 18-gram containers of a hair dye is set so that the average fill is 18.2 grams with a variance of 0.49 grams. Assume that the filling of containers by this machine is normally distributed.
   (a)   What percentage of the containers is not likely to meet the producer's specification of at least 18 grams per container?
   (b)   What is the minimum mass of the heaviest 15% of containers?

   Note: Calculate the results for (a) and (b) using the *z*-table and then the appropriate Excel function (i.e. **NORM.DIST** or **NORM.INV**).

24   The service time of the first service of a BMW is found to be normally distributed, with a mean of 70 minutes and a variance of 81 minutes.
   (a)   If a customer brings her BMW in for its first service, what is the probability that the car will be ready within one hour?
   (b)   What is the probability that the job will take more than an hour and a half?
   (c)   What percentage of first services will be completed between 50 and 60 minutes?
   (d)   The BMW dealer has a policy to give its customers a 15% discount on the cost of the first service if the service is not completed within 80 minutes. From a sample of 80 customers who brought their BMWs in for its first service, how many are likely to receive the 15% discount?
   (e)   If the BMW dealer wants to ensure that no more than 5% of all first services will take longer than 80 minutes, what should the mean service time be?

   Note: Calculate the results using the *z*-table and then the appropriate Excel function (i.e. **NORM.DIST** or **NORM.INV**).

25   A coffee-dispensing machine used in cafeterias is set to dispense coffee with an average fill of 230 ml and a standard deviation of 10 ml per cup. Assume that the volume dispensed is normally distributed.
   (a)   For a randomly selected cup dispensed by the machine, what is the probability that:
      (i)   the cup is filled to more than 235 ml?
      (ii)   the cup is filled to between 235 ml and 245 ml?
      (iii)   the cup is less than 220 ml full?
   (b)   If the company supplying the coffee machines wants only 15% of cups to exceed a given fill level, what level of fill (in ml) does this correspond to?
   (c)   What must the mean fill level (in ml) be set to in order to ensure that no more than 10% of cups are filled to less than 220 ml?

26   Assume that the mean life of a particular brand of car battery is normally distributed with a mean of 28 months and a standard deviation of 4 months.
   (a)   For a randomly selected battery, what is the probability that it will last between 30 and 34 months?
   (b)   What is the probability that a randomly selected battery will fail within two years of the date of purchase?
   (c)   By what time period will 60% of all batteries of this make fail?
   (d)   If a guarantee period is to be set, how many months would it have to be to replace no more than 5% of batteries of this make?

   Note: Calculate the results for (a) and (b) using the *z*-table and then the appropriate Excel function (i.e. **NORM.DIST** or **NORM.INV**).

Sampling and Sampling Distributions

Outcomes

This chapter reviews the different methods of sampling and the concept of the sampling distribution. Both of these topics are important building blocks in inferential statistics. Sampling affects the validity of inferential findings, while the sampling distribution measures the confidence a manager can have in any inferences made.

After studying this chapter, you should be able to:

- describe the purpose of inferential statistics
- distinguish between a sample and a population
- explain the reasons for sampling
- explain the different types of sampling methods
- explain when it is appropriate to choose each sampling method
- understand the concept of the sampling distribution
- explain the importance of the central limit theorem in inferential statistics
- explain the role of the sampling distribution in inferential statistics.

6.1 Introduction

Inferential statistics are statistical methods that use sample findings to either estimate or test values of population parameters of random variables under study. For example, a quality controller can use the mean mass of a sample of 130 cornflakes boxes (descriptive statistics) to determine whether all cornflakes boxes are filled to the correct specification mass by a filling machine (inferential statistics).

There are four pillars that support inferential analysis. Without them, inferential statistics are neither feasible nor valid. These pillars are:
1. descriptive statistics (sample means, proportions and standard deviation)
2. probabilities, especially the normal probability distribution
3. sampling methods (and their influence on sampling error)
4. the concept of the sampling distribution.

Descriptive statistics, probabilities and the normal probability distribution were covered in chapters 2, 3, 4 and 5. This chapter will (i) describe the different sampling methods and relate them to the concept of sampling error, and (ii) derive and explain the significance of the sampling distribution. Chapters 7 to 11 will then draw on these principles and concepts to show how the inferential methods described in these chapters are used to either estimate or test values of population parameter measures.

6.2 Sampling and Sampling Methods

As seen in Chapter 1, a sample is a subset of a population. A sample must be *representative* of its target population if it is to produce *valid* and *reliable* estimates of the population from which it was drawn. There are two basic methods of sampling: non-probability and probability sampling methods.

Non-probability (Non-random) Sampling

Any sampling method where the sample members are *not selected randomly* is called **non-probability sampling**. Criteria other than random selection are used to choose the sample members from the population.

There are four types of non-probability sampling methods:
1. convenience sampling
2. judgement sampling
3. quota sampling
4. snowball sampling.

Convenience Sampling

When a sample is drawn to suit the convenience of the researcher, it is called convenience sampling. For example, it may be more convenient to conduct interviews on textile industry labour practices with employees from only one textile company; or select motorists from only one petrol station to interview on fuel brand preferences; or select items for inspection from only one shift instead of a number of shifts.

Judgement Sampling

When researchers use their judgement alone to select the best sampling units to include in the sample, then judgement sampling has been applied. For example, only professional footballers (instead of any football players) are selected and interviewed on the need for rule changes in the sport; or only labour union leaders are selected (instead of general workers) to respond to a study into working conditions in the mining industry.

Quota Sampling

Quota sampling involves the setting of quotas of sampling units to interview from specific subgroups of a population. When the quota for any one subgroup is met, no more sampling units are selected from that subgroup for interview. This introduces selection bias into the sampling process. For example, a researcher may set a quota to interview 40 males and 70 females from the 25- to 40-year age group on their savings practices. When the quota of interviews for any one subgroup is reached (either the males or the females), no further eligible sampling units from that subgroup are selected for interview purposes. The main feature of quota sampling is the non-random selection of sampling units to fulfil the quota limits. In this respect, quota sampling can be viewed as a non-random version of stratified random sampling.

Snowball Sampling

Snowball sampling is used when it is not easy to identify the members of the target population for reasons of sensitivity or confidentiality (e.g. in studies related to HIV/AIDS, gangster activity, drug addiction, sexuality, poaching or illegal immigrants). If one member can be identified, this person is asked to identify other members of the same target population. Each identified person would be asked to identify other members. In this way, the sample is built up. Again the selection of the sampling units is non-random and potentially biased.

There are two major *disadvantages* of non-probability sampling:

1   The samples are likely to be *unrepresentative* of their target population. This will introduce bias into the statistical findings, because significant sections of the population are likely to have been omitted from the selection process.
2   It is not possible to measure the *sampling error* from data based on a non-probability sample. Sampling error is the difference between the actual population parameter value and its sample statistic. As a result, it is not valid to draw statistical inferences from non-probability sample data.

However, non-probability samples can be useful in *exploratory research* situations or in *less-scientific surveys* to provide initial insights into and profiles of random variables under study.

Probability (Random) Sampling

Probability-based sampling includes any selection method where the sample members (sampling units) are selected from the target population on a *purely random* (chance) basis. Under random sampling, every member of the target population has a chance of being selected for the sample.

There are four *probability-based sampling* methods:

1   simple random sampling
2   systematic random sampling
3   stratified random sampling
4   cluster random sampling.

Simple Random Sampling

> In a **simple random sample**, each member in the target population has an *equal* chance of being selected.

It is assumed that the population is *homogeneous* with respect to the random variable under study (i.e. the sampling units share similar views on the research question(s); or the objects in a population are influenced by a common set of factors).

One way to draw a simple random sample is to assign a number to every element of the population and then effectively 'draw numbers from a hat'. If a database of names exists, a random number generator can be used to draw a simple random sample.

Some examples are given below.

- A simple random sample of taxpayers can be selected from all taxpayers to check on the correctness of their tax return forms. Since the correctness of tax return forms is independent of the age, gender or income of the taxpayer, a simple random sample is likely to be representative of the population of taxpayers.

- The population of Johannesburg motorists is to be surveyed for their views on toll roads. A simple random sample of Johannesburg motorists is assumed to be representative of this population as their views are unlikely to differ significantly across gender, age, car type driven or use of vehicle (i.e. private or business).

- In an 'in-control' production process, parts that come off the same production line can be selected using simple random sampling to check the quality of the entire batch produced.

- A survey of all tourists to Cape Town is to be undertaken to find out their views on service standards (quality and price) in Cape Town with respect to accommodation, transport, attractions and restaurants. A simple random sample of tourists is likely to represent the views of all tourists as it is assumed that their views on 'service standards' will be similar regardless of age, gender or nationality.

Systematic Random Sampling

> **Systematic random sampling** is used to sample items from a continuous (or batch) production process or when a *sampling frame* (i.e. an address list or database of population members) exists. Sampling begins by randomly selecting the first sampling unit. Thereafter subsequent sampling units are selected at a uniform interval relative to the first sampling unit. Since only the first sampling unit is randomly selected, some randomness is sacrificed.

To draw a systematic random sample, first divide the sampling frame by the sample size to determine the size of a sampling block. Randomly choose the first sample member from within the first sampling block. Then choose subsequent sample members by selecting one member from each sampling block at a constant interval from the previously sampled member.

For example, to draw a systematic random sample of 500 property owners from a database of 15 000 property owners, proceed as follows:

- Identify the size of each sampling block = $\frac{15\ 000}{500}$ = 30 property owners.
- Randomly select the first sample member from within the first 30 names on the list. Assume it is the 16th name on the list.
- Thereafter select one property owner from each of the remaining 499 sampling blocks at a uniform interval (every 30th person) relative to the first sampling unit. If the 16th name was initially randomly selected, then the 46th, 76th, 106th, 136th, etc. until the 14 986th name on the list would represent the remaining sample members.
- This will result in a randomly drawn sample of 500 names of property owners.

In a continuous (or batch) production process, systematic random sampling is used for quality control purposes and begins by randomly choosing a sampling point within, say, the first 30 minutes (e.g. randomly select the 19th minute, and then randomly select 8 items). Therefore sampling occurs systematically every 30 minutes after the 19th minute (i.e. at the 49th, 79th, 109th, etc. minutes).

Stratified Random Sampling

Stratified random sampling is used when the population is assumed to be *heterogeneous* with respect to the random variable under study. The population is *divided into segments (or strata)*, where the population members within each stratum are relatively homogeneous. Thereafter, simple random samples are drawn from each stratum.

If the random samples are drawn *in proportion to* the relative size of each stratum, then this method of sampling is called *proportional stratified* random sampling.

The *advantage* of this sampling method is that it generally ensures greater representativeness across the entire population and also results in a smaller sampling error, giving greater precision in estimation. A *disadvantage* is that larger samples are required than in simple random sampling to ensure adequate representation of each stratum. This increases the cost of data collection.

Some examples are given below.

- If age and gender of the motoring public are assumed, *a priori*, to influence their responses to questions on car type preferred and features sought in a car, then stratifying this population by these two characteristics and drawing a simple random sample from each stratum of age/gender combination is likely to produce a more representative sample.
- Ratepayers in Durban could be stratified by the criteria 'property value per square metre'. All 'low-valued' suburbs would form one stratum, all 'medium-valued' suburbs would form a second stratum and all 'high-valued' suburbs would form a third stratum. A simple random sample of households within each stratum would be selected and interviewed. Their responses to questions on rates increases would be assumed to represent the responses of all ratepayers across all strata of property values.

Cluster Random Sampling

Certain target populations form *natural* clusters, which make for easier sampling. For example, labour forces cluster within factories; accountants cluster within accounting firms; lawyers cluster within law firms; shoppers cluster at shopping malls; students cluster at educational institutions; and outputs from different production runs (e.g. margarine tubs) are batched and labelled separately, forming clusters.

> **Cluster random sampling** is used where the target population can be naturally divided into clusters, where each cluster is *similar in profile* to every other cluster. A subset of clusters is then randomly selected for sampling.

The sampling units within these sampled clusters may themselves be randomly selected to provide a representative sample from the population. For this reason, it is also called *two-stage* cluster sampling (e.g. select schools (stage 1) as clusters, then pupils within schools (stage 2); select companies (stage 1) as clusters, then employees within companies (stage 2)).

Cluster sampling tends to be used when the population is large and geographically dispersed. In such cases, smaller regions or clusters (with similar profiles) can be more easily sampled.

The *advantage* of cluster random sampling is that it usually reduces the per unit cost of sampling. One *disadvantage* is that cluster random sampling tends to produce larger sampling errors than those resulting from simple random sampling.

Some examples are given below.

- In a study on mine safety awareness amongst miners, each gold mine could be considered to be a separate cluster. Assume there are 47 mine clusters in the Gauteng area. A randomly drawn sample of, say, eight mine clusters would first be selected. Then a simple random sample of miners within each of the chosen mines would be identified and interviewed. The responses are assumed to be representative of all miners (including those in mine clusters not sampled).
- Each of the 25 major shopping malls in the Cape Peninsula can be classified as a cluster. A researcher may randomly choose, say, seven of these shopping malls, and randomly select customers within each of these selected clusters for interviews on, say, clothing purchase behaviour patterns. Their responses are assumed to reflect the views of all shopping mall shoppers.

Advantages of Random Sampling Methods

- Random sampling *reduces selection bias*, meaning that the sample statistics are likely to be 'better' (*unbiased*) *estimates* of their population parameters.
- The *error in sampling* (sampling error) can be calculated from data that is recorded using random sampling methods. This makes the findings of inferential analysis valid.

Table 6.1 summarises the different sampling methods and highlights valid statistical analysis that can be performed on data derived from each sampling method.

Table 6.1 Summary of sampling methods and valid statistical analysis

Sampling methods	Sample types	Valid statistical analyses
Non-probability (non-random selection)	Convenience Judgement Quota Snowball	Exploratory descriptive statistics only
Probability (random selection)	Simple random Systematic random Stratified random Cluster random	Descriptive statistics Inferential statistics

6.3 The Concept of the Sampling Distribution

In inferential statistics, an important statistical question is: 'How reliable and precise is the sample statistic (e.g. the sample mean) as a true and representative measure of its population parameter (e.g. the population mean)?' We want to know how close a sample statistic lies to its population parameter. The sampling distribution provides the answer to this question.

> A **sampling distribution** shows the relationship between a sample statistic (e.g. sample mean) and its corresponding population parameter (e.g. population mean). It shows how a sample statistic varies about its true population parameter.

From this relationship, the **level of confidence** in estimating the population parameter from a single sample statistic can be established.

The behaviour of four sample statistics with respect to their population parameters are described in this chapter, and then used as the basis for inferential methods from Chapter 7 onwards. These sample statistics and the population parameters to which they relate are given in Table 6.2. The parameters are all measures of central location.

Table 6.2 Selected population parameters and their associated sample statistics

Central location measure	Population parameter	Sample statistic
Single mean	μ	$\bar{x}$
Single proportion	π	p
Difference between two means	$\mu_1 - \mu_2$	$\bar{x}_1 - \bar{x}_2$
Difference between two proportions	$\pi_1 - \pi_2$	$p_1 - p_2$

Only the sampling distribution of the sample mean, $\bar{x}$, will be described and discussed in this chapter. The rationale and interpretation of the sampling distributions for the other three sample statistics are identical to that for the sample mean.

6.4 The Sampling Distribution of the Sample Mean ($\bar{x}$)

This section will describe how the sample mean, $\bar{x}$, is related to the population mean, μ, for any random variable, x. The following explanation is given to provide an understanding of how close sample statistics lie to their population parameters, which we are trying to estimate.

Rationale of a Sampling Distribution

Assume that the Department of Labour wants to determine the average number of years' experience of all professional engineers in South Africa. Consider the hypothetical situation of drawing every possible sample of size n (say $n = 100$ professional engineers) from this population. Assume that there are k such samples. Calculate the mean years of experience for each of these k samples. There will now be k sample means.

Now construct a frequency distribution of these k sample means and also calculate the mean and standard deviation of these k sample means. The following properties will emerge:

(a) The sample mean is itself a *random variable*, as the value of each sample mean is likely to vary from sample to sample. Each separate sample of 100 engineers will have a different sample mean number of years' experience.

(b) The *mean* of all these k sample means will be equal to the *true population mean*, μ.

$$\mu = \frac{\bar{x}_1 + \bar{x}_2 + \bar{x}_3 + \ldots + \bar{x}_k}{k}$$

This tells us that the sample mean, $\bar{x}$, is an *unbiased estimate* of the population mean, μ.

(c) The *standard deviation* of these k sample means is a measure of the *sampling error*. It is called the **standard error of the sample means** and is calculated as follows:

$$\sigma_{\bar{x}} = \frac{\sigma}{\sqrt{n}} \qquad\qquad 6.1$$

It measures the average deviation of sample means about its true population mean.

(d) The histogram of these k sample means will be *normally* distributed.

This distribution of the sample means is called the **sampling distribution** of $\bar{x}$.

To summarise, the sample mean is a random variable that has the following three properties:

1 It is normally distributed.
2 It has a mean equal to the population mean, μ.
3 It has a standard deviation, called the standard error, $\sigma_{\bar{x}}$, equal to $\frac{\sigma}{\sqrt{n}}$.

Based on these three properties and using normal probability distribution theory, it is possible to conclude the following about how sample means behave in relation to their population means:

- 68.3% of all sample means will lie within one standard error of its population mean.
- 95.5% of all sample means will lie within two standard errors of its population mean.
- 99.7% of all sample means will lie within three standard errors of its population mean.

Alternatively, it can be stated as follows:

- There is a 68.3% chance that a single sample mean will lie *no further than one* standard error away from its population mean.
- There is a 95.5% chance that a single sample mean will lie *no further than two* standard errors away from its population mean.
- There is a 99.7% chance that a single sample mean will lie *no further than three* standard errors away from its population mean.

This implies that any sample mean, which is calculated from a randomly drawn sample, has a high probability (up to 99.7%) of being *no more than three* standard errors away from its true, but unknown, population mean value.

These probabilities are found by relating the sampling distribution of $\bar{x}$ to the z-distribution. Any sample mean, $\bar{x}$, can be converted into a z-value through the following z transformation formulae:

$$z = \frac{\bar{x} - \mu}{\sigma_{\bar{x}}} \quad or \quad z = \frac{\bar{x} - \mu}{\frac{\sigma}{\sqrt{n}}} \qquad\qquad 6.2$$

The *sampling distribution of the sample mean* is shown graphically in Figure 6.1.

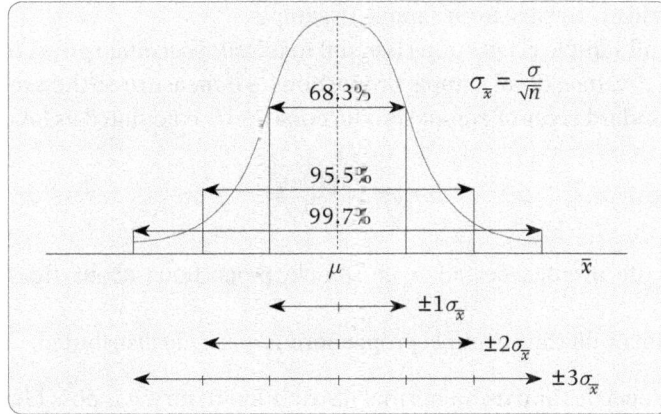

Figure 6.1 Sampling distribution of the sample mean

This relationship between the sample mean and its population mean can be used to:
- find probabilities that a single sample mean will lie within a specified distance of its true but unknown population mean
- calculate probability-based interval estimates of the population mean
- test claims/statistical hypotheses about a value for the true but unknown population mean.

The sampling distribution is the basis for the two inferential techniques of *confidence intervals* and *hypotheses tests*, which are covered in the following chapters.

6.5 The Sampling Distribution of the Sample Proportion (*p*)

The sample proportion, p, is used as the central location measure when the random variable under study is *qualitative* and the data is *categorical* (i.e. nominal/ordinal).

A sample proportion is found by counting the number of cases that have the characteristic of interest, r, and expressing it as a ratio (or percentage) of the sample size, n (i.e. $p = \frac{r}{n}$). See Table 6.3 for illustrations of sample proportions.

Table 6.3 Illustrations of sample proportions for categorical variables

Qualitative random variable	Sample statistic
Gender	Proportion of females in a sample of students
Trade union membership	Proportion of employees who are trade union members
Mobile phone brand preference	Proportion of mobile phone users who prefer Apple

This section will show how the sample proportion, p, is related to the true, but unknown population proportion π for any categorical random variable x.

The sample proportion, p, is related to its population proportion, π, in exactly the same way as the sample mean, $\bar{x}$, is related to its population mean, μ. Thus the relationship between p and π can be described by the **sampling distribution of the sample proportion**.

This relationship can be summarised as follows for a given *categorical* random variable, *x*.

(a) The sample proportion, *p*, is itself a *random variable* as the value of each sample proportion is likely to vary from sample to sample.

(b) The *mean* of all sample proportions is equal to its *true population proportion, π*.

(c) The *standard deviation* of all sample proportions is a measure of the *sampling error*. It is called the **standard error of sample proportions** and is calculated as follows:

$$\sigma_p = \sqrt{\frac{\pi(1-\pi)}{n}}$$

6.3

It measures the average deviation of sample proportions about the true population proportion.

(d) The histogram of all these sample proportions is *normally* distributed.

Based on these properties and using normal distribution theory, it is possible to conclude the following about how sample proportions behave in relation to their population proportion:

- 68.3% of all sample proportions will lie within *one* standard error of its population proportion, π.
- 95.5% of all sample proportions will lie within *two* standard errors of its population proportion, π.
- 99.7% of all sample proportions will lie within *three* standard errors of its population proportion, π.

These probabilities are found by relating the sampling distribution of *p* to the *z*-distribution. Any sample proportion, *p*, can be converted into a *z*-value through the following *z* transformation formulae:

$$z = \frac{p - \pi}{\sigma_p} \quad \text{or} \quad z = \frac{p - \pi}{\sqrt{\frac{\pi(1-\pi)}{n}}}$$

6.4

Figure 6.2 shows the sampling distribution of single sample proportions graphically.

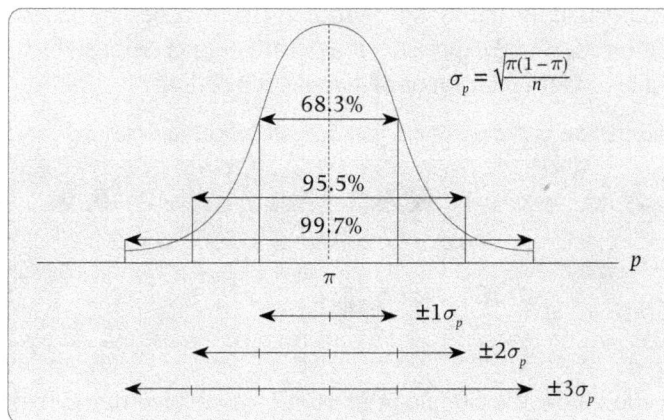

Figure 6.2 Sampling distribution of sample proportions (*p*)

This relationship can now be used to derive probabilities, develop probability-based estimates, and test hypotheses of the population proportion in statistical inference.

6.6 The Sampling Distribution of the Difference between Two Sample Means $(\bar{x}_1 - \bar{x}_2)$

Often the means of two samples are compared to establish if any differences exist between their corresponding population means, as illustrated in Table 6.4.

Table 6.4 Illustrations of the sample statistic – differences between two sample means

Random variable	Two independent samples (derive sample means)	Sample statistic
Age (in years)	Sample 1: Male shoppers Sample 2: Female shoppers	Is there a difference between the mean ages of *male* and *female* shoppers? $(\bar{x}_{male} - \bar{x}_{female}) = 0$?
Turnover (in rand)	Sample 1: Branch 1 monthly turnover Sample 2: Branch 2 monthly turnover	Is branch 1's mean monthly turnover greater than branch 2's mean monthly turnover? $(\bar{x}_{branch1} - \bar{x}_{branch2}) > 0$?
Erf sizes (in m²)	Sample 1: Erf sizes in Durban Sample 2: Erf sizes in Pretoria	Are average erf sizes in Durban smaller than those in Pretoria? $(\bar{x}_{Durban} - \bar{x}_{Pretoria}) < 0$?

Since we need to know whether there is a difference between two unknown population means, it is necessary to know how the sample statistic (i.e. the difference between two sample means) is related to its true but unknown population parameter (i.e. the difference between two population means).

The relationship can be described by the **sampling distribution of the difference between two sample means**. The appropriate sample statistic is $(\bar{x}_1 - \bar{x}_2)$, and its associated population parameter is $(\mu_1 - \mu_2)$.

Using similar rationale to that developed for the sampling distribution of a single mean, the following can be stated:

(a) The difference between two sample means, $(\bar{x}_1 - \bar{x}_2)$, is itself a *random variable*, as its value is likely to vary from sample to sample.

(b) The *mean* of all the differences between two sample means is equal to the *true difference between the two population means*, $(\mu_1 - \mu_2)$.

(c) The *standard deviation* of all the differences between two sample means is a measure of the *sampling error*. It is called the **standard error of the differences between two sample means** and is calculated as follows:

$$c_{\bar{x}_1 - \bar{x}_2} = \sqrt{\frac{\sigma_1^2}{n_1} + \frac{\sigma_2^2}{n_2}}$$

6.5

It measures the average deviation of differences in sample means about the true population difference in means.

(d) The histogram of all the differences between two sample means is *normally* distributed.

Based on these properties, similar probability statements as applied to the sampling distributions for the single mean, and the single proportion, can be made. These relate to

68.26%, 95.5% and 99.73%, respectively, of sample values $(\bar{x}_1 - \bar{x}_2)$ that are likely to fall within one, two and three standard errors about the population parameter $(\mu_1 - \mu_2)$.

In probability calculations, the sample statistic (i.e. the difference between two sample means) is related to the z-distribution through the following z transformation formulae:

$$z = \frac{(\bar{x}_1 - \bar{x}_2) - (\mu_1 - \mu_2)}{\sigma_{\bar{x}_1 - \bar{x}_2}} \quad \text{or} \quad z = \frac{(\bar{x}_1 - \bar{x}_2) - (\mu_1 - \mu_2)}{\sqrt{\frac{\sigma_1^2}{n_1} + \frac{\sigma_2^2}{n_2}}} \qquad 6.6$$

6.7 The Sampling Distribution of the Difference between Two Sample Proportions $(p_1 - p_2)$

If the proportions of a qualitative random variable between two samples are compared to establish if any differences exist between them, the appropriate sample statistic to calculate is the *difference in two sample proportions*, as illustrated in Table 6.5.

Table 6.5 Illustrations of the sample statistic – difference between two sample proportions

Random variable	Two independent samples (derive sample proportions)	Sample statistic
Gender of customers who purchase groceries on credit	Sample 1: Male customers Sample 2: Female customers	Is the proportion of male customers who purchase groceries on credit different from the proportion of female customers who purchase groceries on credit, i.e. $(p_m - p_f) = 0$?
Advertising recall rate	Sample 1: Single persons Sample 2: Married persons	Is the proportion of single persons who recalled a car advertisement greater than the proportion of married persons who recalled the same advertisement, i.e. $(p_s - p_m) > 0$?

The relationship between this sample statistic (the difference between two sample proportions) and its true but unknown population parameter (the difference between two population proportions) is described by the **sampling distribution of the difference between two sample proportions**. The sample statistic is $(p_1 - p_2)$, and its associated population parameter is $(\pi_1 - \pi_2)$.

Using similar rationale to that developed for the sampling distribution of a single mean, the following can be stated:
(a) The differences in two sample proportions is itself a *random variable*, as its value is likely to vary from sample to sample.
(b) The *mean* of all the differences in two sample proportions is equal to the *true difference between the two population proportions*, $(\pi_1 - \pi_2)$.
(c) The *standard deviation* of all the differences between two sample proportions is a measure of the *sampling error*. It is called the **standard error of the differences between two sample proportions** and is calculated as follows:

$$\sigma_{p_1-p_2} = \sqrt{\hat{\pi}(1-\hat{\pi})(\tfrac{1}{n_1}+\tfrac{1}{n_2})}$$
$$\text{where:} \quad \hat{\pi} = \frac{x_1+x_2}{n_1+n_2}$$

6.7

It measures the average deviation of differences in sample proportions about the true population difference in proportions.

(d) The histogram of all the differences between two sample proportions is *normally* distributed.

Based on these properties, similar probability statements as applied to the sampling distributions for the single mean, and the single proportion can be made. These relate to 68.3%, 95.5% and 99.7%, respectively, of sample statistics $(p_1 - p_2)$ that are likely to fall within one, two and three standard errors about the population parameter $(\pi_1 - \pi_2)$.

In probability calculations, the sample statistic – the difference between two sample proportions – is related to the z-distribution through the following z transformation formulae.

$$z = \frac{(p_1-p_2)-(\pi_1-\pi_2)}{\sigma_{p_1-p_2}} \qquad \text{or} \qquad z = \frac{(p_1-p_2)-(\pi_1-\pi_2)}{\sqrt{\hat{\pi}(1-\hat{\pi})(\tfrac{1}{n_1}+\tfrac{1}{n_2})}}$$
$$\text{where:} \quad \hat{\pi} = \frac{x_1+x_2}{n_1+n_2} \qquad p_1 = \frac{x_1}{n_1} \qquad p_2 = \frac{x_2}{n_2}$$

6.8

Finally, Table 6.6 summarises each sample statistic and the properties of its sampling distribution.

Table 6.6 Summary of each sample statistic and its sampling distribution properties

Sample statistic	Population parameter to be estimated	Standard normal (z) distribution formula required in inferential statistics
Sample mean $\bar{x}$ $\longrightarrow$	Population mean μ	$z = \frac{\bar{x}-\mu}{\frac{\sigma}{\sqrt{n}}}$
Sample proportion p $\longrightarrow$	Population proportion π	$z = \frac{p-\pi}{\sqrt{\frac{\pi(1-\pi)}{n}}}$
Difference between two sample means $(\bar{x}_1 - \bar{x}_2)$ $\longrightarrow$	Difference between two population means $(\mu_1 - \mu_2)$	$z = \frac{(\bar{x}_1-\bar{x}_2)-(\mu_1-\mu_2)}{\sqrt{\frac{\sigma_1^2}{n_1}+\frac{\sigma_2^2}{n_2}}}$
Difference between two sample proportions $(p_1 - p_2)$ $\longrightarrow$	Difference between two population proportions $(\pi_1 - \pi_2)$	$z = \frac{(p_1-p_2)-(\pi_1-\pi_2)}{\sqrt{\hat{\pi}(1-\hat{\pi})(\frac{1}{n_1}+\frac{1}{n_2})}}$ where: $\hat{\pi} = \frac{x_1+x_2}{n_1+n_2}, p_1 = \frac{x_1}{n_1}, p_2 = \frac{x_2}{n_2}$

The z-formulae are used in inferential statistics to:
- derive probabilities of closeness to the population parameter
- set up confidence intervals to estimate the population parameter
- test hypotheses about values of the population parameters.

6.8 Central Limit Theorem and Sample Sizes

An important assumption in inferential analysis is that the *sampling distribution* of the sample statistic (mean or proportion) is *normally distributed*. This will always be the case when the sample is drawn from a normally distributed population regardless of the sample size chosen. However, if the underlying population from which a sample is drawn *is not normally distributed* (or its distribution is unknown) then – as proven by the **central limit theorem** – provided the sample size is large enough (usually $n \geq 30$) the sampling distribution of the mean (or proportion) can be assumed to be normal.

The **central limit theorem** states that – regardless of the shape of the underlying population from which the sample is drawn – as the sample size (n) increases, the sampling distribution of the mean (or proportion) approaches the normal distribution. This is illustrated in **Figure 6.3**.

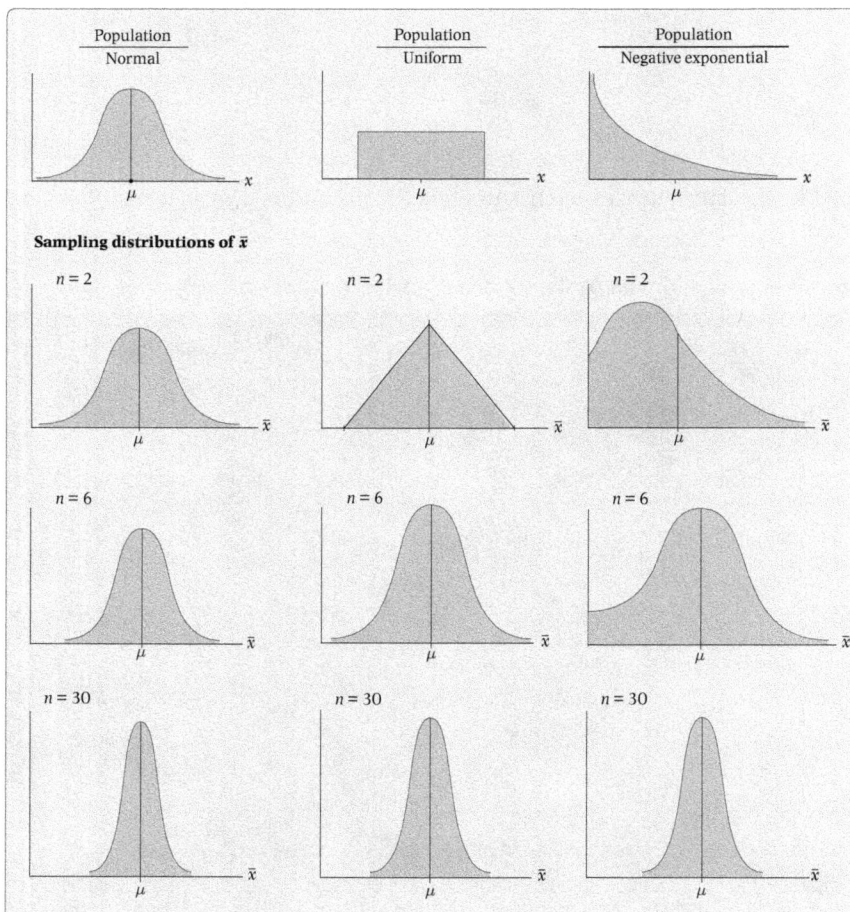

Figure 6.3 Central limit theorem – sampling distribution related to population distribution

The central limit theorem is fundamental to inferential statistics as it allows for valid inferential conclusions to be drawn about population parameter values (e.g. $\mu = k$) or relationships between measures in a population (e.g. $\mu_1 = \mu_2$) based on only a single sample's evidence drawn from any shaped underlying population. The reason for this is because the relevant sample statistic (e.g. $\bar{x}$, $(\bar{x}_1 - \bar{x}_2)$) can be assumed to behave *normally*.

6.9 Summary

This chapter introduced the building blocks of inferential statistics, which will be covered further in chapters 7 to 11. The need for inferential statistical methods arises because most statistical data is gathered from a sample instead of from the population as a whole.

The different types of sampling methods, such as non-probability and probability sampling methods, were reviewed.

An understanding of the different sampling procedures assists with deciding when inferential statistical methods can be applied validly to sample data.

The concept of the sampling distribution was introduced and described for four sample statistics, namely: the single sample mean, the single sample proportion, the difference between two sample means, and the difference between two sample proportions. The sampling distribution describes, in probability terms, how close a sample statistic can lie to its corresponding population parameter. This relationship provides the basis for inferential statistics. The importance of the *central limit theorem* to ensure normality is highlighted.

Exercises

1   What is the purpose of inferential statistics?
2   There are four pillars of inferential statistics. Two of them are (i) descriptive statistics and (ii) probability concepts. Name the other two pillars of inferential statistics.
3   Fill in the missing word: 'A sample is a .... of a population.'
4   Fill in the missing word: 'To produce reliable and valid estimates of a population parameter, a sample must be .... of its target population.'
5   Explain the difference between non-probability and probability sampling methods.
6   Which sampling method is appropriate for inferential analysis? Why?
7   Name the two disadvantages of non-probability sampling.
8   Fill in the missing word: 'Probability-based sampling involves selecting the sample members from the target population on a purely .... basis.'
9   Fill in the missing word: 'In a simple random sample, each member in the target population has an .... chance of being selected.'
10 A wine farmer in Paarl wishes to test the fermentable sugar content (fructose) in a vineyard of chardonnay grapes. All grapes are expected to produce similar fructose levels.
    Which random sampling technique would be appropriate to produce a representative sample of bunches of grapes to test the fructose levels of this vineyard?
11 In a paper milling plant in Sabie, the consistency of the rolled paper is tested at regular hourly intervals. In a given shift, a sample of paper is tested for consistency at a randomly chosen point in time within the first hour after the machine has reached a 'steady-state'. Therefore a sample is tested every half-hour after the first sample was drawn. This method of sampling is known as .... sampling (two words).
12 The BEEE status of a company is determined by its size based on turnover (i.e. turnover under R 5 million; R 5 to R 10 million and above R 10 million per annum). To verify BEEE compliance across all companies, an appropriate sampling method to use to draw a representatives sample would be .... sampling (two words).
13 The National Department of Basic Education wishes to assess the accounting skills of Grade 10 learners in the 92 schools in the Johannesburg metropolitan area that offer this subject. The Department's research staff believe that the range of abilities of Grade 10 learners' accounting skills is likely to be the same across all schools (i.e. each school is a cluster). If a sample of only 15 of these schools is randomly selected (with a further sub-sample of Grade 10 accounting learners selected within each school and tested), then the sampling method used is called .... (three words).
14 Name one advantage of stratified random sampling.
15 A sampling distribution describes the relationship between a .... (two words) and its corresponding .... (two words).
16 Fill in the missing word: 'The standard deviation of all sample means around it population mean is called the ....' (two words).
17 What percentage of sample means lie within two standard errors of the true, but unknown population mean for a given numeric random variable?

18 Fill in the missing word: 'The shape of the distribution of all sample means based on a given sample size around its population mean is ....'

19 If the shape of the population distribution of a variable is non-normal or unknown, how large a sample must be drawn from this population to be sure that the sampling distribution of the sample mean will be normally distribution?

20 Name the theorem that allow statisticians to assume that the sampling distribution of a sample mean approaches a normal distribution as the sample size increases?

21 What does the term 'sampling error' mean?

PART
4

Making Statistical Inferences

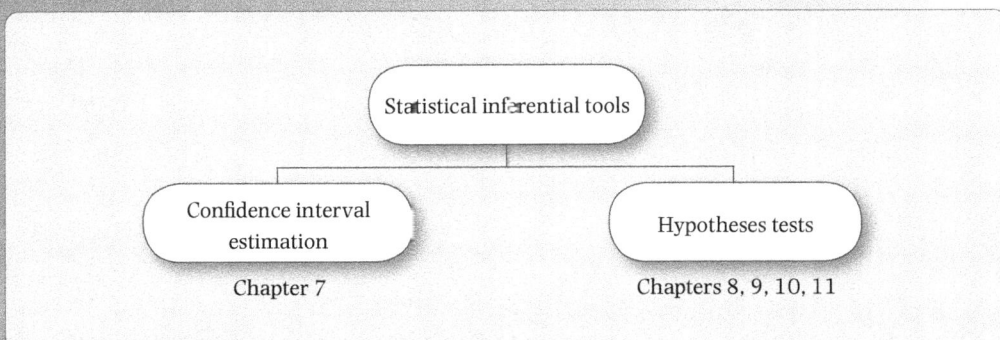

Statistical inferential tools

Confidence interval estimation

Chapter 7

Hypotheses tests

Chapters 8, 9, 10, 11

CHAPTER
7

Confidence Interval Estimation

Outcomes

A useful and reliable method to estimate a population parameter is to use the sample statistic as a reference point and to build an interval of values around it. This interval is likely to cover the true population parameter with a stated level of confidence in a process called confidence interval estimation.

This chapter explains how this is done and how much confidence a manager can have in the most likely value of the population parameter.

After studying this chapter, you should be able to:

- understand and explain the concept of a confidence interval
- calculate a confidence interval for a population mean and a population proportion
- interpret a confidence interval in a management context
- identify factors that affect the precision and reliability of confidence intervals
- determine sample sizes for desired levels of statistical precision.

7.1 Introduction

The role of inferential statistics is to use sample evidence to identify population measures. One approach is to calculate the most likely value for the population parameter based on the sample statistic. This is known as an estimation approach.

This chapter will consider two estimation methods for the true population parameter. They are *point estimation* and *confidence interval estimation*.

The most common population parameters to estimate are the central location measures of the single *population mean*, μ, and single *population proportion*, π.

This chapter will show how each of these population parameters can be estimated using its respective sample statistic: the sample mean, $\bar{x}$, and the sample proportion, p.

7.2 Point Estimation

A **point estimate** is made when the value of a *sample statistic* is taken to be the true value of the population parameter.

Thus a sample mean, $\bar{x}$, is used as a point estimate of its population mean, μ, while a sample proportion, p, is used to represent the true value of its population proportion, π.

Here are two examples:

- A supermarket survey of a random sample of 75 shoppers found that their average shopping time was 28.4 minutes ($\bar{x} = 28.4$), so a point estimate of the actual average shopping time of all supermarket shoppers is expected to be 28.4 minutes ($\mu = 28.4$).
- Suppose 55 out of 350 (15.7%) randomly surveyed coffee drinkers prefer decaffeinated coffee. Then a point estimate of the actual proportion (%) of all coffee drinkers who prefer decaffeinated coffee is assumed to be 0.157 ($\pi = 0.157$ or 15.7%).

A sample point estimate is a highly unreliable measure of a population parameter as the probability that it will exactly equal the true value is extremely small (almost zero). Also, there is no indication of how near or how far a single sample statistic lies from its population measure (i.e. no indication of sampling error).

For these reasons, a point estimate is seldom used to estimate a population parameter. It is better to offer a *range of values* within which the population parameter is expected to fall so that the reliability of the estimate can be measured. This is the purpose of *interval estimation*.

7.3 Confidence Interval Estimation

An **interval estimate** is a range of values defined around a sample statistic. The population parameter is expected to lie within this interval with a specified *level of confidence* (or probability). It is therefore called a **confidence interval**.

Confidence intervals will be constructed for the single population mean, μ, and the single population proportion, π, using their respective sample statistics, $\bar{x}$ and p.

7.4 Confidence Interval for a Single Population Mean (μ) when the Population Standard Deviation (σ) is Known

$$\bar{x} \to \mu$$

The population parameter to be estimated is μ. The appropriate sample statistic to estimate μ is the sample mean, $\bar{x}$.

Typical questions that imply the use of confidence intervals are as follows:

- Construct 95% confidence limits for the average years of experience of all registered financial advisors.
- Estimate, with 99% confidence, the actual average mass of all frozen chickens supplied by County Fair.
- Find the 90% confidence interval estimate for the average duration of all telesales calls.

The following example is used to illustrate the construction of a confidence interval:

Example 7.1 Kimberley Grocery Store Purchase Value Study

A survey of a random sample of 300 grocery shoppers in Kimberley found that the mean value of their grocery purchases was R78. Assume that the population standard deviation of grocery purchase values is R21.

Find the 95% confidence limits for the average value of a grocery purchase by all grocery shoppers in Kimberley.

Solution

To construct confidence limits around a single sample mean, the following sample evidence is required:

- the sample mean, $\bar{x}$ (= R78)
- the sample size, n (= 300)

In addition, the level of confidence and a measure of the sampling error is required.

- The sampling error is represented by the standard error of the sample means:

$$\sigma_{\bar{x}} = \frac{\sigma}{\sqrt{n}} = \frac{21}{\sqrt{300}} = 1.2124 \qquad \text{(Formula 6.1)}$$

It requires that the population standard deviation, σ, is known.

- The 95% confidence level refers to z-limits that bound a symmetrical area of 95% around the mean (centre) of the standard normal distribution.

From the z-table (Appendix 1), a 95% confidence level corresponds to z-limits of ± 1.96. Thus an area of 95% is found under the standard normal distribution between $z = -1.96$ and $z = +1.96$.

These z-limits represent the 95% confidence interval in z terms. To express the confidence limits in the same unit of measure of the random variable under study (i.e. value of grocery purchases), the z-limits must be transformed into $\bar{x}$-limits using the following z transformation formula:

$$z = \frac{\bar{x} - \mu}{\frac{\sigma}{\sqrt{n}}} \qquad\qquad 7.1$$

When re-arranged to isolate μ:

$$\mu = \bar{x} \pm z\frac{\sigma}{\sqrt{n}}$$
$$= 78 \pm 1.96(1.2124)$$
$$= 78 \pm 2.376$$

This gives a lower and an upper confidence limit about μ:

- *lower* 95% confidence limit of $78 - 2.376 = 75.624$ (R75.62)
- *upper* 95% confidence limit of $78 + 2.376 = 80.376$ (R80.38).

Management Interpretation

There is a 95% chance that the true mean value of all grocery purchases by grocery shoppers in Kimberley lies between R75.62 and R80.38.

Thus the confidence interval for a single population mean, μ, is given as:

$$\bar{x} - z\frac{\sigma}{\sqrt{n}} \leq \mu \leq \bar{x} + z\frac{\sigma}{\sqrt{n}}$$
$$\text{(lower limit)} \qquad\qquad \text{(upper limit)}$$

7.2

The term $z\frac{\sigma}{\sqrt{n}}$ in the confidence interval formula is called the *margin of error* in estimation. It determines the *width* of a confidence interval and hence the *precision* of the interval estimate.

7.5 The Precision of a Confidence Interval

The width of a confidence interval is a measure of its *precision*. The narrower the confidence interval, the *more precise* is the interval estimate, and vice versa.

The width of a confidence interval is influenced by its *margin of error* which is determined by:

- the specified confidence level
- the sample size
- the population standard deviation.

The Specified Level of Confidence

The confidence level specifies the probability that the confidence interval will cover the true population mean. The most commonly used confidence levels are 90%, 95% and 99%. Table 7.1 shows the z-limits associated with different confidence levels.

Table 7.1 Typical confidence limits and associated z-limits

Confidence Level	z-limits
90%	±1.645
95%	±1.96
99%	±2.58

Table 7.2 shows how the confidence interval width (and hence the precision of the estimation) varies, according to the chosen confidence level for Example 7.1. The higher

the desired confidence level, the wider the confidence interval becomes to be surer that the interval covers the true population parameter.

Table 7.2 Influence of confidence levels on confidence interval width

Confidence level	Formula	Illustration (applied to Example 7.1)
90%	$\mu = \bar{x} \pm 1.645 \frac{\sigma}{\sqrt{n}}$	$\mu = 78 \pm 1.645(1.2124)$ $76.01 \leq \mu \leq 79.99$
95%	$\mu = \bar{x} \pm 1.96 \frac{\sigma}{\sqrt{n}}$	$\mu = 78 \pm 1.96(1.2124)$ $75.62 \leq \mu \leq 80.38$
99%	$\mu = \bar{x} \pm 2.58 \frac{\sigma}{\sqrt{n}}$	$\mu = 78 \pm 2.58(1.2124)$ $74.87 \leq \mu \leq 81.13$

As the confidence level increases, the interval becomes wider and hence less precise. This shows that there is a trade-off between precision and confidence.

Sample Size

As the sample size increases, the *standard error* becomes smaller resulting in a narrower confidence interval. This leads to a more *precise estimate* of the population parameter. Conversely, smaller sample sizes result in larger standard errors and consequently wider, and therefore less precise, confidence intervals.

This effect of sample size in Example 7.1 is illustrated in Table 7.3. For Example 7.1, the 95% confidence interval limits are illustrated for three different sample sizes (based on z-limits of ± 1.96 and population standard deviation, $\sigma = 21$).

Table 7.3 Effect of sample size on confidence interval precision (using $\sigma = 21$ and $z = \pm 1.96$)

Sample size (n)	Standard error	Confidence limits
50	$\frac{\sigma}{\sqrt{n}} = 2.97$	$78 \pm 1.96(2.970)$ $72.18 \leq \mu \leq 83.82$
300	$\frac{\sigma}{\sqrt{n}} = 1.212$	$78 \pm 1.96(1.212)$ $75.62 \leq \mu \leq 80.38$
500	$\frac{\sigma}{\sqrt{n}} = 0.939$	$78 \pm 1.96(0.939)$ $76.16 \leq \mu \leq 79.84$

The increase in sample size from 50 to 300 and finally to 500 grocery shoppers has significantly improved the precision of the confidence interval estimate for the true mean value of grocery purchases by narrowing the range which is likely to cover μ.

Standard Deviation

If the population standard deviation (σ) is *small* in relation to its mean, variability in the data is low as the data is highly concentrated around its mean. This will produce a *narrower* confidence interval and therefore a *more precise estimate* of the population mean, and vice versa.

Note: Whenever the population standard deviation (σ) is unknown, it is usually estimated by the sample standard deviation(s). The sample standard deviation has the same effect on the estimated standard error as the actual population standard deviation.

Example 7.2 Car Commuter Time Study

From a random sample of 100 Cape Town car commuters, the sample mean time to commute to work daily was found to be 35.8 minutes. Assume that the population standard deviation is 11 minutes and that commuting times are normally distributed.

(a) Set 95% confidence limits for the actual mean time taken by all car commuters in Cape Town to travel to work daily.

(b) Set 90% confidence limits for the actual mean time taken by all car commuters in Cape Town to travel to work daily.

Solution

(a) Given $\bar{x} = 35.8$ minutes, $\sigma = 11$ minutes and $n = 100$ commuters.

- Find the *standard error* of the sample mean.

$$\sigma_{\bar{x}} = \frac{\sigma}{\sqrt{n}}$$
$$= \frac{11}{\sqrt{100}}$$
$$= 1.1 \text{ min}$$

- From the z-table, the 95% confidence level equates to z-limits of ± 1.96.
- Compute the *margin of error* $= 1.96 \times 1.1 = 2.156$
- Thus the lower limit is: $35.8 - 1.96(1.1) = 35.8 - 2.156$
$$= 33.64 \text{ minutes}$$
and the upper limit is: $35.8 + 1.96(1.1) = 35.8 + 2.156$
$$= 37.96 \text{ minutes.}$$

Thus the 95% confidence interval is defined as $33.64 \leq \mu \leq 37.96$ minutes.

Management Interpretation

There is a 95% chance that a Cape Town car commuter takes, on average, between 33.64 and 37.96 minutes to travel to work daily.

Example 7.2 contd.

(b) The measures of $\bar{x} = 35.8$ minutes, $\sigma = 11$ minutes, $n = 100$ commuters and the standard error $= 1.1$ minutes are all unchanged. Only the z-limits will change.

- From the z-table, the 90% confidence level equates to z-limits of ± 1.645.
- Compute the *margin of error* $= 1.645 \times 1.1 = 1.81$
- Thus the lower limit is: $35.8 - 1.645(1.1) = 35.8 - 1.81$
$$= 33.99 \text{ minutes}$$
and the upper limit is: $35.8 + 1.645(1.1) = 35.8 + 1.81$
$$= 37.61 \text{ minutes.}$$

Thus the 90% confidence interval is defined as $33.99 \leq \mu \leq 37.61$ minutes.

Management Interpretation

There is a 90% chance that a Cape Town car commuter takes, on average, between 33.99 and 37.61 minutes to travel to work daily.

Note that the confidence limits are narrower (i.e. more precise) in (b) (90% confidence) than in (a) (95% confidence). Logically, the more confident a decision-maker wishes to be that the true mean is within the derived interval, the wider the limits that must be set. The trade-off that must be made is between setting too high a confidence level and creating too wide an interval to be of any practical use.

Example 7.3 Coalminers' Employment Period Study

A human resources director at the Chamber of Mines wishes to estimate the true mean employment period of all coalminers. From a random sample of 144 coalminers' records, the sample mean employment period was found to be 88.4 months. The population standard deviation is assumed to be 21.5 months and normally distributed.

Find the 95% confidence interval estimate for the actual mean employment period (in months) for all miners employed in coal mines.

Solution

Given $\bar{x} = 88.4$ months, $\sigma = 21.5$ months and $n = 144$ miners.

- Find the *standard error* of the sample mean.

$$\sigma_{\bar{x}} = \frac{\sigma}{\sqrt{n}} = \frac{21.5}{\sqrt{144}}$$
$$= 1.792 \text{ months}$$

- From the z-table, the 95% confidence level equates to z-limits of ± 1.96.
- Compute the *margin of error* $= 1.96 \times 1.792 = 3.51$
- Thus the lower limit is: $88.4 - 1.96(1.792) = 88.4 - 3.51$
$$= 84.89 \text{ months}$$
and the upper limit is: $88.4 + 1.96(1.792) = 88.4 + 3.51$
$$= 91.91 \text{ months.}$$

Thus the 95% confidence interval is defined as $84.89 \le \mu \le 91.91$ months.

Management Interpretation

There is a 95% chance that the average employment period of all coalminers lies between 84.89 and 91.91 months.

Example 7.4 Radial Tyres Tread Life Study

A tyre manufacturer found that the sample mean tread life of 81 radial tyres tested was 52 345 km. The population standard deviation of radial tyre tread life is 4 016 km and is assumed to be normally distributed.

Estimate, with 99% confidence, the true mean tread life of all radial tyres manufactured. Also interpret the results.

Solution

Given $\bar{x} = 52\ 345$ km, $\sigma = 4\ 016$ km and $n = 81$ radial tyres.

- Find the *standard error* of the sample mean.

$$\sigma_{\bar{x}} = \frac{\sigma}{\sqrt{n}} = \frac{4\ 016}{\sqrt{81}}$$
$$= 446.22 \text{ km}$$

- From the z-table, the 99% confidence level equates to z-limits of ± 2.58.

- Compute the *margin of error* = 2.58 × 446.22 = 1151.25
- Lower limit: 52 345 − 2.58(446.22) = 52 345 − 1 151.25
$$= 51\ 193.75\ \text{km}$$
    Upper limit: 52 345 + 2.58(446.22) = 52 345 + 1 151.25
$$= 53\ 496.25\ \text{km}$$

Thus the 99% confidence interval is defined as $51\ 193.75 \le \mu \le 53\ 496.25$ km.

Management Interpretation

The tyre manufacturer can be 99% confident that the actual mean tread life of all their radial tyres is likely to lie between 51 193.75 and 53 496.25 km.

7.6 The Rationale of a Confidence Interval

A common question is: 'How can we be sure that the single confidence interval will cover the true population parameter at the specified level of confidence?' The car commuter time study (Example 7.2) is used to answer this question through illustration.

- We begin by assuming that the population mean time to commute to work daily by Cape Town motorists is 32 minutes (i.e. $\mu = 32$).
- Now construct 95% confidence limits around this true mean, $\mu = 32$. These 95 confidence limits become: $32 − 1.96(1.1) \le \mu \le 32 + 1.96(1.1)$
$$\therefore\quad 32 − 2.156 \le \mu \le 32 + 2.156$$
$$\therefore\quad 29.84 \le \mu \le 34.16\ \text{minutes}$$
- Next construct a set of 95% confidence intervals on the basis of:
$$\bar{x} − 1.96(1.1) \le \mu \le \bar{x} + 1.96(1.1)$$

Use a random selection of sample mean commuting times where:
- some fall *inside* the confidence limits of 29.84 and 34.16 minutes
- others fall *outside* the confidence limits of 29.84 and 34.16 minutes.

Table 7.4 illustrates a selection of sample mean commuting times and their respective 95% confidence intervals.

Table 7.4 Car commuter times – sample means and their 95% confidence intervals

Sample means within the interval $29.84 \le \mu \le 34.16$ minutes	Associated 95% confidence interval (using z-limits = ±1.96)
29.84 (lower limit)	$27.60 \le \mu \le \mathbf{32.00}$
30.6	$28.44 \le \mu \le 32.76$
31.4	$29.24 \le \mu \le 33.56$
32.9	$30.74 \le \mu \le 35.06$
33.5	$31.34 \le \mu \le 35.66$
34.16 (upper limit)	$\mathbf{32.00} \le \mu \le 36.32$
Sample means outside the interval $29.84 \le \mu \le 34.16$ minutes	Associated 95% confidence interval (using z-limits = ±1.96)
28.4	$26.24 \le \mu \le 30.56$
35.5	$33.34 \le \mu \le 37.66$

- From Table 7.4, the following will be observed:
    - Each 95% confidence interval derived from a sample mean that falls *within* or at the limits of the interval $29.84 \leq \mu \leq 34.16$ will *include* the actual mean commuting time of 32 minutes. The sample means that are equal to 29.84 minutes and 34.16 minutes also cover the population mean, but at their upper and lower limits respectively. Since there is a 95% chance that a single sample mean will fall within the limits of $29.84 \leq \mu \leq 34.16$ minutes as shown above, there is a 95% chance that a single confidence interval will cover the true population mean.
    - Each 95% confidence interval derived from a sample mean that falls *outside* the interval $29.84 \leq \mu \leq 34.16$ will *not cover* the actual mean commuting time of 32 minutes. This is likely to happen for only 5% of sample means.

Figure 7.1 illustrates this with numerous intervals based on sample means for a given sample size, n, falling both inside and outside of the 95% confidence limits around the sampling distribution of μ.

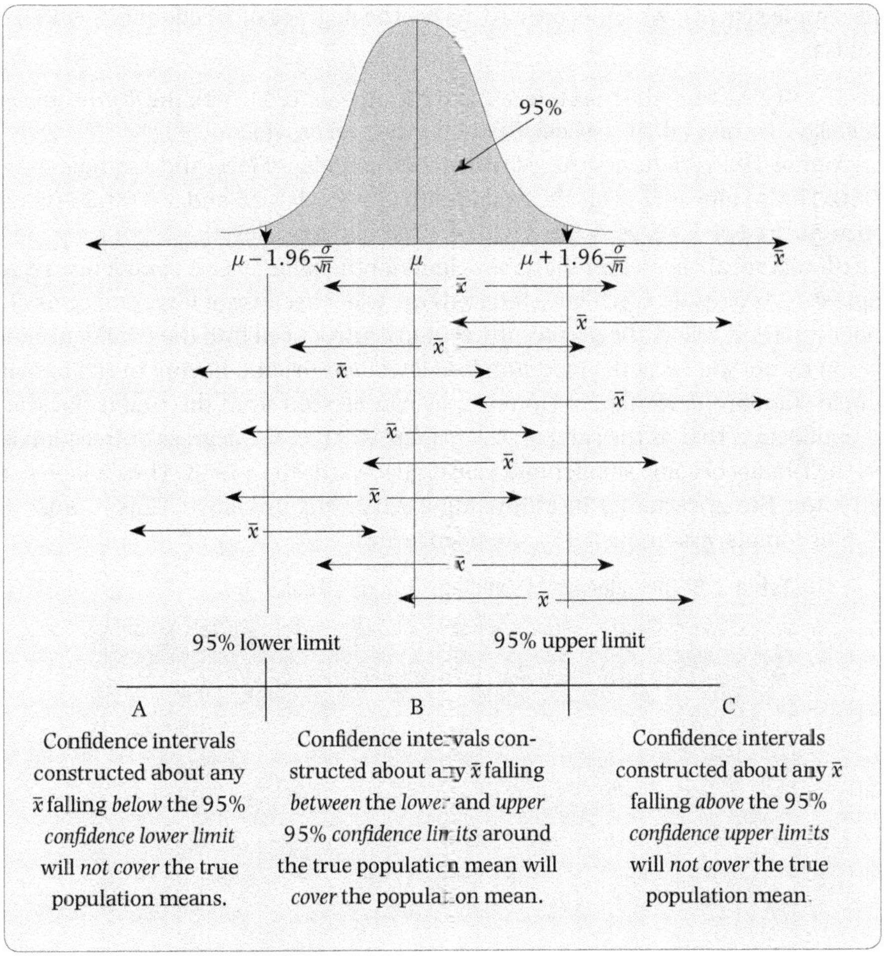

Figure 7.1 Illustration of the confidence interval concept (using a 95% confidence level)

Thus a single confidence interval at, say, a 95% confidence level, can be interpreted as follows: 'There is a 95% chance that the limits of this *single* confidence interval *will cover* the true population mean.'

7.7 The Student *t*-distribution

The confidence intervals constructed in section 7.5 assumed that the population standard deviation, σ, was known. This measure is needed to calculate the standard error of the sample mean. However, it is often the case that the population standard deviation is unknown and needs to be estimated from the sample standard deviation, s. Then the **student *t*-distribution** (or *t*-distribution), instead of the *z*-distribution, is used to derive the limits for the confidence level.

Finding the *t*-limits

To find a *t*-value, the following is required:
- a level of confidence (e.g. 90%, 95% or 99%)
- the sample size (n), which is used to derive the degrees of freedom (df) which equals $n - 1$.

To read off a *t*-value from the **t-table** (see Table 2 in Appendix 1), both the df and an *upper tail area* (called α) are needed. The specified confidence level provides α.

For example, the *t*-limits associated with a 95% confidence level and a sample size $n = 26$ is ±2.060. This *t*-value is read off the *t*-table with $df = n - 1 = 25$ and $\alpha = 0.025$ (where α is the upper tail area of 2.5% associated with a 95% confidence level).

The *t*-limits are always larger than the z-limits for the same level of confidence, regardless of sample size. As a result, confidence intervals are wider because of larger margins of error. The wider intervals reflect the greater uncertainty introduced into the confidence interval calculation by not knowing the true standard deviation (σ) and having to estimate it from the sample standard deviation, s. However, as can be seen from the *t*-table, for the same level of confidence, that as the sample size, n, increases (i.e. the degrees of freedom become bigger), the *t*-limits become smaller and converge towards the z-limit. Thus a larger sample size can lower the uncertainty in estimating μ when σ is unknown. This is illustrated in Table 7.5 of *t*-limits, assuming a 95% confidence level.

Table 7.5 The influence of sample size, n, on *t*-limits

Sample size (n)	Degrees of freedom ($n - 1$)	*t*-limits (read off *t*-table)
6	5	±2.571
11	10	±2.228
26	25	±2.060
41	40	±2.021
61	60	±2.000
121	120	±1.980
∞	∞	±1.960

Note that as n increases towards infinity, the *t*-limits approach ±1.96, which are the z-limits corresponding to a 95% confidence level.

7.8 Confidence Interval for a Single Population Mean (μ) when the Population Standard Deviation (σ) is Unknown

When the population standard deviation, σ, is unknown, a confidence interval estimate for μ with a specified confidence level and based on a given sample size, n, is given by:

$$\bar{x} - t\frac{s}{\sqrt{n}} \leq \mu \leq \bar{x} + t\frac{s}{\sqrt{n}}$$

(lower limit)　　　　(upper limit)

7.3

Where: $\bar{x}$ = sample mean

s = sample standard deviation

n = sample size

t = t-limits for a specified confidence level and $df = n - 1$

Note: The standard error of $\bar{x}$, $\sigma_{\bar{x}}$ $\left(=\frac{\sigma}{\sqrt{n}}\right)$ is now *estimated by* $\frac{s}{\sqrt{n}}$.

Example 7.5 Jed Home Stores Credit Card Purchases Study

Jed Home Stores analysed the value of purchases made on credit card by a random sample of 25 of their credit card customers. The sample mean was found to be R170, with a sample standard deviation of R22. Assume credit card purchase values are normally distributed.

(a) Estimate, with 95% confidence, the actual mean value of credit card purchases by all their credit card customers.

(b) Assume that 46 credit card purchases were sampled. Set 95% confidence limits for the actual mean value of credit card purchases at this home store (σ is unknown).

Solution

(a) Given $\bar{x}$ = R170, s = R22 and n = 25 credit card customers.

The standard error of $\bar{x}$ is *estimated* by　$\sigma_{\bar{x}} \approx \frac{s}{\sqrt{n}} = \frac{22}{\sqrt{25}}$

$$= R4.40$$

Since σ is *unknown*, the t-distribution must be used to find the t-limits for the 95% confidence level. From the t-table (Table 2, Appendix 1) the t-value associated with $\alpha = 0.025$ and $df = n - 1 = 25 - 1 = 24$ is 2.064.

The estimated *margin of error* is 2.064 × 4.4 = R9.08.

Lower limit: 170 − 2.064(4.4) = 170 − 9.08 = 160.92

Upper limit: 170 + 2.064(4.4) = 170 + 9.08 = 179.08

The 95% confidence interval estimate for μ is given by R160.92 $\leq \mu \leq$ R179.08.

Management Interpretation

There is a 95% chance that the actual mean value of all credit card purchases at Jed Home Stores lies between R160.92 and R179.08.

Example 7.5 contd.

(b) The increase in sample size to n = 46 will change the values of both the t-value and the estimated standard error of $\bar{x}$.

The t-limit is now 2.014, since $\alpha = 0.025$ and $df = n - 1 = 45$, and the estimated standard error of $\bar{x}$ is:

$$\sigma_{\bar{x}} \approx \frac{s}{\sqrt{n}} = \frac{22}{\sqrt{46}}$$

$$= R3.24$$

The estimated margin of error is $2.014 \times 3.24 = R6.53$.

Lower limit: $170 - 2.014(3.24) = 170 - 6.53 = 163.47$

Upper limit: $170 + 2.014(3.24) = 170 + 6.53 = 176.53$

Thus the 95% confidence interval estimate for μ is given by $R163.47 \leq \mu \leq R176.53$.

Management Interpretation

There is a 95% chance that the actual mean value of all credit card purchases at Jed Home Stores lies between R163.47 and R176.53.

It can be seen from the above two examples that a larger sample size results in narrower (more precise) confidence limits for the same confidence level. This reflects the greater certainty in estimation as seen in both the *smaller t-limits* (for the same confidence level) and the lower value of the estimated *standard error*.

7.9 Confidence Interval for a Single Population Proportion (π)

$$p \rightarrow \pi$$

If the data of a random variable is categorical (nominal/ordinal scaled), the appropriate measure of central location is a *proportion*. In the same way that the population mean can be estimated from a sample mean, a population proportion π can be estimated from its sample proportion, p.

The following statistical measures are required to construct a confidence interval estimate about the true population proportion, π:

- the sample proportion, p, where $p = \frac{x}{n}$
- the sample size, n
- the z-limits corresponding to a specified level of confidence
- the standard error of the sample proportion, p, which is calculated using:

$$\sigma_p \approx \sqrt{\frac{p(1-p)}{n}} \qquad 7.4$$

Thus the confidence interval for a single population proportion, p, is given by:

$$\underbrace{p - z\sqrt{\frac{p(1-p)}{n}}}_{\text{(lower limit)}} \leq \pi \leq \underbrace{p + z\sqrt{\frac{p(1-p)}{n}}}_{\text{(upper limit)}} \qquad 7.5$$

Where: $z\sqrt{\frac{p(1-p)}{n}}$ is the *margin of error* in estimation.

Example 7.6 Johannesburg Street Vendor By-law Study

A recent survey amongst 240 randomly selected street vendors in Johannesburg showed that 84 of them felt that local by-laws still hampered their trading.

Find the 90% confidence interval for the true proportion, π, of all Johannesburg street vendors who believe that local by-laws still hamper their trading.

Solution

From the data, $x = 84$ (number of 'success' outcomes) and $n = 240$ (sample size), so the sample proportion, $p = \frac{84}{240} = 0.35$.

Using the sample proportion, p, the standard error of p is given by:

$$\sigma_p \approx \sqrt{\frac{p(1-p)}{n}}$$
$$= \sqrt{\frac{0.35(1-0.35)}{240}}$$
$$= 0.0308$$

The z-value is 1.645 for the 90% confidence level (Table 1, Appendix 1).
The estimated *margin of error* is $1.645 \times 0.0308 = 0.0507$ (5.07%).

Thus the 90% confidence interval for the *population* of all street vendors who feel that the local by-laws still hamper their trading is given by:

lower limit: $0.35 - 1.645(0.0308) = 0.35 - 0.0507 = 0.299$
upper limit: $0.35 + 1.645(0.0308) = 0.35 + 0.0507 = 0.401$

The 90% confidence interval estimate for π is given by $0.299 \le \pi \le 0.401$.

Management Interpretation

There is a 90% chance that the true percentage of all Johannesburg street vendors who feel that the local by-laws still hamper their trading lies between 29.9% and 40.1%.

7.10 Sample Size Determination

To estimate a *population mean*, a formula to determine an appropriate *sample size*, n, is derived from the *margin of error* term of a confidence interval for a single mean, i.e. *margin of error* $= \frac{z\sigma}{\sqrt{n}}$. Let margin of error $= e$, then by re-arranging this formula to solve for n, the following *sample size formula* results:

$$n = \frac{z^2\sigma^2}{e^2} \qquad\qquad 7.6$$

This means that the sample size used in any given study depends on:

z – a chosen level of confidence
σ – the standard deviation of the population of the random variable under study
e – an acceptable margin of error (or sampling error) in estimation.

Once these three measures are chosen, the appropriate sample size can be derived.

For example, to be 95% confident (i.e. $z = 1.96$) that a sample estimate will be within, say, 3 units of measure (i.e. $e = 3$) of its true but *unknown population mean* with an assumed known standard deviation of 14 units of measure (i.e. $\sigma = 14$), then the *minimum sample size* required that will satisfy these criteria is:

$n = 1.96^2 \times \frac{14^2}{3^2} = 83.67$ (or 84 objects to be sampled).

A similar sample size formula to estimate a *population proportion* is derived from the *margin of error* term of a single proportion – as shown in Formula 7.7.

$$n = z^2 \frac{p(1-p)}{e^2}$$
7.7

Where: $p =$ the population proportion of the 'success' outcome.

In practice, use a guestimate or prior information for p, or if such information is not available, use $p = 0.5$ as a conservative estimate to avoid underestimating the sample size required.

For example, to be 90% confident (i.e. $z = 1.645$) that a sample estimate will be within 3% (i.e. $e = 0.03$) of its true but unknown *population proportion* (based on a guestimated $p = 0.25$), then the *minimum sample size* required that will satisfy these criteria is:

$n = 1.645^2 \times \frac{0.25(1-0.25)}{0.03^2} = 563.76$ (or 564 objects to be sampled).

7.11 Using Excel (2016) and X-Static to Compute Confidence Interval Limits

Excel can be used to compute both the z- and the t-limits.

z-limits: =NORM.S.INV(probability)

To compute the z-limits corresponding to, say, a 95% confidence level, type =NORM.S.INV **(0.025)** to derive the lower z-limit of -1.96 and =NORM.S.INV(**0.975**) to derive the upper z-limit of $+1.96$.

Note: The value in each bracket (i.e. 0.025 and 0.975) refers to the cumulative area (probability) under the standard normal curve up to the required z-value.

t-limits: =T.INV.2T(probability,degrees of freedom)

To compute the t-limits corresponding to, say, a 95% confidence level and based on a sample size of 36, type =T.INV.2T(**0.05.35**). This will result in the t-value of 2.030. Thus the t-limits will be ±2.030.

Note: The values in the bracket (0.05 and 35) respectively refer to the combined tail areas of a 95% confidence level (i.e. $1 - 0.95 = 0.05$) and the degrees of freedom ($= n - 1 = 36 - 1 = 35$).

Using the CONFIDENCE.NORM Function

The formula =CONFIDENCE.NORM(**alpha,standard_dev,size**) assumes that σ is known. Therefore it computes the *margin of error* using *z-limits* that correspond to a specified confidence level. This value must be subtracted from, and also added to, the sample mean to derive the lower and upper confidence limits.

For Example 7.1, the following values are given:
- alpha = 1 – (the specified confidence level). i.e. $\alpha = 1 - 0.95 = 0.05$ for a 95% confidence level
- the population standard deviation ($\sigma = 21$)
- the sample size ($n = 300$).

Then =CONFIDENCE.NORM(0.05,21,300) produces the result of 2.376.

To find the lower 95% confidence limit: $78 - 2.376 = R75.62$
To find the upper 95% confidence limit $78 + 2.376 = R80.38$

Using the CONFIDENCE.T Function

The formula =CONFIDENCE.T(**alpha,standard_dev,size**) computes a confidence interval range (*margin of error*) using *t-limits*. This is used when the population standard deviation is unknown and the sample standard deviation, s, is used.

Using Excel's Data Analysis

If a sample of numeric (quantitative) data values is available, use the **Data Analysis** add-in in Excel to compute the confidence limits for a population mean.

The confidence limits for a population mean of a numeric random variable is computed in the **Descriptive Statistics** option of **Data Analysis**. Tick the box labelled **Confidence Level** and specify the desired level of confidence.

> *Note*: This **Data Analysis** option always uses the *t*-limits to compute the confidence interval, as it assumes that the population standard deviation, σ, is unknown. It uses the standard deviation derived from the *sample* data to compute the standard error.

Using X-Static

X-Static can derive a confidence interval for both a *single population mean* (**Confidence Interval: Single Mean**) and a *single population proportion* (**Confidence Interval: Single Proportion**).

Confidence Interval: Single Mean

Figure 7.2 illustrates the sample data, input menu and output display for a 95% confidence interval estimate for the *daily amount spent* (in rand) on taxi transport by all commuters in a particular metropolitan district. A sample of 15 commuters were surveyed.

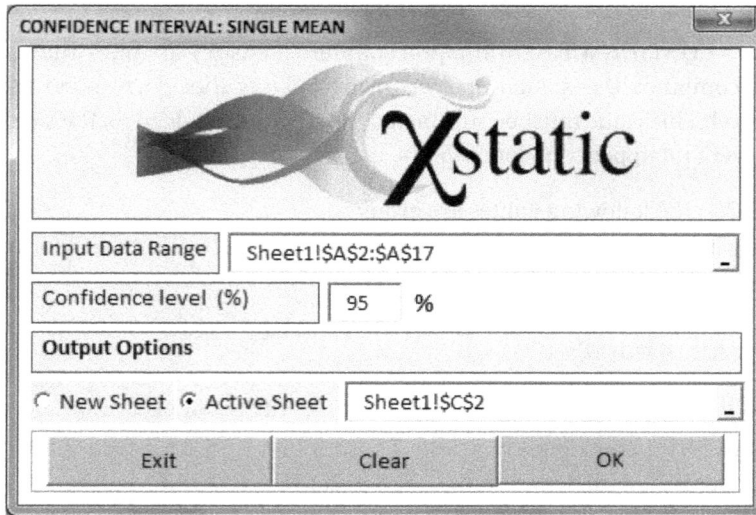

Spend (R)	Confidence level – single mean	Spend (R)
24	Confidence level (%)	95%
32		
45	Sample mean	33.6
28	Sample standard deviation	6.3336
36	Sample size	15
29	Degrees of freedom (df)	14
44	Standard error	1.6353
40	t-statistic	2.1448
30	Margin of error	3.5074
31		
38		
26	**Lower confidence limit**	**30.09**
33	**Upper confidence limit**	**37.11**
30		
38		

Figure 7.2 Illustration of X-Static's Confidence Interval estimate for a single mean

The following management conclusion can be drawn from the findings: 'There is a 95% chance that the actual average daily amount spent by all commuters on taxi transport is likely to lie between R30.09 and R37.11'.

Confidence Interval: Single Proportion

Figure 7.3 illustrates the sample data, input menu and output display for a 90% confidence interval estimate for the *percentage of consumers who prefer brand X* of a product. A sample of 20 commuters were surveyed of whom 6 preferred brand X. Note, in the data, code 1 = prefer brand X and code 2 = do not prefer brand X.

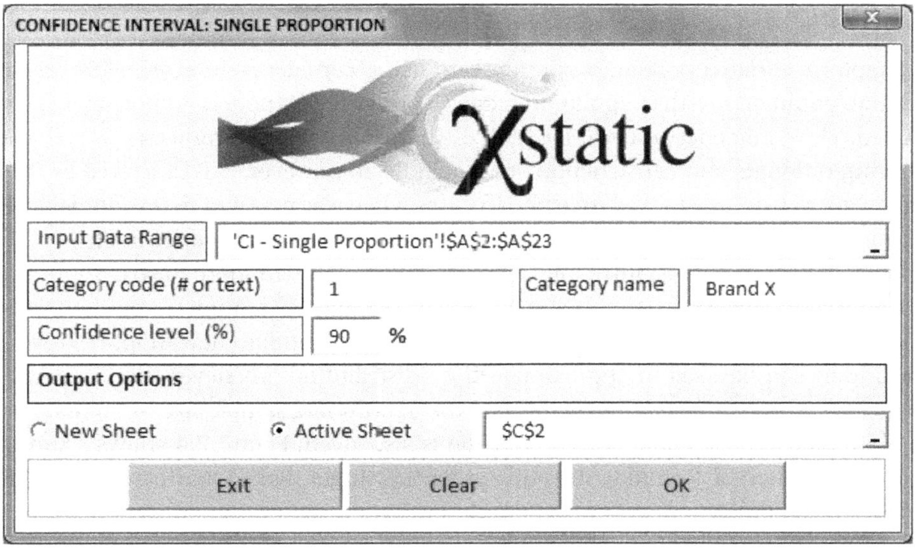

Choice
2
1
2
2
1
1
2
2
1
2
2
2
2
2
2
2
1
2
1
2

Confidence interval – single proportion	
Choice – Brand X	
Confidence level (%)	**90%**
Sample size	20
Category size	6
Sample proportion	0.30
Standard error (p)	0.1025
z-statistic	1.6449
Margin of error	0.1685
Lower confidence limit	**13.15%**
Upper confidence limit	**46.85%**

Figure 7.3 Illustration of X-Static's Confidence Interval estimate for a single proportion

The following management conclusion can be drawn from the findings: 'There is a 90% chance that the actual percentage of consumers who prefer brand X of a product is likely to lie between 13.15% and 46.85%.'

7.12 Summary

This chapter estimated population parameters using confidence intervals. Two separate population parameters – the population mean (μ) and the population proportion (π) – were estimated. The confidence interval for each of these population parameters uses the same underlying rationale and construction approach. Each, however, was described by its own sampling distribution and standard error. In cases where the population standard deviation is known, the z-distribution is used to provide the standardised confidence limits.

The t-distribution was introduced as an alternative standard distribution to the z-distribution whenever the population standard deviation of a numeric random variable is unknown and needs to be estimated using the sample standard deviation. However, the z-distribution can be used to approximate the t-distribution whenever the sample size is large (i.e. above 40). A formula to determine the appropriate sample size to estimate either a population mean or a population proportion is also given. Figure 7.4 shows a summary of confidence interval formulae for both numeric (single mean) and categorical (single proportion) data types.

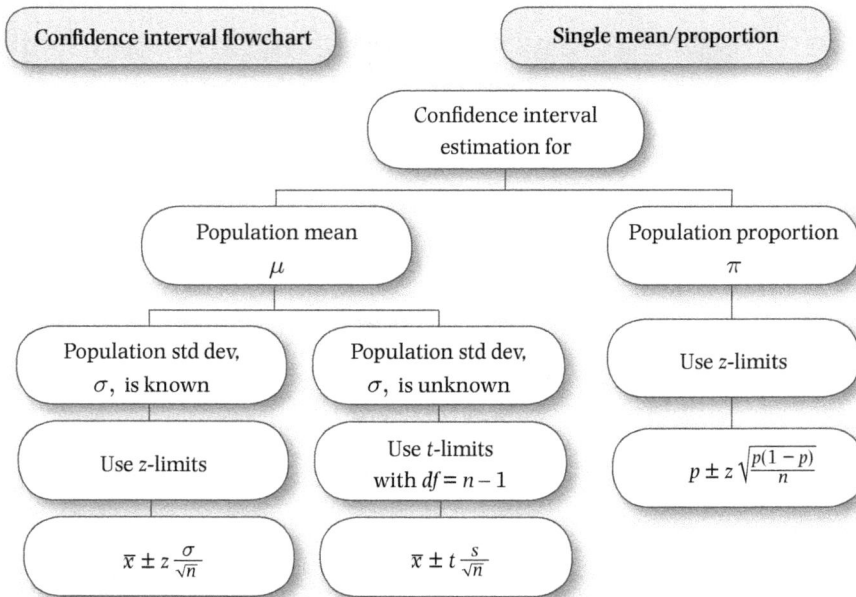

Figure 7.4 Summary of confidence interval formulae

Chapter 8 will examine the second inferential approach of hypothesis testing.

Exercises

This symbol denotes data available online

1 What is the purpose of a confidence interval?

2 If $\bar{x} = 85$, $\sigma = 8$ and $n = 64$, set up a 95% confidence interval estimate of the population mean, μ.

3 If the population standard deviation, σ, is not known, what standardised statistic is used to construct a confidence interval?

4 If $\bar{x} = 54$, $s = 6$ and $n = 25$, set up a 90% confidence interval estimate of the population mean, μ.

5 The Department of Trade and Industry (DTI) conducted a survey to estimate the average number of employees per small and medium-sized enterprises (SME) in Gauteng. A random sample of 144 SMEs in Gauteng found that the average number was 24.4 employees. Assume that the population standard deviation is 10.8 employees and that the number of employees per SME is normally distributed.
   (a) Estimate, with 95% confidence, the actual average number of employees per SME in Gauteng. Interpret the findings for the DTI. Use the z-table.
   (b) Compute the confidence interval in (a) using Excel's **NORM.S.INV** formula to find the z-value.
   (c) Compute the confidence interval in (a) using Excel's **CONFIDENCE.NORM** formula.

6 The operations manager of a sugar mill in Durban wants to estimate the average size of an order received. An order is measured in the number of pallets shipped. A random sample of 87 orders from customers had a sample mean value of 131.6 pallets. Assume that the population standard deviation is 25 pallets and that order size is normally distributed.
   (a) Estimate, with 90% confidence, the mean size of orders received from all the mill's customers. (Use the z-table.)
   (b) Compute (a) using Excel's **NORM.S.INV** formula to find the z-value.
   (c) Use Excel's **CONFIDENCE.NORM** formula to reproduce the findings in (a).
   (d) If the sugar mill receives 720 orders this year, calculate, with 90% confidence, the total number of pallets of sugar that they will ship during the year.

7 For a random sample of 256 owners of medium-sized cars, it was found that their average monthly car insurance premium for comprehensive cover was R356. Assume that the population standard deviation is R44 per month and that insurance premiums are normally distributed.
   (a) Find the 95% confidence interval for the average monthly comprehensive car insurance premium paid by all owners of medium-sized cars. Interpret the result. (Use the z-table.)
   (b) Find the 90% confidence interval for the same problem. Interpret the result and compare it to (a).
   (c) Compute (a) using Excel's **NORM.S.INV** formula to find the z-value.
   (d) Use Excel's **CONFIDENCE.NORM** formula to compute (a).
   (e) If 3 000 car owners are comprehensively insured by the Sun Insurance company, estimate, with 95% confidence, the total monthly premium income of the company.

8   Suppose that a paint supply shop wanted to estimate the correct amount of paint contained in five-litre cans purchased from a manufacturer. It is known from the manufacturer's specifications that the standard deviation of the amount of paint is equal to 0.04 ℓ. A random sample of 50 cans is selected, and the average amount of paint per five-litre can is 4.985 ℓ. Assume a normal distribution of fill.

   (a)   Set up a 99% confidence interval estimate of the true population average amount of paint included in a five-litre can. (Use the z-table.)

   (b)   Based on the results of (a), do you think that the store owner has a right to complain to the manufacturer? Why?

   (c)   Compute (a) using Excel's **NORM.S.INV** formula to find the z-value.

   (d)   Use Excel's **CONFIDENCE.NORM** function to compute (a).

9   The mean annual inventory turnover rate of a random sample of 24 convenience stores was found to be 3.8 times per annum. Assume that the population standard deviation is 0.6 and that the annual inventory turnover rate amongst convenience stores is normally distributed.

   (a)   Calculate the actual average annual inventory turnover rate, with 90% confidence, for all convenience stores. (Use the z-table.) Interpret the result.

   (b)   Compute (a) using Excel's **NORM.S.INV** formula to find the z-value.

   (c)   Use Excel's **CONFIDENCE.NORM** formula to compute (a).

10   A travel agency call centre wants to know the average number of calls received per day by its call centre. A random sample of 21 days is selected and the sample mean number of calls received was found to be 166.2 with a sample standard deviation of 22.8 calls. Assume that calls received daily are normally distributed.

   (a)   Calculate a 95% confidence interval for the mean number of daily calls received by the call centre. Interpret the findings.

   (b)   Find a 99% confidence interval for the mean number of daily calls received by the call centre.

   (c)   Compare the findings of (a) and (b) and explain the reason for the difference.

   (d)   Compute the confidence interval in (a) using Excel's **T.INV.2T** formula.

   (e)   Estimate, with 95% confidence, the total number of calls received over a 30-day period. Interpret the result.

11   The average dividend yield of a random sample of 28 JSE-listed companies last year was found to be 12.5%, with a sample standard deviation of 3.4%. Assume that dividend yields are normally distributed.

   (a)   Calculate, with 90% confidence, the actual mean dividend yield of all JSE-listed companies last year. Interpret the finding.

   (b)   Compute the confidence interval in (a) using Excel's **T.INV.2T** formula.

   (c)   Compute the confidence interval in (a) using the **CONFIDENCE.T** Excel function.

12   Milk cartons are advertised to contain one litre of milk. From a random sample of 18 one-litre cartons whose contents were accurately measured by the South African Bureau of Standards (SABS), it was found that the average fill was 0.981 ℓ with a sample standard deviation of 0.052 ℓ. Assume that the fill of one-litre milk cartons is normally distributed.

   (a)   Using a 99% confidence level, estimate the actual mean fill of all one-litre milk cartons. Interpret your findings and comment on the question: 'Do one-litre cartons of milk contain one litre of milk on average?'

(b) Repeat the exercise in (a) above, but use a 95% confidence level. Explain any differences in the conclusions.

(c) Compute the confidence intervals in (a) and (b) using Excel's **T.INV.2T** formula.

(d) Compute the confidence intervals in (a) and (b) using the **CONFIDENCE.T** Excel function.

13 Before entering into wage negotiations, the workers' representative of the newly formed farm workers trade union wanted to know the average wage of its union members. The average wage of a random sample of 50 members was found to be R2 420 per month with a sample standard deviation of R160 per month. Assume wages are normally distributed.

(a) What is the 90% confidence interval estimate for the true mean monthly wages paid to farm workers?

(b) What is the 99% confidence interval estimate for the true mean monthly wages paid to farm workers?

(c) Compare and comment on the results of (a) and (b).

(d) Compute the confidence intervals in (a) and (b) using Excel's **T.INV.2T** formula.

(e) Compute the confidence intervals in (a) and (b) using the **CONFIDENCE.T** Excel function.

14 The Department of Trade and Industry (DTI) wants to determine the percentage of manufacturing firms that have met the employment equity charter. To assist the department, Statistics South Africa (Stats SA) selected a random sample of 200 manufacturing firms and established that 84 have met the employment equity charter.

Determine, with 95% confidence, the percentage of manufacturing firms that have met the employment equity charter. Prepare a brief report to the DTI detailing your findings.

15 A Spar retailer observed a random sample of 160 customers and found that 68 customers paid for their grocery purchases by cash and the remainder by credit card.

Construct a 95% confidence interval for the actual percentage of customers who pay cash for their grocery purchases. Interpret the findings.

16 A national bank analysed a random sample of 365 cheque accounts at their Tshwane branch and found that 78 of them were overdrawn.

Estimate, with 90% confidence, the percentage of all bank accounts at the Tshwane branch of the bank that were *not* overdrawn. Interpret the findings.

17 A random sample of 300 shoppers in a shopping mall is interviewed to identify their reasons for coming to this particular mall. The factor of 'I prefer the store mix' was the most important reason for 120 of those interviewed.

Estimate the likely percentage of all shoppers who frequent this shopping mall primarily because of the mix of stores in the mall, using 90% confidence limits.

Excel Exercises

Use Excel's **Data Analysis** option or **X-Static** for exercises 18 to 20.

18 X7.18 – cashier absenteeism

A supermarket manager analysed the number of days absent per year for a random sample of 29 cashiers. Assume that days absent are normally distributed.

(a) Compute the mean (average) and standard deviation of days absent for the sample of 29 cashiers using the **Descriptive Statistics** option in **Data Analysis**. Interpret these sample findings for the manager.

(b) Estimate, with a 95% confidence level, the mean number of days absent per year for all supermarket cashiers.

(*Hint*: Tick the **Confidence Level for Mean** box in **Descriptive Statistics**.)

(c) If it is company policy that the average absenteeism level should not exceed 10 days per cashier per year, based on a 95% confidence level, is the company's policy being adhered to? Comment.

(d) Recompute and confirm the 95% confidence limits using the **T.INV.2T** formula to find the *t*-limits.

19 X7.19 – parcel masses

PostNet wants to estimate the actual mass of documents placed in their medium-sized plastic envelopes (parcel masses) that are couriered to clients throughout the country. A random sample of 43 filled medium-sized plastic envelopes were selected and weighed. Assume that parcel masses (in kg) are normally distributed.

(a) Compute the mean (average) and standard deviation of the sample of parcel weights using the **Descriptive Statistics** option in **Data Analysis**. Report these sample findings to the PostNet manager.

(b) Estimate, with a 90% confidence level, the mean parcel mass of all the filled medium-sized plastic envelopes. (*Hint*: Tick the **Confidence Level for Mean** box in **Descriptive Statistics**.)

(c) These envelopes are designed to carry documents that do not exceed 3 kg on average, based on a 90% confidence level. Is PostNet adhering to this requirement? Comment.

(d) Recompute and confirm the 90% confidence limits using the **T.INV.2T** formula to find the *t*-limits.

20 X7.20 – cost-to-income

A company's cost-to-income ratio is a measure of its ability to control its costs. The lower the ratio (expressed as a percentage), the better the company's ability is to control its cost. An analyst recorded the cost-to-income ratio (as a percentage) of 50 randomly selected public companies to study their ability to control their operating cost. Assume that cost-to-income ratios across public companies are normally distributed.

(a) Compute the mean (average) and standard deviation of the sample of the cost-to-income ratios using the **Descriptive Statistics** option in **Data Analysis**. Interpret the profile of this measure across the sample of public companies surveyed.

(b) Find the 95% confidence interval for the mean cost-to-income ratio for all public companies.

(*Hint*: Tick the **Confidence Level for Mean** box in **Descriptive Statistics**.)

(c) Recompute and confirm the 95% confidence limits using the **T.INV.2T** formula to find the *t*-limits.

(d) As a rule of thumb, a public company's cost-to-income ratio should not exceed 75%. Use the **T.DIST.RT** formula and the sample evidence from (a) to determine what percentage of all public companies are likely to be in violation of the rule of thumb.

21 A consumer group wants to estimate the monthly electricity consumption of households in a district. Assume the standard deviation of monthly household electricity usage in the district is 40 kWh. What *sample size* of households should be selected and surveyed to estimate the mean monthly household electricity consumption to within 15 kWh (margin of error) with 95% confidence?

22 A manufacturer of vitamin products wants to estimate the mean number of milligrams (mg) of vitamin A that is inserted into a capsule by its capsule-filling machine. A standard deviation of 1 mg is assumed. To be 99% confident, how many filled capsules should be selected at random from the process and tested to estimate the mean number of mg of vitamin A in all capsules to within a tolerated error of:
(a) 0.1 mg
(b) 0.15 mg
(c) 0.2 mg

23 A washing powder manufacturer wishes to estimate their share of the washing powder market. How many customers who purchase washing powder should be randomly selected and interviewed so that the manufacturer can be 90% confident that the estimate of their share of the washing powder market will be within 3% (i.e. margin of error = 0.03) of their actual market share?

24 X7.24 – export trade
The Department of Trade and Industry (DTI) would like to estimate the percentage of local businesses that export goods to sub-Saharan African countries. A survey was conducted among a random sample of 140 local businesses and each responded either 1 = export – yes, or 2 = export – no.
Find the 90% confidence interval for the true proportion of all local businesses that export good to sub-Saharan African countries. Interpret the findings.

25 X7.25 – traffic offences
A local traffic department has launched a road safety campaign to reduce road accidents. One infringement that they focused on was motorists who drive through red traffic signals. Before the campaign, the proportion of motorists who were fined for this offence was 29%. After the campaign, a review of a random sample of 240 fines issued was undertaken and the nature of the traffic infringement noted. Each fine was coded as: 1 = not a red traffic signal infringement or 2 = a red traffic signal infringement.
(a) Find the 95% confidence interval for the true proportion of all motorists who were fined for red traffic signal violation.
(b) Does the campaign appear to have been effective in significantly reducing the percentage of red traffic signal infringements? Give a brief explanation.

CHAPTER
8

Hypothesis Testing: Single Population (Mean, Proportion and Variance)

Outcomes

When a manager makes a claim (or statement) about the value of a population parameter, it can be tested statistically using the inferential approach of hypothesis testing. Hypothesis testing is a statistical process to test the validity of a manager's claim using sample evidence. A hypothesis test either supports or refutes the manager's claim (or statement) on the basis of the sample evidence.

This chapter covers hypothesis testing for a single population mean, a single population proportion, and a single population variance. In later chapters, hypothesis testing is extended to include two or more population scenarios.

The use of Excel's Data Analysis and X-Static to conduct hypothesis tests will be shown at the end of the chapter.

After studying this chapter, you should be able to:

- understand the concept of hypothesis testing
- perform hypothesis tests for a single population mean
- perform hypothesis tests for a single population proportion
- perform hypothesis tests for a single population variance
- distinguish when to use the z-test statistic or the t-test statistic or the χ^2-test statistic
- correctly interpret the results of a hypothesis test
- correctly translate the statistical results into management conclusions.

8.1 Introduction

Chapter 7 introduced the confidence interval as one approach to estimate the true value of a population parameter. Another approach of inferential statistics is to test, based on sample evidence, whether a claim made about the true value of a population parameter is valid. This inferential approach is known as hypothesis testing.

> To test claims statistically, sample data is gathered and analysed. On the basis of the sample findings, the hypothesised (or claimed) value of the population parameter is either accepted as *probably true* or rejected as *probably false*. This statistical process of testing the validity of a claim about the true value of any population parameter is known as **hypothesis testing.**

The following statements are illustrative *claims* made about specific population parameters.
- An investment company claims that their average return on all investments is 14% p.a.
- A soap manufacturer states that one in four households uses their product.
- A tyre manufacturer believes that the average tread life of their tyres is 75 000 km.
- A tax auditor is convinced that more than 15% of all company tax returns are incorrectly completed.
- An economist is of the view that there is no difference in the mean starting salaries earned between civil engineers and electrical engineers.
- The factory manager of an exhaust manufacturer believes that, on average, worker output is higher during the day shift than during the night shift.

Hypotheses tests will be conducted on six *central location* parameters and two *dispersion (spread)* parameters:
- the single population mean, μ
- the single population proportion, π
- the mean difference between two dependent populations, μ_d
- the difference between two independent population means, $\mu_1 - \mu_2$
- the difference between two independent population proportions, $\pi_1 - \pi_2$
- the equality of means across multiple independent populations, $\mu_1 = \mu_2 = \mu_3 = ... = \mu_k$
- the single population variance, σ^2
- the equality of variances between two independent populations, $\sigma_1^2 = \sigma_2^2$

This chapter will focus on the hypothesis testing process for a *single population parameter* (i.e. a single mean μ, a single proportion π, a single variance σ^2) while chapters 9, 10 and 11 test hypotheses that compare parameters between *two or more populations*.

Refer to Appendix 3 for a *summary flowchart of hypotheses test* scenarios and appropriate test statistics.

8.2 The Hypothesis Testing Process

Hypothesis testing is a process that tests 'how close' a sample statistic lies to a hypothesised population parameter value to decide whether to accept or reject the management claim. The closer the sample statistic lies to the claimed value, the more likely it is that the hypothesised value is true. Similarly, the further away the sample statistic lies from the claimed value, the more likely it is that the hypothesised value is false.

This process is formalised in a *five-step procedure*, as follows:

Step 1: Define the statistical hypotheses (the null and alternative hypotheses).

Step 2: Determine the region of acceptance of the null hypothesis.

Step 3: Calculate the sample test statistic.

Step 4: Compare the sample test statistic to the region of acceptance.

Step 5: Draw statistical and management conclusions.

Step 1: Define the Statistical Hypotheses (Null and Alternative)

Hypothesis testing begins with a value being assumed for a given population parameter. It is derived from a management question or a claim made. Two statistical hypotheses are formulated based on this assumed population parameter value.

The first statistical hypothesis is called the **null hypothesis**, written H_0. This null hypothesis states that the true population parameter value is *equal* to the hypothesised value. It usually represents the *status quo*.

The second hypothesis is called the **alternative hypothesis**, written H_1. This hypothesis is the opposite of the null hypothesis. It states that the true population parameter value is *different* to the null hypothesised value.

The formulation of the null and alternative hypotheses depends on how the management question is stated and can be represented in one of three different ways.

A Two-sided Hypothesis Test

When the claim (or management question) states that the population parameter is *equal to* a specific value, then the hypotheses are formulated as a **two-sided test**.

> H_0: population parameter = specified value
>
> H_1: population parameter ≠ specified value

For example, if a manager asks whether the mean output per worker is *exactly* 46 units per hour, then the null and alternative hypotheses are expressed as follows:

> $H_0: \mu = 46$ This represents the management question.
>
> $H_1: \mu \neq 46$

The null hypothesis will be rejected in favour of the alternative hypothesis if the sample evidence points towards the true population parameter value being either significantly *less than* or significantly *greater than* the null hypothesised population value.

The null hypothesis must always contain the equality sign (e.g. $H_0: \mu = 46$). In this case, the management question will reside in H_0.

A One-sided Upper-tailed Hypothesis Test

When the claim (or management question) states that the population parameter is *more than* a specified value, then the hypotheses are formulated as a **one-sided upper-tailed test**.

> H_0: population parameter ≤ specified value
>
> H_1: population parameter > specified value

For example, if a manager asks whether it can be assumed that the mean output per worker is *more than* 46 units per hour, then the null and alternative hypotheses are expressed as follows:

$H_0: \mu \leq 46$
$H_1: \mu > 46$ This represents the management question.

The manager's claim resides in the alternative hypothesis, because the null hypothesis must always represent the statement that contains the equality sign (i.e. $\leq$). The null hypothesis will be rejected in favour of the alternative hypothesis only when the sample value is significantly *greater than* the population value specified in the null hypothesis.

Note: Words such as *not more than*, *at most* or *does not exceed* also result in the formulation of a one-sided upper-tailed hypothesis test. In such instances, the management question resides in the null hypothesis, since all these statements include the equality sign (i.e. $\leq$).

A One-sided Lower-tailed Hypothesis Test

When the claim states that the population parameter is *less than* a specified value, then the hypotheses are formulated as a **one-sided lower-tailed test**.

H_0: population parameter $\geq$ specified value
H_1: population parameter $<$ specified value

For example, if a manager believes that the mean output per worker is *less than* 46 units per hour, then this belief can be tested using the following null and alternative hypotheses:

$H_0: \mu \geq 46$
$H_1: \mu < 46$ This represents the management question.

The manager's belief (or claim) resides in the alternative hypothesis because the null hypothesis must always represent the statement that contains the equality sign (i.e. $\geq$). The null hypothesis will be rejected in favour of the alternative hypothesis only when the sample value is significantly *less than* (or smaller than) the population value specified in the null hypothesis.

Note 1: Words such as *not less than* or *at least* in the management question also result in the formulation of a one-sided lower-tailed hypothesis test. In such instances, the management question resides in the null hypothesis since all these statements include the equality sign (i.e. $\geq$).

Note 2: The null hypothesis, H_0, must always contain the equality sign (i.e. $\leq$, = or $\geq$). This identifies a specific value against which the alternative hypothesis is being tested.

Note 3: The remaining four steps of hypothesis testing focus only on testing whether the null hypothesis can be *accepted or rejected* based on the sample evidence.[1] Only once a statistical decision is made as to whether to accept or reject the null hypothesis is the validity of the management claim (or question) considered in terms of whether it is likely to be true or not.

---

[1] It is more appropriate to use the term '*do not reject*' the null hypothesis instead of '*accept*' the null hypothesis when the sample evidence is not strong enough to favour the alternative hypothesis. In this text, however, the term '*accept*' the null hypothesis will be used to imply '*do not reject*' the null hypothesis.

A three-step guide to correctly formulate the null and alternative hypotheses:

1. Express the management question as a mathematical relationship (e.g. if the management question asks, 'Is the mean worker output less than 46 units?', this is expressed mathematically as $\mu < 46$).

2. Now set up a complementary mathematical relationship to the management question (e.g. for the management question, $\mu < 46$, a complementary relationship is $\mu \geq 46$).

3. Of the two relationships, the null hypothesis is *always* the one with the equality sign (e.g. in this illustration, H_0: $\mu \geq 46$ and H_1: $\mu < 46$. The management question resides in the alternative hypothesis).

Step 2: Determine the Region of Acceptance of the Null Hypothesis

This step sets up a *decision rule* to determine when to accept or reject the null hypothesis. The null hypothesis is always centred on the sampling distribution of the given sample statistic.

The **region of acceptance** of H_0 is an *interval of sample statistic values* around the centre value of the sampling distribution. The null hypothesis will *not be rejected* if the sample evidence falls *within these limits* around H_0.

The **region of rejection** of H_0, on the other hand, is the *interval of sample statistic values* that lies outside the region of acceptance of H_0. The null hypothesis will be *rejected* in favour of the alternative hypothesis, H_1, if the sample evidence falls *within these limits*. This interval always lies in the tails of the sampling distribution. It never includes the null hypothesis value.

Figures 8.1, 8.2 and 8.3 illustrate the regions of acceptance and rejection about a null hypothesised population mean, μ, for the three different ways of formulating the null and alternative hypothesis.

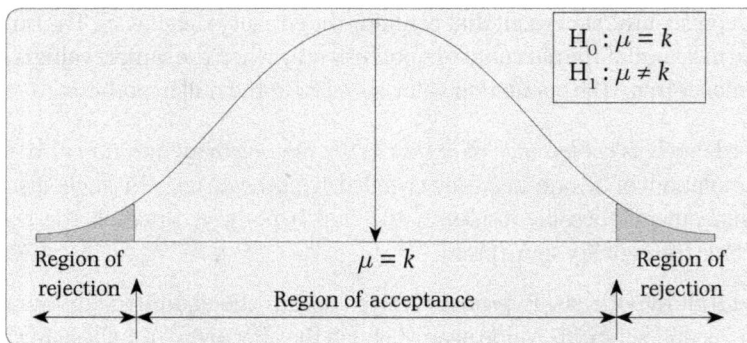

$$H_0 : \mu = k$$
$$H_1 : \mu \neq k$$

Region of rejection $\mu = k$ Region of rejection

Region of acceptance

Figure 8.1 Region of acceptance and rejection for a two-sided hypothesis test

A *two-sided* test has a *region of rejection* both *below and above* the null hypothesised value of the population parameter.

A *one-sided upper-tailed* test means that the *region of rejection* lies only above the null hypothesised value of the population parameter.

A *one-sided lower-tailed* test means that the *region of rejection* lies only *below* the null hypothesised value of the population parameter.

The cut-off (or critical) limits of the regions of acceptance and rejection of the null hypothesis are determined by the *level of risk* acceptable to the decision-maker in drawing an incorrect conclusion.

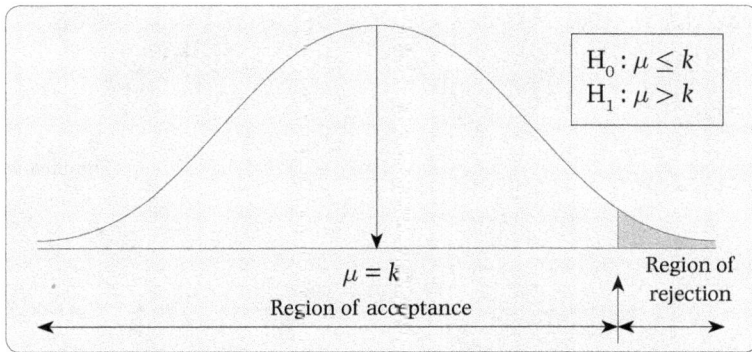

Figure 8.2 Region of acceptance and rejection for a one-sided upper-tailed hypothesis test

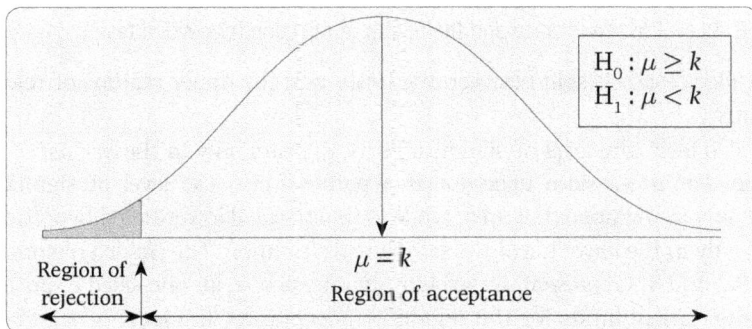

Figure 8.3 Region of acceptance and rejection for a one-sided lower-tailed hypothesis test

There are two risks involved in testing any hypothesis. They are called the Type I error, and the Type II error.

A **Type I error** is the probability of rejecting the null hypothesis when in fact it is true.

A **Type II error** is the probability of accepting the null hypothesis when it is actually false.

These two error types move inversely to each other. By reducing the Type I error, the chances of incurring a Type II error increase, and vice versa. In hypothesis testing, we control the level of the Type I error and set the critical limits of the region of acceptance accordingly.

Level of Significance (α)

A Type I error is called the level of significance and is represented by the symbol α (alpha). The level of significance is the area (probability) in the 'tails' of a sampling distribution, as this is where the rejection region is located. Once the level of significance, α, is set (usually at 1%, 5% or 10%), the critical limits that separate the region of acceptance from the region of rejection are found either from statistical tables or by using an appropriate Excel function.

Figure 8.4 illustrates the relationship between the level of significance and the region of rejection for any sampling distribution for a *two-sided* test.

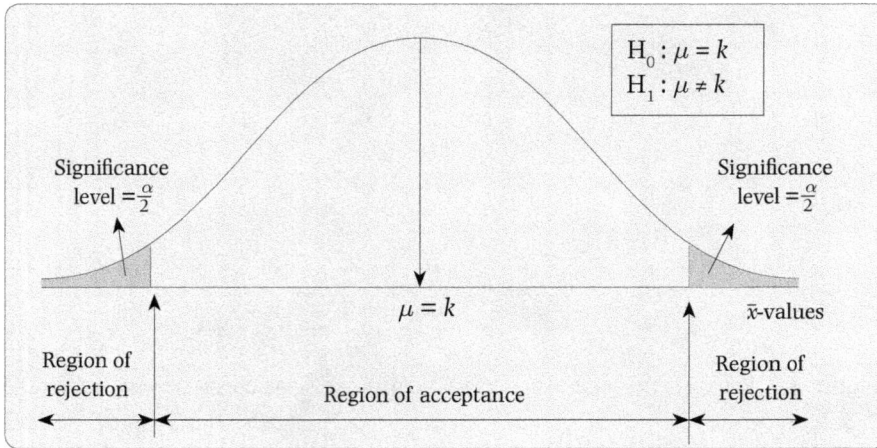

Figure 8.4 Level of significance and the region of rejection (two-sided tests)

- In a two-tailed test, α is split between the lower and the upper regions of rejection. Each tail contains $\frac{\alpha}{2}$.
- For one-tailed tests, the level of significance, α, appears only in the *one tail* of a sampling distribution. For a one-sided upper-tailed hypothesis test, the level of significance, α, is contained only in the upper tail area, while for a one-sided lower-tailed hypothesis test, α is contained only in the lower tail of the sampling distribution. The shaded regions of rejection in figures 8.2 and 8.3 represent the levels of significance, α, for one-sided hypotheses tests.

To find the critical limits for the region of acceptance, the level of significance must be specified. If a 5% level of significance ($\alpha = 0.05$) is specified, it means that there is a 5% chance of rejecting a true null hypothesis. The critical limits for the region of acceptance are always expressed in terms of a test statistic such as the z-statistic (see **Step 3**) and are referred to as **z-crit**. These z-limits are found using the statistical tables in Appendix 1, where the tail area of the distribution is defined by the chosen level of significance, α. Note that these z-critical limits can also be found using the Excel function NORM.S.INV(probability). See section 8.7.

From the z-distribution, these critical limits are:

- either the two z-limits (i.e. $\pm z$-limit) that bound a combined area (probability) of α in the two tails of the sampling distribution if the hypothesis test is two-sided. (Each tail will contain an area of $\frac{\alpha}{2}$.)
- or a single z-limit that bounds an area (probability) of α in only one tail of the sampling distribution if the hypothesis test is one-sided. (Thus α is in the lower tail only if it is a one-sided lower-tailed test and in the upper tail only if it is a one-sided upper-tailed test.)

Critical limits for a two-sided hypothesis test:

> Region of acceptance: $-z$-crit $\leq z \leq +z$-crit

For example, if $\alpha = 0.05$, the z-crit is ± 1.96 and the region of acceptance is $-1.96 \leq z \leq +1.96$.

Critical limit for a one-sided lower-tailed hypothesis test:

> Region of acceptance: $z \geq -z$-crit

For example, if $\alpha = 0.05$, the z-crit is -1.645 and the region of acceptance is $z \geq -1.645$.

Critical limit for a one-sided upper-tailed hypothesis test:

Region of acceptance: $z \leq +z\text{-}crit$

For example, if $\alpha = 0.05$, the z-crit is $+1.645$ and the region of acceptance is $z \leq 1.645$.

Table 8.1 shows commonly used significance levels and their associated z-crit limits for both two-tailed and one-tailed hypotheses tests.

Table 8.1 z-limits for given levels of significance (one-sided and two-sided tests)

Level of significance (α)	Type of hypothesis test	z-limit(s)
0.01 (1%)	two-sided	± 2.58
0.05 (5%)	two-sided	± 1.96
0.10 (10%)	two-sided	± 1.645
0.01	one-sided lower-tailed	-2.33
0.05	one-sided lower-tailed	-1.645
0.10	one-sided lower-tailed	-1.28
0.01	one-sided upper-tailed	$+2.33$
0.05	one-sided upper-tailed	$+1.645$
0.10	one-sided upper-tailed	$+1.28$

Using the defined region of acceptance, a decision rule can be formulated to guide the statistical decision at the conclusion phase (i.e. at Step 5). The *decision rule* would read as follows:

- *Accept* H_0 if the sample test statistic falls *within* the region of acceptance.
- *Reject* H_0 in favour of H_1 if the sample test statistic falls *outside* the region of acceptance (i.e. *within* the region of rejection).

When H_0 is accepted, it means that the sample evidence is close enough to the null hypothesised value, and hence we assume H_c to be true. Alternatively, if H_0 is rejected, it means that the sample evidence lies far enough away from the null hypothesised value, and hence we assume that H_0 is false and that the alternative hypothesis is likely to be the true state of nature.

Step 3: Calculate the Sample Test Statistic

Sample data is used to produce a sample statistic that provides the evidence to test the validity of the null hypothesis. Depending on the type of hypothesis test, the sample statistic is one of the following:

For **central location** measures:
- the single sample mean, $\bar{x}$
- the single sample proportion, p
- the difference between two independent sample means, $\bar{x}_1 - \bar{x}_2$
- the difference between two independent sample proportions, $(p_1 - p_2)$ and
- the paired mean difference, $\bar{x}_d$.

For **dispersion** measures:
- the single sample variance, s^2 and
- the difference between two sample variances, $s_1^2 - s_2^2$.

The sample statistic must be expressed in the same *standardised unit of measure* as the critical limits for the region of acceptance (e.g. in z terms). When the sample statistic is expressed in standardised terms, it is called the **sample test statistic** and is referred to, for example, as *z-stat*.

For a hypothesis test for the single sample mean, $\bar{x}$, the z-statistic transforms the sample mean into its standardised form, using the following standardised z formula:

$$z\text{-}stat = \frac{\bar{x} - \mu}{\frac{\sigma}{\sqrt{n}}}$$

8.1

To decide whether the sample test statistic, *z-stat*, lies 'close enough' to the null hypothesised value to accept H_0 or not, the *z-stat* value must be compared to the decision rule from Step 2. This is the purpose of Step 4.

Step 4: Compare the Sample Test Statistic to the Area of Acceptance

The sample test statistic, *z-stat*, is now compared to the region of acceptance of H_0 (from Step 2). The sample test statistic either lies within (inside) the region of acceptance or it lies outside the region of acceptance (i.e. within the region of rejection of H_0).

For example, if *z-stat* = 1.52 and the region of acceptance is $-1.96 \le z \le +1.96$, based on a 5% level of significance, then *z-stat* = 1.52 lies within the region of acceptance of H_0.

Step 5: Draw Statistical and Management Conclusions

Depending on the outcome of the comparison at Step 4, the course of action, as identified by the decision rule in Step 2, is taken.

First, a *statistical conclusion* must be drawn followed by the *management conclusion*. This ensures that statistical conclusions are correctly translated into valid and consistent management conclusions.

Statistical Conclusion

If the sample test statistic (*z-stat*) falls within the limits of the region of acceptance, the null hypothesis is accepted as being probably true, at the given level of significance.

Alternatively, if the sample test statistic (*z-stat*) falls outside the limits of the region of acceptance (i.e. within the region of rejection), the null hypothesis is rejected at the given level of significance. This means that the alternative hypothesis is probably true.

The level of significance for the test (e.g. $\alpha = 0.05$) must always be stated in the statistical conclusion to reflect the lack of complete certainty that the correct decision was made based on sample (or partial) evidence only.

Management Conclusion

The management conclusion considers the manager's claim in relation to the statistical conclusion.

- If the null hypothesis is *accepted* and the management claim resides in the *null hypothesis*, the management claim is probably *true*.
- If the null hypothesis is *accepted* and the management claim resides in the *alternative hypothesis*, the management claim is probably *false*.
- If the null hypothesis is *rejected* and the management claim resides in the *null hypothesis*, the management claim is probably *false*.
- If the null hypothesis is *rejected* and the management claim resides in the *alternative hypothesis*, then the management claim is probably *true*.

These guidelines that link the statistical conclusion to the management conclusion are summarised in Figure 8.5.

Location of claim	Statistical conclusion	
	Accept H_0	Reject H_0
Claim in H_0	Claim probably true	Claim probably false
Claim in H_1	Claim probably false	Claim probably true

Figure 8.5 Statistical conclusion in relation to the management claim

These management conclusions must also be qualified to reflect the lack of complete certainty of having made the correct decision.

This hypothesis testing procedure will now be applied to testing claims for the population parameter of a *single mean*, a *single proportion*, and a *single variance* in the remainder of this chapter.

8.3 Hypothesis Test for a Single Population Mean (μ) when the Population Standard Deviation (σ) is Known

$$\bar{x} \rightarrow \mu$$

Whenever a management claim or statement is made about the value of a *single population mean*, the claim can be tested using the sampling distribution of $\bar{x}$.

Two illustrative claims for a single population mean are as follows:

- A call-centre manager believes that the mean employment period of call-centre workers is 16 months.
- The Life Office Association (LOA) has claimed that the average value of endowment policies in force is above R125 000.

To conduct a hypothesis test for a single population mean, the following sample and test information is required:

- the sample mean, $\bar{x}$
- the sample size, n

- the population standard deviation, σ
- the level of significance for the test, α.

The z-statistic (as shown in Formula 8.1 above) is the appropriate test statistic.

Example 8.1 Purchase Value of Grocery Baskets Study

The Grocery Retailers Association of South Africa (GRASA) believes that the average amount spent on groceries by Cape Town shoppers on each visit to a supermarket is R175. To test this belief, the association commissioned Market Research e-Afrika to conduct a survey among a random sample of 360 grocery shoppers at supermarkets in Cape Town.

Based on the survey, the average value of grocery purchases was R182.40. Assume that the population of grocery purchase values is normally distributed with a standard deviation, σ, of R67.50.

Management Question

Can GRASA conclude that grocery shoppers spend R175, on average, on each visit to a supermarket? Conduct a test at the 5% level of significance.

Solution

This hypothesis test is a *two-tailed test for a single mean* because the GRASA's belief is that the population mean of the numeric random variable 'value of grocery purchase' is a single value (i.e. R175) only.

Step 1: Define the null and alternative hypotheses
Given that this is a two-tailed test, H_0 and H_1 are formulated as follows:

$H_0: \mu = 175$ This represents the management claim to be tested.
$H_1: \mu \neq 175$

The null hypothesis will be rejected in favour of the alternative hypothesis if the sample evidence shows that the actual mean value of grocery purchases is either *significantly less than* or *significantly more than* the null hypothesised value of R175.

Step 2: Determine the region of acceptance of the null hypothesis
A level of significance is needed to find the critical z-limits between the regions of acceptance and rejection. In this example, $\alpha = 0.05$ (5% level of significance).

Since this is a two-tailed test, the region of acceptance is defined by two limits: a lower and an upper limit around H_0. These two critical z-limits identify a combined area of $\alpha = 0.05$ in the two tails of the z-distribution.

The critical z-limits are z-crit = ± 1.96 (Table 1, Appendix 1). Thus the region of acceptance for H_0 is $-1.96 \leq z \leq +1.96$.

The decision rule for accepting or rejecting H_0 is then stated as follows:
- Accept H_0 if z-stat falls between -1.96 and $+1.96$.
- Reject H_0 if z-stat falls below -1.96 or above $+1.96$.

Step 3: Calculate the sample test statistic (z-stat)
The sample test statistic, z-stat, is calculated using sample data that is substituted into Formula 8.1.

Given $\bar{x} = 182.40$, $\sigma = 67.5$ and $n = 360$. First calculate the standard error:

$$\frac{\sigma}{\sqrt{n}} = \frac{67.5}{\sqrt{360}}$$
$$= 3.558$$

Then: $z\text{-stat} = \frac{182.4 - 175}{3.558} = \frac{7.4}{3.553}$
$$= 2.08$$

This z-$stat$ tells us how many standard errors the sample mean of R182.40 lies away from the null hypothesised population mean of R175. Here, $\bar{x}$ lies 2.08 standard errors above R175. The further away it lies, in standard error terms, the more likely the null hypothesis will be rejected.

Step 4: Compare the sample test statistic to the area of acceptance
This sample test statistic, z-$stat$, must now be compared to the decision rule for the region of acceptance (Step 2) to decide if it is 'close enough' to the null hypothesised population mean.

The sample test statistic z-$stat = 2.08$ lies *outside the region of acceptance* of $-1.96 \leq z \leq +1.96$. Refer to Figure 8.6, which shows the sample test statistic (z-$stat$) in relation to the regions of acceptance and rejection as defined by the z-$crit$ limits.

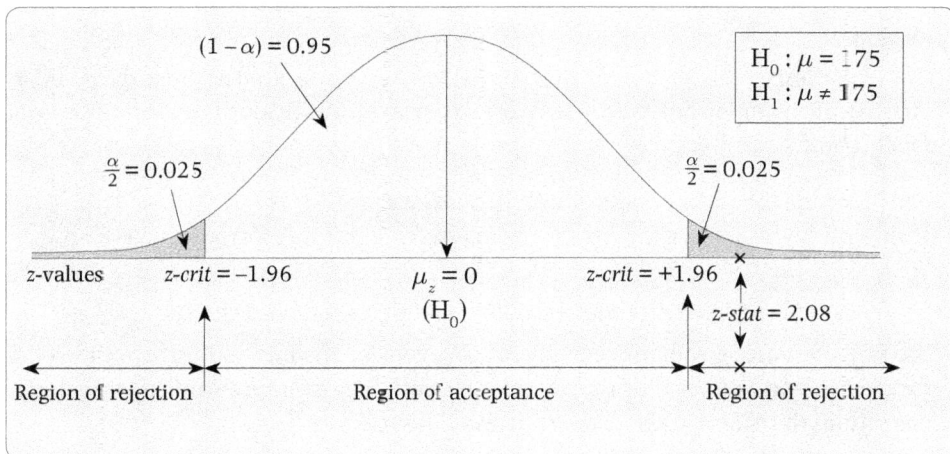

Figure 8.6 Purchase value of grocery baskets study – *z-stat* and region of acceptance

Step 5: Draw statistical and management conclusions

Statistical Conclusion

Since z-$stat$ lies outside the region of acceptance of H_0, the sample evidence is not 'close enough' to the null hypothesised value of R175 to accept H_0. There is sufficient sample evidence at the 5% level of significance to reject H_0 in favour of H_1. The alternative hypothesis is therefore probably true.

Management Conclusion

It can be concluded, with 95% confidence, that the actual mean value of grocery purchases is *not* R175. The GRASA's claim cannot be supported on the basis of the sample evidence presented.

Example 8.2 Executive Hours Worked Study

An international study on executive working hours reported that company CEOs (chief executive officers) worked *more than* 60 hours per week on average. The South African Institute of Management (SAIM) wanted to test whether this norm applied to South African CEOs as well.

A random sample of 90 CEOs from South African companies was drawn, and each executive was asked to record the number of hours worked during a given week. The sample mean number of hours worked per week was found to be 61.3 hours. Assume a normal distribution for weekly hours worked and a population standard deviation of 8.8 hours.

Management Question

Do South African CEOs work *more than* 60 hours per week, on average? Test this claim at the 5% level of significance.

Solution

This hypothesis test is a *one-sided upper-tailed test for a single mean* because the SAIM asks whether the mean number of hours worked per week by all South African CEOs is *more than* 60 hours.

Step 1: Define the null and alternative hypotheses

Given that this is a one-sided upper-tailed test, H_0 and H_1 are formulated as follows:

$H_0 : \mu \leq 60$
$H_1 : \mu > 60$ This represents the management claim to be tested.

The null hypothesis will only be rejected in favour of the alternative hypothesis if the sample evidence shows that the actual mean number of hours worked is *significantly higher* than the null hypothesised value of 60 hours.

Since the management claim is a strict inequality (i.e. *more than 60 hours*), the claim resides in the alternative hypothesis, as the null hypothesis must always contain the equality sign.

Step 2: Determine the region of acceptance of the null hypothesis

The level of significance is given as 5% (i.e. $\alpha = 0.05$). Since this is a one-sided (upper-tailed) test, the 5% level of significance is found only in the upper tail of the sampling distribution for the sample mean. Thus the z-crit limit is that z-value that bounds an area of 5% in the upper tail of the standard normal distribution.

The critical z-limit is z-crit $= 1.645$ (Table 1, Appendix 1). Thus the region of acceptance for H_0 is $z \leq +1.645$.

The decision rule for accepting or rejecting H_0 is then stated as follows:
- Accept H_0 if *z-stat* falls at or below +1.645.
- Reject H_0 if *z-stat* falls above +1.645.

Step 3: Calculate the sample test statistic (*z-stat*)

From the sample data, compute the sample test statistic *z-stat* using Formula 8.1.
Given $\bar{x} = 61.3$, $\sigma = 8.8$ and $n = 90$. First calculate the standard error:

$$\frac{\sigma}{\sqrt{n}} = \frac{8.8}{\sqrt{90}}$$

$$= 0.9276$$

Then $\quad$ $z\text{-}stat = \frac{61.3 - 60}{0.9276} = \frac{1.3}{0.9276}$

$$= 1.4015$$

This *z-stat* value implies that the sample mean of 61.3 hours lies 1.4015 standard errors above the null hypothesised population mean of 60 hours.

Step 4: Compare the sample test statistic to the area of acceptance

Is the sample evidence – expressed in standardised z-units (*z-stat*) – 'close enough' to the null hypothesised population mean to accept the null hypothesis as the true state of nature? 'Close enough' is defined by the limits of the region of acceptance. To accept H_0 as the true state of nature, *z-stat* must not exceed 1.645 standard errors above the null hypothesised value of 60 hours (i.e. the upper limit of the region of acceptance).

Since *z-stat* is 1.4015, it lies *inside the region of acceptance* of $z \leq +1.645$. Refer to Figure 8.7, which shows the sample test statistic (*z-stat*) in relation to the regions of acceptance and rejection.

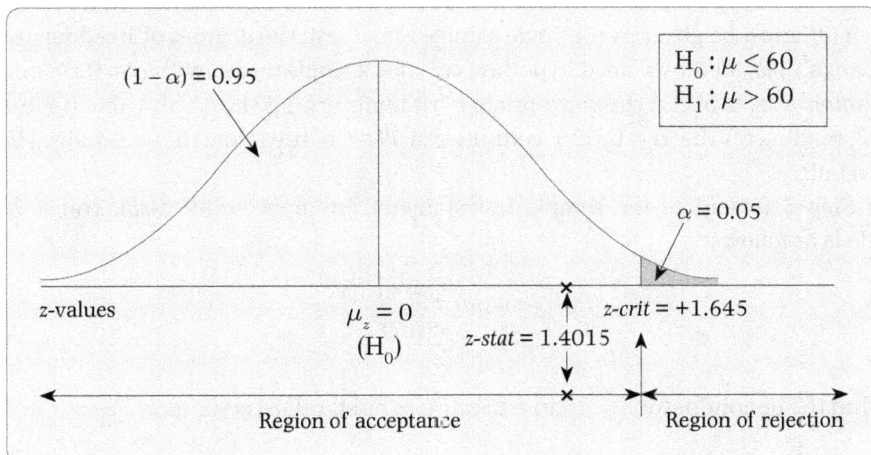

$(1-\alpha) = 0.95$

$H_0 : \mu \leq 60$
$H_1 : \mu > 60$

$\alpha = 0.05$

z-values $\qquad$ $\mu_z = 0$ $\qquad$ z-crit = +1.645
(H_0) $\qquad$ z-stat = 1.4015

Region of acceptance $\qquad$ Region of rejection

Figure 8.7 Executive hours worked study – z-stat and region of acceptance

Step 5: Draw statistical and management conclusions.

Statistical Conclusion

Since z-stat lies *within* the region of acceptance, the sample evidence is not convincing enough to reject H_0 in favour of H_1. Thus accept H_0 at the 5% level of significance.

Management Conclusion

It can be concluded, with 95% confidence, that South African CEOs do not work more than 60 hours per week, on average. The SA Institute of Management (SAIM) can therefore be advised that South African CEOs do *not* appear to be following the international norm of working, on average, more than 60 hours per week.

8.4 Hypothesis Test for a Single Population Mean (μ) when the Population Standard Deviation (σ) is Unknown

$$\bar{x} \to \mu$$

In Chapter 7 (section 7.8), it was seen that if the population standard deviation, σ, is unknown, it can be estimated by its sample standard deviation, s. When this happens, the student t-distribution (instead of the z-distribution) is used to compute the sample test statistic. The sample test statistic is now called *t-stat*.

In hypothesis testing for a single population mean, z-crit and z-stat are replaced by *t-crit* and *t-stat*, respectively, *whenever the population standard deviation is unknown*. This occurs in steps 2 and 3 of the hypothesis testing procedure.

In Step 2 (determine the regions of acceptance and rejection), the critical limits for the region of acceptance (*t-crit*) are found from the ***t*-table** (Table 2, Appendix 1) as illustrated in Chapter 7 (section 7.8).

To revise, to read off the critical t-limit, both a level of significance, α, and degrees of freedom (*df*) must be given. For a single sample mean test, the degrees of freedom are $n - 1$.

For example, for a two-sided hypothesis test for a single mean, with $\alpha = 0.05$ and based on a sample size, n, of 27, the appropriate *t-crit* limits are ± 2.056. This value is found from Table 2, reading off the '$\alpha = 0.025$' column and '$df = 26$' row. Note that α is halved between the two tails.

In Step 3 (calculate the sample test statistic), the appropriate *t-stat* transformation formula is as follows:

$$t\text{-}stat = \frac{\bar{x} - \mu}{\frac{s}{\sqrt{n}}} \qquad \qquad 8.2$$

Note that the denominator, $\frac{s}{\sqrt{n}}$, is an *estimate* for the standard error term, $\frac{\sigma}{\sqrt{n}}$.

Example 8.3 SARS e-Filing Completion Time Study

SARS (the South African Revenue Service) believes that it takes typical salary-earning taxpayers *less than* 45 minutes, on average, to complete their tax return using e-Filing (the online tax return submission system).

To test this claim, SARS randomly selected 12 salary-earning taxpayers who had registered for e-Filing, and recorded their time to complete the e-Filing process. The completion times (in minutes) for the sample of 12 taxpayers are given in the table below.

42	56	29	35	47	37	39	29	45	35	51	53

The sample mean completion time for the 12 taxpayers is 41.5 minutes, with a sample standard deviation of 9.04 minutes. Assume e-Filing completion time is normally distributed.

Management Question

Test at the 5% level of significance whether SARS' claim is likely to be true (i.e. that it takes typical salary-earning taxpayers *less than* 45 minutes, on average, to complete their tax return using e-Filing).

Solution

This hypothesis test is a *one-sided lower-tailed test for a single mean* because SARS claims that the average e-Filing completion time by all salary-earning taxpayers is *less than* 45 minutes.

Step 1: Define the null and alternative hypotheses
Given that this is a one-sided lower-tailed test, H_0 and H_1 are formulated as follows:

$H_0: \mu \geq 45$
$H_1: \mu < 45$ This represents SARS' claim to be tested.

Since SARS claims that the average e-Filing completion time is less than 45 minutes, this strict inequality (<) means that the management question resides in the alternative hypothesis, H_1. The null hypothesis must always contain the equality sign.

Step 2: Determine the region of acceptance of the null hypothesis
The level of significance is given as 5% (i.e. $\alpha = 0.05$). Since this is a one-sided lower-tailed test, the 5% level of significance is found only in the lower tail of the sampling distribution for the sample mean. The region of acceptance is defined by a *critical lower limit only*.

Since the *population standard deviation, σ, is unknown*, the t-statistic is used to find the critical limit for the region of acceptance. The critical t-limit (t-crit) is that t-value that bounds an area of 5% in the lower tail of the t-distribution.

With degrees of freedom of $n - 1 = 11$, and $\alpha = 0.05$, the critical t-limit is $t\text{-}crit = -1.796$ (Table 2, Appendix 1). Thus the region of acceptance for H_0 is $t \geq -1.796$.

The decision rule for accepting or rejecting H_0 is then stated as follows:
- Accept H_0 if *t-stat* falls at or above -1.796.
- Reject H_0 if *t-stat* falls below -1.796.

Step 3: Calculate the sample test statistic (*t-stat*)

From sample data, compute the sample test statistic, *t-stat*, using Formula 8.2.

Given $\bar{x} = 41.5$, $s = 9.04$ and $n = 12$. First calculate the (estimated) standard error:

$$\frac{s}{\sqrt{n}} = \frac{9.04}{\sqrt{12}}$$

$$= 2.6096$$

Then $t\text{-}stat = \frac{41.5 - 45}{2.6096} = \frac{-3.5}{2.6096}$

$$= -1.341$$

This *t-stat* value measures the number of standard errors that the sample mean of 41.5 minutes lies from the null hypothesised population mean of 45 minutes. In this case, $\bar{x} = 41.5$ minutes lies 1.34 standard error units below the hypothesised mean value of 45 minutes. Is this 'far enough' away from the null hypothesised mean of 45 minutes to reject the null hypothesis?

Step 4: Compare the sample test statistic to the area of acceptance

This sample test statistic, *t-stat*, must now be compared to the decision rule (from Step 2) to decide if it is 'close enough' to the null hypothesised population mean to accept H_0.

Since *t-stat* = −1.341, it lies *inside the region of acceptance* of $t \geq -1.796$. Refer to Figure 8.8, which shows the sample test statistic (*t-stat*) in relation to the regions of acceptance and rejection.

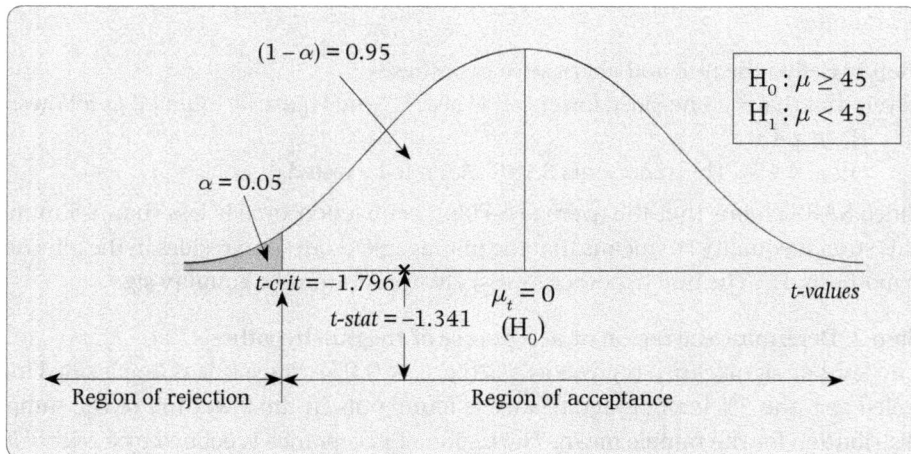

Figure 8.8 SARS e-Filing completion time study – *t-stat* and region of acceptance

Step 5: Draw statistical and management conclusions

Statistical Conclusion

Since *t-stat* lies within the region of acceptance, the sample evidence is not convincing enough to reject H_0 in favour of H_1. Thus accept H_0 at the 5% level of significance.

Management Conclusion

It can be concluded, with 95% confidence, that the mean e-Filing completion time is not less than 45 minutes. Thus SARS' claim cannot be supported.

When to Use the Student *t*-statistic – a Review

The *t*-distribution, theoretically, is the correct standardised distribution to use in place of the *z*-distribution whenever the population standard deviation, σ, is unknown.

However, it can be seen from the *t*-table (Table 2, Appendix 1 and illustrated in Table 7.4 of Chapter 7, section 7.8) that the *t*-value depends on the sample size, *n*. As *n* increases, the *t*-value approaches the *z*-value, for the same level of significance. In practice, if the sample size exceeds 40 for any hypothesis test of means, the *z*-statistic can be used as a good approximation to the *t*-statistic. If, however, the sample size is less than 40, the *t*-value must be used.

This can be summarised as follows:

- If the population standard deviation, σ, is unknown, and the sample size is *small* (i.e. $n \leq 40$), then always use the *t*-statistic (with appropriate degrees of freedom) instead of the *z*-statistic. We also assume a *normally* distributed population.
- If the population standard deviation, σ, is unknown, and the sample size is *large* (i.e. $n > 40$), then the *z*-statistic can be used as a good approximation to the *t*-statistic, with the sample standard deviation, *s*, used as an estimate for the unknown population standard deviation, σ.

8.5 Hypothesis Test for a Single Population Proportion (π)

$$p \to \pi$$

In management, many random variables are qualitative in nature and generate categorical data. When a claim is made about these qualitative random variables, they can be tested statistically by examining the *sample proportion* in relation to the claimed population proportion. Such a hypothesis test is called a test for a **single population proportion**.

The sampling distribution of the single sample proportion, as described in Chapter 6, is used as the basis for this hypothesis test.

The following information is required:

- the single sample proportion, *p*
- the sample size, *n*
- a level of significance, α
- the appropriate *z*-transformation formula, which is:

$$z\text{-}stat = \frac{p - \pi}{\sqrt{\frac{\pi(1-\pi)}{n}}}$$

8.3

Example 8.4 Mobile Phone Service Provider Market Share Study

A mobile phone service provider, Cell D Mobile, claims that it has 15% of the prepaid mobile phone market. A competitor, who commissioned a market research company to conduct a survey amongst prepaid mobile phone users, challenged this claim. The market research company randomly sampled 360 prepaid mobile users and found that 42 users subscribe to Cell D Mobile as a service provider.

Management Questions

1 Test, at the 1% level of significance, Cell D Mobile's claim that they have a 15% share of the prepaid mobile phone market.
2 Test at the 10% level of significance, whether Cell D Mobile's share of the prepaid mobile phone market is significantly *less than* 15%. Use the same market research data as for (1) above.

Solution

1 The hypothesis test is classified as a two-tailed (or two-sided) test for a single proportion because:
   - the random variable (i.e. a Cell D Mobile prepaid phone user or not) is categorical, with the sample proportion summarising the proportion of prepaid mobile phone users who subscribe to Cell D Mobile as their service provider
   - the management question requires us to test if the true proportion (or percentage) of prepaid mobile phone users who use Cell D Mobile as a service provider is *equal* to a specified value only (i.e. 15%).

Step 1: Define the null and alternative hypotheses

$H_0: \pi = 0.15$ Market share = 15%, as claimed by Cell D Mobile.
$H_1: \pi \neq 0.15$

The Cell D Mobile management claim of a 15% market share resides in the null hypothesis.

Step 2: Determine the region of acceptance of the null hypothesis

Given $\alpha = 0.01$ (i.e. 1% level of significance), and since this is a two-tailed test, the region of acceptance will be defined by both a critical lower limit and a critical upper limit around H_0.

The z-distribution is always used for hypothesis tests for proportions. Thus the two critical z-limits are those z-values that identify a combined tail area of 1% in the z-distribution.

These critical z-limits are $z\text{-}crit = \pm 2.58$ (Table 1, Appendix 1). Thus the region of acceptance for H_0 is $-2.58 \leq z \leq +2.58$.

The decision rule for accepting or rejecting H_0 is then stated as follows.
- Accept H_0 if $z\text{-}stat$ falls between -2.58 and $+2.58$ (inclusive).
- Reject H_0 if $z\text{-}stat$ falls either below -2.58 or above $+2.58$.

These critical z-limits define how many standard errors (± 2.58) the sample proportion can fall away from the null hypothesised population proportion before H_0 is rejected in favour of H_1.

Step 3: Calculate the sample test statistic (z-stat)

The sample evidence is represented by the sample proportion, p, which is defined as the proportion of prepaid mobile phone users who subscribe to Cell D Mobile. This statistic, p, must now be converted into the z-test statistic (z-stat) using Formula 8.3.

Given $x = 42$ (number of respondents who subscribe to Cell D Mobile) and $n = 360$:

$$p = \frac{42}{360} = 0.1167$$

and the standard error is:

$$\sqrt{\frac{\pi(1-\pi)}{n}} = \frac{0.15(1-0.15)}{360} = 0.0188$$

Note: The null hypothesised population proportion (in this example, $\pi = 0.15$) is always used to compute the standard error for a single proportion (i.e. the denominator of z-stat).

Then the sample test statistic (z-stat) is calculated as follows:

$$z\text{-stat} = \frac{0.1167 - 0.15}{0.0188} = \frac{-0.0333}{0.0188}$$
$$= -1.771$$

This z-stat value indicates that the sample proportion ($p = 0.1167$) lies 1.771 standard error units below the hypothesised population proportion of $\pi = 0.15$ (i.e. 15%).

Step 4: Compare the sample test statistic to the area of acceptance

This sample test statistic, z-stat, must now be compared to the decision rule (from Step 2) to decide if it is close enough to the null hypothesised population proportion to allow us to accept H_0.

The sample test statistic, z-stat $= -1.771$, lies *inside* the region of acceptance of $-2.58 \leq z \leq +2.58$. Refer to Figure 8.9, which shows the sample test statistic (z-stat) in relation to the regions of acceptance and rejection.

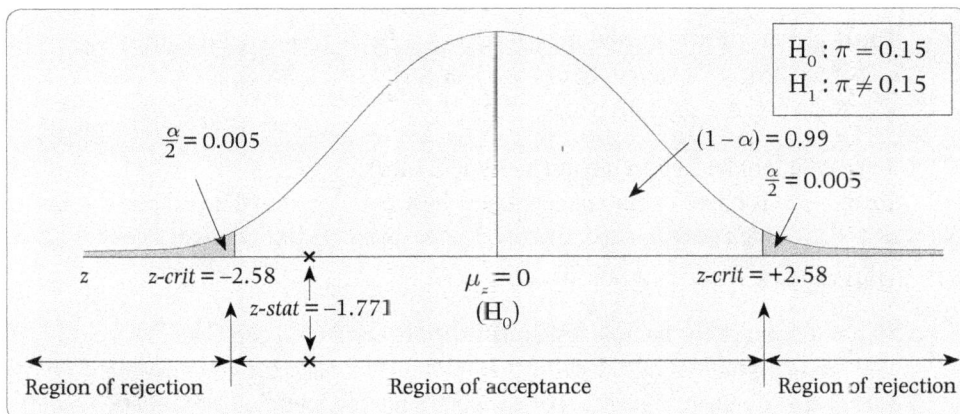

Figure 8.9 Prepaid mobile phone subscribers study – *z-stat* and region of acceptance

Step 5: Draw statistical and management conclusions

Statistical Conclusion

Since *z-stat* lies *inside* the region of acceptance, we accept (do not reject) H_0 at the 1% level of significance. The sample evidence is not convincing (or strong) enough to reject the null hypothesis at the 1% level of significance. The null hypothesis is therefore probably true.

Management Conclusion

It can be concluded, with 99% confidence, that Cell D Mobile's claim about their market share of the prepaid mobile phone market being 15% is probably true. The competitor has no compelling sample evidence to refute Cell D Mobile's claim that their market share is 15%.

Example 8.4 contd.

2 **Step 1: Define the null and alternative hypotheses**

This hypothesis test can be classified as a one-sided lower-tailed test for a single proportion. The management question requires that a strict inequality relationship be tested (i.e. is $\pi < 0.15$?)

$H_0: \pi \geq 0.15$
$H_1: \pi < 0.15$ Cell D Mobile's market share is strictly less than 15%.

The management question now resides in the alternative hypothesis.

Step 2: Determine the region of acceptance of the null hypothesis

Given $\alpha = 0.10$ (i.e. 10% level of significance), and since this is a *one-sided lower-tailed* test, the region of acceptance will be defined by a critical *lower limit* only. Using the z-distribution, the critical z-limit is that z-value that identifies a *lower tail area* of 10% in the z-distribution.

The critical z-limit is *z-crit* $= -1.28$ (Table 1, Appendix 1). Thus the region of acceptance for H_0 is $z \geq -1.28$.

The decision rule for accepting or rejecting H_0 is then stated as follows:
- Accept H_0 if *z-stat* falls at or above -1.28.
- Reject H_0 if *z-stat* falls below -1.28.

Step 3: Calculate the sample test statistic (*z-stat*)

Since *z-stat* is based on sample evidence only and does not depend on whether the test is one-sided or two-sided, the *z-stat* value remains unchanged.

Thus *z-stat* $= -1.771$ (as for (a) above).

Step 4: Compare the sample test statistic to the area of acceptance

The sample test statistic, *z-stat* $= -1.771$ lies *outside the region of acceptance* of $z \geq -1.28$. Refer to Figure 8.10, which shows the sample test statistic (*z-stat*) in relation to the regions of acceptance and rejection.

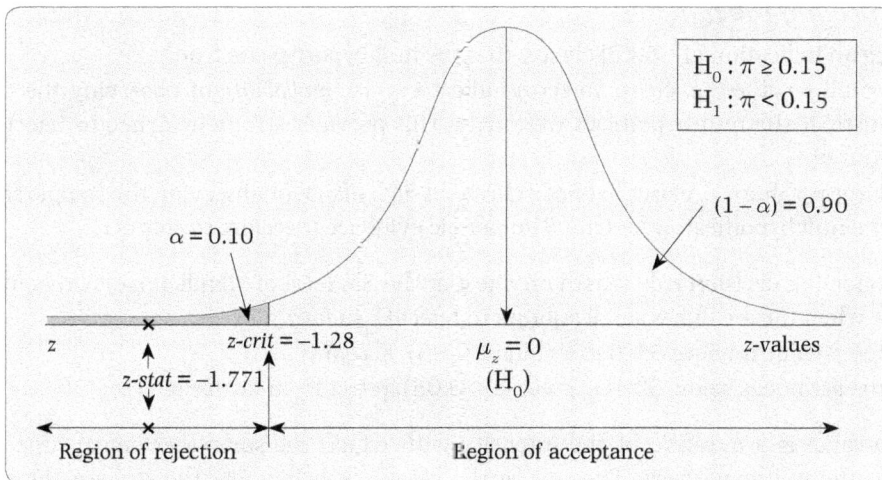

Figure 8.10 Prepaid mobile phone subscribers study – z-stat and region of acceptance

Step 5: Draw statistical and management conclusions

Statistical Conclusion

Since *z-stat* lies *outside* the region of acceptance, reject H_0 at the 10% level of significance. There is strong sample evidence at the 10% level of significance to reject H_0 in favour of H_1. The alternative hypothesis is therefore probably true.

Management Conclusion

It can be concluded, with 90% confidence, that Cell D Mobile's market share is significantly below 15%, and their claim cannot be supported based on the available market research evidence.

8.6 The *p*-value Approach to Hypothesis Testing

An alternative approach to conducting an hypothesis test is to use *probabilities* to decide whether the null hypothesis is likely to be true or false. This is called the *p*-value approach, and is used in all statistical software packages, including Excel and **X-Static**.

A ***p*-value** is the probability of observing the sample statistic (or a more extreme value) if the null-hypothesised population parameter value is assumed to be true.

Interpreting the p-value

It gives an indication of how likely it is that the null hypothesis is true.

- A small p-value (i.e. closer to zero) indicates a *low probability* of observing the sample statistic if the null hypothesis were true. This provides strong evidence to reject H_0 in favour of H_1.
- A large p-value (i.e. closer to one) indicates a *high chance* of observing the sample statistic if the null hypothesis were true. The sample evidence therefore supports H_0.

The following **decision rule** (based on a test at the 5% level of significance) can be used to decide when the p-value is small enough to reject H_0 in favour of H_1:

- If the p-value is above 5% (i.e. p-value ≥ 0.05), accept H_0.
- If the p-value is below 5% (i.e. p-value < 0.05), reject H_0 in favour of H_1.

The p-value is a measure of the intensity with which the sample evidence supports or refutes the null hypothesis. The *smaller* the p-value is below 5%, the *stronger* the sample evidence against the null hypothesis being the true state of nature. The sample evidence then strongly supports the alternative hypothesis.

Figure 8.11 graphically shows the decision rule for accepting/rejecting H_0 based on the p-value.

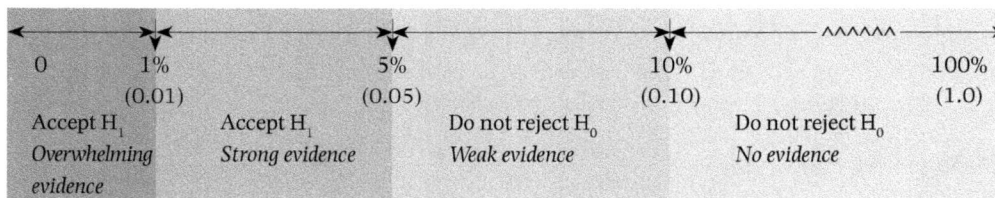

0	1% (0.01)	5% (0.05)	10% (0.10)	100% (1.0)
	Accept H_1 Overwhelming evidence	Accept H_1 Strong evidence	Do not reject H_0 Weak evidence	Do not reject H_0 No evidence

Figure 8.11 Decision rule for interpreting the p-value (based on a 5% level of significance)

Calculating the p-value

The p-value is calculated by finding the *tail area* of a sampling distribution from the *sample test statistic value* (e.g. z-stat or t-stat).

- If the hypothesis test is one-tailed (either upper or lower), then the p-value is the area (or probability) in only the upper or the lower tail.
- If the hypothesis test is two-tailed, then the p-value is the combined areas (or probability) in both the upper and lower tail using the *sample test statistic* (e.g. z-stat or t-stat) and its mirror image in the opposite tail to derive the p-value.

Figures 8.12(a)–(d) show the p-value associated with different z-stat values based on $\alpha = 0.05$.

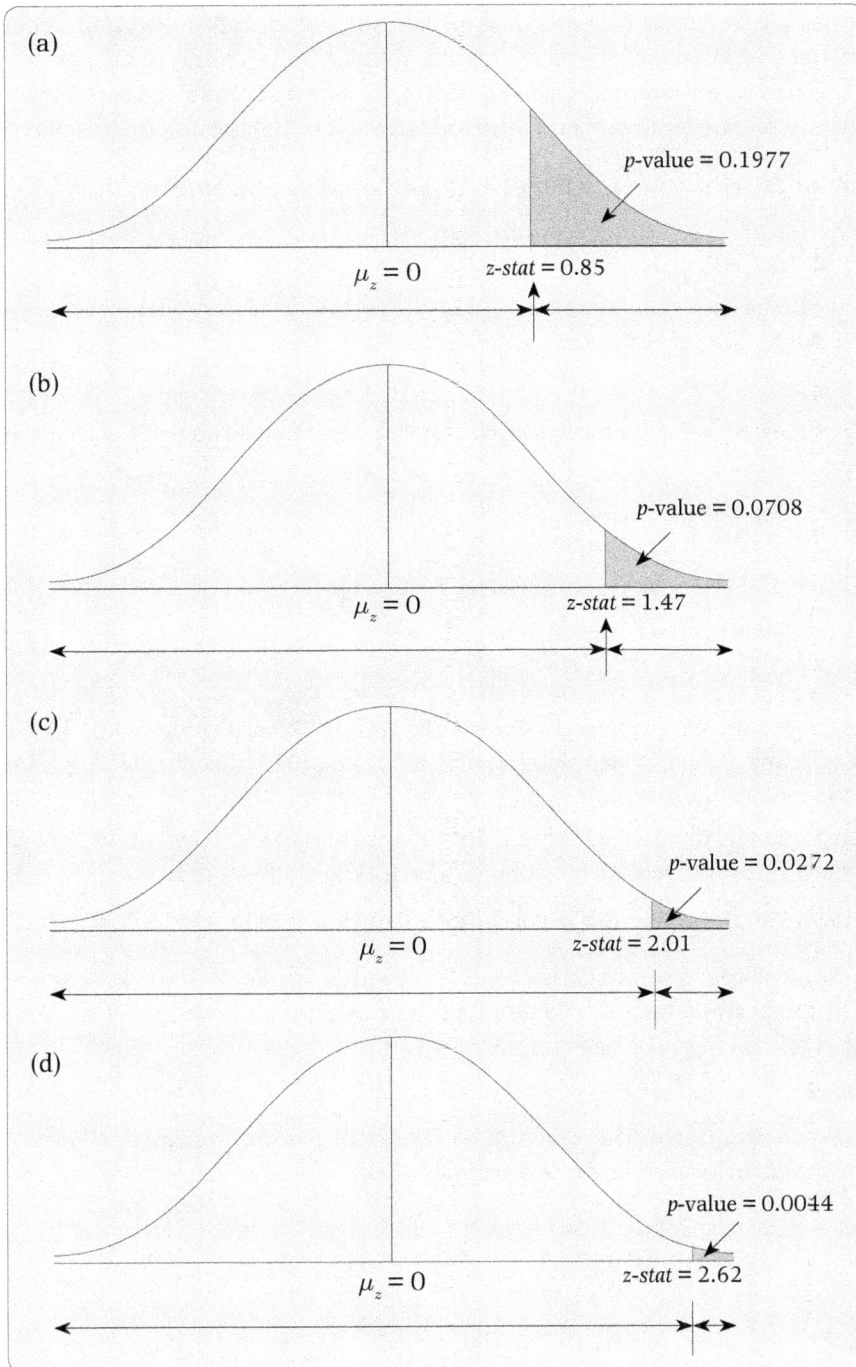

Figure 8.12 Diagrams of *z-stat* values and their associated *p*-values

From Figure 8.12 it can be seen that the *p*-value indicates how close or how far the sample statistic (expressed in *z-stat* terms) is from the null-hypothesised population parameter.

- The *larger* the p-value, the *closer* the sample statistic is to the null hypothesised population parameter and, therefore, the *more likely* it is that the null hypothesis is true.
- The *smaller* the p-value, the *further* the sample statistic is from the null hypothesised population parameter and, therefore, the *less likely* it is that the null hypothesis is true.

Illustration 1: Calculating the p-value for a One-tailed Hypothesis Test

Find the p-value for a one-sided upper-tailed hypothesis test with a sample test statistic z-stat = 2.16.

On the basis of this sample test statistic, can the null hypothesis be accepted or rejected at a 5% level of significance?

Solution

The p-value associated with this sample test statistic is the tail area of the z-distribution above $z = 2.16$.

Thus: p-value $= P(z > 2.16)$
$$= 0.5 - 0.4846$$
$$= 0.0154 \text{ (Table 1, Appendix 1)}$$

Then the p-value is 0.0154 (1.54%).

Statistical Conclusion

Since the p-value for this hypothesis test is less than 5% (i.e. p-value = 0.0154 < 0.05), there is strong sample evidence to reject H_0 in favour of H_1. (Refer to Figure 8.11 for the decision rule for the p-value).

Stated pragmatically, there is only a 1.54% chance that the null hypothesis is true. Since this is a very low probability (less than 5%), reject H_0 in favour of H_1.

Illustration 2: Calculating the p-value for a Two-tailed Hypothesis Test

Find the p-value for a two-tailed hypothesis test with a sample test statistic z-stat = −1.06.

On the basis of this sample test statistic, can the null hypothesis be accepted or rejected at a 5% level of significance?

Solution

The p-value associated with this sample test statistic is the combined tail area of the z-distribution below $z = -1.06$ and above $z = 1.06$.

Thus: p-value $= P(z < -1.06) + P(z > 1.06)$
$$= (0.5 - 0.3554) + (0.5 - 0.3554)$$
$$= 0.1446 + 0.1446$$
$$= 0.2892 \text{ (Table 1, Appendix 1)}$$

Then the p-value is 0.2892 (28.92%).

Statistical Conclusion

Since the p-value for this hypothesis test is greater than 5% (i.e. p-value = 0.2892 > 0.05), there is insufficient evidence to reject H_0. (Refer to Figure 8.11 for the decision rule for the p-value.)

Stated pragmatically, there is a 28.92% chance that the null hypothesis is true. Since this is a relatively high probability (significantly more than 5%), H_0 is accepted.

Management Conclusion

From a management point of view, the p-value of a hypothesis test provides a measure of the *intensity* with which the sample evidence (as reflected in the sample test statistic) supports the alternative hypothesis. Low p-values (below 5%) show strong-to-overwhelming support for the alternative hypothesis, H_1, while high p-values (above 5% and certainly above 10%) show weak-to-no support for the alternative hypothesis, H_1.

If the p-value method is used to test a hypothesis, then Step 2 and Step 4 of the hypothesis testing process are eliminated. Only steps 1, 3 and 5 are required to conduct the hypothesis test.

Example 8.5 Executive Hours Worked Study (Revisited)

Refer to the management scenario in Example 8.2 and use the p-value method to conduct the hypothesis test for a single population mean.

Solution
Step 1: Define the null and alternative hypotheses
For the one-sided upper-tailed test, H_0 and H_1 are formulated as follows:

$$H_0: \mu \le 60$$
$$H_1: \mu > 60 \qquad \text{The management question resides in } H_1.$$

Step 3: Calculate the sample test statistic (z-stat) and the p-value
Given z-stat is 1.4015 (derived from the survey sample evidence).

Then: p-value $= P(z > 1.4015)$
$$= 0.5 - 0.4192$$
$$= 0.0808 \text{ (Table 1, Appendix 1)}$$

Step 5: Draw statistical and management conclusions
Statistical Conclusion

Since the p-value > 0.05, accept H_0 at the 5% level of significance (based on the decision rule in Figure 8.11). This p-value $= 0.0808$ implies that there is only weak sample evidence to reject H_0 in favour of H_1, hence we do not reject H_0.

Management Conclusion

(This will be the same as Example 8.2.) It can be concluded, with 95% confidence, that South African CEOs do not work more than 60 hours per week, on average.

The p-value and Type I and II Errors

When H_0 is rejected (i.e. p-value $< \alpha$), meaning that the sample test statistic (e.g. t-stat) lies in the region of rejection of H_0, the possibility exists that a Type I error (i.e. rejecting a *true* null hypothesis) has been made. This Type I error probability is equal to the level of significance (α) that is set by the statistical analyst. It refers to the area under the null hypothesis sampling distribution over the region of rejection of H_0.

Alternatively, when H_0 is accepted (i.e. *p*-value $> \alpha$), meaning that the sample test statistic (e.g. *t-stat*) lies in the region of acceptance of H_0, the possibility exists that a Type II error (accepting a *false* null hypothesis) has been made. This Type II error probability (referred to as β) relates to the area under a specified alternative hypothesis (H_1) sampling distribution over the region of acceptance of H_0.

Figure 8.13 shows the respective areas that correspond to the Type I and Type II error probabilities.

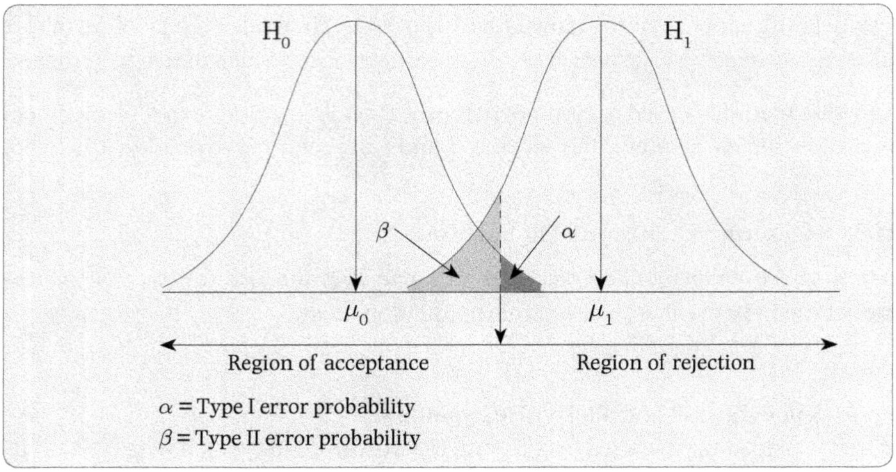

Figure 8.13 Areas that identify Type I (α) and Type II (β) error probabilities

8.7 Hypothesis Test for a Single Population Variance (σ^2)

A hypothesis test can also be conducted on a single population variance. This test is used when the management question relates to the *variability* of a process or a product. For example, a production manager can ask whether the *variability* of the *weights* of a product produced by a machine is no more than, say, 10g around the product specification weight of say, 500g.

The test statistic used for a single population *variance* test is the ***chi-square statistic*** (χ^2).

$$\chi^2 = \frac{(n-1)s^2}{\sigma_0^2}$$ 8.4

Where: n = sample size $n-1$ = degrees of freedom
s^2 = sample variance
σ_0^2 = a null hypothesised value for the population variance

Example 8.6 Mineral water bottle fills Study

A machine is set to fill plastic bottle containers with 750 ml of mineral water. To meet quality standards, the variability of the fills of all the bottles should be *no more* than $\sigma = 5$ ml. To test this quality requirement, a random sample of 20 filled bottles is selected and their volumes measured. The standard deviation of the fills was found to be 5.8 ml. (See Excel file C8.2 – *bottle fills*.)

Test, at the 5% level of significance, whether the filling machine is operating within the quality standards (i.e. filling bottles with a *standard deviation* (σ) of fills of no more than 5 ml (i.e. $\sigma^2 = 25$).

Note: The population parameter being tested is a single population variance (σ^2)

Solution

Step 1: Define the null and alternative hypothesis

$H_0 : \sigma^2 \leq 25$ The management question resides in H_0.

$H_1 : \sigma^2 > 25$

This is a *one-sided upper-tailed* test.

Step 2: Determine the region of acceptance of the null hypothesis (use $\alpha = 0.05$)

The test statistic is the chi-square statistic, χ^2.

The *critical* chi-square limit is $\chi^2\text{-}crit = \chi^2(0.05,19) = 30.14$ (Table 3, Appendix 1).

In Excel, use **CHISQ.INV.RT(0.05,19)**.

Thus the region of acceptance for H_0 is $\chi^2 \leq 30.14$.

The decision rule for accepting or rejecting H_0 is as follows:

- Accept H_0 if $\chi^2\text{-}stat \leq 30.14$
- Reject H_0 in favour of H_1 if $\chi^2\text{-}stat > 30.14$

Step 3: Calculate the sample test statistic ($\chi^2\text{-}stat$)

$$\chi^2\text{-}stat = \frac{(20-1)(5.8)^2}{5^2} = 25.57 \quad \text{Use Formula 8.4}$$

Also, the *p*-value = 0.1427 (In Excel, use **CHISQ.DIST.RT(25.57,19) = 0.1427**)

Step 4: Compare the sample test statistic to the area of acceptance

The sample test statistic, lies *within* the region of acceptance of H_0.

(i.e. $\chi^2\text{-}stat (= 25.57) < \chi^2\text{-}crit (= 30.14)$). Alternatively, *p*-value ($= 0.1427$) $> \alpha = 0.05$. Refer to Figure 8.14 which shows the sample test statistic ($\chi^2\text{-}stat$) in relation to the regions of acceptance and rejection of H_0.

Step 5: Draw statistical and management conclusions

Statistical Conclusion

Since $\chi^2\text{-}stat$ lies within the acceptance region, accept H_0 at the 5% level of significance. There is insufficient sample evidence to reject H_0 in favour of H_1.

Management Conclusion

It can be concluded, with 95% confidence, that the *variability* of bottle fills is no more than $\sigma = 5$ ml. Thus the bottling machine is producing bottled mineral water within the product specification limits of *variability*.

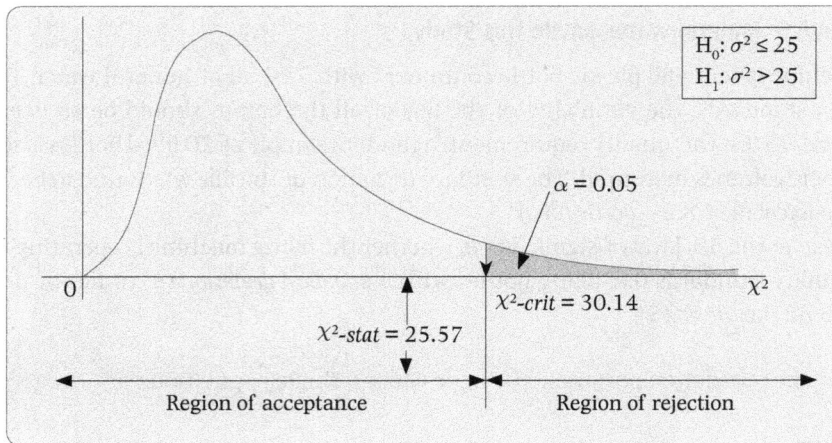

Figure 8.14 One-sided upper tailed chi-square test – region of acceptance and test statistic

Note:

1. To test if a population variance (or standard deviation) has *decreased*, the test would be: $H_0: \sigma^2 \geq k$ versus $H_1 : \sigma^2 < k$. For this *one-sided lower-tailed* test, the region of acceptance will lie to the right of (or above) a *lower* critical χ^2 limit where $\alpha = 0.05$ (for example), would be the area to the left of this lower χ^2-*crit* limit. To find this lower χ^2-*crit* limit, refer to Table 3, Appendix 1. Choose the '$\alpha = 0.95$' column that represents the area to the right of the χ^2-*crit* lower limit. In *Excel*, use **CHISQ.INV(0.05,df)** to find the lower χ^2-*crit* value.

2. To test if a population variance (or standard deviation) equals a given value, k, the test would be: $H_0: \sigma^2 = k$ versus $H_1 : \sigma^2 \neq k$. For this *two-tailed* test, the region of acceptance will lie between a lower χ^2-*crit* and an upper χ^2-*crit*. To find these lower and upper χ^2-*crit* limits, refer to Table 3, Appendix 1. If $\alpha = 0.05$ (for example), the lower critical limit is read from the column '$\alpha = 0.975$' and the upper critical limit from the column '$\alpha = 0.025$'. Note that the level of significance for a two-tailed test must be split between the two tails. In Excel, use **CHISQ.INV(0.025,df)** for the lower critical limit and **CHISQ.INV(0.975,df)** (or **CHISQ.INV.RT(0.025,df)**) for the upper critical limit respectively.

8.8 Using Excel (2016) for Single Population Tests

In hypothesis tests for a single mean and a single proportion, Excel functions can be used to compute the *z-crit* and *t-crit* limits for the regions of acceptance and rejection (Step 2) as well as the *p*-value for a given sample test statistic (Step 3).

*   For the *z-crit* limits, use **NORM.S.INV(probability)** with a given significance level, α.
    For example, for a two-tailed hypothesis test (either for single mean when σ is known, or a single proportion) with $\alpha = 0.05$, the lower *z-crit* limit is found using **NORM.S.INV(0.025)** and upper *z-crit* limit is found using **NORM.S.INV(0.975)**.
    NORM.S.INV(0.025) = −1.96
    NORM.S.INV(0.975) = 1.96

- For *t-crit* limits, use either **T.INV.2T** for a two-tailed test, or **T.INV** for a one-tailed test. For example, for a two-tailed hypothesis test for a single mean when σ is unknown, with $\alpha = 0.05$ and sample size $n = 24$, then the *lower* and *upper t-crit* limits are found using **T.INV.2T(0.05,23)** = 2.069. Thus *t-crit* (lower) = -2.069 and *t-crit* (upper) = $+2.069$.

  If the hypothesis test is one-sided with $\alpha = 0.05$ and $n = 24$, then the *t-crit* limit for a *lower-tailed* test is derived from **T.INV(0.05,23)** = -1.714 while the *t-crit* limit for an *upper-tailed* test is found by using the cumulative probability of 0.95 as follows **T.INV(0.95,23)** = 1.714.

- The *p*-value of a test is computed using either the **NORM.S.DIST(z,cumulative)** if the sample test statistic is *z-stat*; or one of **T.DIST** or **T.DIST.RT** functions, if the sample test statistic is *t-stat*.

  - For *z-stat*: For example, given *z-stat* = 2.43 for a one-sided (upper-tailed) hypothesis test, then the appropriate *p*-value is **1 – NORM.S.DIST(2.43,True)** = $1 - 0.99245$ = 0.00755. If this was a two-tailed hypothesis test, then the *p*-value is 2×0.00755 = 0.0151.

  - For *t-stat*: For example, given *t-stat* = 1.32 with $n = 31$, for a one-sided (upper-tailed) hypothesis test, then the appropriate *p*-value is **T.DIST.RT(1.32,30)** = 0.0984.

    For a one-sided (lower-tailed) hypothesis test with *t-stat* = -1.32 and $n = 31$, the appropriate *p*-value is **T.DIST(–1.32,30,True)** = 0.0984.

    If this was a two-tailed hypothesis test, the *p*-value = **T.DIST.2T(1.32,30)** = 0.1968. Note that this function requires a *positive t-stat* value only.

Note that Excel's Data Analysis add-in *does not offer* one sample tests.

8.9 Using X-Static for Single Population Tests

The following one-sample tests can be conducted using **X-Static**

- Test for a single population mean (σ is known) :   *z*-Test: Single Mean
- Test for a single population mean (σ is unknown):   *t*-Test: Single Mean
- Test for a single population proportion: *z*-Test: Single Proportion
- Test for a single population variance: **Chi-square: Single Variance Test**

8.10 Summary

This chapter introduced the concept of hypothesis testing as a process by which claims/ assertions that are made about population parameter central location values can be tested statistically. Such claims or assertions are supported or refuted on the basis of sample evidence.

The five steps of hypothesis testing were identified and explained. The full hypothesis testing procedure was illustrated on population parameters for a single population: the single population mean, the single population proportion, and the single population variance.

The process of identifying the correct nature of the hypothesis test – whether the test is two-tailed, one-sided lower-tailed or one-sided upper-tailed – was emphasised. In addition, the chapter covered the appropriate formulation of the null hypothesis (which must always contain the equality sign) and the alternative hypothesis, based on the wording of the management question. Incorrect formulations lead to invalid management conclusions at the end of the test procedure.

The chapter showed that the selection of the appropriate sample test statistic for hypothesis tests for a single population mean depends on knowing the population standard deviation. If it is known, the z-distribution is used to derive the sample test statistic. Alternatively, if the population standard deviation is unknown and estimated using the sample standard deviation, then the t-distribution must be used to derive the sample test statistic.

A hypothesis test is also shown for a single population variance where the focus of a management question falls on the variability (standard deviation) of a variable (rather than its mean value). The test statistic for a single variance test is the chi-square statistic (χ^2).

The p-value approach to hypothesis testing was introduced as an alternative way of concluding whether to accept or reject the null hypothesis. It uses probabilities as a measure of the strength (or intensity) of the sample evidence to establish whether H_0 is likely to be true or not.

Finally, Excel functions were introduced to show how Excel can be used to assist in the computations of the hypothesis testing process. The computations of z-crit, t-crit, χ^2-crit and the p-value were illustrated. **X-Static** can be used for all single population tests.

Chapter 9 will extend the hypothesis testing process further by comparing population parameters between two populations. The population parameters covered are both central location measures, namely the difference between two population means and the difference between two population proportions, and variances (equality of test between two variances).

Exercises

This symbol denotes data available online

1   What is meant by the term 'hypothesis testing'?

2   What determines whether a claim about a population parameter value is accepted as probably true or rejected as probably false?

3   Name the five steps of hypothesis testing.

4   What information is required to determine the critical limits for the region of acceptance of a null hypothesis?

5   If $-1.96 \leq z \leq 1.96$ defines the limits for the region of acceptance of a two-tailed hypothesis test and z-stat = 2.44, what statistical conclusion can be drawn from these findings?

6   (a)   For each of the following hypothesis tests, state whether the test is two-tailed, one-sided upper-tailed, or one-sided lower-tailed, and find the appropriate area of acceptance.

   (b)   Calculate the appropriate sample test statistic from the given sample information and decide whether there is sufficient sample evidence to reject the null hypothesis in favour of the alternative hypothesis.

   (c)   Compute the p-value for each of the test statistics using the **NORM.S.DIST**, **NORM.DIST**, or **T.DIST** (or **T.DIST.RT** or **T.DIST.2T**) function in Excel. Interpret the meaning of each p-value.

   (i) $H_0: \mu \leq 560$ $H_1: \mu > 560$
   $\bar{x} = 577$ $c = 86$ $n = 120$ $\alpha = 0.05$

   (ii) $H_0: \pi \geq 0.72$ $H_1: \pi < 0.72$
   $x = 216$ $n = 330$ $\alpha = 0.10$

   (iii) $H_0: \mu = 8.2$ $H_1: \mu \neq 8.2$
   $\bar{x} = 9.6$ $s = 2.9$ $n = 30$ $\alpha = 0.01$

   (iv) $H_0: \mu \geq 18$ $H_1: \mu < 18$
   $\bar{x} = 14.6$ $s = 3.4$ $n = 12$ $\alpha = 0.01$

   (v) $H_0: \pi = 0.32$ $H_1: \pi \neq 0.32$
   $x = 68$ $n = 250$ $\alpha = 0.05$

7   The manager of a large shopping mall in Knysna believes that visitors to the mall spend, on average, 85 minutes in the mall on any one occasion. To test this belief, the manager commissioned a study, which found that, from a random sample of 132 visitors to the mall, the average visiting time was 80.5 minutes. Assume a population standard deviation of 25 minutes and that visiting time is approximately normally distributed.

   (a)   Formulate the null and alternative hypothesis for this test situation.

   (b)   Which test statistic (z or t) is appropriate for this test? Why?

   (c)   Conduct a hypothesis test for a single mean at the 5% significance level to support or refute the manager's belief. What management conclusion would be drawn from the findings?

   (d)   Use Excel's **NORM.S.DIST** function to compute the p-value for the test.

   (e)   What statistical and management conclusion could be drawn from the p-value?

8   A supermarket chain believes that customers to its stores spend half-an-hour *or more*, on average, doing their purchases. A consumer body wants to verify this claim. They observed the entry and departure times of 86 randomly selected customers from

supermarkets in the chain. The sample average time in the store was 27.9 minutes. Assume a population standard deviation of 10.5 minutes and that shopping time is approximately normally distributed.

(a) Formulate the null and alternative hypothesis for this test scenario.
(b) Which test statistic (z or t) is appropriate for this test? Why?
(c) Test the validity of the supermarket's belief by conducting a hypothesis test for a single mean. Use $\alpha = 0.01$. What conclusion can be drawn?
(d) Use Excel's **NORM.S.DIST** function to compute the p-value for the test and draw the appropriate management conclusion based on the p-value.

9   The Port and Customs authorities at Cape Town harbour claim that imported textile consignments are cleared *within* an average of 72 hours of the goods being offloaded from a vessel. A local textile importer is not convinced of this, and believes that the average clearance time is *much longer*. He analysed documents of 46 recent consignments and found that the average clearance time was 75.9 hours. Assume a population standard deviation of 18 hours and that clearance time is approximately normally distributed.

Are the harbour authorities working to their stated clearance times?

(a) Formulate a suitable null and alternative hypothesis for this test situation.
(b) Test whether the local importer's claim is justified using a hypothesis test for a single mean. Use $\alpha = 0.10$. What conclusion can be drawn?
(c) Compute the p-value for this test using Excel's **NORM.S.DIST** function and draw the appropriate management conclusion.

10   The Department of Health is concerned that the average percentage mark-up on a particular vitamin product is *more than* 40%. To test their concern, they sampled 76 pharmacies that sell the product, and found that the mean percentage mark-up was 44.1%. Assume that the population standard deviation of the percentage mark-up is 14.7%.

(a) What is the appropriate test statistic for this management scenario? Why?
(b) Formulate the null and alternative hypothesis for this test situation.
(c) Conduct an appropriate statistical test at the 1% level of significance to determine whether the Department of Health's concern is justified. What conclusion can be drawn from the findings?
(d) Use Excel's **NORM.S.DIST** function to find the p-value for the test and draw the appropriate management conclusion.

11   The mass of a standard loaf of white bread is, by law, meant to be 700 g. The Ryeband Bakery, which supplies outlets throughout the Eastern Cape, regularly checks the masses of its standard loaf of white bread. If their bread is underweight, on average, they are liable to a fine by the provincial Department of Health, whose inspectors undertake random checks; if the bread is overweight, on average, the bakery is wasting its ingredients.

On a given day, a random sample of 64 loaves is selected and weighed. The sample mean mass was found to be 695 g with a sample standard deviation of 21 g. Assume that the mass of bread is approximately normally distributed.

(a) Is Ryeband Bakery complying with provincial government regulations, while also not wasting its own resources? Formulate the null and alternative hypothesis. Conduct a hypothesis test for a single mean at the 5% level of significance. What statistical and management conclusions can be drawn?

(b) Use Excel's **T.DIST** (or **T.DIST.RT** or **T.DIST.2T**) function to compute the *p*-value for the test. Interpret the findings for the Eastern Cape's provincial Department of Health.

(c) Reformulate the null and alterative hypothesis test if it is more important for the bakery to comply with government regulations (i.e. to ensure that the average mass of a standard loaf of white bread is not less than 700 g). Conduct the test at the 5% level of significance and draw the statistical and management conclusions.

12 Moir's recently launched a new-flavoured pudding. The marketing manager now wants to assess the product's success in the marketplace. If average sales per week are *less than* R5 500 per outlet, the product will be withdrawn. The results from a sample of 18 supermarket outlets countrywide showed that average sales per week were R5 275, with a sample standard deviation of R788. Assume weekly sales are normally distributed.

(a) Should the new pudding flavour be withdrawn? Advise the marketing manager by performing an appropriate hypothesis test at the 10% level of significance. Also show the null and alternative hypothesis for this test.

(b) Use Excel's **T.DIST** (or **T.DIST.RT** or **T.DIST.2T**) function to find the *p*-value for this test. Interpret the findings for the marketing manager.

13 A company, Marathon Products, has purchased a large quantity of steel wire from Gate and Fence (Pty) Ltd. The supplier, Gate and Fence (Pty) Ltd, claims that the wire has a mean tensile strength (i.e. breaking strength) of *more than* 80 kg. Marathon Products will only accept the consignment of wire if this claim can be supported. Their quality controller sampled 26 pieces of this wire and found that the sample mean tensile strength was 81.3 kg with a standard deviation of 3.6 kg. Assume that tensile strength is approximately normally distributed.

Should Marathon Products accept this steel wire consignment?

(a) Conduct a hypothesis test for a single mean at the 5% significant level and advise the management of Marathon Products accordingly. Show the null and alternative hypothesis for this test.

(b) Compute the *p*-value for this test using Excel's **T.DIST** (or **T.DIST.RT** or **T.DIST.2T**) function, and interpret the findings in the management context.

14 One-litre cartons of milk are advertised to contain 1 ℓ of milk. To test this claim, the Consumer Council of South Africa measured a random selection of 20 cartons from supermarket shelves. They found that the average fill was 0.982 litres, with a sample standard deviation of 0.068 ℓ. Assume that carton fills are approximately normally distributed.

(a) Formulate the null and alternative hypothesis to test the claim that one-litre cartons of milk are being *underfilled*. Conduct a hypothesis test for a single mean using $\alpha = 0.05$.

(b) Use Excel's **T.DIST** (or **T.DIST.RT** or **T.DIST.2T**) function to find the *p*-value for this test. Interpret the findings for the Consumer Council of South Africa.

15 A local radio station advertises that *at least* 30% of listeners in its reception area tune into its daily news broadcasts. A company that is considering advertising on this radio station in its news slot wants to test the validity of this statement. They will place adverts in the news timeslots if the radio station's statement can be verified.

The company conducted a telephone survey of 400 randomly selected listeners to test the radio station's statement. If 106 listeners in the survey indicated that they tuned into the local radio's news broadcasts, should the company place adverts in the radio station's news timeslots?

(a) Recommend a course of action to the management of the company, based on the results of a hypothesis test for a single proportion conducted at the 5% level of significance.

(b) Compute the *p*-value of the test statistic using Excel's **NORM.S.DIST** function. Interpret the *p*-value for the management of the company.

(c) Confirm the *p*-value found in (b) by using Excel's **NORM.DIST** function.

16 A motor vehicle insurance advisor stated recently in a newspaper report that *more than* 60% of Cape Town motorists do not have motor vehicle insurance. A random survey amongst 150 motorists found that 54 do have motor vehicle insurance.

(a) Is the motor vehicle insurance advisor's claim valid? Formulate the null and alternative hypothesis and conduct a hypothesis test for a single proportion, using $\alpha = 0.05$.

(b) Use the **NORM.S.DIST** function in Excel to compute the *p*-value of the test statistic. Interpret its value in terms of the insurance advisor's claim.

17 'Churn' is a term used to describe the rate at which a company loses customers to its competitors. In the telecommunications industry, it is believed that the churn rate between cellphone service providers (e.g. Vodacom, MTN, Virgin Mobile, 8.ta and Cell C) is *not more than* 15%.

A telecommunications analyst surveyed a random sample of 560 cellphone subscribers and found that 96 of them had changed service provider within the past year.

(a) Is there sufficient statistical evidence at the 10% significance level to conclude that the churn rate in the telecommunications industry exceeds 15%? Perform a hypothesis test for a single proportion and report the findings.

(b) Use the **NORM.S.DIST** function in Excel to compute the *p*-value for the test. Interpret the findings for the telecommunications analyst.

(c) Confirm the *p*-value found in (b) by using Excel's **NORM.DIST** function.

18 A farming cooperative in the Free State buys barley seeds for its farmer members from seed merchants. A particular seed merchant claims that their barley seeds have *at least* a 90% germination rate. Before the farming cooperative will buy from this seed merchant, they want to verify this claim.

A random sample of 300 barley seeds supplied by this seed merchant was tested, and it was found that only 260 seeds germinated.

(a) Is there sufficient statistical evidence at the 1% significance level to justify the purchase of barley seeds from this seed merchant? Conduct a hypothesis test for a single proportion, and report the findings to the Free State farming cooperative.

(b) Use the **NORM.S.DIST** function in Excel to compute the *p*-value for the test. Interpret the findings for the Free State farming cooperative.

(c) Confirm the *p*-value found in (b) by using Excel's **NORM.DIST** function.

For the following Excel-based exercises, use the **Descriptive Statistics** option in Excel's **Data Analysis** to compute appropriate descriptive measures to derive the test statistic, *t-stat*. Then compute the *t-crit* value(s) (using **T.INV** or **T.INV.2T**) based on the given level of significance of each test, and the *p*-value of the test (using **T.DIST** [or **T.DIST.RT** or **T.DIST.2T**]).

19 X8.19 – cost-to-income

A company's cost-to-income ratio is a measure of its ability to control its costs. The lower the ratio (expressed as a percentage), the better the cost management is within the company. For a company to remain profitable and attract investment, a rule of thumb exists that states that the company's cost-to-income ratio should be *less than* 75%.

An investment analyst wished to test this rule of thumb amongst JSE companies, so selected a sample of 50 and recorded their cost-to-income ratios.

Test, at the 5% significance level, whether the average cost-to-income ratio amongst all JSE companies adheres to the rule of thumb. Formulate the null and alternative hypothesis and interpret the findings.

20 X8.20 – kitchenware

The management of a kitchenware company is evaluating the financial viability of one of its stores located in Claremont, Cape Town. One measure they would like to estimate is the mean value of purchases at this store. If the mean value of all purchases (in rand) is likely to be less than R150, the management will consider closing the branch.

The management selected a random sample of 50 invoices of recent sales and recorded each transaction value (in rand).

(a) Construct a histogram using the **Histogram** option in **Data Analysis** to check the assumption of normality. Does the data appear to be normally distributed? Comment.

(b) What recommendation would you make to the management about the continued trading of this Claremont store? Base your recommendation on the results of a hypothesis test for a single mean conducted at the 5% significance level. Show the null and alternative hypothesis.

21 X8.21 – flight delays

The Airports Company of South Africa (ACSA) is investigating the length of flight delays on departure. It is acceptable to have flight delays due to various environmental and operational factors, provided these delays *do not exceed* 10 minutes, on average. ACSA management would conduct an investigation into the causes of lengthy flight delays if the average delay significantly exceeds 10 minutes. To test whether flight delays do not exceed 10 minutes on average, a random sample of 80 delayed flights over the past month were drawn from airport records.

(a) Use the **Histogram** option in **Data Analysis** to check the assumption of normality. Comment on the findings.

(b) What recommendation would you make to ACSA management about the average length of flight delays? Should they conduct a detailed investigation into the causes of flight delays? Base your recommendation on the results of a hypothesis test for a single mean conducted at a 10% level of significance. Show the null and alternative hypothesis for this management question.

22   X8.22 – medical claims

The manager of the claims department of a medical scheme can motivate to employ additional staff if she can show that the average number of claims being received for processing per day is *more than* 180. To motivate her need for additional staff, the manager selected a random sample of 100 days over the past year and recorded the number of claims received on each of these days.

(a)   Use the **Histogram** option in **Data Analysis** to check the assumption of normality. Does the data appear to be normally distributed? Comment.

(b)   Does the claims manager have good statistical evidence to support her request for additional staff? Conduct a hypothesis test for a single mean at the 1% level of significance. Show the null and alternative hypothesis and make a recommendation to the claims manager.

23   X8.23 – newspaper readership

The *Guardian* newspaper claims that it has at least 40% of the readership market. To test this claim, a print media analyst conducted a survey amongst newspaper readers. Each of the 120 randomly sampled readers was asked to identify which newspaper (*Voice, Sun, Mail* or *Guardian*) they buy and read most often.

(a)   Use the **PivotTable** option in the **Data** tab to produce a frequency table (one-pivot table) and then construct a bar chart of newspaper readership preferences using the **Column** option in the **Insert > Chart** tab. Interpret the summary statistics.

(b)   Formulate the null and alternative hypothesis to examine the *Guardian's* claim.

(c)   Test the *Guardian's* claim by conducting a hypothesis test for a single proportion at the 5% level of significance. Is the *Guardian's* claim overstated? Justify.

24   X8.24 – citrus products

Fruitco is an organisation that distributes and markets citrus products throughout the country. It believes that the general awareness of the nutritional value of citrus products is low amongst consumers. Fruitco's current view is that no more than 15% of consumers have a high level of awareness and understanding of the health benefits of consuming citrus products regularly.

  Before conducting a national awareness campaign, Fruitco ran a pilot study amongst a random sample of 170 consumers to gauge their level of awareness of the nutritional value of citrus products. Their awareness responses were classified as low, moderate or high.

(a)   Use the **PivotTable** option in the **Data** tab to produce a frequency table (one-pivot table) of the awareness levels of the nutritional value of citrus products. Then construct a bar chart of these awareness levels using the **Column** option in the **Insert > Chart** tab. Interpret the summary statistics findings.

(b)   Fruitco will launch a national awareness campaign if there is sufficient sample evidence that the level of high consumer awareness is no more than 15% amongst all consumers. Should Fruitco launch a national awareness campaign?

(i)   Formulate the null and alternative hypothesis to Fruitco's management question.

(ii)   Conduct a hypothesis test for a single proportion at the 1% level of significance.

(iii)   What recommendation would you make to the Fruitco management? Justify.

25   X8.25 – aluminium scrap

The plant manager at an aluminium processing plant in KZN recorded the percentage of scrap produced daily by a sheet-rolling machine. Scrap is measured as a percentage of daily machine output.

(a)   Use the **Histogram** option from **Data Analysis** to examine whether the daily percentage scrap from the machine is normally distributed. Comment on the findings.

(b)   Use the **Descriptive Statistics** option from **Data Analysis** to derive the 95% confidence interval estimate for the actual mean percentage of scrap produced daily by the machine. Interpret the findings.

(c)   It is company policy that a machine must be stopped and fully serviced if its average daily percentage scrap is 3.75% *or more*. Test, at the 5% significance level, whether the machine is due for a full service. Use the **T.INV** or **T.INV.RT** function to find the critical test statistic. Use the findings from (b) to compute *t-stat*.

26   A machine is set to produce 5-m-long pipes with a population standard deviation (σ) of 3 cm. For a random sample of $n = 26$ pipes, the sample standard deviation was found to be 3.46 cm. Assume that pipe lengths are normally distributed. Use $\alpha = 0.05$ to test that the product specification on *variability* is being met. i.e. test $H_0: \sigma^2 \leq 9$ versus $H_1: \sigma^2 > 9$.

27   For a random sample of 20 observations, the sample variance $s^2 = 49.3$. Assume that the population is normally distributed. Use $\alpha = 0.1$ to test $H_0: \sigma^2 \leq 30$ versus $H_1: \sigma^2 > 30$.

28   The *variability* in household insurance claim values for lost/damaged/stolen items is believed – by the insurance industry – to be $\sigma^2 = R5\,625$. This measure is used to set annual insurance premium rates. Test at the 5% level of significance whether this is still a valid measure of variability in claim values using a sample of 32 randomly selected claims with $s = R84$. i.e. test $H_0: \sigma^2 = 5\,625$ versus $H_1: \sigma^2 \neq 5\,625$.

29   X8.29 – pain relief

A pharmaceutical company has produced a new headache pill that is claimed to reduce the *variability in time* for the pill to relieve a headache. Their current headache pill has a proven *variability in time* for pain relief of $\sigma^2 = 1.8$ min. A study was conducted on 16 randomly selected headache sufferers and the time to pain relief (based on neurological measurements using sensors) after taking the new headache pill was recorded. Does the sample evidence support the pharmaceutical company's belief that the new headache pill significantly *reduces* the *variability in time* to pain relief relative to their current headache pill? Use $\alpha = 0.01$. (i.e. test $H_0: \sigma^2 \geq 1.8$ versus $H_1: \sigma^2 < 1.8$).

| 6.32 | 5.68 | 7.54 | 7.78 | 5.69 | 5.71 | 8.04 | 5.35 |
| 8.06 | 7.28 | 6.75 | 5.77 | 6.18 | 6.46 | 6.31 | 6.24 |

Note: $\bar{x} = 6.5725$; $s = 0.9004$ (Use **AVERAGE(range)** and **STDEV.S(range)**.)

Hypothesis Testing: Comparison between Two Populations (Means, Proportions and Variances)

Outcomes

When two samples of a random variable are drawn, the question most commonly asked is whether they come from the same population. This chapter uses hypothesis-testing procedures to determine whether two samples represent one population or two distinct populations.

If the sample data is numeric, the hypothesis test compares the differences between the two sample means, or tests for equality of two population variances. If the sample data is categorical, a difference between two sample proportions hypothesis test is conducted. This chapter also illustrates how to set up null and alternative hypotheses for directional tests between two sample means or proportions.

After studying this chapter, you should be able to:

- distinguish between *difference* in *mean*, *variance* and *proportion* tests
- correctly formulate the null and alternative hypotheses from the management question
- recognise when to apply the z-test statistic or the *t-test* statistic for two-sample means tests
- perform the hypothesis test for two-sample tests between population means
- perform the hypothesis test for differences between two population proportions
- perform the hypothesis test for equality of variances
- correctly interpret the statistical findings in a management context.

9.1 Introduction

In Chapter 8 hypothesis tests were conducted for a single population parameter, namely a single population mean, if the random variable was numeric (e.g. age, distance or price), or a single population proportion, if the random variable was categorical (e.g. preferred brand, gender or transport mode).

This chapter uses hypothesis testing to *compare* for differences between two population parameters. The statistical question being asked is whether the samples are drawn from different populations or the same population. If the populations are different (i.e. their central location measures differ), then the factor that distinguishes the samples is assumed to explain the differences in the results. If the populations are the same (i.e. their central location measures are equal), there is no influence from the factor that distinguishes the two samples. This insight could assist managers in decision-making, depending on whether differences exist or not.

In this chapter, hypothesis testing will be used to examine for:

- a difference between two population means $(\mu_1 - \mu_2)$ (for numeric variables)
- a difference between two population proportions $(\pi_1 - \pi_2)$ (for categorical variables)
- the equality of variances between two populations $(\sigma_1^2 = \sigma_2^2)$ (for numeric variables).

Two-sample hypothesis tests are widely applied in management to find out if differences in means, proportions or variances can be attributed to an identifiable influence.

Illustrations

- In marketing, a manager can test the belief that 'proportionately more females than males prefer rooibos tea'. (Influencing factor = 'gender'.)
- In finance, portfolio managers believe that 'an equity-weighted portfolio produces higher mean returns than a bond-weighted portfolio'. (Influencing factor = 'investment types'.)
- In manufacturing, a production manager would like to know whether 'on-the-job training leads to higher worker output, on average, than classroom training'. (Influencing factor = 'training method'.)

Conclusions drawn from hypothesis tests that compare differences between central location measures or variances of two populations provide managers with statistically verified findings on which to base their decisions.

9.2 Hypothesis Test for the Difference between Two Means $(\mu_1 - \mu_2)$ for Independent Samples: Assume Population Standard Deviations are Known

$$(\bar{x}_1 - \bar{x}_2) \to (\mu_1 - \mu_2)$$

When a claim or statement is made about the difference between two population means for the *same* random variable, the claim can be tested using the *sampling distribution of the difference between two sample means*.

Here are some examples:

- Is the mean *monthly turnover* of the Vodacom outlet at Tyger Valley Centre the same as that of the Cavendish Square outlet?
- Is the average *age* of female shoppers at Truworths lower (i.e. are they younger?) than the average age of female shoppers at Foschini?
- Are the mean *years of experience* of technicians at Eskom different from that of those at Telkom?

In each example, a separate sample is drawn from each group and then compared. In this section and in section 9.3, we assume that, in each case, the *two samples drawn* are *independent* of each other (i.e. they are unrelated).

The following information is required to perform such two-sample hypothesis tests:

- the *sample means* for each independent sample, $\bar{x}_1$ and $\bar{x}_2$
- the *sample size* for each sample, n_1 and n_2
- each population's *standard deviation*, σ_1 and σ_2
- a level of significance, α.

The appropriate test statistic, when the population standard deviations are known, is *z-stat*.

The *z* standardisation formula is as follows:

$$z\text{-stat} = \frac{(\bar{x}_1 - \bar{x}_2) - (\mu_1 - \mu_2)}{\sqrt{\frac{\sigma_1^2}{n_1} + \frac{\sigma_2^2}{n_2}}}$$

9.1

Where: $(\bar{x}_1 - \bar{x}_2)$ = the difference in sample means
$(\mu_1 - \mu_2)$ = the difference in population means

The numerator measures the difference between the sample statistic $(\bar{x}_1 - \bar{x}_2)$ and the hypothesised population parameter $(\mu_1 - \mu_2)$. The denominator measures the standard error of the sample statistic. Then, *z-stat* measures how many standard error units that the sample statistic, $(\bar{x}_1 - \bar{x}_2)$, lies from the hypothesised population parameter, $(\mu_1 - \mu_2)$.

Example 9.1 Courier Service Study

PQ Printers is evaluating the delivery time of two courier delivery services in Johannesburg. Their initial belief is that there is no difference between the average delivery times of the two courier services.

To examine this view, PQ Printers used both courier services daily on a random basis over a period of three months for deliveries to similar destinations. A dispatch clerk in the marketing department recorded *delivery times*. Courier A was used 60 times over this period and the sample mean delivery time was 42 minutes. Courier B was used 48 times over the same period and their sample mean delivery time was 38 minutes.

Assume that the population standard deviation of delivery times for courier A is 14 minutes, and for courier B assume it is 10 minutes. Also assume that delivery times are normally distributed.

(See Excel file C9.1 – *courier times*.)

Management Questions

1. PQ Printers wishes to sign a one-year contract with one of the courier companies after this trial period. Test the hypothesis, at the 5% level of significance, that there is *no difference* between the mean delivery times of the two couriers.

2. PQ Printers would like to know whether courier A is *slower*, on average, than courier B in its delivery times to clients. Test statistically, at the 5% level of significance, whether courier A's mean delivery time is *longer than* (i.e. greater than) courier B's mean delivery time.

Solution

1. An inspection of the two sample means indicates that courier A appears to take longer, on average, to deliver printed documents to clients than courier B. The question that needs to be addressed statistically is whether this observed difference in sample means is statistically significant (i.e. a genuine difference), or only due to sampling error (i.e. random sampling or chance sampling). Rigorous hypothesis testing is now used to answer this question.

This hypothesis test can be classified as:

- a *difference between two means test*, because the random variable is numeric and the mean delivery times between two similar, but independent, populations is being measured
- a *two-sided hypothesis test*, because the difference between the mean delivery times of the two courier services is being tested for a specified value only, namely 'no difference'. This implies that the specified value of the population parameter is zero (i.e. $\mu_1 - \mu_2 = 0$).

Step 1: Define the null and alternative hypotheses
Let population 1 = courier service A and population 2 = courier service B. Then:

$H_0: \mu_1 - \mu_2 = 0$ This represents PQ Printers' belief of *no difference*.
$H_1: \mu_1 - \mu_2 \neq 0$

Step 2: Determine the region of acceptance of the null hypothesis
A level of significance is required to find the critical z-limits. We are given $\alpha = 0.05$.

For a two-tailed test, the critical z-limits are given by $z\text{-}crit = \pm 1.96$ (Table 1, Appendix 1). Thus, the region of acceptance for H_0 is $-1.96 \leq z \leq +1.96$.

The following decision rule then applies:

- Accept H_0 if z-*stat* falls within the limits of -1.96 and $+1.96$ (inclusive).
- Reject H_0 if z-*stat* falls either below -1.96 or above $+1.96$.

Step 3: Calculate the sample test statistic (z-*stat*)
The z-*stat* test statistic is derived from the following two sets of sample data:

Sample 1 (courier A)	Sample 2 (courier B)
$n_1 = 60$	$n_2 = 48$
$\bar{x}_1 = 42$ minutes	$\bar{x}_2 = 38$ minutes
$\sigma_1 = 14$ minutes	$\sigma_2 = 10$ minutes

The appropriate z-$stat$ sample statistic is calculated using Formula 9.1 as follows:

$$z\text{-}stat = \frac{(\bar{x}_1 - \bar{x}_2) - (\mu_1 - \mu_2)}{\sqrt{\frac{\sigma_1^2}{n_1} + \frac{\sigma_2^2}{n_2}}}$$

$$= \frac{(42 - 38) - (0)}{\sqrt{\frac{14^2}{60} + \frac{10^2}{48}}} = 1.73$$

This means that the sample statistic $(\bar{x}_1 - \bar{x}_2)$ is 1.73 standard errors above the population parameter $(\mu_1 - \mu_2)$ that it is testing. Step 4 determines whether this is close enough to accept H_0 as the true state of nature.

Step 4: Compare the sample test statistic to the region of acceptance

The sample test statistic, z-$stat = 1.73$ lies *within* the region of acceptance of $-1.96 \le z \le +1.96$.

Figure 9.1 shows the sample test statistic (z-$stat$) in relation to the regions of acceptance and rejection.

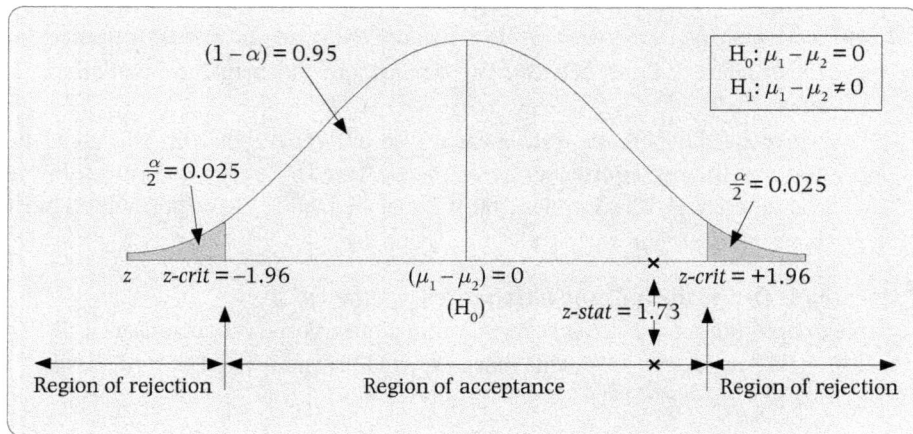

Figure 9.1 Courier service study – z-$stat$ and region of acceptance

Step 5: Draw statistical and management conclusions

Statistical Conclusion

Accept H_0 at the 5% level of significance. The sample evidence is not strong enough to reject H_0 in favour of H_1 at $\alpha = 0.05$. The null hypothesis is therefore probably true.

Management Conclusion

It can be concluded, with 95% confidence, that there is no significance difference in the mean delivery times between the two courier service companies.

2   The hypothesis test can be classified as:
- a *difference between two means test* (same reason as before)
- a *one-sided upper-tailed hypothesis test*, since it is required to show that courier A's mean delivery time is greater (slower) than courier B's mean delivery time (i.e. is $\mu_1 - \mu_2 > 0$?)

Step 1: Define the null and alternative hypotheses

Again, let population 1 = courier A and population 2 = courier B. Then:

$$H_0: \mu_1 - \mu_2 \leq 0$$
$$H_1: \mu_1 - \mu_2 > 0 \qquad \text{This represents the client's management question.}$$

The alternative hypothesis indicates that courier A is slower, on average, than courier B.

Step 2: Determine the region of acceptance of the null hypothesis

Given $\alpha = 0.05$ (5% level of significance).

Since this is a *one-sided upper-tailed* test, the critical z-limit identifies an area of 5% in the *upper tail* only of the z-distribution. Then $z\text{-}crit = +1.645$ (Table 1, Appendix 1). Thus, the region of acceptance for H_0 is $z \leq +1.645$.

The following decision rule then applies:
- Accept H_0 if *z-stat* falls at or below +1.645.
- Reject H_0 if *z-stat* falls above +1.645.

Step 3: Calculate the sample test statistic (z-stat)

Since *z-stat* is based on the same sample evidence as in (a) above, the same *z-stat* value applies to this management question. Thus $z\text{-}stat = 1.73$.

Step 4: Compare the sample test statistic to the region of acceptance

The sample test statistic, $z\text{-}stat = 1.73$ lies *outside* the region of acceptance. Refer to Figure 9.2, which shows *z-stat* in relation to the regions of acceptance and rejection.

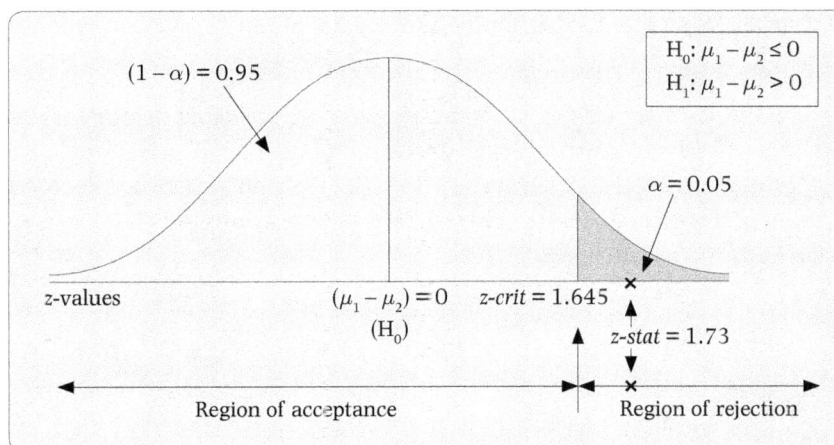

Figure 9.2 Courier service study – *z-stat* and region of acceptance

Step 5: Draw statistical and management conclusions

Statistical Conclusion

Reject H_0 at the 5% level of significance. The sample evidence is strong enough to reject H_0 in favour of H_1 at $\alpha = 0.05$. The alternative hypothesis is therefore probably true.

Management Conclusion

It can be concluded, with 95% confidence, that courier A is significantly slower, on average, than courier B.

As a management recommendation, PQ Printers should sign a contract with courier B, because, on average, it delivers faster to their clients than courier A.

Note that in (1), which was a two-tailed test, H_0 was accepted, while in (2), which was a one-tailed test, H_0 was rejected, for the same level of significance.

The reason for this apparent contradiction is that one-tailed hypothesis tests (directional tests) are more discriminating (sensitive), as all the Type I error is contained in only one tail, instead of being divided between the two tails. This increases the likelihood of rejecting the null hypothesis when it is false.

9.3 Hypothesis Test for the Difference between Two Means $(\mu_1 - \mu_2)$ for Independent Samples: Assume Population Standard Deviations are Unknown, but Equal

$$(\bar{x}_1 - \bar{x}_2) \rightarrow (\mu_1 - \mu_2)$$

When the population standard deviations (σ_1 and σ_2) are *unknown*, but assumed to be equal ($\sigma_1 = \sigma_2$), the appropriate sample test statistic for the difference between two means is the *student t* statistic. (Note that the test for the assumption of *equal population variances* is given in section 9.7).

Thus, in hypotheses tests for the *difference between two population means*, whenever the *population standard deviations* are *unknown* (but *assumed* to be *equal*):

- the *t-stat* statistic replaces the *z-stat* statistic as the test statistic for the hypothesis
- the degrees of freedom (*df*) for two independent sample means tests is ($n_1 + n_2 - 2$)
- the *t-stat* formula (required at Step 3) is:

$$t\text{-}stat = \frac{(\bar{x}_1 - \bar{x}_2) - (\mu_1 - \mu_2)}{\sqrt{s_p^2 \left(\frac{1}{n_1} + \frac{1}{n_2} \right)}} \qquad 9.2$$

Where: $\quad s_p^2 = \dfrac{(n_1 - 1)s_1^2 + (n_2 - 1)s_2^2}{n_1 + n_2 - 2}$

The s_p^2 statistic is called a **pooled variance**. It is a weighted average of the two sample variances and is used to estimate the common population variance, σ^2, when the two *population variances* are unknown, but are assumed to be *equal*. This *t-stat* formula is called the **pooled-variances *t-test***.

Note: If the combined sample size $(n_1 + n_2)$ exceeds 40, then *z-stat* (Formula 9.1) can be used as a good approximation to *t-stat* (Formula 9.2) based on the Central Limit Theorem (CLT).

Example 9.2 Corporate Financial Performance Study

A financial analyst wished to establish whether the mean ROI% (return on investment per cent) of financial companies is *greater than* the mean ROI% of manufacturing companies.

The financial analyst randomly sampled 28 financial companies and found their sample mean ROI% to be 18.714% with a sample standard deviation of 9.645%. For a random sample of 24 manufacturing companies, the sample mean ROI% was 15.125% with a sample standard deviation of 8.823%.
  (See Excel file C9.2 – *ROI performance*.)

Management Question

Can the financial analyst conclude that financial companies have a *higher* ROI%, on average, than manufacturing companies? Conduct a hypothesis test at the 5% level of significance.

Solution

This hypothesis test can be classified as:
- a *difference between two means tests* (i.e. between financial and manufacturing ROI%s)
- a *one-sided upper-tailed test* since it is required to show that the mean ROI% of financial companies is *greater than* the mean ROI% of manufacturing companies.

Step 1: Define the null and alternative hypotheses
Let f = the population of financial companies and m = the population of manufacturing companies. Then:

$$H_0: \mu_f - \mu_m \leq 0$$
$$H_1: \mu_f - \mu_m > 0 \quad \text{This represents the analyst's management question.}$$

Step 2: Determine the region of acceptance of the null hypothesis
Given $\alpha = 0.05$ (5% level of significance).

Also the degrees of freedom (df) for the two-sample test = 28 + 24 − 2 = 50.

Then the critical *t*-limit for this one-sided (upper-tailed) test is given by $t_{(0.05)(50)} = +1.676$ (Table 2, Appendix 1). Thus the region of acceptance for H_0 is $t \leq +1.676$.

The following decision rule then applies:
- Accept H_0 if *t-stat* lies at or below the upper limit of +1.676.
- Reject H_0 if *t-stat* lies above +1.676.

Step 3: Calculate the sample test statistic (t-stat)

Using Formula 9.2 and the sample data summarised in the following table:

Sample 1 (financial)	Sample 2 (manufacturing)
$n_1 = 28$	$n_2 = 24$
$\bar{x}_1 = 18.714\%$	$\bar{x}_2 = 15.125\%$
$s_1 = 9.645\%$	$s_2 = 8.823\%$

$$t\text{-stat} = \frac{(18.714 - 15.125) - (0)}{\sqrt{(86.0468)\left(\frac{1}{28} + \frac{1}{24}\right)}} = 1.391$$

Where: $s_p^2 = \frac{[(28 - 1)(93.026) + (24 - 1)(77.853)]}{(28 + 24 - 2)} = 86.0468$

Thus t-stat $= 1.391$.

Step 4: Compare the sample test statistic to the region of acceptance

The sample test statistic, t-stat $= 1.391$ lies *within* the region of acceptance. Refer to Figure 9.3, which shows t-stat in relation to the regions of acceptance and rejection.

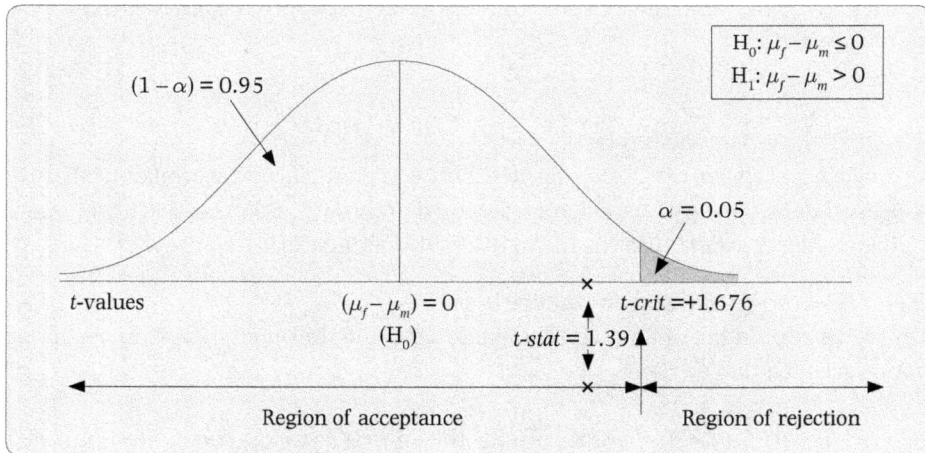

$$H_0: \mu_f - \mu_m \leq 0$$
$$H_1: \mu_f - \mu_m > 0$$

$(1 - \alpha) = 0.95$

$\alpha = 0.05$

t-values

$(\mu_f - \mu_m) = 0$
(H_0)

t-crit $= +1.676$

t-stat $= 1.39$

Region of acceptance

Region of rejection

Figure 9.3 Corporate financial performance study – *t-stat* and region of acceptance

Step 5: Draw statistical and management conclusions

Statistical Conclusion

Accept H_0 at the 5% level of significance. The null hypothesis is probably true.

Management Conclusion

The statistical evidence does not support the view that the mean ROI% of financial companies is greater than the mean ROI% of manufacturing companies.

9.4 Hypothesis Test for the Difference between Two Dependent Sample Means: The Paired *t*-test (μ_d)

$$\bar{x}_d \rightarrow \mu_d$$

When the data from two samples are *related*, the samples are *not independent* of each other. This occurs when data for a given numeric random variable is recorded either:

1   from objects that are *matched* (i.e. objects are paired in a way that makes them as similar as possible in order to isolate the impact of the attribute being tested, and often referred to as *matched pairs* testing or *AB* testing).

For example:

- to test the efficacy of a new drug/new medical procedure, patients in a treatment (experimental) group are matched to similar patients in a control (placebo) group
- to test the sales impact of two different promotion strategies in a retail chain, pairs of outlets with similar sales potential are matched and a different promotion strategy is assigned to each of the paired outlets
- to test which braking systems (hydraulic or electromagnetic) is more effective, pairs of identical 1 600 cc motor vehicles were fitted with each system and measured on stopping distance under controlled driving and road conditions.

or

2   from the *same object* measured at two different points in time or under two different circumstances as a result of an intervention (commonly known as *before/after* testing or *repeated measurements* testing).

For example:

- An employee's job performance is recorded both *before* and *after* a training programme to observe whether any difference in performance has occurred due to the training programme.
- A patient's blood pressure is recorded *before* a drug is administered and then again *after* the treatment to see whether the treatment has had any effect on blood pressure.
- Internet usage of subscribers *last year* is compared to the same subscribers' internet usage *this year* to determine whether there is any change in usage levels.

Regardless of whether the two samples of data are gathered from *matched pairs of objects* or from *repeated measures of the same object*, the hypothesis test that is applied to compare the differences in means between these matched (or dependent) samples is known as the **paired *t*-test**.

The purpose of a *paired t-test* hypothesis test is to determine whether there has been *any significant change* in the mean level of activity of a numeric random variable under study between the two sets of paired measurements.

The Paired *t*-statistic for Dependent Samples

When the samples are dependent, the sample data consists of the *difference between paired observations*.

$$x_d = x_1 - x_2 \qquad \text{(i.e. differences between pairs)}$$

Where: x_1 = first observation for an object or a respondent

x_2 = second observation for the *same* or *matched* object or respondent

This results in a new random sample, x_d, which consists of a sample of *paired difference data*. The descriptive statistics for this random sample of *paired difference* data are as follows:

$$\bar{x}_d = \frac{\Sigma x_d}{n} \qquad\qquad 9.3$$

Where: n = sample size and is equal to the number of paired difference observations.

$$s_d = \sqrt{\frac{\Sigma(x_d - \bar{x}_d)^2}{n-1}} \qquad\qquad 9.4$$

The *t-stat* for paired samples is:

$$t\text{-}stat = \frac{(\bar{x}_d - \mu_d)}{\frac{s_d}{\sqrt{n}}} \qquad\qquad 9.5$$

The *population parameter* being tested is the *population mean* of *paired differences*, μ_d, derived from *all differences in paired data*. It is stated as follows:

$$\mu_d = \mu_1 - \mu_2 \qquad\qquad 9.6$$

Example 9.3 Internet Usage Study

A random sample of 12 home internet users was selected from Telkom's database and their monthly internet usage (in hours) was identified for March last year (period 1) and again for March this year (period 2). The data, together with the difference in paired data, x_d, is shown in Table 9.1.

(See Excel file C9.3 – *internet usage*.)

Table 9.1 Internet usage data (period 1 and period 2) and the difference measure (in hours)

Subscriber	Period 1	Period 2	Difference
A	70	72	−2
B	85	84	1
C	64	68	−4
D	83	88	−5
E	68	68	0
F	91	95	−4
G	65	64	1
H	78	76	2
I	96	102	−6
J	92	94	−2
K	86	89	−3
L	73	75	−2

Note: The 'Difference' column is calculated by subtracting period 2's data from period 1's data (i.e. $x_d = x_1 - x_2$). Therefore a negative difference implies an increase in usage from period 1 to period 2 and a positive difference implies a decrease in usage from period 1 to period 2.

Management Question

Telkom's internet marketing manager asked the question: 'Is internet usage increasing among home users?'

Conduct a hypothesis test, at the 5% significance level to determine if the average monthly internet usage per home user has increased significantly from period 1 (March last year) to period 2 (March this year).

Solution

This is a *paired t-test hypothesis test* because the two samples of internet usage data (period 1 and period 2) are drawn from the *same subscribers* over two time periods. The two samples of data are therefore *related (dependent)*.

The five steps of hypothesis testing also apply to paired tests.

Step 1: Define the null and alternative hypotheses

Since the difference statistic $x_d = (x_1 - x_2)$ is calculated by subtracting period 2's internet usage from period 1's internet usage, a significant increase in internet usage would be represented by negative differences in the paired data. The mean of these differences should be negative if the sample evidence supports the management question (i.e. $\mu_d < 0$).

Thus the statistical test is defined as a *one-sided lower-tailed hypothesis test*, as follows:

$H_0: \mu_d \geq 0$
$H_1: \mu_d < 0$ This represents Telkom management's question.

Step 2: Determine the region of acceptance of the null hypothesis

Since the t-statistic is the test statistic, both a level of significance, α, and degrees of freedom are required to calculate the critical t-limits for the region of acceptance.

The degrees of freedom for matched-pairs samples is as follows:

$$\text{Degrees of freedom } (df) = n - 1 \qquad\qquad 9.7$$

Where: n = the number of pairs of data (or number of respondents).

Given $\alpha = 0.05$ (5% significance level) and degrees of freedom = $12 - 1 = 11$, then the critical t-limit for this one-sided (lower-tailed) test is t-crit = $t_{(0.05)(11)} = -1.796$ (Table 2, Appendix 1). Thus the region of acceptance for H_0 is $t \geq -1.796$.

The decision rule is then stated as follows:
- Accept H_0 if t-stat lies at or above the lower limit of -1.796.
- Reject H_0 if t-stat lies below -1.796.

Step 3: Calculate the sample test statistic (paired t-stat)

The relevant sample data to derive the t-stat test statistic is based on the descriptive statistics computed from the 'difference' data in Table 9.3.

Calculate $\Sigma x_d = -24$ and $n = 12$.

Then $\quad \bar{x}_d = -\frac{24}{12} = -2.0 \qquad$ (Formula 9.3)

and $\quad s_d = 2.5584 \qquad$ (Formula 9.4)

The *standard error* for the difference between two means is:

$$\frac{s_d}{\sqrt{n}} = \frac{2.5584}{\sqrt{12}} = 0.73855$$

Using the above descriptive statistics as applied to Formula 9.5:

$$
\begin{aligned}
t\text{-stat} &= \frac{(-2.00 - 0)}{\frac{2.5584}{\sqrt{12}}} \\
&= \frac{-2.00}{0.73855} \\
&= -2.708
\end{aligned}
$$

This t-stat value implies that the sample mean difference statistic x_d lies 2.708 standard errors *below* the hypothesised population mean difference of *zero*.

Step 4: Compare the sample test statistic to the region of acceptance

The sample test statistic, t-stat $= -2.708$ lies *outside* (*below*) the region of acceptance.

Refer to Figure 9.4, which shows *t-stat* in relation to the regions of acceptance and rejection.

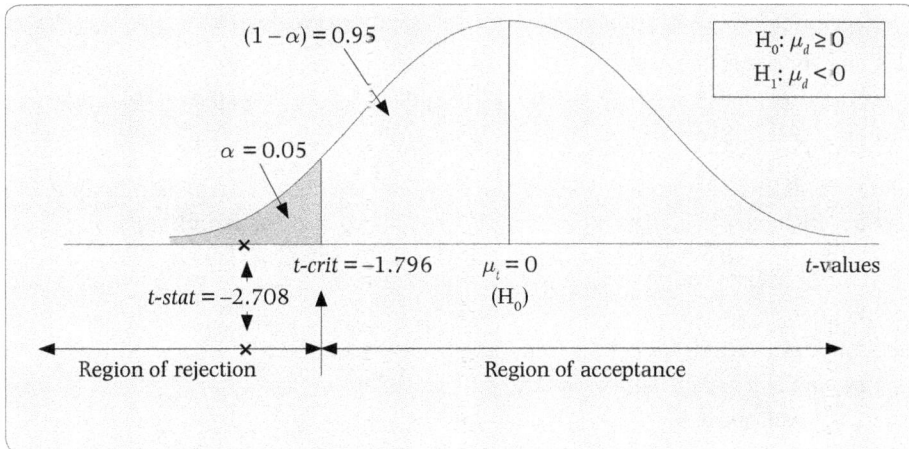

Figure 9.4 Internet usage study – *t-stat* and region of acceptance

Step 5: Draw statistical and management conclusions

Statistical Conclusion

Reject H_0 at the 5% level of significance. The alternative hypothesis is probably true.

Management Conclusion

It can be concluded, with 95% confidence, that mean internet usage has *increased significantly* from March last year (period 1) to March this year (period 2).

Note: Defining the Difference Statistic (x_d)
The formulation of H_0 and H_1 depends on how x_d is defined. If, for example, $x_d = x_2 - x_1$ (i.e. period 2's usage – period 1's usage) in the 'internet usage study', then a *significant increase* in internet usage would be represented by a *positive difference* in the paired data. This would result in H_1 being formulated as $H_1 : \mu_d > 0$ and the hypothesis test would then be classified as a one-sided *upper-tailed* test. The *t-crit* limit for the region of acceptance would be +1.796 and *t-stat* would be +2.708. Either definition of x_d is acceptable, and both will result in the same statistical and management conclusions.

9.5 Hypothesis Test for the Difference between Two Proportions ($\pi_1 - \pi_2$)

$$(p_1 - p_2) \rightarrow (\pi_1 - \pi_2)$$

Similarities or differences between two population proportions can be tested using the *sampling distribution* of the *difference between two sample proportions*.

Illustrations

- In marketing, is there a difference in the *market share* between Olé and Flora brands of margarine?
- In insurance, for all household insurance policyholders, is the *claims ratio* higher in Gauteng than it is in KwaZulu-Natal?
- In production, does stamping machine 1 produce a lower *percentage of defective parts* than stamping machine 2?

The data for all three random variables is *categorical*, hence each management question can be tested statistically using the *difference between two proportions* hypothesis test.

The following information is required to perform such two-sample proportions hypothesis tests:

- the *sample proportions* for each independent sample, p_1 and p_2
- the *sample size* for each sample, n_1 and n_2
- a *level of significance*, α.

The appropriate test statistic is *z-stat*. The z standardisation formula is:

$$z\text{-}stat = \frac{(p_1 - p_2) - (\pi_1 - \pi_2)}{\sqrt{\hat{\pi}(1 - \hat{\pi})\left(\frac{1}{n_1} + \frac{1}{n_2}\right)}}$$

9.8

Where: $\hat{\pi} = \frac{x_1 + x_2}{n_1 + n_2}$ $\quad p_1 = \frac{x_1}{n_1} \quad p_2 = \frac{x_2}{n_2}$

$\hat{\pi}$ = pooled sample proportion

Example 9.4 AIDS Awareness Campaign Study

After a recent AIDS awareness campaign, the National Department of Health commissioned a market research company to conduct a survey on its effectiveness. Their brief was to establish whether the *recall rate of teenagers* differed from that of *young adults* (20–30 years of age).

The market research company interviewed a random sample of 640 teenagers and 420 young adults. It was found that 362 teenagers and 260 young adults were able to recall the AIDS awareness slogan of 'AIDS: don't let it happen'.

Management Question

Test, at the 5% level of significance, the hypothesis that there is an *equal recall rate* between teenagers and young adults (i.e. that the campaign was equally effective for both groups).

Solution

This hypothesis test can be classified as:

- a *difference between two proportions test*, since the random variable measures the proportion of respondents from two independent populations who could recall the AIDS awareness campaign slogan (i.e. the 'recall rate')
- a *two-tailed (two-sided) hypothesis test*, since an 'equal recall rate' implies that there is *no difference* between the two population proportions (i.e. $\pi_1 - \pi_2 = 0$).

Step 1: Define the null and alternative hypotheses

Let population 1 = teenagers and population 2 = young adults. Then:

$H_0: \pi_1 - \pi_2 = 0$ This represents the management question of equal recall rates.

$H_1: \pi_1 - \pi_2 \neq 0$

Step 2: Determine the region of acceptance of the null hypothesis

Given $\alpha = 0.05$ (5% significance level).

Then the critical z-limits for this two-sided hypothesis test is given by $z\text{-}crit = \pm 1.96$ (Table 1, Appendix 1). Thus the region of acceptance for H_0 is $-1.96 \leq z \leq +1.96$.

The decision rule is then stated as follows:

- Accept H_0 if $z\text{-}stat$ lies within the interval -1.96 to $+1.96$ (inclusive).
- Reject H_0 if $z\text{-}stat$ falls below -1.96 or above $+1.96$.

Step 3: Calculate the sample test statistic (z-stat)

From sample data, $p_1 = 0.5656 \left(\frac{362}{640}\right)$ and $p_2 = 0.619 \left(\frac{260}{420}\right)$.
Also, $n_1 = 640$ and $n_2 = 420$.

Using Formula 9.8, the z-stat sample test statistic is computed in three stages, as follows:

(i) The *pooled sample proportion* of p_1 and p_2 is:

$$\hat{\pi} = \frac{362 + 260}{640 + 420} = 0.5868$$

(ii) The *standard error* of p_1 and p_2 is the denominator of z-stat:

$$\text{Standard error} = \sqrt{(0.5868)(1 - 0.5868)\left(\frac{1}{640} + \frac{1}{420}\right)}$$

$$= 0.0309$$

(iii) These results are substituted into the z-stat formula:

$$z\text{-}stat = \frac{(0.5656 - 00.619) - 0}{0.0309} = -1.728$$

This z-stat value means that $(p_1 - p_2)$ lies 1.728 standard errors *below zero*, which is the hypothesised difference in population proportions (i.e. $\pi_1 - \pi_2 = 0$).

Step 4: Compare the sample test statistic to the region of acceptance

The sample test statistic, $z\text{-}stat = -1.728$ lies *within* the region of acceptance. Refer to Figure 9.5, which shows z-stat in relation to the regions of acceptance and rejection.

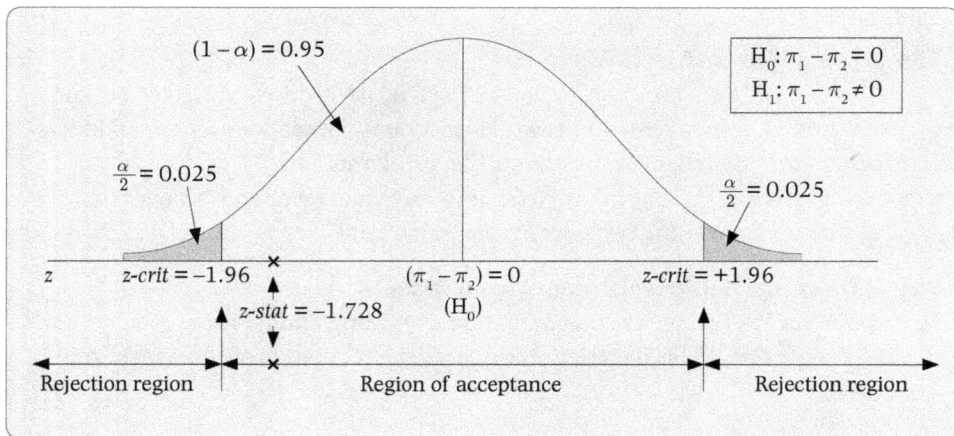

Figure 9.5 AIDS awareness campaign study – *z-stat* and region of acceptance

Step 5: Draw statistical and management conclusions

Statistical Conclusion

Accept H_0 at the 5% level of significance. The sample evidence is 'close enough' to H_0. The null hypothesis is therefore probably true.

Management Conclusion

It can be concluded, with 95% confidence, that there is *no significant difference* in the recall rate of the AIDS awareness slogan 'AIDS: don't let it happen' between teenagers and young adults. The observed difference in sample proportions is due to chance (or sampling error only).

Note: A two-sided hypothesis test does not test for the direction (e.g. higher/lower recall rate) of the relationship between the two population proportions. Statistically, a two-sided test only establishes whether a difference exists or not. To establish a directional relationship between two population parameters, a *one-sided* hypothesis test must be conducted to reach a statistically validated conclusion as to which population group has a lower/higher value for its population parameter. This is illustrated in the next example.

Example 9.5 Online Banking Usage Study

The management of Prime Bank would like to know whether online banking is more popular amongst younger (under 40) banking clients than amongst older banking clients. A random sample of 240 younger clients found that 125 use online banking, while from a random sample of 310 older clients, 140 conducted their banking online.

Management Question

Can the management of Prime Bank conclude, at the 10% level of significance, that *younger* banking clients are *more likely* to use online banking than *older* banking clients?

Solution

This hypothesis test can be classified as:

- a *difference between two proportions test*, because the categorical random variable (use/do not use online banking) measures the proportion between two independent groups of banking clients (younger versus older clients)
- a *one-sided upper-tailed hypothesis test*, because the management question asks whether the proportion of younger clients (population 1) is strictly *greater than* the proportion of older clients (population 2) (i.e. $\pi_1 - \pi_2 > 0$) using online banking.

Step 1: Define the null and alternative hypotheses

Let population 1 = younger banking clients (under 40 years of age) and population 2 = older banking clients. Then:

$H_0: \pi_1 - \pi_2 \leq 0$

$H_1: \pi_1 - \pi_2 > 0$ This represents Prime Bank management's question.

Step 2: Determine the region of acceptance of the null hypothesis

Given $\alpha = 0.10$ (10% significance level).

Then the critical z-limits for this one-sided (upper-tailed) hypothesis test is given by z-*crit* =+1.28 (Table 1, Appendix 1). Thus the region of acceptance for H_0 is z ≤+1.28.

The decision rule is then stated as follows:

- Accept H_0 if z-*stat* lies at or below +1.28.
- Reject H_0 if z-*stat* lies above +1.28.

Step 3: Calculate the sample test statistic (z-*stat*)

From sample data, $p_1 = 0.5208$ $(\frac{125}{240})$ and $p_2 = 0.4516$ $(\frac{140}{310})$.
Also $n_1 = 240$ and $n_2 = 310$.

Using Formula 9.8, the z-*stat* sample test statistic is computed in three stages, as follows:
(i) The *pooled sample proportion* of p_1 and p_2 is:

$$\hat{\pi} = \frac{125 + 140}{240 + 310} = 0.4818$$

(ii) The *standard error* of p_1 and p_2 is the denominator of z-*stat*.

$$\text{Standard error} = \sqrt{(0.4818)(1 - 0.4818)\left(\frac{1}{240} + \frac{1}{310}\right)}$$

$$= 0.04296$$

(iii) These results are substituted into the z-*stat* formula.

$$z\text{-}stat = \frac{(0.5208 - 0.4516) - 0}{0.04296}$$

$$= 1.611$$

Thus the sample test statistic z-*stat* = +1.611

Step 4: Compare the sample test statistic to the region of acceptance

The sample test statistic z-$stat = 1.611$ lies *outside* (*above*) the region of acceptance.

Refer to Figure 9.6, which shows z-$stat$ in relation to the regions of acceptance and rejection.

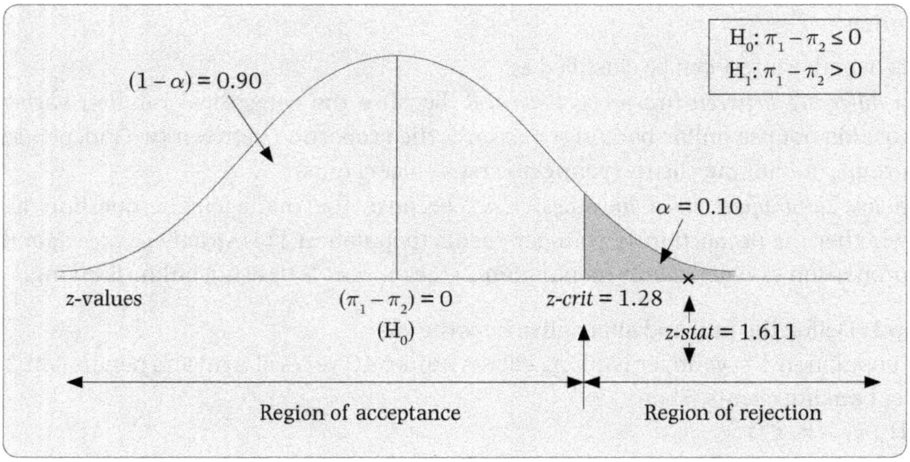

Figure 9.6 Online banking usage study – *z-stat* and region of acceptance

Step 5: Draw statistical and management conclusions

Statistical Conclusion

Reject H_0 at the 10% level of significance. The sample evidence is strong enough to reject H_0 in favour of H_1 at $\alpha = 0.10$. The alternative hypothesis is therefore probably true.

Management Conclusion

It can be concluded, with 90% confidence, that the proportion of younger banking clients who use online banking is *significantly larger* than the proportion of older banking clients who use online banking. The observed sample differences cannot be attributed to chance (or sampling error) alone.

9.6 The *p*-value in Two Population Hypothesis Tests

The *p*-value, introduced in Chapter 8, can also be used in two-population cases to draw statistical conclusions on differences between population means and population proportions.

Calculating the p-value based on z-stat

The same method of computing the *p*-value – as used in Chapter 8 – is appropriate for two sample tests. First the sample test statistic, *z-stat* must be computed (Step 3 of hypothesis testing). Then the *p*-value is the area towards the tail of the standard normal distribution from the *z-stat* point. This area is read off Table 1 in Appendix 1 or by using NORM.S.DIST.

Illustration 1

Refer to Example 9.1(a) (courier service study). This example is a *two-tailed hypothesis test*, with *z-stat* = 1.73 (calculated in Step 3).

To find the *p*-value, first read off the area to the right of 1.73 (Table 1, Appendix 1), i.e. $P(z > 1.73) = 0.5 - 0.4582 = 0.0418$. This area is then doubled to give the *p*-value for a two-tailed test. Thus *p*-value = $2 \times 0.0418 = 0.0836$.

Statistical Conclusion

The statistical conclusion is to accept H_0 as *p*-value = $0.0836 > \alpha = 0.05$.

Illustration 2

Refer to Example 9.5 (online banking usage study). This example is a *one-sided upper-tailed hypothesis test*, with *z-stat* = 1.611.

To find the *p*-value, read off the area to the right of 1.61 (Table 1, Appendix 1) i.e. $P(z > 1.61) = 0.5 - 0.4463 = 0.0537$. Thus *p*-value = 0.0537. (Note: this area is *not* doubled since this is a one-tailed test).

Statistical Conclusion

The statistical conclusion is to reject H_0 as *p*-value = $0.0537 < \alpha = 0.10$.

Calculating the p-value based on t-stat

The *p*-value associated with the *t-stat* test statistic *cannot* be calculated using the *t*-table in Appendix 1. It can only be computed using the Excel function **T.DIST** (for a lower-tailed test), **T.DIST.RT** (for an upper-tailed test) or **T.DIST.2T** (for a two-tailed test). Manual calculation is not possible.

9.7 Two Variances Test ($\sigma_1^2 = \sigma_2^2$)

Test for Equality of Variances between Two Populations ($\sigma^2_1 = \sigma^2_2$)

The **equality of variances** test between **two populations** can be applied in two cases: (i) either to test the assumption – when applying a two-sample *t-test* of means – that the two population variances are equal (as required by the *t-stat* Formula 9.2) or (ii) to examine whether the variability (or volatility) of a numeric variable that is measured in two populations is the same or different.

Case 1: The *t-test* assumption of equal population variances

In a two-sample *t-test* of means (see section 9.3), the *t-stat* Formula 9.2 assumes that the two population variances are equal. This test is known as the **pooled-variances *t-test*.**

If, however, this assumption is not satisfied, a different *t-stat* formula must be used (see Formula 9.9 below) which takes into account that the variances are unequal (i e. different). This test is known as the **unequal-variances *t-test*.**

$$t\text{-stat} = \frac{(\bar{x}_1 - \bar{x}_2) - (\mu_1 - \mu_2)}{\sqrt{\frac{s_1^2}{n_1} + \frac{s_2^2}{n_2}}}$$

9.9

271

With: $df = \dfrac{\left(\dfrac{s_1^2}{n_1} + \dfrac{s_2^2}{n_2}\right)^2}{\dfrac{\left(\dfrac{s_1^2}{n_1}\right)^2}{(n_1 - 1)} + \dfrac{\left(\dfrac{s_2^2}{n_2}\right)^2}{(n_2 - 1)}}$

See the flowchart for the various *two-sample t-test* and *z-test* options in Appendix 3 (Chart 3(a)).

If the incorrect *t-stat* formula is used, the findings of the two-sample *t-test* of means will be misleading. To identify which version of the *t-test* to use when comparing two population means, the hypothesis test for equal variances must always be done first, before the *t-test* for means.

The test statistic for the 'equality of variances' test is called the **F-statistic** and it is always computed as the ratio of **two variances**.

$$F\text{-}stat = \frac{\text{sample variance}_1}{\text{sample variance}_2} = \frac{s_1^2}{s_2^2} \qquad\qquad 9.10$$

Example 9.6 Corporate Financial Performance Study (Refer to Example 9.2)

Before testing for differences in the mean ROI% between the financial and manufacturing companies, we need to test if the *variances* of ROI% is the *same* across the two sectors. This test will identify the correct *t-stat* formula to use (Formula 9.2 or 9.9).

The statistical question is: can we assume, at the 5% level of significance, that the two population variances, σ_f^2 and σ_m^2, are equal?

Table 9.2 Summary statistics – financial and manufacturing companies

	Sample 1 (Financial)	Sample 2 (Manufacturing)
Sample size	28	24
Sample mean	18.714%	15.13%
Sample std dev	9.65%	8.82%

Solution
Step 1: Define the null and alternative hypotheses

$H_0: \sigma_f^2 = \sigma_m^2$ versus $H_1: \sigma_f^2 \neq \sigma_m^2$

or

$H_0: \dfrac{\sigma_f^2}{\sigma_m^2} = 1$ versus $H_1: \dfrac{\sigma_f^2}{\sigma_m^2} \neq 1$ (a two-tailed test)

Step 2: Determine the region of acceptance of the null hypothesis (use $\alpha = 0.05$)
The **test statistic** for equality of variances is called the *F*-statistic. While this is a two-tailed test, only the *upper tailed critical value* is necessary to define the region of acceptance (based on the construction of *F-stat*) (See step 3 below.)

F-crit (upper) $= F(\frac{\alpha}{2}, df_1, df_2) = F(0.025, 27, 23) = 2.266$ (refer to Table 4(b), Appendix 1)
In Excel, use **F.INV.RT(0.025,27,23)**.

> *Note:* $df_1 = (n_f - 1)$ for the *numerator* sample variance (i.e. $df_1 = 28 - 1 = 27$)
> $df_2 = (n_m - 1)$ for the *denominator* sample variance (i.e. $df_2 = 24 - 1 = 23$)
> Use only $\alpha/2$ to find F-crit (upper) (i.e. $\alpha/2 = 0.05/2 = 0.025$)

The following decision rule then applies:
- Accept H_0 if *F-stat* lies at or below ($\leq$) the upper critical value of 2.266
- Reject H_0 if *F-stat* lies above ($>$) 2.266.

Step 3: Calculate the sample test statistic (*F-stat*)
Construct *F-stat* using Formula 9.10 but intentionally put the larger sample variance in the numerator and the smaller sample variance in the denominator. This will result in *F-stat* always being greater than one and hence the need to only test against the upper critical limit.

$$F\text{-stat} = \frac{\text{larger sample variance}}{\text{smaller sample variance}}$$
$$= \frac{9.645^2}{8.823^2} = 1.1949$$

Also: the *p*-value $= 0.6692$ (*p*-value $= 2 \times$ **F.DIST.RT(1.1949,27,23)** $= 2 \times 0.3346$).

Step 4: Compare the sample test statistic to the region of acceptance
The sample test statistic, *F-stat* $= 1.1949$, lies *within* the region of acceptance of H_0. Refer to Figure 9.7, which shows *F-stat* in relation to the regions of acceptance and rejection.

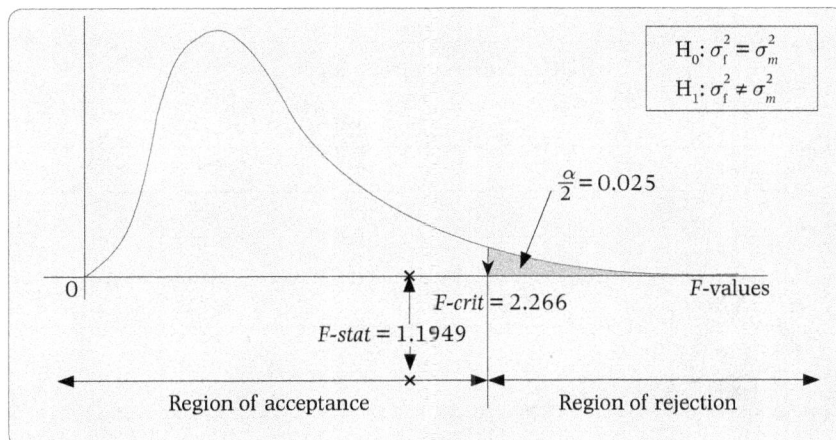

Figure 9.7 Corporate financial performance – *F-stat* and region of acceptance

Step 5: Draw the statistical conclusion

Accept H_0 at the 5% level of significance and conclude that the population variances of ROI% are the same between financial and manufacturing companies. Therefore equal population variances can be assumed and the *pooled-variances t-test* can be used to test for mean ROI% differences between financial and manufacturing companies.

If *F-stat* is computed using *smaller* s^2/*larger* s^2, then *F-stat* would be *less than one*. It must therefore be compared to an *F-crit lower* limit only rather than an *F-crit* upper limit (as was illustrated in Example 9.2).

Table 9.3 shows **X-Static**'s output for Example 9.6. It shows both the lower and upper *F-crit* limits for the region of acceptance. The calculation of the *F-crit* (*lower*) limit is shown at the end of Section 9.7.

Table 9.3 X-Static Output for the *F*-Test: Equality of Variances (Two Populations) – Example 9.6

F-test: Equality of variances (Two populations)		
Descriptive statistics	**Financial**	**Manufacturing**
Sample mean	18.7143	15.1250
Sample standard deviation	9.6450	8.8234
Sample variance	93.0265	77.8533
Sample size	28	24
Degrees of freedom (*df*)	27	23

Hypothesis test results		
Two-tailed test		
F-critical	0.4530	2.2659
F-statistic	1.1949	
p-value	0.6692	
Significance level (α)	0.05	

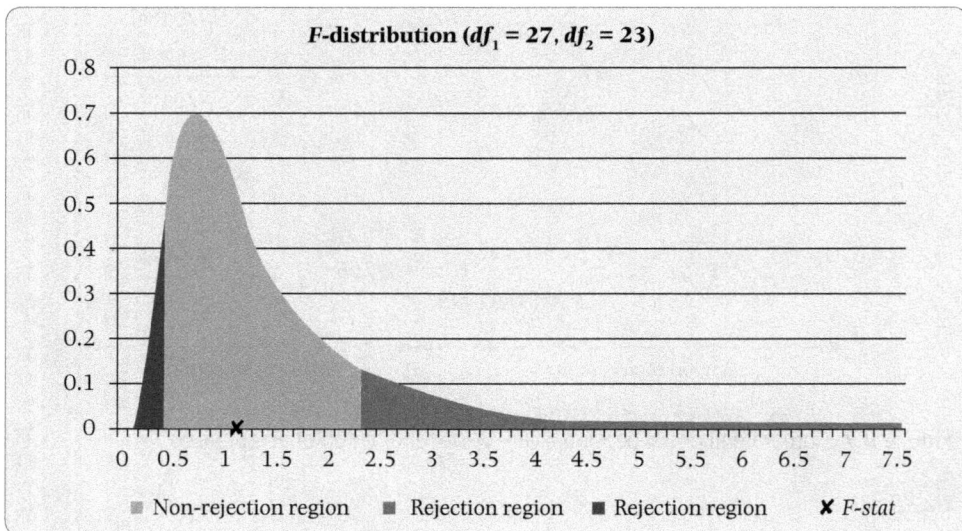

F-distribution ($df_1 = 27$, $df_2 = 23$)

Non-rejection region · Rejection region · Rejection region · ✗ F-stat

Note 1: If H_0: $\sigma_1^2 = \sigma_2^2$ was rejected in favour of H_1, then the *unequal-variances t-test* would be used to test for mean ROI% differences between financial and manufacturing companies. The same hypothesis test procedure (as in section 9.3) is used except, at Step 3, *t-stat* is derived using Formula 9.9 (*unequal-variances t-stat*) in place of Formula 9.2 (*pooled- variances t-stat*). The degrees of freedom formula required for the unequal-variances *t-test* is manually cumbersome, but is worked out in Excel's **Data Analysis** '*t-Test: Two-Sample Assuming Unequal Variances*' or in **X-Static** '*t-Test: Two Means* **(Unequal Variances)**'. The formula is shown in Formula 9.9.

Note 2: As a quick test, use the following rule of thumb to gauge equality of variances (i.e. H_0: $\sigma_1^2 = \sigma_2^2$):

$$If\ \frac{\text{larger sample variance}}{\text{smaller sample variance}} < 3,\ \text{do not reject } H_0.$$

Note 3: The difference between the two *t-stat* formulae (9.2 and 9.9) is in the denominator term (i.e. in the computation of the *standard error* for difference between two means). In an equal variances case, the standard error term is likely to be smaller than in an unequal variances case. This makes the *t-test* more discriminating (i.e. more likely to reject the null hypothesis of equal population means for small differences in sample means). By not accounting for differences in the two population variances in the *t-test* statistic, a possible erroneous conclusion could be drawn. There is a greater likelihood of concluding that no differences in means exist when in fact there may well be a significant difference.

Case 2: Comparing the variances of two independent samples

There are occasions when it is necessary to compare the variances between two independent populations. For example, an investment analyst would like to know if one portfolio of equities shows greater *variability of returns* than a second portfolio made up of similar equities. The focus of a statistical analysis is therefore on the variability within data (as measured by the standard deviation/variance) rather than on the mean.

Consequently a hypothesis test to *compare two sample variances* (instead of two sample means) would be performed. An identical *F-test* approach – as used in Case 1 above – can be applied to the two samples of data to compare the *variability of data* for a numeric variable between two independent populations.

Both one-tailed (one-sided) and two-tailed (two-sided) hypotheses can be formulated depending on the management question. A two-tailed *F-test* would be used if the management question examines whether the variability of data is the *same* between two populations. Alternatively, a one-tailed *F-test* is used if the management question examines whether the variability of data in one population is *greater* (or *less*) *than* the variability in a second population. To illustrate:

1 For the management question, 'Does investment fund A show *greater variability* in quarterly rates of return than investment fund B?', a one-sided upper-tailed *F-test* would be formulated as follows: H_0: $\sigma_A^2 \leq \sigma_B^2$ versus H_1: $\sigma_A^2 > \sigma_B^2$.

2   For the management question, 'Is the *variability* in bottle filling the same between two bottling plants, 1 and 2?', a two-tailed *F*-test would be formulated as follows: $H_0: \sigma_1^2 = \sigma_2^2$ versus $H_1: \sigma_1^2 \neq \sigma_2^2$.

3   For the management question, 'Is there *greater consistency* in the time to perform a given medical procedure using procedure A as opposed to procedure B?', a one-sided lower tailed *F*-test would be formulated as follows: $H_0: \sigma_A^2 \geq \sigma_B^2$ versus $H_1: \sigma_A^2 < \sigma_B^2$.

Example 9.7 Investment Fund Returns Volatility Study

An investment analyst asked the following question: Is Fund A *more volatile* (*riskier*) than Fund B? Test this management question at the 5% level of significance based on a sample of weekly returns for each investment fund. Refer to the data in Table 9.3.

(See Excel file C9.4 – *fund returns*.)

Table 9.3 Sample of weekly fund returns

Fund A	14.14	16.61	10.17	8.74	12.88	9.78	10.09	14.62	9.77	11.38
Fund B	10.42	7.42	10.75	9.89	11.04	13.11	10.64	8.99	6.58	8.76

A hypothesis test on the *variability* of weekly returns between fund A and fund B is conducted using a one-sided *F*-test for variances.

Step 1: Define the null and alternative hypotheses

$$H_0: \sigma_A^2 \leq \sigma_B^2 \qquad H_1: \sigma_A^2 > \sigma_B^2 \qquad \text{or} \qquad H_0: \frac{\sigma_A^2}{\sigma_B^2} \leq 1 \qquad H_1: \frac{\sigma_A^2}{\sigma_B^2} > 1$$

This is a one-sided (upper-tailed) *F*-test for equality of variances.

Step 2: Determine the region of acceptance of the null hypothesis
Given $\alpha = 0.05$, *F*-crit (upper) = F(0.05, 9, 9) = 3.18 (Table 4(a), Appendix 1)
In Excel, use **F.INV.RT(0.05,9,9)**.

The following decision rule then applies:
- Accept H_0 if *F*-stat lies at or below ($\leq$) the upper critical value of 3.18
- Reject H_0 if *F*-stat lies above (>) 3.18.

Step 3: Calculate the sample test statistic (*F*-stat)
Derived from Table 9.3, $s_A^2 = 6.783$ and $s_B^2 = 3.582$.
Thus *F*-stat = 6.783/3.582 = 1.893.   (based on Formula 9.10)
Also, the *p*-value = 0.1778.   (Use Excel's **F.DIST.RT(1.893,9,9)**)

Step 4: Compare the sample test statistic to the region of acceptance
The sample test statistic, *F*-stat = 1.893, lies *within* the region of acceptance of H_0. Also, the *p*-value (0.1778) > $\alpha = 0.05$. Refer to Figure 9.8, which shows *F*-stat in relation to the regions of acceptance and rejection.

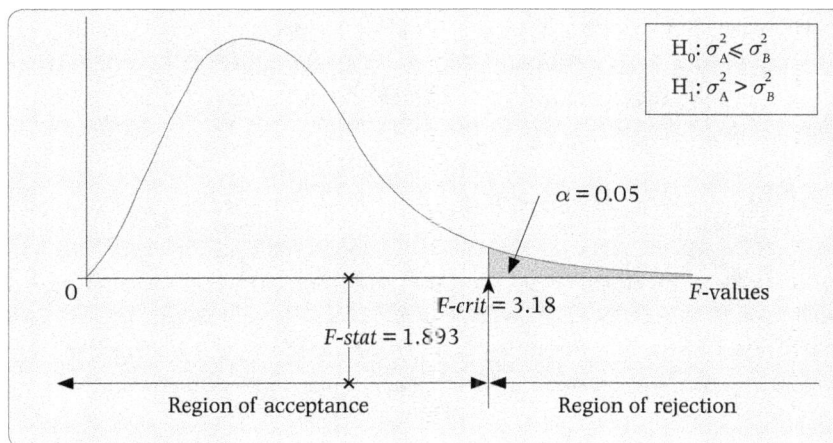

Figure 9.8 Investment fund returns – *F-stat* and region of acceptance

Step 5: Draw the statistical and management conclusions

Statistically, accept H_0 at the 5% level of significance and conclude that Fund A's variance of returns is not greater than the variance of returns of Fund B (i.e. the sample evidence does not support H_1).

The financial analyst can therefore be advised, with 95% confidence, that returns in Fund A are *not* more volatile than returns in Fund B (or that Fund A is not more risky than Fund B).

The statistical evidence at the 5% level of significance is not strong enough to conclude that Fund A is more risky than Fund B.

Note 1: It is desirable to always compute *F-stat* for the above two cases by *dividing* the *larger sample variance* by the *smaller sample variance*. As a result, *F-stat* will always be greater than one. Then, regardless of which hypothesis test scenario of equality of variances is being tested (i.e. lower-tailed, two-tailed, or upper-tailed tests), the correct statistical conclusion can be drawn by comparing *F-stat* (> 1) to the *upper critical F*-limit (*F-crit* [upper]) only. The *p*-value will also always be the area to the right of *F-stat* (i.e. in the upper tail area of the *F* distribution).

Note 2: $F\text{-}crit = F(\alpha, df_1, df_2)$
In one-sided tests (lower- or upper-tailed), use α for the tail area (rejection area) of the *F*-test, while in two-sided tests, use $\frac{\alpha}{2}$ for the rejection area in each tail. Also, df_1 always relates to the sample used in the *numerator* and df_2 to the sample used in the *denominator* of *F-stat*.

Note 3: Use the following approach to manually compute the *F-crit* (lower) limit:
Assume $F\text{-}stat = \dfrac{\text{sample variance}_1}{\text{sample variance}_2}$ and the associated lower
F-crit limit is $F(\alpha, (n_1 - 1), (n_2 - 1))$ where α is the lower tail area of the *F*-distribution.

Now to derive this *F-crit* (lower) limit, first find *F-crit* (upper) $= F(\alpha, (n_2 - 1), (n_1 - 1))$. Note that the numerator and denominator degrees of freedom in *F-crit* (upper) are reversed and that α relates to the upper tail area of the *F*-distribution.

Now apply the following reciprocal formula:

$$\text{\textit{F-crit} (lower)} = \frac{1}{\text{\textit{F-crit} (upper)}} \qquad\qquad 9.11$$

For example: For a one-sided *lower-tailed* test with $\alpha = 0.05$, $n_1 = 10$ and $n_2 = 16$, first find *F-crit* (upper) = F(0.05,15,9) = 3.01 (from Table 4(a) Appendix 1). (Note the *df* are switched around.) Now find *F-crit* (lower) = F(0.05,9,15) = 1/3.01 = 0.3322.
In Excel (2016), use F.INV(0.05,9,15) = 0.3327 (note minor rounding error).

Note 4: Use the following combination of Excel (2016) functions to find *F-crit* and *p-values*:
(i) For a *one-sided upper tailed F*-test:
  – *F-crit* (upper) = F.INV.RT(α, df_1, df_2) and *p-value* = F.DIST.RT(*F-stat*, df_1, df_2)
(ii) For a *one-sided lower tailed F*-test:
  – *F-crit* (lower) = F.INV(α, df_1, df_2) and *p-value* = F.DIST(*F-stat*, df_1, df_2, **cumulative**)
(iii) For a *two-tailed F*-test:
  – If *F-stat* < 1, then compute only *F-crit* (lower) = F.INV(α, df_1, df_2) and *p-value* = 2 × F.DIST(*F-stat*, df_1, df_2) where df_1 = numerator *df* and df_2 = denominator *df*.
  – If *F-stat* > 1, then compute only *F-crit* (upper) = F.INV.RT(α, df_1, df_2) and *p-value* = 2 × F.DIST(*F-stat*, df_1, df_2, **cumulative**) where df_1 = numerator *df* and df_2 = denominator *df*.

Note 5: Using the *p*-value method to draw the statistical conclusion.
In equal variances tests (one-sided or two-sided), it is recommended to draw the statistical conclusion based on the *p*-value only – rather than by comparing an *F-stat* to a *F-crit* value. The reason for this is that in statistical packages, *F-stat* may have been computed using *smaller* s^2/*larger* s^2. When this happens, *F-stat* is less than one and therefore should be compared to an *F-crit* lower limit, rather than an *F-crit* upper limit. The *p*-value avoids this confusion as it will be the *same value* regardless in which order *F-stat* is computed and therefore will result in the correct conclusion being drawn with respect to the null and alternative hypotheses.

9.8 Using *Excel (2016)* and *X-Static* for Two Population Tests

Both the **Data Analysis** add-in module in Excel (refer to Figure 9.9) and **X-Static** (refer to Figure 9.10) can perform all the two-sample tests covered in this chapter (except **Data Analysis** does not offer a difference between two proportions option).
(a) For differences between two independent means (population variances known), i.e.
  $H_0: \mu_1 - \mu_2 = 0$:
  – use the **Data Analysis** module *z*-Test: Two Sample for Means
  – in **X-Static**, use the module: *z*-Test: Two Means

(b) For differences between two independent means (population variances unknown – but assumed equal), i.e. H_0: $\mu_1 - \mu_2 = 0$:
- use the **Data Analysis** module *t-Test*: **Two Sample Assuming Equal Variances.**
- in **X-Static**, use the module: *t*-Test: Two Means (Equal Variances)

(c) For differences between two independent means (population variances unknown – but assumed unequal) i.e. H_0: $\mu_1 - \mu_2 = 0$:
- use the **Data Analysis** module *t-Test*: **Two Sample Assuming Unequal Variances**
- in **X-Static**, use the module: *t*-Test: Two Means (Unequal Variances)

(d) For the matched-pairs test i.e. H_0: $\mu_d = 0$:
- use the **Data Analysis** module *t-Test*: **Paired Two Sample for Means**
- in **X-Static**, use the module: *t*-Test: Matched Pairs

(e) For the equality of variances test, i.e. H_0: $\sigma_1^2 = \sigma_2^2$:
- use the **Data Analysis** module *F*-Test Two Sample for Variances
- in **X-Static**, use the module: *F*-Test: Equality of Variances (Two Populations)

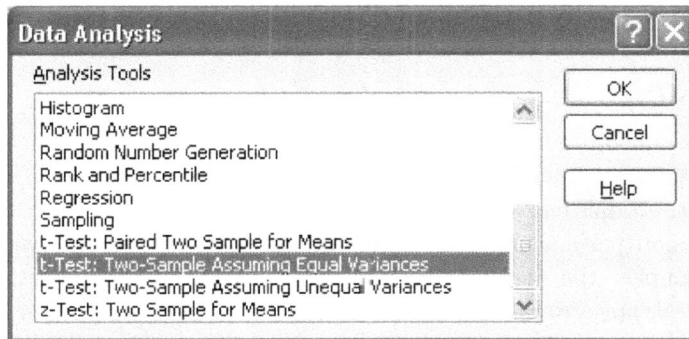

Figure 9.9 Data Analysis add-in module in Excel

(f) For differences between two proportions:
- in **Data Analysis**, this option is not available.
- in **X-Static**, use the module: *z*-Test: Two Proportions

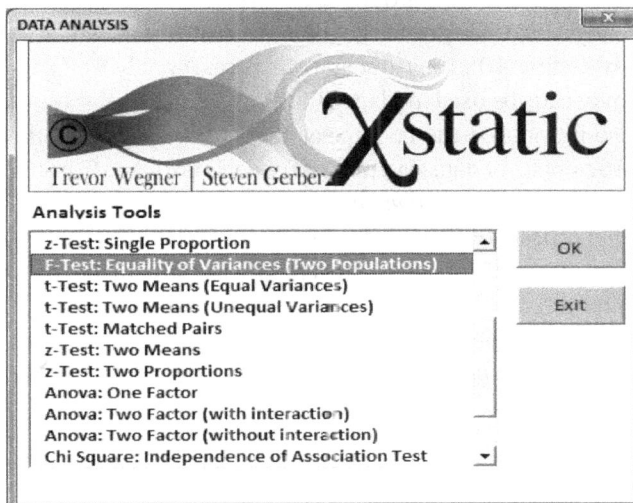

Figure 9.10 X-Static Two Sample Hypotheses Test modules

(g) To identify the *critical limits* for a region of acceptance, use the following Excel functions:
  - For the *z-crit* limits, use **NORM.S.INV(cumulative probability)**.
  - For the *t-crit* limits, use either **T.INV(α,degrees of freedom)** for a one-tailed test, or **T.INV.2T(α, degrees of freedom)** for a two-tailed test.
  - For the *F-stat* limits, use **F.INV(α, df_1, df_2)** for a lower critical limit and/or **F.INV.RT(α, df_1, df_2)** for an upper critical limit.

(h) To compute the *p-value* for a sample test statistic, use the following Excel functions:
  - For a given *z-stat* value, use **NORM.S.DIST(z-stat)**.
  - For a given *t-stat* value, use either **T.DIST(t-stat,df,cumulative)** for a lower-tailed test; **T.DIST.RT(t-stat, df)** for an upper-tailed test; or **T.DIST.2T(t-stat,df)** for a two-tailed test.
  - For a given *F-stat* value, use **F.DIST(F-stat,df_1,df_2,cumulative)** for a *lower-tailed* test; and **F.DIST.RT(F-stat,df_1,df_2)** for an *upper-tailed test*.

Note that *p*-values are automatically shown in both **Data Analysis** and **X-Static** outputs for the hypothesis testing options noted in (a) to (f) above.

9.9 Summary

This chapter extended the *hypothesis testing process* to examine for significant differences between two *population parameters*. The same five steps of hypothesis testing are applied to each of these two-sample test situations.

The population parameters tested were the *difference between two sample means* for independent samples, the *matched-pairs* test for dependent samples, and the *difference between two sample proportions*. For each population parameter, the chapter illustrated the appropriate hypothesis-testing procedure to be applied. This involves deciding whether the test is two-tailed, one-tailed upper or one-tailed lower, and this is determined by the nature of the claim or assertion made in the management question.

In addition to choosing the appropriate tailed test, this chapter also distinguished between cases where the population standard deviation is either known or unknown. If known, the z-test statistic is the appropriate test statistic to calculate at steps 2 and 3 of the hypothesis-testing procedure. Alternatively, the *t-test* statistic would be selected. However, for large samples (exceeding 40), the *t-test* statistic is reasonably well approximated by the z-test statistic and may thus be used in place of it.

This chapter also introduced the concept of the *matched-pairs* hypothesis test, which is appropriate when two samples of data for a random variable are taken from the *same respondents*. In such instances, the two samples are *not independent* of each other and a *difference statistic* (paired *t*-statistic) hypothesis test must then be employed. This test is suitable for many marketing situations where before/after measurements are taken on a given numeric random variable. The test for equal variances was introduced to consider management questions where the focus of the analysis is on the *variability* of a process or a measure.

Finally, the use of Excel's *function operations*, **Data Analysis** and **X-Static** were referenced as a means of conducting two-sample hypothesis tests.

Exercises

This symbol denotes data available online

1   When is the *t-test* statistic used in a hypothesis test for the difference between two means?

2   Given a sample of size $n_1 = 40$ from a population with a standard deviation $\sigma_1 = 20$, and an independent sample of size $n_2 = 50$ from another population with a known standard deviation $\sigma_2 = 10$, what is the value of *z-stat* when testing for the difference in two population means if $\bar{x}_1 = 72$ and $\bar{x}_2 = 66$?

3   When conducting a two-tailed test for equality of means, what is the *t-crit* value:
    (a)   when $n_1 = 14$, $n_2 = 26$ and $\alpha = 0.05$?
    (b)   when $n_1 = 54$, $n_2 = 38$ and $\alpha = 0.05$?

4   When is it appropriate to use a *matched-pairs t-test* to conduct a hypothesis test?

5   A production manager wants to know whether the proportion of defective parts produced by machine 1 is *less than* the proportion of defective parts produced by machine 2. Formulate the null and alternative hypothesis appropriate for this management question.

6   A financial analyst asked the following question: 'Is the *average earnings yield* of *manufacturing companies* the same as the average earnings yield of *retailing companies*?' To examine this question, the analyst randomly sampled 19 manufacturing companies and 24 retailing companies. The descriptive statistics from each sample of companies are as follows:

	Manufacturers	Retailers
Sample mean (%)	8.45	10.22
Sample standard deviation	3.32	4.14
Sample size	19	24

    (a)   Conduct a hypothesis test at the 5% level of significance to test whether the two population variances are equal. Based on this statistical conclusion, would you use the pooled-variances *t-test* or the unequal-variances *t-test* to test the management question?
    (b)   Formulate the null and alternative hypothesis for this management question (i.e. can the financial analyst conclude that there is *no difference* in the average earnings yield between companies in the manufacturing and retailing sectors?)
    (c)   Use the two-sample *t-test* based on the conclusion from (a). Conduct a hypothesis test for the difference between two means to test the null hypothesis at the 5% level of significance. What conclusion can be drawn?

7   The do-it-yourself (DIY) consumer movement has had a profound impact on the retailing business. A recent study conducted by the Centre for Consumer Research examined various traits of persons classified as '*do-it-yourselfers*' and '*non-do-it-yourselfers*'. One factor considered was a person's *age*. Because younger people are generally healthier

but less affluent, it is reasonable to expect do-it-yourselfers to be younger. The ages (in years) of the people in the two groups from the study are summarised as follows:

	DIY consumers	Non-DIY consumers
Sample mean (years)	41.8	47.4
Standard deviation	15.9	16.2
Sample size	29	34

Does the data support the hypothesis that do-it-yourselfers are *younger*, on average, than non-do-it-yourselfers?
(a) Define the two populations and then formulate the appropriate null and alternative hypothesis for the test.
(b) Conduct a hypothesis test at the 10% level of significance to test the null hypothesis.
(c) What statistical and management conclusion can be drawn from the findings?
(d) Will the conclusion differ if the hypothesis test was conducted at the 5% level of significance? Justify your answer statistically.

8   A transport subcommittee of the Cape Town City Council wanted to know if there is any difference in the mean *commuting time* to work between *bus* and *train commuters*. They conducted a small-scale survey amongst bus and train commuters and computed the following descriptive statistics for each sample of commuters:

	Bus commuters	Train commuters
Sample mean (minutes)	35.3	31.8
Sample standard deviation	7.8	4.6
Sample size	22	36

The subcommittee would like to know if it takes bus commuters *longer*, on average, to get to work than train commuters.
(a) Name the two populations and then formulate the null and alternative hypothesis to address the subcommittee's management question.
(b) Test whether the two population variances are equal. Use $\alpha = 0.05$. Would you use the pooled-variances *t-test* or the unequal-variances *t-test* to test the management question?
(c) Use the two-sample *t-test* based on the conclusion from (b). Test the null hypothesis formulated in (a) at the 1% significance level.
(d) Based on the statistical findings in (c), which of the two public transport facilities (bus or train) should the City Council prioritise for upgrading to reduce the average commuting time of workers?

9   A large multi-branch bank is affiliated with both *Mastercard* and *Visa* credit cards. A random sample of 45 *Mastercard* clients found that their average *month-end credit card balance* was R922. For a random sample of 66 *Visa* card clients, their average month-end credit card balance was found to be R828.

   Assume that the population of month-end credit card balances for *Mastercard* and *Visa* card clients is normally distributed, with population standard deviations of

R294 for *Mastercard* clients and R336 for *Visa* card clients respectively. Establish at the 5% level of significance whether there is *any significant difference* in the average month-end credit card balances between *Mastercard* and *Visa* card clients.

10 A national car dealer has been running job-enrichment workshops for its sales consultants over the past three years. To establish if these programmes have been effective, the human resource manager conducted a study amongst the sales consultants to measure their degree of *job satisfaction* on a 10-point rating scale (1 = low job satisfaction; 10 = high job satisfaction).

A random sample of 22 sales consultants who had *not attended* a job-enrichment workshop had a mean rating score on job satisfaction of 6.9. The mean rating score on job satisfaction for 25 randomly selected sales consultants who *had attended* a job-enrichment workshop was 7.5.

Assume that the population of rating scores for each group of sales consultants is normally distributed. Also assume a population standard deviation of rating scores for *non-attendees* of 1.1, and for *attendees* of job-enrichment workshops assume a population standard deviation of rating scores of 0.8.

Can the human resource manager conclude, at the 5% significance level, that the job-enrichment workshops *increase* sales consultants' job satisfaction levels? Present your findings to the human resource manager.

11 The Medical Aid Board wanted to find out if the mean *time to settle medical claims* of members differs between two major medical schemes – the Green-Aid Fund and the Explorer Fund.

Fourteen Green-Aid Fund medical claims received were randomly selected and monitored, and the sample mean time to settlement was 10.8 days. Assume a population standard deviation of 3.2 days for settlement times of Green-Aid Fund claims. For a random sample of 15 Explorer Fund medical claims received, the average time to settlement was 12.4 days. Assume a population standard deviation of 2.3 days for settlement times of Explorer Fund claims. Assume settlement times are normally distributed.

(a) Estimate, with 95% confidence, the actual average settlement time (in days) for claims received by the Explorer Fund only. Interpret the result.

(b) Can the Medical Aid Board conclude that the Green-Aid Fund settles claims *sooner*, on average, than the Explorer Fund? Formulate the null and alternative hypothesis and test this hypothesis at the 5% significance level. What conclusion can be drawn?

12 A consumer testing service compared *gas ovens to electric ovens* by baking one type of bread in five separate ovens of each type. Assume the *baking times* are normally distributed. The electric ovens had an average baking time of 0.89 hours with standard deviation of 0.09 hours and the gas ovens had an average baking time of 0.75 hours with a standard deviation of 0.16 hours.

Test the hypothesis, at the 5% significance level, that gas ovens have a *faster* baking time, on average, than electric ovens. Assume identical population variances. Show suitable null and alternative hypotheses for the test.

13 The operations manager of a computer accessories firm with branches in Cape Town and Durban wants to establish whether their *Cape Town branch* is performing *better* than their *Durban branch* in terms of the average *size of orders* received. Both branches have been operating for only one year.

A random sample of 18 orders from the Cape Town branch had a average value of R335.20 with a standard deviation equal to R121.50. Orders received by the Durban branch of the firm were also randomly sampled. The average of the 15 orders sampled was R265.60 with a sample standard deviation of R152.20.

(a) Use a 'rule-of-thumb' test to determine whether the two population variances are equal. Based on this conclusion, would you use the pooled-variances *t-test* or the unequal-variances *t-test* to test the management question?

(b) Can the operations manager conclude, at the 10% significance level, that the Cape Town branch is *performing better* than the Durban branch? Show the null and alternative hypotheses for the test and draw the appropriate conclusion.

(c) Will the management conclusion to (b) change if the level of significance of the hypothesis test was changed to 5%? Explain your answer.

(d) In which conclusion (b) or (c) would the operations manager have greater confidence? Comment.

14 X9.14 – package designs

A fruit juice producer conducted a study at a large supermarket to determine the possible influence of different *package designs* on the sales volume of their one-litre cartons of pure apple juice. The apple juice was sold in *pyramid-shaped* cartons for the first eight weeks, after which the same product packaged in *barrel-shaped* cartons was sold for a further eight weeks. Weekly sales (in cases) were recorded over each eight-week period.

Assume weekly sales are normally distributed for each carton design and that population variances are equal. If the marketer's decision is to choose the package design that is likely to lead to *larger* national sales, on average, should they use the barrel-shaped carton design?

Conduct a suitable one-sided hypothesis tests of means at the 5% level of significance using the appropriate *t-test* (pooled-variances or unequal-variances *t-test*) to determine if the mean *weekly sales* of pure apple juice in the *barrel-shaped* carton design is *greater* than the mean weekly sales in the *pyramid-shaped* carton. Show the null and alternative hypothesis and make a recommendation to the marketer based on your findings.(For a *variance* test, assume $\alpha = 0.05$.)

	Carton shape	
	Pyramid	Barrel
	27	25
	16	28
	25	34
	32	28
	20	22
	22	35
	26	18
	22	29
Mean	23.750	27.375
Std dev	4.862	5.706

15   Two test products of a new fruit-flavoured wheat cereal were market tested recently. Fifty-four of a consumer test panel of 175 households said that they would buy their test product cereal labelled *Fruit Puffs* if offered on the market. Also, 36 of a separate consumer test panel of 150 households said that they would buy their test product cereal labelled *Fruity Wheat*. Based on these test market responses of product acceptance, the cereal company will decide which one of the two cereals to launch.

After an inspection of the test market data, the marketing manager concluded that *Fruit Puffs* are preferred by a *greater percentage* of households than *Fruity Wheat*. He therefore believes that they should launch the *Fruit Puffs* cereal.

Use a hypothesis test for the difference between two proportions to provide statistical evidence at the 5% significance level to examine the marketing manager's claim. What recommendation would you make? Show appropriate null and alternative hypotheses for the test.

16   A survey amongst a random sample of 250 male and female respondents was conducted into their music listening preferences. Each respondent was asked whether they enjoy listening to jazz.

Of the 140 males surveyed, 46 answered 'Yes'. Of the 110 female respondents, 21 answered 'Yes'.

(a)   Is there statistical evidence at the 5% level of significance that males and females *equally* enjoy listening to jazz? What conclusion do you reach?

(b)   Compute the *p*-value for the test statistic in (a) using the **NORM.S.DIST** function in Excel. Interpret its value in the context of the management question.

17   A random sample of 300 Status cheque accounts at Capital Bank showed that 48 were overdrawn. When 250 Elite cheque accounts at the same bank were randomly checked, it was found that 55 were overdrawn.

(a)   Can the bank manager conclude that *more* Elite cheque account clients, *proportionately*, are likely to be overdrawn than Status cheque account clients? Test this hypothesis at the 5% level of significance. What conclusion can be drawn?

(b)   Compute the *p*-value for the test statistic in (a) using the **NORM.S.DIST** function in Excel. Interpret its value in the context of the management question.

18   X9.18 – aluminium scrap

The plant manager at an aluminium processing plant in KZN recorded the *percentage of scrap produced daily* by each of two sheet-rolling machines. Scrap is measured as a percentage of daily machine output.

(a)   Can the plant manager conclude that machine 1, on average, produces less scrap – as a percentage of its daily output – than machine 2?

(i)   Use the **Data Analysis** add-in **F-Test Two-Sample for Variances** to find out if the two population variances can be assumed to be equal. Use $\alpha = 0.05$.

(ii)   Define the null and alternative hypotheses of the management question.

(iii) Use the appropriate *t-test* from **Data Analysis: *t-Test*: Two Sample Assuming Equal (or Unequal) Variances** option to test the hypotheses in (ii) at the 5% level of significance.

(iv)   What conclusion can be drawn from the findings?

    (b)   Identify the *p*-value for this hypothesis test from the output in (a) and interpret its value in the context of the management question.

19   X9.19 – water purification

The number of impurities per million particles of water is a measure of the quality of drinking water. If the average *number of impurities exceeds* 21 parts per million, water is considered impure and needs further purification before being piped to households for domestic consumption.

    The Department of Health recently conducted a study at two separate water purification plants – one in the Free State and the other in KZN. Impurity readings were recorded for a random sample of 24 days at the Free State plant and for a separate random sample of 29 days at the KZN plant.

    (a)   Is the drinking water produced by the KZN purification plant of a *higher quality* (i.e. *fewer impurities*, on average) than that of the Free State purification plant?

        (i)   Use the **Data Analysis** add-in **F-Test Two-Sample for Variances** to find out if the two population variances can be assumed to be equal. Use $\alpha = 0.05$.

        (ii)   Define the null and alternative hypotheses for this management question.

        (iii)   Use the appropriate *t-test* from **Data Analysis: *t*-Test: Two Sample Assuming Equal** (or **Unequal**) **Variances** option to test the hypotheses in (ii) at the 1% level of significance.

        (iv)   What conclusion can be drawn from the findings?

    (b)   Identify the *p*-value for this hypothesis test from the output in (a) and interpret its value in the context of the management question.

20   X9.20 – herbal tea

Rooibos herbal tea contains the vitamin called 'quercetin', which is known to improve blood circulation. To determine whether two brands of rooibos herbal tea have equal amounts of this vitamin, a chemist examined two randomly drawn samples of rooibos tea from *two different brands* – Freshpak and Yellow Label – and recorded the quercetin content of each tea in mg/kg.

    (a)   Use the **Data Analysis** add-in **F-Test Two-Sample for Variances** to find out if the two population variances can be assumed to be equal. Use $\alpha = 0.05$.

    (b)   Use the appropriate *t-test* from **Data Analysis: *t*-Test: Two Sample Assuming Equal** (or **Unequal**) **Variances** option to answer the management questions in both (i) and (ii).

        (i)   Provide statistical evidence at the 5% significance level that there is *no difference* in the mean quercetin levels between the two brands of rooibos tea tested. Show appropriate null and alternative hypotheses for the test. What conclusion is drawn?

        (ii)   If the producers of the Freshpak brand claim that their brand of rooibos tea contains *more* quercetin, on average, than the Yellow Label brand, test, at the 5% significance level, whether the sample evidence can support their claim. Show the null and alternative hypothesis for this test. Is the Freshpak claim valid?

21   X9.21 – meat fat

The *fat content* (in g/kg) of two large consignments of meat received from *different regions* (one from Namibia and other from the Little Karoo) were analysed by the quality controller of a local meat distributor. Random samples of portions were selected from each consignment and tested. Assume that the data on fat content for the two consignments is normally distributed and that population variances are equal.

(a) The distributor is considering signing an exclusive supply contract with the Namibian meat producer. However, they will only sign the contract if it can be shown statistically that the mean fat content is *significantly lower* for meat supplied by the Namibian producer compared to the Little Karoo meat producer.

   (i) Use the **Data Analysis** add-in *F*-**Test Two-Sample for Variances** to find out if the two population variances can be assumed to be equal. Use $\alpha = 0.05$.

   (ii) Define the null and alternative hypotheses for this management question.

   (iii) Use the appropriate *t-test* from **Data Analysis: *t*-Test: Two Sample Assuming Equal (or Unequal) Variances** option to test the hypotheses in (ii) at the 1% level of significance.

   (iv) Should the distributor sign an exclusive supply contract with the Namibian producer? Justify your recommendation.

(b) Identify the *p*-value for this hypothesis test from the output in (a) and interpret its value in the context of the management question.

22 X9.22 – disinfectant sales

A supplier of a household disinfectant liquid launched a promotional campaign to increase sales of its 500 ml bottles. *Before the campaign*, the average weekly sales (in cases sold) were recorded at 12 randomly chosen retail outlets throughout KwaZulu-Natal. Three weeks *after the campaign*, average weekly sales were again recorded at the *same 12 outlets*. The average weekly sales (in cases sold) are shown for each of the 12 retail outlets as follows:

Outlet	Sales (in cases) Before	After
1	12	12
2	8	11
3	14	14
4	9	9
5	13	11
6	15	16
7	10	11
8	12	13
9	10	11
10	13	13
11	12	14
12	10	11

Can the suppliers of the household disinfectant conclude that the promotional campaign has been a success? Test this management question statistically.

(a) Why is this a matched-pairs *t-test*? Explain.

(b) Formulate the null and alternative hypotheses to answer this management question.

(c)   Conduct a matched-pairs *t-test* at the 5% significance level. What is your conclusion?

(d)   Repeat the test using the *t-Test*: **Paired Two Sample for Means** option in Excel's **Data Analysis**. Interpret the appropriate *p*-value from this output.

23   X9.23 – performance ratings

The human resource department of Eskom – a national electricity supplier – ran a series of workshops and seminars for its field employees aimed at increasing their motivation and productivity. To test the effectiveness of this programme, the training manager randomly selected 18 field employees and recorded their most recent *performance ratings* (conducted *after the workshop* programme) and their ratings *prior* to attending the workshops. Performance ratings are scored from 1 to 20. Assume performance rating scores are normally distributed.

(a)   Are the two samples of performance rating scores independent? Why or why not?

(b)   Has the workshop programme been *effective* for Eskom field workers in general? Conduct a hypothesis test at the 5% level of significance using the *t-Test*: **Paired Two Sample for Means** option in Excel's **Data Analysis**. Formulate the appropriate null and alternative hypotheses for the test. What conclusion is drawn?

(c)   Using the output from (b), interpret the appropriate *p*-value for this test.

Employee	Performance rating	
	Before	After
1	12.8	13.1
2	8.5	9.2
3	10.2	12.6
4	8.3	7.8
5	13.1	14.0
6	11.2	12.1
7	9.3	9.7
8	6.6	7.5
9	14.8	15.2
10	11.2	11.9
11	14.1	13.8
12	7.8	8.1
13	10.6	10.2
14	12.7	12.9
15	9.8	10.2
16	14.3	13.8
17	13.8	13.9
18	10.1	9.6

24   X9.24 – household debt

The *debt ratio* of 10 households was monitored from *a year ago*, when the prime interest rate was 6%, to the *current period*, when the prime interest rate has risen to 11%. The analyst wanted to find out if the increase in prime interest rate has had a significant impact on reducing the average level of household debt. Assume that the household debt ratio is normally distributed.

| | Household debt ratio | |
Household	Year ago	Current
H1	45	43
H2	39	37
H3	46	46
H4	51	48
H5	38	40
H6	31	29
H7	37	36
H8	43	44
H9	41	37
H10	34	33

(a)   Are these two samples independent? Why or why not?

(b)   At the 5% level of significance, can the analyst conclude that the increase in the prime interest rate from 6% a year ago to 11% currently has led to a *significant reduction* in the average *level of household debt*? Formulate a suitable null and alternative hypothesis for the test. Use the *t-Test*: **Paired Two Sample for Means** option in Excel's **Data Analysis** to conduct the test.

(c)   From the output in (b), identify the appropriate *p*-value for the test statistic and interpret its meaning in the context of the analyst's question.

25   Process 1 has a variability of units produced per hour of $s_1^2 = 14.6$ units, while process 2 has a variability of output of $s_2^2 = 23.2$ units. Assume $n_1 = 25$ and $n_2 = 31$. Can it be assumed that the two processes have equal *variability* of units produced per hour? Test at the 5% level of significance.

26   X9.26 – milk yield

A milk producer studied the yield of milk from cows under two feeding practices. One group of randomly selected cows from a herd were fed a controlled diet while a second group of randomly selected cows from the same herd were allowed to graze freely. After three months, the yield of milk from the cows in each sample were recorded (in litres per week). Can the milk producer conclude that the *variability* in milk yield from the 'free grazing' cows is *greater* than that of the 'controlled feed' cows? Test at the 5% significance level.

Free grazing		Feeding programme	
28.6	34.1	38.3	29.7
24.6	24.5	24.7	42.2
20.1	45.8	36.2	44.7
25.3	39.3	36.9	41.5
42.8	28.8	35.8	31.6
27.2	21.1	23.7	42.3
41.7	21.9	26.9	40.9
39.3	35.8	38.2	32.4

27   X9.27 – employee wellness

An organisation encourages its employees to participate in planned exercises on a regular weekly basis to promote employee wellness. Separate exercise routines are planned for 'under 40' and 'over 40' employees. The HR executive responsible for employee wellness believes that the 'over 40' employees are more 'erratic' (or variable) than the 'under 40' employees in the time spent exercising on a weekly basis. A sample of employees from each group were selected and their weekly exercise times recorded (in hours).

Over 40				Under 40			
3.6	2.7	2.1	2.9	2.6	3.3	2.1	3.3
2.9	0.9	2.3	2.1	3.1	2.3	4.2	3.1
1.5	4.1	1.7	2.4	2.6	4.2	2.5	2.7
2.4	2.7	3.7	2.9	3.1	3.4	3.1	
4.3	1.8	3.2	1.5	3.7	3.5	2.5	
1.1	1.6	2.2		2.6	4.1	2.8	

Test, at the 5% level of significance, if there is sufficient sample evidence to support the HR executive's belief (i.e. that the 'over 40' employees show greater variability in time spent on weekly exercise than the 'under 40' employees).

28   X9.28 – attrition rate

A study on the attrition rates of call-centre consultants was conducted between call centres operating in the financial services sector and the health services sector. A random sample of monthly attrition rates of call centres from each sector was recorded. The analyst was interested in the variability of attrition rates between these two sectors.

Financial services				Health services		
7.1	5.9	5.9	5.6	6.9	4.0	4.4
3.6	6.7	6.5	6.7	6.2	5.1	5.0
7.2	6.2	5.6	6.8	3.5	4.9	6.8
5.4	6.9	7.0		4.6	5.5	7.7
5.7	6.1	6.5		5.8	5.9	5.5
5.6	5.5	6.3		5.4	5.6	

Can it be concluded that there is no significant difference in the variability of attrition rates between these two sectors? Conduct a suitable hypothesis test at the 5% level of significance.

29 **X9.29 – operating systems**

A software analyst was testing the efficiency of two operating systems (OS1 and OS2) in terms of the speed with which each opens a document. The analyst conducted an experiment where the same file saved in 8 different document formats (e.g. jpeg, zlsx, pdf, txt, doc, xps, rtf, xml) was read by each operating system separately (running on the same hardware). The *time to open each document* (in seconds) was recorded.

Document type	OS1	OS2
*.jpg	1.7	2.1
*.xlsx	2.9	2.5
*.pdf	1.8	1.5
*.txt	1.4	2.4
*.doc	2.1	2.2
*.xps	2.5	3.3
*.trf	2.2	3.1
*.xml	2.9	2.9

Management question:

Can the software analyst conclude that Operating System 1 is *more efficient* (i.e. faster) on average, than Operating System 2?

(a) Is this a paired *t-test*? Why or why not?

(b) Formulate the null and alternative hypothesis to address this management question.

(c) Conduct a hypothesis test at the 10% level of significance and draw the statistical and management conclusion.

(d) Compute the *p*-value of the test (use T.DIST) and draw a statistical conclusion.

30 **X9.30 – aircraft performance**

South African Airways (SAA) plans to replace its existing 747 fleet of aircraft. Two aircraft manufacturers, *Airbus Industrie* and *Boeing Corporation*, are bidding for the contract. To assist the decision-makers at SAA, each bidder supplied SAA with an 'evaluation' aircraft with the same specifications on which identical performance tests were performed. The performance score on each of **17 in-flight tests** (called **Test Codes**) by SAA flight engineers was recorded for each aircraft. Note that a *higher performance score* means *better performance*.

Test Code	Airbus	Boeing
C2	8.8	8.1
P6	9.1	9.8
D1	9.7	8.9
T7	9.8	9.2
F2	10.6	11.5
F5	9.7	7.6
K5	8.6	9.6
N2	8.4	7.9
C6	9.3	8.1
H7	7.5	7.9
A5	8.1	6.8
S8	9.8	9.3
S1	10.6	9.6
V2	11.5	8.2
V5	10.5	9.6
B5	10.1	10.4
M1	9.4	8.8

Management question:

Can the SAA board conclude that, on *average*, the *Airbus Industrie* aircraft performs *significantly better* than the *Boeing* aircraft in terms of their respective *in-flight performance scores?*

(a) Is this a paired *t-test*? Why or why not?

(b) Formulate the null and alternative hypothesis to address this management question.

(c) Conduct a hypothesis test at the 5% level of significance and draw the statistical and management conclusion. What recommendation would you make to SAA?

(d) Compute the *p*-value of the test (use **T.DIST.RT**) and draw a statistical conclusion.

CHAPTER
10

Chi-square Hypothesis Tests

Outcomes

Hypothesis tests can also be used to examine whether two categorical variables are statistically associated. The test is based on an analysis of the pattern of outcomes as shown in a cross-tabulation table between the two categorical random variables. A *test for independence of association* is conducted on the cross-tabulated table using the *chi-square test statistic*. This test for independence of association is used extensively in marketing, for example to identify which consumer demographic measures are associated with particular consumer buying behaviour.

The chi-square test statistic is also used to conduct goodness-of-fit tests, and tests for equality of proportions across multiple populations.

After studying this chapter, you should be able to:

- understand the concept and rationale of the chi-square statistic
- understand the use of the chi-square statistic in management practice
- perform independence of association hypothesis tests using the chi-square statistic
- perform equality of multiple proportions hypothesis tests using the chi-square statistic
- perform goodness-of-fit hypothesis tests using the chi-square statistic
- interpret the results of the various chi-square tests.

10.1 Introduction and Rationale

The chi-square statistic, written χ^2, is used to test hypotheses on *patterns of outcomes* for *categorical* random variables. These patterns of outcomes are based on *frequency counts*.

It differs from the z-statistic and the t-statistic tests that are used to conduct hypothesis tests on central location measures (i.e. mean values) only. In contrast, chi-square hypothesis tests focus on testing for patterns of outcomes based on frequency counts. They can be used to examine whether a single categorical random variable displays a certain pattern (profile) of outcomes, or whether two categorical random variables are associated (by examining their joint pattern of outcomes).

The chi-square test can be used in three different contexts:
- to test for *independence of association* between two categorical variables, e.g. 'Is the choice of magazine read associated with the reader's gender?'
- to test for *equality of proportions across two or more populations*, e.g. 'Is the percentage of unionised workers per firm the same across four construction firms?'
- as a *goodness-of-fit* test, e.g. 'Is the completion time (in minutes) for a task normally distributed?'

In all three test scenarios, the same five steps of hypothesis testing are used. When formulating the hypotheses (Step 1), the population measure being tested is a *pattern of outcomes*, not a central location parameter. Also, the test statistic used in steps 2 and 3 is the chi-square statistic, χ^2, instead of the z- or the t-statistic.

The Chi-square Statistic

The **chi-square test** is based on *frequency count* data. It always compares a set of *observed frequencies* obtained from a random sample to a set of *expected frequencies* that describes the null hypothesis.

The **chi-square test statistic** (χ^2-*stat*) measures by how much the observed frequencies and the expected frequencies *differ*. If this difference is small, the null hypothesis is likely to be accepted. Conversely, a large difference is likely to result in the null hypothesis being rejected. The chi-square statistic that transforms sample frequencies into a test statistic is given by the following formula:

$$\chi^2 = \sum \frac{(f_o - f_e)^2}{f_e}$$

10.1

Where: f_o = *observed frequency* of a category of a categorical random variable
f_e = *expected frequency* of a category of a categorical random variable.

10.2 The Chi-square Test for Independence of Association

In many management situations, the chi-square statistic is used to test for *independence of association*. This test establishes whether two categorical random variables are statistically related (i.e. dependent or independent of each other). Statistical independence means that the outcome of one random variable in no way influences (or is influenced by) (or associated with) the outcome of a second random variable

A hypothesis test will establish whether the association as observed in a cross-tabulation table is purely a *chance occurrence* or whether it reflects a *genuine association* between the variables in the populations from which the sample data was drawn.

Knowing whether two random variables are associated can influence many decision processes. For example, if market research establishes that consumer brand choices of fruit juices are influenced by the type of packaging or the shelf position in a supermarket, decisions about which packaging to use or which shelf level to select are important. If, however, brand choice is independent of packaging or shelf level, these factors need not be considered in the promotion of fruit juices.

The test for independence of association follows the same five steps of hypothesis testing and is explained by the following example.

Example 10.1 Teenage Magazine Preferences Study

The Abacus Media Company publishes three magazines for the teenage market (male and female readers between 13 and 16 years of age). The management question, which the executive editor of Abacus would like to answer, is the following: 'Are readership preferences for the three magazines independent of gender?'

A survey was carried out amongst 200 teenagers (of both genders and between the ages of 13 and 16 years) in various bookstores. Randomly selected teenagers who bought at least one of the three magazines were interviewed and asked the following question: 'Which one of these three magazines do you most prefer to read?' The gender of the respondent was also noted. The magazine preference responses by gender is summarised in Table 10.1.

(See Excel file C10.1 – *teenage magazines*.)

The sample profile shows that 80 girls and 120 boys were interviewed (column total), and that 46 teenagers prefer *Beat*; 73 prefer *Youth* and 81 prefer *Grow* (row total). Table 10.1 also shows the observed joint frequency count for each combination of gender and magazine preference (e.g. 33 boys most prefer *Beat* magazine, and 28 girls most prefer *Youth* magazine).

Table 10.1 Cross-tabulation table of gender by magazine preference

Gender	Magazine preference			Total
	Beat	Grow	Youth	
Female	13	39	28	80
Male	33	42	45	120
Total	46	81	73	200

Management Question

Are readership preferences for the three magazines independent of gender?

Test, at the 5% level of significance, whether there is a statistical association between gender and magazine preference (i.e. whether or not they are statistically independent).

Solution

The two categorical random variables are 'gender' (female, male) and 'magazine preference' (*Beat, Grow, Youth*).

Exploratory Data Analysis

Initially, inspect the sample magazine preference profiles by gender to get an indication of the likely association between these two variables. To do this, the frequency counts must be converted into percentages (either row or column percentages). In this example, row percentages are selected as it allows an interpretation of magazine preferences by gender. (Column percentages would allow an interpretation of gender profile by magazine type.) Row percentages are calculated by dividing each joint frequency count by its respective row total (given in the 'Total' column) and shown in Table 10.2.

Table 10.2 Row percentage pivot table of gender with magazine preference

Gender	Magazine preference			Total
	Beat	*Grow*	*Youth*	
Female	16%	49%	35%	100%
Male	27%	35%	38%	100%
Total	**23%**	**40%**	**37%**	**100%**

An association exists if the individual gender profiles (i.e. the 'Female' row profile and the 'Male' row profile) differ significantly from the combined gender profile (the 'Total' row profile). From the sample data in Table 10.2, boys are more likely to prefer *Beat* (male: 27%; female: 16%, compared with the combined percentage of 23%), while girls are more keen on *Grow* (female: 49%; male: 35%, compared with the combined percentage of 40%). On the other hand, there is an almost equal preference by girls and boys for *Youth* (female: 35%; male: 38%, compared with the combined percentage of 37%).

The statistical question that hypothesis testing will answer is whether these observed differences in patterns of outcomes are due to *chance* (i.e. sampling error) or due to a *genuine difference* in readership profiles between girls and boys across the three teenage magazines.

Hypothesis test for independence of association

Step 1: Define the null and alternative hypotheses

H_0: There is no association between gender and magazine preference (i.e. they are statistically independent).

H_1: There is an association (i.e. they are not independent).

The null hypothesis always states that the two categorical random variables are independent of (or not associated with) each other. From a management perspective, accepting the null hypothesis would mean that:

- magazine preference profiles are the same for both boys and girls or, alternatively,
- each gender has the same preference across all magazines.

A rejection of the null hypothesis, on the other hand, means that different magazine preferences exist between girls and boys. Management would then develop different promotional strategies for each magazine according to gender preference.

Step 2: Determine the region of acceptance of the null hypothesis

The chi-square hypothesis test is only an *upper-tailed test*, hence only a single critical X^2-limit is required. To find the critical X^2-limit, both a level of significance, α, and degrees of freedom are needed.

Given the level of significance, $\alpha = 0.05$ (5% significance level).

The *degrees of freedom* formula is:

$$df = (r-1)(c-1) \qquad 10.2$$

Where: r = number of rows in the cross-tabulation table

c = number of columns in the cross-tabulation table

In the example, the degrees of freedom is $df = (2-1)(3-1) = 2$.

Then the critical X^2-limit is given by $X^2_{(\alpha = 0.05)(df = 2)} = 5.991$ (Table 3, Appendix 1).

Thus the region of acceptance for H_0 is $X^2 \leq 5.991$.

The decision rule is then stated as follows:

- Accept H_0 if X^2-*stat* lies at or below the upper limit of 5.991.
- Reject H_0 if X^2-*stat* lies above 5.991.

Step 3: Calculate the sample test statistic (X^2-*stat*)

The appropriate sample test statistic is X^2-*stat*, which is calculated using formula 10.1. It requires both observed frequencies (f_o) and expected frequencies (f_e). The observed frequencies (f_o) are based on the sample survey data and are given in Table 10.1.

Deriving the expected frequencies

The formula to calculate the expected *frequency* for each cell ($i; j$) is:

$$\text{Expected frequency}_{i,j} = f_e = \frac{i^{th} \text{ row total} \times j^{th} \text{ column total}}{\text{Sample size } (n)} \qquad 10.3$$

These frequencies are shown in a separate cross-tabulation table that will always have the same row totals and column totals as the observed frequency cross-tabulation table (Table 10.1). Table 10.3 shows the calculated *expected frequencies* for the teenager magazine readership study.

Table 10.3 Expected frequencies for teenage magazine preferences study

Gender	Magazine preference			Total
	Beat	Grow	Youth	
Female	18.4	32.4	29.2	80
Male	27.6	48.6	43.8	120
Total	46	81	73	200

To illustrate, consider the cell 'males who most prefer *Beat* magazine':

$$f_e(males/Beat) = \frac{\text{'Male' row total} \times \text{'Beat' column total}}{\text{Sample size}}$$
$$= \frac{120 \times 46}{200} = 27.6$$

Similarly, consider the cell of 'females who most prefer *Grow* magazine':

$$f_e(females/Grow) = \frac{\text{'Female' row total} \times \text{'Grow' column total}}{\text{Sample size}}$$
$$= \frac{80 \times 81}{200} = 32.4$$

These expected frequencies are constructed to reflect *no statistical association* (i.e. independence) between the two categorical random variables. Each expected frequency cell represents the *theoretical number* of teenagers within each gender that would prefer each type of magazine *if* the two variables were *independent*. For example, out of the sample of 200 teenagers surveyed, 18.4 girls and 27.6 boys are expected to prefer *Beat* magazine, *if* there were *no association* between gender and magazine preference.

To confirm that these expected frequencies reflect the null hypothesis of no association (i.e. independence), we calculate the row (or column) percentages for the expected table as shown in Table 10.4.

Table 10.4 Row percentages for expected frequency pivot table of the teenage magazine preferences study

Gender	Magazine preference			Total
	Beat	*Grow*	*Youth*	
Female	23%	40.5%	36.5%	100%
Male	23%	40.5%	36.5%	100%
Total	**23%**	**40.5%**	**36.5%**	**100%**

Table 10.4 shows independence between magazine preference and gender, because the readership preference profiles (in row percentage terms) are the same for both males and females, and for the sample as a whole (both females and males together).

To derive the X^2-*stat* sample test statistic, use Formula 10.1 as shown in Table 10.5.

Table 10.5 X^2-*stat* for the teenage magazine preferences study

Joint categories		f_o	f_e	$(f_o - f_e)^2$	$\dfrac{(f_o - f_e)^2}{f_e}$
Female	*Beat*	13	18.4	29.16	1.585
	Grow	39	32.4	43.56	1.344
	Youth	28	29.2	1.44	0.049
Male	*Beat*	33	27.6	29.16	1.057
	Grow	42	48.6	43.56	0.896
	Youth	45	43.8	1.44	0.033
				X^2-stat	**4.964**

Thus X^2-*stat* = 4.964.

Also the *p*-value of the test is 0.0836. (Use Excel's function **CHISQ.DIST.RT(4.964,2)**).

Step 4: Compare the sample test statistic to the region of acceptance

The sample test statistic, $X^2\text{-stat} = 4.964$ lies *within* the region of acceptance of $X^2 \leq 5.991$ as shown in Figure 10.1. This is also confirmed with the *p*-value (0.0836) $> \alpha$ (0.05).

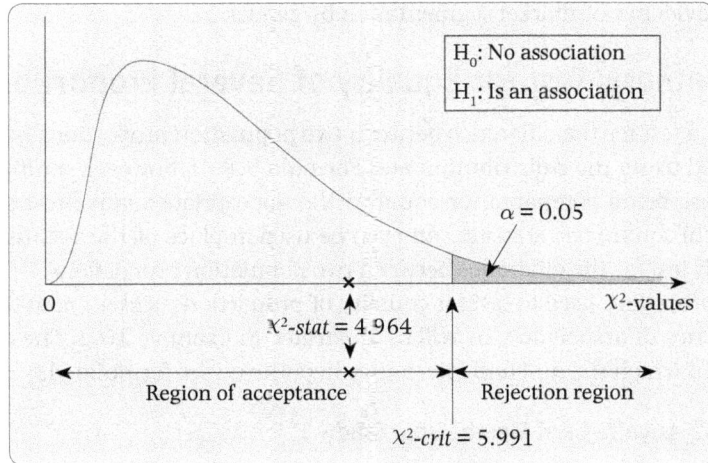

Figure 10.1 Teenage magazine preference study – $X^2\text{-stat}$ and region of acceptance

Step 5: Draw statistical and management conclusions

Statistical Conclusion

Accept H_0 at the 5% level of significance. The sample evidence is not strong enough to reject H_0 in favour of H_1 at $\alpha = 0.05$. The null hypothesis is therefore probably true.

Management Conclusion

It can be concluded, with 95% confidence that magazine preference is independent of gender. Alternatively, it can be stated that there is no association between magazine preference and gender.

The stacked bar chart in Figure 10.2 highlights the similarity of profiles of magazine preferences between girls and boys. Any observed differences in profiles across gender are due purely to chance.

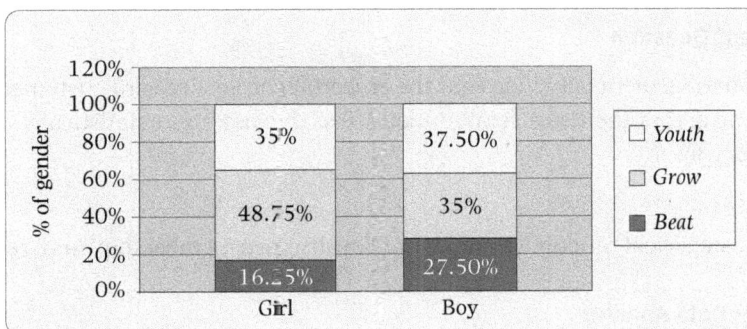

Figure 10.2 Stacked bar chart – teenage magazine preferences by gender

Management Recommendation

Therefore a *common* promotional strategy for both genders can be adopted by each of the three magazines. These findings suggest that there is no perceived product differentiation between the three magazines by the teenage target population, nor is there any evidence of market segmentation by gender.

10.3 Hypothesis Test for Equality of Several Proportions

In Chapter 9, a test for the difference between two population proportions (see section 9.5) was conducted using the z-distribution and Formula 9.8. If, however, multiple population proportions are being compared for equality, the appropriate sample test statistic is chi-square. The chi-square test statistic can even be used in place of the z-statistic to conduct the hypothesis test for the difference between two population proportions.

The test procedure used to test for equality of proportions is *identical* to that for the test for independence of association, as will be illustrated in Example 10.2. The only difference is in the way in which the null and alternative hypotheses are formulated.

Example 10.2 Loyalty Card Membership Study

A ladies' fashion retail company wants to know whether the proportion of their customers who have store loyalty cards is the same across three major retail outlets: Canal Walk, Sandton Mall and Somerset Mall. A random sample of 180 customers across the three stores was selected and the number who had loyalty cards was recorded. The sample findings are shown in Table 10.6.

(See Excel file C10.2 – *loyalty card*.)

Table 10.6 Cross-tabulation of loyalty card membership by retail store

Card	Retail outlet location			Total
	Canal Walk	Sandton Mall	Somerset Mall	
Yes	36	44	26	106
No	16	40	18	74
Total	52	84	44	180

Management Question

Can the management conclude that the *proportion* of loyalty card customers per store is the *same* across the three retail outlets? Test this assertion statistically at the 10% significance level.

Solution

The two categorical random variables are 'loyalty card membership' and 'retail outlet'.

Exploratory Data Analysis

The loyalty membership profile per store can initially be examined by inspection from the column percentages in Table 10.7.

Table 10.7 Column percentage analysis of the proportion of loyalty card members per store

Card	Retail outlet location			Total
	Canal Walk	Sandton Mall	Somerset Mall	
Yes	69%	52%	59%	59%
No	31%	48%	41%	41%
Total	100%	100%	100%	100%

The sample data shows that 69% of all Canal Walk customers are loyalty card members, while only 52% of Sandton Mall customers and 59% of Somerset Mall customers are loyalty card members. Across all stores, 59% of all customers are loyalty card members.

The statistical question is whether these observed *sample proportions* of loyalty members *per store* differ significantly from the overall proportion of loyalty card members *across all stores*, or whether these differences are due purely to *chance* (i.e. random sampling). Hence a hypothesis test for equality of proportion in three populations is conducted.

Hypothesis test for equality of multiple proportions

Step 1: Define the null and alternative hypotheses

Let: π_1 = population proportion of loyalty card members at the Canal Walk store

π_2 = population proportion of loyalty card members at the Sandton Mall store

π_3 = population proportion of loyalty card members at the Somerset Mall store.

Then:

H_0: $\pi_1 = \pi_2 = \pi_3$ (population proportions are equal across all stores)

H_1: At least one population proportion is different.

The null hypothesis states that the population proportion of customers with loyalty cards per store is the *same* across the three stores. This is equivalent to stating that loyalty card membership is *independent* of (or not associated with) store location.

Step 2: Determine the region of acceptance of the null hypothesis

Given the level of significance $\alpha = 0.10$ (i.e. 10%) and degrees of freedom = 2 (where $r = 2$ and $c = 3$, using Formula 10.2).

Then the critical χ^2-limit is given by $\chi^2_{(\alpha = 0.10)(df = 2)} = 4.605$ (Table 3, Appendix 1). Thus the region of acceptance for H_0 is $\chi^2 \leq 4.605$.

The decision rule is then stated as follows:

- Accept H_0 if χ^2-*stat* falls at or below the upper limit of 4.605.
- Reject H_0 if χ^2-*stat* falls above 4.605.

Step 3: Calculate the sample test statistic (χ^2-*stat*)

To calculate the sample test statistic, χ^2-*stat* both an *observed* and an *expected* frequency table are required. The observed frequency table is derived from the sample data as shown in Table 10.6, while the expected frequency table is constructed in the same way as for the independence of association test (using Formula 10.3) and is shown in Table 10.8.

Table 10.8 Expected frequency cross-tabulation table for the loyalty card membership study

Card	Retail outlet location			Total
	Canal Walk	Sandton Mall	Somerset Mall	
Yes	30.6	49.5	25.9	106
No	21.4	34.5	18.1	74
Total	**52**	**84**	**44**	**180**

Table 10.9 shows the calculation of X^2-*stat* using Formula 10.1.

Table 10.9 X^2-*stat* for the loyalty card membership study

Joint categories		f_o	f_e	$(f_o - f_e)^2$	$\dfrac{(f_o - f_e)^2}{f_e}$
Yes	Canal Walk	36	30.6	29.16	0.953
	Sandton Mall	44	49.5	30.25	0.611
	Somerset Mall	26	25.9	0.01	0.0004
No	Canal Walk	16	21.4	29.16	1.363
	Sandton Mall	40	34.5	30.25	0.877
	Somerset Mall	18	18.1	0.01	0.0006
				X^2-stat	**3.805**

Thus X^2-*stat* = 3.805. Also, the *p*-value of the test is 0.1492. (Use Excel's function **CHISQ.DIST.RT(3.805,2)**).

Step 4: Compare the sample test statistic to the region of acceptance

The sample test statistic, X^2-*stat* = 3.805 lies *within* the region of acceptance of $X^2 \le 4.605$, as shown in Figure 10.3. This is also confirmed with the *p*-value (0.1492) > α (0.10).

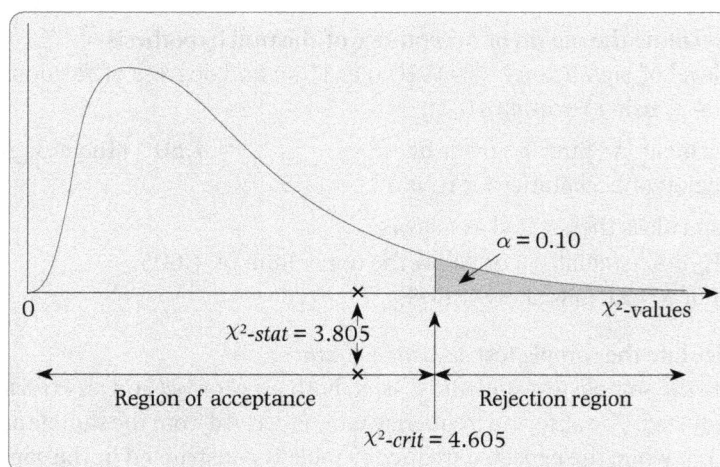

Figure 10.3 Loyalty card membership study – X^2-*stat* and region of acceptance

Step 5: Draw statistical and management conclusions

Statistical Conclusion

Accept H_0 at the 10% level of significance. The sample evidence is not strong enough to reject H_0 in favour of H_1, and any observed differences in sample proportions of loyalty card members between retail outlets is due purely to chance. The null hypothesis is therefore probably true.

Management Conclusion

It can be concluded, with 90% confidence, that the proportion of loyalty card customers per store is the same across all three store locations. The stacked bar chart in Figure 10.4 highlights the similarity of profiles of loyalty card membership across stores. Any observed differences in profiles between stores are due purely to chance.

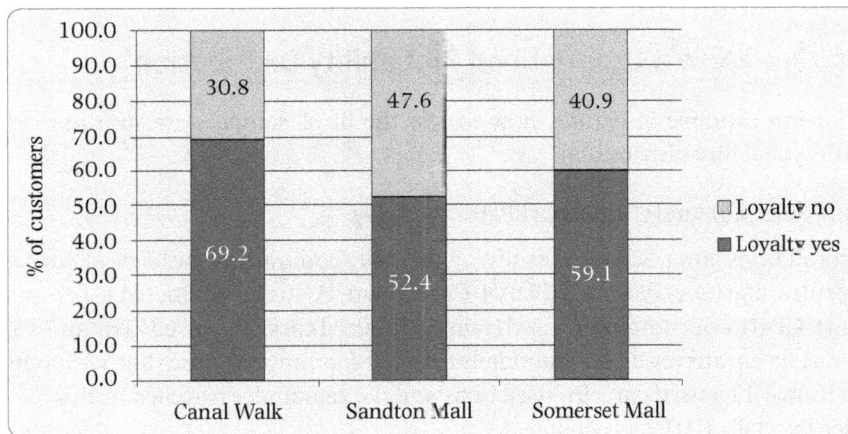

Figure 10.4 Stacked bar chart – loyalty card membership by store location

Comparing the Equality of Multiple Proportions Test and the Independence of Association Test

The test for equality of proportions across multiple populations is *equivalent* to the test for independence of association between two categorical random variables.

In the test for independence of association, the null hypothesis of 'no association' means that for a specific category of one random variable, the proportion of responses is the *same* across all categories of the second random variable. Using Example 10.2 to illustrate: If the *proportion* of customers who have a loyalty card is the *same* across three retail outlets (i.e. Canal Walk, Sandton Mall and Somerset Mall), then this is the same as saying that there is *no association* between loyalty card ownership and retail outlet. Thus no association implies *equality of proportions across multiple populations*.

As a result, the *same hypothesis test procedure* is followed when either a test of *independence of association* or *a test for equality of multiple proportions* is required. The only difference is in the way in which the management question is phrased and therefore how the null hypothesis (Step 1) is defined, and in the manner in which the conclusion (Step 5) is drawn.

10.4 Chi-square Goodness-of-Fit Test

The chi-square statistic can also be used to test whether the *outcomes* for a given random variable follow a certain *specified pattern* (e.g. the normal distribution). The outcomes for a random variable are represented by its frequency distribution.

If a random variable's observed sample frequency distribution can be matched to a specified probability distribution such as the normal, binomial, Poisson or some other user-defined probability distribution, then this specified distribution can be used to describe the behaviour of the random variable in general.

The chi-square statistic measures how well the *observed frequency* distribution of a random variable 'fits' (or matches) an *expected frequency* distribution. The expected frequencies would be based on a particular theoretical or a user-defined distribution, which the random variable is hypothesised to follow. The hypothesis-testing procedure is identical to the procedure followed in the independence of association hypothesis test.

Testing for Fit to a User-defined Probability Distribution

The following example illustrates how to test the fit of sample data to a *user-defined* (or *empirical*) probability distribution.

Example 10.3 Commuter Transport Patterns Study

Metrorail Commuter Service is studying the daily commuting patterns of workers into the central business district (CBD) of Cape Town. A study conducted seven years ago found that 40% of commuters used trains, 25% used cars, 20% used taxis and 15% used buses. A recent survey of 400 randomly selected commuters found that 135 commuters used trains, 115 used cars, 96 used taxis and the remainder travelled by bus.

(See Excel file C10.3 – *commuters*.)

Management Question

Can Metrorail conclude that commuting patterns into the CBD of Cape Town have changed since the study seven years ago? Test the hypothesis at the 5% level of significance.

Solution

Step 1: Define the null and alternative hypotheses
The *null hypothesis* always states that the observed data of the random variable *fits* the proposed theoretical or user-defined probability pattern of outcomes. In this example, the user-defined probability distribution is represented by the commuting patterns of seven years ago.

Thus: H_0: The commuting patterns today are the *same* as they were seven years ago (i.e. the commuting pattern is still 40% trains; 25% cars; 20% taxis; 15% buses).

H_1: The commuting patterns today *differ significantly* from those of seven years ago (i.e. the commuting pattern *is not* 40% trains; 25% cars; 20% taxis; 15% buses).

Step 2: Determine the region of acceptance of the null hypothesis
Given the level of significance $\alpha = 0.05$ (i.e. 5%).
The degrees of freedom formula for goodness-of-fit tests is:

$$df = k - m - 1 \qquad\qquad 10.4$$

Where: k = number of classes (categories)
   m = number of population parameters to estimate from the sample data.

Table 10.10 shows the number of population parameters (m) that need to be estimated from sample data when fitting theoretical or user-defined probability distributions. The m-term has a non-zero value only if the sample data is being fitted to a probability distribution such as the binomial, Poisson or normal distribution. Otherwise its value is zero.

Table 10.10 Population parameters to be estimated (m) for degrees of freedom

Probability distribution	Population parameters to be estimated	m
Normal	μ and σ^2	2
Binomial	π	1
Poisson	a	1
Uniform	None	0
User defined	None	0

Since there are four transport modes, $k = 4$. There are no estimated parameters ($m = 0$) because the distribution to be fitted is a user-defined distribution. Thus the degrees of freedom, $df = 4 - 0 - 1 = 3$.

Then the critical χ^2-limit is given by $\chi^2_{(\alpha = 0.05)(df = 3)} = 7.815$ (Table 3, Appendix 1). Thus the region of acceptance for H_0 is $\chi^2 \leq 7.815$.

The decision rule is then stated as follows:
- Accept H_0 if χ^2-*stat* falls at or below the upper limit of 7.815.
- Reject H_0 if χ^2-*stat* falls above 7.815.

Step 3: Calculate the sample test statistic (χ^2-*stat*)
The *observed frequencies* (f_o) are based on the recent survey data of 400 commuters, as shown in the column labelled f_o in Table 10.5.

The *expected frequencies* (f_e) are calculated from the study of seven years ago. The percentages given for each mode of transport must be converted into *frequencies* by multiplying each transport mode percentage by the sample size of 400 (i.e. $f_e = n \times$ transport mode %). For example, if 40% used trains, then theoretically 160 commuters ($= 400 \times \frac{40}{100}$) out of the 400 surveyed recently would be expected to use trains today if the null hypothesis were true.

Table 10.11 shows the calculation of χ^2-*stat* using formula 10.1.

Table 10.11 χ^2-stat for the commuter transport patterns study

Transport mode	Observed frequencies $\%f_o$	Observed frequencies f_o	Expected frequencies $\%f_e$	Expected frequencies f_e	$\dfrac{(f_o - f_e)^2}{f_e}$
Train	34%	135	40%	160	3.906
Car	29%	115	25%	100	2.25
Taxi	24%	96	20%	80	3.2
Bus	14%	54	15%	60	0.6
Total	**100%**	**400**	**100%**	**400**	**9.956**

Thus χ^2-stat = 9.956. Also, the p-value of the test is 0.0189. (Use Excel's function **CHISQ.DIST.RT(9.956,3)**).

Step 4: Compare the sample test statistic to the region of acceptance
The sample test statistic, χ^2-stat = 9.956 lies *outside* the region of acceptance of $\chi^2 \leq 7.815$, as seen in Figure 10.5. This is also confirmed with the p-value (0.0189) $< \alpha$ (0.05)

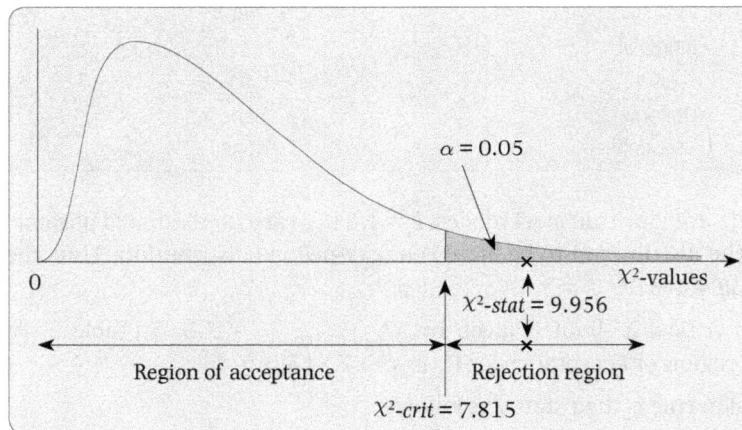

Figure 10.5 Commuter transport patterns study – χ^2-stat and region of acceptance

Step 5: Draw statistical and management conclusions

Statistical Conclusion

Reject H_0 at the 5% level of significance. The sample evidence is strong (convincing) enough to support H_1. Differences between observed and expected (under H_0) commuting profiles are not due purely to chance, but due to changed commuting behaviour. The alternative hypothesis is therefore probably true.

Management Conclusion

It can be concluded, with 95% confidence, that commuting patterns into the CBD of Cape Town have changed significantly from seven years ago.
To determine the nature of the changed pattern of commuting, the current pattern (i.e. the observed frequency percentages) can be compared to the previous pattern

(i.e. study from seven years ago), as shown in Table 10.12 and the multiple bar chart of Figure 10.6 below.

Table 10.12 Current and previous percentages of commuter transport patterns study

Transport mode	Previous pattern (%f_e)	Current pattern (%f_o)
Train	40%	33.75%
Car	25%	28.75%
Taxi	20%	24%
Bus	15%	13.5%
Total	**100%**	**100%**

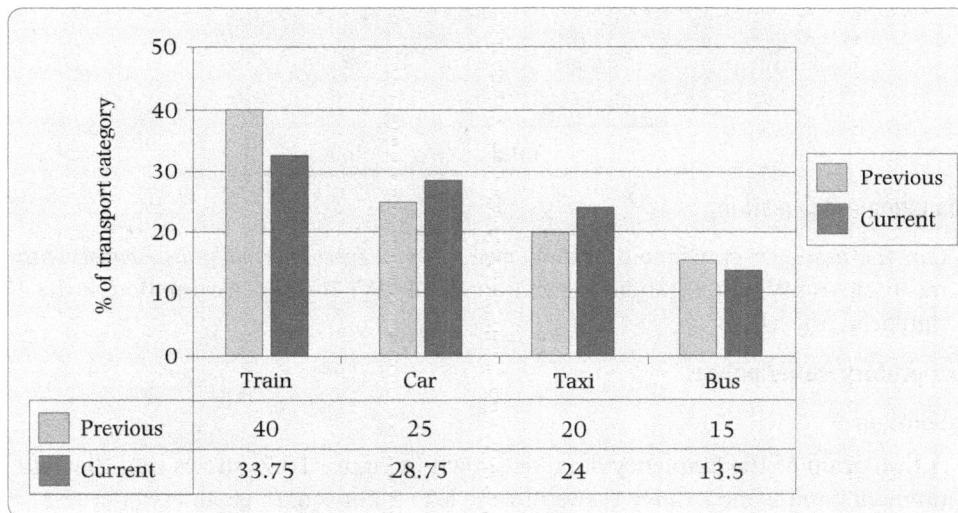

Figure 10.6 Multiple bar chart – commuter transport patterns study

From Table 10.12 and Figure 10.6, it can be seen that train and bus usage have both decreased over the past seven years (train usage more significantly so than bus usage). Car and taxi usage, on the other hand, have both shown about a 20% increase over the past seven years.

Testing for Fit to a Theoretical Probability Distribution

The following example illustrates how to test whether a particular theoretical probability distribution – such as the normal distribution – fits the profile of a given random variable. If a good fit is found, then the theoretical probability distribution can be used to describe the behaviour of this random variable as well as to calculate probabilities of outcomes for this random variable.

Fitting the Normal Probability Distribution

Many continuous numeric random variables are assumed to follow the normal distribution pattern of outcome. Normality is often assumed for the random variable, but it may be necessary to examine this assumption statistically. The **chi-square goodness-of-fit test** can be used to test whether a numeric continuous random variable is normally distributed or not.

Example 10.4 Electricity Usage Study

The manager of a restaurant recorded the daily usage of electricity in kilowatts (kW) for a period of 160 days, as shown in the numeric frequency table (Table 10.13).
(See Excel file C10.4 – *electricity usage*.)

Table 10.13 Frequency table of daily electricity usage by a restaurant

Usage intervals (kW/day)	Number of days (f_o)
Below 20	7
20–35	24
36–50	69
51–65	52
Above 65	8
Total	160

Management Question

Can the manager conclude that daily electricity usage is *normally distributed*, with a mean of 45 kW and a standard deviation of 14 kW? Test this assumption at the 1% significance level.

Exploratory Data Analysis

Solution

A histogram of the frequency data (as shown in Figure 10.7) shows that the data is unimodal and is moderately skewed to the left. A chi-square goodness-of-fit test will establish whether the shape of the histogram is sufficiently normally distributed with $\mu = 45$ and $\sigma = 14$.

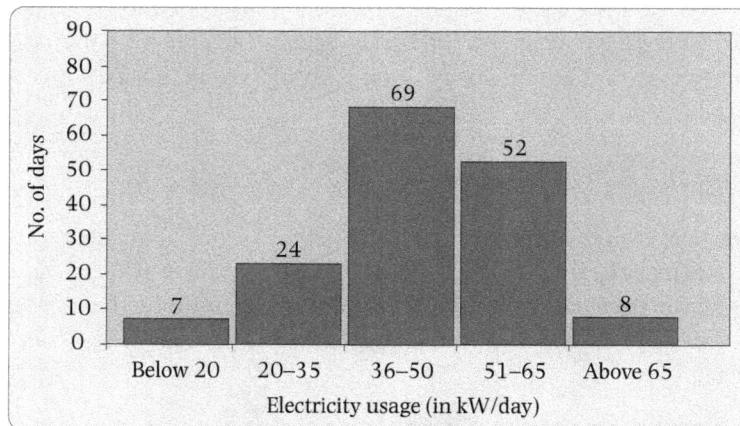

Figure 10.7 Histogram of daily electricity usage by restaurant

Goodness-of-fit test for normal distribution (with $\mu = 45$ and $\sigma = 14$)

Step 1: Define the null and alternative hypotheses

The null hypothesis states that the observed data of the continuous numeric random variable (x = daily electricity usage) fits the normal probability distribution with $\mu = 45$ kW and $\sigma = 14$ kW. Thus:

H_0: *Daily electricity usage* fits the normal distribution with $\mu = 45$ and $\sigma = 14$.

H_1: *Daily electricity usage* does not fit this normal distribution.

Step 2: Determine the region of acceptance of the null hypothesis

Given the level of significance $\alpha = 0.01$ (i.e. 1%).

The degrees of freedom for this normal distribution goodness-of-fit test are given by Formula 10.4 where $k = 5$ usage intervals and $m = 2$ estimated parameters (see Table 10.10). Thus $df = 5 - 2 - 1 = 2$.

Then the critical χ^2-limit is given by $\chi^2_{(\alpha = 0.01)(df = 2)} = 9.21$ (Table 3, Appendix 1). Thus the region of acceptance for H_0 is $\chi^2 \le 9.21$.

The decision rule is then stated as follows:

- Accept H_0 if χ^2-*stat* lies at or below the upper limit of 9.21.
- Reject H_0 if χ^2-*stat* lies above 9.21.

Step 3: Calculate the sample test statistic (χ^2-*stat*)

The *observed frequencies* (f_o) are obtained from the sample data as given in Table 10.13.

The *expected frequencies* (f_e), on the other hand, are derived from the normal distribution for the random variable 'daily electricity usage', with $\mu = 45$ and $\sigma = 14$, as follows:

- Find the *normal probabilities* for each interval of electricity usage (see Table 10.14) with $\mu = 45$ and $\sigma = 14$. The normal probabilities are calculated using the standard normal (z) tables (Table 1, Appendix 1). For example, for the first interval ($x < 20$), $P(x < 20) = P(z < -1.79) = 0.5 - 0.4633 = 0.037$.
- Calculate the *expected frequencies* for each usage interval by multiplying each normal probability by the sample size, $n = 160$.

Table 10.14 shows the calculation of the expected frequencies that follow a normal distribution (with $\mu = 45$ and $\sigma = 14$), and χ^2-*stat* using formula 10.1.

Table 10.14 Normal expected frequencies and χ^2-*stat* calculations for electricity usage study

Usage (kW/day)	Normal probability		Frequency		
	$P(k_1 < x < k_2)$	Probability	Observed frequency f_o	Expected f_e = probability × 160	$\chi^2 = \dfrac{(f_o - f_e)^2}{f_e}$
Below 20	$P(x < 20)$	0.037	7	5.93	0.192
20–35	$P(20 < x < 35)$	0.122	24	19.45	1.063
36–50	$P(36 < x < 50)$	0.533	69	85.25	3.097
51–65	$P(51 < x < 65)$	0.286	52	45.73	0.861
Above 65	$P(x > 65)$	0.023	8	3.60	5.367
Total		**1**	**160**	**160**	**10.58**

Thus χ^2-*stat* = 10.58. Also, the *p*-value of the test is 0.00504. (Use Excel's function **CHISQ.DIST.RT(10.58,2)**).

Step 4: Compare the sample test statistic to the region of acceptance
The sample test statistic, χ^2-*stat* = 10.58 lies *outside* the region of acceptance of $\chi^2 \leq 9.21$, as seen in Figure 10.8. This is also confirmed with the *p*-value (0.00504) < α (0.01).

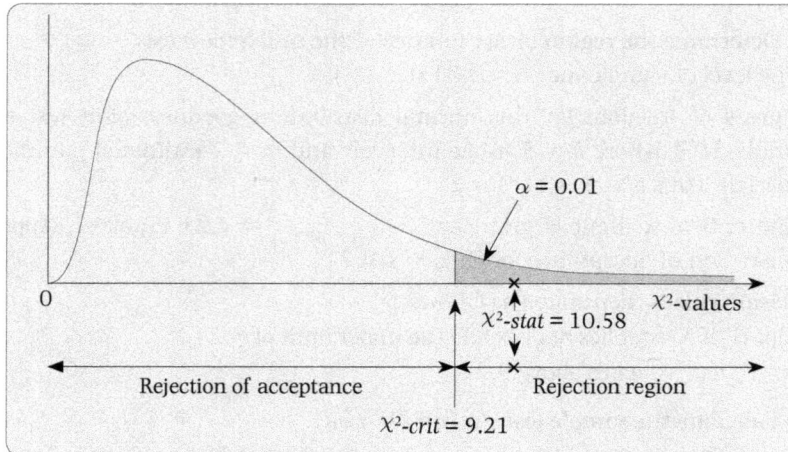

Figure 10.8 Electricity usage study – χ^2-*stat* and region of acceptance

Step 5: Draw statistical and management conclusions

Statistical Conclusion

Reject H_0 at the 1% level of significance. The sample evidence is strong enough to support H_1. The alternative hypothesis is therefore probably true.

Management Conclusion

It can be concluded, with 99% confidence, that the pattern of daily electricity usage by the restaurant does *not* follow a normal probability distribution with $\mu = 45$ kW and $\sigma = 14$ kW.

Note: By rejecting the null hypothesis, it could either mean that:
- the data is sufficiently skewed as to be genuinely non-normal, or
- the pattern of daily electricity usage does actually follow a normal distribution, but with different mean, μ, and standard deviation, σ. Different μ and σ values can be assumed and then tested in further goodness-of-fit tests.

The Rule of Five

When fitting any observed sample frequencies to a set of expected frequencies, the only condition that *must* be satisfied is that each *expected frequency* should be at least five. This condition is necessary to ensure that the χ^2-*stat* test statistic is stable and that reliable conclusions can be drawn. To ensure this condition is met, it may be necessary to *combine* adjacent classes or categories (if meaningful) for both the observed and expected frequency tables.

10.5 Using Excel (2016) and X-Static for Chi-square Tests

Excel does not offer a chi-square option in the **Data Analysis** add-in module. All calculations for the expected frequencies and the chi-square sample test statistic, X^2-*stat*, would have to be done 'manually' in Excel using formulae 10.1 and 10.2. The Excel function keys **CHISQ.INV.RT** and **CHISQ.DIST.RT** can be used to find the critical X^2-limit for the region of acceptance, and the *p*-value for the chi-square test statistic respectively.

The critical X^2-limit for the region of acceptance is given by:

   =CHISQ.INV.RT(upper-tail probability,degrees of freedom)

Where: upper-tail probability = the level of significance, α.

For example, for $\alpha = 0.05$ and degrees of freedom (df) = 2, the critical X^2-limit is:
   =CHISQ.INV.RT(0.05,2) = 5.9915.

The *p*-value for a given sample test statistic, X^2-*stat*, is given by:

   =CHISQ.DIST.RT(x,degrees of freedom)

Where: $x = X^2$-*stat*.

For example, assume X^2-*stat* = 3.964 and degrees of freedom (df) = 2, then the *p*-value is:
   =CHISQ.DIST.RT(3.964,2) = 0.1378.

X-Static, however, has a chi-square option for the *Test for Independence of Association*. Refer to the module: **Chi-square: Independence of Association Test**. The output for Example 10.1 is shown in Figure 10.9. It includes similar chart outputs as shown in Figures 10.1 and 10.2.

The % of X^2 entries in each combination-cell shows what percentage of the X^2-stat value is coming from the deviation between the *observed* and *expected frequency counts*. By inspecting the 'high-percentage cells' and the 'direction' of the deviation between the observed and the expected frequency counts within these cells, it is possible to explain the nature of the statistical association between the categorical variables (e.g. *Beat* is more preferred by males (boys) than females (girls); while *Grow* is more preferred by females (girls) than by males (boys)).

Chi-square – Test for Independence of Association

Chi-square statistic		Magazines			
Gender		*Beat*	*Grow*	*Youth*	**Total**
Female	Observed (f_o)	13	39	28	80
	Expected (f_e)	18.40	32.40	29.20	80
	$(O - E)^2/E$	1.5848	1.3444	0.0493	2.9785
	% of χ^2	31.92%	27.08%	0.99%	60.00%
Male	Observed (f_o)	33	42	45	120
	Expected (f_e)	27.60	48.60	43.80	120
	$(O - E)^2/E$	1.0565	0.8963	0.0329	1.9857
	% of χ^2	21.28%	18.06%	0.66%	40.00%
Total	Observed (f_o)	46	81	73	200
	Expected (f_e)	46.00	81.00	73.00	200
	$(O - E)^2/E$	2.6413	2.2407	0.0822	4.9642
	% of χ^2	53.20%	45.14%	1.65%	100.00%

% of rows total		*Beat*	*Grow*	*Youth*	**Total**
	Female	16.25%	48.75%	35.00%	100.00%
	Male	27.50%	35.00%	37.50%	100.00%
	Total	23.00%	40.50%	36.50%	100.00%

% of columns total		*Beat*	*Grow*	*Youth*	**Total**
	Female	28.26%	48.15%	38.36%	40.00%
	Male	71.74%	51.85%	61.64%	60.00%
	Total	100.00%	100.00%	100.00%	100.00%

Hypothesis test results	
Degrees of freedom (*df*)	2
χ^2-critical	5.9915
χ^2-statistic	4.9642
p-value	0.0836
significance level	0.05

Figure 10.9 X-Static output (Exercise 10.1): Chi-square Test for Independence of Association

10.6 Summary

This chapter introduced the *chi-square* test statistic. It is used to test whether the *observed pattern* of *outcomes* of a random variable follows a specific hypothesised pattern. The chi-square statistic is applied to three hypothesis test situations, namely the test for independence of association between two categorical random variables; the test for *equality of proportions* in two or more populations; and the *goodness-of-fit* test.

The first two tests are equivalent tests and their purpose is to examine whether a relationship exists between two categorical variables. Goodness-of-fit tests, on the other hand, are used when it is necessary to examine whether the response patterns of a random variable follow a given theoretical or user-defined empirical distribution.

In management situations, especially marketing and marketing research, *chi-square tests for association* are regularly applied to cross-tabulated data. The manager is seeking associations between various categorical *demographic measures* and *consumer behaviour attributes* (e.g. usage, attitudes towards brands, perceptions and buying intentions), which are of value for market segmentation purposes.

In all these chi-square test situations, the same five steps of hypothesis testing apply. Excel only offers the function keys **CHISQ.INV.RT** (to find the critical χ^2-limit, which defines the regions of acceptance and rejection) and **CHISQ.DIST.RT** (to find the *p*-value for the test statistic on which a statistical conclusion and management interpretation can be based). There is no function key in Excel to compute the sample test statistic, χ^2-*stat*. However a complete hypothesis test for *independence of association* is available in **X-Static**.

Exercises

This symbol denotes data available online

1. What is the purpose of a chi-square test for independence of association?
2. What type of data (categorical or numerical) is appropriate for a chi-square test for independence of association?
3. What does the null hypothesis say in a test for independence of association?
4. What is the role of the *expected* frequencies in chi-square tests?
5. In a three rows by four columns cross-tabulation table of a chi-square test for independence of association, what is the critical chi-square value (X^2-crit) in a hypothesis test conducted:
   (a) at the 5% level of significance?
   (b) at the 10% level of significance?
6. X10.6 – motivation status

   A company recently conducted a study on motivation levels amongst its clerical employees. The HR manager wished to establish if there was any association between the *gender* of an employee and his/her *level of motivation*. The following cross-tabulation was compiled from the survey data:

Gender	Motivation level		
	High	Moderate	Low
Male	8	8	14
Female	19	12	9

   (a) Calculate a *row percentage* cross-tabulation table to show the motivation level profile for each gender. Interpret each gender's profile. By inspection, would you conclude that an association exists between an employee's gender and his/her motivation level?
   (b) Now conduct a chi-square hypothesis test to identify statistically whether there is an association between employees' gender and motivation level. Use $\alpha = 0.10$. Define the null and alternative hypotheses, and state the statistical and management conclusion.
7. X10.7 – internet shopping

   A large supermarket offers an internet shopping service to its customers. It recently conducted a survey amongst its customers to find out if *full-time employed* customers are more likely to *use the internet shopping facility* than *at-home* customers. The survey findings are summarised in the following cross-tabulation table:

Employment status	Use internet shopping	
	Yes	No
Full-time	35	109
At-home	40	176

   (a) Show the joint frequency counts in the cross-tabulation table as row percentages. Interpret these percentages.

(b)   At the 5% significance level, is there sufficient statistical evidence to conclude that full-time employed customers are *more likely* to use the internet shopping service than at-home customers? (i.e. is employment status and the use of internet shopping statistically dependent?) What conclusion can be drawn?

8   X10.8 – car size

A national motor vehicle distributor wishes to find out if the *size of car* bought is related to the *age of a buyer*. From sales transactions over the past two years, a random sample of 300 buyers was classified by size of car bought and buyer's age. The following cross-tabulation table was constructed.

Buyer's age	Car size bought		
	Smal	Medium	Large
Under 30	10	22	34
30 – 45	24	42	48
Over 45	45	35	40

(a)   Construct a *row percentage* table. Interpret these percentages.

(b)   Test, at the 1% level of significance, whether *car size bought* and *buyer's age* are statistically independent using the chi-square test procedure.

(c)   Interpret your findings and make a recommendation to the marketing manager of the national motor vehicle distributor.

9   X10.9 – sports readership

An advertising agency wanted to establish if the proportion of people who read a particular magazine, *Sports News*, was the same across three geographical regions. A total of 300 readers of sports magazines was randomly sampled from the three regions and their readership of *Sports News* was recorded in the following cross-tabulation table.

Read *Sports News*	Region		
	E Cape	W Cape	KZN
No	84	86	78
Yes	16	10	26

(a)   Formulate the null and alternative hypothesis to test whether the advertising agency can assume *equal proportions* of readership of *Sports News* across the three regions.

(b)   Conduct the hypothesis test formulated in (a). Use $\alpha = 0.01$. What conclusion can be drawn?

(c)   Rephrase the null hypothesis as a test for independence of association between the readership of *Sport News* and *geographical region*.

10   X10.10 – gym activity

In a recent survey, 140 members were randomly interviewed at a gym and asked to indicate their most *preferred gym activity*. The choices were spinning, swimming or circuit. The *gender* of the member was also noted. Their summarised responses are shown in the cross-tabulation table.

Gender	Most preferred activity		
	Spinning	Swimming	Circuit
Male	36	19	30
Female	29	16	10

(a) Calculate *row percentages* from the joint frequency counts. Interpret the preferred gym activity profile of each gender.

(b) Is there a statistical association between *most preferred gym activity* and *gender*? Test at the 10% level of significance. Define the null and alternative hypothesis and draw the management conclusion.

(c) If the hypothesis test was conducted at the 5% significance level, would the conclusion change? Justify your answer.

(d) Now formulate the hypothesis as a test of *equality of proportions*. Draw a management conclusion based on the 'equality of proportions' hypothesis using the results from (b).

11   X10.11 – supermarket visits

The manager of a large supermarket in Brakpan believes that 25% of her customers shop for groceries daily, 35% shop at least three or four times per week, 30% shop twice weekly and the balance shop only once a week. In a survey conducted amongst a random sample of 180 customers, the following shopping frequencies were identified:

Visits per week	Customers
Daily	36
3 – 4 times	55
Twice	62
Once only	27

(a) Based on the survey findings, what is the *percentage profile* of shopping frequencies by customers? Interpret.

(b) Does the survey data support the manager's belief about the frequency of store visits by customers? Conduct a chi-square goodness-of-fit hypothesis test to examine the store manager's belief. Use $\alpha = 0.05$.

(c) In what way, if any, does the current shopping profile of customers differ from the manager's belief? Comment.

12   X10.12 – equity portfolio

An investor on the JSE held a $2 : 3 : 1 : 4$ ratio of equities between the mining, industrial, retail and financial sectors in 2008. In 2012, of the 4 500 shares that she currently holds, 900 shares are in mining companies, 1 400 shares are in industrial companies, 400 shares are in retail companies, and the rest in financial companies. Has this investor changed her portfolio mix substantially since 2008?

Use the chi-square goodness-of-fit test to test the hypothesis, at the 5% significance level, that there has been no significant change in portfolio mix since 2008.

13   X10.13 – payment method

The financial officer of an electronics goods company that sells TVs, sound systems, DVDs, VCRs, etc., knows from past experience that 23% of the store's customers pay cash for their purchases, 35% use debit cards, and the remaining 42% use credit cards. He wants to confirm that this is still the payment method for electronic goods purchases.

Based on a random sample of 200 recent sales receipts, a frequency table showing the breakdown of payment methods was constructed.

Payment method	Customers
Cash	41
Debit card	49
Credit card	110

(a)   Use the chi-square goodness-of-fit test to determine whether the payment patterns of the past are still relevant today. Use $\alpha = 0.05$.

(b)   What should the financial officer conclude about customers' current payment methods for electronic goods?

14   X10.14 – package sizes

Bokomo Breakfast Cereal is sold in three package sizes: large, midsize and small. National sales figures have shown that these sell in the ratio of $3:5:2$. Sales returns for the Limpopo region show that 190 cases, 250 cases and 100 cases, respectively, of the different package sizes have been sold recently.

(a)   Is the Limpopo region's pattern of sales significantly different from the national sales pattern? Test at the 5% level of significance using the chi-square goodness-of-fit test.

(b)   If it is different, based on the conclusion in (a), in what way does it differ from the national sales profile?

15   X10.15 – compensation plan

An insurance company sampled its field sales staff in four provinces concerning their preference for compensation. Employees were given the choice between the present compensation method (fixed salary plus year-end bonus) and a proposed new method (straight commission). The responses of the randomly sampled field sales staff are summarised in the following cross-tabulation table:

Compensation plan	Province			
	Cape	Gauteng	Free State	KZN
Present payment plan	62	140	47	80
New payment plan	38	45	23	30

(a)   Calculate the *column percentage* cross-tabulation table. Interpret the findings.

(b)   Formulate the null and alternative hypothesis to test whether there is any *difference* across the four provinces in the *proportion* of field sales staff who prefer the present compensation method.

(c)   Use the chi-square test to test the hypotheses formulated in (b). Use $\alpha = 0.10$. Interpret your findings in a brief report to the HR manager of the insurance company.

(d) What is an alternative way to formulate the null and alternative hypotheses in (b) above? Show the reformulated null and alternative hypotheses.

(e) If the hypothesis test were conducted at the 5% significance level, would the management conclusion change? Refer to the results in (c) above.

16 X10.16 – tyre defects

The quality control manager of a tyre manufacturing plant in Port Elizabeth wants to test the belief that the nature of defects found in manufactured tyres depends on the shift during which the defective tyre is produced. He compiled the following cross-tabulation table showing the number of defective tyres identified by *shift* and by *nature of defect*, i.e. technical (operator induced), mechanical (machine fault), material (raw material quality):

Shift	Nature of tyre defect		
	Technical	Mechanical	Material
Morning	15	42	11
Afternoon	26	40	20
Night	29	25	14

(a) Compute a *row percentage* pivot table. Interpret the findings.

(b) Is there evidence to substantiate the claim that there is a statistical association between the *nature* of defective tyres and the *shift* on which they are produced? Perform a chi-square test of association at the 5% significance level to establish if these two criteria are statistically independent or not.

(c) What conclusion should the quality control manager communicate to the production manager concerning this issue?

(d) Reformulate the null and alternative hypotheses to test whether the *proportion* of defective tyres caused by *mechanical* factors is the same across all shifts. Conduct this revised hypothesis test. Use $\alpha = 0.05$. What conclusion can be drawn?

17 X10.17 – flight delays

This question investigates the flight delay times of scheduled commercial aircraft.

(a) Use the **Histogram** option in **Data Analysis** to examine the normality of flight delay times by inspection. Comment on the findings.

(b) Use the **Descriptive Statistics** option in **Data Analysis** to compute the mean, standard deviation and skewness coefficient of the sample flight delay times (in minutes). Again comment on whether the distribution of flight delay times is likely to be normal.

(c) Use the chi-square goodness-of-fit test to test, at the 1% level of significance, that the data on flight delays follows a normal distribution with a mean of 10.324 minutes and a standard deviation of 2.333 minutes. What conclusion can be drawn?

Hint:

● Use the interval limits as given in the bin range of Excel file X10.17.

● Compute the expected normal probabilities using the standard normal statistical tables, then use Excel's **NORM.DIST** function to confirm the results.

18   X10.18 – newspaper sections

The *Daily Mail* newspaper conducted a survey amongst a random sample of 180 of its readers to determine which of the three *sections* (namely sport, social or business) they *most prefer to read*. The *gender* of the respondents was also recorded.

(a)   Use the **PivotTable** option in the **Insert > Table** tab to construct a cross-tabulation table between *gender* (row variable) and *section preference* (column variable). Show both the frequency counts and row percentages. Interpret the percentage pivot table.

(b)   Use the **Stacked Column (bar chart)** option in the **Insert > Chart** tab to display the percentage pivot table graphically.

(c)   Are *gender* and *section preference* statistically independent? Test the hypothesis at the 10% level of significance. What conclusion can be drawn?

(d)   Reformulate the hypothesis as a test for *equality of proportions* of *female preferences* across the different newspaper sections. What statistical conclusion can be drawn. Use $\alpha = 0.10$?

19   X10.19 – vehicle financing

Wesbank is a motor vehicle financing company. The financial director wants to know if the pattern of loan amounts that car buyers applied for has changed over the past four years. Four years ago, 10% of car loan applications were for amounts of less than R100 000; 20% of applications were for car loans of between R100 000 and R150 000; 40% of car loan applications were for amounts of between R150 000 and R200 000; 20% were for amounts of between R200 000 and R250 000, and 10% of applications were for amounts above R250 000.

An analysis was undertaken recently. A random sample of 300 car finance applications was selected and their loan sizes were recorded.

(a)   Use the **PivotTable** option in the **Insert > Table** tab to construct a one-way frequency table to show the sample profile of vehicle financing applications received by Wesbank. Show both the frequency counts and percentages. Interpret the percentage frequency table.

(b)   Use the **Column (bar chart)** option in the **Insert > Chart** tab to show the percentage frequency table as a bar chart.

(c)   Formulate the null and alternative hypothesis to test whether the pattern of vehicle loan amounts applied for has changed from four years ago.

(d)   Using the chi-square goodness-of-fit method, test, at the 5% significance level, whether the financial director of Wesbank can conclude that there has been no change in the pattern of vehicle loan amounts requested from four years ago.

20   X10.20 – milk products

In a survey of a random sample of 76 customers at the dairy products section of a supermarket, consumers were asked the following two questions:

Question 1: Do you purchase mainly fat-free milk, low-fat milk or full-cream milk?
Question 2: Do you consider yourself to be a health-conscious consumer? (Yes, No)

(a)   Use the **PivotTable** option in the **Insert > Tables** tab to construct a cross-tabulation table to show the association between *milk type purchased* (row variable) and the *health-conscious status* of a consumer (column variable).

Show both the frequency counts and column percentages. Interpret the percentage pivot table.

(b)   Use the **Stacked Column (bar chart)** option in the **Insert > Chart** tab to display the percentage pivot table graphically as a stacked bar chart.

(c)   Can it be concluded that consumers who are more health conscious are more likely to purchase milk with a lower fat content? Or are they statistically independent? Test the hypothesis at the 5% level of significance. What statistical and management conclusions can be drawn?

(d)   Reformulate the hypothesis as a *test for equality of proportions* of milk type purchased by the health-conscious consumers. What statistical conclusion can be drawn based on the results in (c)? Use $\alpha = 0.05$.

CHAPTER
11

Analysis of Variance: Comparing Means Across Multiple Populations

Outcomes

Analysis of variance (ANOVA) is a hypothesis test approach to test for *equality of means* across *multiple populations* . It is an extension of the z-test or *t-test*, which only test for equality of means between two populations.

Analysis of variance asks whether different sample means of a numeric random variable come from the same population, or whether at least one sample mean comes from a different population. The test statistic used to test this hypothesis is called the *F*-statistic.

If significant differences between sample means are found to exist, it is assumed to be the result of an influencing factor rather than chance This chapter will consider two cases: (i) where only one factor influences the differences in sample means – using the method of *one-factor ANOVA* ; and (ii) where two factors influence the differences in sample means – using the method of *two-factor ANOVA*.

After studying this chapter, you should be able to:

- identify when to apply ANOVA as a hypothesis-testing technique
- understand the rationale of ANOVA and how it tests for equality of means
- calculate the *F*-statistic for a one-factor ANOVA problem
- conduct a two-factor ANOVA hypothesis test
- distinguish between two-factor ANOVA *with* replication and two-factor ANOVA *without* replication
- interpret the findings of an ANOVA application.

11.1 Introduction and the Concept of ANOVA

In Chapter 10, the hypothesis test for the difference between two population means was conducted using either the *z*- or the *t-test* statistic. However, when *more* than two population means are compared for equality, a different test statistic – known as the **F-statistic** – is used. The test procedure that is used to compute the *F*-statistic is called **analysis of variance (ANOVA)**.

In many management areas there is a need to compare the means of a *numeric* random variable across multiple populations.

Illustrations

- Does average *fuel consumption* vary across *five* different makes of 1 600 cc cars?
- Is the average *hourly output* of items the same between *four* models of the same machine?
- Is there a difference in the mean *annual return* between *three* types of unit trusts?

In each illustration, a numeric response variable (e.g. fuel consumption, machine output, annual return) is observed under different conditions (e.g. different makes of cars, different models of a machine, different unit trusts) called a *factor*, with the types of conditions called *factor levels* (or *treatments*). To illustrate, 'unit trust category' is the factor, and the three 'category types' are the factor levels. Each factor level represents a separate sample.

The purpose of ANOVA is to determine whether there is a statistical relationship between the factor and the response variable (i.e. are the two measures *statistically dependent* or not?) Comparing sample means does this. If at least one factor level's sample mean can be shown to be different from the other factor level sample mean, then a statistical relationship has been found between the factor and the response variable.

If, on the other hand, the sample means are not significantly different, then it can be concluded that the factor has no influence on the outcome of the response variable and that the two measures are statistically *independent* of each other (i.e. no statistical relationship). This implies that any observed differences in sample means are due purely to chance and that all sample data was actually drawn from one homogeneous population.

Section 11.2 will examine the influence of only *one factor* to explain differences between sample means (called *one-factor ANOVA*), while section 11.5 will examine the case of two influencing *factors* and their interaction effect to explain differences between sample means (called *two-factor ANOVA*).

11.2 One-factor Analysis of Variance (One-factor ANOVA)

This section will consider the influence of one factor (e.g. unit trust, machine type, make of car) to explain the differences in sample means. This analysis is called **one-factor ANOVA** and its rationale will be explained through a worked example. Since ANOVA is an *inferential* hypothesis-testing technique, it follows the *same five steps* of hypothesis testing as outlined in earlier hypotheses tests.

Example 11.1 Unit Trust Returns Study

A financial analyst studied the annual returns of three different categories of unit trust. She wanted to know whether the average annual returns per category varied across unit trust categories. A random sample of unit trusts from each of three categories (labelled A, B and C) were selected and their annual returns were recorded. The data is shown in Table 11.1.

(See Excel file C11.1 – *ut returns 1*.)

Table 11.1 Sample data of unit trust annual returns

Unit Trusts		
A	B	C
11	7	14
9	10	13
6	8	11
12	13	16
14		10
11		

Management Question

Can the financial analyst conclude that the average annual returns from the three categories of unit trusts are the same? Conduct a hypothesis test at the 5% significance level.

Solution

The response variable is the *annual return* of a unit trust. Each sample in Table 11.1 represents a separate *category of unit trust* and collectively is called the factor in this study. The purpose of ANOVA is to find out if the annual returns of unit trusts are influenced by the category of unit trusts.

There is no influence of unit trust category on annual returns if the population mean annual returns can be shown to be equal across all three categories of unit trusts.

Exploratory Data Analysis

Table 11.2 shows the sample annual returns across the three unit trust categories. By inspection, category C unit trusts appear to have the highest average annual returns (12.8), while category B has the lowest average annual returns (9.5).

Table 11.2 Descriptive statistics for unit trust annual returns study

Unit trust	n	Sum	Average	Std dev
A	6	63	10.5	2.74
B	4	38	9.5	2.65
C	5	64	12.8	2.39

The management question that needs to be addressed through a hypothesis test is whether these observed differences in sample means are 'small enough' to be attributed to chance (i.e. sampling error) or 'large enough' to be due to the influence of the factor (i.e. the different unit trust categories). To conduct a hypothesis test of equality of means, the ANOVA approach is used.

ANOVA – Hypothesis Test for Equality of Means

Step 1: Define the null and alternative hypotheses
The null hypothesis always states that all the population means are equal. Thus:

$H_0: \mu_1 = \mu_2 = \mu_3$
(i.e. the mean annual returns are equal across all categories)
$H_1:$ At least one μ_i differs ($i = 1, 2, 3$)
(i.e. at least one unit trust category has a *different* mean annual return)

Note that the alternative hypothesis only states that *at least one* of the population means must be different. It does *not* imply that they must *all differ* from one another before H_0 is rejected.

If H_0 is accepted, this implies that annual unit trust returns are independent of the category of unit trust. Alternatively, if *at least one* sample mean is found to be significantly different to the rest, then it can be concluded that the mean annual returns do differ by unit trust category, and H_0 is rejected.

Step 2: Determine the region of acceptance of the null hypothesis
The ANOVA test is based on the F-distribution as shown in Figure 11.1. This hypothesis test is always an *upper-tailed test* with a single cut-off point between the region of acceptance and the region of rejection of the null hypothesis (*F-crit*).

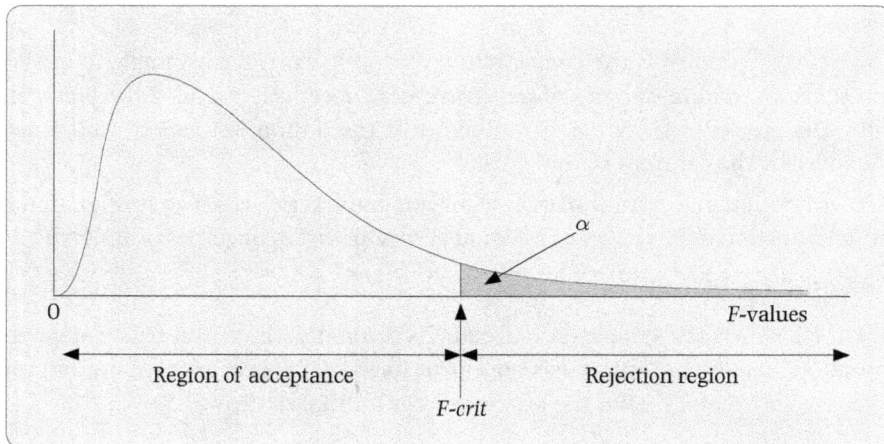

Figure 11.1 The F-distribution, showing the regions of acceptance and rejection

To find *F-crit*, both a level of significance, α, and degrees of freedom must be known. For this example, the level of significance is given as $\alpha = 0.05$.

There are two values for the degrees of freedom of an F-statistic. They are called the *numerator* degrees of freedom and the *denominator* degrees of freedom.
- The numerator degrees of freedom, $df_1 = k - 1$, where k = number of samples (or factor levels).
- The denominator degrees of freedom, $df_2 = N - k$, where k = number of samples (or factor levels) and N = total (combined) sample size.

The *critical F*-value is defined as:

$$F\text{-}crit = F_{(\alpha)(k-1, N-k)}$$ **11.1**

In the example, with $k = 3$ samples and $N = 15$ data values in total, the degrees of freedom are $(3 - 1, 15 - 3) = (2, 12)$.

The *F-crit* limit is read off Table 4 in Appendix 1. To read off the F-table:
- select the table for $\alpha = 0.05$
- identify the *column* for the *numerator* degrees of freedom, and the *row* for the *denominator* degrees of freedom
- the value at the intersection of the row and column is the F-crit statistic.

Thus $F_{(0.05)(2, 12)} = 3.89$. Hence the region of acceptance for H_0 is $F \leq 3.89$.

The decision rule is then stated as follows:
- Accept H_0 if *F-stat* lies at or below the upper limit of 3.89.
- Reject H_0 if *F-stat* lies above 3.89.

Step 3: Calculate the sample test statistic (*F-stat*)
The appropriate sample test statistic is *F-stat*. Unlike the two-sample means test, which compares the sample means directly using either z or t, the ANOVA test compares sample means by examining variances *within* and *between* the different samples.

Constructing the F-stat test statistic using ANOVA
The *F-stat* sample test statistic is calculated in three stages based on sources of variability within the total sample data. Variability is a measure of how far data values lie from their mean and is based on the concept of the standard deviation (see Chapter 3, Formula 3.9). It is called **sum of squares (SS)**.

- **Stage 1: Deriving sums of squares**
  ANOVA identifies *three* sources of variability in the total sample data:
  – total sample variability (SSTotal)
  – between-sample (between treatments) variability (SST)
  – within-sample variability (SSE).

  (i) *Total sample variability (SSTotal)*
       To calculate SSTotal, first combine all the different samples into one overall sample and calculate $\bar{\bar{x}}$, which is the overall grand mean, calculated as follows: if x_{ij} = each individual data value across all the samples, N = the combined sample size ($n = n_1 + n_2 + n_3 + ... + n_k$) and $\Sigma\Sigma x_{ij}$ = the sum of all data values across all the samples, then the overall grand mean is:

$$\bar{\bar{x}} = \frac{\Sigma\Sigma x_{i}}{n}$$ **11.2**

Now calculate a measure of deviation (variability) of each data value, x_{ij}, from the overall grand mean, $\overline{\overline{x}}$. When these deviations are squared and summed, the result is *total sample variability*. It is called the **total sum of squares** (SSTotal).

$$\text{Total sum of squares (SSTotal)} = \sum_i \sum_j (x_{ij} - \overline{\overline{x}})^2 \qquad \textbf{11.3}$$

In the example, SSTotal = 108, which is derived using Formula 11.2 and Formula 11.3 as follows:

$$\sum\sum x_{ij} = 11 + 9 + 6 + 12 + 14 + 11 + 7 + 10 + 8 + 13 + 14 + 13 + 11 + 16 + 10$$
$$= 165$$
$$n = 6 + 4 + 5 = 15$$
$$\overline{\overline{x}} = \frac{165}{15} = 11$$

Then SSTotal $= (11 - 11)^2 + (9 - 11)^2 + (6 - 11)^2 + ... + (16 - 11)^2 + (10 - 11)^2$
$$= 108$$

SSTotal is now divided into two components: variability *between* samples and variability *within* samples as follows:

(ii) *Between-sample (explained) variability (SST)*

Calculate the deviation (variability) *between* each sample (or treatment) mean and the overall grand mean. The extent to which the sample means deviate about the overall *grand mean* explains the influence of the factor levels (i.e. the *categories of unit trusts*). This measure of variability is called the **between treatments sum of squares** (SST).

$$\text{SST} = \sum_j^k n_j (\overline{x}_j - \overline{\overline{x}})^2 \qquad \textbf{11.4}$$

Where: n_j = sample size of the the jth sample (treatment)
$\overline{x}_j$ = j^{th} sample mean
k = number of different samples (or treatments)

In the example, SST = 26.7, which is derived using Formula 11.4 as follows:
$$\text{SST} = 6(10.5 - 11)^2 + 4(9.5 - 11)^2 + 5(12.8 - 11)^2 = 26.7$$

This means that 26.7 units (i.e. SST) of the 108 units of *total variability* (SSTotal) in unit trust returns across all samples is *explained* by the different unit trust categories (i.e. the factor treatments). This variation is also called **explained variation** or variation *due to the factor effect*.

(iii) *Within-sample (error) variability (SSE)*

For each sample separately, calculate the deviation (variability) of data values from their respective sample mean. Then sum these within-sample deviations across all samples. This is the variability that occurs between data values *within* each sample. It represents the *error* (or chance) variation, since the different treatments cannot explain it. This measure of variability is called the **error sum of squares** (SSE) and is calculated as follows:

$$SSE = \sum_j \sum_i (x_{ij} - \bar{x}_j)^2$$

11.5

In the example, SSE = 81.3, which is derived as follows, using Formula 11.5:

$$
\begin{aligned}
SSE = &[(11 - 10.5)^2 + (9 - 10.5)^2 + ... + (11 - 10.5)^2] \quad \text{(sample A squared deviations)}\\
&+ [(7 - 9.5)^2 + ... + (10 - 9.5)^2] \qquad\qquad\quad \text{(sample B squared deviations)}\\
&+ [(14 - 12.8)^2 + (13 - 12.8)^2 + ... + (16 - 12.8)^2] \quad \text{(sample C squared deviations)}\\
= &\ 81.3
\end{aligned}
$$

The SSE value of 81.3 measures the amount of variation *within* each sample (and summed across all samples) that cannot be 'explained' by the factor. Since it represents unexplained variation, it is called the **error sum of squares** (SSE).

The Sum of Squares Principle

These three measures of variability are related as follows:

$$SSTotal = SST + SSE$$

11.6

This shows that the sums of squares are *additive:*

> *total* sample variation = *between* sample variation + *within* sample variation
>
> or
>
> *total* sum of squares = *explained* sum of squares + *unexplained* sum of squares.

In the example, 108 (SSTotal) = 26.7 (SST) + 81.3 (SSE).

- **Stage 2: Calculating variances from the sum of squares**

  Each sum of squares term is the numerator of a variance formula (see the variance Formula 3.9 in Chapter 3). Thus when each sum of squares term (SSTotal, SST and SSE) is divided by its respective degrees of freedom (based on its sample size), the resultant measure is a *variance*. A variance is also called a *mean square* – representing the *average of a sum of squares.*

The different variances are calculated as follows:

(i) *Total sample variance (also called mean square total (MSTotal))*

$$MSTotal = \frac{SSTotal}{n - 1}$$

11.7

The degrees of freedom for the combined sample size is $n - 1$. In the example, $n = 15$ ($n_1 + n_2 + n_3 = 6 + 4 + 5$) and its degrees of freedom = $15 - 1 = 14$. Given SSTotal = 108 and $df = 14$, then the combined sample variance (MST) = 7.71.

(ii) *Between groups variance (also called mean square treatment (MST)).*

$$MST = \frac{SST}{k-1}$$ 11.8

Here, k = the number of samples (factor levels).

In the example, $k = 3$ and $df = 2$, so MSB = $\frac{26.7}{2}$ = 13.35.

(iii) *Within (error) samples variance (also called mean square error (MSE)).*

$$MSE = \frac{SSE}{n-k}$$ 11.9

Here, $n - k$ is the 'within samples' degrees of freedom.

For the example, $k = 3$ and $n = 15$, so MSE = $\frac{81.3}{15-3}$ = 6.775.

- **Stage 3: Calculating the *F-stat* sample test statistic**

  The *F-stat* sample test statistic is defined as a *ratio of two variances*, in this case, MST and MSE.

$$F\text{-}stat = \frac{MST}{MSE}$$ 11.10

Thus $F\text{-}stat = \frac{13.35}{6.775} = 1.97048$.

For ease of reference, the above calculations are usually set out in an **ANOVA table**, as shown in Table 11.3. The general layout for an ANOVA table is shown in Table 11.4.

Table 11.3 One-factor ANOVA output for unit trust annual returns study

Source of variation	Sum of squares	Degrees of freedom	Mean square	F-stat	F-crit
Between groups (treatments)	26.7	2	13.35	1.97048	3.89
Within groups (error)	81.3	12	6.775		
Total	108.0	14	7.714		

Table 11.4 The general layout of a one-factor ANOVA table

Source of variation	SS	df	MS	F-stat
Between groups (explained variation)	SST	$(k-1)$	$MST = \frac{SST}{(k-1)}$	$\frac{MST}{MSE}$
Within groups (unexplained variation)	SSE	$(n-k)$	$MSE = \frac{SSE}{(n-k)}$	
Total sample variation	SSTotal	$(n-1)$	$s_y^2 = \frac{SSTotal}{(n-1)}$	

Note: The Sum of Squares values and the degrees of freedom values are always additive. This additive property does not apply to mean square values. This means that SSTotal = SST + SSE and $(n-1) = (k-1) + (n-k)$, but that $s_y^2 \neq$ MST + MSE. Refer to the ANOVA findings in Table 11.3 to confirm these relationships.

The *p*-value for the ANOVA test is defined as the *right-tail area* under the *F-distribution* starting from the *F-stat* value. To find this area (probability), use the Excel function $\textbf{F.DIST.RT}(x, df_1, df_2) = \textbf{F.DIST.RT}(1.97048, 2, 12) = 0.18197$.

Step 4: Compare the sample test statistic to the region of acceptance
The sample test statistic, *F-stat* = 1.97048, lies *inside* the region of acceptance of H_0, as shown in Figure 11.2.

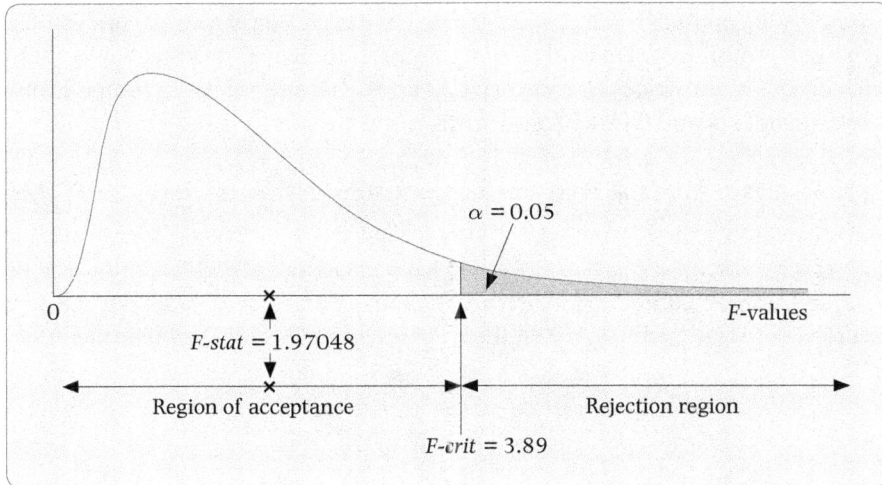

Figure 11.2 Unit trusts study – *F-stat* and region of acceptance

Step 5: Draw statistical and management conclusions

Statistical Conclusion

Since *F-stat* (= 1.97048) < *F-crit* (3.89) and *p*-value (0.18197) > α (0.05), we accept H_0 at the 5% level of significance. The sample evidence is not strong enough to reject H_0 in favour of H_1 at $\alpha = 0.05$. The null hypothesis is therefore probably true.

Management Conclusion

It can be concluded, with 95% confidence, that the average annual returns across the three categories of unit trusts are the same. This implies that the mean annual returns on unit trusts are independent of the category in which the unit trusts are classified.

Note: It is possible to compute the percentage of variation in the response variable that can be explained by the factor. *Divide the treatment sum of squares* (SST) by *the total sum of squares* (SSTotal). In example 11.1, SST = 26.7 and SSTotal = 108, thus $\frac{\text{SST}}{\text{SSTotal}} = 24.72\%$. This tells us that 24.72% of the variation in annual unit trust returns (the response variable) can be explained by (or attributed to) the different categories of unit trusts (the factor).

How to Interpret the Influence of the Factor of the Response Variable

When the null hypothesis is rejected in favour of the alternative hypothesis, the response variable is assumed to be influenced by the factor (i.e. there is a statistical relationship between the factor and the response variable – they are statistically dependent).

However, ANOVA does not identify the nature of the relationship between the response variable and the factor (i.e. it does not identify which means differ from each other). The nature of the relationship can be found either by inspecting the sample means and observing how they differ from each other; or by using a more rigorous **post hoc analysis** hypothesis testing approach called *multiple pairwise comparison of means*. For example, if the null hypothesis was rejected in worked example 11.1, then by inspecting Table 11.2, it may be concluded that unit trusts in category C (12.8%) have significantly outperformed unit trusts in categories A and B (10.5% and 9.5%, respectively).

Post Hoc Analysis: Multiple Pairwise Comparison of Means (Tukey's HSD Method)

A modified version of the two-sample t-test (called *Tukey's Honestly Significant Difference (HSD) test*) is conducted on *each pair* of sample means to identify which pairs of population means differ from each other and which are the same. This then makes it possible to explain the nature of the relationship between the response variable and the single factor.

$$\text{Tukey's } t\text{-stat} = \frac{(\bar{x}_i - \bar{x}_j)}{\sqrt{\text{MSE}(\frac{1}{n_i} + \frac{1}{n_j})}}$$

11.11

where i and j represent each pair of samples being compared
        MSE is the mean square error from the ANOVA table
        n_i and n_j are the respective sample sizes for samples i and j

$$\text{Tukey's } t\text{-crit} = \frac{q(\alpha,\, k,\, (n-k))}{\sqrt{2}}$$

11.12

where k = number of samples in the ANOVA test
        n = combined sample size across all samples
        α = combined level of significance across all tests (called experiment-wise α)
        q = *q-critical* value read from the *Studentized Range q* Table in **Appendix 1**

To compute the *p*-value for each *pairwise t*-test, use **T.DIST.2T**(t-stat,$df = (n - k)$).

Decision rule: For each pairwise test, if t-stat > t-crit, or p-value < significance level (α), we reject H_0: $\mu_i = \mu_j$ and conclude that the two corresponding population means differ significantly (i.e. the samples come from different populations).

Example 11.2 Absenteeism Rate Study

The *absenteeism rate* (as a %) amongst employees across three sectors (mining, construction, manufacturing) was analysed. Random samples of companies from each sector were selected and their absenteeism rate for the past quarter was recorded. The data are shown in Table 11.5.

(See Excel file C11.2 – *absenteeism rate*)

Table 11.5 Sample data on quarterly absenteeism rates by sector

Mining	Construction	Manufacturing
5.0	5.2	4.7
5.2	5.8	4.9
5.8	5.1	4.5
5.3	6.2	4.6
5.8	5.9	5.0
	5.1	4.9
		4.5
		5.8
		5.3

Management Question

The Bureau of Labour Statistics (BLS) which commissioned the study would like to know whether the *absenteeism rate* was the same across all three sectors, or if not, how absenteeism rates differed across sectors. Conduct hypotheses tests at the 5% level of significance.

Solution

The ANOVA and post hoc analysis output from **X-Static** is given in Tables 11.6 – 11.8. From the ANOVA output (Table 11.6), the null hypothesis of equal means is rejected (p-value = 0.0237 < α = 0.05). Thus *at least* one sector's mean absenteeism rate differs from the rest.

Table 11.6 ANOVA: Comparison of mean absenteeism rates across sectors

One-factor ANOVA

Summary

Groups	Count	Sum	Mean	Variance
Mining	5	27.1	5.4200	0.1320
Construction	6	33.3	5.5500	0.2270
Manufacturing	9	44.2	4.9111	0.1786
Combined	20	104.6	5.2300	0.2527

ANOVA ($\alpha = 0.05$)						
Source of variation	**SS**	**df**	**MS**	**F-stat**	**p-value**	**F-crit**
Explained (Between)	1.7101	2	0.8551	4.7013	0.0237	3.5915
Unexplained (Within)	3.0919	17	0.1819			
Total	4.8020	19	0.2527			

The **post hoc analysis** shows (i) the 95% confidence interval estimate of each sector's mean absenteeism rate in a *multiple box plot* display and (ii) the multiple pairwise *t-tests* (Tukey's HSD). Each pairwise *t-test* tests the following hypothesis: H_0: $\mu_i - \mu_j = 0$ versus H_1: $\mu_i - \mu_j \neq 0$ and the *p*-value of each test is found using Excel's function **T.DIST.2T**.

A visual inspection of the multiple box plots (Table 11.7) indicates a lower absenteeism rate for the manufacturing sector compared to the other two sectors. To examine this more rigorously, Tukey's HSD hypotheses tests (Table 11.8) show that there is no statistically significant difference in the mean absenteeism rates between the mining and construction sectors (mean sample difference = 0.13% is insignificant (status = NS) since the *p*-value = 0.6211), while there are statistically significant mean differences (status = S) between mining and manufacturing (mean sample difference = 0.5089% with *p*-value = 0.0472) and between construction and manufacturing (mean sample difference = 0.6389% with *p*-value = 0.0113).

The overall statistical conclusion is that there is a statistical relationship between absenteeism rate (the response variable) and sector (the influencing factor). The management conclusion is that the absenteeism rate is likely to be significantly lower in the manufacturing sector than in the other two sectors (mining and construction).

Table 11.7 95% Confidence interval estimate of mean absenteeism rates per sector

95% Confidence intervals			
	Mining	**Construction**	**Manufacturing**
Lower confidence limit	5.0	5.1	4.6
Upper confidence limit	5.9	6.0	5.2

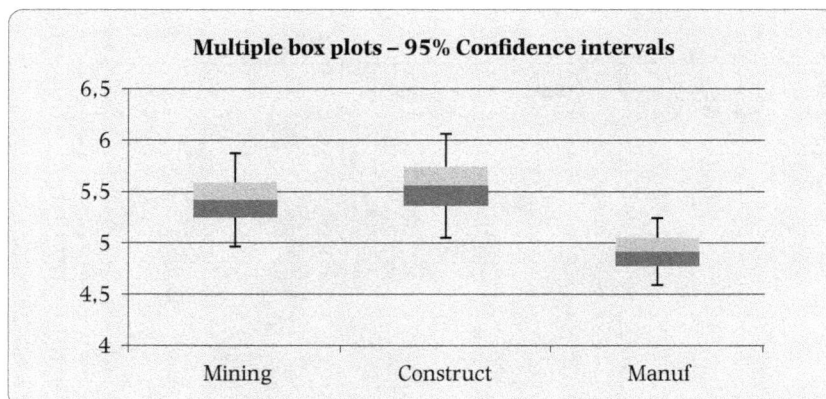

Multiple box plots – 95% Confidence intervals

Table 11.8 Multiple comparison test of mean absenteeism rate across sectors

Post hoc analysis					
Multiple pairwise comparison of means (Tukey's HSD Method)					
df =	17	α =	0.05		
Pairs	**Difference**	**Std error**	**t-stat**	**t-crit**	**p-value**	**Status**
Mining – Construction	0.1300	0.2582	0.5034	2.5654	0.6211	NS
Mining – Manufacturing	0.5089	0.2379	2.1393	2.5654	0.0472	S
Construction – Manufacturing	0.6389	0.2248	2.8424	2.5654	0.0113	S

11.3 How ANOVA Tests for Equality of Means

The test statistic *F-stat* is the ratio of two variances (refer to Formula 11.10). The numerator variance measures variability *between* sample means and the denominator variance measures variability *within* each sample.

$$F = \frac{\text{Between samples variance}}{\text{Within samples variance}} = \frac{\text{Explained source of variation}}{\text{Unexplained source of variation}} = \frac{\text{Treatment sum of squares}}{\text{Error sum of squares}}$$

$$= \frac{\frac{\text{SST}}{(k-1)}}{\frac{\text{SSE}}{(n-k)}}$$

$$= \frac{\text{MST}}{\text{MSE}}$$

Recall that SSTotal = SST + SSE. For a given set of data across multiple samples, SSTotal will be a fixed value, while SST and SSE will vary, depending on the data values within each sample.

If SST is *large* in relation to SSE, this implies that there are some *large differences* between sample means. This will result in a *large F-stat* value. Alternatively, if SST is *small* in relation to SSE, this implies that the sample means are *close* to each other. This will result in a *small F-stat* value.

Thus a small *F-stat* value (i.e. close to zero) implies that H_0 is probably true and that all the population means are equal. This indicates no statistical relationship between the response variable and the factor. Conversely, a large *F-stat* value implies that H_0 is probably false, and that at least one population mean is different from the rest. The factor is therefore assumed to have an influence on the outcome of the response variable, confirming that a statistical relationship exists between them.

11.4 Using Excel (2016) and X-Static for One-factor ANOVA

Excel's **Data Analysis** add-in module can perform one-factor ANOVA and produce the ANOVA table, as shown in Table 11.3 and Table 11.4. Refer to the **ANOVA: Single-factor** option from **Data Analysis**.

Table 11.9 shows the ANOVA output from Excel for Example 11.1.

Using Excel to Derive the Critical F-limit (F-crit)

The Excel function **F.INV.RT(probability,df$_1$,df$_2$)** can be used to generate the *F-crit* value for the region of acceptance in an ANOVA test.

The probability is α (the level of significance of the test), df_1 = numerator (between groups) degrees of freedom and df_2 = denominator (within groups) degrees of freedom. For Example 11.1, given $\alpha = 0.05$ with $df_1 = 2$ and $df_2 = 12$, the critical F-value = *F-crit* =F.INV.RT(0.05,2,12) = **3.885**.

Table 11.9 ANOVA output for Example 11.1 using **Data Analysis**

ANOVA: Single factor				
Summary				
Groups	**Count**	**Sum**	**Average**	**Variance**
A	6	63	10.5	7.5
B	4	38	9.5	7.0
C	5	64	12.8	5.7

ANOVA						
Source of variation	**SS**	**df**	**MS**	**F-stat**	**p-value**	**F-crit**
Between groups	26.7	2	13.35	1.97048	0.18197	3.885294
Within groups	81.3	12	6.775			
Total	**108.0**	**14**				

X-static also has a one-factor ANOVA module (called **Anova: One Factor**). Optional outputs include 95% confidence interval multiple box plots and post hoc analysis (multiple pairwise comparisons of means based on Tukey's HSD test) as seen in worked example 11.2.

11.5 Two-factor Analysis of Variance (Two-factor ANOVA)

Two-factor ANOVA is an extension of one-factor ANOVA. It includes a second factor (or treatment) as a possible influencing factor (or source of variation) to explain the differences in observed sample means. For example, is *worker productivity* (the numeric response variable) influenced by either their *level of training* {limited, extensive} (Factor 1) and/or their *working conditions* {poor, average, good} (Factor 2) or *both factors* together?

In two-factor ANOVA, the response variable is always numerical and both the factors are categorical. Two-factor ANOVA examines the impact on the response variable of *each factor separately* (called the *factor* [or main] *effect*) and in *combination* (called the *interaction effect*). As a result, the hypothesis testing procedure involves *three separate hypotheses*:

- **Hypothesis 1:** Are there significant differences in sample means between the levels of Factor 1? (Alternatively, is there an *effect* due to Factor 1 on its own?)
- **Hypothesis 2:** Are there significant differences in sample means between the levels of Factor 2? (Alternatively, is there an *effect* due to Factor 2 on its own?)
- **Hypothesis 3:** The *interaction hypothesis*: Are there significant differences in sample means across combinations of the levels of Factor 1 and Factor 2. (Alternatively, is there an *interaction effect* between the levels of Factor 1 and Factor 2?)

Example 11.3 Unit Trust Returns Study

A financial analyst wanted to know whether *unit trust returns* are related to their *sector focus* (A = retail, B = services, C = manufacturing) and their *management's strategy* (X = passively managed portfolio; Y = actively managed portfolio). The analyst stratified the population of all unit trust funds by *sector* (i.e. retail, services, manufacturing) and *management strategy* (into passively versus actively managed). She then randomly sampled five unit trust funds from each strata. The *annual % returns* of these sampled funds is shown in Table 11.10.

(See Excel file C11.3 – *ut returns 2*.)

Management Question

Can the financial analyst conclude that *unit trust returns* vary by *sector* and *management strategy*? Conduct the hypothesis tests at the 5% level of significance.

Table 11.11 Sample data of unit trusts annual % returns

Strategy	A (Retail)	B (Services)	C (Manuf)
X (Passive)	14	14	9
	13	12	10
	11	9	8
	15	15	12
	11	11	10
Y (Active)	11	11	15
	12	9	12
	14	12	15
	15	13	18
	16	10	14

The analysis is performed using Excel's **Data Analysis** module **ANOVA: Two-factor with replication**. The findings are shown in Table 11.12 and Table 11.13.

Exploratory Data Analysis

Before conducting the rigorous hypotheses tests, it is useful to inspect the sample descriptive statistics (i.e. *sample means* and *standard deviations*) within and between the different factors to form an initial impression of possible factor influences. Refer to Table 11.12.

The following observational conclusions can be drawn:

1   With reference to sector only, unit trust funds that are focused on the retail sector appear to have the highest average annual % returns (13.2% ± 1.87% (SD)), while the services sector unit trusts have the lowest (11.7% ± 1.95% (SD)). When the size of the standard deviations is also considered, the difference in sample means (of 1.5% between the highest and the lowest) may not be large enough to be significantly different from each other in the population. This indicates that mean annual % returns are likely to be similar across sectors, implying that 'sector focus' is unlikely to have a statistically significant influence on unit trust % returns.

2   Actively managed unit trusts (regardless of sector focus) appear to have a higher average annual % return (13.5% ± 2.32% (SD)) than passively managed unit trusts (11.3% ± 1.95% (SD)). Even when the standard deviations are taken into account, the wider difference between the sample means (of 2.2%) shows evidence of significant differences in average % returns due to the effect of management's strategy.

3   Examining combinations of sample means across sector focus and management strategy shows that average annual % returns vary from (9.8% ± 1.48% (SD)) (manufacturing and passively managed funds) to (14.8% ± 2.17 (SD)) (manufacturing and actively managed funds). The wide differences in sample means show that different combinations of the two factor levels appear to result in different unit trust performances. As a result, there is a possible interaction effect of the two factors on the annual % returns.

Table 11.12 Exploratory data analysis – unit trust annual % returns

X (Passive)	A (Retail)	B (Services)	C (Manuf)	Total
Count	5	5	5	15
Sum	64	61	49	174
Average	**12.8**	**12.2**	**9.8**	**11.6**
Variance	3.2	5.7	2.2	4.97
Y (Active)				
Count	5	5	5	15
Sum	68	55	74	197
Average	**13.6**	**11**	**14.8**	**13.13**
Variance	4.3	2.5	4.7	5.98
Total				
Count	10	10	10	
Sum	132	116	123	
Average	**13.2**	**11.6**	**12.3**	
Variance	3.51	4.04	10.01	

However, these observational conclusions have to be tested rigorously using the hypotheses testing approach. This statistical evidence is shown in Table 11.13.

Hypotheses Testing

The various statistical tests in two-factor ANOVA are based on the same *F*-test statistic as used in one-factor ANOVA. Each application tests whether the observed differences in sample means are statistically significant (caused by the influencing factors), or due purely to chance (called sampling error).

Table 11.13 Two-factor ANOVA – annual % returns by sector and strategy

ANOVA						
Source of variation	SS	df	MS	F-stat	p-value	F-crit
Strategy (F_2)	17.63	1	17.633	4.681	0.0407	4.26
Sector (F_1)	12.87	2	6.433	1.708	0.2025	3.40
Interaction $(F_1 \times F_2)$	50.07	2	25.033	6.646	0.0050	3.40
Error (within)	90.40	24	3.767			
Total	**170.97**	**29**				

Step 1: Define the null and alternative hypotheses

The management question translates into the following three statistical hypotheses:

Hypothesis 1 $\quad$ H_0: $\mu_1 = \mu_2 = \mu_3$ (means are all equal across all sectors)
Sector focus: $\quad$ (i.e. no influence on the mean annual % returns due to a fund's sector focus.)

(Factor 1 effect) $\quad$ H_1: At least one *sector's mean annual % returns* differs from the others.

Hypothesis 2 $\quad$ H_0: $\mu_1 = \mu_2$ (means are all equal across management strategy options)
Strategy: $\quad$ (i.e. no influence on the mean annual % returns due to the management strategy.)

(Factor 2 effect) $\quad$ H_1: At least one management strategy's mean differs from the others.

Hypothesis 3: $\quad$ H_0: There is *no interaction effect* on mean annual % returns of funds from different sectors combined with different management strategies.
Sector $\times$ Strategy: $\quad$ (i.e. all means are the same across all combinations of the two factors.)
(Interaction effect) H_1: There is an interaction effect.
$\quad$ (i.e. at least one mean from the different combinations of sector and management strategy differs significantly from the others.)

Step 2: Determine the region of acceptance of each null hypotheses (use $\alpha = 0.05$)

A separate rejection region applies to each null hypothesis (as shown in Table 11.8).

Sector focus $\quad$ F-crit = 3.40 $\quad$ (Also see the F-Table with $df_1 = 2$, $df_2 = 24$)
(Factor 1 effect) $\quad\quad\quad\quad\quad$ ($df_1 = (sectors - 1) = (3 - 1) = 2$)
Strategy $\quad\quad$ F-crit = 4.26 $\quad$ (Also see the F-Table with $df_1 = 1$, $df_2 = 24$)
(Factor 2 effect) $\quad\quad\quad\quad\quad$ ($df_1 = (strategy - 1) = (2 - 1) = 1$)
Sector $\times$ Strategy $\quad$ F-crit = 3.40 $\quad$ (Also see the F-Table with $df_1 = 2$, $df_2 = 24$)
(Interaction effect) $\quad\quad\quad\quad\quad$ ($df_1 = (sectors - 1)(strategy - 1) = (2 \times 1) = 2$)

For each hypotheses, $df_2 = (sectors \times strategy \times (sample\ size - 1))$ is the same (i.e. $(3 \times 2 \times (5-1)) = 24$.

In each case, the *decision rule* is to reject H_0 in favour of H_1 when F-stat > F-crit.

Step 3: Calculate the sample test statistic (*F-stat* (and its *p*-value))
Again, a separate sample *F-test* statistic is derived for each of the three hypotheses:

Sector focus	*F-stat* = 1.708	(Refer to the *Sector* (F_1) row)
(Factor 1 effect)	*p*-value = 0.2025	
Strategy	*F-stat* = 4.681	(Refer to the *Strategy* (F_2) row)
(Factor 2 effect)	*p*-value = 0.0407	
Sector × Strategy	*F-stat* = 6.646	(Refer to the *Interaction* ($F_1 \times F_2$) row)
(Interaction effect)	*p*-value = 0.0050	

Computing *F-stat*:
The *F-stat* value for each hypothesis is computed in the same way as for one-factor ANOVA (see section 11.2) by *dividing* its respective MST (mean square treatment) by the MSE (mean square error). For example, for Factor 2, $MST(F_2) = 17.633$; $MSE = 3.77$ giving *F-stat* = 4.681.

> *Note:* The two-factor ANOVA table is seldom computed manually. The calculations of the SS values are tedious and in practice are always computed using statistical software such as Excel's **Data Analysis** add-in (ANOVA) on **X-Static**. See section 11.7 for the relevant SS formulae for a two-factor ANOVA.

Finding the *p*-value:
The *p*-value for each hypothesis test is found by finding the *right-tail area* under the *F-distribution* from the *F-stat* value. This calculation is only done using Excel's **F.DIST.RT** function key. For example, for Factor 1 (*Sector*), its *p*-value is found using **F.DIST.RT**(x, df_1, df_2) = **F.DIST.RT**(1.708,2,24) = 0.2025.

Step 4: Compare the sample test statistic (*F-stat*) to the region of acceptance (or compare the *p*-value to the chosen level of significance, α)

For the *Sector focus* (*Factor 1*) effect:	*F-stat* < *F-crit* (within the acceptance region) or *p*-value (= 0.2025) > 0.05
For the *Strategy* (*Factor 2*) effect:	*F-stat* > *F-crit* (within the rejection region) or *p*-value (= 0.0407) < 0.05
For the *Interaction* effect:	*F-stat* > *F-crit* (within the rejection region) or *p*-value (= 0.0050) << 0.05

These findings are shown graphically in Figure 11.3.

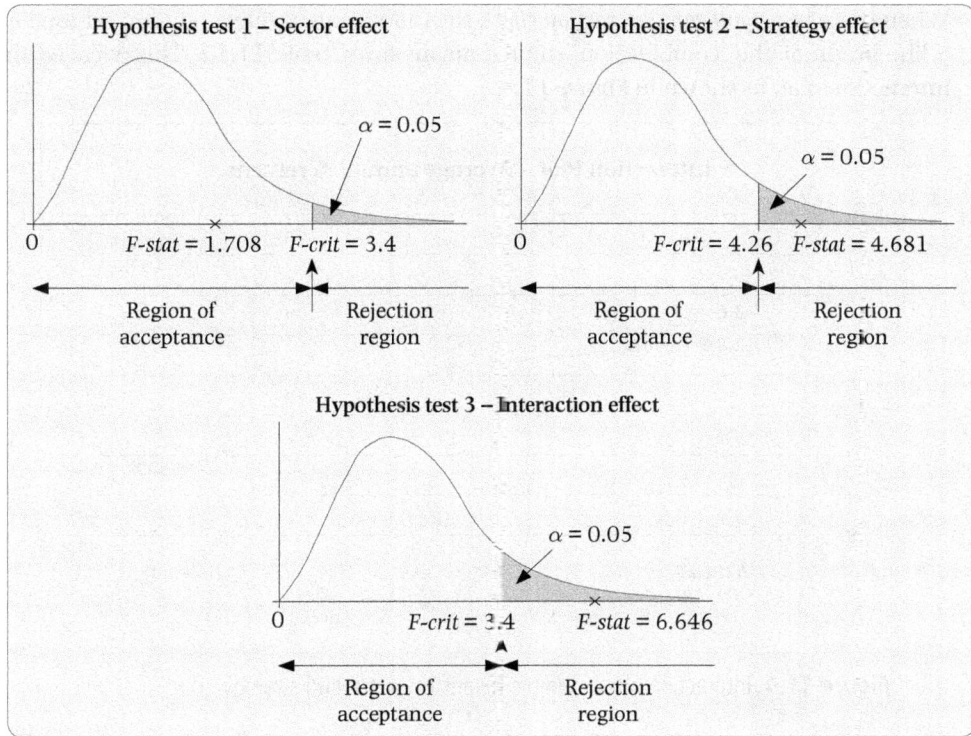

Figure 11.3 Sample test statistic (*F-stat*) and the region of acceptance

Step 5: Draw statistical and management conclusions

The following conclusions can now be drawn:

1   For the *sector focus* (main effect – *Factor 1*) effect:
Since *F-stat* < *F-crit* (or its *p*-value > 0.05), there is *insufficient sample evidence* to reject H_0 in favour of H_1 at the 5% level of significance. The *mean annual % returns* of unit trust funds across the three sectors is the same.

2   For the *management strategy* (main effect – *Factor 2*) effect:
Since *F-stat* > *F-crit* (or its *p*-value < 0.05), there is *strong sample evidence* at the 5% level of significance to reject H_0 in favour of H_1.
There is a significant difference in the *mean annual % returns* of unit trust funds between the two management strategies.

3   For the *sector focus × management strategy (Interaction)* effect:
Since *F-stat* > *F-crit* (or its *p*-value < 0.05), there is *overwhelmingly strong sample evidence* to reject H_0 in favour of H_1 at the 5% level of significance. There is therefore *at least one interaction effect* (combination) that has a very *different mean annual % return* to the other combinations.

Management Interpretation – Using the Interaction Plot of Means

When there is a *significant interaction effect*, the management interpretation is based on a line graph of the 'combination' sample means from Table 11.12. This is called the **interaction plot**, as shown in Figure 11.4.

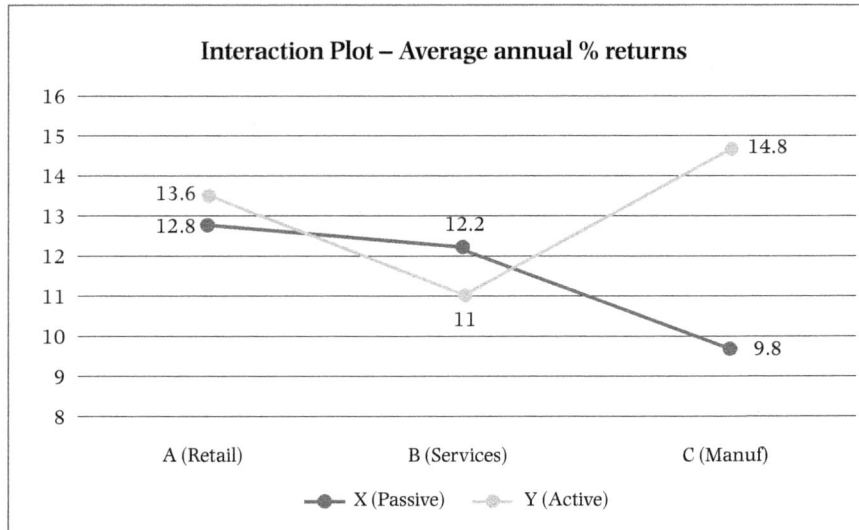

Interaction Plot – Average annual % returns

Figure 11.4 Interaction plot – sample means by sector and strategy

The presence of a significant interaction effect means that the average annual % returns of unit trust funds vary across different sector focus/management strategy combinations. A line graph of the interaction effects assists in identifying the *most profitable combination*.

From the line graphs, it is clear that in the retail and manufacturing sectors, the actively managed unit trust funds produce higher average annual % returns; while in the services sector, passively managed unit trust funds are likely to be more profitable.

Note: The extent to which the line graphs overlap each other, is evidence of interaction. The more they intersect, the stronger the evidence in favour of an interaction effect, and vice versa.

Use the following process to interpret a two-factor ANOVA table:
- The interaction effect takes precedence over the individual main (or treatment) effects. Thus, always examine the interaction effect first for statistical significance.
- If the interaction effect is *statistically significant* (i.e. reject H_0), interpret the statistically significant interaction and do not continue to examine each of the factor effects (also called main effects) individually for statistical significance. (Even if a main effect is significant, it is superceded by the interaction effect.)
- If the interaction effect is *not statistically significant* (i.e. do not reject H_0), only then examine the statistically significance of each of the factor effects (i.e. main effects) individually.

Note: A descriptive statistical measure to identify the *explanatory power* of each factor can be derived by dividing its respective sum of squares by the total sum of squares. In Example 11.3, the total sum of squares (i.e. total amount of variation in the sample data of annual % returns) is 170.97. Of this total amount of variation, the *strategy* factor accounts for 17.63. Thus its *percentage of explained variation* of the annual % returns is 10.3% (17.63/170.97). For the *sector* factor, it is 7.5% (12.87/170.97), while the *percentage of explained variation* of the annual % returns from the interaction effect (strategy × sector) is 29.3% (50.07/170.97). This also highlights the fact that 52.9% of the total variation in the numeric response variable – annual % returns – is not being explained by these two factors. This 52.9% represents variation in annual % returns that can be attributed to other 'external' factors and/or pure chance variation.

11.6 The Rationale of Two-factor ANOVA

In one-factor ANOVA, only one factor (Factor A) is assumed to influence the outcome of the numeric response variable. Recall from section 11.2 that its *explained variation* is captured in the SST term and the remaining *unexplained variation* in the SSE term. (The notation SSA – in place of SST – can also be used to identify this *explained variation* of Factor A.)

Now in two-factor ANOVA, it is assumed that a *second influencing factor effect* is present in the unexplained variation component of one-factor ANOVA (i.e. within SSE of a one-factor ANOVA). The rationale of two-factor ANOVA is therefore to *extract the additional explained variation* (additional structural effects of factors) from the unexplained variation term of one-factor ANOVA. Ideally the purpose of including additional factors into ANOVA is to reduce the amount of unexplained variation to pure chance variation only and therefore be able to attribute as much of the variation in the numerical response variable as possible to the identified factor(s).

Thus the SSE from one-factor ANOVA is *partitioned* into an additional *Factor B (main effect)* explained variation component (and called SSB) and an *interaction* explained variation component (called SS(AB)). The remaining balance becomes the unexplained variation in a two-factor ANOVA model (called SSE).

i.e. SSE (one-factor ANOVA) = SSB + SS(AB) + SSE (two-factor ANOVA)

Figure 11.5 shows the partitioning of the one-factor SSE into three new variation components, SSB, SS(AB)-Interaction, and SSE (reduced from the original SSE).

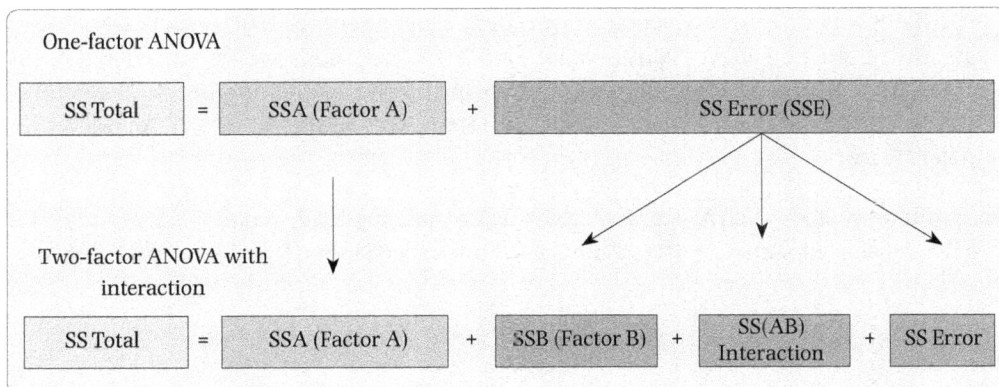

Figure 11.5 Diagrammatic view of one-factor and two-factor ANOVA

Example 11.3 is used to illustrate the extension of one-factor ANOVA into two-factor ANOVA using Excel's **Data Analysis** add-in.

Conducting a one-factor ANOVA. Assume that only the 'sector focus' factor was used to explain any differences in sample mean annual % returns of unit trust funds. Table 11.14 shows the one-factor ANOVA for unit trust fund % returns by sector focus.

Table 11.14 One-factor ANOVA – annual % returns with factor 'sector focus' only

ANOVA						
Source of variation	*SS*	*df*	*MS*	*F-stat*	*p*-value	*F-crit*
Sector focus (F_1)	12.87	2	6.43	1.099	0.3478	3.35
Error (within)	158.1	27	5.86			
Total	**170.97**	**29**				

Table 11.15 shows the two-factor ANOVA for unit trust fund % returns by sector focus and management strategy adopted toward fund management.

Table 11.15 Two-factor ANOVA – annual % returns with 'sector focus' and 'strategy'

ANOVA						
Source of variation	*SS*	*df*	*MS*	*F-stat*	*p*-value	*F-crit*
Strategy (F_2)	17.63	1	17.633	4.681	0.0407	4.26
Sector focus (F_1)	12.87	2	6.433	1.708	0.2025	3.40
Interaction ($F_1 \times F_2$)	50.07	2	25.033	6.646	0.0050	3.40
Error (within)	90.40	24	3.767			
Total	**170.97**	**29**				

The following can now be observed:

- SSTotal and SST for the 'sector focus' factor is exactly the same values in both tables (i.e. SSTotal = 170.97 and SST(F_1) = 12.87).
- In Table 11.14, SSE = 158.1. This amount of 'unexplained variation' in a one-factor ANOVA is split up into two 'explained variation' components (SST(F_2 – strategy) = 17.63 and the interaction effect (SS Interaction) = 50.07. The balance of the variation (i.e. SSE = 90.40) remains as unexplained variation in the two-factor ANOVA. So Error (one-factor ANOVA) = 158.1 = SS(F_2) (17.63) + SS Interaction (50.07) + SSE (in two-factor ANOVA) (90.40).

Thus in two-factor ANOVA, some of the original unexplained variation in a one-factor ANOVA is being explained by the second factor introduced into a two-factor ANOVA study.

11.7 Formulae for Two-factor ANOVA

In notation terms:

Let a = the number of levels of Factor A

Let b = the number of levels of Factor B

Let k = the sample size for each combination of levels of factors A and B (called replicates)

$$\text{SSTotal} = \sum_a \sum_b \sum_k (x_{ijk} - \bar{x})^2 \quad \textit{Total variation} - \text{same as for one-factor ANOVA} \quad \textbf{11.13}$$

$$\text{SSA} = bk \sum_j^a (\bar{x}_j[A] - \bar{x})^2 \quad \textit{Explained variation due to Factor A} \quad \textbf{11.14}$$

Where: $\bar{x}_j[A]$ = j^{th} sample mean of Factor A level j

$$\text{SSB} = ak \sum_i^b (\bar{x}_i[B] - \bar{x})^2 \quad \textit{Explained variation due to Factor B} \quad \textbf{11.15}$$

Where: $\bar{x}_i[B]$ = i^{th} sample mean of Factor B level i

$$\text{SS(AB)} = \text{SSTotal} - \text{SSA} - \text{SSB} - \text{SSE} \quad \textit{Explained variation due to interaction} \quad \textbf{11.16}$$

Finally, the remaining *unexplained variation* is given by SSE, which is computed as follows:

$$\text{SSE} = \sum_a \sum_b \sum_k (x_{ijk} - \bar{x}_{ij}[AB])^2 \quad \textbf{11.17}$$

These partitioned sums of squares can be represented in a two-factor ANOVA table and each explained variation component tested for statistical significance using the F-statistic as shown in Table 11.16. Note that n = total sample size = $a \times b \times k$.

Table 11.16 Two-factor ANOVA table

Source of variation	Degrees of freedom	Sums of squares	Mean squares	F-statistic
Factor A	$(a-1)$	SSA	$MSA = \dfrac{SSA}{(a-1)}$	$F_A = \dfrac{MSA}{MSE}$
Factor B	$(b-1)$	SSB	$MSB = \dfrac{SSB}{(b-1)}$	$F_B = \dfrac{MSB}{MSE}$
Interaction (A x B)	$(a-1)(b-1)$	SS(AB)	$MS(AB) = \dfrac{SS(AB)}{[(a-1)(b-1)]}$	$F_{AB} = \dfrac{MS(AB)}{MSE}$
Error (residual)	$n - ab$	SSE	$MSE = \dfrac{SSE}{(n-ab)}$	
Total	$n-1$	**SSTotal**		

Note 1: If there is only *one data value for each combination* of factor levels, it is not possible to examine an interaction effect since a measure of variability for a combination cannot be computed based on a single value. This occurs in studies where it is either too expensive or too time-consuming or even too dangerous to collect more than one observation for each combination of factor levels. Then only the significance of each main effect (the factors) can be tested. In Excel, use the **Data Analysis** module **ANOVA: Two-Factor Without Replication**. In **X-Static**, use the module **ANOVA: Two Factor (without interaction)**.

Note 2: If there are *multiple data values* for *each combination* of factor levels (i.e. replicates), then it is possible to test for an interaction effect. In Excel's **Data Analysis**, the *sample sizes* for each combination of factor levels *must be equal* to run a two-factor ANOVA analysis. In **X-Static**, use the module **ANOVA: Two Factor (with interaction)**. **X-Static**, however, can accommodate *unequal sample sizes* for each combination of factor levels.

11.8 Assumptions for Analysis of Variance

There are a few assumptions that need to be satisfied to give *validity* to the statistical findings from analysis of variance. They are:

- the populations from which the samples of each factor level are drawn must be *normally distributed*
- the *population variances* must be *equal*
- the samples for each factor level must be *randomly selected* and *independent* of each other.

Statistical tests can be performed on the sample data to examine both the normality and equal population variances assumptions. While the tests for both of these assumptions are beyond the scope of this text, the following 'rule of thumb' can be applied as a test for equality of variances across multiple populations: 'divide the largest sample variance by the smallest sample variance, and if the ratio is less than 3, equal population variances across all populations can be assumed'.

11.9 Summary

Analysis of variance (ANOVA) is the method used to compare sample means across multiple populations to determine if any significant differences exist. If differences in means are found, these differences are attributed to various influencing factors. One-factor ANOVA examines the influence of only one factor to explain possible differences in sample means; while two-factor ANOVA looks at the influence of two factors simultaneously to explain possible differences in sample means across multiple populations.

Separate samples of data of the numerical response variable are gathered for each treatment (or factor) level. In two-factor ANOVA, separate samples of data must be gathered for each combination of factor levels between the two factors. ANOVA follows the same five-step hypothesis-testing procedure as outlined in earlier chapters.

It calculates a test statistic called *F-stat*, which is the ratio of two variances. The *numerator variance* measures variability *between* the sample means of the different treatments. As such, it is termed the 'explained variance', since any observed differences could be explained' by the different treatments applied to each sample separately. The *denominator variance*, on the other hand, measures the variability *within* the different samples, and averaged across all samples. It is termed the 'unexplained' variance, since variability within samples cannot be explained by the different treatments. In two-factor ANOVA, a separate *F-stat* value is computed for each factor separately as well as for the interaction effect between the two factors.

ANOVA works on the principle that large *F-stat* values imply significant differences between at least two population means, giving sufficient evidence to reject H_0 in favour of H_1. Alternatively, small *F-stat* values imply no significant differences between population means and hence the sample evidence indicates that H_0 (i.e. that all the population means are equal) is probably true.

Finally, both Excel and **X-Static** can be used to perform ANOVA tests. In Excel's **Data Analysis**, the options are: **ANOVA: Single Factor** (for one-factor ANOVA); **ANOVA: Two-factor without Replication** (for a two-factor ANOVA with *only one data value* per combination – and, therefore, no interaction effect); and **ANOVA: Two-factor with Replication** (for a two-factor ANOVA with *multiple data values* of equal size samples for each combination that allows for an interaction effect to be examined). In addition, the **F.INV.RT** and **F.DIST.RT** function keys can be used to compute the *critical* F-limit (*F-crit*) for the region of acceptance and the *p*-value for a test respectively. **X-Static** offers similar modules but includes multiple box plots and post hoc analysis in its **one-factor ANOVA** module, as well as accommodates *unequal sample sizes* for **two-factor ANOVA with interaction** tests.

Exercises

This symbol denotes data available online

1   Explain the purpose of one-factor ANOVA.
2   Give an example of a business problem where one-factor ANOVA can apply.
3   Why is the variation between groups (samples) also called the 'explained' source of variation?
4   If four samples (groups) each consisting of 10 observations are being compared, with SST = 25.5 and SSTotal = 204.6, calculate F-stat.
5   Refer to Question 4. Identify F-crit, given a 5% level of significance.
6   Refer to questions 4 and 5. Conduct a hypothesis test to test whether the population means are equal across the four groups. What conclusion is drawn?
7   X11.7 – car fuel efficiency
    A car magazine tested the fuel efficiency of three makes of 1 600 cc motor vehicle (Peugeot, VW and Ford). A sample of 1 600 cc motor vehicles from each make was road tested under identical driving conditions and their consumption in litres/100 km was recorded.

Peugeot	VW	Ford
7.0	6.8	7.6
6.3	7.4	6.8
6.0	7.9	6.4
6.4	7.2	7.0
6.7		6.6

(a)   Calculate the sample average fuel consumption for each make of motor vehicle. Display the results in a bar chart.
(b)   Can the car magazine editor conclude that the average fuel consumption across the three makes of 1 600 cc motor vehicles is the same? Conduct an appropriate hypothesis test at the 5% level of significance, assuming that the three populations are normally distributed with equal variances (these are two assumptions required for ANOVA). Which make of motor vehicle, if any, is the most fuel efficient?
(c)   If the significance level of the test was 1%, would this change the conclusion reached in (b)? Support your answer with statistical evidence.
8   X11.8 – package design
    A cereal manufacturer evaluated three different package designs (A, B and C) to test market their new muesli breakfast cereal. Each design was tested in randomly selected convenience grocery stores in locations with similar customer profiles. The number of cartons sold (where each carton contains 50 packs of cereal) was recorded for a one-month trial period in each store.

Sales of cereal packs					
Design A		Design B		Design C	
35	30	35	34	38	34
37	39	34	32	34	33
39	36	30	34	32	
36	34	31		34	

(a)   Is any package design more effective in generating higher sales of packs of the muesli? Test this statement at the 5% significance level using one-factor ANOVA. Set up the null and alternative hypotheses and show the ANOVA table.

(b)   Which one package design should the cereal producer use to market the product? Explain your answer using the evidence from (a).

9   X11.9 – bank service

Random samples of customers from each of three banks were asked to rate the level of service of their bank on a 10-point rating scale (1 = extremely poor; 10 = extremely good). Assume that the three populations of rating scores are normally distributed with equal variances.

(a)   Test the hypothesis that the mean service level rating scores are the same across all three banks. Use $\alpha = 0.10$. Show the null and alternative hypotheses and the ANOVA table. Interpret the findings.

(b)   If the significance level of the test was 5%, would this change the conclusion reached in (a)? Support your answer with statistical evidence.

Bank service levels ratings					
Bank X		Bank Y		Bank Z	
8	6	5	5	8	6
6	7	6	7	7	5
6	9	7	5	6	6
7		5	7	7	5
6		5		6	6

10   X11.10 – shelf height

The manager of a grocery retail chain wished to find out if shelf height played a role in influencing a product's sales. A drinking chocolate product was displayed at four different shelf heights for equal periods of time and the volume of sale (units sold) was recorded.

Shelf height							
Bottom		Waist		Shoulder		Top	
78	80	78	75	83	88	69	75
84	74	85	94	86	90	76	
74		76	80	75	78	74	
75		82		78	84	72	
68		81		80		83	

Can the manager of the grocery retail chain conclude that mean product sales are independent of shelf height? Test at the 5% significance level. Assume the populations are normally distributed with equal variances. What conclusion can the manager draw from the findings?

11   X11.11 – machine evaluation

A company that produces labelled packaging (e.g. cereal boxes) plans to buy a new shaping and labelling machine. They are considering three different machines. Each machine's method of operation differs, and therefore so does its processing time to complete tasks. The company subjected each machine to five randomly selected shaping and labelling tasks, and recorded the processing time of each machine (in minutes).

Processing time by machine		
Machine A	Machine B	Machine C
11	10	15
13	11	13
12	13	15
9	8	17
14	14	12

(a)   Can it be concluded that there is no difference in the mean processing time between the three different machines? Use $\alpha = 0.10$. Formulate the null and alternative hypotheses, and complete the ANOVA table. Interpret the findings for the company.

(b)   Use the *t-test* for equal means (assuming equal population variances) to test the hypothesis that there is no difference in the processing speeds between the *two fastest* processing machines. Use $\alpha = 0.10$. Interpret the findings.

(c)   Based on the findings of the two hypotheses tests in (a) and (b), which shaping and labelling machine would you recommend that the company purchases? Why?

(d)   Use **X-Static** to perform a one-factor ANOVA with **post hoc analysis** (multiple box plots and pairwise comparison *t-tests* using Tukey's HSD method). Perform all tests at $\alpha = 0.10$. Is there one shaping and processing machine that is significantly faster than the other machines? Reference appropriate statistical evidence to support your conclusion.

Use the **ANOVA: Single Factor** option in Excel's **Data Analysis** for the following exercises.

12   X11.12 – earnings yields

A business analyst recorded the earnings yields of a random sample of public companies from each of four economic sectors (industrial, retail, financial and mining). She wanted to know if the average earnings yields are different across sectors.

Earnings yields by sector							
Industrial		Retail		Financial		Mining	
3.4	3.8	6.4	5.0	4.6	7.2	7.2	4.4
5.0	4.2	3.6	4.0	6.2	5.4	5.4	5.0
4.0	5.2	4.4	3.6	3.8	5.8	5.8	3.8
4.0	4.0	4.4	4.2	4.6	6.0	6.0	5.0
4.2	4.0	3.8	5.2	4.2	7.6	7.6	3.6
5.2	6.8	4.0	6.8	6.6	7.6	6.8	6.0
5.0	7.2	5.8	3.4	4.4	7.2	4.0	7.6
3.8	5.2	6.0	5.0	5.0	5.4	3.6	6.8
5.7	5.0	7.6	4.0	3.8	5.8	4.2	4.0
6.2	4.2	3.8	3.4	4.8	7.2	6.6	7.6

(a) Formulate the null and alternative hypothesis to test whether there is any difference in the mean earnings yields across the four economic sectors.
(b) Perform the hypothesis test at the 5% level of significance.
(c) Interpret the findings for the business analyst.

13 X11.13 – advertising strategy
A deodorant manufacturer test marketed a new women's deodorant under three different advertising strategies. The same deodorant was marketed over three consecutive periods of 20 weeks, first each as 'sophisticated', then as 'athletic' and finally as 'trendy'. The level of sales achieved each week under each advertising strategy was recorded.

Deodorant sales by advertising strategy					
Sophisticated		Athletic		Trendy	
428	477	424	475	444	458
259	441	280	429	310	405
394	503	349	392	340	408
435	415	362	234	379	419
517	356	342	296	447	438
302	553	253	527	298	532
463	373	407	314	413	364
338	454	417	308	362	444
428	426	430	252	434	280
437	381	401	349	445	410

(a) Formulate the null and alternative hypothesis to test whether mean deodorant sales differ according to advertising strategy used.
(b) Conduct the hypothesis test at the 5% level of significance.
(c) Which advertising strategy should the company adopt for maximum sales impact? Explain.
(d) Use the **t-Test: Two-Sample Assuming Equal Variances** option in **Data Analysis** to test for equality of mean sales between the two advertising strategies that generated the two highest sample average sales volumes of deodorant. Use $\alpha = 0.05$. What conclusion can be drawn?

(e)   Based on the statistical findings in (b) – (d), which advertising strategy would you recommend that the deodorant manufacturer should adopt to achieve maximum sales impact?

14   X11.14 – leverage ratio

A financial investor recorded the leverage ratios of a random selection of companies from four different economic sectors (technology, construction, banking and manufacturing). The leverage ratio is the ratio of company debt to the value of shareholder equity and is a measure of financial risk. The higher the leverage ratio, the greater the risk is to shareholders. The investor wants to invest in a low-risk economic sector.

Leverage ratios by economic sector							
Technology		Construction		Banking		Manufacturing	
83	86	70	69	66	68	44	75
62	71	75	60	87	84	59	80
61	60	72	80	55	69	47	81
85	88	68	61	41	55	60	87
60	68	72	89	68	78	79	84
78	82	92	97	49	99	62	85
68	85	70	98	52	87	73	83
66	86	71	79	57	57	64	94
83	71	74	80	66	84	69	89
81	72	80	84	62	93	81	77
63	77	71	58	78	64	70	94
67	73	88	79	75	70	80	92
88	68	90	86	68	80	78	82
60	75	85	91	75	64	72	93
71	77	78	75	57	84	71	86

(a)   Compute the descriptive statistics of leverage ratio for each sector using the **Descriptive Statistics** option in **Data Analysis**. By inspection, what conclusions can the financial investor draw about differences in mean leverage ratios between the four economic sectors?

(b)   What statistical and management conclusions can the financial investor draw about differences in the mean leverage ratios between the different economic sectors? Use the **ANOVA: Single Factor** option in **Data Analysis** to perform the hypothesis test at the 5% level of significance. In which economic sector should the financial investor invest his funds? Provide statistical evidence.

(c)   Use the **t-Test: Two-Sample Assuming Equal Variances** option in **Data Analysis** to test the hypothesis that there is no difference in the mean leverage ratios between the *two sectors* with the *lowest risk* in terms of sample mean leverage ratios. Use $\alpha = 0.05$. Interpret the findings.

(d)   Based on the findings of the two hypotheses tests in (b) and (c), into which economic sector would you recommend that the financial investor invests his funds? Why?

15 X11.15 – training methods

The HR department of a telecommunications organisation (such as MTN or Vodacom) wants to find the most effective training method for their employees to deal with their customers. A random sample of 56 employees was selected from their various client services departments, and randomly assigned to one of *four* training methods (on-the-job training, lectures, role play and audio-visual). After the assigned training, each employee was assessed by a training evaluator using a score out of 10, as shown in the table.

Method of employee training							
On-the-job		Lectures		Role play		Audio-visual	
9.3	9.0	9.1	9.0	9.6	9.4	8.7	8.9
8.9	8.6	8.3	8.5	9.0	8.8	9.0	9.3
8.7	9.0	8.2	8.6	9.2	8.9	8.4	8.6
9.1	9.0	9.0	8.9	9.7	9.2	7.7	9.0
8.6	8.5	9.2	9.7	9.6		9.2	9.1
9.1	8.8	8.5	8.3	8.9		8.8	8.9
9.5	9.0	8.7		8.8		8.9	
9.7	9.2	8.5		9.3		9.4	

(a) Compute the descriptive statistics of performance scores for each training method using the **Descriptive Statistics** option in **Data Analysis**. By inspection, what conclusions can the HR manager draw about differences in mean performance scores using the different training methods?

(b) What statistical and management conclusions can the HR manager draw about differences in the mean performance scores using the different training methods? Use the **ANOVA: Single Factor** option in **Data Analysis** to test the hypothesis at the 5% significance level. Is there any one training method that is more effective than the rest in producing superior employee performance levels when dealing with the company's customers? Provide statistical evidence. Formulate appropriate null and alternative hypotheses for this hypothesis test.

(c) Use the **t-Test: Two-Sample Assuming Equal Variances** option in **Data Analysis** to test the hypothesis that there is no difference in the mean performance scores between the two training methods with the highest sample mean performance scores. Use $\alpha = 0.05$. Interpret the finding.

(d) Based on the findings of the two hypotheses tests in (b) and (c), which single training method, if any, would you recommend that the HR manager adopts for all company employees? Why?

Two-factor ANOVA Exercises

16 Explain the key difference between one-factor ANOVA and two-factor ANOVA.

17 Identify the data types for each of the variables in a two-factor ANOVA study (i.e. the response variable and each of the two factors).

18 What is meant by the interaction term in two-factor ANOVA?

19 What is the purpose of the interaction plot? How is it constructed?

20 Construct a two-factor ANOVA table for the following problem: Factor A = PC operating system, Factor B = make of laptop, and response measure = 'boot up time (in seconds)'.

   (a) If Factor A has 3 levels and Factor B has 4 levels with a sample size of 5 data values per combination of factor levels, what are the degrees of freedom for SSA, SSB, SS(AB) and SSE?

   (b) Assume the total variation (SSTotal) is 482. If SSA = 68, SSB = 42 and SS(AB) = 132, how much of total variation is unexplained by the two Factors A and B collectively?

   (c) What are the values of MSA, MSB, MS(AB) and MSE?

   (d) What are the *F-stat* values for Factor A, Factor B and the interaction effect of Factor A and B respectively?

   (e) What are the values of *F-crit* for each hypotheses being tested based on a 1% level of significance?

   (f) Use the Excel function **F.DIST.RT** to find the *p*-value for each test.

   (g) Is Factor A significant? is Factor B significant? is the interaction effect between Factor A and Factor B significant?

Use the **ANOVA: Two-Factor with Replication** option in Excel's **Data Analysis** for the following exercises.

21 X11.21 – sales ability

   Grant Insurance employs graduates as sales consultants in the area of client benefits. The HR manager would like to know whether there are differences in sales abilities of these client-service graduate employees based on their *undergraduate qualification (Arts, Business, or Social Sciences)* (Factor A) and their *work experience* (classified as *under 3 years*, or *over 3 years*) (Factor B). No employee has more than 6 years of work experience. The findings will be used to review their recruitment practices.

   Random samples of 10 client-service graduate employees were selected from each grouping of *qualification type* and *experience level* and their *sales ability* (measured in terms of *commission earned* (in R10 000) in the last financial year) was recorded.

Experience (categorised)					
Under 3 years			Over 3 years		
Business	Arts	Social	Business	Arts	Social
42.8	40.4	29.8	47.7	47.5	45.8
25.9	28.0	31.0	44.1	42.9	40.5
39.4	39.9	25.0	50.3	39.2	40.8
43.5	36.2	32.9	41.5	23.4	41.9
51.7	34.2	36.1	42.6	29.6	43.8
30.2	32.4	29.8	55.3	52.7	53.2
46.3	40.7	32.2	37.3	31.4	36.4
33.8	41.7	36.2	45.4	30.8	44.4
42.8	43.0	36.4	42.6	25.2	28.0
43.7	40.1	36.5	39.4	34.9	41.0

(a) Conduct a two-factor ANOVA hypothesis test at the 5% level of significance.
   (i) Formulate the null and alternative hypothesis for each test.
   (ii) Is *experience* a statistically significant influence on a consultant's *sales ability*?
   (iii) Is *qualification* a statistically significant influence on a consultant's *sales ability*?
   (iv) Does *sales ability* vary by *graduate type* and *experience* together?
(b) Construct an interaction plot and describe the nature of any interaction effect.
(c) How should the HR manager of Grant Insurance revise their recruitment practice?

22 X11.22 – dropped calls

A key quality characteristic of a mobile phone service provider is its *rate of dropped calls*. This is assumed to be influenced by the type of *switching device* used to transfer calls through the network (of which there are 4 different types – labelled SW1, SW2, SW3 and SW4) (Factor A) and the transmission type (voice or data transfer) (Factor B).

The engineers responsible for maintaining the integrity of the service provider's network would like to determine statistically which combination of these two factors (*switching device type* and the *transmission type*), if any, is likely to result in the lowest average *rate of dropped calls* on the network. Sample data was collected on *dropped call rates* (% of daily dropped calls) for each transmission type routed through each switching device type.

Transmission type							
Voice				Data			
SW1	SW2	SW3	SW4	SW1	SW2	SW3	SW4
0.74	0.16	0.32	0.77	1.08	0.64	0.95	0.47
1.15	0.82	0.65	0.62	0.44	0.93	0.65	1.05
0.47	0.32	0.21	1.14	0.69	0.38	1.31	0.78
0.93	0.51	0.58	0.71	0.72	0.88	1.02	1.35
1.23	0.53	1.12	0.81	1.02	1.06	1.35	0.8
0.81	1.05	0.44	1.08	0.66	0.68	0.77	0.93
0.95	0.35	0.86	0.95	0.54	1.29	1.07	0.99
1.48	0.61	0.51	0.31	0.68	0.96	1.04	0.73

(a) Conduct a two-factor ANOVA hypothesis test to identify the influence that each factor has on the mean dropped call rates. Use a 1% level of significance.
   (i) Formulate the null and alternative hypothesis for each test.
   (ii) Is the *transmission type* an influencing factor on *dropped call rates*?
   (iii) Does *switching device type* statistically influence *dropped call rates*?
   (iv) Do both factors in combination statistically influence *dropped call rates*?
(b) Construct an interaction plot and describe the nature of any interaction effect.
(c) Advise the chief engineer on the most reliable switching devices to use for different transmission types based on the findings of this analysis.

23 X11.23 – rubber wastage

The *percentage of rubber wastage* generated from the production of vehicle tyres produced by a local tyre manufacturer based in Port Elizabeth has been recorded for three different tyre-processing *machines* (referred to as TAM1, TAM2 and TAM3) (Factor A) and for two different *tyre types* (*radial* and *bias*) (Factor B). The data was reported weekly (and included scrap, repairs and buffing figures).

Tyre type					
Radial			Bias		
TAM1	TAM2	TAM3	TAM1	TAM2	TAM3
3.53	7.44	2.97	2.81	6.63	5.03
2.88	6.86	3.42	1.30	3.37	11.27
2.47	4.05	3.72	1.83	11.48	12.18
3.41	4.66	2.27	3.31	9.92	6.79
7.42	10.51	7.06	4.22	7.20	8.50

(a) Conduct a two-factor ANOVA hypotheses test to identify which operational factors (*machine type used* or *tyre type manufactured*) influence the *rubber wastage levels*. Use a 5% level of significance. Formulate the relevant null and alternative hypotheses for each test and drawn the appropriate statistical and management conclusions.

(b) Construct an interaction plot and describe the nature of any interaction effect.

(c) Advise the production manager on an optimum production strategy (which includes work allocation practices and possible machine replacement) to minimise rubber wastage in the plant.

24 X11.24 – quality assurance

A company that manufactures safety-harness equipment sources its raw material (canvas) from three different suppliers. To determine whether the quality of the canvas is consistent across all three suppliers, the company's quality controller sampled six recent consignments of canvas from each supplier and measured its *tensile strength*.

Supplier 1	Supplier 2	Supplier 3
85	70	68
75	74	73
82	72	71
76	73	78
71	68	84
85	81	76

The descriptive statistics and partially completed one-factor ANOVA table is given below:

Summary				
Groups	**Count**	**Sum**	**Mean**	**Variance**
Supplier 1	6	474	79	34
Supplier 2	6	438	73	20
Supplier 3	6	450	75	32
Combined	18	1362	75.67	31.88

ANOVA ($\alpha = 0.05$)						
Source of variation	**SS**	**df**	**MS**	**F-stat**	**p-value**	**F-crit**
Explained (between)	[1]?	2	[4]?	[5]?	0.1762	[6]?
Unexplained (within)	430	[2]?	28.6667			
Total	542	[3]?	31.8824			

(a) Complete the empty cells labelled [1] to [6] in the ANOVA table to find *F-stat* and *F-crit*.
(b) Formulate the null and alternative hypothesis to test whether the mean tensile strength of the canvas raw material is the same from all three suppliers.
(c) Draw the statistical conclusion at the 5% level of significance using *F-stat* and *F-crit* to examine H_0.
(d) What is the management conclusion that can be drawn from these findings?

25 **X11.25 – work stress**

The *Journal of Work Psychology* published a research paper that examined the stress levels of employees in different professions. The study examined pilots, lawyers and stockbrokers. 5-point rating scales were used to measure 20 work items and then summed (maximum score = 100) The *unit of measure* is a *summed rating score* out of 100. A higher score denotes greater stress levels. A random sample of 15 workers from each profession participated in the study.

Summary				
Groups	**Count**	**Sum**	**Mean**	**Variance**
Pilots	15	1076	71.7333	117.6381
Lawyers	15	897	59.8000	170.4571
Stockbrokers	15	1032	68.8000	137.1714
Combined	45	3005	66.7778	161.67677

ANOVA ($\alpha = 0.05$)						
Source of Variation	**SS**	**df**	**MS**	**F-stat**	**p-value**	**F-crit**
Explained (between)	1160.04	[2]?	580.02	[5]?	[6]?	[7]?
Unexplained (within)	[1]?	[3]?	[4]?			
Total	7113.78	44	161.68			

Post hoc analysis

Multiple pairwise comparison of means (Tukey's HSD Method)

	df =	42	α =	0.05		
Pairs	**Difference**	**Std error**	**t-stat**	**t-crit**	**p-value**	**Status**
Pilots – Lawyers	11.9333	4.3475	[8]?	2.4295	0.0089	[12]?
Pilots – Stockbrokers	2.9333	4.3475	0.6747	2.4295	[10]?	[13]?
Lawyers – Stockbrokers	9.0000	4.3475	[9]?	2.4295	[11]?	[14]?

(a) Complete the empty cells labelled [1] to [7] in the ANOVA table to find *F-stat*, *F-crit* and the *p*-value.

(b) Formulate the null and alternative hypothesis to test whether the mean stress levels are the same across all three professions.

(c) Based on the ANOVA findings, draw the statistical conclusion at the 5% level of significance using *F-stat* compared to *F-crit* and the *p*-value compared to the level of significance to examine H_0.

(d) Complete the empty cells labelled [8] to [14] in the Post hoc analysis table to find the *t-stat* and *p*-values as well as identify the 'status'(significant or not significant) of each test.

(e) What conclusion, based on the statistical evidence from the ANOVA table and the Post hoc analysis table, can the researcher draw about work stress levels across the three professions?

CHAPTER
12

Simple Linear Regression and Correlation Analysis

Outcomes

In many business decisions it is necessary to predict the unknown values of a numeric variable using other numeric variables that are related to it and for which values are known.

Regression analysis is a statistical technique that quantifies the relationship between a single response variable and one or more predictor variables. This relationship, which is called a statistical model, is used for prediction purposes. Correlation analysis, on the other hand, identifies the strength of the relationships and determines which variables are useful in predicting the response variable.

After studying this chapter, you should be able to:

- explain the meaning of regression analysis
- identify practical examples where regression analysis can be used
- construct a simple linear regression model
- use the regression line for prediction purposes
- calculate and interpret the correlation coefficient
- calculate and interpret the coefficient of determination
- conduct a hypothesis test on the regression model to test for significance.

12.1 Introduction

In management, many numeric measures are related (either strongly or loosely) to one another. For example:
- *advertising expenditure* is assumed to influence *sales volumes*
- a company's *share price* is likely to be influenced by its *return on investment*
- the number of *hours of operator training* is believed to impact positively on *productivity*
- the *operating speed* of a bottling machine affects the *reject rate* of under-filled bottles.

Regression analysis and **correlation analysis** are two statistical methods that aim to *quantify the relationship* between these variables and *measure the strength* of this relationship.

The relationship between any pair of variables – labelled x and y – can be examined graphically by producing a **scatter plot** of their data values, as illustrated in Figure 12.1.

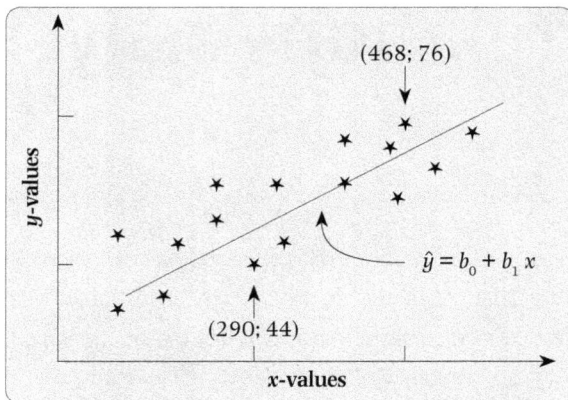

Figure 12.1 A scatter plot between pairs of x and y data values

The scatter plot illustrates the idea behind regression and correlation analysis. Each scatter point represents a pair of data values from the two random variables, x and y. The pattern of the scatter points indicates the nature of the relationship, which is represented by the straight line, calculated by regression analysis. The degree of closeness of the scatter points to the straight line is a measure of the strength of the relationship and is described by correlation analysis.

To perform regression and correlation analysis, the *data* for both variables must be *numeric*.

12.2 Simple Linear Regression Analysis

Simple linear regression analysis finds a *straight-line equation* that represents the relationship between the values of *two numeric variables*.

One variable is called the **independent** or **predictor variable**, x, and the other is called the **dependent** or **response variable**, y.

The x-variable influences the outcome of the y-variable. Its values are usually known or easily determined. The dependent variable, y, is influenced by (or responds to) the independent variable, x. Values for the dependent variable are estimated from values of the independent variable.

Figure 12.2 shows pairs of random variables between which possible relationships exist. Some relationships are simple and strong, while others may be more complex and weak.

Independent variable (x) (predictor of y)	Dependent variable (y) (variable estimated from x)
Advertising	Company turnover
Training	Labour productivity
Speed	Fuel consumption
Hours worked	Machine output
Daily temperature	Electricity demand
Hours studied	Statistics grade
Amount of fertiliser used	Crop yield
Product price	Sales volume
Bond interest rate	Number of bond defaulters
Cost of living	Poverty

Figure 12.2 Possible relationships between sets of numeric random variables

In simple linear regression, there is only one independent variable, x, that is used to estimate or predict values of the dependent variable, y. The process of building a simple linear regression model is illustrated using Example 12.1.

Example 12.1 Flat-screen TV Sales Study

Music Technologies, an electronics retail company in Durban, has recorded the number of flat-screen TVs sold each week and the number of advertisements placed weekly for a period of 12 weeks.

Table 12.1 Database of flat-screen TV sales and newspaper advertisements placed

Advertisements	4	4	3	2	5	2	4	3	5	5	3	4
Sales	26	28	24	18	35	24	36	25	31	37	30	32

Management Question

Can the manager predict flat-screen TV sales from the number of advertisements placed each week?

Statistical Questions

1 Find the straight-line regression equation to estimate the number of flat-screen TVs that Music Technologies can expect to sell each week, based on the number of advertisements placed.
2 Estimate the mean sales of flat-screen TVs when three advertisements are placed.

Solution

Step 1: Identify the dependent and independent variables
An essential first step is to correctly identify the independent and dependent variables. A useful rule of thumb is to ask the following question: 'Which variable is to be estimated?'

The answer will identify the dependent variable, y. In the example:

x = the number of advertisements placed weekly

y = the number of flat-screen TVs sold in the week.

Step 2: Construct a scatter plot between x and y

A scatter plot graphically displays both the nature and strength of the relationship between the independent variable (x) and the dependent variable (y), as is illustrated in Figure 12.1. A visual inspection of the scatter plot will show whether the pattern is linear or not, whether it is direct or inverse, and its strength. Refer to figures 12.3 to 12.7 to interpret the relationship between x and y.

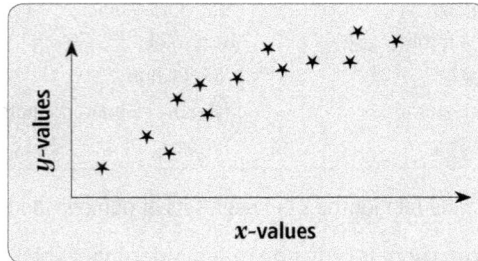

Figure 12.3 Strong – direct linear relationship with small dispersion (for any given x-value, the range in y-values is small)

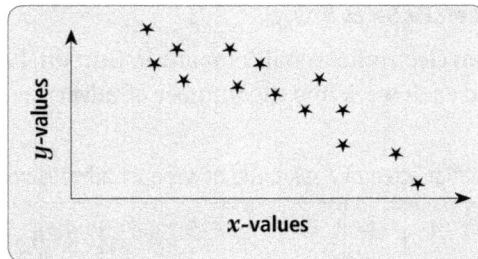

Figure 12.4 Strong – inverse linear relationship with small dispersion (for any given x-value, the range in y-values is small)

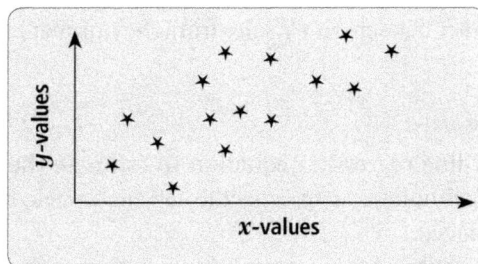

Figure 12.5 Moderate – direct linear relationship with greater dispersion (for any given x-value, the range in y-values is larger)

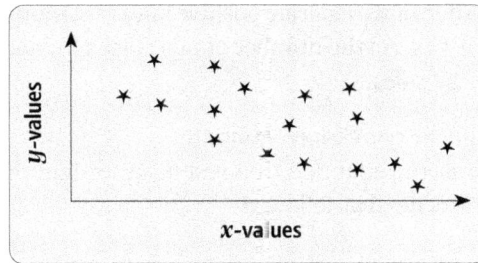

Figure 12.6 Moderate – inverse linear relationships with greater dispersion (for any given x-value, the range in y-values is larger)

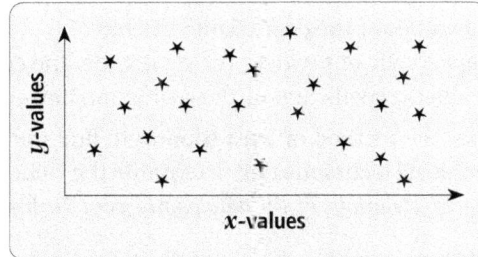

Figure 12.7 No linear relationship (values of x and y are randomly scattered: for any given x-value, y can have any value over a wide range)

The patterns in figures 12.3 and 12.4 show *strong linear relationships* between x and y. Estimates of y based on these relationships will be highly reliable. The patterns shown in figures 12.5 and 12.6 are evidence of *moderate to weak linear relationships* and are of less value for estimation purposes. Finally, the pattern shown in Figure 12.7 is evidence of *no statistical relationship* between the two numeric measures. In such cases, regression analysis is of little value to estimate y based on x-values. These estimates of y will be unreliable.

In the example, the scatter plot between ads placed and sales recorded is shown in Figure 12.8.

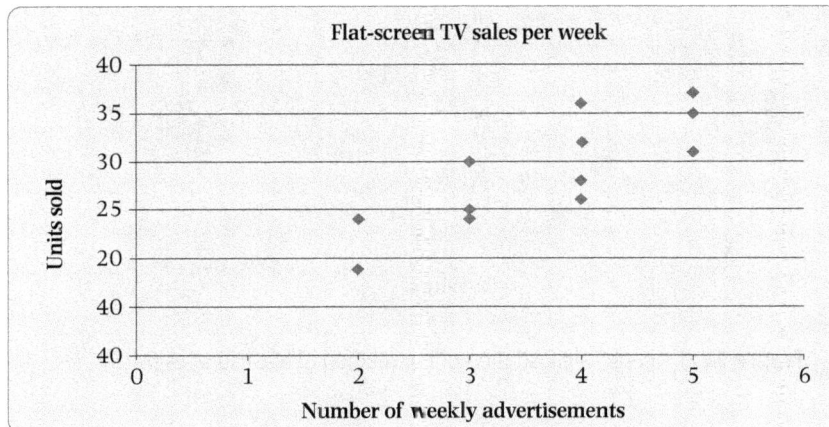

Figure 12.8 Scatter plot of ads placed (x) against sales recorded (y) for flat-screen TVs

From the scatter plot, there is a moderate positive linear relationship between ads placed and sales of flat-screen TVs. As the number of ads placed increases, there is a moderate increase in flat-screen TV sales.

Step 3: Calculate the linear regression equation

Regression analysis finds the equation that *best fits* a straight line to the scatter points. A straight-line graph is defined as follows:

$$\hat{y} = b_0 + b_1 x$$

12.1

Where: x = values of the independent variable

$\hat{y}$ = estimated values of the dependent variable

b_0 = y-intercept coefficient (where the regression line cuts the y-axis)

b_1 = slope (gradient) coefficient of the regression line

Regression analysis uses the **method of least squares** to find the best-fitting straight-line equation. It is a mathematical technique that determines the values b_0 and b_1, such that:

the sum of the squared deviations of the data points from the fitted line is minimised.

A brief explanation of this method is given and illustrated using Figure 12.9.

(a) First, calculate the deviation (e_i) of each y_i-value from its estimated value $\hat{y}_i$.
$$e_i = y_i - \hat{y}_i$$

(b) Square each deviation to avoid positive and negative deviations cancelling each other out when summed.
$$e_i^2 = (y_i - \hat{y}_i)^2$$

(c) Sum the squared deviations to obtain a measure of *total squared deviations*.
$$\Sigma e_i^2 = \Sigma(y_i - \hat{y}_i)^2 \quad \text{or} \quad \Sigma e_i^2 = \Sigma(y_i - (b_0 + b_1 x_i))^2$$

(d) Values for b_0 and b_1 are now found mathematically by minimising the total squared deviations in (c). The calculation is called the **method of least squares (MLS)**.

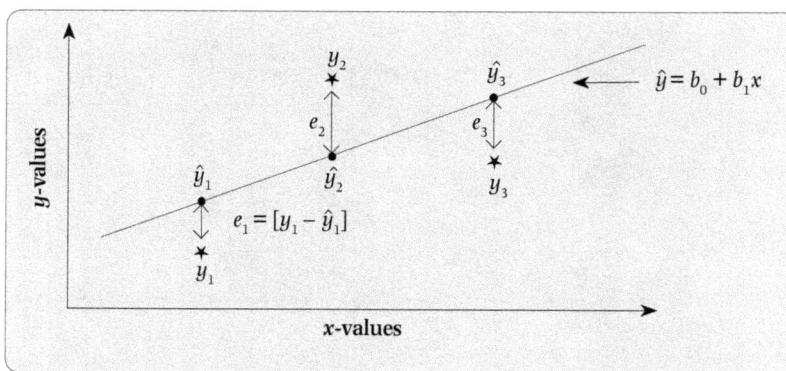

Figure 12.9 Graphical illustration of the method of least squares (MLS)

Without showing the mathematical calculations, the coefficients b_0 and b_1 that result from this *method of least squares* are given as follows:

$$b_1 = \frac{n\Sigma xy - \Sigma x \Sigma y}{n\Sigma x^2 - (\Sigma x)^2}$$

12.2

$$b_0 = \frac{\Sigma y - b_1 \Sigma x}{n}$$

12.3

The values of b_0 and b_1 define the best-fitting linear regression line. This means that no other straight-line equation will give a better fit (i.e. a smaller sum of squared deviations) than the regression line. For the example, Table 12.2 shows the calculations of the regression coefficients using Formula 12.2 and Formula 12.3.

Table 12.2 Calculation of the regression coefficients b_0 and b_1 for flat-screen TV sales

Ads (x)	Sales (y)	x^2	xy
4	26	16	104
4	28	16	112
3	24	9	72
2	18	4	36
5	35	25	175
2	24	4	48
4	36	16	144
3	25	9	75
5	31	25	155
5	37	25	185
3	30	9	90
4	32	16	128
Total	**44**	**346**	**174**	**1 324**

From Table 12.2, we have $\Sigma x = 44$, $\Sigma y = 346$, $\Sigma x^2 = 174$, $\Sigma xy = 1\,324$ and $n = 12$. Then:

$$b_1 = \frac{12(1\,324) - (44)(346)}{12(174) - (44)^2} = \frac{664}{152} = 4.368$$

$$b_0 = \frac{346 - 4.368(44)}{12} = 12.817$$

The simple linear regression equation to estimate flat-screen TV sales is given by:

$\hat{y} = 12.817 + 4.368x$ for $2 \leq x \leq 5$

The interval of x-values (i.e. $2 \leq x \leq 5$) is called the **domain** of x. It represents the set of x-values that were used to construct the regression line. Thus to produce valid estimates of y, only values of x from within the domain should be substituted in the regression equation.

Step 4: Estimate y-values using the regression equation

The regression equation can now be used to estimate y-values from (known) x-values by substituting a given x-value into the regression equation. In the example, management question 2 asks for a sales *estimate* of the average number of flat-screen TVs in a week when three advertisements are placed.

Thus substitute $x = 3$ into the regression equation:

$$\hat{y} = 12.817 + 4.368(3)$$
$$= 12.817 + 13.104$$
$$= 25.921$$
$$= 26 \text{ (rounded)}$$

The management of Music Technologies can therefore expect to sell, on average, 26 flat-screen TVs in a week when three newspaper advertisements are placed.

It is statistically more valid to *estimate* the average y-value using a *confidence interval* instead of a point estimate. The *confidence interval formula* of a forecasted average y value, $\hat{y}_0$ based on a given x_0 value is:

$$\hat{y}_0 \pm t\text{-}crit \times \text{s.e.} \qquad\qquad 12.4$$

where s.e. = the *standard error* of the confidence interval

$$\text{s.e.} = \sqrt{\text{MSE}\left(\frac{1}{n} + \frac{(x_0 - \bar{x})^2}{\Sigma(x_i - \bar{x})^2}\right)} \qquad\qquad 12.5$$

and $t\text{-}crit = t(\alpha, df = n - p - 1)$ Use the Excel function **T.INV.2T**(α, df)

A simpler, but only an *approximate* value for s.e. is: s.e. $\approx \sqrt{\left(\frac{\text{MSE}}{n}\right)}$

MSE (mean square error) is the *average squared deviation* of the scatter points (x's) around the fitted regression line (refer to **step 3(c)** in the calculation of the regression equation). The smaller the MSE, the closer the scatter points are to the fitted regression line (the better the fit), and vice versa.

$$\text{MSE} = \frac{\Sigma e_i^2}{(n - p - 1)} \qquad\qquad 12.6$$

where n = sample size and p = number of independent variables.

Table 12.3 shows the calculation of the confidence interval for $x_0 = 3$ using formulae 12.4 to 12.6.

Table 12.3 Confidence interval calculations to estimate the average y value

Ads (x)	Sales (y)	$\hat{y}$	$c_i = (y - \hat{y})^2$	$(x - \bar{x})^2$
4	26	30.29	18.4	0.111
4	28	30.29	5.242	0.111
3	24	25.92	3.69	0.444
2	18	21.55	12.621	2.778
5	35	34.66	0.117	1.778
2	24	21.55	5.99	2.778
4	36	30.29	32.61	0.111
3	25	25.92	0.848	0.444
5	31	34.66	13.38	1.778
5	37	34.66	5.485	1.778
3	30	25.92	16.638	0.444
4	32	30.29	2.926	0.111
			117.947	**12.667**

For $x_0 = 3$, the point estimate for the average $y = \hat{y}_0 = 25.92$

$n = 12$ and $p = 1$, then MSE $= \dfrac{117.947}{(12-1-1)} = 11.7947$.

Also $\bar{x} = 3.67$ $\Sigma(x_i - \bar{x})^2 = 12.667$ $(x_0 - \bar{x})^2 = (3 - 3.67)^2 = 0.4489$

Now s.e. $= \sqrt{11.7947 \times \left(\frac{1}{12} + \frac{0.4489}{12.667}\right)} = \sqrt{(11.7947 \times 0.1188)} = 1.1835$

Also t-crit $= t(0.05, df = 12 - 1 - 1) = t(0.05,10) = $ **T.INV.2T**$(0.05,10) = 2.2281$

Lower 95% confidence interval limit $= 25.92 - (2.2281 \times 1.1835) = 23.3$

Upper 95% confidence interval limit $= 25.92 + (2.2281 \times 1.1835) = 28.6$

Thus, there is a 95% chance that the average number of flat-screen TV's that Music Technologies can expect to sell in any week where three advertisements are placed is between 23 and 29.

Interpreting the b_1 Coefficient

The b_1 regression coefficient is the slope of the regression line. It is a *marginal rate of change* measure. It is interpreted as follows: for a unit change in x, y will change by the value of b_1. For Example 12.1, with $b_1 = 4.368$, this means that if one additional newspaper advertisement is placed, weekly flat-screen TV sales can be expected to increase by 4.368 units.

The Danger of Extrapolation

Extrapolation occurs when x-values are chosen from *outside* the domain to substitute into the regression equation to estimate y.

If a y-value is estimated for x-values that lie outside the domain (i.e. extrapolation has taken place), the y estimates are unreliable and possibly even *invalid*. The reason for this is that the relationship between x and y *outside* the domain limits is unknown. The relationship may in fact be quite different from that which is defined between x and y within the domain. Extrapolation can sometimes lead to absurd and meaningless estimates of y.

In the example, extrapolation occurs if $x = 10$ ads is substituted into the regression line to estimate sales of $y = 57$ flat-screen TVs. This result is untested in the data, and very unreliable.

12.3 Correlation Analysis

The reliability of the estimate of y depends on the *strength* of the relationship between the x and y variables. A strong relationship implies a more accurate and reliable estimate of y.

> **Correlation analysis** measures the strength of the *linear association* between two numeric (ratio-scaled) variables, x and y.

This measure is called **Pearson's correlation coefficient**. It is represented by the symbol r when it is calculated from sample data.

The following formula is used to calculate the sample correlation coefficient:

$$r = \frac{n\Sigma xy - \Sigma x \Sigma y}{\sqrt{[n\Sigma x^2 - (\Sigma x)^2] \times [n\Sigma y^2 - (\Sigma y)^2]}}$$

12.7

Where: r = the sample correlation coefficient
x = the values of the independent variable
y = the values of the dependent variable
n = the number of paired data points in the sample

Example 12.2 Flat-screen TV Sales Study

Refer to the management scenario of Example 12.1. Find the sample correlation coefficient, r, between the number of ads placed and flat-screen TV sales. Comment on the strength of the linear relationship.

Solution

Table 12.4 shows the calculations for Pearson's sample correlation coefficient, r.

Table 12.4 Pearson's correlation coefficient for the flat-screen TV sales study

Ads (x)	Sales (y)	x^2	xy	y^2
4	26	16	104	676
4	28	16	112	784
3	24	9	72	576
2	18	4	36	324
5	35	25	175	1 225
2	24	4	48	576
4	36	16	144	1 296
3	25	9	75	625
5	31	25	155	961
5	37	25	185	1 369
3	30	9	90	900
4	32	16	128	1 024
44	346	174	1 324	10 336

Table 12.4 gives $\Sigma x = 44$, $\Sigma y = 346$, $\Sigma x^2 = 174$, $\Sigma xy = 1\,324$, $\Sigma y^2 = 10\,336$ and $n = 12$.

Then: $r = \dfrac{12(1\,324) - (44)(346)}{\sqrt{[12(174) - (44)^2][12(10\,336) - (346)^2]}} = \dfrac{664}{\sqrt{(152)(4\,316)}}$

$= 0.8198$ (Formula 12.5)

How to Interpret a Correlation Coefficient

A correlation coefficient is a proportion that lies between -1 and $+1$ *only*.

$$-1 \leq r \leq +1$$

12.8

Figure 12.10 shows how the strength of the linear association between two numeric variables is represented by the correlation coefficient.

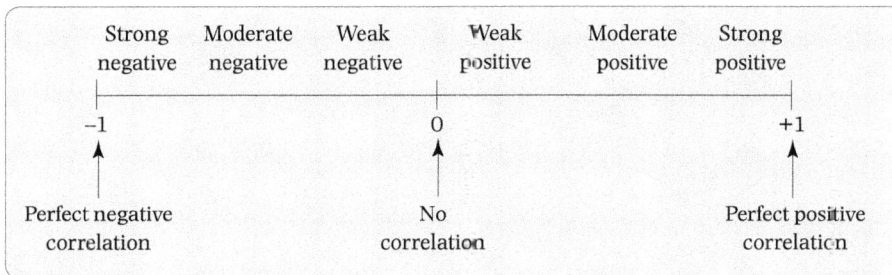

Figure 12.10 Graphical display of interpretation of a correlation coefficient

Figures 12.11 to 12.17 show both the *direction* and *strength* of a correlation coefficient associated with various scatter plots of two numeric random variables.

Perfect associations

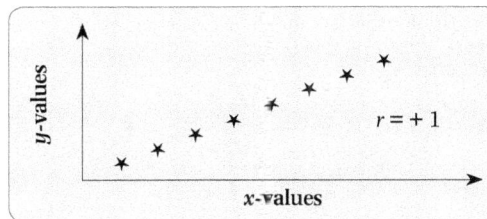

Figure 12.11 Perfect positive linear correlation ($r = +1$)

All the data points of a scatter plot lie exactly on a positively sloped straight line.

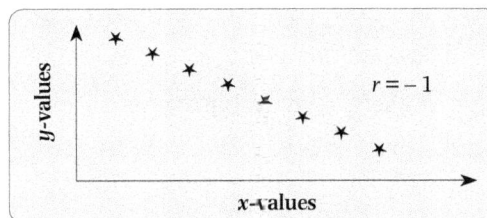

Figure 12.12 Perfect negative linear correlation ($r = -1$)

All the data points will again lie exactly on a straight line, but in an inverse direction (i.e. as x increases, y decreases, and vice versa). It is thus a negatively sloped straight line.

In both cases, the values of x *exactly predict* the values of y.

Strong associations

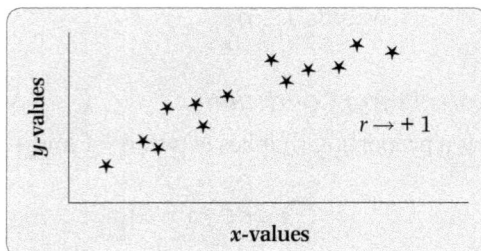

Figure 12.13 Positive linear correlation ($0 < r < +1$), with r being closer to $+1$

This is a *direct relationship*. As x increases (or decreases), y will also increase (or decrease).

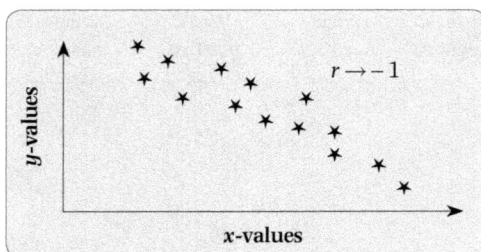

Figure 12.14 Negative linear correlation ($-1 < r < 0$), with r being closer to -1

This is an *inverse relationship*, since as x increases (or decreases), y will decrease (or increase).

The *close grouping* of the scatter points in both diagrams implies a *strong linear relationship*, with the correlation coefficient r being close to $+1$ if the relationship is positive (or direct), or close to -1 if the relationship is negative (or inverse).

Moderate to weak associations

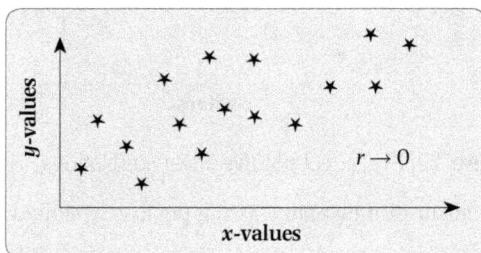

Figure 12.15 Positive linear correlation ($0 < r < +1$), with r being closer to 0

This illustrates a *direct* – but weaker – relationship between x and y.

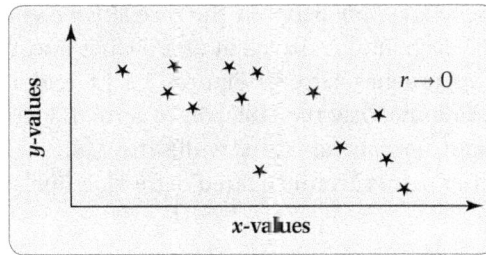

Figure 12.16 Negative linear correlation ($-1 < r < 0$), with r being closer to 0

This illustrates an *inverse* – but weaker – relationship between x and y.

The more widely spread scatter points in both cases show a *moderate to weak linear relationship*, with the correlation coefficient, r, lying closer to 0.

No association

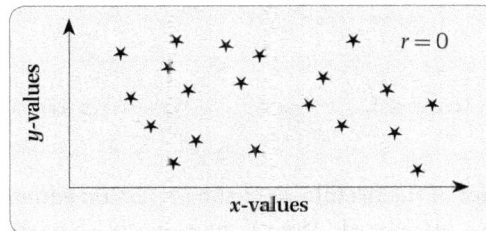

Figure 12.17 No linear correlation ($r = 0$)

The values of x are of *no value* in estimating values of y. The data points are randomly scattered.

From the above illustrations, it can be seen that the closer r is to -1 or $+1$, the stronger the association. Similarly, the closer r is to 0, the weaker the linear relationship between x and y.

Any interpretation should take the following two points into account:
- A low correlation does not necessarily imply that the variables are unrelated, only that the relationship is poorly described by a straight line. A non-linear relationship may well exist. Pearson's correlation coefficient does not measure non-linear relationships.
- A correlation does not imply a cause-and-effect relationship. It is merely an observed statistical association.

For Example 12.2, the Pearson's sample correlation coefficient $r = 0.8198$. This implies a strong, direct (positive) statistical association between the number of ads placed and the sales of flat-screen TVs. Thus the number of newspaper advertisements placed is a *good estimator* of the actual number of flat-screen TVs that the company can expect to sell in the following week.

Note: There is an *inverse relationship* between the *correlation coefficient*, r, and the *mean square error*, MSE. As the correlation coefficient approaches one, the mean square error of the regression line approaches zero. In Figures 12.11 and 12.12, the correlation coefficient is ± 1 and simultaneously the MSE will be zero. In Figures 12.15 and 12.16, the correlation coefficient approaches zero, while the MSE becomes larger showing greater variation of scatter points around a fitted regression line.

12.4 The r^2 Coefficient

When the sample correlation coefficient, r, is squared (r^2), the resultant measure is called the coefficient of determination.

The **coefficient of determination** measures the proportion (or percentage) of variation in the dependent variable, y, that is explained by the independent variable, x. The coefficient of determination ranges between 0 and 1 (or 0% and 100%).

$$0 \leq r^2 \leq 1 \qquad \text{or} \qquad 0\% \leq r^2 \leq 100\% \qquad\qquad 12.9$$

r^2 is an important indicator of the usefulness of the regression equation because it measures *how strongly* x and y are associated. The closer r^2 is to 1 (or 100%), the stronger the association between x and y. Alternatively, the closer r^2 is to 0, the weaker the association between x and y. This interpretation is shown in Figure 12.18.

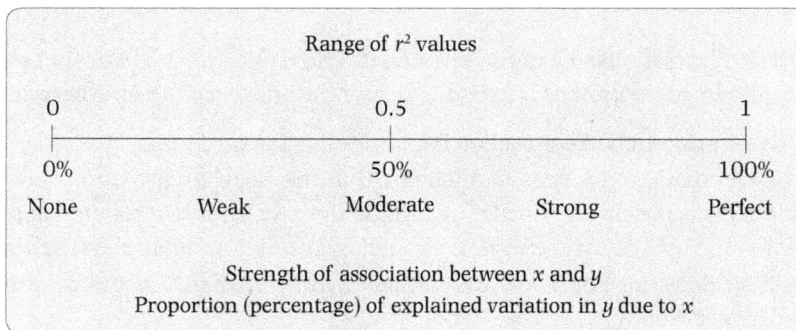

Figure 12.18 Interpretation of the r^2 coefficient

When: $r^2 = 0$ There is *no association* between x and y (as shown in Figure 12.17).

$r^2 = 1$ There is *perfect association* between x and y (as shown in Figures 12.11 and 12.12). In both cases, y is *completely* (100%) explained by x.

$0 < r^2 < 1$ The strength of association depends on how close r^2 lies to either 0 or 1.
- When r^2 lies closer to 0 (or 0%), it indicates a weak association between x and y (as shown in Figures 12.15 and 12.16).
- When r^2 lies closer to 1 (or 100%), it indicates a *strong* association between x and y (as shown in Figures 12.13 and 12.14).

Example 12.3 Flat-screen TV Sales Study

Refer to the management scenario of Example 12.1. Calculate the sample coefficient of determination, r^2, between the number of ads placed and flat-screen TV sales. Comment on the strength of the linear relationship.

Solution

The coefficient of determination, r^2, between x (number of ads placed) and y (weekly sales of flat-screen TVs) is found by squaring the correlation coefficient, r.

Given $r = 0.8198$, then $r^2 = (0.8198)^2 = 0.6721$ (or 67.21%).

This means that the number of newspaper advertisements placed, x, explains 67.21% of the variation in flat-screen TV sales, y. Newspaper advertisements therefore have a *moderate to strong* impact on weekly flat-screen TV sales.

The r^2 coefficient is more useful than the correlation coefficient when interpreting the strength of association between two random variables, because it measures the strength as a percentage.

12.5 Testing the Regression Model for Significance

An important question in regression analysis is the following: 'Is the statistical relationship between x and y, as given by the regression equation, a genuine relationship or is it due purely to chance?'

Since the regression equation is constructed from sample data, it is possible that there is no genuine relationship between the x and y variables in the population and that any observed relationship from the sample is due purely to chance. A hypothesis test can be conducted to determine whether the sample-based regression relationship is genuine or not.

To test the regression equation for significance, the sample correlation coefficient, r, is tested against its population correlation coefficient, ρ, which is hypothesised to be 0. In the test, the null hypothesis states that there is *no relationship* between x and y in the population. The hypothesis test will be illustrated using Example 12.1.

Example 12.4 Testing the Correlation Coefficient

Refer to the management scenario of Example 12.1. At the 5% level of significance, test whether the population correlation coefficient, ρ, between the number of advertisements placed and weekly flat-screen TV sales is actually zero.

Solution

The same five steps of hypothesis testing are used. The test statistic is *t-stat*.

Step 1: Define the null and alternative hypotheses

$H_0: \rho = 0$ (newspaper advertisements and TV sales are not related)
$H_1: \rho \neq 0$ (newspaper advertisements and TV sales are related)

This is a two-tailed hypothesis test that shows *no relationship* in the null hypothesis.

Note: The closer *r* is to zero, the more likely it is that the null hypothesis will be accepted.

Step 2: Determine the region of acceptance of the null hypothesis
The test is based on the *t* statistic (as used in chapters 7 and 8). To read off the critical *t*-limits for the region of acceptance, both a level of significance and degrees of freedom for the test are required.

Given $\alpha = 0.05$. For a simple regression equation:

$$\text{Degrees of freedom } (df) = n - 2$$

12.10

In this example, $df = 12 - 2 = 10$. Then $t\text{-}crit = \pm 2.228$ (Table 2, Appendix 1). Thus the region of acceptance for H_0 is $-2.228 \leq t \leq +2.228$.

The decision rule is then stated as follows:
- Accept H_0 if *t-stat* lies between -2.228 and $+2.228$ inclusive.
- Reject H_0 if *t-stat* lies below -2.228 or above $+2.228$.

Step 3: Calculate the sample test statistic (*t-stat*)
The sample test statistic is *t-stat*, which is calculated using the following formula:

$$t\text{-}stat = r\sqrt{\frac{(n-2)}{1-r^2}}$$

12.11

In the example, $r = 0.8198$ and $n = 12$. Then:

$$t\text{-}stat = 0.8198\sqrt{\frac{(12-2)}{(1-0.8198^2)}} = 0.8198 \times \sqrt{\frac{10}{0.3279}} = 4.527$$

The *p*-value can be found using **T.DIST.2T**(*t-stat,df* $= n - 2$)
i.e. *p*-value = **T.DIST.2T**(4.527,10) = 0.0011

Step 4: Compare the sample test statistic to the region of acceptance
The sample test statistic, $t\text{-}stat = 4.527$ *lies outside* (well above) the region of acceptance of H_0, as shown in Figure 12.19.

Step 5: Draw statistical and management conclusions
Since $t\text{-}stat > + t\text{-}crit$ (and *p*-value $<< \alpha$), we reject H_0 at the 5% level of significance. There is strong enough sample evidence to conclude that the population correlation coefficient is *not* zero. The alternative hypothesis is probably true.

From a management viewpoint, the sample evidence indicates that there is a genuine *strong positive* statistical relationship between the number of advertisements placed (*x*) and the weekly flat-screen TV sales (*y*) in the population.

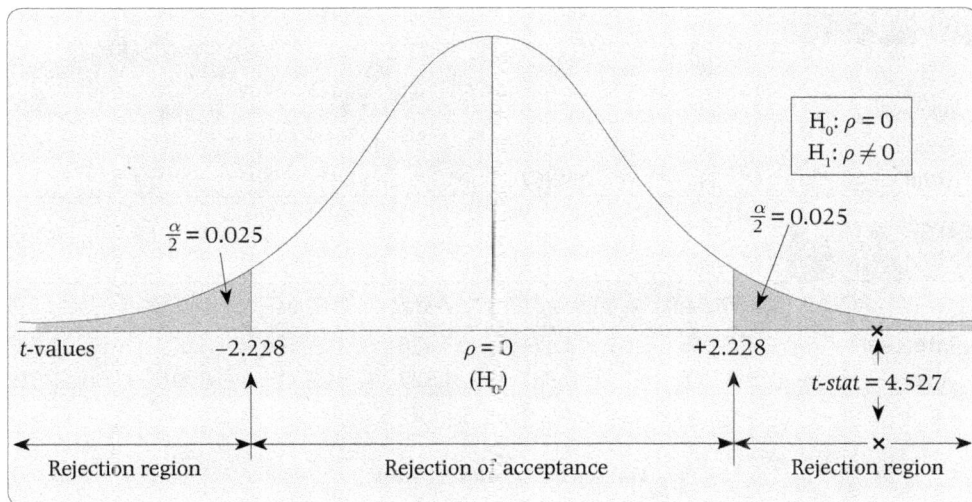

Figure 12.19 *t-stat*: Regions of acceptance/rejection for the flat-screen TV sales study

12.6 Using Excel (2016) and X-Static for Regression Analysis

Regression and correlation analysis can be performed in Excel using the **Regression** option in the **Data Analysis** add-in module. The output for Example 12.1 is shown in Table 12.5, with the regression equation coefficients (b_0 and b_1), the correlation coefficient, r, the coefficient of determination, r^2, and *t-stat* test statistic for the hypothesis test highlighted in **bold**.

A scatter plot between x and y can also be produced using the **Chart – Scatter** option in the **Insert** tab. A scatter plot of the x–y data in Example 12.1 is shown in Figure 12.19.

In addition, the regression equation can be computed and superimposed on the scatter plot, together with the coefficient of determination. To do this, right-click on any scatter point, select **Add Trendline** from the drop-down option list. Then select the **Linear** option, and tick the boxes **Display Equation** on the chart and **Display R-squared** on the chart. The graph, regression equation and R^2 are shown in Figure 12.21.

Insert the y-axis label 'Number of units sold per week' and the x-axis label 'Number of weekly advertisements placed'.

Table 12.5 Regression output for Example 12.1 using the **Data Analysis** add-in

Summary output	
Regression statistics	
Multiple R	**0.8198**
R square	**0.6721**
Adjusted R square	0.6393
Standard error	3.4343
Observations	12

ANOVA

	df	SS	MS	F-stat	p-value
Regression	1	241.72	241.72	20.494	0.0011
Residual	10	117.95	11.79		
Total	**11**	**359.67**			

Regression

	Coefficients	Standard error	t-stat	p-value	Lower 95%	Upper 95%
Intercept	**12.816**	3.674	3.488	0.0058	4.629	21.003
Ads	**4.368**	0.965	**4.527**	0.0011	2.218	6.519

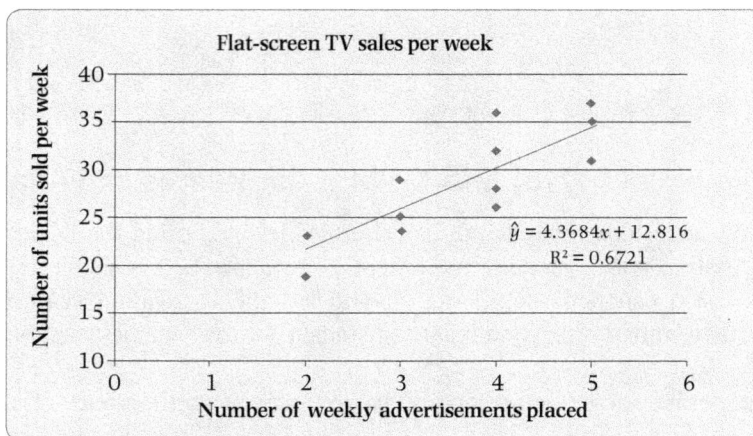

Figure 12.21 Scatter plot of ads and TV sales, with superimposed regression equation

X-Static can also be used to generate similar linear regression results as **Data Analysis**. In addition to the standard regression output (as shown in Table 12.5), there are options for correlation analysis, scatter plots and residual analysis.

Note: The **coefficient of determination**, r^2, can also be derived from the *Sum of Squares* (SS) calculations in the ANOVA table of Table 12.5. *SS Regression* represents the amount of total variation in the dependent variable, y, that is explained by the independent variable, x, while the *SS Total* represents the total amount of variation in the dependent variable, y. By dividing SS Regression by SS Total, we obtain the percentage of total variation in y that can be explained by the independent variable, x. i.e. $r^2 = 241.72/359.67 = 0.6721$ (67.21%).

12.7 Summary

Simple linear regression analysis is a technique that builds a straight-line relationship between a single independent variable, x, and a dependent variable, y. The purpose of the regression equation is to estimate y-values from known, or assumed, x-values by substituting the x-value into a regression equation. The data of all the independent variable and the dependent variable must be *numeric*.

The *method of least squares* is used to find the *best-fit* equation to express this relationship. The coefficients of the regression equations, b_0 and b_1, are weights that measure the importance of each of the independent variables in estimating the y-variable.

Two descriptive statistical measures were identified to indicate the usefulness of the regression equation to estimate y-values. They are the coefficient of correlation, r, and the coefficient of determination, r^2.

The simple linear regression equation, which is always based on sample data, must be tested for statistical significance before it can be used to produce valid and reliable estimates of the true mean value of the dependent variable. In simple linear regression, a test of significance of the simple correlation coefficient, r, between x and y will establish whether x is significant in estimating y.

The use of Excel through the **Regression** option in **Data Analysis** was illustrated using the worked example in the chapter. **X-Static** can also be used to generate similar output.

This regression analysis technique is of real value to managers, because it is used as a forecasting and planning tool.

Exercises

This symbol denotes data available online

1   What is regression analysis? What is correlation analysis?
2   What name is given to the variable that is being estimated in a regression equation?
3   What is the purpose of an independent variable in regression analysis?
4   What is the name of the graph that is used to display the relationship between the dependent variable and the independent variable?
5   What is the name given to the method used to find the regression coefficients?
6   Explain the *strength and direction* of the association between two variables, x and y, that have a correlation coefficient of -0.78.
7   Given a regression equation $\hat{y} = 2.35 + 6.82x$, with $n = 18$ and a correlation coefficient, $r = 0.42$, conduct a hypothesis test to determine if the regression relationship between x and y is statistically significant at the 5% level of significance. What conclusion can be drawn from the hypothesis test?
8   X12.8 – training effectiveness

The training manager of a company that assembles and exports pool pumps wants to know if there is a link between the *number of hours* spent by assembly workers in *training* and their *productivity* on the job. A random sample of 10 assembly workers was selected and their performances evaluated.

Training hours	20	36	20	38	40	33	32	28	40	24
Output	40	70	44	56	60	48	62	54	63	38

(a)   Construct a scatter plot of the sample data and comment on the relationship between hours of training and output.
(b)   Calculate a simple regression line, using the method of least squares, to identify a linear relationship between the *hours of training* received by assembly workers and their *output* (i.e. number of units assembled per day).
(c)   Calculate the coefficient of determination between training hours received and worker output. Interpret its meaning and advise the training manager.
(d)   *Estimate* the average daily output of an assembly worker who has received only 25 hours of training.

9   X12.9 – capital utilisation

A business analyst believes that capital utilisation (as measured by inventory turnover) has a direct effect on a company's earnings yield. To examine this belief, the analyst randomly surveyed nine JSE-listed companies and recorded their *inventory turnover* and their *earning yield*.

Inventory turnover	3	5	4	7	6	4	8	6	5
Earnings yield	10	12	8	13	15	10	16	13	10

(a)   Graphically display the relationship between inventory turnover and earnings yield for the sample of nine companies. What relationship can be observed?
(b)   Calculate a linear regression equation to express the relationship between the inventory turnover and earnings yields of companies.
(c)   Construct the correlation coefficient between inventory turnover and earnings yield. Does this value support the business analyst's view? Comment.

(d)   Find the coefficient of determination between earnings yield and inventory turnover.

(e)   Test the significance of the correlation coefficient between inventory turnover and earnings yield. Conduct a hypothesis test at the 5% level of significance. What conclusion can be drawn?

(f)   What earnings yield can a company expect to achieve if they have an inventory turnover of six next year?

10   X12.10 – loan applications

A bank wanted to find out whether the number of loan applications received are influenced by the current loan interest rate. The manager selected 11 monthly periods for which different *interest rates* applied and recorded the *number of loan applications received.*

Loan applications received											
Interest rate (%)	7.0	6.5	5.5	6.0	8.0	8.5	6.0	6.5	7.5	8.0	6.0
Loan applications	18	22	30	24	16	18	28	27	20	17	21

(a)   Identify the independent variable and the dependent variable.

(b)   Show the data graphically in a scatter plot. What relationship is observed?

(c)   Calculate the correlation coefficient between the rate of interest and the number of loan applications received. Comment on the strength of the association.

(d)   Test the association between the rate of interest and number of loan applications received for statistical significance. Use $\alpha = 0.05$. Show the null and alternative hypotheses and interpret the findings of the hypothesis test.

(e)   Derive the least squares regression line between the rate of interest and the number of loan applications received.

(f)   Interpret the meaning of the regression coefficient (b_1) of the independent variable.

(g)   How many loan applications can the bank expect to receive when the interest rate is 6%?

11   X12.11 – maintenance costs

A company that manufacturers wooden products (e.g. garden furniture, ladders, benches) regularly maintains its lathe machines, which are used for cutting and shaping components. The manager would like to know whether the *cost of machine maintenance* is related to the *age of the machines*. For a random sample of 12 lathe machines in the company's factory, the *annual maintenance cost* (in R100s) and *age of each machine* was recorded.

Maintenance costs analysis												
Machine	1	2	3	4	5	6	7	8	9	10	11	12
Age (yrs)	4	3	3	8	6	7	1	1	5	2	4	6
Annual cost (R)	45	20	38	65	58	50	16	22	38	26	30	35

(a) Identify the independent variable and the dependent variable.

(b) Show the data graphically in a scatter plot. What relationship is observed?

(c) Calculate the correlation coefficient between the age of lathe machines and their annual maintenance costs. Comment on the strength of the association.

(d) Is the correlation statistically significant? Test at the 5% significance level. What conclusion can be drawn?

(e) Use the method of least squares to find the best fitting line between the age of lathe machines and their annual maintenance costs.

(f) Interpret the meaning of the regression coefficient (b_1) of the independent variable.

(g) What is the expected average maintenance cost of a lathe machine that is five years old?

12 X12.12 – employee performance

A call centre requires all new employees to undertake an aptitude test when hired. A year later, their job performance is evaluated. The call centre manager would like to know if aptitude test scores can be used to predict job performance. The aptitude scores (measured out of 10) and job performance scores (measured out of 100) of 12 randomly selected employees is recorded below.

Employee performance ratings												
Employee	1	2	3	4	5	6	7	8	9	10	11	12
Aptitude score	7	6	5	4	5	8	7	8	9	6	4	6
Performance rating	82	74	82	68	75	92	86	69	85	76	72	64

(a) Show the relationship between aptitude score (x) and performance rating (y) graphically. What relationship is observed?

(b) Measure the strength of the statistical relationship by calculating the correlation coefficient between the aptitude score and performance ratings of call centre employees.

(c) Test the sample correlation for statistical significance. Use $\alpha = 0.05$. Interpret the findings for the call centre manager.

(d) Calculate the simple linear regression equation between aptitude score and performance rating.

(e) Estimate the average performance rating score for call centre employees with an aptitude score of 8. How much confidence can the call centre manager have in this estimate? Comment using the findings of the hypothesis test in (c).

13 X12.13 – opinion polls

Opinion polls are often criticised for their lack of predictive validity (i.e. the ability to reliably estimate the actual election results). In a recent election in each of 11 regions, the *percentage of votes predicted* by opinion polls for the winning political party are recorded together with the *actual percentage of votes* received.

Region	1	2	3	4	5	6	7	8	9	10	11
Opinion poll (%)	42	34	59	41	53	40	65	48	59	38	62
Actual election (%)	51	31	56	49	68	35	54	52	54	43	60

(a) Determine the degree of association between the opinion poll results and the results of the actual election by calculating Pearson's correlation coefficient.

(b) Test the sample correlation for statistical significance at the 5% level. Comment on the findings in the context of this study.

(c) Set up a least squares regression equation to estimate actual election results based on opinion poll results.

(d) Calculate the coefficient of determination for this regression equation. Interpret its value.

(e) If an opinion poll showed 58% support for the winning party, what is the actual election result likely to be?

(f) If an opinion poll showed 82% support for the winning party, what is the actual election result likely to be? Is this a valid and reliable result? Comment.

Use Excel to generate the statistical results for questions 14 and 15.

14 X12.14 – capital investment

Companies regularly need to invest capital into their business operations to continue to grow and generate profits. A business analyst examined the relationship within companies between their *level of capital investment* (expressed as a percentage of turnover) and their *return on investment* (recorded in the financial period after the capital investment). A random sample of 45 companies were included in the study.

(a) Define the independent and dependent variables in this study. Explain.

(b) Use the **XY (Scatter)** option from the **Insert > Charts** tab to graphically display the relationship between capital investment and ROI.

(c) Use the **Regression** option in **Data Analysis** to derive the correlation coefficient and regression line between a company's level of capital investment and its return on investment.

(d) Identify the coefficient of determination and interpret its value.

(e) Test the regression equation for statistical significance. Use $\alpha = 0.05$. State the null and alternative hypotheses and the appropriate test statistic. Interpret the findings of the hypothesis test for the business analyst.

(f) Interpret the meaning of the regression coefficient (b_1) of the independent variable.

(g) Estimate the expected return on investment for a company that is planning a 55% level of capital investment.

Capital investment analysis					
Company	Capital investment	ROI	Company	Capital investment	ROI
1	62.3	5.1	24	64.2	6.8
2	45.8	1.8	25	59.3	5.0
3	70.3	3.7	26	52.3	8.2
4	43.2	3.3	27	76.7	8.2
5	33.7	4.4	28	44.6	5.8
6	55.1	4.8	29	49.0	5.1
7	28.6	3.3	30	49.1	7.7
8	63.6	4.5	31	23.3	0.2
9	63.0	5.6	32	62.9	3.9
10	48.2	9.5	33	52.1	1.0
11	73.2	3.7	34	46.5	3.1
12	43.4	8.7	35	67.3	7.4
13	42.1	2.1	36	37.6	5.3
14	55.7	3.8	37	41.6	3.0
15	32.8	1.1	38	47.1	2.3
16	66.2	8.8	39	21.1	3.6
17	64.4	8.0	40	61.9	5.3
18	53.1	2.4	41	51.2	6.2
19	79.5	5.2	42	38.6	6.3
20	50.2	4.6	43	58.8	2.8
21	52.0	4.4	44	29.5	1.5
22	53.2	6.7	45	32.8	5.8
23	31.7	1.9			

15 X12.15 – property valuations

A property analyst wished to examine the relationship between the town council's valuation of residential property in Bloemfontein and the market value (selling price) of the properties. A random sample of 40 recent property transactions was examined. All data values are expressed in R10 000s.

Property market analysis					
Property	Council valuations	Market values	Property	Council valuations	Market values
1	54	156	21	154	225
2	144	189	22	68	147
3	96	110	23	95	162
4	150	198	24	77	139
5	84	144	25	133	244
6	132	226	26	108	228
7	62	106	27	82	185
8	120	182	28	56	115
9	114	147	29	129	158
10	98	198	30	144	216
11	138	198	31	88	188
12	94	178	32	64	158
13	102	145	33	154	242
14	123	231	34	74	128
15	131	255	35	85	165
16	54	126	36	135	204
17	76	118	37	93	164
18	48	98	38	125	186
19	102	175	39	152	226
20	129	214	40	68	178

(a) Define the independent and dependent variables in this study. Explain.

(b) Use the **XY (Scatter)** option from the **Insert > Charts** tab to graphically display the relationship between council valuations and market values.

(c) Use the **Regression** option in **Data Analysis** to derive the correlation coefficient and regression line between council valuations and market values.

(d) Identify the coefficient of determination and interpret its value.

(e) Test the regression equation for statistical significance. Use $\alpha = 0.05$. State the null and alternative hypotheses and the appropriate test statistic. Interpret the findings of the hypothesis test for the business analyst.

(f) Interpret the meaning of the regression coefficient (b_1) of the independent variable.

(g) Estimate the average market value of properties in Bloemfontein that have a council valuation of R100 (in R10 000s).

CHAPTER
13

Multiple Regression

Outcomes

This chapter describes the modelling process of multiple linear regression where multiple independent variables are used to estimate a numeric response variable that represents a key performance measure in a management situation. Its purpose and some illustrative applications are initially outlined, followed by a description of the structure of a multiple linear regression model. The data requirement for a valid regression model is also identified.

The process of developing a useful and statistically validated multiple regression model is explained through a six-step methodology that covers scoping the management problem; performing pre-analysis data checks; the construction and testing of the model for statistical significance and validity; and the use of the validated model for estimation purposes. The emphasis of the chapter is on understanding the concepts of multiple regression and being able to interpret the findings correctly in a management context.

The chapter concludes with an explanation of how to include category independent variables as regressors into a regression model. The method of binary coded variables is introduced, illustrated and interpreted through two worked examples.

After studying this chapter, you should be able to:

- explain the difference between simple and multiple linear regression
- give practical examples from management of possible uses of multiple regression
- develop and interpreted a multiple regression model using the six step approach
- describe how to include categorical independent variables into a regression model
- describe two methods on variable selection.

13.1 Purpose and Applications

Multiple linear regression analysis is an extension of simple linear regression analysis. It assumes that *more than one* (or multiple) independent variable is related to the outcome of the dependent variable, y. Its aim is to identify the set of independent variables (x_1, x_2, x_3, ... x_p) that are significantly related to the dependent variable, y, that can then be used to predict values of the y-variable through a multiple linear regression equation.

Multiple linear regression analysis is arguably the most widely used statistical prediction modelling tool in practice. It is used in, inter alia, *econometrics* to build statistical models to estimate macroeconomic activity levels using various economic indicators as predictors; in *finance* to estimate risks and returns; and as a general *forecasting* tool in business (e.g. marketing to model consumer purchase behaviour; in human resource management to identify 'drivers' of employee productivity; and production management to identify factors responsible for machine downtime).

13.2 Structure of a Multiple Linear Regression Model

A **multiple linear regression equation** is an extension of a simple linear equation to include more independent variables, x_i, as shown mathematically as follows:

$$\hat{y} = b_0 + b_1 x_1 + b_2 x_2 + b_3 x_3 + \ldots\ldots + b_p x_p$$
13.1

Where: $\hat{y}$ = *the estimated y-value* computed from the regression equation

b_0, b_1, b_2, b_3, etc. are called the *regression coefficients*. They are *weights* that measure the relative importance (or strength of relationship) between each independent variable x_i, and the dependent variable, y.

In multiple linear regression analysis, both the *dependent variable*, y, and the set of *independent variables* (x_1, x_2, x_3, ... x_p) must be *numeric* in nature. Refer to section 13.5 to show how categorical independent variables are included into a regression model.

13.3 The Six-phase Regression Model-building Methodology

Model-building is a process that involves defining, building and testing the model. The following six phases can be used to structure this process.

Phase 1: Scope the management problem in statistical terms
- Identify and define the key dependent and independent variables.
- Source the relevant data.

Phase 2: Data preparation and pre-regression analysis data checks
- Consider the relevancy (appropriateness) and suitability (data format) of each variable
- Consider data enrichment to enhance the explanatory power of an x-variable
- Use the tools of descriptive statistics to profile the sample data
- Use scatter plots between y and each x to
  - examine the direction; nature (linear; non-linear); strength of the relationships
  - identify possible outliers

- Compute a correlation matrix to
    - measure the strength of association between y and each x variable
    - check for the presence of multi-collinearity between the x variables

Phase 3: Build the multiple regression model
- Use the method of Ordinary Least Squares to derive the regression coefficients
- Interpret the meaning of each regression coefficient, b_i.

Phase 4: Test the model for usefulness
- Identify and interpret the R^2 statistic (i.e. the overall percent of explained variation)
- Test the significance of the overall regression model (use aSER one-factor ANOVA test)
  $H_0: \beta_1 = \beta_2 = \beta_3 = \dots = \beta_p = 0$ versus H_1: At *least one* $\beta_i \neq 0$
- Test the significance of each x_i (use a one-sample t-test)
  $H_0: \beta_i = 0$ versus H_1: At least one $\beta_i \neq 0$
- Finalise the model by excluding statistically insignificant x-variables

Phase 5: Test the validity of the regression model (Is a linear fit the best fitting model?)
- Use residual analysis (i.e. plots of residual values against y-values)
Phase 6: Use the regression model to estimate/predict the dependent variable, y
- Compute an initial point estimate of the dependent variable, $\hat{y}$
- Construct confidence interval estimates for $\hat{y}$
- Present the findings in a non-technical management style report.

The modelling process is *iterative* and *repetitive*. At any stage of the modelling process, revisions to the model can be made, which will require revisiting earlier phases of the modelling process. In practice, modifications and enhancements to any regression model are continually made to improve the model's *overall usefulness* and increase its *predictive validity*.

13.4 The Modelling Process – Applying the Six-phase Approach

The six-phase model-building process will be illustrated using Example 13.1.
(See Excel file C13.1 – *security lock sales*.)

Example 13.1 Sure Safe Security Locks Sales Analysis Study

Safeguard Security manufactures and markets the Sure Safe security locks for external doors. The marketing manager would like to identify any significant factors that could influence the sales level of their brand of security locks. Sales and other marketing data is recorded for each of 26 stores selling the Sure Safe locks.

Table 13.1 shows the sample data set consisting of one numeric dependent (response) variable, *sales* (in units of 100); and four independent numeric predictor variables, *adspend* (in R1 000s), the number of regional *representatives*, the number of *competing brands* and a *crime index*.

Table 13.1 Dataset – Sure Safe security locks

Adspend	Reps	Brands	Crimedx	Sales
5.5	31	10	8	79.3
2.5	45	8	9	200.1
8.0	67	12	9	163.2
3.0	42	7	16	200.1
3.0	38	8	15	146.0
2.9	71	12	17	177.7
8.0	30	12	8	30.9
9.0	48	5	10	291.9
4.0	42	8	4	160.0
6.5	63	5	16	339.4
5.5	60	8	7	159.6
5.0	44	12	12	86.3
6.0	50	6	6	237.5
5.0	39	10	4	107.2
3.5	55	10	4	155.0
8.0	52	6	7	291.4
6.0	40	8	6	100.2
4.0	50	11	8	135.8
7.5	60	9	13	223.3
7.0	59	9	11	195.0
6.7	58	7	5	72.4
6.1	46	10	10	47.7
3.6	43	9	8	104.7
4.2	26	8	3	93.5
4.5	75	8	19	259.0
5.6	68	4	9	331.2

Management Question

Which of the above factors, if any, can be used to estimate the level of sales of Sure Safe security locks?

Solution

Phase 1: Identify and define the variables of the regression model – scope the problem
This initial step identifies the dependent variable (y), and a set of potential influencing factors (x's). A process of brainstorming with relevant stakeholders involved in the management question can lead to the identification of the *most relevant* variables to use. Data availability on these identified variables must also be considered.

Phase 2: Data preparation – use exploratory data analysis
The data on all the variables should be reviewed to examine its suitability for regression analysis. The following two checks should be conducted:

- **Scatter plots:** Prepare *scatter plots* between y and each x_i variable. Use the scatter plot to (i) check the degree of *linearity* between y and each x and, if necessary, transform either x or y to achieve a better linear fit (e.g. logs, square roots); (ii) check the *direction* of the relationship (positive or negative); (iii) check the *strength* of the relationship (weak, moderate, strong); and (iv) identify any possible outliers (influential or non-influential).

- **Correlations:** Compute the correlation between each pair of x variables to identify if the problem of *multicollinearity* exists. Multicollinearity is present when independent variables are highly correlated with each other. When this happens, they overlap in their explained variation of y, resulting in a regression model that is unreliable in its estimation.

  As a rule of thumb, if pairwise correlations between the x's are less than 0.4, multi-collinearity does not adversely affect the regression model's predictive validity.

Phase 3: Build the multiple regression model

To build a (sample) multiple linear regression model, find the *estimated regression coefficients* b_0, b_1, b_2, b_3 etc. of the linear equation as shown in Formula 13.1. As with simple linear regression, the method of ordinary least squares (OLS), which minimises the sum of squared errors, is used to find the b_i coefficients for each independent x-variable (see section 12.2 for a review of the OLS method). The formulae to calculate the b_i coefficients are complicated and are never computed manually. The derived equation of b_i coefficients represents the 'best-fit' linear relationship between all the x's and y.

A sample-derived regression equation is not a guarantee that the overall model is useful to estimate y. Also, not all the independent variables may be related to the y-variable. Therefore before the sample regression equation can be used for estimation purposes, it must be tested for statistical significance. This is the purpose of *Step 4*.

Phase 4: Test the regression model for statistical signficance (usefulness)

The most important measure of the model's overall statistical significance (or usefulness) is its R^2 statistic – the *coefficient of determination* (see section 12.4). This is only a sample-derived descriptive measure and must, therefore, be tested for statistical significance in the population.

Two sets of *hypotheses tests* are conducted on the regression model: (i) a hypothesis test to determine the *overall significance* of the model and (ii) a set of hypotheses tests to determine the significance of each *individual* x-variable. The final 'working' model will *exclude* the *insignificant* x-variables.

Phase 5: Test the validity of the model

A valid regression model assumes a *linear* relationship between y and each of the x-variables. This *assumption* is examined through *residual analysis*. Residual analysis examines the pattern of residuals (e_i) between the observed y-values and their model-predicted (estimated) y-values ($e_i = y - \hat{y}$).

The residual pattern should possess the following characteristics for the assumption of linearity-of-fit to be satisfied: (i) the mean of the residuals must be zero, (ii) the variance of the residuals must be a constant across all y_i, (iii) the residuals must be normally distributed for each y_i, and (iv) the residuals must be independent of each other. These assumptions are examined graphically by the inspection of graphs known as *residual plots*.

Phase 6: Use the derived regression model for estimation/prediction purposes

Once the multiple regression model has largely *satisfied* the above criteria of statistical *significance* (Phase 4) and *validity* (Phase 5), the model can then be *used* to estimate *y*-values. A *confidence interval* approach is used.

Interpretation of Phases 1 to 6 for security lock sales

Refer to the scatter plots and correlations in Figure 13.1 and Table 13.2 respectively, and the multiple regression analysis output in Table 13.3 using Excel's **Data Analysis** module **Regression**.

Phase 1: Scoping the problem

The variables of this study and the relevant data is described and defined in Example 13.1.

Phase 2: Exploratory data analysis

By an inspection of each scatter plot, *adspend* shows a weak relationship with *sales*; *brands* shows a relatively strong inverse relationship with *sales*; *reps* shows a moderate to strong positive relationship with *sales*; and the *crime index* shows a moderate to weak relationship with *sales*.

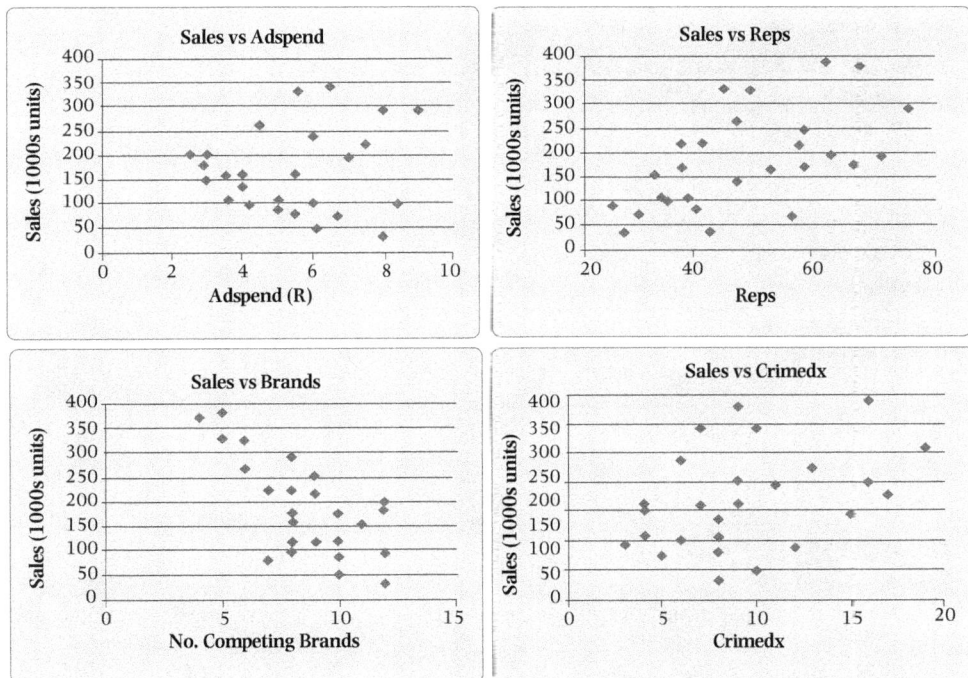

Figure 13.1 Scatter plots: *Sales* (*y*) versus x_1 (*adspend*), x_2 (*reps*), x_3 (*brands*), x_4 (*crimedx*)

By an inspection of the simple (linear) correlations between each pair of variables (*x*'s and *y*), it can be seen that:

- the **dependent variable**, *y* (*sales*) is strongly and inversely associated with the variable *brands* ($r = -0.70$); moderately associated with *reps* ($r = 0.59$) and weakly associated with both *adspend* ($r = 0.17$) and *crimedx* ($r = 0.39$). High correlations are desirable, as they show strong relationships between *y* and the *x*-variables.

- the *independent variables* are largely uncorrelated with each other, except for *reps* and *crimedx* which shows a moderate association ($r = 0.46$). Moderate *multicollinearity* is therefore present in the model, but is not a serious problem in this example.

Table 13.2 Correlations between each pair of variables (n = 26)

	Adspend	Reps	Brands	Crimedx	Sales
Adspend	1				
Reps	0.13773	1			
Brands	−0.15805	−0.14746	1		
Crimedx	−0.12866	0.45651	−0.00155	1	
Sales	0.17361	0.59146	−0.69659	0.38727	1

These pre-analysis checks provide both insight into the nature (direction and strength) of the likely relationships between y and the x's and can also be used to highlight further data preparation (outlier treatment and possible data transformations) to ensure that the most useful and valid regression model is produced.

Table 13.3 Regression summary for dependent variable – sales

Summary output	
Regression statistics	
Multiple R	0.874
R square	0.763
Adjusted R square	0.718
Standard error	45.332
Observations	26

ANOVA	df	SS	MS	F-stat	p-value
Regression	4	139 121.7	34 780.4	16.925	0.00000243
Residual (Error)	21	43 155.0	2 055.000457		
Total	25	182 276.7			

Regression	Coefficients	Std error	t-stat	p-value	Lower 95%	Upper 95%
Intercept	190.45	61.018	3.121	0.0052	63.56	317.35
Adspend (x_1)	2.18	5.161	0.422	0.6771	−8.55	12.91
Reps (x_2)	2.61	0.816	3.200	0.0043	0.91	4.31
Brands (x_3)	−23.75	4.089	−5.809	0.0000	−32.26	−15.25
Crimedx (x_4)	4.12	2.380	1.731	0.0982	−0.83	9.07

Phase 3: Fit (derive) the Multiple Linear Regression Model

From Table 13.3 the sample multiple linear regression model to estimate lock sales (y) is defined by the *regression coefficients* of the independent variables, *adspend* (x_1), *reps* (x_2), *brands* (x_3) and *crimedx* (x_4). It is as follows:

$$\hat{y} = 190.45 + 2.18x_1 + 2.61x_2 - 23.75x_3 + 4.12x_4$$

Interpretation of the Regression Coefficients

A regression coefficient, b_i, is interpreted as a *marginal rate of change in y for a unit change in the associated x-variable*. For example, consider $b_1 = 2.18$, which is the coefficient of x_1 (*adspend*). This means that sales (y) can be expected to increase by 2.18 units, on average, for every additional unit increase (i.e. for each additional R1 000) allocated to *adspend* (x_1), holding all other variables constant – and vice versa. Similarly, for x_3 (*brands*, $b_3 = -23.75$), assuming all other x-variables are held constant, then *sales* can be expected to decrease by 23.75 units, on average, for every additional competing brand (x_3) that enters the market place – and vice versa. Similar interpretations apply to the coefficients of *reps* ($b_2 = 2.61$) and *crimedx* ($b_4 = 4.12$).

Phase 4: Testing the usefulness/significance of the regression equation

The *overall strength* and *significance* of the regression model is assessed initially by an inspection and interpretation of the R^2 statistic, and then, more rigorously, by a hypothesis test to test R^2 for statistical significance – as described in Chapter 12.5.

1   **R^2 – the coefficient of determination ($0 \leq R^2 \leq 1$) or ($0\% \leq R^2 \leq 100\%$)**

R^2 is *the percentage of total variation in the y that can be collectively explained by all the independent variables (x_i's) in the model*. In this example, $R^2 = 0.763$ (76.3%) (see Table 13.2). This means that 76.3% of the variation in *sales* can be explained by the four regressors (*adspend, reps, brands* and *crimedx*).

R^2 can be computed from the *sum of squares* terms in the ANOVA table. Since SS(Regression) is the *amount of variation* in y that can be explained due to the *regression effect* (i.e. the influence of the x-variables), and SS(Total) is the total amount of variation that can be *explained* in y, then:

$$R^2 = \frac{SS(Regression)}{SS(Total)} \qquad \text{13.2}$$

In the example, $R^2 = \frac{139\,121.7}{182\,276.7} = 0.7632$

The **standard error** = 45.332 is inversely related to R^2. Standard error is a measure of the average deviation of the y-values about the regression equation and is derived from the SS(Error) term in the **ANOVA** table of Table 13.3. The smaller the standard error, the better the fit of the model and the higher the R^2 value; and vice versa.

From the ANOVA table, the standard error is calculated as follows:

Standard error (SE) = $\sqrt{MSError} = \sqrt{2\,055} = 45.33$.

$$S_e = \sqrt{\frac{\Sigma(y_i - \hat{y}_i)^2}{n - p - 1}} \qquad \text{13.3}$$

Where: y_i = each observed data value of y

$\hat{y}_i$ = estimated y value from regression equation

n = sample size

p = number of independant variables (x_i's)

This inverse relationship is shown by the sum of squares formula of SS(Total) = SS(Regression) + SS(Error). If SS(Regression) increases, SS(Error) must decrease (and vice versa) since SS(Total) is a constant value for a given set of y data in a regression model.

R^2 is only a *descriptive statistical measure* derived from sample data. It must be tested for statistical significance in the population to determine whether its value is due purely to chance or whether there is a genuine structural relationship between y and *at least one* of the independent x-variables. This is the purpose of the following hypothesis tests.

2   **Hypotheses tests on the regression model**

(a) **Test the overall regression model for statistical significance (i.e. test that $R^2 \neq 0$)**

The *F-test statistic* that is derived from the ANOVA table (in Table 13.3) is used to test the overall significance of the regression model.

To test R^2 for statistical significance (i.e. that $R^2 \neq 0$ and that its value is not due to chance) is equivalent to testing whether *at least one population* regression coefficient (β_i) is not zero. If all the regression coefficients (β_1, β_2, β_3, ... β_p) are zero, it implies that none of the x-variables are significantly related to the dependent variable, y.

Step 1: Define the null and alternative hypotheses

H_0: $\beta_1 = \beta_2 = \beta_3 = \beta_4 = 0$ All the x's are insignificant.

H_1: At least one $\beta_i \neq 0$ *At least one x_i regressor is significant.*

This is always a *one-sided, upper tailed test* using the **F-distribution**.

Step 2: Determine the region of acceptance of H_0. Use $\alpha = 0.05$.

$F\text{-crit} = F(\alpha, df_1 = p, df_2 = n-p-1) = F(0.05, 4, 21) = 2.84$ (Table 4(a), Appendix 1)

Where: $df_1 = df$(numerator) = p (the number of independent variables) (= 4)

$df_2 = df$(denominator) = $(n-p-1)$ (=26−4−1 = 21), where $n = 26$.

In Excel, use **F.INV.RT(0.05,4,21)** to find the *F-crit* (upper) limit.

Decision rule: Do not reject H_0 if *F-stat* $\leq$ *F-crit* (= 2.84); else reject H_0 in favour of H_1.

Step 3: Compute the sample test statistic (*F-stat*)

From the ANOVA table in Table 13.3, the following test statistics are derived:

$F\text{-stat} = 16.925$ and p-value = 0.00000243

In this one-factor ANOVA test, *F-stat* is always computed from the *ratio* of the **explained** variation (due to regression) to the **unexplained** variation (due to other factors and/or chance).

$$F\text{-stat} = \frac{\text{Variation explained by regression}}{\text{Unexplained variation}} = \frac{\text{MS Regression}}{\text{MS Error}} \qquad \textbf{13.4}$$

In the example, $F\text{-stat} = \frac{34\,780.4}{2\,055} = 16.925$

Step 4: Compare *F-stat* to the region of acceptance of H$_0$

Since *F-stat* (= 16.925) > *F-crit* (=2.84), *F-stat* lies in the *rejection region* of H$_0$.
Alternatively, the *p*-value (=0.00000243) < α (0.05).

Step 5: Draw the statistical and management conclusions

There is overwhelmingly strong statistical evidence to reject H$_0$ in favour of H$_1$. This means that there is *at least one* regressor that is significantly related to *y*. Thus the derived regression model is statistically significant – and so therefore is the R^2 measure.

Having concluded that there is value in the overall regression model by virtue of *at least one* regressor (x_i) being statistically significant, the model must now be tested further to identify which independent variables are statistically significant and which are not.

(b) Test the significance of individual regressors

The significance of each regressor is examined separately by a one-sample *t-test* hypothesis test. This is a *two-tailed* test.

Step 1: Define the null and alternative hypotheses

$\quad\quad$ H$_0$: $\beta_i = 0$ $\quad$ The ith regressor is insignificant
$\quad\quad$ H$_1$: $\beta_i \neq 0$ $\quad$ The ith regressor is significant.

Step 2: Determine the region of acceptance of H$_0$

The acceptance region of H$_0$ is defined by *t-crit* = $\pm$ t ($\frac{\alpha}{2}$, $df = n - p - 1$).
For $\alpha = 0.05$, $n = 26$ and $p = 4$; *t-crit* = $t(0.025, 21) = \pm 2.08$ $\quad\quad$ (Table 2, Appendix 1)
In Excel, use **T.INV.2T(0.05,21)**.

Steps 3, 4 and 5 Sample test statistics (*t-stat*) and *p*-values obtained from Table 13.3.

The following statistical conclusions are drawn.

For *adspend*: $\quad$ t-stat = 0.422 lies *inside* the region of acceptance of H$_0$
$\quad\quad\quad\quad\quad\quad$ Also, its *p*-value = 0.6771 > 0.05 $\quad\quad\quad$ Hence, do not reject H$_0$.

For *reps*: $\quad\quad$ t-stat = 3.200 lies *outside* the region of acceptance of H$_0$
$\quad\quad\quad\quad\quad\quad$ Also, its *p*-value = 0.0043 < 0.05 $\quad\quad\quad$ Hence, reject H$_0$.

For *brands*: $\quad$ t-stat = -5.809 lies *outside* the region of acceptance of H$_0$
$\quad\quad\quad\quad\quad\quad$ Also, its *p*-value = 0.00003912 < 0.05 $\quad$ Hence, reject H$_0$.

For *crimedx*: $\quad$ t-stat = 1.731 lies *inside* the region of acceptance of H$_0$
$\quad\quad\quad\quad\quad\quad$ Also, its *p*-value = 0.0982 > 0.05 $\quad\quad\quad$ Hence, do not reject H$_0$.

Note: For each independent variable x_i, its *t-stat* value is derived from:

$$t\text{-}stat = \frac{(b_i - \beta_i)}{s_{b_i}}$$

$\quad\quad\quad\quad\quad\quad\quad\quad\quad\quad\quad\quad\quad\quad\quad\quad\quad\quad\quad\quad\quad\quad\quad$ **13.5**

Where: $\quad$ s_{b_i} = standard error of the regression coefficient, b_i

Its formula is not provided, but its value is always given in the regression output.

To calculate the p-value for each regressor (x_i) use **T.DIST.2T**(t-stat, $df = 21$).

A **confidence interval** approach can also be used to test the *significance of individual regressors*. For each x_i, a confidence interval can be constructed to estimate its true population regression coefficient, β_i using the following formula:

$$b_i - (t\text{-}crit) \times std\,error\,(b_i) \leq \beta_i \leq b_i + (t\text{-}crit) \times std\,error\,(b_i) \qquad 13.6$$

Where: $t\text{-}crit = t(\frac{\alpha}{2}, df = (n - p - 1))$. It is the same t-crit value as used in the hypothesis test for β_i.

To illustrate for *adspend*:
using $b_1 = 2.18$, $std\,error(b_1) = 5.161$ and $t\text{-}crit = t(\frac{\alpha}{2} = 0.025, df = 21) = \pm 2.08$, then the 95% confidence interval estimate for β_1 is $2.18 \pm 2.08(5.161)$ resulting in a lower 95% confidence limit of -8.55 and an upper 95% confidence limit of 12.91, so $(-8.55 \leq \beta_i \leq 12.91)$.

The following decision rule is then applied:
- If the confidence interval *includes zero*, then do not reject H_0.
- If the confidence interval does *not include zero*, then reject H_0 in favour of H_1.

If zero falls within the confidence limits, it implies that H_0: $\beta_i = 0$ is probably true. The corresponding independent variable, x_i, is therefore statistically insignificant as a predictor of y.

For the above example (refer to Table 13.3):
- zero falls within the 95% confidence limits of β_i for *adspend* $(-8.55 < \beta_1 < 12.91)$ and *crimedx* $(-0.83 < \beta_4 < 9.07)$, therefore do not reject H_0 in both cases.
- zero does not fall within the 95% confidence limits of β_i for *reps* $(0.91 < \beta_2 < 4.31)$ and *brands* $(-32.26 < \beta_3 < -15.25)$, therefore reject H_0 in favour of H_1 in both cases.

Overall Management Conclusion

It can be stated with 95% confidence, that the statistically significant regressors are *brands* and *reps*. *Adspend* and *crimedx* are not statistically significant and can be removed from the regression model. Thus only *brands* and *reps* could be used to provide reliable estimates of *sales* of Sure Lock products.

Phase 5: Check the regression assumptions – residual analysis
The *validity* of a multiple linear regression model is based on the following assumptions:
- the residuals (error term defined by $(y - \hat{y})$) must be *normally distributed*
- the *mean* of the residuals is *zero*
- the *variance* of the residuals is constant across all values of y (homoscedasticity)
- the residuals are *independent* across all values of y.

These assumptions can be examined by inspecting the pattern of residuals of the linear regression model as shown in a *scatter plot of residuals* (on the y-axis) against the actual *values of y* (on the x-axis). Figure 13.2 shows such a residual plot.

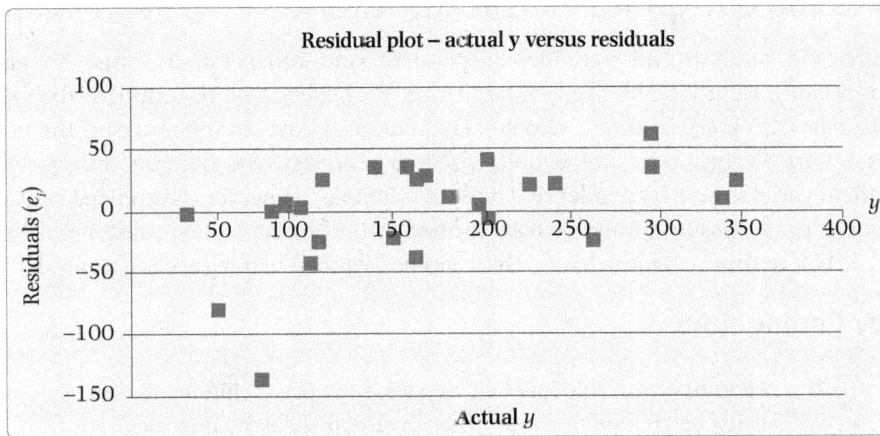

Figure 13.2 Sure Safe locks – residual plot of actual versus residuals

For all four assumptions to be satisfied, the residuals should be *concentrated* around the horizontal line at zero on the *y*-axis and then fan out evenly on either side of the zero line. Apart from an outlier (residual = −138), the model appears to satisfy all the regresssion assumptions.

Phase 6: Use the regression model to estimate *y*-values

Initially, a *point estimate* of the dependent variable, *y*, can be found by substituting *x*-values into the regression model

For example, what is the expected (mean) level of security lock sales ($\hat{y}$) when *adspend* is budgeted at 8% ($x_1 = 8$); the number of *representatives* is expected to be 60 ($x_2 = 60$); the number of competing *brands* is expected to be 10 ($x_3 = 10$); and the *crime index* is expected to be 7 ($x_4 = 7$)?

$$\hat{y} = 190.45 + 2.18(8) + 2.61(60) - 23.75(10) + 4.12(7) = \mathbf{155.8}$$

To provide a more useful estimate, a 95% confidence interval estimate of the mean of *y* can be computed using the following formula:

$$\hat{y} \pm t\left(\tfrac{\alpha}{2}, n-p-1\right)\left(\frac{\text{standard error}}{\sqrt{n}}\right) \qquad \textbf{13.7}$$

For the example: $155.8 \pm 2.08 \dfrac{(45.33)}{\sqrt{26}} = 155.8 \pm 18.49$

giving   [lower limit = 137.3; upper limit = 174.29]

Thus there is a 95% chance that the average sales volume per outlet for Sure Safe locks is expected to lie between 137.3 units and 174.29 units (in 1 000s of units).

13.5 Using Categorical Independent Variables in Regression

In regression analysis, all variables (dependent and independent) must be *numeric*. However, categorical variables (e.g. *region* (A, B, C), *qualification* (BCom, BA, BSc, BProc), *machine type* (X, Y), *gender* (male, female), etc.) can also have an influence on the numeric response variable, y. Codes are usually used to represent the different categories of a categorical variable (e.g. for gender, 1 = male, 2 = female). However these coded values have no *numeric* properties and must be transformed into numeric values using binary coding (0 and 1) before these categorical variables can be included in a regression analysis.

Binary Coding Rule

If a categorical variable has k categories, then $(k - 1)$ binary variables must be created to *numerically* represent these k categories.

For example, for *gender* (1 = male; 2 = female)) with $k = 2$ categories, one binary variable must be created to represent this categorical variable numerically (see Table 13.4).

Table 13.4 Binary coding for a two-category categorical variable

Categorical variable		Binary variable
Gender	Codes	Gen1
Male	1	1
Female	2	0

Similarly, for *qualification* (1 = BA, 2 = BSc, 3 = BCom) with $k = 3$ categories, two binary variables must be created to represent this categorical variable as shown in Table 13.5.

Table 13.5 Binary coding for a three-category categorical variable

Categorical variable		Binary variables	
Qualification	Code	Qual1	Qual2
BA	1	1	0
BSc	2	0	1
BCom	3	0	0

The category with *all zeros* for the binary variables is called the *base category*. In Table 13.4, it is the *female* category of *gender*; in Table 13.5, it is the *BCom qualification*. The base category is arbitrarily chosen by the analyst. The binary-coded variables must now replace the categorical variables (with their original codes) in the dataset for regression analysis.

Note: It may seem intuitive to use as many binary-coded dummy variables are there are categories of the independent variable (e.g. for three categories, Dummy1 = 1 0 0, Dummy2 = 0 1 0 and Dummy3 = 0 0 1). This coding system brings redundant information into the regression model and results in the undesirable effect of perfect multicollinearity.

The following example illustrates regression analysis with a single categorical independent variable with two categories.

Example 13.2 Financial Planning Consultant Performance Study (Case 1)

Management Question

Are *performance scores* of financial planning consultants related to their *training* exposure and years of relevant work *experience?* The *training* variable is *categorical* as it is defined as 'Has a consultant attended a training programme within the past two years?' (1 = No, 2 = Yes).

Table 13.6(a) shows the source data with the *training* variable represented by its original arbitrary codes of 1 = No and 2 = Yes. These codes are replaced with binary values 0 = No and 1 = Yes as shown in Table 13.6(b). Note that the binary *base category* represents 'no training'.

(See Excel file C13.2 – *consultant performance* (case 1).)

Table 13.6(a)

Training	Exper	Perf
2	5	50
1	4	36
2	5	25
2	8	58
1	8	38
2	7	58
2	1	30
1	1	26
1	7	32
2	2	38
2	4	46
1	3	30
2	5	35
2	3	40
2	7	48
2	2	39
1	3	44
2	6	50
1	2	25
2	6	36

Table 13.6(b)

Trainx	Exper	Perf
1	5	50
0	4	36
1	5	25
1	8	58
0	8	38
1	7	58
1	1	30
0	1	26
0	7	32
1	2	38
1	4	46
0	3	30
1	5	35
1	3	40
1	7	48
1	2	39
0	3	44
1	6	50
0	2	25
1	6	36

Table 13.7 shows the partial output of a regression analysis based on the data of Table 13.6(b).

Table 13.7 Regression analysis with a two-level categorical variable (Training)

Descriptive statistics	
R square	0.454
Observations	20

Regression						
	Coefficients	Std Error	t-stat	p-value	Lower 95%	Upper 95%
Intercept	24.272	4.37	5.56	0.0000	15.06	33.49
Training	8.028	3.73	2.15	0.0460	0.16	15.90
Experience	2.182	0.80	2.73	0.0143	0.49	3.87

Interpretation of the regression coefficient for the categorical variable

The *regression coefficient* of a non-base category must always be *interpreted in relation to the base category*. The non-base category's regression coefficient reflects the change in the y-variable as a result of belonging to this non-base category instead of the base category, holding all other variables constant.

The *regression coefficient* of the categorical *training* variable ($b_1 = 8.028$) is interpreted as follows: A financial planning consultant who has received training within the past two years (i.e. 1 = Yes) is likely to have a performance score that is 8.028 points higher, on average, than a consultant who has not received training within the past two years (i.e. 0 = No), holding *experience* constant. It therefore represents the change from the base category (0 = No) as a result of having received training (i.e. 1 = Yes).

Hypothesis test of the statistical significance of the categorical variable

The same hypothesis *t-test* approach is applied to the categorical variable as for the numerical independent variables (i.e. $H_0: \beta_1 = 0$ versus $H_1: \beta_1 \neq 0$).

For the *training* variable:

If $H_0: \beta_1 = 0$ is not rejected, this means that consultants who had received training (1 = Yes) have a mean performance score that is no *different* from the mean performance score of consultants who have not had training in the past two years. This would mean that the training variable does not significantly influence performance scores and can be removed from the regression model.

On the other hand, if $H_0: \beta_1 = 0$ is rejected in favour of $H_1: \beta_1 \neq 0$, then this means that having received training (1 = Yes) does significantly influence performance scores of consultants.

In Example 13.2, (as seen from Table 13.7), for the *training* variable, its p-value = 0.046 < α = 0.05, resulting in a rejection of H_0 in favour of H_1 at the 5% level of significance. The management conclusion is, therefore, that 'training attendance *does significantly influence* performance scores of financial planning consultants'.

This management conclusion is also supported by the statistical evidence that shows
- *t-stat* (= 2.15) lies outside the limits of ± 2.11 ($t(\frac{\alpha}{2} = 0.025, df = 20–2–1)$).
- the confidence interval for β_1 ($0.16 \leq \beta_1 \leq 15.9$) does not include zero.

The following example illustrates regression analysis with a single categorical independent variable with three categories.

Example 13.3 Financial Planning Consultant Performance Study (Case 2)

Management Question

Are *performance scores* of financial planning consultants related to their undergraduate *qualification* (1 = BA, 2 = BSc, 3 = BCom) and years of relevant work *experience*?

Solution

Using the binary coding scheme as shown in Table 13.5, the three categories of arbitrary codes (1, 2, 3) of the *qualifications* variable (as seen in Table 13.8(a)) are transformed into two binary variables (*Qual1* and *Qual2*) as shown in the database of Table 13.8(b).
(See Excel file C13.3 – *consultant performance (case 2)*.

Table 13.8(a)

Qual	Exper	Perf
3	5	50
3	4	36
1	5	25
2	8	58
1	8	38
2	7	58
1	1	30
2	1	26
1	7	32
3	2	38
2	4	46
2	3	30
3	5	35
3	3	40
2	7	48
3	2	39
2	3	44
2	6	50
1	2	25
3	6	36

Table 13.8(b)

Qual1	Qual2	Exper	Perf
0	0	5	50
0	0	4	36
1	0	5	25
0	1	8	58
1	0	8	38
0	1	7	58
1	0	1	30
0	1	1	26
1	0	7	32
0	0	2	38
0	1	4	46
0	1	3	30
0	0	5	35
0	0	3	40
0	1	7	48
0	0	2	39
0	1	3	44
0	1	6	50
1	0	2	25
0	0	6	36

Qual1 = 1 identifies a consultant with a BA degree while *Qual2* = 1 identifies a consultant with a BSc degree. The base category is a consultant with a BCom degree. The partial regression results are shown in Table 13.9.

Table 13.9 Regression analysis with a three-level categorical variable (Qualifications)

Descriptive statistics	
R square	0.6437
Observations	20

Regression						
	Coefficients	Std Error	t-stat	p-value	Lower 95%	Upper 95%
Intercept	29.873	3.585	8.332	0.0000	22.273	37.474
Qual1	−10.928	3.868	−2.825	0.0122	−19.128	−2.728
Qual2	3.411	3.459	0.986	0.3387	−3.921	10.743
Experience	2.403	0.672	3.574	0.0025	0.978	3.828

The *regression equation* to estimate consultant *performance scores* is as follows:

$$\hat{y} = 29.873 - 10.928 Qual1 + 3.411 Qual2 + 2.403 Experience$$

For each coefficient's significance test, we use: $H_0: \beta_i = 0$ versus $H_1: \beta_i \neq 0$.

Experience (numeric) $b_3 = 2.403$

For every one additional year of relevant work *experience*, the *performance* score of financial planning consultants is likely to rise by 2.403 points, on average, holding all other variables constant.

Since its *p*-value = 0.0025 < α = 0.05, we reject H_0 in favour of H_1 and conclude that *experience* (x_3) is a statistically *significant estimator* of *performance* scores (*y*) of financial planning consultants.

Qualification (categorical)

For binary coded categorical variables, their regression coefficients always measure a change in the *y*-variable from the *base category* of the variable. In this example, the base category is a BCom qualification.

(a) **Qual1** $b_1 = -10.928$ (*Qual1* = 1 identifies a consultant with a BA degree)
Thus $b_1 = -10.928$ means that consultants with a BA degree, as opposed to a B Com degree (the base category), are likely to have performance scores that are 10.928 points *lower*, on average, than consultants with a BCom degree, holding all other variables constant.

Since its *p*-value = 0.0122 < α = 0.05, we reject $H_0: \beta_1 = 0$ in favour of $H_1: \beta_1 \neq 0$ and conclude that *qual1* is a *statistically significant* independent variable. This means that consultants with a BA degree have *significantly lower* performance scores than consultants with a BCom degree, on average.

(b) *Qual2* $b_2 = 3.411$ (*Qual2* = 1 identifies a consultant with a BSc degree)
Thus $b_2 = 3.411$ means that consultants with a BSc degree, as opposed to a BCom degree (the base category), are likely to have performance scores that are 3.411 points *higher*, on average, than consultants with a B Com degree, holding all other variables constant.

Since its *p*-value = 0.3387 > α = 0.05, we do not reject H$_0$: β_1 = 0. It can be concluded that *qual2* is a statistically *insignificant* independent variable.

This means that the average performance scores of consultants with a BSc degree are *no different* to consultants with a BCom degree.

The implication of this finding is that the categorical variable, *qualification*, is statistically significant as an estimator of *y*. However, the variable need only be represented by two significant categories, i.e. BA (category 1) and BSc/BCom (category 2). The BSc and BCom can be merged into a single category, as there is no statistically significant difference between them

13.6 Variable Selection Approaches

When a large number of independent variables are being considered for inclusion in the final regression model (e.g. 15 variables), there is likely to be high intercorrelations between some of these variables. To find the model that 'best' explains the dependent variable, without the confounding effect of interconnected independent variables (i.e. *multicollinearity*), a variable selection approach should be used. Two common variable selection approaches are *stepwise regression* and *best subsets regression*. Both aim to find a parsimonious model (i.e. a model that can explain the most amount of variation in the dependent variable with the least number of predictor variables).

Stepwise Regression

Stepwise regression is a step-by-step model-building approach. It begins at step 0 with no independent variables in the model. At step 1, the independent variable with the highest significant R^2 is entered into the model. At each subsequent step, the independent variable that significantly increases R^2 the most is added to the model (i.e. the *incremental increase* in R^2 by including this variable is statistically significant – it *p*-value is the smallest and below the level of significance). The process stops when no independent variable outside the model can make a statistically significant incremental increase in R^2. At each step, stepwise regression also considers removing independent variables from the model if they become statistically insignificant when a new variable is added to the model (i.e. the variable's *p*-value is greater than the level of significant). The independent variable with the largest *p*-value greater than the level of significance is removed. In this way, this step-by-step process ensures that the subset of independent variables in the final model are all statistically significant (i.e. their *p*-values < α) and largely uncorrelated with each other.

All Subsets Regression (also known as All Possible Regressions)

This approach of variable selection builds every possible model from the set of independent variables. For each model, it also shows its adjusted R^2 value. The total number of models built is always $(2^p - 1)$ where p = number of independent variables. For example, if there are 4 independent variables, it builds $15 (= 2^4 - 1)$ separate linear regression models each with its adjusted R^2 value. They are:

One-variable category:

$$\hat{y} = x_1 \quad \hat{y} = x_2 \quad \hat{y} = x_3 \quad \hat{y} = x_4$$

Two-variable category:

$$\hat{y} = x_1 + x_2 \quad \hat{y} = x_1 + x_3 \quad \hat{y} = x_1 + x_4 \quad \hat{y} = x_2 + x_3 \quad \hat{y} = x_2 + x_4 \quad \hat{y} = x_3 + x_4$$

Three-variable category:

$$\hat{y} = x_1 + x_2 + x_3 \quad \hat{y} = x_1 + x_2 + x_4 \quad \hat{y} = x_1 + x_3 + x_4 \quad \hat{y} = x_2 + x_3 + x_4$$

Four-variable category:

$$\hat{y} = x_1 + x_2 + x_3 + x_4$$

To identify the overall 'best-fitting' regression model, only the 'best' model (based on the highest adjusted R^2 value) from each variable category is considered. The choice of the final model is based on judgement where one is looking for the model with the fewest number of independent variables, but with the highest adjusted R^2 value.

13.7 Summary

Multiple linear regression is an extension of simple linear regression with multiple independent variables potentially influencing the outcome of a single numeric dependent variable.

This chapter introduced a six-step approach to build and evaluate the usefulness of a sample-derived multiple regression model. These steps provide a framework to ensure that the design and assessment of the modelling process is methodical and rigorous. These steps include (i) scoping the regression problem, (ii) pre-analysis data preparation, (iii) construction of the model, (iv) evaluating the model's usefulness using various hypotheses tests (one-factor ANOVA and single sample t-tests), (v) testing assumptions that impact on the model's validity, and finally (vi) using the tested and evaluated model for estimation and prediction purposes using a confidence interval estimation approach.

This chapter also discussed and illustrated the manner in which regression analysis can include categorical independent variables in the regression model through binary coded variables. Each binary variable's regression coefficient is a measure of its 'distance' from its base category. If the 'distance' is not statistically significant, the binary variable is merged with its base category as it is seen as being no different to the base category in terms of its relationship to the dependent variable.

Finally, multiple linear regression analysis is always performed using statistical software. Both Excel's **Data Analysis** add-in module **Regression** and the **X-Static** moduler **Multiple Regression** can be used to generate multiple regression models. Neither offer the stepwise regression option but both can be used to generate the various models for the **All Subsets Regression** approach to *variable selection*.

Exercises

This symbol denotes data available online.

1   What is the key difference between simple linear regression and multiple linear regression analysis?

2   A multiple regression model with five numeric independent variables with $n = 46$ records has the following results: SS(Regression) = 84 and SS(Total) = 232.

   (a)   Find the R^2 of this model and interpret its meaning.

   (b)   Formulate the null and alternative hypothesis to test the overall model for statistical significance (i.e. test the statistical significance of R^2).

   (c)   Find F-stat and F-crit to conduct the hypothesis test in (b). Use $\alpha = 0.05$.

   (d)   Draw the statistical conclusion about the significance of the overall model.

3   Use the following table of four numeric independent variables in a regression model based on a sample of 24 data records to identify which of the independent variables are statistically significant at the 5% level of significance.

   (a)   For each variable, formulate the null and alternative hypothesis.

   (b)   Conduct each variable's hypothesis test by comparing t-stat and t-crit.

   (c)   Repeat each variable's hypothesis test based on the p-value of the test.

   (d)   Repeat each variable's hypothesis test using the 95% confidence limits for the variable's regression coefficient, β_i.

	Coefficients	Std Error	t-stat	p-value	Lower 95%	Upper 95%
Intercept	1.82	1.12	1.63	0.1215	−0.53	3.92
A	0.68	0.28	2.44	0.0253	0.09	2.78
B	−2.35	0.984	−2.39	0.0140	−4.42	−0.25
C	0.017	0.012	1.42	0.1737	−0.01	2.12
D	1.96	1.16	1.69	0.1083	−0.48	4.06

4   For a given independent variable, x_3, in a multiple regression model of four x-variables based on a sample of 35 sets of observations, assume t-stat = 2.44.

   (a)   Define the null and alternative hypothesis to test x_3 for statistical significance.

   (b)   Identify the region of acceptance for H_0. Use $\alpha = 0.05$.

   (c)   Draw the statistical conclusion for this hypothesis test.

   (d)   Conclude whether x_3 is a statistically significant estimator of the y-variable.

5   Assume that $b_2 = -1.6$ and that the 95% confidence interval estimate for the regression coefficient β_2 lies between −2.34 and −0.86 for the numeric independent variable x_2 in a multiple regression model consisting of five independent variables.

   (a)   Interpret the meaning of the sample regression coefficient b_2.

   (b)   Is the independent variable x_2 statistically significant? Explain.

6   Provide a binary coding scheme for the categorical independent variable, *fuel type used* (leaded, unleaded, lean) to monitor a machine's vibration level (vibrations per minute).

7   Show a binary coding scheme to include the *seasonal effect* (of summer, autumn, winter and spring) in a multiple regression model to predict product sales.

Use Excel's **Data Analysis** module **Regression** for each of the following exercises.

8   X13.8 – employee absenteeism

The human resources manager at SA Knitting Mills (SAKM) is concerned about *employee absenteeism*. She believes that *job tenure* is probably the most significant contributing factor. However, she is also interested in the possible effect that other, more subjective, factors such as *job satisfaction* and *organisational commitment* have on the level of employee absenteeism. These last two factors are employee attitudes that are measured by indexes. Score for the indexes are determined by the employees' responses to questions on questionnaires. Higher scores for the indexes are associated with greater job satisfaction or greater degrees of organisational commitment.

A random sample of 35 employee records was selected and their *level of absenteeism* (in days p.a.) noted, as well as the *duration of their job tenure* (in months). Each was also sent a confidential questionnaire from which a *job satisfaction index* and an *organisational commitment index* were derived. Only the first 10 employee records are shown below.

Employee	Tenure	Satisfaction	Commitment	Absence
1	37	46.3	41.9	23
2	53	42.5	35.6	26
3	30	45.9	24.4	29
4	40	41.8	55.4	18
5	59	49.9	43.5	27
6	49	62.4	48.9	19
7	53	44.9	45.1	23
8	36	50.1	63.8	12
9	37	42.3	41.3	25
10	42	55.2	41.8	23

Construct a multiple linear regression model of *absenteeism* using *tenure*, the *satisfaction index* and the *organizational commitment index* as 'drivers'.

(a) What percentage of variation in absenteeism can be explained by the three independent variables?

(b) Test whether the overall regression model is statistically significant. Formulate the null and alternative hypotheses, identify *F-crit* and *F-stat* and draw the statistical conclusion. Use $\alpha = 0.05$.

(c) Test the statistical significance of each independent variable separately. Use $\alpha = 0.05$. For each hypothesis test, formulate the null and alternative hypotheses, identify *t-crit* and *t-stat* and draw the statistical conclusion. Use $\alpha = 0.05$.

(d) Test each of the independent variables for statistical significance based on their *p*-values.

(e) Test each of the independent variables for statistical significance using the 95% confidence interval estimate for their regression coefficients, β_i.

(f) Answer the following management questions:

(i) Is job *tenure* the most important contributor to employee absenteeism?

(ii) Does *job satisfaction* and *organisational commitment* play any role in explaining employee absenteeism?

(g) Estimate, with 95% confidence, the average level of absenteeism for employees with tenure of 48 months; a satisfaction index score of 50 and organisational commitment index score of 60.

9   X13.9 – plastics wastage

A plastics moulding manufacturer is evaluating factors that could affect the level of % *wastage* from an injection moulding process. He identified three possible 'drivers', namely *operator dexterity* (0 = min score, 30 = max score), *machine speed* (rpm), and *plastic viscosity* (PA.s). A *regression model* was built to examine the possible influence of these independent variables (drivers) on the % *wastage* per shift measure.

A random sample of 31 shifts was selected and the above data recorded. Only the data for the first 10 shifts are shown in the table below.

The production manager wishes to identify which of these factors are significant 'drivers' of plastic wastage. Conduct all tests at the 5% level of significance.

Dexterity	Speed	Viscosity	Wastage
24.5	218	0.25	2.5
19.6	187	0.18	2.9
16.4	194	0.21	3.6
20.4	201	0.32	4.1
27.2	165	0.16	1.8
24.8	158	0.18	1.6
27.6	194	0.36	3.1
19.5	188	0.19	2.7
25.7	224	0.18	4.2
22.8	200	0.27	4.2

Construct a multiple linear regression model of % *plastics wastage* per shift using *operator dexterity, machine speed* and *plastic viscosity* as drivers.

(a) What percentage of variation in % plastic wastage per shift can be explained by the three independent variables?

(b) Test whether the overall regression model is statistically significant. Formulate the null and alternative hypotheses, identify *F-crit* and *F-stat* and draw the statistical conclusion. Use $\alpha = 0.05$.

(c) Test the statistical significance of each regressor separately. For each hypothesis test, formulate the null and alternative hypotheses, identify *t-crit* and *t-stat* and draw the statistical conclusion. Use $\alpha = 0.05$.

(d) Test each of the independent variables for statistical significance based on their *p*-values.

(e) Test each of the independent variables for statistical significance using the 95% confidence interval estimate for their regression coefficients, β_i.

(f) Advise the production manager on the most important influencing factors of plastics wastage in the machine injection moulding process.

(g) Estimate, with 95% confidence, the average % of plastic wastage per shift when the operator dexterity's score is 25, the machine speed is 200 rpm and the viscosity level is 0.25 units.

10   X13.10 – employee performance

A work study analyst was contracted by a banking organisation to identify key work-performance criteria of their marketing consultants whose primary function was to market the bank's services to clients. The analyst recorded for a sample of 20 marketing consultants, their *productivity* (deals closed per month); their number of years of relevant work *experience*; and which of three *marketing methods* each consultant used in negotiating with potential clients (identified as method A, method B and method C).

Consultant	Productivity	Experience	Method
1	24	9	A
2	30	4	B
3	26	10	A
4	37	12	B
5	29	10	C
6	28	6	C
7	34	12	C
8	28	10	C
9	29	12	B
10	30	13	A
11	29	14	A
12	32	11	C
13	30	12	B
14	32	12	B
15	31	5	B
16	32	9	B
17	22	7	A
18	27	8	A
19	33	14	B
20	26	3	A

(a) For the categorical variable, *method*, set up a binary coding scheme to recode the data.

(b) Construct a multiple linear regression model to estimate productivity levels of marketing consultants based on their *experience* and preferred *marketing method*.

(c) What percentage of variation in productivity levels (deals closed per month) can be explained by the two independent variables?

(d) Test whether the overall regression model is statistically significant. Formulate the null and alternative hypotheses, identify *F-crit* and *F-stat* and draw the statistical conclusion. Use $\alpha = 0.05$.

(e) Test whether *work experience* is a statistically significant regressor to estimate productivity. Formulate the null and alternative hypotheses, identify *t-crit* and *t-stat* and draw the statistical conclusion. Use $\alpha = 0.05$.

(f) Is the *marketing method* adopted by a marketing consultant statistically significant? Test each binary coded variable separately and conclude about the overall significance of the marketing approach variable. Formulate the null and alternative hypotheses, identify *t-crit* and *t-stat* and draw the statistical conclusion. Use $\alpha = 0.05$.

(g) Test each of the independent variables for statistical significance based on their *p*-values.

(h) Test each of the independent variables for statistical significance using the 95% confidence interval estimate for their regression coefficients, β_i.

(i) What recommendation can the work study analyst make to the banking organisation about productivity performance measures? Provide a brief report.

(j) Estimate, with 95% confidence, the average productivity of marketing consultants who have eight years of relevant work experience and who prefer marketing method B to negotiate with potential clients.

11 **X13.11 – corporate performance**

An investment analyst studied the relationship between corporate *return on capital* (%) and a number of *performance* and *demographic characteristics* of business entities. The performance measures are *sales*, *margin* % and *debt ratio* (%) and the demographic measures are the *region* (Gauteng, Cape, KZN) and *sector* (agriculture, construction).

The data gathered from annual financial reports are shown in the table below for a sample of 25 business entities.

(a) For each of the categorical variables, *region* and *sector*, set up a binary coding scheme to recode the data.

(b) Construct a multiple linear regression model to estimate corporate *return on capital* (%) based on the selected performance and demographic measures

(c) What percentage of variation in *return on capital* (%)) can be explained by all the independent variables?

(d) Test whether the overall regression model is statistically significant. Formulate the null and alternative hypotheses, identify *F-crit* and *F-stat* and draw the statistical conclusion. Use $\alpha = 0.05$.

(e) Test whether the *performance measures* (*sales*, *margin* %, *debt ratio* (%)) are each individually statistically significant independent variables to estimate *return on capital* %. For each, formulate the null and alternative hypotheses, identify *t-crit* and *t-stat* and draw the statistical conclusion. Use $\alpha = 0.05$.

(f) Is *region* statistically significant? Test each binary coded variable separately and conclude about the overall significance of *region* as a useful regressor. Formulate the null and alternative hypotheses, identify *t-crit* and *t-stat* and draw the statistical conclusion. Use $\alpha = 0.05$.

(g) Is *sector* statistically significant? Test each binary coded variable separately and conclude about the overall significance of *sector* as a useful regressor. Formulate the null and alternative hypotheses, identify *t-crit* and *t-stat* and draw the statistical conclusion. Use $\alpha = 0.05$.

(h)   Test each of the independent variables for statistical significance based on their *p*-values.

(i)   Test each of the independent variables for statistical significance using the 95% confidence interval estimate for their regression coefficients, β_i.

(j)   Prepare a brief report of the overall findings of this study.

(k)   Estimate, with 95% confidence, the average return on capital % of business entities with a sales volume of 8 862; a margin % of 10%; a debt ratio (%) of 22% and which operates primarily in the construction sector in the Cape region.

y	Performance measures			Demographic measures	
ROC (%)	Sales	Margin %	Debt ratio (%)	Region	Sector
19.7	7 178	18.7	28.5	1	1
17.2	1 437	18.5	24.3	1	1
17.1	3 948	16.5	65.6	1	1
16.6	1 672	16.2	26.4	1	1
16.6	2 317	16.0	20.1	1	2
16.5	4 123	15.6	46.4	2	1
15.9	4 418	15.3	60.3	2	2
15.4	6 804	14.0	17.7	3	1
15.3	3 592	14.0	17.0	2	1
15.1	1 570	13.3	14.1	2	2
15.0	3 802	13.0	26.1	2	2
14.7	2 594	12.7	19.2	2	2
14.7	1 414	13.8	0.0	2	1
14.6	1 991	9.8	21.9	2	2
13.8	3 379	8.6	10.7	2	1
13.7	1 910	9.9	21.4	3	2
13.4	7 548	5.2	29.5	3	2
12.9	1 858	7.8	5.1	2	2
11.9	3 085	1.4	14.6	3	2
11.9	15 197	1.9	39.6	3	2
11.3	2 453	10.2	21.7	3	2
17.7	2 485	17.7	38.6	1	1
15.5	9 564	7.5	22.4	2	2
14.1	3 912	16.1	19.3	2	1
12.5	2 006	14.9	17.9	2	2

CHAPTER

14

Index Numbers: Measuring Business Activity

Outcomes

An index is a summary value that reflects how business or economic activity has changed over time. The CPI is the most commonly understood economic index. Index numbers are used to measure either price or quantity changes over time. They play an important role in the monitoring of business performance, as well as in the preparation of business forecasts.

After studying this chapter, you should be able to:

- define and explain the purpose of index numbers
- describe applications of index numbers in management practice
- develop and interpret indexes to measure price changes over time
- develop and interpret indexes to measure quantity changes over time
- distinguish between the Laspeyres and Paasche methods of index number construction
- distinguish between the weighted aggregates method and the weighted average of relatives method in composite index construction
- identify pitfalls of index number construction
- move the base index of a time series to a different time period
- construct and interpret link relatives
- calculate the average rate of change of link relatives over a period of time
- distinguish between price/quantity relatives and link relatives
- transform monetary values into constant values using index numbers.

14.1   Introduction

> An **index number** is a summary measure of the overall change in the level of activity of a *single item* or a *basket of related items* from one time period to another.

Index numbers are most commonly used to monitor *price* and *quantity* changes over time. They can also monitor changes in *business performance* levels and are therefore a useful planning and control tool in business. The best-known and most widely used index number in any country is the **consumer price index**, or *inflation* indicator (CPI). This index measures the general changes of retail prices from month to month and from year to year.

Illustrations of index numbers in practice in South Africa include:

- a wide range of *financial performance indicators* (over 60 indicators), supplied by I-Net Bridge from JSE data (www.inet.co.za) (e.g. JSE All Share Index; JSE Gold Index; JSE Industrial Index; JSE Technologies Index; JSE Mining Index; JSE Bond Index)
- over 100 *economic indicators* made available monthly, quarterly and annually by Statistics South Africa (Stats SA) – the central government statistical service (www.statssa.gov.za) (e.g. CPI, CPIX [CPI excluding mortgage payments]; PPI (production price index); manufacturing output index)
- the Business Confidence Index (BCI), produced monthly by the South African Chamber of Business (SACOB) (www.sacob.co.za) as a measure of the level of business confidence within the South African economy.

An index number is *constructed* by dividing the value of an item (or a basket of items) in the *current period* by its value in a *base period*, expressed as a percentage.

$$\text{Index number} = \frac{\text{Current period value}}{\text{Base period value}} \times 100\% \qquad 14.1$$

How to Interpret an Index Number

An index number measures the percentage change from a base period, which has an index value of 100. Index values *above* 100 indicate an *increase* in the level of activity being monitored, while index values *below* 100 reflect a *decrease* in activity relative to the base period. The magnitude of the change is shown by the difference between the index number and the base index of 100.

For example, if the index for electronic goods (TVs, sound systems, DVDs, MP3s, iPods, etc.) stands at 94 in January 2012 with January 2011 as base (100), it means that overall prices of electronic goods have fallen by 6% *on average* over the past year. However, if the index was 105 in January 2012, the overall prices of electronic goods have risen by 5% *on average* over the past year.

Classification of Index Numbers

There are two major categories of index numbers. Within each category, an index can be calculated for either a single item or a basket of related items. These categories are:

1   price indexes
   - single price index
   - composite price index

2   quantity indexes
-   single quantity index
-   composite quantity index.

The monthly percentage adjustment in the fuel price per litre is an example of a single price index, the CPI is an example of a composite price index, and the manufacturing output index is an example of a composite quantity index.

The following notation is used in the construction of price and quantity index numbers:

p_0 = base period price
q_0 = base period quantity
p_1 = current period price
q_1 = current period quantity

14.2 Price Indexes

A **price index** measures the *percentage change* in price between any *two time periods* either for a single item (e.g. car tyres), or a basket of items (e.g. car maintenance items).

Simple Price Index (Price Relative)

The **simple price index** is the change in price from a base period to another time period for a *single item*. It is also called a *price relative*.

$$\text{Price relative} = \frac{p_1}{p_0} \times 100\%$$ 14.2

This relative price change is multiplied by 100 to express it in percentage terms.

Example 14.1 95-octane Fuel Price Study

In January 2008, the pump price of 95-octane fuel in Cape Town was R6.87 per litre. In January 2009 it cost R7.18 per litre, in January 2010 it cost R7.58 per litre and in January 2011 it cost R8.44 per litre.
    (See Excel file C14.1 – *fuel price*.)

Using 2008 as the base period, find the *price relatives* for 95-octane fuel in Cape Town for each year: 2009, 2010 and 2011 respectively. Interpret the results.

Solution

Since 2008 is chosen as the base period, p_0 = R6.87, with the base price relative being 100. Table 14.1 shows the calculation of price relatives for 95-octane fuel in Cape Town for each year from 2009 to 2011. To illustrate, the price relative for 2010 is calculated as follows:

Price relative (2010) = $\frac{7.58}{6.87} \times 100 = 110.3$ (Formula 14.2)

Table 14.1 Price relatives for 95-octane fuel price per litre

Year	Price/litre	Price relative
2008	R 6.87	100.0
2009	R 7.18	104.5
2010	R 7.58	110.3
2011	R 8.44	122.9

Since the price relative for 2009 was 104.5, this means that the price of a litre of 95-octane fuel increased by 4.5% between January 2008 (with base index of 100) and January 2009. The increase from January 2008 to January 2010 was 10.3%, while the price of a litre of 95-octane fuel increased by 22.9% over the three-year period from January 2008 to January 2011.

Composite Price Index for a Basket of Items

A **composite price index** measures the *average price change* for a basket of related items (activities) from one time period (the base period) to another period (the current period).

To illustrate, a basket of groceries consists of milk, bread, cheese, margarine, eggs and chicken. The price of each item varies over time. A composite price index will summarise and report the average 'price' change for the same basket of groceries over a given time period.

Weighting the Basket

To calculate a composite index, each item must be *weighted* according to its importance in the basket. Importance is determined by the value of each item in the basket (i.e. unit price × quantity consumed).

A composite price index measures only price changes in a basket of related items over time. Since the quantities consumed can also change over time, it is necessary to hold all quantities consumed constant. This allows price changes to be monitored without the confounding effect of simultaneous quantity changes.

Laspeyres versus Paasche Weighting Method

Quantities can be held constant either at base period or current period levels. This results in two approaches to determining weights:
- The *Laspeyres approach* holds quantities constant at *base* period levels.
- The *Paasche approach* holds quantities constant at *current* period levels.

One of these approaches must be adopted when calculating a composite price index. Unless explicitly stated, the Laspeyres approach to weighting items is usually assumed.

Constructing a Composite Price Index

There are two methods to derive a composite price index once the weighting method (Laspeyres or Paasche) has been decided. Both methods produce the same index value, but differ only in their reasoning. The two computational methods are:

- the method of *weighted aggregates*
- the method of *weighted average* of *price relatives*.

Weighted Aggregates Method – Using the Laspeyres Weighting Approach

The construction of the Laspeyres composite price index using the weighted aggregates method is illustrated in Example 14.2 based on the data shown in Table 14.2.

Example 14.2 Toiletries Usage Study (1)

The data in Table 14.2 shows the usage of a basket of three toiletry items in two-person households in Tshwane for 2010 and 2011 respectively. The data was collected from household surveys.
(See Excel file C14.2 – *toiletries basket*.)

Table 14.2 Annual household consumption of a basket of toiletries (2010–2011)

Toiletry items	Base year (2010)		Current year (2011)	
	Unit price p_0	Quantity q_0	Unit price p_1	Quantity q_1
Soap	R1.95	37	R2.10	40
Deodorant	R14.65	24	R15.95	18
Toothpaste	R6.29	14	R6.74	16

Management Question

Use 2010 as the base period and find the *Laspeyres weighted aggregate* composite price index for this basket of toiletries for 2011.

Solution

Using the Laspeyres weighted aggregates method:

Step 1: Find the base period value for the basket of items
The base period value is what the basket of items would have cost in the base period. It is found by multiplying each item's *base period price with its base period quantity* ($p_0 \times q_0$) and then summing over all items in the basket.

$$\text{Base period value} = \sum (p_0 \times q_0) \qquad\qquad \textbf{14.3}$$

In the example, the base period value is:
$$(1.95 \times 37) + (14.65 \times 24) + (6.29 \times 14) = R511.8$$

Step 2: Find the current period value for the basket of items
Using Laspeyres, the current period value is the cost of the basket of items in the current period paying current prices (p_1), but consuming base period quantities (q_0). The *current period value* is found by multiplying each item's *current period price* with its *base period quantity* ($p_1 \times q_0$) and then summing over all items in the basket.

$$\text{Current period value} = \sum(p_1 \times q_0)$$ **14.4**

In the example, the current period value is:

$$(2.10 \times 37) + (15.95 \times 24) + (6.74 \times 14) = R554.86$$

Step 3: Calculate the composite price index

Divide the *current period value* by the *base period value* to derive the composite price index.

$$\text{Laspeyres (weighted aggregates) price index} = \frac{\Sigma(p_1 \times q_0)}{\Sigma(p_0 \times q_0)} \times 100\%$$ **14.5**

Thus the Laspeyres (weighted aggregates) price index is:

$$\frac{554.86}{511.81} \times 100 = 108.4$$

The calculations for these three steps are summarised in Table 14.3.

Table 14.3 Laspeyres (weighted aggregates) composite price index for the toiletries basket

Toiletry items	Base year (2010)		Current year (2011)		Value in period	
	Unit price p_0	Quantity q_0	Unit price p_1	Quantity q_1	Base value $p_0 \times q_0$	Current value $p_1 \times q_0$
Soap	R1.95	37	R2.10	40	R72.15	R77.70
Deodorant	R14.65	24	R15.95	18	R351.60	R382.80
Toothpaste	R6.29	14	R6.74	16	R88.06	R4.36
					R511.81	**R554.86**
		Laspeyres (weighted aggregates) price index				108.4

Management Interpretation

For this basket of toiletry items, the base period value is R511.81 and the current period value is R554.86. This means that in 2010, a typical two-person household in Tshwane spent R511.81 on the toiletries basket, while a year later, in 2011, they spent R554.86 on the same basket. Overall, the average price of this basket of toiletries has increased by 8.4% from 2010 to 2011, while holding quantities consumed constant at 2010 levels.

Weighted Aggregates Method – Using the Paasche Weighting Approach

The Paasche composite price index uses the *current period quantities* (consumption levels) to weight the basket. This is illustrated in Example 14.3 based on the data shown in Table 14.2.

Example 14.3 Toiletries Usage Study (2)

Refer to the problem scenario of Example 14.2.

Management Question

Use 2010 as the base period and find the *Paasche weighted aggregate* composite price index for this basket of toiletries for 2011.

Solution

Using the Paasche weighted aggregates method:

The same three steps in calculating the weighted aggregates composite price index are used.

Step 1: Find the base period value for the basket of items

The base period value is what the basket of items would have cost in the base period, but consuming *current period quantities*. It is found by multiplying each item's *base period price* with its *current period quantity* ($p_0 \times q_1$) and then summing over all items in the basket.

$$\text{Base period value} = \sum (p_0 \times q_1) \qquad \text{14.6}$$

In the example, the base period value is:

$$(1.95 \times 40) + (14.65 \times 18) + (6.29 \times 16) = 442.34$$

Step 2: Find the current period value for the basket of items

Using Paasche, the *current period value* of a basket is the *current* cost of the basket of items based on current prices and current consumption. It is found by *multiplying* each item's *current period price* with its *current period quantity* ($p_1 \times q_1$) and then summing over all items in the basket.

$$\text{Current period value} = \sum (p_1 \times q_1) \qquad \text{14.7}$$

In the example, the current period value is:

$$(2.1 \times 40) + (15.95 \times 18) + (6.74 \times 16) = 478.94$$

Step 3: Calculate the composite price index

Divide the *current period value* by the *base period value* to derive the composite price index.

$$\text{Paasche (weighted aggregates) price index} = \frac{\Sigma(p_1 \times q_1)}{\Sigma(p_0 \times q_1)} \times 100\% \qquad \text{14.8}$$

Thus the Paasche (weighted aggregates) price index is:

$$\frac{478.94}{442.34} \times 100 = 108.3$$

The calculations for these three steps are summarised in Table 14.4.

Table 14.4 Paasche (weighted aggregates) composite price index for the toiletries basket

Toiletry items	Base year (2010)		Current year (2011)		Value in period	
	Unit price p_0	Quantity q_0	Unit price p_1	Quantity q_1	Base value $p_0 \times q_1$	Current value $p_1 \times q_1$
Soap	R1.95	37	R2.10	40	R78.00	R84.00
Deodorant	R14.65	24	R15.95	18	R263.70	R287.10
Toothpaste	R6.29	14	R6.74	16	R100.64	R107.84
					R442.34	R478.94
Paasche (weighted aggregates) price index						108.3

Management Interpretation

For this basket of toiletry items that is based on the quantity of items consumed in 2011 (i.e. the current period), the base period value is R442.34 and the current period value is R478.94. This means that in 2010, a typical two-person household in Tshwane spent R442.34 on the toiletries basket, while a year later, in 2011, they spent R478.94 on the same basket. Overall, the average price of this basket of toiletries has increased by 8.3% from 2010 to 2011, while holding quantities consumed constant at 2011 levels.

Weighted Average of Price Relatives Method

This method highlights the fact that the composite price index is a *weighted average of* the individual items' *price relatives* in the basket. An item's relative value is its percentage contribution to the total basket's value. High-valued items will weight (or influence) the composite price index more than low-valued items. The *benefit* of this weighted average of price relatives method over the weighted aggregates method is the *added insight* that it provides into the *price changes of individual items*.

The construction of a composite price index using the weighted average of price relatives method is given in the following three-step approach.

Step 1: Find the *price relative* for each item in the basket ($\frac{p_1}{p_0}$%)
A price relative for each separate item in a basket is found using Formula 14.2.

Step 2: Find the *base period value* of each item in the basket
The base period value for each item is found by ($p_0 \times q_0$) if the *Laspeyres* approach is used, or by ($p_0 \times q_1$) if the *Paasche* approach is used.

Step 3: *Weight* the *price relative* for each item by its importance in the basket
Multiply each item's *price relative* by its *own base period value*. Then sum these weighted price relatives over all items. Finally, divide this sum by the base period value of the basket. These three steps are summarised in the following formulae:

- If *base period quantities* are used as *weights*, then:

$$\text{Laspeyres (price relatives) composite price index} = \frac{\Sigma\left[\left(\frac{p_1}{p_0}\right) \times 100 \times (p_0 \times q_0)\right]}{\Sigma(p_0 \times q_0)} \qquad 14.9$$

- If *current period quantities* are used as weights, then:

$$\text{Paasche (price relatives) composite price index} = \frac{\Sigma\left[\left(\frac{p_1}{p_0}\right) \times 100 \times (p_0 \times q_1)\right]}{\Sigma(p_0 \times q_1)} \qquad 14.10$$

The construction of a Laspeyres and a Paasche composite price index using the weighted average of price relatives method is illustrated using the data shown in Table 14.2.

Example 14.4 Toiletries Usage Study (3)

Refer to the problem scenario of Example 14.1.

Management Questions

1   Using 2010 as the base period, find the composite price index for the toiletries basket for 2011 using the *Laspeyres weighted average of price relatives* method.
2   With 2010 as the base period, find the composite price index for the toiletries basket for 2011 using the *Paasche weighted average of price relatives* method.

Solution

1   Using the Laspeyres weighted average of price relatives method:
    Table 14.5 shows the calculations of the above three steps based on the data in Table 14.2.

Table 14.5 Laspeyres (price relatives) composite price index of toiletries basket

Toiletry items	Base year (2010)		Current year (2011)		Price relatives $\frac{p_1}{p_0} \times 100$	Base value $p_0 \times q_0$	Weighted price relatives
	Unit price p_0	Quantity q_0	Unit price p_1	Quantity q_1			
Soap	R1.95	37	R2 10	40	107.7	R72.15	R7 770.56
Deodorant	R14.65	24	R15 95	18	108.9	R351.60	R38 289.24
Toothpaste	R6.29	14	R6 74	16	107.2	R88.06	R9 440.03
						R511.81	R55 499.83
Laspeyres (weighted average of price relatives) price index							108.4

Management Interpretation

The 'Price relatives' column in Table 14.5 shows that a bar of soap increased in price by 7.7% from 2010 to 2011. Similarly, deodorant increased by 8.9% over the same period, while a tube of toothpaste increased in price by 7.2% over the past year.

In terms of the base period values, deodorant is the highest-valued item in the toiletries basket (i.e. R351.60 out of R511.81 = 68.7%), followed by toothpaste (R88.06 out of R511.81 = 17.2%), with soap being the lowest-valued item (i.e. only R72.15 out of R511.81 = 14.1%).

The weighting of each individual item's *price relative* by its respective base period weight is shown in the 'Weighted price relatives' column. Finally, to derive the composite price index, the sum of the weighted price relatives (R55 499.83) is divided by the base value of the basket (R511.81).

Thus the Laspeyres (price relatives) composite price index is $\frac{55\,499.83}{511.81} = 108.4$ (using Formula 14.9). Note that this index value is exactly the same as for the Laspeyres method of weighted aggregates.

This calculation is equivalent to working out the *percentage value of each item* in the basket (i.e. for soap: $\frac{R72.15}{R511.81}$ = 14.1%; for deodorant: $\frac{R351.6}{R511.81}$ = 68.7%; and for toothpaste: $\frac{R88.06}{R511.81}$ = 17.2%) and then calculating a weighted average of the price relatives.

Weighted average index = $(107.7 \times 0.141) + (108.9 \times 0.687) + (107.2 \times 0.172)$

$$= 108.4$$

2 Using the Paasche weighted average of price relatives method:

Table 14.6 summarises the above three steps based on the data in Table 14.2.

Table 14.6 Paasche (price relatives) composite price index of toiletries basket

Toiletry items	Price relatives $\frac{p_1}{p_0} \times 100$	Base value $p_0 \times q_1$	Weighted price relatives
Soap	107.7	78.00	8 400.60
Deodorant	108.9	263.70	28 716.93
Toothpaste	107.2	100.64	10 788.61
		442.34	47 906.14
Paasche (weighted average of price relatives) price index			**108.3**

From Table 14.6, it can be seen that the *price relative for each toiletries item* is the same as in Table 14.5, since it is based on the same Formula 14.2.

The calculation of the base period value for each item in the basket, however, changes. It is found by multiplying each *base period price*, p_0, by its *current period quantity* consumed, q_1, to give the *value (weight) of each item* in the basket (i.e. $p_0 \times q_1$). As seen from these base period values, deodorant is the highest-valued item in the toiletries basket (i.e. R263.7 out of R442.34 = 59.6%), while soap is the least-valued item (i.e. only R78 out of R442.34 = 17.6%).

The last column first multiplies each item's price relative by its base value to produce a *weighted price relative* per item, and then divides the sum of these weighted price relatives (47 906.14) by the value of the basket (442.34) to give the composite price index.

Thus the Paasche (price relatives) composite price index is $\frac{47\,906.14}{442.34}$ = 108.3 (using Formula 14.10). Note that this index value is the same as for the Paasche method of weighted aggregates.

14.3 Quantity Indexes

A **quantity index** measures the *percentage change* in *consumption level*, either for a single item (e.g. milk) or a basket of items (e.g. hardware tools), from *one time period to another*.

The methods of calculation for quantity indexes are similar to those for price indexes. When constructing quantity indexes, it is necessary to hold *price levels constant* over time in order to isolate the effect of quantity (consumption level) changes only.

Simple Quantity Index (Quantity Relative)

For a single item, the change in units consumed from a base period to another time period is found by calculating its *quantity relative*.

$$\text{Quantity relative} = \frac{q_1}{q_0} \times 100\%$$

14.11

This relative quantity change is multiplied by 100 to express it in percentage terms.

Example 14.5 Door Sales Study

In 2009, a hardware store sold 143 doors. In 2010, door sales were only 122 units, while in 2011, sale of doors rose to 174 units.
(See Excel file C14.3 – *door sales*.)

Management Question

Find the quantity relative of door sales for each year 2010 and 2011C respectively, using 2009 as base period.

Solution

Table 14.7 shows the *quantity relatives* calculated for sales of the single item – doors – for 2010 and 2011 respectively, based on Formula 14.11.

Table 14.7 Quantity relatives for door sales

Item – doors		
Year	Units sold	Quantity relative
2009	$q_0 = 143$	100
2010	$q_1 = 122$	85.3
2011	$q_1 = 174$	121.7

In 2010, the number of doors sold by this hardware store decreased by 14.7% from 2009 sales levels. In 2011, however, sales were 21.7% higher than their 2009 (base year) levels.

Composite Quantity Index for a Basket of Items

A **composite quantity index** measures the *average consumption (quantity) change* for a basket of related items from one time period (the base period) to another period (the current period).

A composite quantity index must reflect only *consumption changes*, without the confounding effect of simultaneous price changes. As a result, prices must be *held constant* to monitor quantity changes only. Either the Laspeyres approach (holding prices constant in the *base period*), or the Paasche approach (holding prices constant in the *current period*) can be chosen to determine the relative weights (or importance) of items in a basket.

The construction of a composite quantity index is similar to that of a composite price index. It can be calculated using either the *weighted aggregates method* or the *weighted average of quantity relatives method*. Both methods produce the same composite quantity index.

Weighted Aggregates Method – Composite Quantity Index

This method compares the *aggregate value* of the basket between the *current* period and the *base* period. The composite quantity index will reflect overall consumption changes while holding prices constant at either the base period (Laspeyres approach) or current period (Paasche approach).

- The Laspeyres approach holds prices constant in the *base* period.

$$\text{Laspeyres (weighted aggregates) quantity index} = \frac{\Sigma(p_0 \times q_1)}{\Sigma(p_0 \times q_0)} \times 100\%$$

14.12

- The Paasche approach holds prices constant in the *current* period.

$$\text{Paasche (weighted aggregates) quantity index} = \frac{\Sigma(p_1 \times q_1)}{\Sigma(p_1 \times q_0)} \times 100\%$$

14.13

Weighted Aggregates Method – Using the Laspeyres Weighting Approach

The following example illustrates the construction of both the Laspeyres composite quantity index and the Paasche composite quantity index using the *weighted aggregates* method.

Example 14.6 Cupboard Manufacturer Study (1)

The data in Table 14.8 refers to a basket of three carpentry items (cold glue, wooden boards and paint) used by a joinery company in the manufacture of cupboards for 2010 and 2011 respectively. The data was collected from the company's financial records.
    (See Excel file C14.4 – *carpentry material*.)

Table 14.8 Data on carpentry material usage for joinery company (2010–2011)

Carpentry items	Year 2010		Year 2011	
	p_0	q_0	p_1	q_1
Cold glue (1 ℓ)	R13	45	R15	52
Boards (m²)	R63	122	R77	110
Paint (5 ℓ)	R122	16	R125	20

Management Questions

1   Using the *Laspeyres weighted aggregates* method, construct a composite *quantity* index for the average change in the quantity of carpentry materials used (cold glue, wooden boards, paint) between 2010 (as base period) and 2011.

2   Using the *Paasche weighted aggregates* method, construct a composite *quantity* index for the average change in the quantity of carpentry materials used (cold glue, wooden boards, paint) between 2010 (as base period) and 2011.

Solution

1   Using the Laspeyres weighted aggregates method:
    A three-step approach similar to that applied to the weighted aggregrates composite price index is used. Table 14.9 summarises the three-step approach based on Formula 14.12.

Step 1
The *base period value* is found using $\Sigma(p_0 \times q_0) = $ R10 223. This means that in 2010 (base period), the joinery used R10 223 worth of raw materials (cold glue, boards and paint).

Step 2
The *current period value* is found using $\Sigma(p_0 \times q_1) = $ R10 046. This means that in 2011 (current period), the joinery used R10 046 worth of raw materials (cold glue, boards and paint), assuming 2010 prices were paid.

Step 3
The *composite quantity index* is found by dividing the current period value by the base period value.

Table 14.9 Laspeyres (weighted aggregates) composite quantity index

Carpentry raw material	p_0	q_0	p_1	q_1	Base value $(p_0 \times q_0)$	Current value $(p_0 \times q_1)$
Cold glue (1 ℓ)	13	45	15	52	585	676
Boards (m²)	63	122	77	110	7 686	6 930
Paint (5 ℓ)	122	16	125	20	1 952	2 440
					10 223	**10 046**
Laspeyres (weighted aggregates) quantity index						**98.3**

Thus the Laspeyres (weighted aggregates) quantity index $= \frac{10\,046}{10\,223} \times 100 = 98.3$ (using Formula 14.12).

Management Interpretation

If prices are held constant at 2010 (base period) levels, the composite quantity index stands at 98.3 in 2011. This means that the joinery company used 1.7% less of all raw materials, on average, from 2010 to 2011.

2   Using the Paasche weighted aggregates method:
    The Paasche method holds prices constant at *current period* levels. The 'weighted aggregates' three-step approach is summarised in Table 14.10 on the next page and is based on Formula 14.13.

Table 14.10 Paasche (weighted aggregates) composite quantity index

Carpentry raw material	p_0	q_0	p_1	q_1	Base value $(p_1 \times q_0)$	Current value $(p_1 \times q_1)$
Cold glue (1 ℓ)	13	45	15	52	675	780
Boards (m²)	63	122	77	110	9 394	8 470
Paint (5 ℓ)	122	16	125	20	2 000	2 500
					12 069	**11 750**
Paasche (weighted aggregates) quantity index						**97.4**

Thus Paasche (weighted aggregates) quantity index $= \frac{11\ 750}{12\ 069} \times 100 = 97.4$ (using Formula 14.13).

Management Interpretation

If prices are held constant at 2011 (current period) levels, the composite quantity index stands at 97.4 in 2011. This means that the joinery company used 2.6% less of all raw materials, on average, from 2010 to 2011.

Weighted Average of Quantity Relatives Approach

This approach is similar to the weighted average of price relatives approach used in the construction of the composite price index. Again, either a Laspeyres weighting method or a Paasche weighting method can be used to derive the composite quantity index.

- Using the *Laspeyres weighting method*, the *quantity relative* of an item is weighted by its value in the basket derived from its *base period price*, p_0, i.e. $(p_0 \times q_0)$.

$$\text{Laspeyres (quantity relatives) quantity index}$$
$$= \frac{\Sigma\left[\left(\frac{q_1}{q_0}\right) \times 100 \times (p_0 \times q_0)\right]}{\Sigma(p_0 \times q_0)}$$

14.14

- Using the Paasche weighting method, the quantity relative of an item is weighted by its value in the basket derived from its current period price, p_1, i.e. $(p_1 \times q_0)$.

$$\text{Paasche (quantity relatives) quantity index}$$
$$= \frac{\Sigma\left[\left(\frac{q_1}{q_0}\right) \times 100 \times (p_1 \times q_0)\right]}{\Sigma(p_1 \times q_0)}$$

14.15

Example 14.6 (cupboard manufacturer) is used to illustrate the construction of a composite quantity index using the method of *weighted average of quantity relatives* based on (i) the Laspeyres weighting method (Formula 14.14); and (ii) the Paasche weighting method (Formula 14.15).

Example 14.7 Cupboards Manufacture Study (2)

Refer to Example 14.6 for the problem description.

Management Questions

1 Using the *Laspeyres weighted average of quantity relatives* method, construct a composite *quantity* index for the average change in the quantity of carpentry materials used (cold glue, wooden boards, paint) between 2010 (as base period) and 2011.

2 Using the *Paasche weighted average of quantity relatives* method, construct a composite *quantity* index for the average change in the quantity of carpentry materials used (cold glue, wooden boards, paint) between 2010 (as base period) and 2011.

Solution

1 Using the Laspeyres weighted average of quantity relatives method:
Table 14.11 summarises the three-step approach (similar to the weighted average of price relatives method) using Formula 14.14, where the base value is found using $(p_0 \times q_0)$.

Step 1: Find the *quantity relative* for each item in the basket, $(\frac{q_1}{q_0}\%)$. Use Formula 14.11

Step 2: Find the *base period value* of each item in the basket
The base period value *for each item* is found using $(p_0 \times q_0)$ if the *Laspeyres method* is used, or using $(p_1 \times q_0)$ if the *Paasche method* is used.

Step 3: *Weight* the *quantity relative* for each item by its importance in the basket
Multiply each item's *quantity relative* by its own *base period value*. Then sum these weighted relatives over all items. Finally, divide this sum by the base period value of the basket.

Table 14.11 Laspeyres (weighted average of quantity relatives) composite quantity index

Carpentry raw material	p_0	q_0	p_1	q_1	Quantity relatives $(\frac{q_1}{q_0}\%)$	Base value $(p_0 \times q_0)$	Weighted quantity relatives
Cold glue (1 ℓ)	13	45	15	52	115.56	585	67 600
Boards (m²)	63	122	77	110	90.16	7 686	693 000
Paint (5 ℓ)	122	16	125	20	125.00	1 952	244 000
						10 223	1 004 600
Laspeyres (weighted average of quantity relatives) quantity index							98.3

Management Interpretation

The 'Quantity relatives' column in Table 14.11 shows that the joinery used 15.56% more cold glue in 2011 than in 2010. Usage of paint also increased by 25% from 2010 to 2011. However, wooden board usage dropped by 9.84% over this same period.

In terms of the base period values, wooden boards are the highest-valued item in the carpentry raw materials basket (R7 686 out of R10 223 = 75.2%), followed by paint (R1 952 out of R10 223 = 19.1%), with cold glue being the lowest-valued item (only R585 out of R10 223 = 5.7%).

The weighting of each individual item's *quantity relative* by its respective base period weight is shown in the 'Weighted quantity relatives' column. Finally, to derive the composite quantity index, the sum of the weighted quantity relatives (1 004 600) is divided by the base value of the basket (10 223).

Thus the Laspeyres (quantity relatives) quantity index = $\frac{1\ 004\ 600}{10\ 223}$ = 98.3 (using Formula 14.14).

This result is the same as for the Laspeyres (weighted aggregates) composite quantity index (Example 14.6, Solution 1).

2   *Using the Paasche weighted average of quantity relatives method*
Table 14.12 summarises the three-step approach (similar to 1 above) using Formula 14.15 where the *base value* is found by weights derived from current prices $(p_1 \times q_0)$.

Table 14.12 Paasche (weighted average of quantity relatives) composite quantity index

Carpentry raw material	p_0	q_0	p_1	q_1	Quantity relatives ($\frac{q_1}{q_0}$%)	Base value ($p_1 \times q_0$)	Weighted quantity relatives
Cold glue (1 ℓ)	13	45	15	52	115.56	675	78 000
Boards (m²)	63	122	77	110	90.16	9 394	847 000
Paint (5 ℓ)	122	16	125	20	125.00	2 000	250 000
						12 069	1 175 000
Paasche (weighted average of quantity relatives) quantity index							97.4

Thus the Paasche (quantity relatives) quantity index = $\frac{1\ 175\ 000}{12\ 069}$ = 97.4.

This result is the same as for the Paasche (weighted aggregates) composite quantity index (Example 14.6, Solution 2).

14.4 Problems of Index Number Construction

Five primary factors require careful consideration when planning the construction of index numbers. These are:
- the purpose (scope) of the index
- the selection of the items
- the choice of weights
- the choice of a base year
- an item substitution rule.

The Purpose (Scope) of the Index

A clear understanding of the purpose and scope of a proposed index is necessary. This determines the choice of items, the frequency of measurement, the degree of accuracy required, the choice of the weights and the choice of the base year.

If the proposed mix of items is not readily measurable in the time frame required, or if it is not possible to achieve the desired accuracy from the data available, it may be necessary to rethink the purpose of the index.

It must also be established whether the choice of items to be included in the basket will measure that which is desired by the index (i.e. that the index has *construct validity*).

The Selection of the Basket (Mix of Items)

It is generally impractical, from a cost and time point of view, to include every relevant item in the construction of the required index. A *sample of items* is generally selected for inclusion. Considerable care must be taken in the selection of a *representative* sample of relevant items. This may not always be an easy task.

Judgement sampling, in preference to simple random sampling, tends to be used to ensure representativeness for the purpose of the index. In this regard, it must first be decided which items best relate to the purpose of the index and then which set of products best represents a given item (e.g. cereals are included in a consumer price index, but which brand of cereal and what quantity?).

Choice of Item Weights

Each item's relative importance must be reflected in the construction of composite indexes. The problem faced in index number construction is to decide on *typical quantities* (consumption levels) and *prices* to compute *values* that measure the relative importance of items. These typical quantities and prices are obtained either through observation or investigation (e.g. 'pantry audits').

Choice of a Base Year

The base period should be a period of relative economic stability. Defining a normal economic period is difficult. If a period of excessive (severely depressed) economic activity is selected, all indexes will appear to indicate good (poor) performance relative to this base period.

The chosen base period should also be fairly recent, so that changing technology, product quality and/or purchasing habits do not excessively affect comparisons. For example, the base period for the CPI is currently 2008, and is reset every five years.

Item Substitution Rule

Every index should have substitution rules. These rules define when items become obsolete or new trends emerge (technology changes), resulting either in existing products being removed from the basket or new products being added. It is essential to have valid substitution rules to ensure *continuity validity*. The *weighting* of an item in a basket (for items in the current mix), or the need to maintain *construct validity* of the index (for items not in the current basket), are factors that influence the nature of substitution rules.

The following extracts from the CPI statistical release of Stats SA show how the CPI addresses some of the above issues. Stats SA (www.statssa.gov.za) conducts a 'Survey of

Income and Expenditure of Households' every five years to '*identify the goods and services bought* by a typical consumer or household and which should be included in the basket of goods and services used to monitor price changes ... The current CPI basket covers approximately 1 500 goods and services'. In addition, this survey 'is used to *determine the weights* of the indicator products in the basket. The CPI is a Laspeyres weighted index, with the weights remaining constant for the five-year period until the next "Survey of Income and Expenditure of Households" results become available.'

14.5 Limitations on the Interpretation of Index Numbers

Index numbers are generally based on samples of items. For example, the CPI uses a *sample* of 1 500 products and services, and the FTSE/JSE Overall Index is based on only a *sample* of the approximately 390 companies listed on the JSE, hence sampling errors are introduced. This raises questions of *representativeness and construct validity.*

In addition, technological changes, product quality changes and changes in consumer purchasing patterns can individually and collectively make comparisons of index number series over time both unreliable and incompatible.

Index numbers are useful summary measures of the historical performance of items or groups of related items, and are also useful for the tracking (or monitoring) of past performance, but have limited forecasting capabilities due to their inability to 'predict' turning points in economic activity.

14.6 Additional Topics of Index Numbers

Changing the Base of an Index Series

The base of an index number series can be shifted from one time period to another to make the interpretation of recent values of the index number series more meaningful. Since index numbers are expressed relative to the base period (with index = 100), the base period should not be too far removed from the current levels of activity being monitored by the index number series. This may require repositioning of the base year to bring it in line with more recent periods.

To *re-base* an index number series to a new base period, k, multiply each index number in the series by the following adjustment factor:

$$\text{Adjustment factor} = \frac{100}{\text{Index in period } k} \qquad\qquad 14.16$$

Example 14.8 Electrical Appliances Study

Revise the base period of the price index series shown in Table 14.13 from 2007 to 2009. (See Excel file C14.5 – *electrical appliances.*)

Table 14.13 Electrical appliances price index series (base = 2007)

Year	2005	2006	2007	2008	2009	2010	2011
Price index	78	87	100	106	125	138	144

Solution

Calculate the adjustment factor:

$$\frac{100}{\text{Price index in 2009}} = \frac{100}{125} = 0.80 \quad \text{(Formula 14.16)}$$

Now multiply each price index in the series by the adjustment factor of 0.80.

2005: $78 \times 0.8 = 62.4$

2006: $87 \times 0.8 = 69.6$, etc.

This results in the following *revised* price index series, with 2009 as the new base year (Table 14.14).

Table 14.14 Re-based electrical appliances price index series (base = 2009)

Year	2005	2006	2007	2008	2009	2010	2011
Price index	62.4	69.6	80.0	84.8	100.0	110.4	115.2

In the revised price index series, price changes are now interpreted relative to 2009. For example, 2008 prices were 84.8% (or 15.2% below those) of 2009 prices, on average. In the previous price index series, 2008 and 2009 prices could not be compared directly.

Note: When re-basing an index series, the relative relationship between the individual indexes does not change.

Link Relatives

Link relatives are indexes that reflect price or quantity changes on a period-by-period basis.

Each period's level of activity (price or quantity) is expressed as a percentage of the *immediately preceding* period's level of activity. A link relative is calculated by dividing the *current value* (unit price, quantity or basket value) by its corresponding *immediate preceding value* and expressing the result as a percentage

$$\text{Price link relative} = \frac{p_i}{p_{i-1}} \times 100\% \qquad \text{14.17}$$

$$\text{Quantity link relative} = \frac{q_i}{q_{i-1}} \times 100\% \qquad \text{14.18}$$

$$\text{Composite link relative} = \frac{\text{Basket value}_i}{\text{Basket value}_{i-1}} \times 100\%$$

or

$$= \frac{\text{Composite index}_i}{\text{Composite index}_{i-1}} \times 100\% \qquad \text{14.19}$$

Where: i is any given period, and $(i - 1)$ is the preceding period.

The consumer price index (CPI) is always calculated as a composite price index, but is transformed into a link relative to highlight the year-on-year changes in the general level of prices in the economy.

Example 14.9 Standard White Bread Loaf Study

The prices of a standard loaf of white bread between 2004 and 2011 are given in Table 14.15. Calculate both the *link relatives* and *price relatives* for this white bread price index series.

(See Excel file C14.6 – *white bread loaf*.)

Solution

The calculated link relatives (using Formula 14.17) and price relatives (using Formula 14.2) are shown in Table 14.15.

Table 14.15 Link relatives and price relatives for a standard loaf of white bread

Year	Bread price (R)	Link relative	Price relative (base 2004 = 100)
2004	3.15	100.0	100.0
2005	3.45	109.5	109.5
2006	3.70	107.2	117.5
2007	3.95	106.8	125.4
2008	4.10	103.8	130.2
2009	4.45	108.5	141.3
2010	4.85	109.0	154.0
2011	5.05	104.1	160.3

Management Interpretation

The 'Link relative' column shows that the price of a standard loaf of white bread increased by 9.5% from 2004 to 2005, by 7.2% from 2005 to 2006, by 6.8% from 2006 to 2007, etc. The smallest *year-on-year* increase in the price of a standard loaf of white bread was 3.8% from 2007 to 2008.

On the other hand, the 'Price relative' column shows how the price of a standard loaf of white bread has increased *relative to the base period price* of 2004. From 2004 to 2007 the price of white bread rose by 25.4%. From 2004 to 2010 the price of a standard loaf of white bread increased by 54%. In 2011, a standard loaf of white bread cost 60.3% more than in 2004.

For a *basket of items*, a *link relative* is found by dividing each period's *composite index* (price or quantity) by the preceding period's *composite index*. The interpretation is similar to that for a single item's link relative, as illustrated in Example 14.10.

Example 14.10 Paint and Painting Accessories Study (1)

Calculate and interpret the link relative (i.e. *year-on-year average price changes*) for a basket consisting of paint and painting accessories (brushes, cleansing agents, sandpaper, etc.) from 2005 to 2011, using the composite price indexes given in Table 14.16.

(See Excel file C14.7 – *paint prices*.)

Table 14.16 Paint and painting accessories composite price index series (base = 2008)

Year	2005	2006	2007	2008	2009	2010	2011
Composite price index	79	88	91	100	114	138	151

Solution

Table 14.17 shows the link relatives for the above composite price index series for a basket of paint and paint accessories (using Formula 14.19).

Table 14.17 Link relatives – paint and painting accessories composite price index series

Year	2005	2006	2007	2008	2009	2010	2011
Composite price index	79	88	91	100	114	138	151
Link relative	—	111.4	103.4	109.9	114	121.1	109.4

To illustrate, the link relative for $2007 = \frac{91}{88} \times 100 = 103.4$ (using Formula 14.19).

Management Interpretation

The year-on-year average price increases in paint and painting accessories have been 11.4% (2006); 3.4% (2007); 9.9% (2008), etc. The largest *annual* average percentage increase has been 21.1% from 2009 to 2010, while the smallest *annual* average percentage increase was 3.4% from 2006 to 2007.

Averaging Link Relatives

The *average* period-on-period change is found by *averaging the link relatives* of an index series. Since link relatives represent '*rate of change*' data, their average is found using the *geometric mean* instead of the arithmetic mean. (The geometric mean was covered in Chapter 3.)

A geometric mean is defined as the nth root of the product of n link relatives.

$$\text{Geometric mean} = \sqrt[r]{(x_1 x_2 x_3 \dots x_n)} \qquad \textbf{14.20}$$

Where: x_i is the ith period's link relative.

Example 14.11 Paint and Painting Accessories Study (2)

Refer to Example 14.10 for the problem description and the annual price index series for a basket of paint and painting accessories from 2005 to 2011. Find the average annual percentage price change in the basket from 2005 to 2011.

Solution

Calculate the annual link relatives from the composite price indexes (see tables 14.16 and 14.17 above).

Apply the geometric mean formula (Formula 13.20) to the annual link relatives:

Geometric mean $= \sqrt[6]{(111.4 \times 103.4 \times 109.9 \times 114 \times 121.1 \times 109.4)}$

$= 111.41$

The average annual percentage price change $= 111.41 - 100 = 11.41\%$.

Management Interpretation

The prices of paint and painting accessories have increased by *an average* of 11.41% annually from 2005 to 2011.

Transforming Monetary Values into Real (Constant) Values

As the prices of products and services change over time, the monetary value of their sales (turnover) also changes. Index numbers can be used to *remove* the influence of the *price adjustments* on sales of products and services to reveal the *real change* in turnover.

These *real values* will reflect the *actual growth* (or *decline*) in sales volumes that are free of the confounding influence of price changes. Real values – also called *constant values* – show the actual level of business activity in a particular period on the assumption that *base period prices* are paid for products and services in this current period.

To remove the influence of price adjustments from current monetary values, *divide* each period's *monetary value* (e.g. turnover) by its *corresponding composite price index number*. This results in real (or constant) values.

These real values can then be compared to values in the base period to reveal the extent to which the level of activity (e.g. sales volumes, salary adjustments) have changed relative to the base period levels. Real values that are *below* base period values show that the activity has declined relative to base period levels, while real values that are *above* base period values show that the activity has increased relative to base period levels.

This conversion to constant prices of monetary prices is also applied to salary adjustments to reflect whether they have lagged behind or exceed the CPI. Such adjustments to salaries will reveal the *real purchasing power of earnings*. By adjusting *company turnover* in a similar way, a company can determine real changes (either real growth or real decline) in turnover due to increased or decreased demand, without the confounding influence of price changes.

The 'price inflation indicator' – namely the consumer price index (CPI) or, in the case of industrial products, the producer price index (PPI) – which is published monthly by Stats South Africa (www.statssa.gov.za), is used to deflate monetary values such as salaries and turnover to generate real (or constant) values which are more comparable over time.

Example 14.12 Limpopo Province Gross National Product (GNP) Study

The gross national product (GNP) for the Limpopo province for the period 2006 to 2010, together with the CPI for that region, as computed by Stats SA, is given in Table 14.18. (See Excel file C14.8 – *provincial gnp*.)

Management Question

Calculate the *real growth in GNP* from 2006 to 2010 for the Limpopo province.

Table 14.18 GNP (in R million) and CP for Limpopo province (2006–2010)

Year	CPI	GNP (monetary)
2006	100.0	778
2007	104.3	806
2008	110.2	889
2009	112.2	930
2010	118.6	974

Solution

To convert the *monetary* GNP values into *constant* (or *real*) GNP values, divide the actual GNP by the CPI and multiply by 100 to express it as a percentage. The calculations are shown in Table 14.19.

Table 14.19 Real (constant) GNP (in R million) for Limpopo province

Year	CPI	GNP (monetary)	GNP (constant)
2006	100.0	773	778.0
2007	104.3	805	772.8
2008	110.2	889	806.7
2009	112.2	930	828.9
2010	118.6	974	821.2

To illustrate, for 2009, real GNP = $\frac{930}{112.2} \times 100 = 828.9$.

Management Interpretation

Real GNP decreased marginally in 2007 from 2006 levels from R778 to R772.80 (0.67%), but showed real growth (year-on-year) of 4.39% during 2008 (from R772.80 to R806.70) and 2.75% growth during 2009 (from R806.70 to R828.90), but declined again in real terms in 2010 (by 0.92%).

Example 14.13 Technicians' Earnings Study

The monthly earnings of technicians over a five-year period (2006–2010) and the CPI for the corresponding periods, with 2006 as base period, are shown in Table 14.20.
(See Excel file C14.9 – *technicians earnings*.)

Management Questions

1 Find the technicians' real monthly earnings relative to 2006.
2 Calculate the price relatives of technicians' earnings using 2006 as the base.
3 Have technicians' annual salary adjustments kept ahead of annual inflation?

Solution

Table 14.20 shows technicians' *real earnings* over this five-year period, and the price relatives of the real monthly earnings (i.e. earnings at constant prices).

Table 14.20 Real monthly earnings and price relatives (2006–2010)

Year	Monthly earnings (R)	Consumer price index (base 2006 = 100)	Real earnings at 2006 prices (R)	Price (earnings) relative
2006	R12 400	100	R12 400	100.0
2007	R13 100	109	R12 018	96.9
2008	R15 200	120	R12 667	102.2
2009	R15 700	130	R12 077	97.4
2010	R17 600	135	R13 037	105.1

Note: The 'Real earnings' column reflects the purchasing power of monthly income in 2006 terms.

Management Interpretation

Monetary income showed an increase for each of the five years. However, *real income* (purchasing power) declined in 2007 (relative to 2006) by 3.1% and again in 2009 (relative to 2006) by 2.6%. On the other hand, salary increases in 2008 resulted in real income being 2.2% above the base level of 2006, and increases in 2010 pushed real income 5.1% ahead of the base year incomes of 2006.

14.7 Summary

This chapter described the basic concept of an index number as a *summary measure* of the overall *change in the level of activity* of a single item or basket of items from one time period to another. It is always expressed as a ratio relative to a base period. Common South African index numbers were identified.

The chapter focused on the construction and interpretation of both *price* and *quantity indexes*. In each case, an index was calculated for a single item (called price/quantity relative) and a basket of related items (called a composite price/quantity index). With the construction of a composite index, a set of *weights* for each item in the basket must be determined. This measure of relative importance was identified as the *Laspeyres* approach, for which prices/quantities are held constant at base period levels, and the *Paasche* approach, for which prices/quantities are held constant at current period levels. Both the method of *weighted aggregates* and the method of *weighted average of relatives* were demonstrated in the construction of composite indexes.

Problems in index number construction, as well as limitations in respect of their interpretation, were discussed. Three useful applications of index numbers were illustrated, namely: (i) *changing the base* of a series of indexes to a different time period to keep an index series manageable in terms of its economic interpretation; (ii) calculating *period-on-period changes for indexes*, which are called *link relatives*, and finding the average period-on-period change over a number of periods using the *geometric mean*; and (iii) *transforming monetary values into real values*. The difference in interpretation of link relatives and price/quantity relative index numbers was highlighted.

Exercises

This symbol denotes data available online

1   What is an index number? Give a practical example of an index number.
2   Distinguish between a price index and a quantity index.
3   In a composite index, why must a basket of items be 'weighted'?
4   Name two methods of weighting items in a basket.
5   Name five factors that must be considered when planning the construction of an index number.
6   How does a link relative differ from a price relative?
7   Explain how monetary values are transformed into real (constant) values. What do constant values mean?
8   X14.8 – motorcycle sales
    A motorcycle dealer has recorded the unit prices and quantities sold of three models of the Suzuki motorcycle for 2009 and 2010. The quantities sold and unit selling prices for both these years are given in the following table:

Motorcycle model	2009		2010	
	Unit price (R1 000s)	Quantity (units sold)	Unit price (R1 000s)	Quantity (units sold)
A	25	10	30	7
B	15	55	19	58
C	12	32	14	40

(a) Find the *price relative* for each motorcycle model. Use 2009 as the base period. Interpret.
(b) Calculate the *composite price* index for 2010 with 2009 as the base period using each of the following methods:
     (i)   the Laspeyres weighted aggregates method
     (ii) the Laspeyres weighted average of price relatives method.
(c) Interpret the composite price index for the motorcycle dealer.

9   X14.8 – motorcycle sales
    Refer to the data given in Exercise 8.
(a) Find the *quantity relative* for each motorcycle model. Use 2009 as the base period. Interpret.
(b) Calculate the *composite quantity* index for 2010 with 2009 as the base period using each of the following methods:
     (i)   the Laspeyres weighted aggregates method
     (ii) the Laspeyres weighted average of quantity relatives method.
(c) By how much has the motorcycle dealer's *volume of sales* (i.e. quantities sold) for all three models changed between 2009 and 2010?

10 X14.8 – motorcycle sales
    Refer to the data given in Exercise 8.
(a) Calculate the composite quantity index for 2010 with 2009 as the base period using each of the following methods:

        (i)   the Paasche weighted aggregates method

        (ii)   the Paasche weighted average of quantity relatives method.

    (b)   By how much has the motorcycle dealer's *volume of sales* (i.e. quantities sold) for all three models changed between 2009 and 2010?

11   X14.11 – Telkom services

Telkom offers a range of telecommunication services to small businesses. A small printing business has used the services of *TalkPlus* (a value-added telephone service), *SmartAccess* (an advertising service) and *ISDN* (an internet connection) for the past three years. Their annual usage and the unit price of each service are given in the following table:

Telkom services	2009		2010		2011	
	Unit price (cents/call)	Quantity (100s calls)	Unit price (cents/call)	Quantity (100s calls)	Unit price (cents/call)	Quantity (100s calls)
TalkPlus	65	14	70	18	55	17
SmartAccess	35	27	40	29	45	24
ISDN	50	16	45	22	40	32

    (a)   Calculate the *price relatives* for 2010 and 2011 for the ISDN service. Use 2009 as the base period. Interpret the meaning of each of these indexes.

    (b)   Use Laspeyres weighted aggregates method (with 2009 as the base period) to calculate the *composite price indexes* for 2010 and 2011. By what percentage, on average, has the cost of telecommunications services for this printing company changed in 2010 and 2011 relative to 2009?

    (c)   Calculate the Paasche composite quantity indexes for 2010 and 2011, using 2009 as the base period.

    (d)   Has the printing company's overall usage of the different telecommunication services changed significantly in 2010 and 2011 relative to 2009?

12   X14.12 – computer personnel

The average annual salary and number of employees for each of three IT job categories in a large IT consultancy organisation based in Johannesburg are shown in the table below.

IT job category	Annual salary (R10 000s)		No. of employees	
	2008	2011	2008	2011
Systems analyst	42	50	84	107
Programmer	29	36	96	82
Network manager	24	28	58	64

    (a)   Calculate a Laspeyres composite index for 2011 to reflect the overall average change in the annual salaries of IT personnel from 2008. Use 2008 as the base period with index of 100. Apply the method of weighted aggregates.

    (b)   What does the composite index calculated in (a) mean in terms of the change of overall remuneration paid to these three IT job categories from 2008 to 2011?

    (c)   Calculate price relatives for each category of IT personnel. Which category has shown the largest increase in annual salary between 2008 and 2011?

13   X14.12 – computer personnel
     Refer to the data given in Exercise 12.
     (a)   Find the quantity relative for each IT job category using 2008 as the base
           period. Define the meaning of each quantity relative and interpret its value.
     (b)   Calculate the composite quantity index for 2011, with 2008 as the base period,
           using each of the following methods:
           (i)   the Laspeyres weighted aggregates method
           (ii)   the Laspeyres weighted average of quantity relatives method.
     (c)   On average, by how much has the overall staff complement across the three IT
           job categories changed from 2008 to 2011?

14   X14.14 – printer cartridges
     A printing company that specialises in business stationery (i.e. letterheads,
     business cards, reports, invitations) has recorded its usage and cost of printer
     cartridges for its four different printers. The printer cartridges are identified as HQ21,
     HQ25, HQ26 and HQ32.

Printer cartridge	2008		2009		2010	
	Unit price	Quantity used	Unit price	Quantity used	Unit price	Quantity used
HQ21	145	24	155	28	149	36
HQ25	172	37	165	39	160	44
HQ26	236	12	255	12	262	14
HQ32	314	10	306	8	299	11

     (a)   Using 2008 as the base period, calculate the price relatives of the HQ26 and
           HQ32 printer cartridges for 2010 only. Interpret the meaning of these two price
           relatives.
     (b)   Calculate the composite price indexes for 2009 and 2010, with 2008 as the
           base period, using each of the following methods:
           (i)   the Paasche weighted aggregates method
           (ii)   the Paasche weighted average of price relatives method.
     (c)   What was the overall average *change in the cost* to the printing company of
           printer cartridges used between 2008 and 2009 and between 2008 and 2010?
           Explain.
     (d)   Use the composite price indexes computed in (b) to derive the composite *link
           relatives* from 2008 to 2010 of printer cartridges used.

15   X14.15 – electrical goods
     The composite price indexes for electrical goods (e.g. kettles, toasters,
     refrigerators, stoves, microwave ovens, blenders) for the period 2004 to 2010 are
     shown in the following table:

	2004	2005	2006	2007	2008	2009	2010
Composite price index	88	96	100	109	114	112	115

Give all calculations correct to one decimal place.
(a) Reset the base period index for electrical goods from 2006 to 2009. Interpret the revised index number series.
(b) Calculate the *link relatives* for electrical goods and interpret.
16 X14.16 – insurance claims
Two insurance companies (Federal Insurance and Baltic Insurance) both use the Laspeyres index number approach to represent how the number of claims processed annually have either increased or decreased. In 2010 the two companies merged, but decided to maintain separate records of claims processed annually. To make comparisons possible between the two companies, management agreed that their respective index series should have a common base period of 2010. The index series of claims processed for each company is given below.

	2006	2007	2008	2009	2010	2011
Federal Insurance (base = 2008)	92.3	95.4	100.0	102.6	109.4	111.2
Baltic Insurance (base = 2009)	93.7	101.1	98.2	100.0	104.5	107.6

(a) Calculate the revised index series for both companies, with 2010 as the common base period. Calculate to one decimal place.
(b) Which company showed a bigger increase in claims processed between 2008 and 2010? Use the results of (a) to justify your answer.
(c) Using the original index series, compute *link relatives* between successive years for each company.
(d) Which company showed a bigger increase in claims processed between 2010 and 2011? Refer to the link relatives calculated in (c).
(e) Derive the *average annual percentage* change in claims processed for each insurance company using a *geometric mean* (refer to Chapter 3). (*Hint:* Apply the link relative indexes computed in (c) to calculate each geometric mean.)
(f) Which insurance company experienced a larger average annual increase in insurance claims processed between 2006 and 2011?
17 X14.17 – micro-market basket
A micro-market basket price index can be calculated for a household by including several food items typically consumed by that household in one basket. Consider the basic food items in the following table, with their unit price and per capita annual consumption.

Food item in micro-market basket	Unit prices (R)		Consumption	
	2010	2011	2010	2011
Milk (litres)	7.29	7.89	117	98
Bread (loaves)	4.25	4.45	56	64
Sugar (kg)	2.19	2.45	28	20
Maize meal (kg)	5.59	5.25	58	64

Give all calculations correct to one decimal place.

(a)   Find the *price relative* for each food item. Interpret the results. Which food item showed the largest price change (increase or decrease) from 2010 to 2011? Justify your answer.

(b)   Calculate the Paasche *composite price index* for 2011 (2010 = base period). Use the weighted average of price relatives method. What is the average percentage change in 2011 prices over those in 2010?

(c)   Find the *quantity relative (or consumption relative)* for each food item. Interpret the results. Which food item showed the largest consumption change (increase or decrease) from 2010 to 2011?

(d)   Calculate the Paasche *composite consumption index* for 2011 (2010 = base period). Use the weighted average of quantity relatives method. What is the average percentage change in household consumption between 2010 and 2011?

18   X14.18 – utilities usage

A random sample of 100 households was selected to participate in a study to establish a composite price index for *household utilities usage* (i.e. electricity, sewerage, water, telephone). The following average annual figures have been obtained:

Household utility	Price (R/unit)			Consumption (no. of units)		
	2008	2009	2010	2008	2009	2010
Electricity	1.97	2.05	2.09	745	812	977
Sewerage	0.62	0.68	0.72	68	56	64
Water	0.29	0.31	0.35	296	318	378
Telephone	1.24	1.18	1.06	1 028	1 226	1 284

(a)   Find the *price relative* for each household utility for 2010. Use 2008 as the base period. Interpret the meaning of each price relative value. Which utility showed the smallest change in price from 2008 to 2010? Justify.

(b)   Calculate the *composite price indexes* for 2009 and 2010, with 2008 as the base period. Use each of the following methods:
    (i)   the Laspeyres weighted aggregates method
    (ii)   the Laspeyres weighted average of price relatives method.

(c)   Interpret the values of these composite price indexes for 2009 and 2010.

19   X14.18 – utilities usage

Refer to the data given in Exercise 18.

(a)   Find the *quantity relative* for each household utility for 2010, with 2008 as the base period. Which utility showed the largest change in consumption from 2008 to 2010? Justify.

(b)   Calculate the *composite quantity (consumption)* index for 2009 and 2010, with 2008 as the base period. Use each of the following methods:
    (i)   the Laspeyres weighted aggregates method
    (ii)   the Laspeyres weighted average of quantity relatives method.

(c)   Refer to the answers in (b) and explain how overall consumption of utilities in the sampled households changed from 2008 to 2010.

20   X14.20 – leather goods

A leather goods manufacturer has kept records of the annual costs of inputs used in the manufacture of its leather products (briefcases, satchels, belts, hats, etc.). The accountant has developed an annual Laspeyres composite cost index, with 2007 as the base period, as shown in the following table:

	2005	2006	2007	2008	2009	2010	2011
Composite cost index	97	92	100	102	107	116	112

(a)   The accountant would like to move the base of the index series to 2009. Prepare the revised cost index series with base period of 100 in 2009.

(b)   Plot the revised cost index series in a line graph. Comment on the pattern of overall costs of inputs changes over the seven-year period from 2005 to 2011.

(c)   By how much have overall costs of inputs changed, on average, from 2009 to 2011?

(d)   Use the original cost index series to prepare *link relatives* for the period 2005 to 2011. Between which two consecutive years has the change in the costs of inputs been the largest?

(e)   Use the *geometric mean* (refer to Chapter 3) to calculate the average annual percentage change in the overall costs of inputs from 2005 to 2011. Interpret its value.

21   X14.21 – accountants' salaries

The following table shows the average annual salary package of chartered accountants with three years' work experience, and the consumer price index (CPI) for the period 2005 to 2011. The base year for CPI is 2006 (i.e. CPI = 100).

(a)   Use the consumer price index (CPI) to calculate the *real* annual salary package of chartered accountants for each of the years.

(b)   Based on the answer to (a), discuss whether chartered accountants' salary packages have kept pace with 'headline' inflation (CPI) relative to the base period.

(c)   Calculate the *salary link relatives* and *CPI link relatives* and determine whether salary adjustments have maintained the real purchasing power of chartered accountants' incomes on a year-on-year basis.

Accountants' salaries (annual)		
Year	Salary package (R1 000s)	CPI
2005	387	95
2006	406	100
2007	422	104
2008	448	111
2009	466	121
2010	496	126
2011	510	133

22 X14.22 – school equipment
Consider the following cost index series for school equipment supplied by the
Limpopo Education Department to schools in the province.

	2003	2004	2005	2006	2007	2008	2009	2010
Composite cost index	94.8	97.6	100	105.2	108.5	113.9	116.7	121.1

(a) Change the base year index from 2005 to 2008. Show the revised composite
cost index series for school equipment.
(b) Interpret the pattern of overall cost changes in school equipment provided by
the Limpopo Education Department.
(c) Use the original cost index series and calculate *link relatives* to identify year-on-
year cost changes. Interpret the link relatives index series.
(d) If the department budgeted R 5 million in 2003 for school equipment for the
province's schools, what should the budgets have been in each year from 2004
to 2010 to provide at least the same level of service to schools?
(e) **Excel task:** Plot the revised composite cost index series from (a) on a line graph
using the **Line with Markers** option in the **Insert > Chart** tab in Excel.

23 X14.23 – coffee imports
House of Coffees is a coffee wholesaler that imports and distributes ground
coffee to over 300 retailers countrywide. The company has kept records of the unit
price paid per kilogram and the number of kilograms imported of its four major
coffee types (Java, Colombia, Sumatra and Mocha). Only data for 2007 and 2010 is
shown in the following table:

Coffee type	2007		2010	
	Unit price (R/kg)	Quantity (1 000 kg)	Unit price (R/kg)	Quantity (1 000 kg)
Java	85	52	98	46
Colombia	64	75	74	90
Sumatra	115	18	133	20
Mocha	38	144	42	168

(a) Calculate the *price relative* for 2010 for each coffee type. Interpret.
(b) Calculate, to one decimal place, the Laspeyres *composite price index* for coffee
imports for 2010, using 2007 as the base year. Interpret its meaning.
(c) If the economy's producer price index (PPI), which measures raw material cost
changes to producers/wholesalers, increased by 15% from 2007 to 2010,
has the cost of coffee imports become cheaper or more expensive in real cost
terms?
(d) Calculate, to one decimal place, the Laspeyres *composite quantity index* for
coffee imports for 2010, using 2007 as the base year. Interpret its meaning.

24 **X14.24 – medical claims**

Hydrogen is a medical aid fund with over 450 000 members. Data on the *number of claims received* and the *average value* of these claims by the different medical categories (GPs, specialists, dentists and medicines) is given for 2008 and 2010 in the following table.

Claim type	2008		2010	
	Claims (1 000s)	Ave. value (R)	Claims (1 000s)	Ave. value (R)
GPs	20	220	30	255
Specialists	30	720	25	822
Dentists	10	580	15	615
Medicines	50	400	70	438

(a) The management of the medical aid fund would like you to provide them with one overall figure to represent how the *number of claims* (i.e. quantities) have increased over the three years from 2008 to 2010. Use 2008 as the base year.

(b) Calculate the quantity relative for *each claim type* to identify which claim type showed the largest increase in the *number of claims* over this three-year period.

(c) Determine the change in the overall *value of claims* received from 2008 to 2010. Use the Laspeyres approach with 2008 as the base year.

(d) Interpret the result of (c) for the management of the Hydrogen medical aid fund.

25 **X14.25 – tennis shoes**

A sports equipment company sells three models of tennis shoes (Trainer, Balance and Dura). Company records for 2009 and 2010 show the unit price and quantities sold of each model of tennis shoe. See the table below.

The company's financial plan requires that *sales volumes* (i.e. quantities sold) of all models of tennis shoes must show an increase of at least 12% per annum.

Shoe model	2009		2010	
	Unit price (R)	Pairs sold	Unit price (R)	Pairs sold
Trainer	320	96	342	110
Balance	445	135	415	162
Dura	562	54	595	48

(a) Calculate *quantity relatives* for each of the three models of tennis shoes. Which model showed the smallest increase in sales volumes?

(b) Calculate a Laspeyres *composite quantity index* for 2010, using 2009 as the base period.

(c) Has the company achieved its sales volume target for tennis shoes? What conclusion can be drawn from the index?

26   X14.26 – energy fund

The Central Energy Fund (CEF) monitors the price of crude oil imports and uses it as a basis for setting local fuel prices. The fuel-cost indexes of crude oil imports are given in the table below for the period 2001 to 2010.

	2001	2002	2003	2004	2005	2006	2007	2008	2009	2010
Fuel cost index	100	116.2	122.4	132.1	135.7	140.3	142.8	146.9	153.4	160.5

(a)   Every 10 years, the CEF resets the base five years on from the current base. Calculate the revised fuel-cost index series, with 2006 as the new base year.

(b)   Calculate the *link relatives* and plot the annual percentage changes on a line graph.

(c)   Find the *average annual percentage change* in the fuel cost index from 2001 to 2010. Use the geometric mean formula.

(d)   Comment on the trend in price changes of crude oil imports between 2001 and 2010.

27   X14.27 – motorcycle distributor

A motorcycle distributor has recorded the average unit selling prices and quantities sold of three models of a particular make of motorcycle in South Africa from 2007 to 2011. The data is given in the following tables:

Model	Average selling price (R)				
	2007	2008	2009	2010	2011
Blitz	18 050	19 235	21 050	21 950	22 400
Cruiser	25 650	26 200	27 350	28 645	31 280
Classic	39 575	42 580	43 575	43 950	46 750

Model	Units sold				
	2007	2008	2009	2010	2011
Blitz	205	185	168	215	225
Cruiser	462	386	402	519	538
Classic	88	70	111	146	132

Use an Excel worksheet to perform the following calculations:

(a)   Calculate a *price relative* index series for the Cruiser model, using 2007 as base period. Interpret the findings.

(b)   Calculate a Laspeyres *composite price index series* from 2007 to 2011, using 2007 as base period. Use the **Line with Markers** option in the **Insert > Chart** tab to display this price index series graphically.

(c)   Based on 2007 prices, describe how motorcycle prices have changed from 2008 to 2011.

(d)   Calculate a *link relative* series for the selling price of the Classic model, using 2007 as base period. Interpret the findings.

(e)   Use the *geometric mean* to find the *average annual change* in motorcycle prices from 2007 to 2011.

(f)   Calculate a Laspeyres *composite quantity index* series from 2007 to 2011, using 2007 as base period. Use the **Line with Markers** option in the **Insert > Chart** tab to display this quantity index series graphically.

(g)   By how much have motorcycle *sales volumes* in these three models changed between 2007 and 20011? Interpret the findings for the motorcycle distributor.

28   X14.28 – tyre production

The Uitenhage Plant of Hillstone (SA) has recorded unit production costs and volumes for the three makes of tyres (passenger, light truck and giant truck) produced and sold on a monthly basis for 2010. Refer to the Excel file for the data.

Use an Excel worksheet to perform the following calculations:

(a)   Calculate a *cost relative* index series for the passenger tyre data, using January 2010 as the base period. Interpret the findings.

(b)   Calculate a Laspeyres *composite cost index* series from January to December 2010, using January 2010 as base period. Use Excel's **Line with Markers** option in the **Insert > Chart** tab to display this cost index series graphically. What has been the average cost changes for these three makes of tyres from the beginning to the end of 2010? Interpret the findings for the production manager.

(c)   Calculate a *link relative* index series for the light-truck tyres, using January 2010 as the base period. Interpret the findings.

(d)   Calculate a Laspeyres *composite production volume index* series from January 2010 to December 2010, using January 2010 as the base period. Use Excel's **Line with Markers** option in the **Insert > Chart** tab to display this production volume index series graphically.

(e)   By how much have production volumes of tyres in these three makes changed from the beginning of 2010 to the end of 2010? Interpret the findings for the production manager.

Time Series Analysis: A Forecasting Tool

Outcomes

In addition to analysing survey data, managers also need to know how to treat *time series data*. Time series data are invaluable for plotting and tracking trends in business performance.

Time series analysis is a statistical approach to quantify the factors that influence and shape time series data. This understanding can then be applied to prepare forecasts of future levels of activity of the time series variables.

After studying this chapter, you should be able to:

- explain the difference between cross-sectional (survey) and time series data
- explain the purpose of time series analysis
- identify and explain the components in time series analysis
- calculate and interpret the trend values in a time series
- calculate and interpret the seasonal influence in a time series
- de-seasonalise a time series and explain its value
- prepare seasonally adjusted forecast values of a time series.

15.1 Introduction

Most data used in statistical analysis is called *cross-sectional* data, meaning that it is gathered from *sample surveys* at one point in time. However, data can also be collected over time. For example, when a company records its daily, weekly or monthly turnover, or when a household records its daily or monthly electricity usage, they are compiling a time series of data.

> A **time series** is a set of numeric data of a random variable that is *gathered over time* at *regular intervals* and arranged in chronological (time) order.

Examples of time series data include:
- the daily closing *share price* of Pick n Pay quoted on the JSE
- the weekly *absenteeism rates* for an organisation
- the daily *occupancy rates* at the Southern Sun, Newlands
- the weekly *pedestrian flows* through the Eastgate Shopping Mall
- the monthly *company turnover* for Woolworths
- the quarterly *value of new car sales* published by NAAMSA
- the annual *net immigration* figures from the Department of Home Affairs.

Each time series can be analysed to examine trends, identify patterns and prepare forecasts of *future values* of the time series variable that is essential for budgeting and operational planning in a company.

This chapter will describe an approach to analyse time series data – called time series analysis.

> The purpose of **time series analysis** is to identify any *recurring patterns* in a time series, quantify these patterns through building a statistical model and then use the statistical model to prepare forecasts to estimate future values of the time series.

Some of the limitations of time series analysis will also be highlighted.

Plotting Time Series Data

The *trendline graph* (see Chapter 2, Section 2.3) is used to display time series data visually. A visual inspection of a time series line graph will highlight possible patterns and trends inherent in the data over time.

Example 15.1 Monsoon Shoes Sales Study

Monsoon Shoes (Pty) Ltd, a retail shoe company with eight branches nationwide, has recorded the quarterly sales volumes (in R10 000s) since they began trading in January 2008. This sales data is shown in Table 15.1.
   (See Excel file C15.1 – *shoe sales*.)

Table 15.1 Monsoon Shoes quarterly sales data

Quarterly period	2008	2009	2010	2011
Q1 (Jan–Mar)	54	55	49	60
Q2 (Apr–Jun)	58	61	69	72
Q3 (Jul–Sep)	94	84	95	99
Q4 (Oct–Dec)	70	76	88	80

Management Question

Produce a line graph of the quarterly sales data for Monsoon Shoes. Visually establish whether any patterns occur over time.

Solution

The line graph is shown in Figure 15.1.

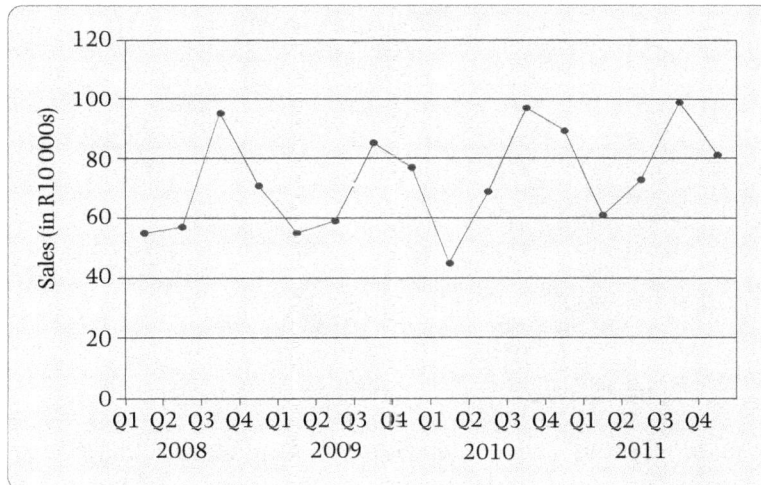

Figure 15.1 Line graph of Monsoon Shoes quarterly sales (in R10 000s)

Management Interpretation

The line graph clearly reveals a fairly regular pattern over time, with sales peaking in the third quarter (July to September) and bottoming out in the first quarter (January to March) of each year. There is also a moderate but steady upward rise in the series.

15.2 The Components of a Time Series

Time series analysis assumes that data values of a time series variable are determined by *four* underlying *environmental forces* that operate both individually and collectively *over time*. They are:
1   trend (T)
2   cycles (C)
3   seasonality (S)
4   irregular (random) influences (I).

Time series analysis attempts to isolate each of these components and *quantify* them statistically. This process is known as *decomposition* of the time series. Once identified and quantified, these components are combined and used to estimate future values of the time series variable.

Trend (T)

Trend is defined as a long-term smooth underlying movement in a time series.

It measures the effect that long-term factors have on the series. These long-term factors tend to operate fairly gradually and in one direction for a considerable period of time. Consequently, the trend component is usually described by a smooth, continuous curve or a straight line, as illustrated in Figure 15.2.

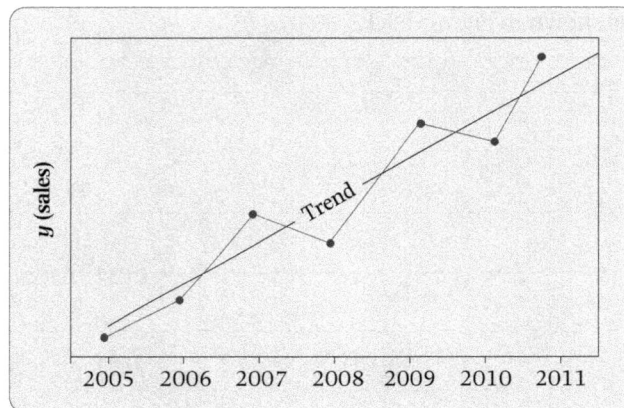

Figure 15.2 Illustration of a trendline in time series data

Some of the more important *causes* of long-term trend movements in a time series include: population growth, urbanisation, technological improvements, economic advancements and developments, and consumer shifts in habits and attitudes.

The statistical technique of *trend analysis* is used to isolate underlying long-term movement.

Cycles (C)

Cycles are medium- to long-term deviations from the trend. They reflect alternating periods of relative expansion and contraction of economic activity.

Cycles are wave-like movements in a time series, which can vary greatly in both duration and amplitude, as illustrated in Figure 15.3. Consequently, while historical patterns of cycles can be measured, these past patterns are of little use in forecasting the future patterns of cycles.

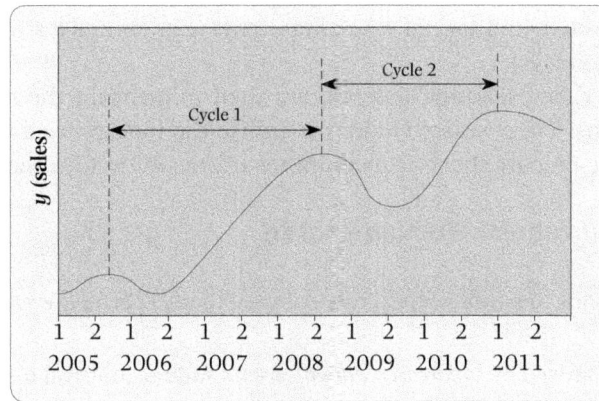

Figure 15.3 Illustration of economic cycles in time series data

The *causes* of cycles are difficult to identify and explain, but their impact on a time series is either to stimulate or depress its levels of activity. Generally stated, cycles are caused by 'mass psychological hysteria'. Certain actions by bodies such as governments (e.g. changes in fiscal, monetary policies, sanctions), trade unions, world organisations and financial institutions can induce levels of pessimism or optimism of varying intensity and duration into an economy, which are reflected in changes in the time series levels (e.g. the world financial crisis in 2008).

Index numbers are used to describe and quantify cyclical fluctuations. However, their usefulness as a forecasting tool is limited as they cannot predict turning points in cycles.

Seasonality (S)

> **Seasonal variations** are fluctuations in a time series that are repeated at regular intervals within a year (e.g. daily, weekly, monthly, quarterly).

These fluctuations tend to occur with a *high degree of regularity* and can be readily isolated through statistical analysis. Figure 15.4 illustrates the highly regular nature of seasonal variations.

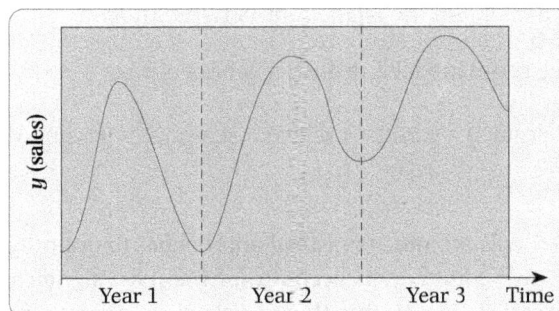

Figure 15.4 Illustration of seasonal variations in time series data

Seasonal variations are caused by recurring environmental influences, such as climatic conditions (the seasons), and special recurring events (e.g. annual festivals, and religious, public and school holidays).

Index numbers, called **seasonal indexes**, are used to measure the regular pattern of seasonal fluctuations. These seasonal indexes, unlike the indexes used to quantify cycles, can be very useful to prepare short- to medium-term forecasts in time series data.

Random Effects (Irregular Fluctuations) (I)

Irregular fluctuations in a time series are attributed to *unpredictable events*.

They are generally caused by *unforeseen one-off events* such as natural disasters (e.g. floods, droughts, fires) or human-made disasters (e.g. strikes, boycotts, accidents, acts of violence [war, riots]). Since these occurrences are totally unpredictable and follow no specific pattern, they cannot be harnessed through statistical analysis or incorporated into statistical forecasts. Irregular behaviour in a time series is illustrated graphically in Figure 15.5.

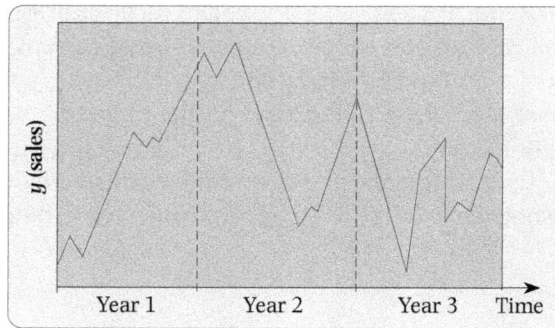

Figure 15.5 Irregular (or random) fluctuations in time series data

15.3 Decomposition of a Time Series

Time series analysis aims to *isolate the influence* of each of the *four components* on the actual time series. The time series model used as the basis for analysing the influence of these four components assumes a *multiplicative relationship* between them.

The multiplicative time series model is defined algebraically as:

$$\text{Actual } y = \text{trend} \times \text{cyclical} \times \text{seasonal} \times \text{irregular}$$
$$y = T \times C \times S \times I$$

15.1

Sections 15.4 and 15.5 will examine statistical approaches to quantify trend and seasonal variations *only*. These two components account for the most significant proportion of an actual value in a time series. By isolating them, most of an actual time series value will be explained.

15.4 Trend Analysis

The long-term trend in a time series can be isolated by removing the medium- and short-term fluctuations (i.e. cycles, seasonal and random) in the series. This will result in either a smooth curve or a straight line, depending on the method chosen.

Two methods for trend isolation can be used:
1   *the moving average* method, which produces a smooth curve
2   *regression analysis*, which results in a straight-line trend.

Method 1: The Moving Average Method

A moving average removes the short-term fluctuations in a time series by taking successive averages of groups of observations. Each time period's actual value is replaced by the average of observations from time periods that surround it. This results in a *smoothed time series*. Thus the moving average technique *smoothes* a time series by removing short-term fluctuations.

The number of observations, k, which are summed and averaged in each group, is determined by the number of periods that are believed to span the short-term fluctuations. To illustrate, if it is assumed that a time series pattern repeats itself every three consecutive time periods within a year, then a three-period moving average is appropriate to remove the short-term fluctuations, thus $k = 3$.

The following four steps are used to calculate a three-period moving average series.

Step 1
Sum the first three periods' observations, and position the *total* opposite the middle (median) time period (i.e. period 2).

Step 2
Repeat the summing of three periods' observations by removing the first period's observation (i.e. period 1) and including the next period's observation (i.e. period 4). This second *moving total* (using periods 2, 3 and 4) is again positioned opposite the middle (median) time period, which is now period 3.

Step 3
Continue producing these *moving (or running) totals* until the end of the time series is reached. This process of positioning each moving total opposite the middle (or median) time period of each sum of the three observations is called **centring**.

Step 4
The *moving average* series is now calculated by dividing each *moving total* by $k = 3$ (i.e. the number of observations that are summed in each group).

This four-step procedure is applied whenever the term, k, of a moving average is *odd*. The calculation of a moving average when k is *even* will be illustrated after the following example.

Example 15.2 Fire Insurance Claims Study

Table 15.2 shows the number of fire insurance claims received by an insurance company in each four-month period from 2008 to 2011.

(See Excel file C15.2 – *fire insurance claims*.)

Table 15.2 Number of fire insurance claims received by an insurance company (2008–2011)

	2008			2009			2010			2011		
Period	P1	P2	P3	P1	P2	P3	P1	P2	P3	P1	P2	P3
Claims (y)	7	3	5	9	7	9	12	4	10	13	9	10

Management Question

Calculate a three-period moving average for the number of insurance claims received.

Solution

Table 15.3 shows the four-step approach outlined above and the resulting three-period moving average of fire insurance claims received.

Table 15.3 Three-period moving average of the number of fire insurance claims received

Period		Claims (y)	Three-period moving total (centred)	Three-period moving average
2008	P1	7	—	—
	P2	3	$7 + 3 + 5 = 15$	$\frac{15}{3} = 5$
	P3	5	$3 + 5 + 9 = 17$	$\frac{17}{3} = 5.67$
2009	P1	9	$5 + 9 + 7 = 21$	$\frac{21}{3} = 7$
	P2	7	$9 + 7 + 9 = 25$	$\frac{25}{3} = 8.33$
	P3	9	$7 + 9 + 12 = 28$	$\frac{28}{3} = 9.33$
2010	P1	12	$9 + 12 + 4 = 25$	$\frac{25}{3} = 8.33$
	P2	4	$12 + 4 + 10 = 26$	$\frac{26}{3} = 8.67$
	P3	10	$4 + 10 + 13 = 27$	$\frac{27}{3} = 9$
2011	P1	13	$10 + 13 + 9 = 32$	$\frac{32}{3} = 10.67$
	P2	9	$13 + 9 + 10 = 32$	$\frac{32}{3} = 10.67$
	P3	10	—	—

The *moving average series* is a smooth curve, which has 'ironed out' the short-term fluctuations.

Example 15.3 Fire Insurance Claims Study

Refer to the problem scenario of Example 15.2 and the time series data set in Table 15.2.

Management Question

Calculate and graph the three-period and five-period moving average series for the number of fire insurance claims. Compare the two moving average series.

Solution

Table 15.4 shows both the three-period and five-period moving average values of fire insurance claims received.

Table 15.4 Three-period and five-period moving averages of fire insurance claims received

Period	Claims (y)	Three-period moving average	Five-period moving total	Five-period moving average
2008 P1	7	—	—	—
P2	3	5.00	—	—
P3	5	5.67	31	6.2
2009 P1	9	7.00	33	6.6
P2	7	8.33	42	8.4
P3	9	9.33	41	8.2
2010 P1	12	8.33	42	8.4
P2	4	8.67	48	9.6
P3	10	9.00	48	9.6
2011 P1	13	10.67	46	9.2
P2	9	10.67	—	—
P3	10	—	—	—

Figure 15.6 is a line plot of the original y-values, and both the three-period and five-period moving average value of the time series of fire insurance claims received. It highlights the effect of different terms ($k = 3$ and then $k = 5$) on the smoothing process.

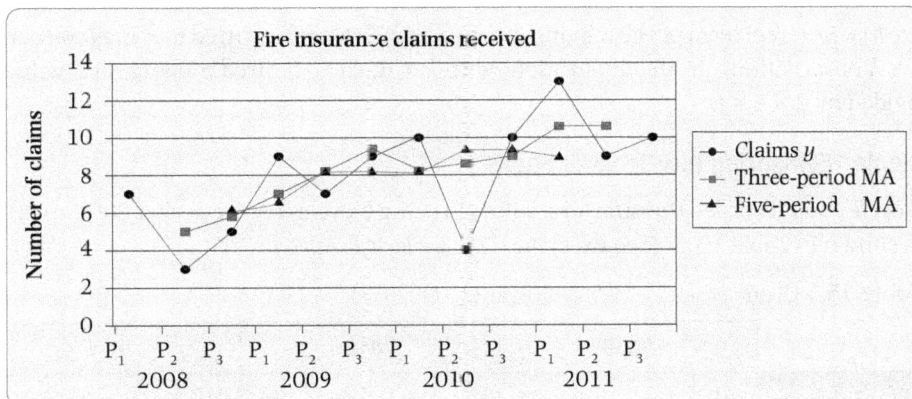

Figure 15.6 Moving average plots of fire insurance claims received

From a comparison of the line plots of the three-period and five-period moving average values, it can be seen that there is *less fluctuation* (*greater smoothing*) in the five-period moving average series than in the three-period moving average series.

The term, k, for the moving average affects the degree of smoothing:

- A shorter term produces a more jagged moving average curve.
- A longer term produces a smoother moving average curve.

Centring an Uncentred Moving Average

A moving average value must always be *centred* on a middle time period.

When the term k (the number of periods to be averaged) is *odd*, centring occurs directly when the moving average value is placed in the median (middle) time period of k observations.

However, when a moving average is calculated for an *even* number of time periods (i.e. the term k is even), then the moving totals will be *uncentred* (i.e. lie between two time periods) when positioned opposite the middle time period of the summed values.

This is illustrated by a four-period moving average (i.e. $k = 4$) calculation below.

Step 1: Calculate the uncentred moving totals

- The first moving total will lie between periods 2 and 3 (i.e. at period 2.5).
- The second moving total will lie between periods 3 and 4 (i.e. at period 3.5).
- The third moving total will lie at period 4.5, and so on.

Step 2: Centre the uncentred moving totals

Calculate a *second* moving total series consisting of *pairs* of the *uncentred moving totals*. Each second moving total value is centred between the two uncentred moving total values. This positions these second moving totals on an actual time period.

Thus the sum of the first pair of uncentred moving totals (in positions 2.5 and 3.5 respectively) will be positioned opposite period 3. The sum of the second pair of uncentred moving totals (in positions 3.5 and 4.5 respectively) will be positioned opposite period 4, the sum of the third pair opposite period 5, etc.

Step 3: Calculate the centred moving averages

A *centred moving average* is calculated by dividing the *centred* moving total values by $2 \times k$, where k is the (*even*) term of the moving average. In effect, each centred moving total consists of $2 \times k$ observations. In the illustration, with $k = 4$, each centred moving total value will be divided by $2 \times 4 = 8$.

Example 15.4 Racing Bicycle Sales Study

A cycle shop recorded the quarterly sales of racing bicycles for the period 2009 to 2011, as shown in Table 15.5. (See Excel file C15.3 – *bicycle sales*.)

Table 15.5 Quarterly sales of racing bicycles (2009–2011)

	2009				2010				2011			
Period	Q1	Q2	Q3	Q4	Q1	Q2	Q3	Q4	Q1	Q2	Q3	Q4
Sales (y)	17	13	15	19	17	19	22	14	20	23	19	20

Management Question

Produce a four-period centred moving average for the quarterly sales of racing bicycles sold by the cycle shop during the period 2009 to 2011.

Solution

The resulting calculations are shown in Table 15.6.

Table 15.6 Quarterly moving average of racing bicycle sales (2009–2011)

Period		Sales y	Uncentred four-period moving total	Centred 2 × four-period moving total	Centred four-period moving average
2009	Q1	17	–	–	–
	Q2	13		–	–
	Q3	15	64	128	16.000
	Q4	19	64	134	16.750
2010	Q1	17	70	147	18.375
	Q2	19	77	149	18.625
	Q3	22	72	147	18.375
	Q4	14	75	154	19.250
2011	Q1	20	79	155	19.375
	Q2	23	76	158	19.750
	Q3	19	82		
	Q4	20			

Interpretation of a Moving Average

A moving average time series is a *smoother* series than the original time series values. It has removed the effect of *short-term fluctuations* (i.e. *seasonal* and *irregular* fluctuations) from the original observations, y, by averaging over these short-term fluctuations. The moving average value can be seen as reflecting mainly the combined trend and *cyclical* movements.

In symbol terms for the multiplicative model:

$$\text{Moving average} = \frac{T \times C \times S \times I}{S \times I} = T \times C \qquad \textbf{15.2}$$

Drawback and Benefit of a Moving Average

As seen from these moving average calculations, its primary *drawback* is a *loss of information* (data values) at both ends of the original time series. Moving averages cannot be found for the first and last $\frac{k}{2}$ periods. This is caused by the centring process of moving average values. However, this is not a significant drawback if the time series is long, say 50 time periods or more.

The major *benefit* of a moving average is the opportunity it affords a manager to focus more clearly on the long-term trend (and cyclical) movements in a time series, without the obscuring effect of short-term 'noise' influences.

Method 2: Trendline Using Regression Analysis

A trendline isolates the *trend* (T) component only. It shows the general direction (upward, downward, constant) in which the series is moving. It is therefore best represented by a *straight line*.

The *method of least squares* from regression analysis (see Chapter 12) is used to find the trendline of best fit to a time series of numeric data.

The dependent variable, y, is the actual time series (e.g. sales, breakdowns, absentees) and the independent variable, x, is *time*. To use time as an independent variable in regression analysis, it must be numerically coded. Any *sequential numbering* system can be used, but the most common choice of coding is the set of *natural numbers* ($x = 1; 2; 3; 4; 5; ... n$, where n = number of time periods in the time series). Each time period (x) of the time series (y) is sequentially assigned an integer value beginning with 1 for the first time period, 2 for the second, 3 for the third, etc. The calculation of the trendline using regression is illustrated in the following example.

Example 15.5 Valley Estates Quarterly House Sales – Trend Analysis Study

The number of houses sold quarterly by Valley Estates in the Cape Peninsula is recorded for the 16 quarters from 2008 to 2011, as shown in Table 15.7.
(See Excel file C15.4 – *house sales*.)

Table 15.7 Quarterly house sales by Valley Estates (2008–2011)

Quarter	2008	2009	2010	2011
Q1	54	55	49	60
Q2	58	61	55	64
Q3	94	87	95	99
Q4	70	66	74	80

The sales director has requested a *trend analysis* of this sales data to determine the general direction (trend) of future quarterly housing sales, and an *estimate* of house sales for the first quarter of 2012.

Management Questions

1   Construct the trendline for the quarterly house sales data (2008–2011) for Valley Estates.
2   Use the regression trendline to *estimate* the level of house sales for the first quarter of 2012.

Solution

1   Calculate the trendline equation using the sequential numbering system, $x = 1, 2, 3, ...$

Table 15.8 shows the intermediate calculations for the trendline coefficients, b_0 and b_1, using the least squares regression formulae from Chapter 12 (Formula 12.2 for b_1 and Formula 12.3 for b_0).

Table 15.8 Intermediate calculations for trendline coefficients – house sales

Period ($n = 16$)	House sales (y)	Time (x)	x^2	xy
2008 Q1	54	1	1	54
Q2	58	2	4	116
Q3	94	3	9	282
Q4	70	4	16	280
2009 Q1	55	5	25	275
Q2	61	6	36	366
Q3	87	7	49	609
Q4	66	8	64	528
2010 Q1	49	9	81	441
Q2	55	10	100	550
Q3	95	11	121	1 045
Q4	74	12	144	888
2011 Q1	60	13	169	780
Q2	64	14	196	896
Q3	99	15	225	1 485
Q4	80	16	256	1 280
Totals	**1 121**	**136**	**1 496**	**9 875**

The regression slope (or gradient), b_1:

$$b_1 = \frac{16(9\ 875) - (136)(1\ 121)}{16(1\ 496) - (136)^2} = \frac{5\ 544}{5\ 440} = 1.019 \qquad \text{(using Formula 12.2)}$$

The y-intercept, b_0:

$$b_0 = \frac{1\ 121 - 1.019(136)}{16} = \frac{982.416}{16} = 61.4 \qquad \text{(using Formula 12.3)}$$

The regression trendline (T) is now defined by the following straight-line equation:

$$T = 61.4 + 1.019x$$

Where: $x = 1$ in 2008 Q1; 2 in 2008 Q2; 3 in 2008 Q3; etc.

2 Estimate trend value for the 2012 quarter 1.

To estimate the trend value of house sales for quarter 1 of 2012, the value of x that would correspond to 2012 quarter 1 is $x = 17$. Substitute $x = 17$ into the trendline equation as follows.

Trend $y = 61.4 + 1.019(17) = 61.4 + 17.32 = 78.72$ (rounded to 79).

Thus, the sales director of Valley Estates can be advised that the estimated trend value of house sales in quarter 1, 2012 is likely to be 79.

Note: The numerical coding scheme used to code x must always be shown together with the trendline, otherwise the trendline coefficients are meaningless. They are determined by the choice of x-values. It also assists in determining the appropriate values of x to substitute into the trendline when trend projections are performed.

Interpretation of the Trendline

- The regression trendline is 'free' of cyclical, seasonal and irregular influences. The 'other' influences have been removed by trend analysis, leaving only the long-term trend influence.
- The 'strength' of the trend influence (i.e. growth/decline) can be gauged by the magnitude of the slope coefficient, b_1. A strong (upward/downward) trend is shown by a large positive/negative value of b_1, while values of b_1 close to zero indicate no strong upward/downward pressure on the values of the time series due to trend forces.

15.5 Seasonal Analysis

Seasonal analysis isolates the influence of seasonal forces on a time series.

The **ratio-to-moving-average method** is used to measure and quantify these seasonal influences. This method expresses the seasonal influence as an *index number*. It measures the percentage deviation of the actual values of the time series, y, from a base value that excludes the short-term seasonal influences. These base values of a time series represent the trend/cyclical influences only.

Ratio-to-Moving-Average Method

Step 1: Identify the trend/cyclical movement

The *moving average* approach, as described earlier, is used to isolate the combined trend/cyclical components in a time series.

The choice of an appropriate moving average term, k, is determined by the number of periods that span the short-term seasonal fluctuations. In most instances, the term k corresponds to the number of observations that span a *one-year* period.

Figure 15.7 identifies the appropriate term to use to remove short-term seasonal fluctuations in time series data that occur annually.

Time interval	Appropriate term (k)
Weekly	52-period term
Monthly	12-period term
Bi-monthly	6-period term
Quarterly	4-period term
Four-monthly	3-period term
Half-yearly	2-period term

Figure 15.7 Choice of moving average term, k, to remove seasonal fluctuations

The resultant smoothed moving average series that reflects the combined trend and cyclical influences represents a *base measure* of the time series.

To illustrate, if quarterly data is given, a four-period moving average will isolate the trend/cyclical movements in the time series and produce a base set of time series values. The steps are:

- finding the *uncentred* four-period *moving total* series
- finding the *centred* 2 × four-period *moving total* series

- dividing the centred 2 × four-period moving total series by 8 to give the *centred* four-period *moving average*.

Step 2: Find the seasonal ratios

A seasonal ratio for each period is found by dividing each actual time series value, y, by its corresponding moving average value (its base value).

$$\text{Seasonal ratio} = \frac{\text{Actual } y}{\text{Moving average } y} \times 100$$

$$= \frac{T \times C \times S \times I}{T \times C} = S \times I \times 100$$

15.3

A **seasonal ratio** is an *index* that measures the percentage deviation of each actual y (which includes seasonal influences) from its moving average (base) value (which represents trend and cyclical influences only).

This deviation from the base level (which is the trend/cyclical influence, with index of 100) is a measure of the seasonal impact, and to a lesser extent, irregular forces, on the time series for each time period. (The interpretation of a seasonal ratio is similar to that of a price relative, as discussed in Chapter 14.)

Step 3: Produce the median seasonal indexes

Average the *seasonal ratios* across *corresponding periods* within the years to smooth out the irregular component inherent in the seasonal ratios.

Generally, the *median* is used to find the average of seasonal ratios for corresponding periods within the years. The arithmetic mean is not used as it could be influenced by the presence of any outlier seasonal ratios, resulting in unrepresentative seasonal indexes.

Step 4: Calculate the adjusted seasonal indexes

Each seasonal index has a base index of 100. Therefore, the sum of the k median seasonal indexes must equal $100 \times k$. If this is not the case, each median seasonal index must be adjusted to a base of 100. The *adjustment factor* is determined as follows:

15.4

$$\text{Adjustment factor} = \frac{k \times 100}{\sum (\text{Median seasonal indexes})}$$

Each median seasonal index is multiplied by the adjustment factor to ensure a base of 100 for each index. These *adjusted seasonal indexes* are a (average) *measure of the seasonal influences* on the actual values of the time series for each given time period within a year.

Example 15.6 Valley Estates Quarterly House Sales Study

Refer to the quarterly house sales data in Table 15.7 (reproduced in Table 15.9). The sales director of Valley Estates would like to identify the impact of quarterly seasonal influences on house sales.

Table 15.9 Quarterly house sales by Valley Estates (2008–2011)

Quarter	2008	2009	2010	2011
Q1	54	55	49	60
Q2	58	61	55	64
Q3	94	87	95	99
Q4	70	66	74	80

Management Question

Calculate the quarterly *seasonal indexes* for the house sales data and interpret the results for the sales director of Valley Estates.

Solution

The four-step process to calculate the seasonal indexes is shown in Table 15.10 (steps 1 and 2), Table 15.11 (Step 3) and Table 15.12 (Step 4) respectively. Since the time series data given (house sales) is *quarterly*, a four-period term ($k = 4$) is chosen to smooth out short-term seasonal and irregular variations (since four periods span a year).

Table 15.10 Valley Estates house sales study – calculation of seasonal ratios (steps 1 and 2)

Period		House sales (y)	Uncentred four-quarter moving total	Centred (2 × 4) quarter moving total	Four-quarter moving average	Seasonal ratios
2008	Q1	54		—	—	—
	Q2	58		—	—	—
			276			
	Q3	94		553	69.125	135.99
			277			
	Q4	70		557	69.625	100.54
			280			
2009	Q1	55		553	69.125	79.57
			273			
	Q2	61		542	67.750	90.04
			269			
	Q3	87		532	66.500	130.83
			263			
	Q4	66		520	65.000	101.54
			257			
2010	Q1	49		522	65.250	75.10
			265			
	Q2	55		538	67.250	81.78
			273			
	Q3	95		557	69.625	136.45
			284			
	Q4	74		577	72.125	102.60
			293			
2011	Q1	60		590	73.750	81.36
			297			
	Q2	64		600	75.000	85.33
			303			
	Q3	99		—	—	—
	Q4	80		—	—	—

Table 15.11 shows the averaging of the seasonal ratios (Step 3) using the *median* as a central location measure to derive the median seasonal indexes for each quarter.

Table 15.11 Valley Estate house sales – median seasonal indexes (Step 3)

Year	Quarter 1	Quarter 2	Quarter 3	Quarter 4	Total
2008	—	—	135.99	100.54	
2009	79.57	90.04	130.83	101.54	
2010	75.10	81.78	136.45	102.60	
2011	81.36	85.33	—	—	
Median seasonal index	**79.57**	**85.33**	**135.99**	**101.54**	**402.43**

These median seasonal indexes are also called *unadjusted seasonal indexes*.

Finally, Table 15.12 adjusts each median seasonal index to a base of 100 (Step 4).

Table 15.12 Valley Estate house sales – adjusted seasonal indexes (Step 4)

Adjustment factor $= \dfrac{400}{402.43} = 0.994$

Period	Median seasonal index	Adjustment factor	Adjusted seasonal index
Quarter 1	79.57	0.994	**79.1**
Quarter 2	85.33	0.994	**84.8**
Quarter 3	135.99	0.994	**135.2**
Quarter 4	101.54	0.994	**100.9**
Total	**402.43**		**400**

Management Interpretation

Each (adjusted) seasonal index measures the average magnitude of the seasonal influence on the actual values of the time series for a given period within the year. By subtracting the base index of 100 (which represents the trend/cyclical component) from each seasonal index, the extent of the influence of seasonal forces can be gauged. For Example 15.6, the following interpretation applies:

- In quarter 1 of each year, the seasonal index of 79.1 means that, on average, Valley Estates house sales are depressed by the presence of seasonal forces by approximately 21%. Alternatively stated, house sales would be about 26% *higher* ($\frac{21}{79} \times 100$) had seasonal influences not been present.
- Quarter 2's interpretation is similar to that of quarter 1, since the seasonal index is also below 100, namely 84.8.
- In quarter 3 of each year, the seasonal index of 135.2 means that, on average, Valley Estates house sales are stimulated by the presence of seasonal forces to the extent of approximately 35%. Alternatively stated, house sales would be about 35% *lower* had seasonal influences not been present.
- In quarter 4 of each year, seasonal influence is negligible, as the seasonal index of 100.9 is almost equal to its base index of 100, which contains only trend and cyclical measurements. Seasonal influences account for less than 1% of Valley Estates' house sales, y, on average, in quarter 4.

15.6 Uses of Time Series Indicators

Time series indicators are important planning aids to managers in two ways. They can be used:

1 to *de-seasonalise* a time series (i.e. removal of seasonal influences), and so provide a clearer vision of the longer-term trend/cyclical movements emerges
2 to produce *seasonally adjusted trend projections* of future values of a time series.

De-seasonalising Time Series Values

The removal of seasonal influences, which represent short-term fluctuations in a time series, results in a smoother time series that makes it easier to identify long-term trend/cyclical movements. Seasonal influences are removed from a time series by *dividing the actual y-value for each period by its corresponding seasonal index*.

$$\text{De-seasonalised } y = \frac{\text{Actual } y}{\text{Seasonal index}} \times 100 \qquad\qquad \textbf{15.5}$$

These *de-seasonalised* y-values, which will be measured in the same physical units as the actual y-values, reflect the collective influence of the *trend* and *cyclical* (and to a lesser extent, irregular) *forces only*.

Interpretation of De-seasonalised Time Series Values

The values of a de-seasonalised time series show a time series without the influence of (short-term) seasonal forces, allowing attention to be focused on the long-term trend/cyclical movements of the time series.

- If the seasonal index was *less than* 100 (showing that seasonal forces dampen (or reduce) the level of activity of the time series), the de-seasonalised y-values will be *inflated* (*higher*) when seasonal influences are removed.
- Conversely, if the seasonal index was *more than* 100 (showing that seasonal forces stimulated [or raised] the level of activity of the time series), the de-seasonalised y-values will be *depressed* (*lower*) when seasonal influences are removed.

Example 15.7 De-seasonalised Valley Estates Quarterly House Sales Study

Refer to the house sales time series data shown in Table 15.9. The sales director of Valley Estates would like to observe the *general direction* of house sales without the effect of short-term seasonal influences.

Management Question

Derive a *de-seasonalised time series* of the quarterly house sales for the sales director of Valley Estates for the period 2008 to 2011. Use the seasonal indexes from Table 15.12.

Solution

Table 15.13 shows the de-seasonalised house sales, while Figure 15.8 shows the plot of the two line graphs (*actual house sales* versus *de-seasonalised house sales*).

Table 15.13 De-seasonalised house sales for Valley Estates and plots

Period		House sales	Seasonal index	De-seasonalised house sales
2008	Q1	54	79.1	68.3
	Q2	58	84.8	68.4
	Q3	94	135.2	69.5
	Q4	70	100.9	69.4
2009	Q1	55	79.1	69.5
	Q2	61	84.8	71.9
	Q3	87	135.2	64.3
	Q4	66	100.9	65.4
2010	Q1	49	79.1	61.9
	Q2	55	84.8	64.9
	Q3	95	135.2	70.3
	Q4	74	100.9	73.3
2011	Q1	60	79.1	75.9
	Q2	64	84.8	75.5
	Q3	99	135.2	73.2
	Q4	80	100.9	79.3

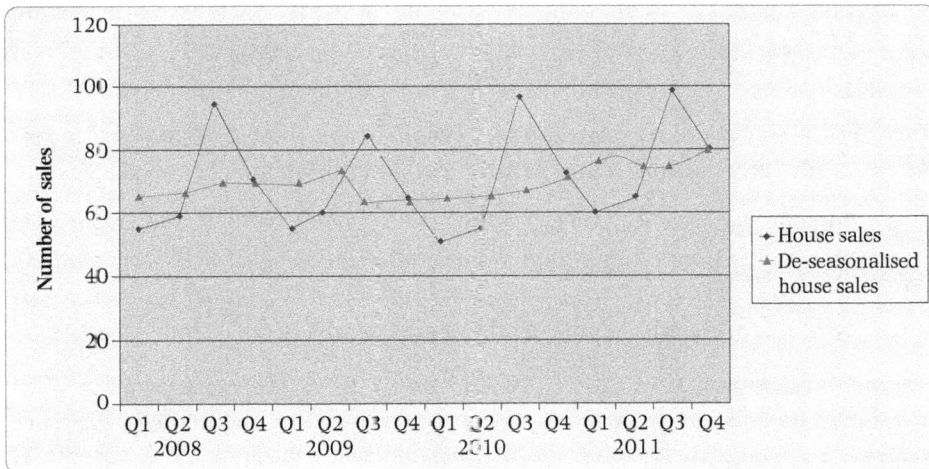

Figure 15.8 Line plots of actual versus de-seasonalised quarterly house sales

Management Interpretation

Quarter 1 2008 house sales, for example, would have been higher at 68 units instead of the actual sales of 54 units had seasonal influences not been present. Similarly, house sales for quarter 3 2009, would have been lower at 64 units instead of the actual sales of 87 units had seasonal influences not been present.

In addition, the *de-seasonalised* quarterly house sales *line graph* for Valley Estates shows a very modest growth over the past four years.

Constructing Seasonally Adjusted Trend Projections

Since the actual time series values are assumed to be a function of trend, cyclical, seasonal and irregular movements (i.e. actual y = T × C × S × I), these components, if known or estimated, can be used to reconstruct values of the actual time series.

However, since only the *trend* and *seasonal* influences have been quantified through time series analysis, only these two influences are used to estimate future values of the actual time series, y.

Step 1: Estimate the trend value of the time series (T)

Estimates of the trend value (T) over the forecasting period are found by substituting the appropriate x-value of the numerically coded time variable into the regression-derived trendline equation. The x-values of the future time periods are found by continuing the sequence of x-values.

Step 2: Incorporate the seasonal influence (S)

The seasonal influence can be built into the trend value by *multiplying* the trend value (found in Step 1) by the seasonal index for the appropriate time period. This is known as *seasonalising the trend value*.

Example 15.8 Valley Estates Quarterly House Sales Forecasts for 2011 Study

Estimate the seasonally adjusted trend value of house sales for Valley Estates for quarters 1, 2, 3 and 4 of 2012. Use the trendline equation and seasonal indexes from examples 15.5 and 15.6.

Solution

Table 15.14 shows the construction of forecasts using trend and seasonal measures derived from time series analysis. The following two-step approach is used:

Step 1: Identify the trend values (T)

From Example 15.5, the straight-line trend equation is given as:

$$T = 61.4 + 1.019x$$

Where: x = 1 in 2008 Q1; 2 in 2008 Q2; 3 in 2008 Q3; etc.

For the forecast periods of Q1, Q2, Q3 and Q4 of 2012, the corresponding x-values are shown in Table 15.14, which are found by continuing the numeric sequence of x-values to span the forecast periods. For each forecast quarter of 2012, substitute the appropriate x-value into the trendline equation as seen in Table 15.14 to produce the *trend estimate* of house sales.

Table 15.14 Seasonally adjusted 2012 trend estimates for house sales

Period	Time (x)	Trend equation $T = b_0 + b_1 x$	Trend estimate (T)	Seasonal index	Seasonally adjusted trend estimates
2012 Q1	17	61.4 + 1.019(17)	78.7	79.1	62.3
Q2	18	61.4 + 1.019(18)	79.7	84.8	67.6
Q3	19	61.4 + 1.019(19)	80.8	135.2	109.2
Q4	20	61.4 + 1.019(20)	81.8	100.9	82.5

The resultant values (e.g. 81.8 [or rounded to 82] for quarter 4 2012) are the expected house sales in the Cape Peninsula by Valley Estates in each quarter of 2012, based on *trend estimates* alone.

Step 2: Seasonalise the trend values (i.e. incorporate the seasonal indexes)
Using the seasonal indexes derived in Table 15.12, the *trendline estimates* for each quarter of 2012 are *multiplied* by their respective *quarterly seasonal indexes* to include seasonal influences in the forecasted values. These values are referred to as *seasonally adjusted trend estimates*, as shown in the last column of Table 15.14.

Management Interpretation

Valley Estates can expect to sell 62 houses in quarter 1, 68 houses in quarter 2, 109 houses in quarter 3, and 83 houses in quarter 4 of 2012 respectively.

Cautionary Notes

These statistical forecasts do not include a cyclical or an irregular component. It is assumed that these forces exert a minimal influence on the actual values of the time series. The validity of this forecasting process depends on the extent to which this assumption holds true. If trend and seasonal forces do account for the majority of the final actual time series values, these statistical forecasts could be of great benefit in practice.

Also, the usefulness and validity of these time series forecasts depend upon the continuation of the historical environmental patterns on which the trend and seasonal indicators are based over the forecasting period. If environmental patterns are reasonably stable, which may be a reasonable assumption in the short-to-medium future, the forecast values can be considered reliable, and vice versa. Hence, time series forecasting is of more value for short- to medium-term forecasting as the short- to medium-term future is likely to exhibit similar patterns to the immediate past. The long-term future is less predictable (in terms of environmental forces). Long-term time series forecasting is thus of less value as there is greater uncertainty that historical patterns will continue into the long-term future.

15.7 Using Excel (2016) for Time Series Analysis

Excel can be used in the analysis of time series data. It can:

- produce the *trendline graph* of time series data using the **Insert > Chart > Line** option, as illustrated in Chapter 2
- construct and superimpose the *regression trendline equation* on the line graph, as illustrated in Chapter 12.

Excel does not offer an option to compute either the moving averages or the seasonal indexes using the ratio-to-moving-average method.

15.8 Summary

This chapter considered an approach to analyse time series data as opposed to cross-sectional data. The analysis and harnessing of time series data is useful for short- to medium-term forecasting. This chapter identified and described the nature of each of four possible influences on the values of a time series, y. These forces were identified as trend, cyclical, seasonal and irregular influences. Time series analysis is used to decompose a time series into these four constituent components, using a multiplicative model. Only the trend and seasonal components were examined in this chapter.

Trend analysis can be performed using either the method of moving averages, or by fitting a straight line using the method of least squares from regression analysis. The natural numbering method for coding the time variable x is the common and preferred coding scheme.

The seasonal component is described by finding seasonal indexes using the ratio-to-moving-average approach. The interpretation of these seasonal indexes was also given in the chapter.

Two applications of trend analysis and seasonal indexes which managers might find useful were described. Firstly, it was shown how to de-seasonalise a time series using seasonal indexes to obtain a clearer vision of the trend of a time series variable such as sales. Finally, the use of time series analysis to prepare short- to medium-term forecasts was illustrated using trendline estimates modified by seasonal indexes.

Exercises

1   Explain the difference between cross-sectional and time series data.
2   Give two practical examples of time series data.
3   What type of graph is used to plot time series data?
4   Name the components of a time series. Which component shows the most regularity?
5   What is the purpose of the moving average method in trend analysis?
6   Is a five-period moving average graph smoother than a three-period moving average graph? Why?
7   If a seasonal index has a value of 108, what does this mean?
8   If a seasonal index has a value of 88, what does this mean?
9   X15.9 – coal tonnage
    The following table represents the annual tonnage (in 100 000s) of coal mined in the Limpopo province over 16 consecutive years.

Year	Tonnage	Year	Tonnage	Year	Tonnage	Year	Tonnage
1	118	5	132	9	160	13	191
2	124	6	115	10	188	14	178
3	108	7	122	11	201	15	146
4	120	8	148	12	174	16	161

   (a)   Calculate the four-yearly moving average of coal tonnage mined.
   (b)   Calculate the five-yearly moving average of coal tonnage mined.
   (c)   Manually plot both the four-yearly and five-yearly moving averages together with the original data, on the same graph.
   (d)   Use Excel's **Insert > Chart > Line** option to produce the plots in (c).
   (e)   Describe the pattern of the three line plots.

10 X15.10 – franchise dealers
    The number of new franchise dealers recorded over 10 periods by the Franchise Association of South Africa is shown below.

Period	1	2	3	4	5	6	7	8	9	10
New dealers	28	32	43	31	38	47	40	45	55	42

   (a)   Draw a time series graph to represent this data.
   (b)   Calculate the trendline $\hat{y} = b_0 + b_1 x$.
   (c)   Calculate trend estimates of the number of new franchise dealers in periods 11, 12 and 13.

11 X15.11 – policy claims
    The number of claims per quarter on household policies submitted to the George branch of an insurance company is as follows:

Year	Q1	Q2	Q3	Q4
2008	84	53	60	75
2009	81	57	51	73
2010	69	37	40	77
2011	73	46	39	63

(a) Plot the time series of household policy claims on a line graph.
(b) Isolate the trend effect by calculating a least squares trendline. Describe the trend in claims.
(c) Calculate the quarterly seasonal indexes for household policy claims. Interpret the seasonal impact.
(d) Calculate the seasonally adjusted trend estimate of the number of claims on household policies for the first and second quarters of 2012.

12   X15.12 – hotel occupancy
A hotel's monthly occupancy rate (measured as a percentage of rooms available) is reported as follows for a 10-month period:

Months	Sep	Oct	Nov	Dec	Jan	Feb	Mar	Apr	May	Jun
Occupancy (%)	74	82	70	90	88	74	64	69	58	65

(a) Produce a line graph of the hotel's occupancy rate per month.
(b) Fit a least squares trendline to the hotel occupancy rate data.
(c) What is the trend estimate of the hotel's occupancy rate for July and August? Comment on your findings.

13   X15.13 – electricity demand
Consider the following quarterly demand levels for electricity (in 1 000 megawatts) in Cape Town from 2008 to 2011.

Months	2008	2009	2010	2011
Jan–Mar	21	35	39	78
Apr–Jun	42	54	82	114
Jul–Sep	60	91	136	160
Oct–Dec	12	14	28	40

(a) Plot the time series of quarterly electricity demand graphically.
(b) Find the least squares trendline for quarterly electricity demand in Cape Town.
(c) Find the seasonal index for each quarter.
(d) Estimate the seasonally adjusted trend values of quarterly electricity demand for quarters 3 and 4 of 2012.

Excel tasks
(e) Use the **Insert > Chart** tab (line with markers) to plot the time series data in (a).
(f) Use the **Add Trendline** option (by right clicking on any data value in the line graph) to compute the least squares trendline for electricity demand in (b).

14   X15.14 – hotel turnover

The seasonal indexes and actual quarterly turnover (in R million) for 2008, 2009 and 2010 in the hotel industry in Cape Town are as follows:

Season	Seasonal index	2008	2009	2010
Summer	136	568	604	662
Autumn	112	495	544	605
Winter	62	252	270	310
Spring	90	315	510	535

(a)   De-seasonalise the hotel industry turnover data for 2008 to 2010.
(b)   Plot both the original and the de-seasonalised quarterly turnover data for the Cape Town hotel industry from 2008 to 2010 on the same axis.
(c)   Calculate a trendline equation for the quarterly turnover.
(d)   Estimate the seasonally adjusted turnover in the Cape Town hotel industry for the summer and autumn seasons in 2011.
(e)   Repeat (b) above using the **Insert > Chart > Line** option in Excel.
(f)   Recompute the trendline equation in (c) using Excel's **Add Trendline** option.

15   X15.15 – farming equipment

The marketing manager of a company that manufactures and distributes farming equipment (such as combine harvesters, ploughs and tractors) recorded the number of farming units sold quarterly for the period 2008 to 2011.

Quarter	2008	2009	2010	2011
Summer	57	60	65	64
Autumn	51	56	60	62
Winter	50	53	58	58
Spring	56	61	68	70

(a)   Find the quarterly seasonal indexes for farming equipment sold.
(b)   Do seasonal forces significantly influence the sale of farming equipment? Comment.
(c)   Calculate the least squares trendline for the sales of farming equipment.
(d)   Prepare seasonally adjusted trend estimates of the number of farming units that this company can expect to sell in each quarter of 2012.
(e)   Use Excel to prepare the quarterly seasonal indexes and derive the seasonally adjusted trend estimates as required in (d).

16   X15.16 – energy costs

The management of an office complex in central Johannesburg wants to understand the pattern of energy consumption (i.e. energy costs related to heating and air-conditioning) in the complex. They have assembled quarterly data on energy costs for the past three years (in R100 000s).

Year	Quarter			
	Summer	Autumn	Winter	Spring
2009	2.4	3.8	4.0	3.1
2010	2.6	4.1	4.1	3.2
2011	2.6	4.5	4.3	3.3

(a) Plot the pattern of energy costs graphically.

(b) Calculate seasonal indexes for the complex's energy costs by the ratio-to-moving-average method.

(c) Find the least squares trendline for energy usage in this office complex.

(d) How much should the financial manager of this office complex budget for energy costs for each quarter of 2012, based on seasonally adjusted trend estimates?

(e) Plot the pattern of energy costs graphically using Excel's **Insert > Chart > Line**.

(f) Recompute the least squares trendline for energy usage in (b) using the **Line graph** and **Add Trendline** option in Excel.

17 X15.17 – business registrations

The number of *new business registrations* in the Gauteng region was recorded by the Department of Trade and Industries for the period 2007 to 2011.

Year	Quarter			
	1	2	3	4
2007	1 005	1 222	1 298	1 199
2008	1 173	1 371	1 456	1 376
2009	1 314	1 531	1 605	1 530
2010	1 459	1 671	1 762	1 677
2011	1 604	1 837	1 916	1 819

Use Excel to perform the following calculations:

(a) Plot the number of new business registrations in the Gauteng region for the period 2007 to 2011.

(b) Calculate a four-period centred moving average and plot it on the same axis.

(c) Calculate quarterly seasonal indexes for new business registrations in the Gauteng region using the ratio-to-moving-average method.

(d) Are new business registrations significantly influenced by seasonal forces? Comment.

(e) Calculate the least squares trendline.

(f) Calculate the seasonally adjusted trend estimates of the number of new business registrations in the Gauteng region for the historical data (i.e. from 2007 quarter 1 to 2011 quarter 4).

(g) Plot the actual time series and the seasonally adjusted trend estimates from (f) on the same axis. How close are the two sets of time series data?

(h) Estimate the number of new business registrations in the Gauteng region for each quarter of 2012.

18 X15.18 – engineering sales
An engineering company estimates its next year's sales will be R48 million.
If the company's sales follow the seasonal pattern of sales in the engineering
industry (as shown in the table below), derive the sales forecast for this company for
each quarter of next year.

Quarter	1	2	3	4
Seasonal index	95	115	110	80

Note: Assume that trend and cyclical influences are negligible during the year.

19 X15.19 – Table Mountain
The Table Mountain Cable Car Company recorded the following data on the
number of tourists (in thousands) who visited Table Mountain, Cape Town, in
each quarter of 2009 and 2010:

Season	Seasonal index	2009	2010
Winter	62	18.1	22.4
Spring	89	26.4	33.2
Summer	162	41.2	44.8
Autumn	87	31.6	32.5

(a) Plot the quarterly number of tourists to Table Mountain for 2009 and 2010.
(b) Calculate the de-seasonalised values for each quarter and plot on the same axis.
     Comment on the trend in the number of tourists visiting Table Mountain.
(c) If the projected total number of tourists to visit Table Mountain in 2011 is 150
     (in thousands), how many visitors can the Cable Car Company expect to carry
     in each quarter of 2011?

20 X15.20 – gross domestic product
The following table gives the gross domestic product (GDP) in R100 millions
for a certain African country from 2001 to 2011.

Year	2001	2002	2003	2004	2005	2006	2007	2008	2009	2010	2011
GDP	45	47	61	64	72	74	84	81	93	90	98

(a) Plot the GDP time series graphically.
(b) Calculate the least squares trendline for GDP.
(c) Use this equation to predict the country's GDP for 2012 and 2013.

21 X15.21 – pelagic fish
The Department of Marine Resources reports the number of tonnes of pelagic fish
caught off the west coast during each four-month period over four years as follows:

Period	2007	2008	2009	2010
Jan–Apr	44	45	38	40
May–Aug	36	42	32	31
Sep–Dec	34	34	27	28

(a) Calculate the three-period moving average trend of pelagic fish caught off the west coast.

(b) Plot the actual catches of pelagic fish and the moving average trend on the same graph. Comment on the pattern of pelagic fish catches over the past four years.

(c) Calculate the seasonal indexes for each of the four-month periods. Give an interpretation of each seasonal index.

(d) Find the least squares trendline for pelagic fish caught off the west coast for the past four years.

(e) Estimate the seasonally adjusted expected number of tonnes of pelagic fish to be caught off the west coast for each four-month period of 2011.

22 X15.22 – share price

A share trader has a policy of selling a share if its share price drops more than one-third of its purchase price. In January, the investor bought shares in Netron (an electronics company) for 90c per share. The table below shows the price of the Netron share at the end of each month.

   If the trend in the under-performance of the Netron share price continues, identify, using the least square trendline method, when the investor is likely to sell his holdings in Netron shares.

Month	Jan	Feb	Mar	Apr	May	Jun	Jul
Share price (c)	90	82	78	80	74	76	70

23 X15.23 – Addo National Park

The following table reports both the seasonal indexes for all national park visitors and the number of visitors to the Addo National Park, near Port Elizabeth, on a quarterly basis (in 1 000s) for 2008, 2009 and 2010.

Season	Seasonal indexes	2008	2009	2010
Summer	112	196	199	214
Autumn	94	147	152	163
Winter	88	124	132	145
Spring	106	177	190	198

Assume that the seasonal pattern of visitors to the Addo National Park follows the national profile of visitors to all national parks.

(a) Remove the influence of seasonal factors on the number of visitors to the Addo National Park for each of the periods from 2008 to 2010.

(b) Plot both the original data series and the de-seasonalised data series of the number of visitors to the Addo National Park over the three-year period on the same axis.

(c) Is any significant trend evident from the de-seasonalised data? Comment.

(d) Use Excel's **Line with Marker** option in the **Insert > Chart** tab to plot the data in (b).

24 X15.24 – healthcare claims

The following table represents the quarterly value of healthcare claims (in R million) against all medical health schemes for the period 2007 to 2010.

Year	Quarter 1	Quarter 2	Quarter 3	Quarter 4
2007	11.8	13.2	19.1	16.4
2008	10.9	12.4	22.4	17.8
2009	12.2	16.2	24.1	14.6
2010	12.8	14.5	20.8	16.1

(a) Calculate quarterly seasonal indexes for healthcare claims using the ratio-to-moving-average method.
(b) Derive a trendline using the method of least squares.
(c) Estimate the seasonally adjusted trend value of healthcare claims for each quarter of 2011.
(d) Use Excel's **Line with Marker** option from the **Insert > Chart** tab to plot the actual healthcare claims values and the seasonally adjusted trend estimates of healthcare claims values.

25 X15.25 – financial advertising

The level of advertising expenditure in the financial services sector (i.e. banks, insurance, investments) to promote products and services has steadily increased in recent years. The annual expenditure levels (in R10 millions) for the financial services sector from 2005 to 2011 are shown in the following table.

Year	2005	2006	2007	2008	2009	2010	2011
Expenditure	9.6	11.8	12.0	13.6	14.1	15.0	17.8

(a) Use the least squares regression to calculate the trendline equation for advertising expenditure in the financial services sector.
(b) Predict the level of advertising expenditure for the sector for 2012.
(c) Use Excel to plot a line graph of advertising expenditure in the financial services sector from 2005 to 2011.
(d) Use the **Add Trendline** option in Excel to compute the trendline equation for annual advertising expenditure levels in the financial services sector.
(e) Use Excel's **Trendline** equation to estimate advertising expenditure levels from 2005 to 2011 and show these estimates on the same graph as the plot of the original series in (c).

26 X15.26 – policy surrenders

An insurance company reported the number of policyholders who applied to surrender their endowment policies for each quarter from 2008 to 2010. The insurance company has been communicating with its policyholders over the past three years to discourage them from surrendering their policy prior to maturity because of the reduced payout on early surrender.

Year	Q1	Q2	Q3	Q4
2008	212	186	192	205
2009	186	165	169	182
2010	169	158	162	178

Note: Q1 = Jan–Mar; Q2 = Apr–Jun; Q3 = Jul–Sep; Q4 = Oct–Dec.

(a) Plot the pattern of surrendered policies from 2008 to 2010. Does the company's communication with policyholders appear to be working? Comment.

(b) Calculate the quarterly seasonal indexes using the ratio-to-moving-average method. Comment on the seasonal pattern of policy surrenders.

(c) Derive the least squares trendline for the number of surrendered policies per quarter for the period 2008 to 2010.

(d) Estimate the number of endowment policies that are likely to be surrendered by policyholders during each of the quarters of 2011, using the seasonal indexes and trend equation calculated in (b) and (c).

27 X15.27 – company liquidations

The Economic Statistics Bureau has recorded the number of company liquidations over 27 time periods as follows:

Period	Liquidations	Period	Liquidations	Period	Liquidations
1	246	10	273	19	234
2	243	11	284	20	162
3	269	12	305	21	240
4	357	13	293	22	298
5	163	14	348	23	264
6	154	15	423	24	253
7	109	16	291	25	293
8	162	17	320	26	302
9	222	18	253	27	188

(a) Use Excel to compute both a three-period and a five-period moving average time series of company liquidations.

(b) Plot the original time series of company liquidations and the three-period and five-period moving average values on the same graph. Use Excel's **Line** graph option in the **Insert > Chart** tab.

(c) Comment on the pattern of company liquidations over this time period.

28 X15.28 – passenger tyres

Hillstone SA manufactures and sells tyres to the passenger vehicle market in southern Africa. The quarterly sales (in 1 000s of units) are shown in the following table. The marketing department wishes to apply time series analysis to estimate future quarterly passenger vehicle tyre sales for 2012 and 2013.

Tyres sold per quarter							
Quarter	2005	2006	2007	2008	2009	2010	2011
Jan – Mar	64 876	68 746	78 788	77 659	84 563	91 556	102 923
Apr – June	58 987	66 573	71 237	76 452	81 243	85 058	96 456
July – Sept	54 621	60 927	68 098	73 456	74 878	77 035	
Oct – Dec	62 345	71 234	74 444	78 908	86 756	80 145	

(a) Use Excel to develop a time series model that Hillstone can use to prepare seasonally adjusted trend forecasts of passenger vehicle tyre sales on a quarterly basis.

(b) Prepare seasonally adjusted trend forecast estimates for 2012 and 2013 on a quarterly basis.

(c) What confidence could the Hillstone management have in the estimates produced? Comment briefly.

29 X15.29 – outpatient attendance

The Medical Officer of Health in charge of day clinics in the Butterworth district is planning for the expansion of the medical facilities at these clinics based on the growth in demand for the clinics' services

She therefore asked a statistical analyst to assist in preparing a forecast of future demand for the clinics' services based on the attendance at these clinics over the past six years. The Medical Officer was able to supply the analyst with quarterly attendance records for the period 2006 to 2011.

Outpatient visits to day clinics per quarter						
Quarters	2006	2007	2008	2009	2010	2011
Q1	12 767	14 198	14 641	14 075	12 412	17 417
Q2	16 389	19 868	20 204	21 259	21 824	20 568
Q3	19 105	20 899	21 078	20 967	22 150	24 310
Q4	15 780	18 304	16 077	16 183	17 979	23 118

(a) Use Excel to conduct a time series analysis (i.e. line plots, seasonal indexes and trendlines) of outpatient attendance at the Butterworth day clinics.

(b) Prepare seasonally adjusted quarterly forecasts of likely outpatient attendance for 2012 and the first half of 2013.

(c) Draft a brief report to the management of Medical Officer discussing your findings, especially (i) the trend in outpatient attendance, and (ii) the influence of seasonality on attendance (where quarter 1 is summer and quarter 3 is winter).

30   X15.30 – construction absenteeism

The construction industry in the Western Cape is very dependent upon reliable labour to ensure that it meets its project deadlines and avoids incurring late-delivery penalties. The Construction Federation undertook an analysis of the absenteeism levels amongst construction workers over the past six years. The number of person-days lost (based on the number of workers absent), aggregated quarterly, is summarised in the table below.

Quarters	Person-days lost per quarter					
	2006	2007	2008	2009	2010	2011
Q1	933	967	892	815	822	785
Q2	865	936	845	715	856	715
Q3	922	931	907	779	762	740
Q4	864	902	801	711	722	704

(a)   Use Excel to conduct a time series analysis of absenteeism levels over the six-year period. Identify seasonal indexes and produce a trendline of absenteeism levels. Also construct a plot (using the **Insert > Chart** tab) of the actual time series and the seasonally adjusted trend estimates for the six years of historical data.

(b)   Prepare seasonally adjusted trend estimates of absenteeism levels for all quarters of 2012.

(c)   Present your findings in a brief management report.

Solutions
to Exercises

Chapter 1

1.1 It is a decision support tool. It generates evidence-based information through the analysis of data to inform management decision-making.

1.2 Descriptive statistics summarise (profile) sample data, inferential statistics generalise sample findings to a broader population.

1.3 Statistical modelling explores and quantifies relationships between variables for estimation or prediction purposes.

1.4 Data source; data-collection method; data type

1.5 Different statistical methods are valid for different data types.

1.6 Data relevancy; data cleaning; data enrichment

1.7 (a) Performance appraisal system used
    (b) All JSE companies
    (c) The 68 HR managers surveyed
    (d) A JSE-listed company
    (e) 46% is a sample statistic
    (f) Random sampling is necessary to allow valid inferences to be drawn based on the sample evidence.

1.8 (a) Women's magazine readership
    (b) All women's magazine readers
    (c) The 2 000 randomly selected women's magazine readers
    (d) A reader of a women's magazine
    (e) 35% ($\frac{700}{2000}$) is a sample statistic
    (f) Inferential statistics. Its purpose is to test the belief that market share is 38%.

1.9 (a) Three random variables: weekly sales volume; number of ads placed per week; advertising media used
    (b) Dependent variable: weekly sales volume
    (c) Independent variables: number of ads placed per week; advertising media used
    (d) Statistical model-building (predict sales volume from ads placed and media used)

1.10 Scenario 1 Inferential statistics
     Scenario 2 Descriptive statistics
     Scenario 3 Descriptive statistics
     Scenario 4 Inferential statistics
     Scenario 5 Inferential statistics
     Scenario 6 Inferential statistics
     Scenario 7 Inferential statistics

1.11 (a) numeric, ratio-scaled, continuous {21.4 years; 34.6 years}
     (b) numeric, ratio-scaled, continuous {416.2 m²; 3 406.8 m²}
     (c) categorical, ordinal-scaled, discrete {matric; diploma}
     (d) categorical, nominal-scaled, discrete {married; single}
     (e) categorical, nominal-scaled, discrete {Boeing; Airbus}
     (f) categorical, nominal-scaled, discrete {verbal; emotional}
     (g) numeric, ratio-scaled, discrete {41; 62}
     (h) categorical, ordinal-scaled, discrete {salary only; commission only}
     (i) (i) categorical, ordinal-scaled, discrete {1 = apple; 2 = orange}
         (ii) categorical, nominal-scaled, discrete {yes; no}
         (iii) categorical, nominal-scaled, discrete {train; bus}
         (iv) numeric, interval-scaled, discrete {2; 5}
     (j) numeric, ratio-scaled, continuous {12.4 kg; 7.234 kg}
     (k) categorical, nominal-scaled, discrete {Nescafé; Jacobs}
     (l) numeric, ratio-scaled, continuous {26.4 min; 38.66 min}
     (m) categorical, ordinal-scaled, discrete {super; standard}
     (n) numeric, ratio-scaled, continuous {R85.47; R2 315.22}
     (o) numeric, ratio-scaled, discrete {75; 23}
     (p) numeric, ratio-scaled, discrete {5; 38}
     (q) numeric, ratio-scaled, continuous {9.54 hours; 10.12 hours}
     (r) numeric, interval-scaled, discrete {2; 6}
     (s) numeric, ratio-scaled, discrete {75; 238}
     (t) categorical, nominal-scaled, discrete {growth funds; industrial funds}

1.12　(a)　11 random variables

(b)	Economic sector	categorical, nominal-scaled, discrete	{retail}
	Head office region	categorical, nominal-scaled, discrete	{Gauteng}
	Company size	numeric, ratio-scaled, discrete	{242}
	Turnover	numeric, ratio-scaled, continuous	{R3 432 562}
	Share price	numeric, ratio-scaled, continuous	{R18,48}
	Earnings per share	numeric, ratio-scaled, continuous	{R2,16}
	Dividends per share	numeric, ratio-scaled, continuous	{R0,86}
	Number of shares	numeric, ratio-scaled, discrete	{12 045 622}
	ROI (%)	numeric, ratio-scaled, continuous	{8,64%}
	Inflation index (%)	numeric, ratio-scaled, continuous	{6,75%}
	Year established	numeric, ratio-scaled, discrete	{1988}

1.13　(a)　20 random variables

(b)	Gender	categorical, nominal-scaled, discrete	{female}
	Home language	categorical, nominal-scaled, discrete	{Xhosa}
	Position	categorical, ordinal-scaled, discrete	{middle}
	Join	numeric, ratio-scaled, discrete	{1998}
	Status	categorical, ordinal-scaled, discrete	{gold}
	Claimed	categorical, nominal-scaled, discrete	{yes}
	Problems	categorical, nominal-scaled, discrete	{yes}
	Yes problem	categorical, nominal-scaled, discrete	{online access difficult}
	Services – airlines	numeric, interval-scaled, discrete	{2}
	Services – car rentals	numeric, interval-scaled, discrete	{5}
	Services – hotels	numeric, interval-scaled, discrete	{4}
	Services – financial	numeric, interval-scaled, discrete	{2}
	Services – telecommunications	numeric, interval-scaled, discrete	{2}
	Quality – statements	numeric, interval-scaled, discrete	{2}
	Quality – guide	numeric, interval-scaled, discrete	{4}
	Quality – centres	numeric, interval-scaled, discrete	{5}
	Quality – communication	numeric, interval-scaled, discrete	{2}
	Quality – queries	numeric, interval-scaled, discrete	{3}
	Quality – product	numeric, interval-scaled, discrete	{4}
	Facilities	categorical, ordinal-scaled, discrete	{1 = holiday specials}

1.14　Financial Analysis data: mainly numeric (quantitative), ratio-scaled.
Voyager Services Quality data: mainly categorical (qualitative), and when numeric, mainly interval-scaled, discrete (rating responses).

Chapter 2

2.1　A picture is worth a *thousand words*.
2.2　(a)　Bar (or pie) chart
　　(b)　Multiple (or stacked) bar chart
　　(c)　Histogram
　　(d)　Scatter plot
2.3　Cross-tabulation table (or joint frequency table; or two-way pivot table)

2.4　Bar chart: displays categorical data only; categories can be displayed in any order; width of category bars is arbitrary (but equal width).
Histogram: displays numeric data only; intervals must be continuous and sequential; bar widths determined by interval width.
2.5　Line graph

2.6 % pie chart: *True Love* (19%); *Seventeen* (29.2%); *Heat* (23.6%); *Drum* (11%); *You* (17.2%)

2.7 (a) % bar chart: same % as 2.6.

(b) *Heat* = 23.6%

2.8 (a) and (b) Grades: A – 14 (35%); B – 11 (27.5%); C – 6 (15%); D – 9 (22.5%)

(c) Grade D: 22.5% of all employees.

(d) Use Excel to construct % pie chart and % bar chart.

2.9 (a) and (b) ≤ 200 (4; 13.3%; 13.3%); 201 – ≤ 250 (8; 26.7%; 40%); 251 – ≤ 300 (9; 30%; 70%); 301 – ≤ 350 (6; 20%; 90); 351 – ≤ 400 (3; 10%; 100%)

(c) (i) 13.3% (ii) 70%
(iii) 10% (iv) 9 (30%) of buildings

2.10 (b) (i) Voëlvlei = 26%

(ii) Wemmershoek + Steenbras = 27.1%

2.11 (a) A (18%); B (10.4%); C (25.6%); D (15.2%); E (30.8%)

(b) Liqui-Fruit (A) = 18%

(c) Yum Yum (C) or Go Fruit (E) = 56.4%

2.12 (b) Toyota (19.4%); Nissan (12.6%); VW (17.6%); Delta (12.6%); Ford (14.8%); MBSA (7.5%); BMW (10.4%); MMI (5.1%)

(c) Top three manufacturers (by unit sales) = Toyota + VW + Ford = 51.8%

2.13 (b) Nissan, Volkswagen, MBSA, MMI

(c) Delta = 34.7% increase in unit sales from first half year to second half year.

2.14 (a) Daewoo – 20 (16%); LG – 38 (30.4%); Philips – 13 (10.4%); Sansui – 30 (24%); Sony – 24 (19.2%)

(c) Philips = 10.4%

(d) LG = 30.4%

2.15 (a) Houses sold: 3 (12) (25%); 4 (15) (31.3%); 5 (6) (12.5%); 6 (7) (14.6%); 7 (5) (10.4%); 8 (3) (6.3%)

(c) Modal number of houses sold = 4 (31.3%)

2.16 (a) Fast-food outlet preferences: KFC (17.2%); St Elmo's (17.8%); Steers (13.8%); Nando's (19.7%); Ocean Basket (7.4%); Butler's (24%)

(b) Food type preferences: Chicken (120) (36.9%); Pizza (136) (41.8%); Beef (45) (13.8%); Fish (24) (7.4%)

(c) Butler's most preferred fast-food outlet (24%); Ocean Basket least preferred (7.4%)
Pizza most preferred fast-food type (41.8%); fish least preferred fast-food type (7.4%)

2.17 (d) 42.9% of all travellers prefer SAA.

(e) Most tourists prefer to fly kulula (47.1% of all tourists prefer kulula).

(f) No, most business travellers prefer to fly SAA (55.6% of all business travellers).

2.18 (a) Random variable: Number of occupants per car
Data type: numeric, ratio, discrete

(b) Occupants: 1 (23) (38.3%); 2 (15) (25%); 3 (10) (16.7%); 4 (5) (8.3%); 5 (7) (11.7%)
Cumulative %: (1) 38.3%; (≤2) 63.3; (≤3) 80%; (≤4) 88.3%; (≤5) 100%

(c) (i) 38.3% (ii) 36.7%
(iii) 63.3%

2.19 (a) Random variable: Distance travelled (km)
Data type: numeric, ratio, continuous

(b) ≤10: (4) (8%); 10–15: (7) (14%); 15–20: (15) (30%); 20–25: (12) (24%); 25–30: (9) (18%); 30–35: (3) (6%)

(c) (i) 18% (9 trips)
(ii) 76% (38 trips)
(iii) 48% (24 trips)
(iv) Below 20 km
(v) Above 25 km

(d) Yes, only 6% are above 30 km.

2.20 (a) Random variable: Monthly fuel bill (R) per motorist
Data type: numeric, ratio, continuous

(b) ≤300: (7) (14%); 300–400: (15) (30%); 400–500: (13) (26%); 500–600: (7) (14%); 600–700: (5) (10%); 700–800: (3) (6%)

(c) 14% (7 motorists)

(d) ≤300: (7) (14%); ≤400: (22) (44%); ≤500: (35) (70%); ≤600: (42) (84%); ≤700: (47) (94%); ≤800: (3) (6%)

(e) Approximately 77% spend less than R550 per month on fuel.

(f) 30% (15 motorists) spend more than R500 per month on fuel.

2.21 (b) Yes, Corsa car sales are showing a (relatively strong) upward trend.

2.22 (b) Volkswagen showed faster but more erratic growth over the periods. Toyota has shown a steady and consistent growth but not at the same rate as VW.

(c) Choice is not clear-cut. Suggest choosing Toyota because of its consistent growth.

2.23 (b) Yes, there is a moderately strong positive linear relationship.

2.24 (b) Yes, there is a moderately strong positive linear relationship.

2.25 (a)

Sector	Average	Std dev
Mining	9.87	4.58
Services	11.33	2.99
Grand Total	10.70	3.78

(b) Services sector produces higher average roi% and with lower volatility than the mining sector.

2.26 (a)

Aisle		Shelf position		
		Bottom	Top	Total
Back	Average	4.66	4.1	4.38
	Std dev	1.193	0.648	0.952
Front	Average	6.08	5.08	5.58
	Std dev	0.892	0.622	0.895
Middle	Average	4.24	2.74	3.49
	Std dev	1.387	0.297	1.232
	Average	4.99	3.97	4.48
	Std dev	1.359	1.114	1.327

(b) Front of aisle (mostly top, but also bottom shelf positions) generates highest average sales.

2.27 (b) and (c)

Region		Type of business usage			
		Commercial	Industrial	Retail	Total
A	Average	7.5	4.3	10.2	7.9
	Std dev	2.5	3.1	3.6	3.5
	Minimum	−2.4	−4.2	0.8	−4.2
	Maximum	14.6	8.1	18.4	18.4
	Count	104	40	70	214
B	Average	12.3	6.8	8.5	9.8
	Std dev	3.1	4.2	1.8	3.5
	Minimum	2.7	−3.4	4.4	−3.4
	Maximum	20.3	10.2	13.2	20.3
	Count	46	16	48	110
	Average	9.0	5.4	9.5	8.6
	Std dev	3.5	3.5	3.1	3.6
	Minimum	−2.4	−4.2	0.8	−4.2
	Maximum	20.3	10.2	18.4	20.3
	Count	150	56	118	324

(e) Best performing properties in the portfolio are commercial in region B and retail in region A. Worst performing properties are industrial, mainly in region A.

Chapter 3

3.1 (a) median   (b) mode
     (c) mean

3.2 Upper quartile

3.3 Statements (c) and (f). The mode would be more appropriate (both are categorical).

3.4 (a) False   (b) False
     (c) True   (d) False
     (e) False

3.5 Correct method is (b).

3.6 Mean = 9.3%; standard deviation = 0.849%

3.7 (a) Hand luggage mass (kg): average = 10.57 kg; standard deviation = 1.718 kg
     (c) Coefficient of variation (CV) = 16.25%
     (d) Low relative variability in hand luggage masses (data closely grouped).

3.8 (a) Monthly bicycle sales: mean = 23.6 units; median = 22 units
     (b) Range (R) = 20 (R = 21 if using Excel); variance = 43.6; standard deviation = 6.603
     (c) Lower quartile (Q_1) = 18 units; upper quartile (Q_3) = 30 units
     (d) Skewness (approx.) = 0.727. Positively skewed distribution of monthly bicycle sales.
     (e) Opening stock level next month = 23.6 + 6.6 = 30.2 (30 bicycles). Will meet demand.

3.9 (a) Glue setting time (min): mean = 24 min; standard deviation = 4.18 min
     (b) Coefficient of variation (CV) = 17.43%
     (c) No, the relative variability (consistency index) is above 10%.

3.10 (a) % wage increases: mean = 6.43%; median = 6.25%
     (b) Variance = 1.921; standard deviation = 1.386
     (c) Lower limit = 3.66%; upper limit = 9.2%. 95.5% of all values lie within this interval.
     (d) Coefficient of variation (CV) = 21.55%. Agreed wage increases moderately consistent.

3.11 (a) CV_1 = 13.8%; CV_2 = 14.66%
     (b) Group 1 trainees' exam scores are marginally more consistent.

3.12 (a) Random variable: Meal value (rand) Data type: numeric, ratio, continuous
     (b) Mean = R55.95; standard deviation = R14.33

     (c) Median = R53. 50% of meals cost less than R53, the other 50% cost more than R53.
     (d) Modal meal value = R44
     (e) Since mean > median, implies outliers (a few high-valued meals) are present in data. Therefore choose median as the representative central location measure.

3.13 (a) Days absent: mean = 10.3 days; median = 9 days; mode = 5 days
     (b) Lower quartile (Q_1) = 5 days; upper quartile (Q_3) = 15 days
     (c) Since mean > median, implies high-valued outliers. Use median to as central location. Hence average absenteeism/month = 1 day (9/9). Policy successfully applied.

3.14 (a) Bad debts %: average = 4.665%; standard deviation = 1.852%
     (b) Median = 5.4%
     (c) Since mean < median, a few low-valued outliers exist. Use median as central location.
     (d) Mode = 2.2% or 5.7% as both occur with equal frequency of 2.
     (e) Skewness (approximation) = −1.19. Excessive negative skewness (a few retailers with very low % of bad debts).
     (f) Lower quartile (Q_1) = 2.5%; upper quartile (Q_3) = 6.2%
     (g) Use median (see (c)). Since median % of bad debts exceeds 5%, send advisory note.

3.15 (a) Daily turnover (rand): average = R1 390.83
     (b) Median = R1 404.89
     (c) Mode = R1 394.53
     (d) Lower quartile Q_1 = R1 168.18
     (e) Upper quartile Q_3 = R1 653.85

3.16 (a) Grocery spend %: average = 33.4%
     (b) (i) Median = 33.125%
         (ii) Lower quartile Q_1 = 24.64%
     (c) Upper quartile Q_3 = 41.5%

3.17 Average equity price = R14.29

3.18 Average car price = R34 900

3.19 Average annual increase in office rentals (%) = 11.955%

3.20 (a) Average annual increase in sugar price (%) = 6.456%
     (b) The base value of each percentage change is different.

3.21 (a) Water usage per household (kl/month): mean = 21.2 kl; median = 19.5 kl; mode = 25 kl
(b) Variance = 91.959 kl²; standard deviation = 9.59 kl
(c) Lower quartile (Q_1) = 14.75 kl; upper quartile (Q_3) = 26 kl
(e) (i) Expected total monthly usage = 15 900 kl
(ii) Expected total annual usage = 190 800 kl

3.22 (a) Price of a veal cordon bleu dish
Data type: numeric, ratio, continuous
(b) Mean = R61.25; median = R59
(c) Mode = R48. Frequency of occurrence unknown. Unsure of representativeness.
(d) Standard deviation = R10.54
(e) Skewness coefficient (approximate) = 0.64. Evidence of moderate skewness to the right.
(f) Median (since skewness is relatively large, and mean > median)
(g) Upper quartile Q_3 = R68 per dish
(h) Lower quartile Q_1 = R54.25 per dish
(i) 90th percentile = R75.50

3.23 (a) Monthly fuel bill per motorist (R): mean = R418; median = R398; variance = R12 926.05; standard deviation = R113.69; skewness (approx.) = 0.528
(c) Moderate skewness to the right (caused by a few large monthly fuel bills).
(d) CV = 27.2% (Fuel bills show moderate (not low) relative variability about the mean.)
(e) Lower quartile (Q_1) = R330; upper quartile (Q_3) = R510
(f) Five number summary table: R256; R332.50; R398; R502.50: R676
(i) Average fuel consumption per motorist per month = 41.8 litres. Expected (most likely) total fuel consumption = 1 045 000 litres.

3.24 (a) Experience (years): mean = 7 years; median = 6 years; standard deviation = 3.838 years; skewness (approx.) = 0.782
(c) Histogram (frequencies – based on bin intervals): 21; 30; 24; 15; 8; 2
(d) Lower limit = 3.16 years; upper limit = 10.84 years.
68.3%
(e) < three years experience = 21% of engineers; >12 years experience = 10% of engineers. Mix not achieved – too few experienced members.

3.25 (a) Dividend yields (%)
Data type: numeric, ratio, continuous
(b) Mean = 4.27%; median = 4.1%; mode = 2.8%; standard deviation = 1.44%; skewness (approx.) = XXX
(d) Mean (no evidence of significant skewness (outliers))
(e) Histogram (frequencies – based on bin intervals): 3; 11; 16; 11; 3
(f) Five number summary table: 1.5%; 3.125%; 4.1%; 5.25%; 7.6%
(g) Minimum dividend yield by top 10% = 6.25%
(h) Cumulative % frequency (up to second interval upper limit of 3.5%) = 31.8%

3.26 (a) Selling price per rosebud (c)
Data type: numeric, ratio continuous
(b) Mean = 60.31c; standard deviation = 3.188c; median = 59.95c; skewness (approx.) = 0.341
(c) Coefficient of variation (CV) = 5.29% (low relative variability about the mean)
(d) Lower quartile (Q_1) = 57.7c; upper quartile (Q_3) = 62.55c
(e) 57.7c (lower quartile)
(f) 62.55c (upper quartile)
(g) 90% percentile selling price = 64.6c
(h) 10% percentile selling price = 56.6c
(i) Five number summary table: 55.2c; 57.7c; 59.95c; 62.55c; 73.5c

3.27 a(ii) Q_1 = R266; Q_3 = R522 a(iii) and a(iv)

		Marital Status		
Gender		**Married**	**Single**	**Row totals**
Female	average	512.6	563.7	545.3
	count	23	41	64
Male	average	368.0	299.3	350.7
	count	83	28	111
Column totals	average	399.4	456.4	421.9
	count	106	69	175

b(i)	gender (categorical, nominal)
	marital status (categorical, nominal)
	month-end savings balances
	(numerical, ratio)

b(ii)	Female clients have a significantly
	higher average month-end savings
	balance (R545.3) than male clients
	(R350.7), but comprise only 36%
	of all clients. Single female clients
	have the highest average month-

end savings balance of R563.7 of all
clients but represent only 23% of the
bank's client base. The lowest average
month-end savings balance is held by the
single male clients (R299.3) who make
up 16% of the client base. Married males
comprise the largest grouping of clients
(47%) but save only R368 on average
per month compared to female clients
(R545.3).

3.28	a(ii) $Q_1 = 0.4586$; $Q_3 = 1.4298$; a(iii) and a(iv)

Marital		Age 26 – 35	36 – 45	46 – 55	row totals
Married	average	1.326	0.915	1.123	1.112
	std dev	0.552	0.589	0.629	0.610
	minimum	0.147	0.051	0.013	0.013
	maximum	2.685	1.989	2.408	2.685
	count	23	27	35	85
Single	average	0.919	0.474	0.947	0.793
	std dev	0.543	0.356	0.500	0.524
	minimum	0.014	0.024	0.218	0.014
	maximum	1.905	1.262	1.814	1.905
	count	36	19	10	65
column totals	average	1.078	0.733	1.084	0.974
	std dev	0.577	0.547	0.602	0.594
	minimum	0.014	0.024	0.013	0.013
	maximum	2.685	1.989	2.408	2.685
	count	59	46	45	150

b(i)	age category (categorical, ordinal)
	marital status (categorical, nominal)
	claims ratio (numerical, ratio)

b(ii)	The overall average claims ratio is
	0.974 (just below the breakeven
	ratio of 1). Married members claim
	more than their contributions
	(1.112) and are subsidised by the
	single members who only claim
	0.793, on average. Members in
	the (36 – 45) year age group, with
	an average claims ratio of only
	0.733 also tend to subsidize
	members in the other two age
	groups (26 – 35 and 46 – 55)
	whose claims ratios of 1.078
	and 1.084 respectively both exceed
	the breakeven level of 1. The
	younger married members (26 –
	35) have the highest claims ratio,
	on average (1.326) and represent

15.3% of all members; while single
members in the 36 – 45 year age group
have the lowest average claims ratio of
0.474 and represent only 12.7% of all
members.

Chapter 4

4.1	$P(A) = 0.2$ means that an event has a
	20% chance of occurring.
4.2	Mutually exclusive events
4.3	The outcome of one event does not
	influence, nor is influenced by, the
	outcome of the other event.
4.4	$P(A \text{ or } B) = 0.47$
4.5	$P(X|Y) = 0.75$. No, since $P(Y|X) = 0.5$.
4.6	(a)	Frequency table: Mining (18%);
		Financial (28.8%); IT (12.8%);
		Production (40.4%)
	(b)	$P(\text{Financial}) = 0.288$

(c) P(Not production) = 0.596

(d) P(Mining or IT) = 0.308

(e) In (c): complementary rule.
In (d): addition rule for mutually exclusive events.

4.7 (a) Frequency table: Apple grades
A (18%); B (28.8%); C (12.8%)
D (40.4%)

(b) P(Grade A) = 0.53

(c) P(Grade B or Grade D) = 0.399

(d) P(Export Grade A or Grade B) = 0.803

(e) In both (c) and (d): addition rule for mutually exclusive events.

4.8 (a) Frequency table: Sector Employment
Business (formal) (53%);
Agricultural (commercial) (11.8%);
Agricultural (subsistence) (5.2%);
Business (informal) (22.7%);
Domestic service (7.3%)

(b) P(Domestic service) = 0.073

(c) P(Agriculture (commercial) or Agriculture (subsistence)) = 0.17

(d) P(Informal trader/Business sector (formal and informal)) = 0.30

(e) In (c): addition rule for mutually exclusive events.
In (d): conditional probability.

4.9 (a) Managerial level
Data type: categorical, ordinal, discrete
Qualification level
Data type: categorical, ordinal, discrete

(b) Matric & division head = 8
Degree & section head = 5
Dept head = 48

(c) (i) P(Matric) = 38.75%
Marginal probability

(ii) P(Section head and degree) = 3.88%
Joint probability

(iii) P(Dept head | diploma) = 48%
Conditional probability

(iv) P(Division head) = 21.71%
Marginal probability

(v) P(Division head or section head) = 62.79%
Addition rule (mutually exclusive events)

(vi) P(Matric or diploma or degree) = 100%
Collectively exhaustive events and addition rule for mutually exclusive events

(vii) P(Degree | dept head) = 20.83%
Conditional probability

(viii) P(Division head or diploma, or both) = 55.81%
Addition rule for non-mutually exclusive events

(d) See (c) above.

(e) Yes

4.10 (a) P(Cash bonus) = 0.28
Marginal probability

(b) P(Tax-free option (i.e. share option)) = 0.323
Marginal probability

(c) P(Production and cash bonus) = 0.187
Joint probability

(d) P(Share option | admin) = 0.486
Conditional probability

(e) P(Production | cash bonus) = 0.667
Conditional probability

(f) P(A) = 0.323 ≠ P(A|B) = 0.486
Events are statistically dependent

(g) See (a) to (e) above.

4.11 (a) (i) P(<30 years) = 0.343
Marginal probability

(ii) P(Production worker) = 0.533
Marginal probability

(iii) P(Sales and 30–50 years) = 0.097
Joint probability

(iv) P(>50 | administration) = 0.449
Conditional probability

(v) P(Production or <30 years, or both) = 0.677
Addition rule for non-mutually exclusive events

(b) No, both events can occur simultaneously for a single employee.

(c) A = Event(<30 years) and B = Event(Sales)
P(A) = 0.343 ≠ P(A|B) = 0.403
Events are statistically dependent

(d) See (a) above.

4.12 (a) P(Professional user) = 0.321

(b) P(Nikon brand) = 0.393

(c) P(Pentax brand | personal user) = 0.342

(d) A = Event(Canon) and B = Event(Personal user)
P(A) = 0.279 ≠ P(A|B) = 0.158
Events are statistically dependent

(e) P(Canon brand and professional user) = 0.171

(f) P(Either professional user or Nikon brand (or both)) = 0.661

(g) No. Both can occur simultaneously. P(Professional user and Nikon brand) = 0.054 ≠ 0.

4.13 (b) P(A fails and B fails) = 0.030 (i.e. a 3% chance of both failing together)

(c) P(Not needing replacing) = 1 − P(A fails or B fails or both A and B fail) = 1 − (0.2 + 0.15 − 0.03) = 0.68 (68%)

4.14 (b) (i) P(Pass and attend) = 0.24
(ii) P(Pass) = 0.66

4.15 (a) 720 (b) 720
(c) 288 (d) 35
(e) 84 (f) 336
(g) 20 (h) 1
(i) 840

4.16 $_{12}C_7 = 792$ different newspaper designs

4.17 $_5P_3 = 60$ different displays

4.18 (a) $_9C_4 = 126$ portfolios
(b) P(One particular portfolio) = $\frac{1}{126}$ = 0.00794 (0.794%)

4.19 P(Replacing screws in same holes) = $\frac{1}{5!}$ = $\frac{1}{120}$ = 0.00833 (0.833%)

4.20 (a) $_{10}C_3 = 120$ different tourist attraction selections of 3 from 10
(b) P(Any 3 attractions) = $\frac{1}{120}$ = 0.00833 (0.833%)

4.21 (a) 210 different committee formations
(b) 420 different committee formations

4.22 P(On-time completion | scope change) = 0.5385

4.23 P(Husband participates in sport | wife participates in sport) = 0.6667

4.24 P(Airline A | flight left on time) = 0.6486

4.25 P(Graduate | New business failed) = 0.4615

4.26 P(e-Ticket purchased | business traveller) = 0. 5424

Chapter 5

5.1 Binomial; Poisson
5.2 (a) continuous (b) discrete
(c) discrete (d) continuous
5.3 (a) (i) 0.1147 (ii) 0.0881
(iii) 0.7237 (iv) 0.0851
(v) 0.3215
5.4 (a) Binomial (b) 0.3932
(c) 0.9011 (d) 0.2621
(e) 1.2

5.5 (a) 0.1422 (b) 0.6042
5.6 (a) 0.2668 (b) 0.9984
5.7 (a) 0.2793 (b) 0.9942
(c) 0.6634 (d) 3.2
5.8 (a) 0.2621 (b) 0.0973
(c) 0.9011
5.9 (a) 0.2835 (b) 0.0532
(c) 0.0194
5.10 (a) 0.7361; 0.0860 (b) 182
5.11 (a) 0.1008 (b) 0.3528
(c) 0.0498
5.12 (a) 0.2381 (b) 0.5665
5.13 (a) (i) 0.0149 (ii) 0.1512
(iii) 0.9380
(b) 0.1494 (c) 6; 2.449
5.14 (a) 0.2694 (b) 0.8913
5.15 (a) 0.3007 (b) 0.2504
(c) 0.0479
5.16 (a) (i) 0.4664 (ii) 0.6844
(iii) 0.4878 (iv) 0.1112
(v) 0.7169 (vi) 0.2483
(vii) 0.3039
5.17 (a) (i) 1.3703 (ii) −0.08005
(iii) 1.2901 (iv) −2.05998
(v) 1.2901 (vi) −0.6692
(vii) −0.34008
5.18 (a) (i) 0.2119 (ii) 0.0869
(iii) 0.2764 (iv) 67.167
(v) 59.0023 (vi) 65.5279
5.19 (a) 0.02275 (b) 0.1587
(c) 74.93 minutes
5.20 (a) 2.8125%
(b) 20.663%; 1.456%
(c) 1.29 years
5.21 (a) (i) 3.772% (ii) 0.383%
(iii) 173.36 litres
(iv) 257.873 litres
5.22 (a) (i) 0.0082 (ii) 0.2881
(iii) 0.02275 (iv) 0.0546
(b) 5.48%; 6.58 (7) drivers
(c) 11.51%; 41.425 (42) drivers
5.23 (a) 38.755% (b) 18.9255 g
5.24 (a) 0.1333 (b) 0.0131
(c) 12.013%
(d) 13.326%; 10.66 (11) customers
(e) z = 1.645 and μ = 65.195 minutes
5.25 (a) (i) 0.3085 (ii) 0.2417
(iii) 0.1587
(b) 240.36 ml
(c) z = −1.28 and μ = 232.8 ml
5.26 (a) 0.2412 (b) 0.1587
(c) 29.01 months (d) 21.42 months

Chapter 6

6.1 To generalise sample findings to the target population

6.2 Sampling methods; Concept of the sampling distribution

6.3 subset

6.4 representative

6.5 Non-probability sampling: sample members are chosen using non-random criteria meaning that some members of the target population are excluded from being included in the sample.

Probability sampling: sample members are chosen using random selection processes so that each target population member stands a chance of being included in the sample.

6.6 Random (probability) sampling methods. Every member of the target population has a chance of being included in the sample. This is likely to result in a more representative sample than if a non-probability sampling method was used.

6.7 Unrepresentativeness of the target population;

Not possible to measure sampling error.

6.8 random (chance)

6.9 equal

6.10 Simple random sampling

6.11 Systematic random sampling

6.12 Stratified random sampling

6.13 Cluster random sampling

6.14 It results in a smaller sampling error

6.15 sample statistic; population parameter

6.16 standard error

6.17 95.5%

6.18 Normal

6.19 $n = 30$ or larger

6.20 Central Limit Theorem.

6.21 Sampling error is the error made when estimating a population parameter (e.g. population mean) from a sample statistic (e.g. sample mean).

Chapter 7

7.1 To estimate a population parameter value by defining an interval within which the true value is likely to fall at a stated level of confidence.

7.2 95% confidence: LCL = 83.04; UCL = 86.96

7.3 t-statistic

7.4 90% confidence: LCL = 51.95; UCL = 56.05

7.5 (a) 95% confidence: LCL= 22.636; UCL = 26.164

(b) =NORMSINV(0.975) = 1.95996

(c) =CONFIDENCE(0.05,10.8,144) = confidence level = 1.764
LCL = 24.2 − 1.764 = 22.636
UCL = 24.4 + 1.764 = 26.164

7.6 (a) 90% confidence: LCL = 127.191; UCL = 136.009

(b) =NORMSINV(0.95) = 1.64485

(c) =CONFIDENCE(0.10,25,87) = confidence level = 4.409
LCL = 131.6 − 4.409 = 127.191
UCL = 131.6 + 4.409 = 136.009

(d) 90% confidence: LCL = 91577.76; UCL = 97926.24

7.7 (a) 95% confidence: LCL = R350.61; UCL = R361.39

(b) 90% confidence: LCL = R351.48; UCL = R360.52

(c) =NORMSINV(0.975) = 1.95996

(d) =CONFIDENCE(0.05,44,256) = confidence level = 5.39
LCL = 356 − 5.39 = 350.61
UCL = 356 + 5.39 = 361.39

(e) 95% confidence: LCL = R1 051 830; UCL = R1 084 170

7.8 (a) 99% confidence: LCL = 4.9704 ℓ; UCL = 4.9996 ℓ

(b) Yes, since the confidence limits do not include 5 ℓ.

(c) =NORMSINV(0.995) = 2.5758

(d) =CONFIDENCE(0.01,0.04,50) = confidence level = 0.0146
LCL = 4.985 − 0.0146 = 4.9704
UCL = 4.985 + 0.0146 = 4.9996

7.9 (a) 90% confidence: LCL = 3.5985 times; UCL = 4.0015 times

(b) =NORMSINV(0.95) = 1.64485

(c) =CONFIDENCE(0.10,0.6,24) = confidence level = 0.2015
LCL = 3.8 − 0.2015 = 3.5985
UCL = 3.8 + 0.2015 = 4.0015

7.10 (a) 95% confidence: LCL = 155.82 calls; UCL = 176.58 calls

(b) 99% confidence: LCL = 152.04 calls; UCL = 180.36 calls

(d) =TINV(0.05,20) = 2.0860

(e) 95% confidence: LCL = 4674.6 calls; UCL = 5297.4 calls

7.11 (a) 90% confidence: LCL = 11.4056%;
UCL = 13.5944%

(b) =TINV(0.10,27) = 1.7033

7.12 (a) 99% confidence: LCL = 0.9455
litres; UCL = 1.0165 litres

(b) 95% confidence: LCL = 0.9551
litres; UCL = 1.0069 litres

(c) =TINV(0.01,17) = 2.8982;
=TINV(0.05,17) = 2.1098

7.13 (a) 90% confidence: LCL = R2382.06;
UCL = R2457.94

(b) 99% confidence: LCL = R2359.36;
UCL = R2480.64

(d) =TINV(0.10,49) = 1.67655;
=TINV(0.01,49) = 2.67995

7.14 95% confidence: LCL = 35.16%;
UCL = 48.84%

7.15 95% confidence: LCL = 34.84%;
UCL = 50.16%

7.16 90% confidence: LCL = 75.1%;
UCL = 82.16%

7.17 90% confidence: LCL = 35.35%;
UCL = 44.65%

7.18 (a) $\bar{x} = 9.379$ days; $s = 3.364$ days

(b) 95% confidence: LCL = 8.1 days;
UCL = 10.66 days

(c) On average, yearly absenteeism does
not exceed 10 (i.e. 11 or more days).

(d) =TINV(0.05,28) = 2.0484

7.19 (a) $\bar{x} = 2.8286$ kg; $s = 0.59985$ kg

(b) 90% confidence: LCL = 2.675 kg;
UCL = 2.982 kg

(c) On average, parcel weights do not
exceed 3 kg.

(d) =TINV(0.10,42) = 1.68195

7.20 (a) $\bar{x} = 71.24\%$; $s = 14.1227\%$

(b) 95% confidence: LCL = 67.226%;
UCL = 75.254%

(c) =TINV(0.05,49) = 2.009575

(d) $P(x > 75) = P(t > 0.266238)$,
where $t = \frac{75 - 71.24}{14.1227}$
From Excel:
=TINV(0.266238,49,1) = 0.3956
Thus 39.56% of all companies are
in violation of the rule of thumb
cost-to-income ratio.

7.21 $n = 96$

7.22 (a) $n = 666$

(b) $n = 296$

(c) $n = 166$

7.23 $n = 752$

Chapter 8

8.1 Test whether a claim made about a
population parameter value is probably
true or false.

8.2 The 'closeness' of the sample statistics to
the claimed population parameter value.

8.3 See text.

8.4 Level of significance (and sample size
when the population standard deviation
is unknown)

8.5 Reject H_0 in favour of H_1 at the 5% level
of significance.

8.6 (i) One-sided upper-tailed
$A = \{z > 1.645\}$ z-stat = 2.165
p-value = 0.0152 Reject H_0 at 5%
level of significance

(ii) One-sided lower-tailed
$A = \{z < -1.28\}$ z-stat = −2.5
p-value = 0.0062 Reject H_0 at 10%
level of significance

(iii) Two-tailed
$A = \{-2.756 < t < 2.756\}$
t-stat = 2.644 p-value = 0.0131
Do not reject H_0 at 1% level of
significance

(iv) One-sided lower-tailed
$A = \{t < -2.718\}$ t-stat = −3.464
p-value = 0.00265 Reject H_0 at 1%
level of significance

(v) Two-tailed
$A = \{-1.96 < z < 1.96\}$
z-stat = −1.706 p-value = 0.0881
Do not reject H_0 at 5% level of
significance

8.7 (a) $H_0: \mu = 85$ $H_1: \mu \neq 85$

(b) z-test statistic (σ is known; data
normally distributed)

(c) z-stat = −2.068 z-crit = ±1.96
Reject H_0 at 5% level of significance

(d) p-value = 0.0387

(e) Strong evidence to reject H_0.
Average shopping time ≠ 85 minutes.

8.8 (a) $H_0: \mu \geq 30$ $H_1: \mu < 30$

(b) z-test statistic (σ is known; data
normally distributed)

(c) z-stat = −1.855 z-crit = −2.33
Do not reject H_0 at 1% level of
significance.

(d) p-value = 0.0318. Insufficient
evidence to reject H_0.
Average shopping time is at least 30
minutes.

8.9 (a) $H_0: \mu \leq 72$ $H_1: \mu > 72$
(b) $z\text{-stat} = 1.4695$ $z\text{-crit} = 1.28$
Reject H_0 ($\alpha = 0.1$)
(c) p-value $= 0.0708$ Strong evidence to reject H_0. Average clearing time exceeds 72 hours.

8.10 (a) z-test statistic (σ is known)
(b) $H_0: \mu \leq 40$ $H_1: \mu > 40$
(c) $z\text{-stat} = 2.432$ $z\text{-crit} = 2.33$
Reject H_0 at 1% level of significance.
(d) p-value $= 0.0075$. Overwhelming evidence to reject H_0. Average % mark-up far exceeds 40%.

8.11 (a) $H_0: \mu = 700$ $H_1: \mu \neq 700$
$t\text{-stat} = -1.905$ $t\text{-crit} = \pm 2.00$
Do not reject H_0 ($\alpha = 0.05$)
Average loaf of bread is neither overweight nor underweight.
(b) p-value $= 0.0614$ Insufficient evidence to reject H_0. Bakery is complying with the law.
(c) $H_0: \mu \geq 700$ $H_1: \mu < 700$
$t\text{-stat} = -1.905$ $t\text{-crit} = -1.671$
Reject H_0 ($\alpha = 0.05$)
The average loaf of bread is underweight. Bakery is not complying with the law.

8.12 (a) $H_0: \mu \geq 5\,500$ $H_1: \mu < 5\,500$
$t\text{-stat} = -1.211$ $t\text{-crit} = -1.33$
Do not reject H_0 ($\alpha = 0.10$)
(b) p-value $= 0.1212$ Insufficient evidence to reject H_0.
Average sales not less than R5 500 per week. Product should not be withdrawn.

8.13 (a) $H_0: \mu \leq 80$ $H_1: \mu > 80$
$t\text{-stat} = 1.841$ $t\text{-crit} = 1.708$
Reject H_0 ($\alpha = 0.05$)
(b) p-value $= 0.0387$ Strong evidence to reject H_0.
Average tensile strength is more than 80 kg. Accept consignment.

8.14 (a) $H_0: \mu \geq 1$ $H_1: \mu < 1$
$t\text{-stat} = -1.184$ $t\text{-crit} = -1.729$
Do not reject H_0 ($\alpha = 0.05$)
(b) p-value $= 0.1255$ Insufficient evidence to reject H_0. Average carton fills is at least 1 litre.

8.15 (a) $H_0: \pi \geq 0.3$ $H_1: \pi < 0.3$
$z\text{-stat} = -1.528$ $z\text{-crit} = -1.645$
Do not reject H_0 ($\alpha = 0.05$).
(b) p-value $= 0.0633$. Insufficient evidence to reject H_0. Radio listenership is at least 30%. Recommend placing ads in news timeslot.

8.16 (a) $H_0: \pi \leq 0.6$ $H_1: \pi > 0.6$ $p = 0.64$
$z\text{-stat} = 1.00$ $z\text{-crit} = 1.645$
Do not reject H_0 ($\alpha = 0.05$).
(b) p-value $= 0.1587$ Insufficient evidence to reject H_0. Insurance advisor's claim invalid.

8.17 (a) $H_0: \pi \leq 0.15$ $H_1: \pi > 0.15$
$p = 0.171$ $z\text{-stat} = 1.42$
$z\text{-crit} = 1.28$ Reject H_0 ($\alpha = 0.10$).
(b) p-value $= 0.0778$. Sufficient evidence to reject H_0. Churn rate exceeds 15%.

8.18 (a) $H_0: \pi \geq 0.9$ $H_1: \pi < 0.9$ $p = 0.867$
$z\text{-stat} = -1.925$ $z\text{-crit} = -2.33$
Do not reject H_0 ($\alpha = 0.01$).
(b) p-value $= 0.0271$. Insufficient evidence to reject H_0.
Seed germination rate is at least 90%. Recommend purchase of seeds.

8.19 $H_0: \mu \geq 75$ $H_1: \mu < 75$
$t\text{-stat} = -1.883$ $t\text{-crit} = -1.677$
Reject H_0 ($\alpha = 0.05$).
p-value $= 0.0329$. Sufficient evidence to reject H_0. Cost-to-income ratio not less than 75%.

8.20 (a) Transaction values do not appear to be normally distributed.
(b) $H_0: \mu \geq 150$ $H_1: \mu < 150$
$t\text{-stat} = -1.937$ $t\text{-crit} = -1.677$
Reject H_0 ($\alpha = 0.05$).
Average transaction value is less than R150. Recommend store closure.

8.21 (a) Flight delay times do appear to be normally distributed.
(b) $H_0: \mu \leq 10$ $H_1: \mu > 10$
$t\text{-stat} = 1.241$ $t\text{-crit} = -1.292$
Do not reject H_0 ($\alpha = 0.10$).
Average flight delay time does not exceed 10 minutes. No further investigation needed.

8.22 (a) Number of claims received daily does appear to be normally distributed.
(b) $H_0: \mu \leq 180$ $H_1: \mu > 180$
$t\text{-stat} = 2.275$ $t\text{-crit} = 2.365$
Do not reject H_0 ($\alpha = 0.01$).
Average claims received daily do not exceed 180. Additional staff motivation not supported.

8.23 (a) Frequencies: *Sun* $= 19$
Guardian $= 42$ *Mail* $= 31$
Voice $= 28$
(b) $H_0: \pi \geq 0.4$ $H_1: \pi < 0.4$

(c) $p = 0.35$ z-stat $= -1.118$
z-crit $= -1.645$
Do not reject H_0 ($\alpha = 0.05$).
Guardian's claim not overstated (its
readership market is at least 40%).

8.24 (a) Frequencies: Low $= 72$
Moderate $= 64$ High $= 34$
(b) (i) H_0: $\pi \leq 0.15$ H_1: $\pi > 0.15$
(ii) $p = 0.2$ z-stat $= 1.826$
z-crit $= 2.326$
(iii) Do not reject H_0 ($\alpha = 0.01$).
High consumer awareness is
no more than 15%.
Recommend launch of
national awareness campaign.

8.25 (a) Daily percentage scrap appears
to be normally distributed.
(b) LCL $= 3.34\%$ UCL $= 3.63\%$
(c) H_0: $\mu \geq 3.75$ H_1: $\mu < 3.75$
t-stat $= -3.698$ t-crit $= -1.677$
Reject H_0 ($\alpha = 0.05$).
Average daily percentage scrap is
less than 3.75%. No service
maintenance necessary.

8.26 H_0: $\sigma^2 \leq 9$ H_1: $\sigma^2 > 9$
Upper X^2-crit $= 37.652$ X^2-stat $=$
33.254 p-value $= 0.1248$
Do not reject H_0 ($\alpha = 0.05$).
Pipe length *variability* is within product
specification.

8.27 H_0: $\sigma^2 \leq 30$ H_1: $\sigma^2 > 30$
Upper X^2-crit $= 27.204$
X^2-stat $= 31.223$ p-value $= 0.0382$
Reject H_0 ($\alpha = 0.10$).
Population variance is *significantly greater*
than 30.

8.28 H_0: $\sigma^2 = 5625$ H_1: $\sigma^2 \neq 5625$
Lower X^2-crit $= 17.539$; upper X^2-crit $=$
48.232
X^2-stat $= 38.886$ p-value $= 0.1561$
Do not reject H_0 ($\alpha = 0.05$).
Insurance claims value variability is still
valid (i.e. $\sigma^2 = $ R5625).

8.29 H_0: $\sigma^2 \geq 1.8$ H_1: $\sigma^2 < 1.8$
Lower X^2-crit $= 5.229$ X^2-stat $= 6.756$
p-value $= 0.0359$
Do not reject H_0 ($\alpha = 0.01$).
New headache pill does *not reduce
variability in time* to pain relief.

Chapter 9

9.1 When the population standard deviations
of the two populations are unknown.

9.2 z-stat $= 1.7321$
9.3 (a) t-crit $(0.05,38) = 2.024$
(b) t-crit $(0.05,90) = 1.987$
9.4 When the two samples are not independent.
9.5 H_0: $\pi_1 \geq \pi_2$
H_1: $\pi_1 < \pi_2$
9.6 (a) H_0: $\mu_1 = \mu_2$
H_1: $\mu_1 \neq \mu_2$
(b) t-crit $(0.025,41) = \pm 2.0195$
t-stat $= -1.5161$ Do not reject H_0.
Conclude that there is no difference
in mean earnings yield between the
two sectors.
9.7 (a) H_0: $\mu_D \geq \mu_{ND}$
H_1: $\mu_D < \mu_{ND}$
(b) t-crit $(0.10,61) = -1.2956$
t-stat $= -1.3792$ Reject H_0.
(c) Conclude that DIY consumers
are younger, on average, than non-
DIY consumers.
(d) t-crit $(0.05,61) = -1.6702$
t-stat $= -1.3792$ Do not reject H_0.
No differences in mean ages.
9.8 (a) H_0: $\mu_B \leq \mu_T$
H_1: $\mu_B > \mu_T$
(b) t-crit $(0.01,56) = 2.3948$
t-stat $= 2.1544$ Do not reject H_0.
(c) No difference in mean commuting
times between busses and trains.
Prioritise either mode.
9.9 H_0: $\mu_M = \mu_V$
H_1: $\mu_M \neq \mu_V$
z-crit $(0.05) = \pm 1.96$ z-stat $= 1.5599$
Do not reject H_0.
No difference in mean month-end
balances between *Mastercard* and *Visa*
cardholders.
9.10 H_0: $\mu_A \leq \mu_{NA}$
H_1: $\mu_A > \mu_{NA}$
z-crit $(0.05) = 1.645$ z-stat $= 2.1134$
Reject H_0.
Seminar attendees have a significantly
higher mean job satisfaction score than
non-attendees.
9.11 (a) Explorer Fund: 95% confidence
limits (11.236 days; 13.564 days)
(b) H_0: $\mu_G \geq \mu_E$
H_1: $\mu_G < \mu_E$
z-crit $(0.05) = -1.645$
z-stat $= -1.5367$ Do not reject H_0.
No difference in mean claims
settlement times between the two
medical funds.

9.12 H_0: $\mu_G \geq u_E$
H_1: $\mu_G < \mu_E$
t-crit $(0.05,8) = -1.86$ *t-stat* $= -1.7053$
Do not reject H_0.
Baking times of gas ovens are not faster, on average, than electric ovens.

9.13 (a) H_0: $\mu_C \leq \mu_D$
H_C: $\mu_C > \mu_D$
t-crit $(0.10,31) = 1.309$
t-stat $= 1.4614$ Reject H_0.
Average order value at the Cape Town branch is significantly higher than the Durban branch.

(b) *t-crit* $(0.05,31) = 1.696$
t-stat $= 1.4614$ Do not reject H_0.
There is no significant difference in the mean order value between the Cape Town and the Durban branches.

(c) In the (b) conclusion ($\alpha = 0.05$) as the sample evidence of a 'difference' must be stronger before H_0 is rejected in favour of H_1.

9.14 H_0: $\mu_P \geq \mu_B$
H_1: $\mu_P < \mu_B$
t-crit $(0.05,14) = -1.761$
t-stat $= -1.3677$ Do not reject H_0.
No difference in mean weekly sales of the apple juice between the two package designs.
Either package design can be used.

9.15 H_0: $\pi_P \leq \pi_B$
H_1: $\pi_P > \pi_B$
z-crit $(0.05) = 1.645$ *z-stat* $= 1.377$
Do not reject H_0.
The percentage of households who would prefer *Fruit Puffs* is not significantly larger than the percentage of households who prefer *Fruity Wheat*. The manager's belief is not justified.

9.16 (a) H_0: $\pi_M = \pi_F$
H_1: $\pi_M \neq \pi_F$
z-crit $(0.05) = \pm 1.96$
z-stat $= 2.4394$ Reject H_0.
There is a significant difference in the percentage of males and females who enjoy jazz music.

(b) *p-value* $= 0.0147 < \alpha = 0.05$. Use (=(1-**NORM.S.DIST(2.4394)**)*2).
There is strong sample evidence to conclude that male and female proportions differ.

9.17 (a) H_0: $\pi_S \geq \pi_E$
H_1: $\pi_S < \pi_E$

z-crit $(0.05) = -1.645$
z-stat $= -1.7959$ Reject H_0.
Significantly larger percentage of Elite accounts than Status accounts are overdrawn.

(b) *p-value* $= 0.03625 < \alpha = 0.05$. Use (=**NORM.S.DIST(–1.7959)**).
There is strong sample evidence to conclude that more Elite accounts, proportionately, than Status accounts are overdrawn.

9.18 (a) H_0: $\mu_1 \geq \mu_2$
H_1: $\mu_1 < \mu_2$
t-crit $(0.05,78) = -1.6646$
t-stat $= -1.7027$ Reject H_0.
Machine 1 produces significantly less daily percentage scrap, on average, than machine 2.

(b) *p-value* $= 0.0463 < \alpha = 0.05$. There is strong sample evidence to confirm the conclusion in (a).

9.19 (a) H_0: $\mu_F \leq \mu_K$
H_1: $\mu_F > \mu_K$
t-crit $(0.01,51) = 2.4017$
t-stat $= 2.9764$ Reject H_0.
The KZN purification plant produces water of a higher quality, on average, than the Free State.

(b) *p-value* $= 0.0022 < \alpha = 0.01$. There is overwhelmingly strong sample evidence to confirm the conclusion in (a).

9.20 (a) H_0: $\mu_F = \mu_Y$
H_1: $\mu_F \neq \mu_Y$
t-crit $(0.025,40) = \pm 2.021$
t-stat $= 1.784$ Do not reject H_0.
The mean quercetin levels are the same between the two brands of rooibos tea.

(b) H_0: $\mu_F \leq \mu_Y$
H_1: $\mu_F > \mu_Y$
t-crit $(0.05,51) = 1.6839$
t-stat $= 1.784$ Reject H_0.
The mean quercetin level of Freshpak tea is significantly higher than that of Yellow Label tea.

9.21 (a) H_0: $\mu_N \geq \mu_K$
H_1: $\mu_N < \mu_K$
t-crit $(0.01,46) = -2.4102$
t-stat $= -2.0186$ Do not reject H_0.
There is no difference in the mean fat content of meat supplied by the two meat producers.

There is no statistical justification to sign an exclusive contract with the Namibian producer.

(b) p-value $= 0.0247 > \alpha = 0.01$. This confirms the conclusion in (a).

9.22 (a) The same stores were used to record sales data both before and after the campaign.

(b) $d = x_{before} - x_{after}$
$H_0: \mu_d \geq 0$
$H_1: \mu_d < 0$

(c) t-crit $(0.05,11) = -1.7958$
t-stat $= -1.8762$ Reject H_0.
The promotional campaign has been successful ('after' sales are significantly higher than 'before' sales, on average).

(d) p-value $= 0.0437 < \alpha = 0.05$.
This confirms the conclusion in (a).

9.23 (a) Not independent. the *same employees* were measured both before and after the programme.

(b) $d = x_{before} - x_{after}$
$H_0: \mu_d \geq 0$
$H_1: \mu_d < 0$
t-crit $(0.05,17) = -1.7396$
t-stat $= -2.1203$ Reject H_0.
The mean performance score of workers is significantly higher after the workshop than before it. The programme has been effective in raising worker performance.

(c) p-value $= 0.0245 < \alpha = 0.05$. This confirms the conclusion in (b).

9.24 (a) Not independent. The *same household* was monitored both a year ago and currently.

(b) $d = x_{year\ ago} - x_{current}$
$H_0: \mu_d \leq 0$
$H_1: \mu_d > 0$
t-crit $(0.05,9) = 1.8331$
t-stat $= 2.0925$ Reject H_0.
The average debt ratio of households is significantly lower today (currently) than it was a year ago. The prime rate increase has been effective in reducing the average household debt ratio.

(c) p-value $= 0.033 < \alpha = 0.05$.
This confirms the conclusion in (b).

9.25 $H_0: \sigma^2(1) = \sigma^2(2)$ $H_1: \sigma^2(1) \neq \sigma^2(2)$
Upper F-crit $= 1.939$ F-stat $= 1.589$
p-value $= 0.1240$
Do not reject H_0 ($\alpha = 0.05$).

The two processes' output variability are likely to be the same.

9.26 $H_0: \sigma^2(f) \leq \sigma^2(c)$ $H_1: \sigma^2(f) > \sigma^2(c)$
Upper F-crit $= 2.403$ F-stat $= 1.673$
p-value $= 0.1647$
Do not reject H_0 ($\alpha = 0.05$).
Variability in free-grazing cows' milk yield is no greater than that of controlled feed cows.

9.27 $H_0: \sigma^2(over\ 40) \leq \sigma^2(under\ 40)$
$H_1: \sigma^2(over\ 40) > \sigma^2(under\ 40)$
Upper F-crit $= 2.102$ F-stat $= 2.24$
p-value $= 0.0373$
Reject H_0 ($\alpha = 0.05$).
Variability in exercise times amongst 'over 40's greater than 'under 40's.

9.28 $H_0: \sigma^2(fin) = \sigma^2(health)$
$H_1: \sigma^2(fin) \neq \sigma^2(health)$
Upper F-crit $= 2.184$ F-stat $= 1.715$
p-value $= 0.1263$
Do not reject H_0 ($\alpha = 0.05$).
The variability of attrition rates between the two call centre types is the same.

9.29 (a) Matched pairs: Same document type subjected to each operating system.

(b) difference $= x(OS1) - x(OS2)$.
Negative differences mean OS1 *is faster* than OS2.
$H_0: \mu_d \geq 0$ vs $H_1: \mu_d < 0$

(c) t-crit $(0.1,7) = -1.4149$
t-stat $= -1.6181$ Reject H_0 ($\alpha = 0.1$)
OS1 is significantly faster, on average, than OS2 in reading various document types.

(d) p-value $= 0.0748$. Since p-value $< \alpha = 0.1$, reject H_0.

9.30 (a) Matched pairs: Identical aircraft subjected to the same in-flight test codes.

(b) difference $= x(airbus) - x(boeing)$.
Positive differences mean Airbus *performs* better than Boeing.
$H_0: \mu_d \leq 0$ vs $H_1: \mu_d > 0$

(c) t-crit $(0.05,17) = 1.7459$
t-stat $= 2.269$ Reject H_0 ($\alpha = 0.05$)
Airbus performs significantly better, on average, than Boeing on the in-flight performance tests.

(d) p-value $= 0.0187$. Since p-value $< \alpha = 0.05$, reject H_0.

Chapter 10

10.1 See text.

10.2 Categorical (nominal- or ordinal-scaled) data

10.3 There is no statistical association between the two categorical variables.

10.4 Expected frequencies represent the null hypothesis of no association.

10.5 X^2-crit $(0.05,6) = 12.592$
X^2-crit $(0.10,6) = 10.645$

10.6 (b) H_0: No association (independent)
H_1: An association (not independent)
X^2-crit $(0.10,2) = 4.605$
Do not reject H_0 if X^2-stat ≤ 4.605
X^2-stat $= 5.0428$ Reject H_0.
Conclude that an association exists between gender and motivation level.

10.7 (b) H_0: No association (independent)
H_1: An association (not independent)
X^2-crit $(0.05,1) = 3.8415$
Do not reject H_0 if X^2-stat ≤ 3.8415
X^2-stat $= 1.7544$
Do not reject H_0. Conclude that there is no association between employment status and the use of the internet shopping facility.

10.8 (a) Under 30: 15% 33% 52%;
30–45: 21% 37% 42%
Over 45: 38% 29% 33%
By inspection of the row percentages, older buyers appear to buy smaller cars.

(b) H_0: No association (independent)
H_1: An association (not independent)
X^2-crit $(0.01,4) = 13.277$
Do not reject H_0 if X^2-stat ≤ 13.277
X^2-stat $= 14.6247$ Reject H_0.
Conclude that there is an association between the age of a buyer and the car size bought.

(c) Older buyers are more likely to buy smaller cars, while younger buyers prefer larger cars.

10.9 (a) p_1 (Yes/E Cape) = 16%
p_2 = (Yes/W Cape) = 10.4%
p_3 = (Yes/KZN) = 25%
H_0: $\pi_1 = \pi_2 = \pi_3$
H_1: At least one π_i differs $(i = 1, 2, 3)$

(b) X^2-crit $(0.01,2) = 9.21$
Do not reject H_0 if X^2-stat ≤ 9.21
X^2-stat $= 7.5954$ Do not reject H_0.

Conclude that there is no difference in the proportion of *Sports News* readers across regions.

(c) H_0: No association (readership is independent of region)
H_1: An association (not independent)

10.10 (a) Male: 42% 22% 35%
Female: 53% 29% 18%
By inspection, both genders prefer spinning, while marginally more males prefer 'doing the circuit' compared to marginally more females, who prefer swimming.

(b) H_0: No association (independent)
H_1: An association (not independent)
X^2-crit $(0.10,2) = 4.605$
Do not reject H_0 if X^2-stat ≤ 4.605
X^2-stat $= 4.803$ Reject H_0.
Conclude that there is an association between gender and gym activity preferred. (This is only a weak association.)

(c) X^2-crit $(0.05,2) = 5.991$
Do not reject H_0 if X^2-stat ≤ 5.991
X^2-stat $= 4.803$ Do not reject H_0.
Conclude that there is no association between gender and gym activity preferred.

(d) p_1 (Males/spin) = 55.4%
p_2 = (Males/swim) = 54.3%
p_3 = (Males/circuit) = 75%
H_0: $\pi_1 = \pi_2 = \pi_3$ H_1: At least one π_i differs $(i = 1, 2, 3)$
Based on (b), males are more likely to prefer 'doing the circuit' than females while preferences for the other two activities are reasonably similar across genders.

10.11 (a) Profile: daily = 20%
3–4 times = 30.6%
twice = 34.4%
once = 15%

(b) H_0: Shopping profile as per manager's belief H_1: Profile differs, or
H_0: $\pi_1 = 0.25$ $\pi_2 = 0.35$ $\pi_3 = 0.3$ $\pi_4 = 0.1$ H_1: At least one π_i differs $(i = 1, 2, 3, 4)$
X^2-crit $(0.05,3) = 7.815$
Do not reject H_0 if X^2-stat ≤ 7.815
X^2-stat $= 8.501$ Reject H_0.

Conclude that the shoppers' profile differs from the manager's belief.

(c) Customers tend to be shopping less frequently than believed by the manager.
Daily 20% (25%); 2–4 times 31% (35%); twice 34% (30%); once 15% (10%)

10.12 H_0: No change in equity portfolio mix
H_1: Equity portfolio mix differs, or
H_0: $\pi_1 : \pi_2 : \pi_3 : \pi_4 = 2 : 3 : 1 : 4$
H_1: At least one π_i differs $(i = 1, 2, 3, 4)$
X^2-crit $(0.05,3) = 7.815$ Do not reject H_0.
if X^2-stat ≤ 7.815 X^2-stat $= 7.4074$
Do not reject H_0.
Conclude that there is no significant change to the equity portfolio mix in 2012.

10.13 (a) H_0: No change in payment method
H_1: Payment method has changed
or
H_0: $\pi_1 = 0.23$ $\pi_2 = 0.35$ $\pi_3 = 0.42$
H_1: At least one π_i differs
$(i = 1, 2, 3)$
X^2-crit $(0.05,2) = 5.991$
Do not reject H_0 if X^2-stat ≤ 5.991
X^2-stat $= 14.8911$ Reject H_0.

(b) Conclude that there is a significant shift towards credit card payment.

10.14 (a) H_0: Limpopo same as national sales profile
H_1: Limpopo sales profile differs, or
H_0: $\pi_1 : \pi_2 : \pi_3 = 3 : 5 : 2$
H_1: At least one π_i ratio differs
$(i = 1, 2, 3)$
X^2-crit $(0.05,2) = 5.991$
Do not reject H_0 if X^2-stat ≤ 5.991
X^2-stat $= 6.9136$ Reject H_0.

(b) Limpopo consumers are buying more large-sized cereal packages.

10.15 (b) H_0: $\pi_1 = \pi_2 = \pi_3 = \pi_4$
H_1: At least one π_i differs
$(i = 1, 2, 3, 4)$

(c) X^2-crit $(0.10,3) = 6.2514$
Do not reject H_0 if X^2-stat ≤ 6.2514
X^2-stat $= 6.5169$ Reject H_0.
Compensation preferences differ across provinces.

(d) H_0: No association between compensation preferences and province H_1: Preferences vary according to province (there is an association)

(e) X^2-crit $(0.05,3) = 7.815$
Do not reject H_0 if X^2-stat ≤ 7.815
X^2-stat $= 6.5169$ Do not reject H_0.
Compensation preferences do not differ across provinces.

10.16 (a) Row percentages: Morn $= 22\%$ 62% 16%; Aft $= 30\%$ 47% 23%; Night $= 43\%$ 37% 21%

(b) H_0: No association (independent)
H_1: An association (not independent)
X^2-crit $(0.05,4) = 9.488$
Do not reject H_0 if X^2-stat ≤ 9.488
X^2-stat $= 10.0812$
Reject H_0. Conclude that an association exists between the nature of tyre defects and shift.

(c) On morning and afternoon shifts, mechanical causes are more common, while technical causes are more likely during the night shift.

(d) p_1 (mech/morn) $= 61.8\%$
$p_2 =$ (mech/aft) $= 46.5\%$
$p_3 =$ (mech/night) $= 36.6\%$
H_0: $\pi_1 = \pi_2 = \pi_3$
H_1: At least one π_i differs $(i = 1, 2, 3)$.
Same conclusion as (b) and (c).

10.17 (b) $\bar{x} = 10.324$ minutes
$s = 2.333$ minutes

(c) H_0: Flight delay times are normally distributed with $\mu = 10.324$ min and $\sigma = 2.333$ min.
H_1: Flight delay times do not follow this normal distribution.
Expected normal probabilities:
0.01125 0.10184 0.33173
0.3797 0.15296 0.02147
X^2-crit $(0.01,3) = 11.345$
Do not reject H_0 if X^2-stat ≤ 11.345.
X^2-stat $= 1.1397$
Do not reject H_0. Flight delay times follow the normal distribution
$(\mu = 10.324; \sigma = 2.333)$.

10.18 (c) H_0: No association (independent)
H_1: An association (not independent)
X^2-crit $(0.10,2) = 4.6052$
Do not reject H_0 if X^2-stat ≤ 4.6052.
X^2-stat $= 5.5525$
Reject H_0. Conclude that an association exists between gender and newspaper section preferred.

(d) p_1 (female/sport) $= 25.45\%$
$p_2 =$ (female/social) $= 44.44\%$

p_3 = (female/business) = 29.03%
H_0: $\pi_{Sport} = \pi_{Social} = \pi_{Bus}$
H_1: At least one π_i differs (i = 1, 2, 3)
Same conclusion as (c).

10.19 (c) H_0: No change in pattern of vehicle loans H_1: There is a pattern change

(d) X^2-crit (0.05,4) = 9.488
Do not reject H_0 if X^2-stat ≤ 9.488.
X^2-stat = 13.9 Reject H_0.
Conclude that a change in loan application patterns has taken place.

10.20 (c) H_0: No association (independent)
H_1: An association (not independent)
X^2-crit (0.05,2) = 5.991
Do not reject H_0 if X^2-stat ≤ 5.991.
X^2-stat = 7.5831
Reject H_0. Conclude that an association exists between the milk type purchased and the health-conscious status of consumer.

(d) p_1 (yes/fat free) = 80%
p_2 (yes/low fat) = 60%
p_3 (yes/full cream) = 42.3%
H_0: $\pi_1 = \pi_2 = \pi_3$
H_1: At least one π_i differs (i = 1, 2, 3).
Same conclusion as (c).

Chapter 11

11.1 See text.
11.2 Example: compare the output performance of five identical machines.
11.3 See text.
11.4 F-stat = 1.7085
11.5 F-crit (0.05,3,36) = 2.84 (approx) (actual = 2.866)
11.6 H_0: $\mu_1 = \mu_2 = \mu_3 = \mu_4$
H_1: At least one μ_i differs
Do not reject H_0 if F-stat ≤ 2.7249.
Since F-stat = 1.7085, do not reject H_0.
All population means are equal.
11.7 (a) Sample means (l/100km): Peugeot = 6.48 VW = 7.325 Ford = 6.88

(b) H_0: $\mu_1 = \mu_2 = \mu_3$
H_1: At least one μ_i differs
F-crit (0.05,2,11) = 3.98
F-stat = 4.234
Reject H_0. At least one make of vehicle has a different mean consumption level. By inspection, Peugeot is the most fuel efficient vehicle of those tested.

(c) If α = 0.01, then F-crit (0.01,2,11) = 7.21 F-stat = 4.234
Do not reject H_0.
No difference. All makes of vehicles are equally fuel efficient.

11.8 (a) H_0: $\mu_A = \mu_B = \mu_C$
H_1: At least one μ_i differs
F-crit (0.05,2,18) = 3.5546
F-stat = 2.7995
Do not reject H_0.

(b) No difference in mean sales per package design. Select any design as all are equally effective.

11.9 (a) H_0: $\mu_X = \mu_Y = \mu_Z$
H_1: At least one μ_i differs
F-crit (0.10,2,24) = 2.5383
F-stat = 2.574
Reject H_0. At least one bank has a different mean service rating score. By inspection, Bank X has the highest mean service rating score (marginal evidence).

(b) If α = 0.05, then F-crit (0.05,2,24) = 3.4028 F-stat = 2.574
Do not reject H_0.
No difference. All banks have an equal mean service rating score.

11.10 H_0: $\mu_B = \mu_W = \mu_S = \mu_T$
H_1: At least one μ_i differs
F-crit (0.05,3,26) = 2.9752
F-stat = 3.7199
Reject H_0. Shelf height and product sales are *not* statistically independent. At least one shelf height generates a different mean sales level. By inspection, shelves at waist and shoulder height generate higher mean sales than bottom and top shelves.

11.11 (a) H_0: $\mu_A = \mu_B = \mu_C$
H_1: At least one μ_i differs
F-crit (0.10,2,12) = 2.8068
F-stat = 3.2879
Reject H_0. Machine processing time varies by machine type (i.e. *not* independent). At least one machine has a different mean processing time. By inspection, machine A appears to have the fastest mean processing time.

(b) H_0: $\mu_A = \mu_B$
H_1: $\mu_A \neq \mu_B$
t-crit (0.10,8) = 1.8596
t-stat = 0.4376 Do not reject H_0.

No difference in mean processing times between machines A and B.

(c) Choose either machine A or machine B (definitely not machine C). A and B are equally fast, and machine C is significantly slower.

11.12 (a) $H_0: \mu_I = \mu_R = \mu_F = \mu_M$
$H_1:$ At least one μ_i differs

(b) F-crit $(0.05, 3, 76) = 2.7249$
Do not reject H_0 if F-stat ≤ 2.7249
F-stat $= 3.0757$
Reject H_0. At least one economic sector has a different mean earnings yield.

(c) By inspection, the financial and mining sectors have the higher earnings yields.

11.13 (a) $H_0: \mu_S = \mu_A = \mu_T$
$H_1:$ At least one μ_i differs

(b) F-crit $(0.05, 2, 57) = 3.1588$
Do not reject H_0 if F-stat ≤ 3.1588
F-stat $= 3.3907$
Reject H_0. At least one advertising strategy has a different mean sales level.

(c) By inspection, the 'sophisticated' strategy appears to make the largest mean sales impact.

(d) Compare 'sophisticated' and 'trendy' sales.
$H_0: \mu_S = \mu_T$
$H_1: \mu_S \neq \mu_T$
t-crit $(0.05, 38) = 2.0244$
t-stat $= 0.8316$
Do not reject H_0.
No difference in mean sales between the 'sophisticated' and 'trendy' strategies.

(e) Recommend either the 'sophisticated' or the 'trendy' advertising strategy as they are likely to produce equal mean sales volumes.

11.14 (a) Sample means: T = 73.83
C = 78.07 B = 69.73 M = 76.37
By inspection, the banking sector has the lowest mean leverage ratio, while the construction and manufacturing sectors have the highest.

(b) $H_0: \mu_T = \mu_B = \mu_C = \mu_M$
$H_1:$ At least one μ_i differs
F-crit $(0.05, 3, 116) = 2.6828$
Do not reject H_0 if F-stat ≤ 2.6828.
F-stat $= 2.8486$

Reject H_0. At least one economic sector has a different mean leverage ratio. By inspection, recommend investing in the banking sector as it appears to have the lowest financial risk.

(c) Compare the technology and banking sectors.
$H_0: \mu_T = \mu_B$
$H_1: \mu_T \neq \mu_{TB}$
t-crit $(0.05, 58) = 2.0017$
t-stat $= 1.3469$ Do not reject H_0.
No difference in mean leverage ratios between the technology and banking sectors.

(d) Based on statistical tests of (b) and (c) above, either the technology or the banking sector can be chosen as an investment option.

11.15 (a) Sample means: OJ = 9 L = 8.75
RP = 9.2 AV = 8.85
By inspection, mean differences appear to exist with OJ and RP producing the higher mean performance scores.

(b) $H_0: \mu_{OJ} = \mu_L = \mu_{RP} = \mu_{AV}$
$H_1:$ At least one μ_i differs
F-crit $(0.05, 3, 52) = 2.7826$
Do not reject H_0 if F-stat ≤ 2.7826
F-stat $= 3.4787$
Reject H_0. At least one training method has a different mean performance score. By inspection, role play and on-the-job training methods produce higher performance scores on average.

(c) Compare on-the-job and role play training methods.
$H_0: \mu_{OJ} = \mu_{RP}$
$H_1: \mu_{OJ} \neq \mu_{RP}$
t-crit $(0.05, 26) = -2.0555$
t-stat $= -1.6074$
Do not reject H_0.
No difference in mean performance scores between on-the-job and role play training methods.

(d) Based on statistical tests of (b) and (c) above, the HR manager can choose between either on-the-job or role play training as they produce similar performance scores on average.

11.16 See text.

11.17 Data types: response variable (numerical); Factor 1 (categorical); Factor 2 (categorical)

11.18 It measures the combined influence of the two categorical factors on the numeric response variable.

11.19 It is a plot of the sample means for the levels of Factor 1, split into the levels of Factor 2. It shows how the sample means vary with different combinations of the levels of the two factors.

11.20 (a)–(f)

Source of Variation	df	SS	MS	F-stat	p-value	F-crit
Factor A: PC O.S.	2	68	34	6.8	0.0025	5.08
Factor B: Laptop	3	42	14	2.8	0.0499	4.22
Interaction (AxB)	6	132	22	4.4	0.0013	3.20
Error (Residual)	48	240	5			
Total	59	482				

(g) Factor A and interaction effect are significant. Factor B is not statistically significant.

11.21 (a)
(i) Experience: H_0: μ(under 3) = μ(over 3)
H_1: At least one μ_i differs (i = under 3, over 3)
Qualifications: H_0: μ(B) = μ(A) = μ(S)
H_1: At least one μ_i differs (i = B, A, S)
Interaction: H_0: No interaction effect is present
H_1: Interaction effect present

(ii) Experience is statistically significant (F-stat (5.22) > F-crit (4.02)). Graduates (over 3) generate significantly higher average sales (40.65) than (under 3) graduates (36.75).

(iii) Qualification is statistically significant (F-stat (4.494) > F-crit (3.168)). Business graduates generate significantly higher average sales (42.32) than Arts graduates (36.71) or Social Science graduates (37.09).

(iv) Interaction effect: statistically significant (F-stat (3.436) > F-crit (3.168)). Business graduates, over 3 years, highest average sales (44.62); Social Science graduates, under 3 years, lowest average sales (32.59).

11.22 (a)
(i) Transmission: H_0: μ(voice) = μ(data)
H_1: At least one μ_i differs (i = voice, data)
Switch type: H_0: $\mu(1) = \mu(2) = \mu(3) = \mu(4)$

H_1: At least one μ_i differs (i = 1,2,3,4)
Interaction: H_0: No interaction effect is present
H_1: Interaction effect present

(ii) Transmission is statistically significant (F-stat (4.73) > F-crit (4.01)). Data transmission is likely to lead to a significantly higher average dropped call rate (0.872) than voice transmission (0.725) regardless of switch type used.

(iii) Switch type *is not* statistically significant (F-stat (1.063) > F-crit (2.769)).

All switch devices are likely to experience the same average dropped call rate.

(iv) Interaction effect: statistically significant (F-stat (4.75) > F-crit (2.769)).

SW2 and SW3, both transmitting voice (0.544 and 0.586) have the lowest average dropped call rate, while SW1 transmitting voice (0.97) and SW3 transmitting data (1.02) have the highest average dropped call rate.

11.23 (a) Tyre type : H_0: μ(radial) = μ(bias)
H_1: At least one μ_i differs (i = radial, bias)
TAM used: H_0: $\mu(1) = \mu(2) = \mu(3)$
H_1: At least one μ_i differs (i =1,2,3,4)
Interaction: H_0: No interaction effect present
H_1: Interaction effect is present

Tyre type produced is not statistically significant (F-stat (3.15) < F-crit (4.26)).

Average rubber wastage is likely to be the same for both tyre types, regardless of TAM use.

TAM used is statistically significant (F-stat (7.318) > F-crit (3.403)). Regardless of tyre type produced, average rubber wastage is likely to be lowest on TAM1 (3.318) compared to TAM2 (7.212) and TAM3 (6.321).

The *Interaction effect* is statistically significant (*F-stat* (4.199) > *F-crit* (3.403)). Average rubber wastage for bias tyres is lowest on TAM1 (2.694) but highest on TAM3 (8.754). By contrast average rubber wastage of radial tyres is lowest on TAM3 (3.888) and highest on TAM2 (6.704).

11.24 (a) [1] = 112 [2] = 15 [3] = 17 [4] = 56 [5] = 1.9535 [6] = 3.6823

    (b) $H_0: \mu_1 = \mu_2 = \mu_3$ H_1: At least one μ_i differs (i = 1, 2, 3)

    (c) Since F-stat < F-crit, do not reject H_0 in favour of H_1 at the 5% significance level.

    (d) Management conclusion: The quality of canvas raw material is the same from all three suppliers.

11.25 (a) [1] = 5953.73 [2] = 2 [3] = 42 [4] = 141.76 [5] = 4.0917 [6] = 0.0238 [7] = 3.2199

    (b) $H_0: \mu_1 = \mu_2 = \mu_3$ H_1: At least one μ_i differs (i = pilots, lawyers, stockbrokers)

    (c) Since F-stat > F-crit and *p*-value < 0.05, reject H_0 in favour of H_1 at the 5% significance level.

    (d) [8] = 2.7449 [9] = 2.0702 [10] = 0.5036 [11] = 0.0446 [12] = S (Signif); [13] = NS (Not signif) [14] = S (Signif)

    (e) Management conclusion: Pilots and stockbrokers have similar high mean stress levels while lawyers have significantly lower mean stress levels than the other two professions.

Chapter 12

12.1 See text.

12.2 Dependent variable, y

12.3 An independent variable is used as a predictor of the dependent variable.

12.4 Scatter plot

12.5 Method of least squares

12.6 Strong inverse relationship

12.7 $H_0: \rho = 0$
$H_1: \rho \neq 0$
Accept H_0 if $-2.12 \leq$ *t-stat* ≤ 2.12
t-stat = 1.851
Do not reject H_0. There is no significant relationship between x and y.

12.8 (a) Strong positive association
    (b) $\hat{y} = 18.916 + 1.112x$
        for $20 \leq x \leq 40$
    (c) $r^2 = 0.6516$
    (d) $y(est) = 46.716$ for $x = 25$
        (expected output of 47 units)

12.9 (a) Very strong positive association
    (b) $\hat{y} = 4.333 + 1.4167x$ for $3 \leq x \leq 8$
    (c) $r = 0.8552$
    (d) $r^2 = 0.7313$
    (e) *t-crit* = ± 2.364
        t-stat = 4.3655
        Reject H_0
    (f) $y(est) = 12.833$ for $x = 6$ (expected earnings yield %)

12.10 (a) x = interest rate y = number of loan applications
    (b) Strong negative (inverse) relationship
    (c) $r = -0.8302$
    (d) $H_0: \rho = 0$
        $H_1: \rho \neq 0$
        Accept H_0 if $-2.262 \leq$ *t-stat* ≤ 2.262.
        t-stat = -4.4677 Reject H_0.
        There is a significant relationship between x and y.
    (e) $\hat{y} = 48.991 - 3.9457x$
        for $5.5 \leq x \leq 8.5$
    (f) $b_1 = -3.9457$
        A 1% increase in interest rates will lead to 3.95 fewer loan applications.
    (g) $y(est) = 25.32$ for $x = 6$ (expected number of loan applications = 25)

12.11 (a) x = machine age (years)
        y = annual maintenance cost
    (b) Very strong positive (direct) relationship
    (c) $r = 0.870028$
    (d) $H_0: \rho = 0$
        $H_1: \rho \neq 0$
        Accept H_0 if $-2.228 \leq$ *t-stat* ≤ 2.228.
        t-stat = 5.58 Reject H_0.
        There is a significant relationship between x and y.
    (e) $\hat{y} = 12.627 + 5.8295x$ for $1 \leq x \leq 8$

(f) $b_1 = 5.8295$ For every additional year, the machine maintenance cost rises by R5.8295.

(g) $y(est) = $ R41.77 for $x = 5$ (expected maintenance costs for five-year-old machines)

12.12 (a) Moderate positive relationship

(b) $r = 0.5194$

(c) $H_0: \rho = 0$
$H_1: \rho \neq 0$
Accept H_0 if $-2.228 \leq t\text{-}stat \leq 2.228$.
$t\text{-}stat = 1.922$ Do not reject H_0.
There is no significant relationship between x and y.

(d) $\hat{y} = 60.1032 + 2.7168x$
for $4 \leq x \leq 9$

(e) $y(est) = 81.84$ for $x = 8$ (expected performance rating score)

12.13 (a) $r = 0.7448$

(b) $H_0: \rho = 0$
$H_1: \rho \neq 0$
Accept H_0 if $-2.262 \leq t\text{-}stat \leq 2.262$.
$t\text{-}stat = 3.3484$ Reject H_0.
There is a significant relationship between x and y.

(c) $\hat{y} = 14.4174 + 0.729x$
for $34 \leq x \leq 65$

(d) $r^2 = 0.5547$

(e) $y(est) = 56.7\%$ for $x = 58$ (expected election percentage)

(f) $y(est) = 74.2\%$ for $x = 82$ (extrapolated (untested) estimate – outside domain of x)

12.14 (a) $x = $ capital investment
$y = $ return on investment

(c) $r = 0.4145$
$\hat{y} = 1.2741 + 0.0678x$
for $21.1 \leq x \leq 79.5$

(d) $r^2 = 0.1718$

(e) $H_0: \rho = 0$
$H_1: \rho \neq 0$
Accept H_0 if $-2.014 \leq t\text{-}stat \leq 2.014$ (approximate).
$t\text{-}stat = 2.9865$ Reject H_0.
There is a significant relationship between x and y.

(f) $b_1 = 0.0678$ For every 1% change (up/down) in capital investment, ROI will change (up/down) by 0.0678%.

(g) $y(est) = 5.005$ for $x = 55$ (expected ROI)

12.15 (a) $x = $ council valuations
$y = $ market values

(c) $r = 0.7810$
$\hat{y} = 71.362 + 1.0151x$
for $48 \leq x \leq 154$

(d) $r^2 = 0.61$

(e) $H_0: \rho = 0$
$H_1: \rho \neq 0$
Accept H_0 if $-2.024 \leq t\text{-}stat \leq 2.024$.
$t\text{-}stat = 7.70975$ Reject H_0.
There is a significant relationship between x and y.

(f) $b_1 = 1.0151$ For every R1 change (up/down) in council valuations, the market value of a property will change (up/down) by R1.0151.

(g) $y(est) = $ R172.87 for $x = 100$ (expected market value)

Chapter 13

13.1 SLR has only one independent variable. MLR has two or more independent variables.

13.2 (a) $R^2 = 36.21\%$

(b) $H_0: \beta_1 = \beta_2 = \beta_3 = \beta_4 = \beta_5 = 0$
vs H_1: At least one $\beta_i \neq 0$ ($i = 1,2,3,4,5$)

(c) $F\text{-}stat = 4.5412$ and $F\text{-}crit = F(0.05,5,40) = 2.45$

(d) Reject H_0. Conclude that the overall model is statistically significant. (i.e. at least one x_i is statistically significant in estimating y)

13.3 (a) For each x_i variable (A, B, C and D), test: $H_0: \beta_i = 0$ against $H_1: \beta_i \neq 0$ for i = A, B, C and D.

(b), (c), (d) $t\text{-}crit = t(0.05,19) = \pm 2.093$
For A: Since $t\text{-}stat$ (2.44) > $t\text{-}crit$ (+2.093); or p-value (0.0253) < α (0.05), or $\{0.09 \leq \beta_A \leq 2.78\}$ does not cover zero, conclude variable A is statistically significant.

For B: Since $t\text{-}stat$ (−2.39) < -$t\text{-}crit$ (−2.093); or p-value (0.014) < α (0.05), or $\{-4.42 \leq \beta_B \leq -0.25\}$ does not cover zero, conclude variable B is statistically significant.

For C: Since $t\text{-}stat$ (1.42) < -$t\text{-}crit$ (+2.093); or p-value (0.1737) > α (0.05), or $\{-0.01 \leq \beta_C \leq 2.12\}$ covers zero, conclude variable C is not statistically significant.

For D: Since $t\text{-}stat$ (1.69) < -$t\text{-}crit$ (+2.093); or p-value (0.1083) > α

(0.05), or $\{-0.48 \leq \beta_D \leq 4.06\}$ covers zero, conclude variable D is *not* statistically significant.

13.4 (a) For x_3 variable, test: $H_0: \beta_3 = 0$ against $H_1: \beta_3 \neq 0$

(b) $t\text{-}crit = t(0.05, 30) = \pm 2.042$. Hence, do not reject H_0 if $-2.042 \leq t\text{-}stat \leq +2.042$.

(c) Since $t\text{-}stat$ (2.44) > $t\text{-}crit$ (+2.042), hence reject H_0 in favour of H_1 at $\alpha = 0.05$.

(d) Conclude that the x_3 variable is statistically significant.

13.5 (a) Holding all other variables constant, a unit increase in x_2 will result in a 1.6 reduction in $\hat{y}$.

(b) Yes, since the 95% confidence interval for β_2 does not cover zero.

13.6 Let fuel category *'lean'* = base category.

Fuel type	F1	F2
Leaded	1	0
Unleaded	0	1
Lean	0	0

13.7 Let the category *'spring'* = base category.

Season	S1	S2	S3
summer	1	0	0
autumn	0	1	0
winter	0	0	1
spring	0	0	0

13.8 (a) $R^2 = 54.53\%$

(b) $H_0: \beta_T = \beta_S = \beta_C = 0$
H_1: At least one $\beta_i \neq 0$
$F\text{-}crit = F(0.05, 3, 31) = 2.92$
$F\text{-}stat = 12.39$ and
p-value $= 0.00001707$
Reject H_0. Conclude the overall model is statistically significant. (i.e. at least one x_i is statistically significant in estimating y).

(c), (d) and (e)
For each x_i variable, test:
$H_0: \beta_i = 0$ against $H_1: \beta_i \neq 0$
with $t\text{-}crit = t(0.05, 31) = \pm 2.04$

Tenure: Since $t\text{-}stat$ (3.376) > $t\text{-}crit$ (+2.04); or p-value (0.001997) < α (0.05), or $\{0.087 \leq \beta_T \leq 0.352\}$ does not cover zero, conclude *Tenure* is statistically significant.

Satisfaction: Since $t\text{-}stat$ (−1.692) lies within $t\text{-}crit$ (± 2.04); or p-value (0.100765) > α (0.05), or $\{-0.406 \leq \beta_S \leq 0.038\}$ covers zero, conclude *Satisfaction* is not statistically significant.

Commitment: Since $t\text{-}stat$ (−4.13) < $t\text{-}crit$ (-2.04); or p-value (0.000254) < α (0.05), or $\{-0.497 \leq \beta_C \leq -0.168\}$ does not cover zero, conclude *Commitment* is statistically significant.

(f) (i) No, *organisational commitment* is the most important explanatory factor. It has a larger $t\text{-}stat$ value (−4.13) and a smaller p-value (0.000254) than job tenure.

(ii) No, for job satisfaction; yes, for organisational commitment.

(g) $\{16.518 \leq \hat{y} \leq 19.083\}$ using $t\text{-}crit = t(0.025, 31) = \pm 2.04$; standard error = 3.7204; $n = 35$

13.9 (a) $R^2 = 64.98\%$

(b) $H_0: \beta_D = \beta_S = \beta_V = 0$
H_1: At least one $\beta_i \neq 0$
$F\text{-}crit = F(0.05, 3, 27) = 2.99$
$F\text{-}stat = 16.70$ and
p-value $= 0.000002466$

Reject H_0. Conclude the overall model is statistically significant. (i.e. at least one x_i is statistically significant in estimating y).

(c), (d) and (e)
For each x_i variable, test:
$H_0: \beta_i = 0$ against $H_1: \beta_i \neq 0$ with $t\text{-}crit = t(0.05, 27) = \pm 2.052$

Dexterity: Since $t\text{-}stat$ (−3.886) < $t\text{-}crit$ (−2.052); or p-value (0.0006) < α (0.05), or $\{-0.17 \leq \beta_D \leq -0.0524\}$ does not cover zero, conclude *dexterity* is statistically significant.

Speed: Since $t\text{-}stat$ (3.677) > $t\text{-}crit$ (+2.052); or p-value (0.001) < α (0.05), or $\{0.0077 \leq \beta_S \leq 0.027\}$ does not cover zero, conclude *speed* is statistically significant.

Viscosity: Since $t\text{-}stat$ (1.525) < $t\text{-}crit$ (+2.052); or p-value (0.1388) > α (0.05), or $\{-0.6625 \leq \beta_V \leq 4.5\}$ covers zero, conclude *viscosity is not* statistically significant.

(f) Most important factor is *operator dexterity* (p-value (0.0006)), then *machine speed* (*p*-value = 0.001). *Plastic viscosity* is not a significant influencing factor (*p*-value = 0.1388).

(g) $\{2.79\% \le \hat{y} \le 3.17\%\}$
using *t-crit* = $t(0.025,27)$ = ±2.052; standard error = 0.516; n = 31

13.10 (a) A suggested binary coding scheme with marketing method C as the base category

Coding Scheme		
Method	**MA**	**MB**
A	1	0
B	0	1
C	0	0

(b) $\hat{y}$ = 26.387 + 0.389 *Experience* – 3.659 MA + 1.472 MB (based on data recoded as in (a))

(c) R^2 = 62.31%

(d) $H_0: \beta_E = \beta_{MA} = \beta_{MB} = 0$
H_1: At least one $\beta_i \ne 0$
F-crit = $F(0.05,3,16)$ = 3.24
F-stat = 8.817 and
p-value = 0.001108
Reject H_0. Conclude the overall model is statistically significant. (i.e. at least one x_i is statistically significant in estimating y).

(e) For *Experience*, test: $H_0: \beta_E = 0$
against $H_1: \beta_E \ne 0$
with *t-crit* = $t(0.05,16)$ = ±2.12

Since *t-stat* (2.335) > *t-crit* (2.12), conclude *work experience* is statistically significant.

(f) For MA and MB, test: $H_0: \beta_i = 0$ vs $H_1: \beta_i \ne 0$ (*i* = MA, MB), with *t-crit* = $t(0.05,16)$ = ±2.12

MA: Since *t-stat* (−2.659) < lower *t-crit* (−2.12), conclude *MA* is statistically significant (i.e. adopting marketing method A results in significantly lower consultant productivity levels compared to using marketing method C (base category).

MB: Since −*t-crit* (−2.12) < *t-stat* (1.102) < +*t-crit* (+2.12), conclude MB is not statistically significant (i.e. consultant productivity levels are the same, on average, for marketing methods B and C (base category).

Overall conclusion: the independent variable 'marketing method' is statistically significant, but only for method A (when compared to method C). Methods B and C can be combined as there is no statistically significant difference between them with regards to consultant productivity levels.

(g) and (h)
Experience: Since its *p*-value (0.0329) < α = 0.05, or $\{0.036 \le \beta_E \le 0.742\}$ does not cover zero, conclude that *work experience* is statistically significant.

MA: Since its *p*-value (0.0172) < α = 0.05, or $\{-6.576 \le \beta_{MA} \le -0.742\}$ does not cover zero, conclude that *marketing method A* is significantly different from marketing method C (base category) in terms of consultant productivity levels.

MB: Since its *p*-value (0.2867) > α = 0.05, or $\{-1.36 \le \beta_{MA} \le 4.304\}$ covers zero, conclude *marketing method B* is not significantly different from marketing method C (base category) in terms of consultant productivity levels.

(i) Employ consultants with longer work experience and avoid using marketing method A as it produces lower productivity levels, on average, than either methods B or C.

(j) $\{29.86 \le \hat{y} \le 32.08\}$ using *t-crit* = $t(0.05,16)$ = ±2.12; standard error = 2.3425; n = 20

13.11 (a) A suggested binary coding scheme: *Region*, base category = KZN; *Sector*, base category = Construction

Region	Code	R1	R2	Sector	Code	S1
Gauteng	1	1	0	Agriculture	1	1
Cape	2	0	1	Construction	2	0
KZN	3	0	0			

(b) $\hat{y}$ = 11.0146 + 0.0002 *Sales* + 0.1791 *Margin%* + 0.0091 *Debt ratio%* + 3.1453 *R1* + 0.9213 *R2* − 0.923 *S* (based on data recoded as in (a))

(c) R^2 = 83.27%

(d)　H_0: $\beta_S = \beta_{M\%} = \beta_{DR} = \beta_{R1} = \beta_{R2}$
$= \beta_S = 0$
H_1: At least one $\beta_i \neq 0$
$F\text{-}crit = F(0.05,6,18) = 2.66$
$F\text{-}stat = 14.932$ and
$p\text{-}value = 0.000004076$

Reject H_0. Conclude the overall model is statistically significant. (i.e. at least one x_i is statistically significant in estimating y).

(e), (h), (i)

For all variable, test: H_0: $\beta_i = 0$ vs H_1: $\beta_i \neq 0$ with $t\text{-}crit = t(0.05,18)$ $= \pm 2.101$

Sales: Since $t\text{-}stat$ (2.1668) > $t\text{-}crit$ (2.101), or $p\text{-}value$ (0.0439) < $\alpha = 0.05$ or $\{0.00001 \leq \beta_S \leq 0.00033\}$ does not cover zero, conclude sales is statistically significant.

Margin%: Since $t\text{-}stat$ (2.6656) > $t\text{-}crit$ (2.101), or $p\text{-}value$ (0.0158) < $\alpha = 0.05$ or $\{0.0379 \leq \beta_{M\%} \leq 0.3203\}$ does not cover zero, conclude *margin %* is statistically significant.

Debt ratio%: Since $-t\text{-}crit$ (-2.101) < $t\text{-}stat$ (0.593) < $t\text{-}crit$ (2.101), or $p\text{-}value$ (0.5606) > $\alpha = 0.05$ or $\{-0.0232 \leq \beta_{DR\%} \leq 0.0415\}$ covers zero, conclude *debt ratio%* is *not* statistically significant.

(f)　*Region:* For *R1* and *R2*, test: R1 (*Gauteng*): Since $t\text{-}stat$ (3.7494) > $t\text{-}crit$ (2.101); or $p\text{-}value$ (0.0015) < $\alpha = 0.05$, or $\{1.38288 \leq \beta_{R1} \leq 4.9077\}$ does not cover zero, conclude that *R1* is statistically significant. Gauteng-based companies have a significantly higher ROC (%) on average than KZN-based companies (i.e. base region).
R2 (*Cape*): Since $t\text{-}stat$ (1.5716) < $t\text{-}crit$ (2.101); or $p\text{-}value$ (0.1335) > $\alpha = 0.05$, or $\{-0.31031 \leq \beta_{R2} \leq 2.15295\}$ covers zero, conclude that *R2* is not statistically significant. Cape-companies have the *same* average ROC (%) as KZN-based companies (i.e. base region). *Region* is statistically significant since Gauteng differs from KZN. Cape and KZN can be merged.

(g)　*Sector:* For S, test: S (*Agriculture*): Since $t\text{-}stat$ (-2.195) < $t\text{-}crit$ (-2.101); or $p\text{-}value$ (0.0415) < $\alpha = 0.05$, or $\{-1.80651 \leq \beta_S \leq -0.03956\}$ does not cover zero, conclude agricultural-sector companies have a significantly *lower* ROC (%) on average than construction-sector companies (i.e. base category). *Sector* is therefore statistically significant.

(j)　Significant performance measures of ROC% are: Sales, Margin%, but not Debt ratio%.

For *region*, Gauteng has a significantly positive impact on ROC% compared to Cape and KZN. The *agricultural* sector has a significant negative impact on ROC% compared to the construction sector.

(k)　$\{15.3\% \leq \hat{y} \leq 16.1\%\}$ using $t\text{-}crit = t(0.05,18) = \pm 2.101$; standard error = 0.9524; n = 25

Chapter 14

14.1 – 14.7　See text.

14.8　(a)　Price relatives: A = 120　B = 126.7　C = 116.7

　　　(b)　Composite (Laspeyres) price index (using both methods) = 122.9

14.9　(a)　Quantity relatives: A = 70　B = 105.45　C = 125

　　　(b)　Composite (Laspeyres) quantity index (using both methods) = 104.5

　　　(c)　Motorcycle units sold (volumes) have increased by 4.5% only from 2009 to 2010.

14.10　(a)　Composite (Paasche) quantity index (using both methods) = 104.41

　　　(b)　Motorcycle units sold (volumes) have increased by 4.41% only from 2009 to 2010.

14.11　(a)　Price relative (ISDN): (2010) 90 (2011) 80

　　　(b)　Composite price index: (2010) 104.71　(2011) 98.87

　　　(c)　Composite quantity index: (2010) 122.7　(2011) 125.5

14.12　(a)　Composite salary (price) index: (2011) 120.46

(c) Salary relatives: Programmers have had the largest salary increase.
Systems analyst = 119.05
Programmer = 124.14
Network manager = 116.67

14.13 (a) Staff (quantity) relatives: Systems analysts have shown the largest increase in staff.
Systems analyst = 127.38
Programmer = 85.42
Network manager = 110.34

(b) Composite staff (quantity) index: (2011) 109.14

14.14 (a) Price relatives: (2010)
HQ26 = 11.02   HQ32 = 95.22

(b) Composite price (cost) index: (2009) = 101.06   (2010) = 99.05

(c) Overall costs increased by 1.06% from 2008 to 2009, but showed a overall decrease of 0.95% from 2008 to 2010.

(d) Composite link relatives: (2009) 101.06   (2010) 98.01

14.15 (a) Re-based to 2009   78.6   85.7   89.3   97.3   101.8   100   102.7

(b) Link relatives 100   109.1   104.2   109   104.6   98.2   102.7

14.16 (a) Federal (base = 2010) 84.4   87.2   91.4   93.8   100   101.6
Baltic (base = 2010)   89.7   96.7   94   95.7   100   103

(b) Federal = 9.4% increase;
Baltic = 6.4% increase only

(c) Link relatives: Federal   100   103.4   104.8   102.6   106.6   101.6
Baltic   100   107.9   97.1   101.8   104.5   103

(d) Baltic = 3% increase;
Federal = 1.6% increase only

(e) Geometric mean:
Federal = 1.03785 (3.785%);
Baltic = 1.02799 (2.799%)

(f) Federal Insurance's claims grew by an average of 3.785% annually between 2006 and 2011.

14.17 (a) Price relatives: Milk = 108.2
Bread = 104.7 Sugar = 111.9
Maize = 106.5

(b) Composite price index (2011) = 107.2 (an overall 7.2% price increase from 2010)

(c) Quantity relatives: Milk = 83.8
Bread = 114.3 Sugar = 71.4
Maize = 110.3

(d) Composite consumption index (2011) = 93.6 (an overall 6.4% drop in consumption from 2010)

14.18 (a) Price relatives (2010)
Electricity = 106.1
Sewage = 116.1 Water = 120.7
Telephone = 85.5

(b) Composite price index: (2009) = 100.3 (2010) = 97.5

(c) In 2009, overall utility costs increased by 0.3% from 2008; while in 2010, overall utility costs decreased by 2.5% from 2008.

14.19 (a) Consumption relatives (2010)
Electricity = 14..1 Sewage = 94.1
Water = 127.7 Telephone = 124.9

(b) Composite consumption index: (2009) = 113.1 (2010) = 127.7

(c) Relative to 2008, overall usage of utility increased by 13.1% in 2009; while in 2010, overall utility usage increased by 27.7% relative to 2008.

14.20 (a) Re-based to 2009 90.7 86 93.5   95.3 100 108.4 104.7

(c) From 2009 to 2011: 4.7% increase

(d) Link relatives 100 94.9 108.7   102 104.9 108.4 96.6
Largest annual increase of 8.7% from 2006 to 2007.

(e) Geometric mean: Leather cost = 102.4244 (2.424% annual increase on average)

14.21 (a) CPI-adjusted salaries R407.4   R406 R405.8 R403.6 R385.1   R393.7 R383.5

(b) Salaries have been below base-period salaries from 2007 to 2011.

(c) Salary link relatives 100 104.9   103.9 106.2 104.0 106.4   102.8
CPI link relatives   100 105.3   104   106.7 109   104.1 105.6

14.22 (a) Re-based to 2008   83.2 85.7   87.8 92.4 95.3 100 102.5   106.3

(c) Link relatives: 100 102.95   102.46 105.2 103.14 104.98   102.46 103.77

(d) Budgets: R5 000 000   R5 147 500   R5 274 129   R5 548 384   R5 722 603   R6 007 589   R6 155 376   R6 387 434

14.23 (a) Price relatives (2010):
Java = 115.3 Colombia = 115.6
Sumatra = 115.7 Mocha = 110.5
   (b) Composite price index (2010) =
113.9
   (c) Cheaper. Coffee imports have
increased by only 13.9% since
2007.
   (d) Composite quantity index (2010) =
109.5

14.24 (a) Composite claims index (2010)
= 118.34 (claims have increased by
18.34% since 2008.)
   (b) Quantity relatives (2010):
GPs = 150 Specialists = 83.33
Dentists = 150 Medicines = 140
   (c) Composite price index (2010) =
111.6

14.25 (a) Quantity relatives (2010):
Trainer = 114.6 Balance = 120
Dura = 88.9
Dura's sales volume is down by
11.1% from 2009.
   (b) Composite quantity (volume) index
(2010) = 110.83 (10.83% increase)
   (c) Overall sales volumes do not meet
the required growth rate of 12% p.a.

14.26 (a) Re-based to 2006: 71.28 82.82
87.24 94.16 96.72 100 101.78
104.7 109.3 114.4
   (b) Link relatives: 100 116.2 105.34
107.92 102.73 103.39 101.78
102.87 104.42 104.63
   (c) Geometric mean = 1.053974
(5.3974% p.a.)

14.27 (a) Price relatives (Cruiser model):
100 102.1 106.6 111.7 121.9
   (b) Composite price index: 100 104
109.2 113.5 121.7
   (c) On average, motorcycle prices have
increased by 21.7% from 2007 to
2011.
   (d) Link relatives (Classic model):
100 107.6 102.3 100.9 106.4
   (e) Geometric mean (Classic model):
1.04263 (4.263%)
   (f) Composite quantity index:
100 84.1 93.2 120.7 121.3
   (g) Motorcycle sales volumes have risen
by 21.3% from 2007 to 2011.

14.28 (a) Cost relative index series (passenger
tyres) (base = January 2010)
100 100.8 100 103.5 104
102.6 107.2 111.1 109.1 105.7
106.3 95.1

   (b) Composite cost index series (base =
January 2010)
100 98 97.4 99.8 100.3 99.3
103.4 105.9 104.2 102.7 102.8
96.8
Overall monthly production costs
have fluctuated from 3.2% below to
5.9% above January 2010 costs.
   (c) Link relative index series (light
truck radial tyres)
100 96.1 100 100.6 99.9 100.1
103.5 99.6 100 99.9 100.1
100.2
   (d) Composite volume index series
(base = January 2010)
100 133.7 123 106.8 141.6
138.3 156.5 146.4 138.3 143.7
129.2 53.2
   (e) Production volumes from
February to November have
fluctuated between 6.8% to 56.5%
higher than January 2010. In
December, output slumped by
46.8% from January 2006 (possibly
due to the factory closing for the
holiday period).
Monthly production volumes of
tyres are more volatile than
production costs.

Chapter 15

15.1 Cross-sectional data is gathered at one
point in time; time series data is recorded
at fixed intervals over time.
15.2 Monthly national new car sales; daily
temperature for Cape Town.
15.3 A line graph
15.4 See text.
15.5 See text.
15.6 Yes, averaging occurs over a longer
period (i.e. five periods) producing a
smoother curve.
15.7 Seasonal influences stimulate the time
series values by 8% above the trend/
cyclical level.
15.8 Seasonal influences depress the time
series values by 12% below the trend/
cyclical level.
15.9 (a) Four-yearly moving average:
119.25   119.875   120.5
125.75   132.75 ...
   (b) Five-yearly moving average:
120.4   119.8   119.4   127.4
135.4 ...

(e) Pattern: upward cyclical trend

15.10 (b) y(trend) = 29 + 2.0182x

(c) $x = 11$ y(trend) = 51.20 (51)
$x = 12$ y(trend) = 53.22 (53)
$x = 13$ y(trend) = 55.24 (55)

15.11 (b) y(trend) = 71.475 − 1.21765x
where $x = 1$ in Q1, 2008;
$x = 2$ in Q2, 2008

(c) Seasonal indexes:
Q1 = 121.4   Q2 = 79.7
Q3 = 78.7   Q4 = 120.2

(d) Q1, 2012 ($x = 17$)
y(trend-adj) = 61.64 (62);
Q2, 2012 ($x = 18$)
y(trend-adj) = 39.5 (40)

15.12 (b) y(trend) = 84.933 − 2.097x
where $x = 1$ in Sept; $x = 2$ in Oct

(c) Estimated occupancy rate (%):
y(est) = 61.866% ($x = 11$);
y(est) = 59.769% ($x = 12$)

15.13 (b) y(trend) = 20.8 + 4.95x where
$x = 1$ in Q1, 2008; $x = 2$ in Q2, 2008

(c) Seasonal indexes:
Q1 = 77.97   Q2 = 115.98
Q3 = 175.61   Q4 = 30.44

(d) Estimated electricity demand:
y(est) = 201.69 mw ($x = 19$);
y(est) = 36.47 mw ($x = 20$)

15.14 (a) 2008
Summer 417.6   Autumn 442
Winter 406.5   Spring 350
2009
Summer 444.1   Autumn 485.7
Winter 435.5   Spring 566.7
2010
Summer 486.8   Autumn 540.2
Winter 500   Spring 594.4

(c) y(trend) = 435.64 + 5.6713x
where $x = 1$ (summer 2008); $x = 2$
(autumn 2008)

(d) Estimated hotel turnover:
y(est) = R692.74m ($x = 13$);
y(est) = R576.84m ($x = 14$)

15.15 (a) Seasonal indexes:
Summer = 107.4   Autumn = 97
Winter = 92.63   Spring = 102.97

(b) Seasonal forces have a moderate
quarterly influence

(c) y(trend) = 52.05 + 0.8544x
where $x = 1$ (summer 2008);
$x = 2$ (autumn 2008)

(d) Estimated farming unit sales (2012)
Summer = 71.5 (72)
Autumn = 65.41 (66)

Winter = 63.25 (64)
Spring = 71.19 (72)

15.16 (b) Seasonal indexes:
Summer = 73   Autumn = 119.5
Winter = 117.6   Spring = 90

(c) y(trend) = 3.1091 + 0.0601x
where $x = 1$ (summer 09);
$x = 2$ (autumn 09)

(d) Estimated energy costs (2012)
(using $x = 13, 14, 15, 16$)
Summer = R2.84
Autumn = R4.7215
Winter = R 4.7172
Spring = R 3.6642

15.17 (c) Seasonal indexes:
Q1 = 91.72   Q2 = 103.46
Q3 = 106.41   Q4 = 98.41

(e) y(trend) = 1078.2 + 39.338x
where $x = 1$ (Q1, 2007); $x = 2$
(Q2, 2007)

(h) Estimates (2012) 1747; 2011;
2110; 1990

15.18 Estimated quarterly sales:
Q1 = R11.4   Q2 = R13.8
Q3 = R13.2   Q4 = R9.6

15.19 (b) (2009) 29.19; 29.66; 25.43; 36.32
(2010) 36.13; 37.3; 27.65; 37.36

(c) Estimated visitors (2011)
Q1 = 23.25   Q2 = 33.375
Q3 = 60.75   Q4 = 32.625

15.20 (b) y(trend) = 41.964 + 5.2636x
where $x = 1$ (2001); $x = 2$ (2002)

(c) Estimates (2012) R105.1
(2013) R110.4

15.21 (c) Seasonal indexes
Period 1 = 112.65
Period 2 = 97.79
Period 3 = 89.56

(d) y(trend) = 42.621 − 1.0315x
where $x = 1$ (Jan – Apr 2007);
$x = 2$ (May – Aug 2007)

(e) Estimates (2011)
Period 1 = 32.907
Period 2 = 27.558
Period 3 = 24.313

15.22 y(trend) = 89.429 − 2.7143x
where $x = 1$ (Jan); $x = 2$ (Feb)
Selling policy: If share price falls below
60c.
Estimates:
Aug = 67.71c   Sept = 65c
Oct = 62.286c   Nov = 59.572c
Sell Netron shares in November.

15.23 De-seasonalised number of visitors
  (a) 2008
     Summer 175   Autumn 156.4
     Winter 140.9   Spring 167
     2009
     Summer 177.7   Autumn 161.7
     Winter 150   Spring 179.2
     2010
     Summer 191.1   Autumn 173.4
     Winter 164.8   Spring 186.8

15.24 (a) Seasonal indexes
     Q1 = 70.37   Q2 = 89.19
     Q3 = 136.28   Q4 = 104.15
  (b) y(trend) = 14.2 + 0.2066x
     where $x = 1$ (Q1, 2007);
     $x = 2$ (Q2, 2007)
  (c) Estimates (2011)
     Q1 = R12.46m   Q2 = R15.98m
     Q3 = R24.7m   Q4 = R19.09m

15.25 (a) y(trend) = 8.6857 + 1.1821x
     where $x = 1$ (2005); $x = 2$ (2006);
     $x = 3$ (2007)
  (b) Estimate (2012) = R18.143

15.26 (b) Seasonal indexes
     Q1 = 100.77   Q2 = 93.62
     Q3 = 97.99   Q4 = 107.62
  (c) y(trend) = 203.42 – 3.5524x
     where $x = 1$ (Q1, 2008);
     $x = 2$ (Q2, 2008)
  (d) Estimates (2011)
     Q1 = 158.45   Q2 = 143.88
     Q3 = 147.12   Q4 = 157.75

15.27 (a) Three-yearly moving average: (period 2)
     252.7; 289.7; 263; 224.7;
     142; 141.7 ...
     Five-yearly moving average: (period 3)
     255.6; 237.2; 210.4; 189.0;
     162; 184 ...

15.28 (a) Seasonal indexes
     Q1 = 107.76   Q2 = 100.61
     Q3 = 90.72   Q4 = 100.91
     y(trend) = 58 114 + 1302x
     where $x = 1$ (Q1, 2005);
     $x = 2$ (Q2, 2005)
  (b) Estimates (2012)
     Q1 = 103 312   Q2 = 97 767
     Q3 = 89 337   Q4 = 100 686
     Estimates (2013)
     Q1 = 108 924   Q2 = 103 007
     Q3 = 94 062   Q4 = 105 941
  (c) High confidence in estimates as
     trend and seasonal patterns are
     very stable.

15.29 (a) Seasonal indexes
     Q1 = 79.1   Q2 = 110.69
     Q3 = 117.46   Q4 = 92.75
     y(trend) = 15 591 + 224.66x
     where $x = 1$ (Q1, 2006);
     $x = 2$ (Q2, 2006)
  (b) Estimates (2012)
     Q1 = 16 775   Q2 = 23 723
     Q3 = 25 438   Q4 = 20 295
     Estimates (2013)
     Q1 = 17 486   Q2 = 24 718

15.30 (a) Seasonal indexes
     Q1 = 104.21   Q2 = 96.98
     Q3 = 102.88   Q4 = 95.93
     y(trend) = 952.75 – 9.917x
     where $x = 1$ (Q1, 2006);
     $x = 2$ (Q2, 2006)
  (b) Estimates (2012)
     Q1 = 734   Q2 = 674
     Q3 = 705   Q4 = 648

Appendices

APPENDIX 1: LIST OF STATISTICAL TABLES

$z \sim N(0;1)$

TABLE 1 The standard normal distribution (z)

This table gives the area under the standard normal curve between 0 and z

$P[0 < Z < z]$

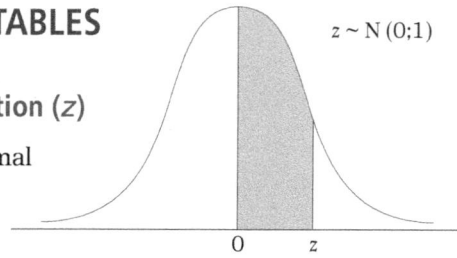

In Excel (2016): use NORM.S.DIST(z, cumulative = True) to find $P(-\infty < Z < z)$

Z	0.00	0.01	0.02	0.03	0.04	0.05	0.06	0.07	0.08	0.09
0.0	0.0000	0.0040	0.0080	0.0120	0.0160	0.0199	0.0239	0.0279	0.0319	0.0359
0.1	0.0398	0.0438	0.0478	0.0517	0.0557	0.0596	0.0636	0.0675	0.0714	0.0753
0.2	0.0793	0.0832	0.0871	0.0910	0.0948	0.0987	0.1026	0.1064	0.1103	0.1141
0.3	0.1179	0.1217	0.1255	0.1293	0.1331	0.1368	0.1406	0.1443	0.1480	0.1517
0.4	0.1554	0.1591	0.1628	0.1664	0.1700	0.1736	0.1772	0.1808	0.1844	0.1879
0.5	0.1915	0.1950	0.1985	0.2019	0.2054	0.2088	0.2123	0.2157	0.2190	0.2224
0.6	0.2257	0.2291	0.2324	0.2357	0.2389	0.2422	0.2454	0.2486	0.2517	0.2549
0.7	0.2580	0.2611	0.2642	0.2673	0.2703	0.2734	0.2764	0.2793	0.2823	0.2852
0.8	0.2881	0.2910	0.2939	0.2967	0.2995	0.3023	0.3051	0.3078	0.3106	0.3133
0.9	0.3159	0.3186	0.3212	0.3238	0.3264	0.3289	0.3315	0.3340	0.3365	0.3389
1.0	0.3413	0.3438	0.3461	0.3485	0.3508	0.3531	0.3554	0.3557	0.3599	0.3621
1.1	0.3643	0.3665	0.3686	0.3708	0.3729	0.3749	0.3770	0.3790	0.3810	0.3830
1.2	0.3849	0.3869	0.3888	0.3907	0.3925	0.3944	0.3962	0.3980	0.3997	0.4015
1.3	0.4032	0.4049	0.4066	0.4082	0.4099	0.4115	0.4131	0.4147	0.4162	0.4177
1.4	0.4192	0.4207	0.4222	0.4236	0.4251	0.4265	0.4279	0.4292	0.4306	0.4319
1.5	0.4332	0.4345	0.4357	0.4370	0.4382	0.4394	0.4406	0.4418	0.4429	0.4441
1.6	0.4452	0.4463	0.4474	0.4484	0.4495	0.4505	0.4515	0.4525	0.4535	0.4545
1.7	0.4554	0.4564	0.4573	0.4582	0.4591	0.4599	0.4608	0.4616	0.4625	0.4633
1.8	0.4641	0.4649	0.4656	0.4664	0.4671	0.4678	0.4686	0.4693	0.4699	0.4706
1.9	0.4713	0.4719	0.4726	0.4732	0.4738	0.4744	0.4750	0.4756	0.4761	0.4767
2.0	0.4772	0.4778	0.4783	0.4788	0.4793	0.4798	0.4803	0.4808	0.4812	0.4817
2.1	0.4821	0.4826	0.4830	0.4834	0.4838	0.4842	0.4846	0.4850	0.4854	0.4857
2.2	0.4861	0.4864	0.4868	0.4871	0.4875	0.4878	0.4881	0.4884	0.4887	0.4890
2.3	0.48928	0.48956	0.48983	0.49010	0.49036	0.49061	0.49086	0.49111	0.49134	0.49158
2.4	0.49180	0.49202	0.49224	0.49245	0.49266	0.49286	0.49305	0.49324	0.49343	0.49361
2.5	0.49379	0.49396	0.49413	0.49430	0.49446	0.49461	0.49477	0.49492	0.49506	0.49520
2.6	0.49534	0.49547	0.49560	0.49573	0.49585	0.49598	0.49609	0.49621	0.49632	0.49643
2.7	0.49653	0.49664	0.49674	0.49683	0.49693	0.49702	0.49711	0.49720	0.49728	0.49736
2.8	0.49744	0.49752	0.49760	0.49767	0.49774	0.49781	0.49788	0.49795	0.49801	0.49807
2.9	0.49813	0.49819	0.49825	0.49831	0.49836	0.49841	0.49846	0.49851	0.49856	0.49861
3.0	0.49865	0.49869	0.49874	0.49878	0.49882	0.49886	0.49889	0.49893	0.49897	0.49900
3.1	0.49903	0.49906	0.49910	0.49913	0.49916	0.49918	0.49921	0.49924	0.49926	0.49929
3.2	0.49931	0.49934	0.49936	0.49938	0.49940	0.49942	0.49944	0.49946	0.49948	0.49950
3.3	0.49952	0.49953	0.49955	0.49957	0.49958	0.49960	0.49961	0.49962	0.49964	0.49965
3.4	0.49966	0.49968	0.49969	0.49970	0.49971	0.49972	0.49973	0.49974	0.49975	0.49976
3.5	0.49977	0.49978	0.49978	0.49979	0.49980	0.49981	0.49981	0.49982	0.49983	0.49983
3.6	0.49984	0.49985	0.49985	0.49986	0.49986	0.49987	0.49987	0.49988	0.49988	0.49989
3.7	0.49989	0.49990	0.49990	0.49990	0.49991	0.49991	0.49991	0.49992	0.49992	0.49992
3.8	0.49993	0.49993	0.49993	0.49994	0.49994	0.49994	0.49994	0.49995	0.49995	0.49995
3.9	0.49995	0.49995	0.49996	0.49996	0.49996	0.49996	0.49996	0.49996	0.49997	0.49997
4.0	0.49997	0.49997	0.49997	0.49997	0.49997	0.49997	0.49998	0.49998	0.49998	0.49998

TABLE 2 The t distribution

This table gives the value of $t_{(\alpha, n)}$ with n degrees of freedom

[gray box] $= P[t \geq t_{(\alpha, n)}]$

In Excel (2016) use:

- T.INV(α, df) for a one-sided lower limit
- T.INV($1 - \alpha$, df) for a one-sided upper limit
- T.INV.2T(α, df) for two-sided limits where α = combined tail areas

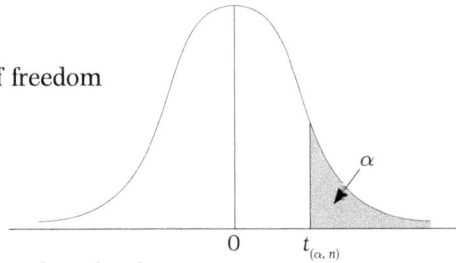

α df	0.100	0.050	0.025	0.010	0.005	0.0025
1	3.078	6.314	12.706	31.821	63.657	127.322
2	1.886	2.920	4.303	6.965	9.925	14.089
3	1.638	2.353	3.182	4.541	5.841	7.453
4	1.533	2.132	2.776	3.747	4.604	5.598
5	1.476	2.015	2.571	3.365	4.032	4.773
6	1.440	1.943	2.447	3.143	3.707	4.317
7	1.415	1.895	2.365	2.998	3.499	4.029
8	1.397	1.860	2.306	2.896	3.355	3.833
9	1.383	1.833	2.262	2.821	3.250	3.690
10	1.372	1.812	2.228	2.764	3.169	3.581
11	1.363	1.796	2.201	2.718	3.106	3.497
12	1.356	1.782	2.179	2.681	3.055	3.428
13	1.350	1.771	2.160	2.650	3.012	3.372
14	1.345	1.761	2.145	2.624	2.977	3.326
15	1.341	1.753	2.131	2.602	2.947	3.286
16	1.337	1.746	2.120	2.583	2.921	3.252
17	1.333	1.740	2.110	2.567	2.898	3.222
18	1.330	1.734	2.101	2.552	2.878	3.197
19	1.328	1.729	2.093	2.539	2.861	3.174
20	1.325	1.725	2.086	2.528	2.845	3.153
21	1.323	1.721	2.080	2.518	2.831	3.135
22	1.321	1.717	2.074	2.508	2.819	3.119
23	1.319	1.714	2.069	2.500	2.807	3.104
24	1.318	1.711	2.064	2.492	2.797	3.091
25	1.316	1.708	2.060	2.485	2.787	3.078
26	1.315	1.706	2.056	2.479	2.779	3.067
27	1.314	1.703	2.052	2.473	2.771	3.057
28	1.313	1.701	2.048	2.467	2.763	3.047
29	1.311	1.699	2.045	2.462	2.756	3.038
30	1.310	1.697	2.042	2.457	2.750	3.030
31	1.309	1.696	2.040	2.453	2.744	3.022
32	1.309	1.694	2.037	2.449	2.738	3.015
33	1.308	1.692	2.035	2.445	2.733	3.008
34	1.307	1.691	2.032	2.441	2.728	3.002
35	1.306	1.690	2.030	2.438	2.724	2.996
36	1.306	1.688	2.028	2.434	2.719	2.990
37	1.305	1.687	2.026	2.431	2.715	2.985
38	1.304	1.686	2.024	2.429	2.712	2.980
39	1.304	1.685	2.023	2.426	2.708	2.976
40	1.303	1.684	2.021	2.423	2.704	2.971
45	1.301	1.679	2.014	2.412	2.690	2.952
50	1.299	1.676	2.009	2.403	2.678	2.937
60	1.296	1.671	2.000	2.390	2.660	2.915
70	1.294	1.667	1.994	2.381	2.648	2.899
80	1.292	1.664	1.990	2.374	2.639	2.887
90	1.291	1.662	1.987	2.369	2.632	2.878
100	1.290	1.660	1.984	2.364	2.626	2.871
120	1.289	1.658	1.980	2.358	2.617	2.860
140	1.288	1.656	1.977	2.353	2.611	2.852
160	1.287	1.654	1.975	2.350	2.607	2.847
180	1.286	1.653	1.973	2.347	2.603	2.842
200	1.286	1.653	1.972	2.345	2.601	2.839
∞	1.282	1.645	1.960	2.327	2.576	2.807

TABLE 3   The Chi-square distribution (χ^2)

The entries in this table are critical χ^2
limits where α is the area to the
right of the critical limit.

In Excel (2016): CHISQ.INV.RT(α, df)

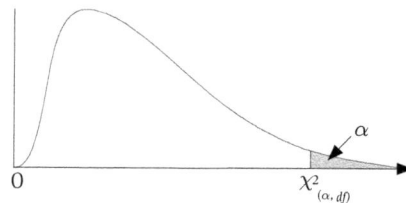

α / df	0.005	0.01	0.025	0.05	0.1	0.9	0.95	0.975	0.99	0.995
1	7.879	6.635	5.024	3.841	2.706	0.016	0.004	0.001	0.000	0.000
2	10.597	9.210	7.378	5.991	4.605	0.211	0.103	0.051	0.020	0.010
3	12.838	11.345	9.348	7.815	6.251	0.584	0.352	0.216	0.115	0.072
4	14.860	13.277	11.143	9.488	7.779	1.064	0.711	0.484	0.297	0.207
5	16.750	15.086	12.833	11.070	9.236	1.610	1.145	0.831	0.554	0.412
6	18.548	16.812	14.449	12.592	10.645	2.204	1.635	1.237	0.872	0.676
7	20.278	18.475	16.013	14.067	12.017	2.833	2.167	1.690	1.239	0.989
8	21.955	20.090	17.535	15.507	13.362	3.490	2.733	2.180	1.646	1.344
9	23.589	21.666	19.023	16.919	14.684	4.168	3.325	2.700	2.088	1.735
10	25.188	23.209	20.483	18.307	15.987	4.865	3.940	3.247	2.558	2.156
11	26.757	24.725	21.920	19.675	17.275	5.578	4.575	3.816	3.053	2.603
12	28.300	26.217	23.337	21.026	18.549	6.304	5.226	4.404	3.571	3.074
13	29.819	27.688	24.736	22.362	19.812	7.042	5.892	5.009	4.107	3.565
14	31.319	29.141	26.119	23.685	21.064	7.790	6.571	5.629	4.660	4.075
15	32.801	30.578	27.488	24.996	22.307	8.547	7.261	6.262	5.229	4.601
16	34.267	32.000	28.845	26.296	23.542	9.312	7.962	6.908	5.812	5.142
17	35.718	33.409	30.191	27.587	24.769	10.085	8.672	7.564	6.408	5.697
18	37.156	34.805	31.526	28.869	25.989	10.865	9.390	8.231	7.015	6.265
19	38.582	36.191	32.852	30.144	27.204	11.651	10.117	8.907	7.633	6.844
20	39.997	37.566	34.170	31.410	28.412	12.443	10.851	9.591	8.260	7.434
21	41.401	38.932	35.479	32.671	29.615	13.240	11.591	10.283	8.897	8.034
22	42.796	40.289	36.781	33.924	30.813	14.041	12.338	10.982	9.542	8.643
23	44.181	41.638	38.076	35.172	32.007	14.848	13.091	11.689	10.196	9.260
24	45.559	42.980	39.364	36.415	33.196	15.659	13.848	12.401	10.856	9.886
25	46.928	44.314	40.646	37.652	34.382	16.473	14.611	13.120	11.524	10.520
26	48.290	45.642	41.923	38.885	35.563	17.292	15.379	13.844	12.198	11.160
27	49.645	46.963	43.195	40.113	36.741	18.114	16.151	14.573	12.879	11.808
28	50.993	48.278	44.461	41.337	37.916	18.939	16.928	15.308	13.565	12.461
29	52.336	49.588	45.722	42.557	39.087	19.768	17.708	16.047	14.256	13.121
30	53.672	50.892	46.979	43.773	40.256	20.599	18.493	16.791	14.953	13.787
31	55.003	52.191	48.232	44.985	41.422	21.434	19.281	17.539	15.655	14.458
32	56.328	53.486	49.480	46.194	42.585	22.271	20.072	18.291	16.362	15.134
33	57.648	54.776	50.725	47.400	43.745	23.110	20.867	19.047	17.074	15.815
34	58.964	56.061	51.966	48.602	44.903	23.952	21.664	19.806	17.789	16.501
35	60.275	57.342	53.203	49.802	46.059	24.797	22.465	20.569	18.509	17.192
36	61.581	58.619	54.437	50.998	47.212	25.643	23.269	21.336	19.233	17.887
37	62.883	59.893	55.668	52.192	48.363	26.492	24.075	22.106	19.960	18.586
38	64.181	61.162	56.896	53.384	49.513	27.343	24.884	22.878	20.691	19.289
39	65.476	62.428	58.120	54.572	50.660	28.196	25.695	23.654	21.426	19.996
40	66.766	63.691	59.342	55.758	51.805	29.051	26.509	24.433	22.164	20.707
45	73.166	69.957	65.410	61.656	57.505	33.350	30.612	28.366	25.901	24.311
50	79.490	76.154	71.420	67.505	63.167	37.689	34.764	32.357	29.707	27.991
55	85.749	82.292	77.380	73.311	68.796	42.060	38.958	36.398	33.570	31.735
60	91.952	88.379	83.298	79.082	74.397	46.459	43.188	40.482	37.485	35.534
65	98.105	94.422	89.177	84.821	79.973	50.883	47.450	44.603	41.444	39.383
70	104.215	100.425	95.023	90.531	85.527	55.329	51.739	48.758	45.442	43.275
75	110.286	106.393	100.839	96.217	91.061	59.795	56.054	52.942	49.475	47.206
80	116.321	112.329	106.629	101.879	96.578	64.278	60.391	57.153	53.540	51.172
85	122.325	118.236	112.393	107.522	102.079	68.777	64.749	61.389	57.634	55.170
90	128.299	124.116	118.136	113.145	107.565	73.291	69.126	65.647	61.754	59.196
95	134.247	129.973	123.858	118.752	113.038	77.818	73.520	69.925	65.898	63.250
100	140.169	135.807	129.561	124.342	118.498	82.358	77.929	74.222	70.065	67.328
110	151.948	147.414	140.917	135.480	129.385	91.471	86.792	82.867	78.458	75.550
120	163.648	158.950	152.211	146.567	140.233	100.624	95.705	91.573	86.923	83.852
130	175.278	170.423	163.453	157.610	151.045	109.811	104.662	100.331	95.451	92.222
150	198.360	193.208	185.800	179.581	172.581	128.275	122.692	117.985	112.668	109.142
160	209.824	204.530	196.915	190.516	183.311	137.546	131.756	126.870	121.346	117.679
170	221.242	215.812	207.995	201.423	194.017	146.839	140.849	135.790	130.064	126.261
180	232.620	227.056	219.044	212.304	204.704	156.153	149.969	144.741	138.820	134.884
190	243.959	238.266	230.064	223.160	215.371	165.485	159.113	153.721	147.610	143.545
200	255.264	249.445	241.058	233.994	226.021	174.835	168.279	162.728	156.432	152.241

TABLE 4(a)   *F* distribution ($\alpha = 0.05$)

The entries in this table are critical values of *F* for which the area under the curve to the right of *F* is equal to 0.05.

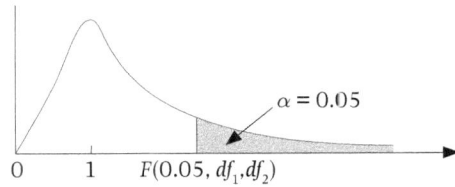

$\alpha = 0.05$

$F(0.05, df_1, df_2)$

In Excel (2016): F.INV.RT(0.05, df_1, df_2)

		Degrees of freedom for numerator (df_1)									
		1	2	3	4	5	6	7	8	9	10
	1	161.4	199.5	215.7	224.6	230.2	234	236.8	238.9	240.5	241.9
	2	18.5	19.0	19.2	19.2	19.3	19.3	19.4	19.4	19.4	19.4
	3	10.1	9.55	9.28	9.12	9.01	8.94	8.89	8.85	8.81	8.79
	4	7.71	6.94	6.59	6.39	6.26	6.16	6.09	6.04	6.00	5.96
	5	6.61	5.79	5.41	5.19	5.05	4.95	4.88	4.82	4.77	4.74
	6	5.99	5.14	4.76	4.53	4.39	4.28	4.21	4.15	4.10	4.06
	7	5.59	4.74	4.35	4.12	3.97	3.87	3.79	3.73	3.68	3.64
	8	5.32	4.46	4.07	3.84	3.69	3.58	3.50	3.44	3.39	3.35
	9	5.12	4.26	3.86	3.63	3.48	3.37	3.29	3.23	3.18	3.14
	10	4.96	4.10	3.71	3.48	3.33	3.22	3.14	3.07	3.02	2.98
	11	4.84	3.98	3.59	3.36	3.20	3.09	3.01	2.95	2.90	2.85
	12	4.75	3.89	3.49	3.26	3.11	3.00	2.91	2.85	2.80	2.75
	13	4.67	3.81	3.41	3.18	3.03	2.92	2.83	2.77	2.71	2.67
	14	4.60	3.74	3.34	3.11	2.96	2.85	2.76	2.70	2.65	2.60
	15	4.54	3.68	3.29	3.06	2.90	2.79	2.71	2.64	2.59	2.54
	16	4.49	3.63	3.24	3.01	2.85	2.74	2.66	2.59	2.54	2.49
	17	4.45	3.59	3.20	2.96	2.81	2.70	2.61	2.55	2.49	2.45
	18	4.41	3.55	3.16	2.93	2.77	2.66	2.58	2.51	2.46	2.41
	19	4.38	3.52	3.13	2.90	2.74	2.63	2.54	2.48	2.42	2.38
	20	4.35	3.49	3.10	2.87	2.71	2.60	2.51	2.45	2.39	2.35
	21	4.32	3.47	3.07	2.84	2.68	2.57	2.49	2.42	2.37	2.32
	22	4.30	3.44	3.05	2.82	2.66	2.55	2.46	2.40	2.34	2.30
	23	4.28	3.42	3.03	2.80	2.64	2.53	2.44	2.37	2.32	2.27
	24	4.26	3.40	3.01	2.78	2.62	2.51	2.42	2.36	2.30	2.25
	25	4.24	3.39	2.99	2.76	2.60	2.49	2.40	2.34	2.28	2.24
	30	4.17	3.32	2.92	2.69	2.53	2.42	2.33	2.27	2.21	2.16
	40	4.08	3.23	2.84	2.61	2.45	2.34	2.25	2.18	2.12	2.08
	60	4.00	3.15	2.76	2.53	2.37	2.25	2.17	2.10	2.04	1.99
	120	3.92	3.07	2.68	2.45	2.29	2.18	2.09	2.02	1.96	1.91
	∞	3.84	3.00	2.60	2.37	2.21	2.10	2.01	1.94	1.88	1.83

Degrees of freedom for denominator (df_2)

TABLE 4(a) continued F distribution ($\alpha = 0.05$)

		12	15	20	24	30	40	60	120	∞
	1	243.9	245.9	248	249.1	250.1	251.1	252.2	253.3	254.3
	2	19.4	19.4	19.4	19.5	19.5	19.5	19.5	19.5	19.5
	3	8.74	8.70	8.66	8.64	8.62	8.59	8.57	8.55	8.53
	4	5.91	5.86	5.80	5.77	5.75	5.72	5.69	5.66	5.63
	5	4.68	4.62	4.56	4.53	4.50	4.46	4.43	4.40	4.37
	6	4.00	3.94	3.87	3.84	3.81	3.77	3.74	3.70	3.67
	7	3.57	3.51	3.44	3.41	3.38	3.34	3.30	3.27	3.23
	8	3.28	3.22	3.15	3.12	3.08	3.04	3.01	2.97	2.93
	9	3.07	3.01	2.94	2.90	2.86	2.83	2.79	2.75	2.71
	10	2.91	2.85	2.77	2.74	2.70	2.66	2.62	2.58	2.54
	11	2.79	2.72	2.65	2.61	2.57	2.53	2.49	2.45	2.40
	12	2.69	2.62	2.54	2.51	2.47	2.43	2.38	2.34	2.30
	13	2.60	2.53	2.46	2.42	2.38	2.34	2.30	2.25	2.21
	14	2.53	2.46	2.39	2.35	2.31	2.27	2.22	2.18	2.13
	15	2.48	2.40	2.33	2.29	2.25	2.20	2.16	2.11	2.07
	16	2.42	2.35	2.28	2.24	2.19	2.15	2.11	2.06	2.01
	17	2.38	2.31	2.23	2.19	2.15	2.10	2.06	2.01	1.96
	18	2.34	2.27	2.19	2.15	2.11	2.06	2.02	1.97	1.92
	19	2.31	2.23	2.16	2.11	2.07	2.03	1.98	1.93	1.88
	20	2.28	2.20	2.12	2.08	2.04	1.99	1.95	1.90	1.84
	21	2.25	2.18	2.10	2.05	2.01	1.96	1.92	1.87	1.81
	22	2.23	2.15	2.07	2.03	1.98	1.94	1.89	1.84	1.78
	23	2.20	2.13	2.05	2.01	1.96	1.91	1.86	1.81	1.76
	24	2.18	2.11	2.03	1.98	1.94	1.89	1.84	1.79	1.73
	25	2.16	2.09	2.01	1.96	1.92	1.87	1.82	1.77	1.71
	30	2.09	2.01	1.93	1.89	1.84	1.79	1.74	1.68	1.62
	40	2.00	1.92	1.84	1.79	1.74	1.69	1.64	1.58	1.51
	60	1.92	1.84	1.75	1.70	1.65	1.59	1.53	1.47	1.39
	120	1.83	1.75	1.66	1.61	1.55	1.50	1.43	1.35	1.25
	∞	1.75	1.67	1.57	1.52	1.46	1.39	1.32	1.22	1.00

Degrees of freedom for numerator (df_1)

Degrees of freedom for denominator (df_2)

TABLE 4(b) *F* distribution ($\alpha = 0.025$)

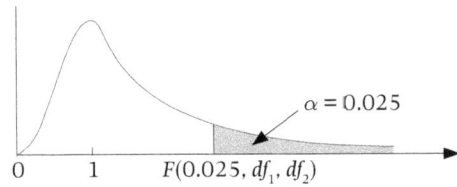

In Excel (2016): F.INV.RT(0.025, df_1, df_2)

		Degrees of freedom for numerator (df_1)								
	1	**2**	**3**	**4**	**5**	**6**	**7**	**8**	**9**	**10**
1	647.8	799.5	864.2	899.6	921.8	937.1	948.2	956.7	963.3	968.6
2	38.51	39.00	39.17	39.25	39.30	39.33	39.36	39.37	39.39	39.40
3	17.44	16.04	15.44	15.10	14.88	14.73	14.62	14.54	14.47	14.42
4	12.22	10.65	9.98	9.60	9.36	9.20	9.07	8.98	8.90	8.84
5	10.01	8.43	7.76	7.39	7.15	6.98	6.85	6.76	6.68	6.62
6	8.81	7.26	6.60	6.23	5.99	5.82	5.70	5.60	5.52	5.46
7	8.07	6.54	5.89	5.52	5.29	5.12	4.99	4.90	4.82	4.76
8	7.57	6.06	5.42	5.05	4.82	4.65	4.53	4.43	4.36	4.30
9	7.21	5.71	5.08	4.72	4.48	4.32	4.20	4.10	4.03	3.96
10	6.94	5.46	4.83	4.47	4.24	4.07	3.95	3.85	3.78	3.72
11	6.72	5.26	4.63	4.28	4.04	3.88	3.76	3.66	3.59	3.53
12	6.55	5.10	4.47	4.12	3.89	3.73	3.61	3.51	3.44	3.37
13	6.41	4.97	4.35	4.00	3.77	3.60	3.48	3.39	3.31	3.25
14	6.30	4.86	4.24	3.89	3.66	3.50	3.38	3.29	3.21	3.15
15	6.20	4.77	4.15	3.80	3.58	3.41	3.29	3.20	3.12	3.06
16	6.12	4.69	4.08	3.73	3.50	3.34	3.22	3.12	3.05	2.99
17	6.04	4.62	4.01	3.66	3.44	3.28	3.16	3.06	2.98	2.92
18	5.98	4.56	3.95	3.61	3.38	3.22	3.10	3.01	2.93	2.87
19	5.92	4.51	3.90	3.56	3.33	3.17	3.05	2.96	2.88	2.82
20	5.87	4.46	3.86	3.51	3.29	3.13	3.01	2.91	2.84	2.77
21	5.83	4.42	3.82	3.48	3.25	3.09	2.97	2.87	2.80	2.73
22	5.79	4.38	3.78	3.44	3.22	3.05	2.93	2.84	2.76	2.70
23	5.75	4.35	3.75	3.41	3.18	3.02	2.90	2.81	2.73	2.67
24	5.72	4.32	3.72	3.38	3.15	2.99	2.87	2.78	2.70	2.64
25	5.69	4.29	3.69	3.35	3.13	2.97	2.85	2.75	2.68	2.61
30	5.57	4.18	3.59	3.25	3.03	2.87	2.75	2.65	2.57	2.51
40	5.42	4.05	3.46	3.13	2.90	2.74	2.62	2.53	2.45	2.39
60	5.29	3.93	3.34	3.01	2.79	2.63	2.51	2.41	2.33	2.27
120	5.15	3.80	3.23	2.89	2.67	2.52	2.39	2.30	2.22	2.16
∞	5.02	3.69	3.12	2.79	2.57	2.41	2.29	2.19	2.11	2.05

Degrees of freedom for denominator (df_2)

TABLE 4(b) continued   F distribution ($\alpha = 0.025$)

	Degrees of freedom for numerator (df_1)								
	12	15	20	24	30	40	60	120	∞
1	976.7	984.9	993.1	997.2	1001.4	1005.6	1009.8	1014.0	1018.3
2	39.41	39.43	39.45	39.46	39.46	39.47	39.48	39.49	39.50
3	14.34	14.25	14.17	14.12	14.08	14.04	13.99	13.95	13.90
4	8.75	8.66	8.56	8.51	8.46	8.41	8.36	8.31	8.26
5	6.52	6.43	6.33	6.28	6.23	6.18	6.12	6.07	6.02
6	5.37	5.27	5.17	5.12	5.07	5.01	4.96	4.90	4.85
7	4.67	4.57	4.47	4.41	4.36	4.31	4.25	4.20	4.14
8	4.20	4.10	4.00	3.95	3.89	3.84	3.78	3.73	3.67
9	3.87	3.77	3.67	3.61	3.56	3.51	3.45	3.39	3.33
10	3.62	3.52	3.42	3.37	3.31	3.26	3.20	3.14	3.08
11	3.43	3.33	3.23	3.17	3.12	3.06	3.00	2.94	2.88
12	3.28	3.18	3.07	3.02	2.96	2.91	2.85	2.79	2.72
13	3.15	3.05	2.95	2.89	2.84	2.78	2.72	2.66	2.60
14	3.05	2.95	2.84	2.79	2.73	2.67	2.61	2.55	2.49
15	2.96	2.86	2.76	2.70	2.64	2.59	2.52	2.46	2.40
16	2.89	2.79	2.68	2.63	2.57	2.51	2.45	2.38	2.32
17	2.82	2.72	2.62	2.56	2.50	2.44	2.38	2.32	2.25
18	2.77	2.67	2.56	2.50	2.44	2.38	2.32	2.26	2.19
19	2.72	2.62	2.51	2.45	2.39	2.33	2.27	2.20	2.13
20	2.68	2.57	2.46	2.41	2.35	2.29	2.22	2.16	2.09
21	2.64	2.53	2.42	2.37	2.31	2.25	2.18	2.11	2.04
22	2.60	2.50	2.39	2.33	2.27	2.21	2.14	2.08	2.00
23	2.57	2.47	2.36	2.30	2.24	2.18	2.11	2.04	1.97
24	2.54	2.44	2.33	2.27	2.21	2.15	2.08	2.01	1.94
25	2.51	2.41	2.30	2.24	2.18	2.12	2.05	1.98	1.91
30	2.41	2.31	2.20	2.14	2.07	2.01	1.94	1.87	1.79
40	2.29	2.18	2.07	2.01	1.94	1.88	1.80	1.72	1.64
60	2.17	2.06	1.94	1.88	1.82	1.74	1.67	1.58	1.48
120	2.05	1.94	1.82	1.76	1.69	1.61	1.53	1.43	1.31
∞	1.94	1.83	1.71	1.64	1.57	1.48	1.39	1.27	1.00

Degrees of freedom for denominator (df_2)

TABLE 4(c)   *F* distribution ($\alpha = 0.01$)

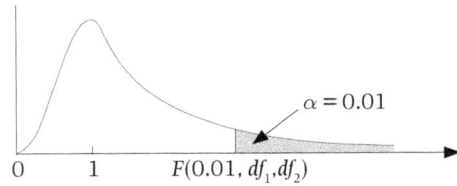

$\alpha = 0.01$

$0 \quad 1 \quad F(0.01, df_1, df_2)$

In Excel (2016): F.INV.RT(0.01, df_1, df_2)

				Degrees of freedom for numerator (df_1)						
	1	**2**	**3**	**4**	**5**	**6**	**7**	**8**	**9**	**10**
1	4052	4999.5	5403	5525	5764	5859	5928	5982	6022	6056
2	98.5	99.0	99.2	99.2	99.3	99.3	99.4	99.4	99.4	99.4
3	34.1	30.8	29.5	28.7	28.2	27.9	27.7	27.5	27.3	27.2
4	21.2	18.0	16.7	16.0	15.5	15.2	15.0	14.8	14.7	14.5
5	16.3	13.3	12.1	11.4	11.0	10.7	10.5	10.3	10.2	10.1
6	13.7	10.9	9.78	9.15	8.75	8.47	8.26	8.10	7.98	7.87
7	12.2	9.55	8.45	7.85	7.46	7.19	6.99	6.84	6.72	6.62
8	11.3	8.65	7.59	7.01	6.63	6.37	6.18	6.03	5.91	5.81
9	10.6	8.02	6.99	6.42	6.06	5.80	5.61	5.47	5.35	5.26
10	10.0	7.56	6.55	5.99	5.64	5.39	5.20	5.06	4.94	4.85
11	9.65	7.21	6.22	5.67	5.32	5.07	4.89	4.74	4.63	4.54
12	9.33	6.93	5.95	5.41	5.06	4.82	4.64	4.50	4.39	4.30
13	9.07	6.70	5.74	5.21	4.86	4.62	4.44	4.30	4.19	4.10
14	8.86	6.51	5.56	5.04	4.70	4.46	4.28	4.14	4.03	3.94
15	8.68	6.36	5.42	4.89	4.56	4.32	4.14	4.00	3.89	3.80
16	8.53	6.23	5.29	4.77	4.44	4.20	4.03	3.89	3.78	3.69
17	8.40	6.11	5.19	4.67	4.34	4.10	3.93	3.79	3.68	3.59
18	8.29	6.01	5.09	4.58	4.25	4.01	3.84	3.71	3.60	3.51
19	8.19	5.93	5.01	4.50	4.17	3.94	3.77	3.63	3.52	3.43
20	8.10	5.85	4.94	4.43	4.10	3.87	3.70	3.56	3.46	3.37
21	8.02	5.78	4.87	4.37	4.04	3.81	3.64	3.51	3.40	3.31
22	7.95	5.72	4.82	4.31	3.99	3.76	3.59	3.45	3.35	3.26
23	7.88	5.66	4.76	4.26	3.94	3.71	3.54	3.41	3.30	3.21
24	7.82	5.61	4.72	4.22	3.90	3.67	3.50	3.36	3.26	3.17
25	7.77	5.57	4.68	4.18	3.86	3.63	3.46	3.32	3.22	3.13
30	7.56	5.39	4.51	4.02	3.70	3.47	3.30	3.17	3.07	2.98
40	7.31	5.18	4.31	3.83	3.51	3.29	3.12	2.99	2.89	2.80
60	7.08	4.98	4.13	3.65	3.34	3.12	2.95	2.82	2.72	2.63
120	6.85	4.79	3.95	3.48	3.17	2.96	2.79	2.66	2.56	2.47
∞	6.63	4.61	3.78	3.32	3.02	2.80	2.64	2.51	2.41	2.32

Degrees of freedom for denominator (df_2)

513

TABLE 4(c) continued   F distribution ($\alpha = 0.01$)

		12	15	20	24	30	40	60	120	∞
		\multicolumn{9}{c}{Degrees of freedom for numerator (df_1)}								
	1	6 106	6 157	6 209	6 235	6 261	6 287	6 313	6 339	6 366
	2	99.4	99.4	99.4	99.5	99.5	99.5	99.5	99.5	99.5
	3	27.1	26.9	26.7	26.6	26.5	26.4	26.3	26.2	26.1
	4	14.4	14.2	14.0	13.9	13.8	13.7	13.7	13.6	13.5
	5	9.89	9.72	9.55	9.47	9.38	9.29	9.20	9.11	9.02
	6	7.72	7.56	7.40	7.31	7.23	7.14	7.06	6.97	6.88
	7	6.47	6.31	6.16	6.07	5.99	5.91	5.82	5.74	5.65
	8	5.67	5.52	5.36	5.28	5.20	5.12	5.03	4.95	4.86
	9	5.11	4.96	4.81	4.73	4.65	4.57	4.48	4.40	4.31
	10	4.71	4.56	4.41	4.33	4.25	4.17	4.08	4.00	3.91
	11	4.40	4.25	4.10	4.02	3.94	3.86	3.78	3.69	3.60
	12	4.16	4.01	3.86	3.78	3.70	3.62	3.54	3.45	3.36
	13	3.96	3.82	3.66	3.59	3.51	3.43	3.34	3.25	3.17
	14	3.80	3.66	3.51	3.43	3.35	3.27	3.18	3.09	3.00
	15	3.67	3.52	3.37	3.29	3.21	3.13	3.05	2.96	2.87
	16	3.55	3.41	3.26	3.18	3.10	3.02	2.93	2.84	2.75
	17	3.46	3.31	3.16	3.08	3.00	2.92	2.83	2.75	2.65
	18	3.37	3.23	3.08	3.00	2.92	2.84	2.75	2.66	2.57
	19	3.30	3.15	3.00	2.92	2.84	2.76	2.67	2.58	2.49
	20	3.23	3.09	2.94	2.86	2.78	2.69	2.61	2.52	2.42
	21	3.17	3.03	2.88	2.80	2.72	2.64	2.55	2.46	2.36
	22	3.12	2.98	2.83	2.75	2.67	2.58	2.50	2.40	2.31
	23	3.07	2.93	2.78	2.70	2.62	2.54	2.45	2.35	2.26
	24	3.03	2.89	2.74	2.66	2.58	2.49	2.40	2.31	2.21
	25	2.99	2.85	2.70	2.62	2.53	2.45	2.36	2.27	2.17
	30	2.84	2.70	2.55	2.47	2.39	2.30	2.21	2.11	2.01
	40	2.66	2.52	2.37	2.29	2.20	2.11	2.02	1.92	1.80
	60	2.50	2.35	2.20	2.12	2.03	1.94	1.84	1.73	1.60
	120	2.34	2.19	2.03	1.95	1.86	1.76	1.66	1.53	1.38
	∞	2.18	2.04	1.88	1.79	1.70	1.59	1.47	1.32	1.00

Degrees of freedom for denominator (df_2)

TABLE 5 Binomial Probability Distribution $P(x = r) = {}_nC_r \, p^r \, (1-p)^{n-r}$

The Table shows **marginal probabilities** of a binomial process. In Excel (2016): BINOM.DIST(r, n, p, False).

n	r	0.05	0.1	0.15	0.2	0.25	0.3	0.35	0.4	0.45	0.5	0.55	0.6	0.65	0.7	0.75	0.8	0.85	0.9	0.95
2	0	0.9025	0.8100	0.7225	0.6400	0.5625	0.4900	0.4225	0.3600	0.3025	0.2500	0.2025	0.1600	0.1225	0.0900	0.0625	0.0400	0.0225	0.0100	0.0025
	1	0.0950	0.1800	0.2550	0.3200	0.3750	0.4200	0.4550	0.4800	0.4950	0.5000	0.4950	0.4800	0.4550	0.4200	0.3750	0.3200	0.2550	0.1800	0.0950
	2	0.0025	0.0100	0.0225	0.0400	0.0625	0.0900	0.1225	0.1600	0.2025	0.2500	0.3025	0.3600	0.4225	0.4900	0.5625	0.6400	0.7225	0.8100	0.9025
3	0	0.8574	0.7290	0.6141	0.5120	0.4219	0.3430	0.2746	0.2160	0.1664	0.1250	0.0911	0.0640	0.0429	0.0270	0.0156	0.0080	0.0034	0.0010	0.0001
	1	0.1354	0.2430	0.3251	0.3840	0.4219	0.4410	0.4436	0.4320	0.4084	0.3750	0.3341	0.2880	0.2389	0.1890	0.1406	0.0960	0.0574	0.0270	0.0071
	2	0.0071	0.0270	0.0574	0.0960	0.1406	0.1890	0.2389	0.2880	0.3341	0.3750	0.4084	0.4320	0.4436	0.4410	0.4219	0.3840	0.3251	0.2430	0.1354
	3	0.0001	0.0010	0.0034	0.0080	0.0156	0.0270	0.0429	0.0640	0.0911	0.1250	0.1664	0.2160	0.2746	0.3430	0.4219	0.5120	0.6141	0.7290	0.8574
4	0	0.8145	0.6561	0.5220	0.4096	0.3164	0.2401	0.1785	0.1296	0.0915	0.0625	0.0410	0.0256	0.0150	0.0081	0.0039	0.0016	0.0005	0.0001	0.0000
	1	0.1715	0.2916	0.3685	0.4096	0.4219	0.4116	0.3845	0.3456	0.2995	0.2500	0.2005	0.1536	0.1115	0.0756	0.0469	0.0256	0.0115	0.0036	0.0005
	2	0.0135	0.0486	0.0975	0.1536	0.2109	0.2646	0.3105	0.3456	0.3675	0.3750	0.3675	0.3456	0.3105	0.2646	0.2109	0.1536	0.0975	0.0486	0.0135
	3	0.0005	0.0036	0.0115	0.0256	0.0469	0.0756	0.1115	0.1536	0.2005	0.2500	0.2995	0.3456	0.3845	0.4116	0.4219	0.4096	0.3685	0.2916	0.1715
	4	0.0000	0.0001	0.0005	0.0016	0.0039	0.0081	0.0150	0.0256	0.0410	0.0625	0.0915	0.1296	0.1785	0.2401	0.3164	0.4096	0.5220	0.6561	0.8145
5	0	0.7738	0.5905	0.4437	0.3277	0.2373	0.1681	0.1160	0.0778	0.0503	0.0313	0.0185	0.0102	0.0053	0.0024	0.0010	0.0003	0.0001	0.0000	0.0000
	1	0.2036	0.3281	0.3915	0.4096	0.3955	0.3602	0.3124	0.2592	0.2059	0.1563	0.1128	0.0768	0.0488	0.0284	0.0146	0.0064	0.0022	0.0005	0.0000
	2	0.0214	0.0729	0.1382	0.2048	0.2637	0.3087	0.3364	0.3456	0.3369	0.3125	0.2757	0.2304	0.1811	0.1323	0.0879	0.0512	0.0244	0.0081	0.0011
	3	0.0011	0.0081	0.0244	0.0512	0.0879	0.1323	0.1811	0.2304	0.2757	0.3125	0.3369	0.3456	0.3364	0.3087	0.2637	0.2048	0.1382	0.0729	0.0214
	4	0.0000	0.0005	0.0022	0.0064	0.0146	0.0284	0.0488	0.0768	0.1128	0.1563	0.2059	0.2592	0.3124	0.3602	0.3955	0.4096	0.3915	0.3281	0.2036
	5	0.0000	0.0000	0.0001	0.0003	0.0010	0.0024	0.0053	0.0102	0.0185	0.0313	0.0503	0.0778	0.1160	0.1681	0.2373	0.3277	0.4437	0.5905	0.7738

_p_

TABLE 5 (continued) Binomial Probability Distribution $P(x = r) = {}_nC_r\, p^r (1 - p)^{n-r}$

n	r	0.05	0.1	0.15	0.2	0.25	0.3	0.35	0.4	0.45	0.5	0.55	0.6	0.65	0.7	0.75	0.8	0.85	0.9	0.95
6	0	0.7351	0.5314	0.3771	0.2621	0.1780	0.1176	0.0754	0.0467	0.0277	0.0156	0.0083	0.0041	0.0018	0.0007	0.0002	0.0001	0.0000	0.0000	0.0000
	1	0.2321	0.3543	0.3993	0.3932	0.3560	0.3025	0.2437	0.1866	0.1359	0.0938	0.0609	0.0369	0.0205	0.0102	0.0044	0.0015	0.0004	0.0001	0.0000
	2	0.0305	0.0984	0.1762	0.2458	0.2966	0.3241	0.3280	0.3110	0.2780	0.2344	0.1861	0.1382	0.0951	0.0595	0.0330	0.0154	0.0055	0.0012	0.0001
	3	0.0021	0.0146	0.0415	0.0819	0.1318	0.1852	0.2355	0.2765	0.3032	0.3125	0.3032	0.2765	0.2355	0.1852	0.1318	0.0819	0.0415	0.0146	0.0021
	4	0.0001	0.0012	0.0055	0.0154	0.0330	0.0595	0.0951	0.1382	0.1861	0.2344	0.2780	0.3110	0.3280	0.3241	0.2966	0.2458	0.1762	0.0984	0.0305
	5	0.0000	0.0001	0.0004	0.0015	0.0044	0.0102	0.0205	0.0369	0.0609	0.0938	0.1359	0.1866	0.2437	0.3025	0.3560	0.3932	0.3993	0.3543	0.2321
	6	0.0000	0.0000	0.0000	0.0001	0.0002	0.0007	0.0018	0.0041	0.0083	0.0156	0.0277	0.0467	0.0754	0.1176	0.1780	0.2621	0.3771	0.5314	0.7351
7	0	0.6983	0.4783	0.3206	0.2097	0.1335	0.0824	0.0490	0.0280	0.0152	0.0078	0.0037	0.0016	0.0006	0.0002	0.0001	0.0000	0.0000	0.0000	0.0000
	1	0.2573	0.3720	0.3960	0.3670	0.3115	0.2471	0.1848	0.1306	0.0872	0.0547	0.0320	0.0172	0.0084	0.0036	0.0013	0.0004	0.0001	0.0000	0.0000
	2	0.0406	0.1240	0.2097	0.2753	0.3115	0.3177	0.2985	0.2613	0.2140	0.1641	0.1172	0.0774	0.0466	0.0250	0.0115	0.0043	0.0012	0.0002	0.0000
	3	0.0036	0.0230	0.0617	0.1147	0.1730	0.2269	0.2679	0.2903	0.2918	0.2734	0.2388	0.1935	0.1442	0.0972	0.0577	0.0287	0.0109	0.0026	0.0002
	4	0.0002	0.0026	0.0109	0.0287	0.0577	0.0972	0.1442	0.1935	0.2388	0.2734	0.2918	0.2903	0.2679	0.2269	0.1730	0.1147	0.0617	0.0230	0.0036
	5	0.0000	0.0002	0.0012	0.0043	0.0115	0.0250	0.0466	0.0774	0.1172	0.1641	0.2140	0.2613	0.2985	0.3177	0.3115	0.2753	0.2097	0.1240	0.0406
	6	0.0000	0.0000	0.0001	0.0004	0.0013	0.0036	0.0084	0.0172	0.0320	0.0547	0.0872	0.1306	0.1848	0.2471	0.3115	0.3670	0.3960	0.3720	0.2573
	7	0.0000	0.0000	0.0000	0.0000	0.0001	0.0002	0.0006	0.0016	0.0037	0.0078	0.0152	0.0280	0.0490	0.0824	0.1335	0.2097	0.3206	0.4783	0.6983

TABLE 5 (continued)   Binomial Probability Distribution $P(x = r) = {}_nC_r\, p^r\,(1-p)^{n-r}$

n	r	0.05	0.1	0.15	0.2	0.25	0.3	0.35	0.4	0.45	0.5	0.55	0.6	0.65	0.7	0.75	0.8	0.85	0.9	0.95
8	0	0.6634	0.4305	0.2725	0.1678	0.1001	0.0576	0.0319	0.0168	0.0084	0.0039	0.0017	0.0007	0.0002	0.0001	0.0000	0.0000	0.0000	0.0000	0.0000
	1	0.2793	0.3826	0.3847	0.3355	0.2670	0.1977	0.1373	0.0896	0.0548	0.0313	0.0164	0.0079	0.0033	0.0012	0.0004	0.0001	0.0000	0.0000	0.0000
	2	0.0515	0.1488	0.2376	0.2936	0.3115	0.2965	0.2587	0.2090	0.1569	0.1094	0.0703	0.0413	0.0217	0.0100	0.0038	0.0011	0.0002	0.0000	0.0000
	3	0.0054	0.0331	0.0839	0.1468	0.2076	0.2541	0.2786	0.2787	0.2568	0.2188	0.1719	0.1239	0.0808	0.0467	0.0231	0.0092	0.0026	0.0004	0.0004
	4	0.0004	0.0046	0.0185	0.0459	0.0865	0.1361	0.1875	0.2322	0.2627	0.2734	0.2627	0.2322	0.1875	0.1361	0.0865	0.0459	0.0185	0.0046	0.0054
	5	0.0000	0.0004	0.0026	0.0092	0.0231	0.0467	0.0808	0.1239	0.1719	0.2188	0.2568	0.2787	0.2786	0.2541	0.2076	0.1468	0.0839	0.0331	0.0515
	6	0.0000	0.0000	0.0002	0.0011	0.0038	0.0100	0.0217	0.0413	0.0703	0.1094	0.1569	0.2090	0.2587	0.2965	0.3115	0.2936	0.2376	0.1488	0.2793
	7	0.0000	0.0000	0.0000	0.0001	0.0004	0.0012	0.0033	0.0079	0.0164	0.0313	0.0548	0.0896	0.1373	0.1977	0.2670	0.3355	0.3847	0.3826	0.2793
	8	0.0000	0.0000	0.0000	0.0000	0.0000	0.0001	0.0002	0.0007	0.0017	0.0039	0.0084	0.0168	0.0319	0.0576	0.1001	0.1678	0.2725	0.4305	0.6634
9	0	0.6302	0.3874	0.2316	0.1342	0.0751	0.0404	0.0207	0.0101	0.0046	0.0020	0.0008	0.0003	0.0001	0.0000	0.0000	0.0000	0.0000	0.0000	0.0000
	1	0.2985	0.3874	0.3679	0.3020	0.2253	0.1556	0.1004	0.0605	0.0339	0.0176	0.0083	0.0035	0.0013	0.0004	0.0001	0.0000	0.0000	0.0000	0.0000
	2	0.0629	0.1722	0.2597	0.3020	0.3003	0.2668	0.2162	0.1612	0.1110	0.0703	0.0407	0.0212	0.0098	0.0039	0.0012	0.0003	0.0000	0.0000	0.0000
	3	0.0077	0.0446	0.1069	0.1762	0.2336	0.2668	0.2716	0.2508	0.2119	0.1641	0.1160	0.0743	0.0424	0.0210	0.0087	0.0028	0.0006	0.0001	0.0000
	4	0.0006	0.0074	0.0283	0.0661	0.1168	0.1715	0.2194	0.2508	0.2600	0.2461	0.2128	0.1672	0.1181	0.0735	0.0389	0.0165	0.0050	0.0008	0.0006
	5	0.0000	0.0008	0.0050	0.0165	0.0389	0.0735	0.1181	0.1672	0.2128	0.2461	0.2600	0.2508	0.2194	0.1715	0.1168	0.0661	0.0283	0.0074	0.0077
	6	0.0000	0.0001	0.0006	0.0028	0.0087	0.0210	0.0424	0.0743	0.1160	0.1641	0.2119	0.2508	0.2716	0.2668	0.2336	0.1762	0.1069	0.0446	0.0629
	7	0.0000	0.0000	0.0000	0.0003	0.0012	0.0039	0.0098	0.0212	0.0407	0.0703	0.1110	0.1612	0.2162	0.2668	0.3003	0.3020	0.2597	0.1722	0.2985
	8	0.0000	0.0000	0.0000	0.0000	0.0001	0.0004	0.0013	0.0035	0.0083	0.0176	0.0339	0.0605	0.1004	0.1556	0.2253	0.3020	0.3679	0.3874	0.2985
	9	0.0000	0.0000	0.0000	0.0000	0.0000	0.0000	0.0001	0.0003	0.0008	0.0020	0.0046	0.0101	0.0207	0.0404	0.0751	0.1342	0.2316	0.3874	0.6302

TABLE 5 (continued) Binomial Probability Distribution $P(x = r) = {}_nC_r\, p^r\, (1-p)^{n-r}$

n	r	0.05	0.1	0.15	0.2	0.25	0.3	0.35	0.4	0.45	0.5	0.55	0.6	0.65	0.7	0.75	0.8	0.85	0.9	0.95
10	0	0.5987	0.3487	0.1969	0.1074	0.0563	0.0282	0.0135	0.0060	0.0025	0.0010	0.0003	0.0001	0.0000	0.0000	0.0000	0.0000	0.0000	0.0000	0.0000
	1	0.3151	0.3874	0.3474	0.2684	0.1877	0.1211	0.0725	0.0403	0.0207	0.0098	0.0042	0.0016	0.0005	0.0001	0.0000	0.0000	0.0000	0.0000	0.0000
	2	0.0746	0.1937	0.2759	0.3020	0.2816	0.2335	0.1757	0.1209	0.0763	0.0439	0.0229	0.0106	0.0043	0.0014	0.0004	0.0001	0.0000	0.0000	0.0000
	3	0.0105	0.0574	0.1298	0.2013	0.2503	0.2668	0.2522	0.2150	0.1665	0.1172	0.0746	0.0425	0.0212	0.0090	0.0031	0.0008	0.0001	0.0000	0.0000
	4	0.0010	0.0112	0.0401	0.0881	0.1460	0.2001	0.2377	0.2508	0.2384	0.2051	0.1596	0.1115	0.0689	0.0368	0.0162	0.0055	0.0012	0.0001	0.0000
	5	0.0001	0.0015	0.0085	0.0264	0.0584	0.1029	0.1536	0.2007	0.2340	0.2461	0.2340	0.2007	0.1536	0.1029	0.0584	0.0264	0.0085	0.0015	0.0001
	6	0.0000	0.0001	0.0012	0.0055	0.0162	0.0368	0.0689	0.1115	0.1596	0.2051	0.2384	0.2508	0.2377	0.2001	0.1460	0.0881	0.0401	0.0112	0.0010
	7	0.0000	0.0000	0.0001	0.0008	0.0031	0.0090	0.0212	0.0425	0.0746	0.1172	0.1665	0.2150	0.2522	0.2668	0.2503	0.2013	0.1298	0.0574	0.0105
	8	0.0000	0.0000	0.0000	0.0001	0.0004	0.0014	0.0043	0.0106	0.0229	0.0439	0.0763	0.1209	0.1757	0.2335	0.2816	0.3020	0.2759	0.1937	0.0746
	9	0.0000	0.0000	0.0000	0.0000	0.0000	0.0001	0.0005	0.0016	0.0042	0.0098	0.0207	0.0403	0.0725	0.1211	0.1877	0.2684	0.3474	0.3874	0.3151
	10	0.0000	0.0000	0.0000	0.0000	0.0000	0.0000	0.0000	0.0001	0.0003	0.0010	0.0025	0.0060	0.0135	0.0282	0.0563	0.1074	0.1969	0.3487	0.5987
11	0	0.5688	0.3138	0.1673	0.0859	0.0422	0.0198	0.0088	0.0036	0.0014	0.0005	0.0002	0.0000	0.0000	0.0000	0.0000	0.0000	0.0000	0.0000	0.0000
	1	0.3293	0.3835	0.3248	0.2362	0.1549	0.0932	0.0518	0.0266	0.0125	0.0054	0.0021	0.0007	0.0002	0.0000	0.0000	0.0000	0.0000	0.0000	0.0000
	2	0.0867	0.2131	0.2866	0.2953	0.2581	0.1998	0.1395	0.0887	0.0513	0.0269	0.0126	0.0052	0.0018	0.0005	0.0001	0.0000	0.0000	0.0000	0.0000
	3	0.0137	0.0710	0.1517	0.2215	0.2581	0.2568	0.2254	0.1774	0.1259	0.0806	0.0462	0.0234	0.0102	0.0037	0.0011	0.0002	0.0000	0.0000	0.0000
	4	0.0014	0.0158	0.0536	0.1107	0.1721	0.2201	0.2428	0.2365	0.2060	0.1611	0.1128	0.0701	0.0379	0.0173	0.0064	0.0017	0.0003	0.0000	0.0000
	5	0.0001	0.0025	0.0132	0.0388	0.0803	0.1321	0.1830	0.2207	0.2360	0.2256	0.1931	0.1471	0.0985	0.0566	0.0268	0.0097	0.0023	0.0003	0.0000
	6	0.0000	0.0003	0.0023	0.0097	0.0268	0.0566	0.0985	0.1471	0.1931	0.2256	0.2360	0.2207	0.1830	0.1321	0.0803	0.0388	0.0132	0.0025	0.0001
	7	0.0000	0.0000	0.0003	0.0017	0.0064	0.0173	0.0379	0.0701	0.1128	0.1611	0.2060	0.2365	0.2428	0.2201	0.1721	0.1107	0.0536	0.0158	0.0014
	8	0.0000	0.0000	0.0000	0.0002	0.0011	0.0037	0.0102	0.0234	0.0462	0.0806	0.1259	0.1774	0.2254	0.2568	0.2581	0.2215	0.1517	0.0710	0.0137
	9	0.0000	0.0000	0.0000	0.0000	0.0001	0.0005	0.0018	0.0052	0.0126	0.0269	0.0513	0.0887	0.1395	0.1998	0.2581	0.2953	0.2866	0.2131	0.0867
	10	0.0000	0.0000	0.0000	0.0000	0.0000	0.0000	0.0002	0.0007	0.0021	0.0054	0.0125	0.0266	0.0518	0.0932	0.1549	0.2362	0.3248	0.3835	0.3293
	11	0.0000	0.0000	0.0000	0.0000	0.0000	0.0000	0.0000	0.0000	0.0002	0.0005	0.0014	0.0036	0.0088	0.0198	0.0422	0.0859	0.1673	0.3138	0.5688

TABLE 5 (continued) Binomial Probability Distribution $P(x = r) = {}_nC_r\, p^r (1 - p)^{n-r}$

n	r	0.05	0.1	0.15	0.2	0.25	0.3	0.35	0.4	0.45	0.5	0.55	0.6	0.65	0.7	0.75	0.8	0.85	0.9	0.95
12	0	0.5404	0.2824	0.1422	0.0687	0.0317	0.0138	0.0057	0.0022	0.0008	0.0002	0.0001	0.0000	0.0000	0.0000	0.0000	0.0000	0.0000	0.0000	0.0000
	1	0.3413	0.3766	0.3012	0.2062	0.1267	0.0712	0.0368	0.0174	0.0075	0.0029	0.0010	0.0003	0.0001	0.0000	0.0000	0.0000	0.0000	0.0000	0.0000
	2	0.0988	0.2301	0.2924	0.2835	0.2323	0.1678	0.1088	0.0639	0.0339	0.0161	0.0068	0.0025	0.0008	0.0002	0.0000	0.0000	0.0000	0.0000	0.0000
	3	0.0173	0.0852	0.1720	0.2362	0.2581	0.2397	0.1954	0.1419	0.0923	0.0537	0.0277	0.0125	0.0048	0.0015	0.0004	0.0001	0.0000	0.0000	0.0000
	4	0.0021	0.0213	0.0683	0.1329	0.1936	0.2311	0.2367	0.2128	0.1700	0.1208	0.0762	0.0420	0.0199	0.0078	0.0024	0.0005	0.0001	0.0000	0.0000
	5	0.0002	0.0038	0.0193	0.0532	0.1032	0.1585	0.2039	0.2270	0.2225	0.1934	0.1489	0.1009	0.0591	0.0291	0.0115	0.0033	0.0006	0.0000	0.0000
	6	0.0000	0.0005	0.0040	0.0155	0.0401	0.0792	0.1281	0.1766	0.2124	0.2256	0.2124	0.1766	0.1281	0.0792	0.0401	0.0155	0.0040	0.0005	0.0000
	7	0.0000	0.0000	0.0006	0.0033	0.0115	0.0291	0.0591	0.1009	0.1489	0.1934	0.2225	0.2270	0.2039	0.1585	0.1032	0.0532	0.0193	0.0038	0.0002
	8	0.0000	0.0000	0.0001	0.0005	0.0024	0.0078	0.0199	0.0420	0.0762	0.1208	0.1700	0.2128	0.2367	0.2311	0.1936	0.1329	0.0683	0.0213	0.0021
	9	0.0000	0.0000	0.0000	0.0001	0.0004	0.0015	0.0048	0.0125	0.0277	0.0537	0.0923	0.1419	0.1954	0.2397	0.2581	0.2362	0.1720	0.0852	0.0173
	10	0.0000	0.0000	0.0000	0.0000	0.0000	0.0002	0.0008	0.0025	0.0068	0.0161	0.0339	0.0639	0.1088	0.1678	0.2323	0.2835	0.2924	0.2301	0.0988
	11	0.0000	0.0000	0.0000	0.0000	0.0000	0.0000	0.0001	0.0003	0.0010	0.0029	0.0075	0.0174	0.0368	0.0712	0.1267	0.2062	0.3012	0.3766	0.3413
	12	0.0000	0.0000	0.0000	0.0000	0.0000	0.0000	0.0000	0.0000	0.0001	0.0002	0.0008	0.0022	0.0057	0.0138	0.0317	0.0687	0.1422	0.2824	0.5404
13	0	0.5133	0.2542	0.1209	0.0550	0.0238	0.0097	0.0037	0.0013	0.0004	0.0001	0.0000	0.0000	0.0000	0.0000	0.0000	0.0000	0.0000	0.0000	0.0000
	1	0.3512	0.3672	0.2774	0.1787	0.1029	0.0540	0.0259	0.0113	0.0045	0.0016	0.0005	0.0001	0.0000	0.0000	0.0000	0.0000	0.0000	0.0000	0.0000
	2	0.1109	0.2448	0.2937	0.2680	0.2059	0.1388	0.0836	0.0453	0.0220	0.0095	0.0036	0.0012	0.0003	0.0001	0.0000	0.0000	0.0000	0.0000	0.0000
	3	0.0214	0.0997	0.1900	0.2457	0.2517	0.2181	0.1651	0.1107	0.0660	0.0349	0.0162	0.0065	0.0022	0.0006	0.0001	0.0000	0.0000	0.0000	0.0000
	4	0.0028	0.0277	0.0838	0.1535	0.2097	0.2337	0.2222	0.1845	0.1350	0.0873	0.0495	0.0243	0.0101	0.0034	0.0009	0.0001	0.0000	0.0000	0.0000
	5	0.0003	0.0055	0.0266	0.0691	0.1258	0.1803	0.2154	0.2214	0.1989	0.1571	0.1089	0.0656	0.0336	0.0142	0.0047	0.0011	0.0001	0.0000	0.0000
	6	0.0000	0.0008	0.0063	0.0230	0.0559	0.1030	0.1546	0.1968	0.2169	0.2095	0.1775	0.1312	0.0833	0.0442	0.0186	0.0058	0.0011	0.0001	0.0000

TABLE 5 (continued)   Binomial Probability Distribution $P(x = r) = {}_nC_r\, p^r\,(1-p)^{n-r}$

n	r	0.05	0.1	0.15	0.2	0.25	0.3	0.35	0.4	0.45	0.5	0.55	0.6	0.65	0.7	0.75	0.8	0.85	0.9	0.95
	7	0.0000	0.0001	0.0011	0.0058	0.0186	0.0442	0.0833	0.1312	0.1775	0.2095	0.2169	0.1968	0.1546	0.1030	0.0559	0.0230	0.0063	0.0008	0.0000
	8	0.0000	0.0000	0.0001	0.0011	0.0047	0.0142	0.0336	0.0656	0.1089	0.1571	0.1989	0.2214	0.2154	0.1803	0.1258	0.0691	0.0266	0.0055	0.0003
	9	0.0000	0.0000	0.0000	0.0001	0.0009	0.0034	0.0101	0.0243	0.0495	0.0873	0.1350	0.1845	0.2222	0.2337	0.2097	0.1535	0.0838	0.0277	0.0028
	10	0.0000	0.0000	0.0000	0.0001	0.0001	0.0006	0.0022	0.0065	0.0162	0.0349	0.0660	0.1107	0.1651	0.2181	0.2517	0.2457	0.1900	0.0997	0.0214
	11	0.0000	0.0000	0.0000	0.0000	0.0000	0.0001	0.0003	0.0012	0.0036	0.0095	0.0220	0.0453	0.0836	0.1388	0.2059	0.2680	0.2937	0.2448	0.1109
	12	0.0000	0.0000	0.0000	0.0000	0.0000	0.0000	0.0000	0.0001	0.0005	0.0016	0.0045	0.0113	0.0259	0.0540	0.1029	0.1787	0.2774	0.3672	0.3512
	13	0.0000	0.0000	0.0000	0.0000	0.0000	0.0000	0.0000	0.0000	0.0000	0.0001	0.0004	0.0013	0.0037	0.0097	0.0238	0.0550	0.1209	0.2542	0.5133
14	0	0.4877	0.2288	0.1028	0.0440	0.0178	0.0068	0.0024	0.0008	0.0002	0.0001	0.0000	0.0000	0.0000	0.0000	0.0000	0.0000	0.0000	0.0000	0.0000
	1	0.3593	0.3559	0.2539	0.1539	0.0832	0.0407	0.0181	0.0073	0.0027	0.0009	0.0002	0.0001	0.0000	0.0000	0.0000	0.0000	0.0000	0.0000	0.0000
	2	0.1229	0.2570	0.2912	0.2501	0.1802	0.1134	0.0634	0.0317	0.0141	0.0056	0.0019	0.0005	0.0001	0.0000	0.0000	0.0000	0.0000	0.0000	0.0000
	3	0.0259	0.1142	0.2056	0.2501	0.2402	0.1943	0.1366	0.0845	0.0462	0.0222	0.0093	0.0033	0.0010	0.0002	0.0000	0.0000	0.0000	0.0000	0.0000
	4	0.0037	0.0349	0.0998	0.1720	0.2202	0.2290	0.2022	0.1549	0.1040	0.0611	0.0312	0.0136	0.0049	0.0014	0.0003	0.0000	0.0000	0.0000	0.0000
	5	0.0004	0.0078	0.0352	0.0860	0.1468	0.1963	0.2178	0.2066	0.1701	0.1222	0.0762	0.0408	0.0183	0.0066	0.0018	0.0003	0.0000	0.0000	0.0000
	6	0.0000	0.0013	0.0093	0.0322	0.0734	0.1262	0.1759	0.2066	0.2088	0.1833	0.1398	0.0918	0.0510	0.0232	0.0082	0.0020	0.0003	0.0000	0.0000
	7	0.0000	0.0002	0.0019	0.0092	0.0280	0.0618	0.1082	0.1574	0.1952	0.2095	0.1952	0.1574	0.1082	0.0618	0.0280	0.0092	0.0019	0.0002	0.0000
	8	0.0000	0.0000	0.0003	0.0020	0.0082	0.0232	0.0510	0.0918	0.1398	0.1833	0.2088	0.2066	0.1759	0.1262	0.0734	0.0322	0.0093	0.0013	0.0000
	9	0.0000	0.0000	0.0000	0.0003	0.0018	0.0066	0.0183	0.0408	0.0762	0.1222	0.1701	0.2066	0.2178	0.1963	0.1468	0.0860	0.0352	0.0078	0.0004
	10	0.0000	0.0000	0.0000	0.0000	0.0003	0.0014	0.0049	0.0136	0.0312	0.0611	0.1040	0.1549	0.2022	0.2290	0.2202	0.1720	0.0998	0.0349	0.0037
	11	0.0000	0.0000	0.0000	0.0000	0.0000	0.0002	0.0010	0.0033	0.0093	0.0222	0.0462	0.0845	0.1366	0.1943	0.2402	0.2501	0.2056	0.1142	0.0259
	12	0.0000	0.0000	0.0000	0.0000	0.0000	0.0000	0.0001	0.0005	0.0019	0.0056	0.0141	0.0317	0.0634	0.1134	0.1802	0.2501	0.2912	0.2570	0.1229
	13	0.0000	0.0000	0.0000	0.0000	0.0000	0.0000	0.0000	0.0001	0.0002	0.0009	0.0027	0.0073	0.0181	0.0407	0.0832	0.1539	0.2539	0.3559	0.3593
	14	0.0000	0.0000	0.0000	0.0000	0.0000	0.0000	0.0000	0.0000	0.0000	0.0001	0.0002	0.0008	0.0024	0.0068	0.0178	0.0440	0.1028	0.2288	0.4877

TABLE 5 (continued) Binomial Probability Distribution $P(x = r) = {}_nC_r\, p^r (1 - p)^{n-r}$

n	r	p																		
		0.05	0.1	0.15	0.2	0.25	0.3	0.35	0.4	0.45	0.5	0.55	0.6	0.65	0.7	0.75	0.8	0.85	0.9	0.95
15	0	0.4633	0.2059	0.0874	0.0352	0.0134	0.0047	0.0016	0.0005	0.0001	0.0000	0.0000	0.0000	0.0000	0.0000	0.0000	0.0000	0.0000	0.0000	0.0000
	1	0.3658	0.3432	0.2312	0.1319	0.0668	0.0305	0.0126	0.0047	0.0016	0.0005	0.0001	0.0000	0.0000	0.0000	0.0000	0.0000	0.0000	0.0000	0.0000
	2	0.1348	0.2669	0.2856	0.2309	0.1559	0.0916	0.0476	0.0219	0.0090	0.0032	0.0010	0.0003	0.0001	0.0000	0.0000	0.0000	0.0000	0.0000	0.0000
	3	0.0307	0.1285	0.2184	0.2501	0.2252	0.1700	0.1110	0.0634	0.0318	0.0139	0.0052	0.0016	0.0004	0.0001	0.0000	0.0000	0.0000	0.0000	0.0000
	4	0.0049	0.0428	0.1156	0.1876	0.2252	0.2186	0.1792	0.1268	0.0780	0.0417	0.0191	0.0074	0.0024	0.0006	0.0001	0.0000	0.0000	0.0000	0.0000
	5	0.0006	0.0105	0.0449	0.1032	0.1651	0.2061	0.2123	0.1859	0.1404	0.0916	0.0515	0.0245	0.0096	0.0030	0.0007	0.0001	0.0000	0.0000	0.0000
	6	0.0000	0.0019	0.0132	0.0430	0.0917	0.1472	0.1906	0.2066	0.1914	0.1527	0.1048	0.0612	0.0298	0.0116	0.0034	0.0007	0.0001	0.0000	0.0000
	7	0.0000	0.0003	0.0030	0.0138	0.0393	0.0811	0.1319	0.1771	0.2013	0.1964	0.1647	0.1181	0.0710	0.0348	0.0131	0.0035	0.0005	0.0000	0.0000
	8	0.0000	0.0000	0.0005	0.0035	0.0131	0.0348	0.0710	0.1181	0.1647	0.1964	0.2013	0.1771	0.1319	0.0811	0.0393	0.0138	0.0030	0.0003	0.0000
	9	0.0000	0.0000	0.0001	0.0007	0.0034	0.0116	0.0298	0.0612	0.1048	0.1527	0.1914	0.2066	0.1906	0.1472	0.0917	0.0430	0.0132	0.0019	0.0000
	10	0.0000	0.0000	0.0000	0.0001	0.0007	0.0030	0.0096	0.0245	0.0515	0.0916	0.1404	0.1859	0.2123	0.2061	0.1651	0.1032	0.0449	0.0105	0.0006
	11	0.0000	0.0000	0.0000	0.0000	0.0001	0.0006	0.0024	0.0074	0.0191	0.0417	0.0780	0.1268	0.1792	0.2186	0.2252	0.1876	0.1156	0.0428	0.0049
	12	0.0000	0.0000	0.0000	0.0000	0.0000	0.0001	0.0004	0.0016	0.0052	0.0139	0.0318	0.0634	0.1110	0.1700	0.2252	0.2501	0.2184	0.1285	0.0307
	13	0.0000	0.0000	0.0000	0.0000	0.0000	0.0000	0.0001	0.0003	0.0010	0.0032	0.0090	0.0219	0.0476	0.0916	0.1559	0.2309	0.2856	0.2669	0.1348
	14	0.0000	0.0000	0.0000	0.0000	0.0000	0.0000	0.0000	0.0000	0.0001	0.0005	0.0016	0.0047	0.0126	0.0305	0.0668	0.1319	0.2312	0.3432	0.3658
	15	0.0000	0.0000	0.0000	0.0000	0.0000	0.0000	0.0000	0.0000	0.0000	0.0000	0.0001	0.0005	0.0016	0.0047	0.0134	0.0352	0.0874	0.2059	0.4633

TABLE 6 Poisson Probability Distribution $P(x) = \dfrac{e^{-\lambda}\lambda^x}{x!}$

The Table shows **marginal probabilities** of the **Poisson** process.
In Excel (2016): POISSON.DIST(x, λ, False)

λ x	0.1	0.2	0.3	0.4	0.5	0.6	0.7	0.8	0.9	1
0	0.9048	0.8187	0.7408	0.6703	0.6065	0.5488	0.4966	0.4493	0.4066	0.3679
1	0.0905	0.1637	0.2222	0.2681	0.3033	0.3293	0.3476	0.3595	0.3659	0.3679
2	0.0045	0.0164	0.0333	0.0536	0.0758	0.0988	0.1217	0.1438	0.1647	0.1839
3	0.0002	0.0011	0.0033	0.0072	0.0126	0.0198	0.0284	0.0383	0.0494	0.0613
4	0.0000	0.0001	0.0003	0.0007	0.0016	0.0030	0.0050	0.0077	0.0111	0.0153
5	0.0000	0.0000	0.0000	0.0001	0.0002	0.0004	0.0007	0.0012	0.0020	0.0031
6	0.0000	0.0000	0.0000	0.0000	0.0000	0.0000	0.0001	0.0002	0.0003	0.0005
7	0.0000	0.0000	0.0000	0.0000	0.0000	0.0000	0.0000	0.0000	0.0000	0.0001

λ x	1.1	1.2	1.3	1.4	1.5	1.6	1.7	1.8	1.9	2
0	0.3329	0.3012	0.2725	0.2466	0.2231	0.2019	0.1827	0.1653	0.1496	0.1353
1	0.3662	0.3614	0.3543	0.3452	0.3347	0.3230	0.3106	0.2975	0.2842	0.2707
2	0.2014	0.2169	0.2303	0.2417	0.2510	0.2584	0.2640	0.2678	0.2700	0.2707
3	0.0738	0.0867	0.0998	0.1128	0.1255	0.1378	0.1496	0.1607	0.1710	0.1804
4	0.0203	0.0260	0.0324	0.0395	0.0471	0.0551	0.0636	0.0723	0.0812	0.0902
5	0.0045	0.0062	0.0084	0.0111	0.0141	0.0176	0.0216	0.0260	0.0309	0.0361
6	0.0008	0.0012	0.0018	0.0026	0.0035	0.0047	0.0061	0.0078	0.0098	0.0120
7	0.0001	0.0002	0.0003	0.0005	0.0008	0.0011	0.0015	0.0020	0.0027	0.0034
8	0.0000	0.0000	0.0001	0.0001	0.0001	0.0002	0.0003	0.0005	0.0006	0.0009
9	0.0000	0.0000	0.0000	0.0000	0.0000	0.0000	0.0001	0.0001	0.0001	0.0002

λ x	2.1	2.2	2.3	2.4	2.5	2.6	2.7	2.8	2.9	3
0	0.1225	0.1108	0.1003	0.0907	0.0821	0.0743	0.0672	0.0608	0.0550	0.0498
1	0.2572	0.2438	0.2306	0.2177	0.2052	0.1931	0.1815	0.1703	0.1596	0.1494
2	0.2700	0.2681	0.2652	0.2613	0.2565	0.2510	0.2450	0.2384	0.2314	0.2240
3	0.1890	0.1966	0.2033	0.2090	0.2138	0.2176	0.2205	0.2225	0.2237	0.2240
4	0.0992	0.1082	0.1169	0.1254	0.1336	0.1414	0.1488	0.1557	0.1622	0.1680
5	0.0417	0.0476	0.0538	0.0602	0.0668	0.0735	0.0804	0.0872	0.0940	0.1008
6	0.0146	0.0174	0.0206	0.0241	0.0278	0.0319	0.0362	0.0407	0.0455	0.0504
7	0.0044	0.0055	0.0068	0.0083	0.0099	0.0118	0.0139	0.0163	0.0188	0.0216
8	0.0011	0.0015	0.0019	0.0025	0.0031	0.0038	0.0047	0.0057	0.0068	0.0081
9	0.0003	0.0004	0.0005	0.0007	0.0009	0.0011	0.0014	0.0018	0.0022	0.0027
10	0.0001	0.0001	0.0001	0.0002	0.0002	0.0003	0.0004	0.0005	0.0006	0.0008
11	0.0000	0.0000	0.0000	0.0000	0.0000	0.0001	0.0001	0.0001	0.0002	0.0002

TABLE 6 (continued) Poisson Probability Distribution $P(x) = \dfrac{e^{-\lambda}\lambda^x}{x!}$

λ / x	3.1	3.2	3.3	3.4	3.5	3.6	3.7	3.8	3.9	4
0	0.0450	0.0408	0.0369	0.0334	0.0302	0.0273	0.0247	0.0224	0.0202	0.0183
1	0.1397	0.1304	0.1217	0.1135	0.1057	0.0984	0.0915	0.0850	0.0789	0.0733
2	0.2165	0.2087	0.2008	0.1929	0.1850	0.1771	0.1692	0.1615	0.1539	0.1465
3	0.2237	0.2226	0.2209	0.2186	0.2158	0.2125	0.2087	0.2046	0.2001	0.1954
4	0.1733	0.1781	0.1823	0.1858	0.1888	0.1912	0.1931	0.1944	0.1951	0.1954
5	0.1075	0.1140	0.1203	0.1264	0.1322	0.1377	0.1429	0.1477	0.1522	0.1563
6	0.0555	0.0608	0.0662	0.0716	0.0771	0.0826	0.0881	0.0936	0.0989	0.1042
7	0.0246	0.0278	0.0312	0.0348	0.0385	0.0425	0.0466	0.0508	0.0551	0.0595
8	0.0095	0.0111	0.0129	0.0148	0.0169	0.0191	0.0215	0.0241	0.0269	0.0298
9	0.0033	0.0040	0.0047	0.0056	0.0066	0.0076	0.0089	0.0102	0.0116	0.0132
10	0.0010	0.0013	0.0016	0.0019	0.0023	0.0028	0.0033	0.0039	0.0045	0.0053
11	0.0003	0.0004	0.0005	0.0006	0.0007	0.0009	0.0011	0.0013	0.0016	0.0019
12	0.0001	0.0001	0.0001	0.0002	0.0002	0.0003	0.0003	0.0004	0.0005	0.0006
13	0.0000	0.0000	0.0000	0.0000	0.0001	0.0001	0.0001	0.0001	0.0002	0.0002

λ / x	4.1	4.2	4.3	4.4	4.5	4.6	4.7	4.8	4.9	5
0	0.0166	0.0150	0.0136	0.0123	0.0111	0.0101	0.0091	0.0082	0.0074	0.0067
1	0.0679	0.0630	0.0583	0.0540	0.0500	0.0462	0.0427	0.0395	0.0365	0.0337
2	0.1393	0.1323	0.1254	0.1188	0.1125	0.1063	0.1005	0.0948	0.0894	0.0842
3	0.1904	0.1852	0.1798	0.1743	0.1687	0.1631	0.1574	0.1517	0.1460	0.1404
4	0.1951	0.1944	0.1933	0.1917	0.1898	0.1875	0.1849	0.1820	0.1789	0.1755
5	0.1600	0.1633	0.1662	0.1687	0.1708	0.1725	0.1738	0.1747	0.1753	0.1755
6	0.1093	0.1143	0.1191	0.1237	0.1281	0.1323	0.1362	0.1398	0.1432	0.1462
7	0.0640	0.0686	0.0732	0.0778	0.0824	0.0869	0.0914	0.0959	0.1002	0.1044
8	0.0328	0.0360	0.0393	0.0428	0.0463	0.0500	0.0537	0.0575	0.0614	0.0653
9	0.0150	0.0168	0.0188	0.0209	0.0232	0.0255	0.0281	0.0307	0.0334	0.0363
10	0.0061	0.0071	0.0081	0.0092	0.0104	0.0118	0.0132	0.0147	0.0164	0.0181
11	0.0023	0.0027	0.0032	0.0037	0.0043	0.0049	0.0056	0.0064	0.0073	0.0082
12	0.0008	0.0009	0.0011	0.0013	0.0016	0.0019	0.0022	0.0026	0.0030	0.0034
13	0.0002	0.0003	0.0004	0.0005	0.0006	0.0007	0.0008	0.0009	0.0011	0.0013
14	0.0001	0.0001	0.0001	0.0001	0.0002	0.0002	0.0003	0.0003	0.0004	0.0005
15	0.0000	0.0000	0.0000	0.0000	0.0001	0.0001	0.0001	0.0001	0.0001	0.0002

TABLE 6 (continued) Poisson Probability Distribution $P(x) = \dfrac{e^{-\lambda}\lambda^x}{x!}$

	λ	5.1	5.2	5.3	5.4	5.5	5.6	5.7	5.8	5.9	6
x	0	0.0061	0.0055	0.0050	0.0045	0.0041	0.0037	0.0033	0.0030	0.0027	0.0025
	1	0.0311	0.0287	0.0265	0.0244	0.0225	0.0207	0.0191	0.0176	0.0162	0.0149
	2	0.0793	0.0746	0.0701	0.0659	0.0618	0.0580	0.0544	0.0509	0.0477	0.0446
	3	0.1348	0.1293	0.1239	0.1185	0.1133	0.1082	0.1033	0.0985	0.0938	0.0892
	4	0.1719	0.1681	0.1641	0.1600	0.1558	0.1515	0.1472	0.1428	0.1383	0.1339
	5	0.1753	0.1748	0.1740	0.1728	0.1714	0.1697	0.1678	0.1656	0.1632	0.1606
	6	0.1490	0.1515	0.1537	0.1555	0.1571	0.1584	0.1594	0.1601	0.1605	0.1606
	7	0.1086	0.1125	0.1163	0.1200	0.1234	0.1267	0.1298	0.1326	0.1353	0.1377
	8	0.0692	0.0731	0.0771	0.0810	0.0849	0.0887	0.0925	0.0962	0.0998	0.1033
	9	0.0392	0.0423	0.0454	0.0486	0.0519	0.0552	0.0586	0.0620	0.0654	0.0688
	10	0.0200	0.0220	0.0241	0.0262	0.0285	0.0309	0.0334	0.0359	0.0386	0.0413
	11	0.0093	0.0104	0.0116	0.0129	0.0143	0.0157	0.0173	0.0190	0.0207	0.0225
	12	0.0039	0.0045	0.0051	0.0058	0.0065	0.0073	0.0082	0.0092	0.0102	0.0113
	13	0.0015	0.0018	0.0021	0.0024	0.0028	0.0032	0.0036	0.0041	0.0046	0.0052
	14	0.0006	0.0007	0.0008	0.0009	0.0011	0.0013	0.0015	0.0017	0.0019	0.0022
	15	0.0002	0.0002	0.0003	0.0003	0.0004	0.0005	0.0006	0.0007	0.0008	0.0009

	λ	6.1	6.2	6.3	6.4	6.5	6.6	6.7	6.8	6.9	7
x	0	0.0022	0.0020	0.0018	0.0017	0.0015	0.0014	0.0012	0.0011	0.0010	0.0009
	1	0.0137	0.0126	0.0116	0.0106	0.0098	0.0090	0.0082	0.0076	0.0070	0.0064
	2	0.0417	0.0390	0.0364	0.0340	0.0318	0.0296	0.0276	0.0258	0.0240	0.0223
	3	0.0848	0.0806	0.0765	0.0726	0.0688	0.0652	0.0617	0.0584	0.0552	0.0521
	4	0.1294	0.1249	0.1205	0.1162	0.1118	0.1076	0.1034	0.0992	0.0952	0.0912
	5	0.1579	0.1549	0.1519	0.1487	0.1454	0.1420	0.1385	0.1349	0.1314	0.1277
	6	0.1605	0.1601	0.1595	0.1586	0.1575	0.1562	0.1546	0.1529	0.1511	0.1490
	7	0.1399	0.1418	0.1435	0.1450	0.1462	0.1472	0.1480	0.1486	0.1489	0.1490
	8	0.1066	0.1099	0.1130	0.1160	0.1188	0.1215	0.1240	0.1263	0.1284	0.1304
	9	0.0723	0.0757	0.0791	0.0825	0.0858	0.0891	0.0923	0.0954	0.0985	0.1014
	10	0.0441	0.0469	0.0498	0.0528	0.0558	0.0588	0.0618	0.0649	0.0679	0.0710
	11	0.0244	0.0265	0.0285	0.0307	0.0330	0.0353	0.0377	0.0401	0.0426	0.0452
	12	0.0124	0.0137	0.0150	0.0164	0.0179	0.0194	0.0210	0.0227	0.0245	0.0263
	13	0.0058	0.0065	0.0073	0.0081	0.0089	0.0099	0.0108	0.0119	0.0130	0.0142
	14	0.0025	0.0029	0.0033	0.0037	0.0041	0.0046	0.0052	0.0058	0.0064	0.0071
	15	0.0010	0.0012	0.0014	0.0016	0.0018	0.0020	0.0023	0.0026	0.0029	0.0033
	16	0.0004	0.0005	0.0005	0.0006	0.0007	0.0008	0.0010	0.0011	0.0013	0.0014
	17	0.0001	0.0002	0.0002	0.0002	0.0003	0.0003	0.0004	0.0004	0.0005	0.0006

TABLE 6 (continued) Poisson Probability Distribution $P(x) = \dfrac{e^{-\lambda}\lambda^x}{x!}$

	λ	7.1	7.2	7.3	7.4	7.5	7.6	7.7	7.8	7.9	8
x	0	0.0008	0.0007	0.0007	0.0006	0.0005	0.0005	0.0005	0.0004	0.0004	0.0003
	1	0.0059	0.0054	0.0049	0.0045	0.0041	0.0038	0.0035	0.0032	0.0029	0.0027
	2	0.0208	0.0194	0.0180	0.0167	0.0155	0.0145	0.0134	0.0125	0.0116	0.0107
	3	0.0492	0.0464	0.0438	0.0413	0.0389	0.0366	0.0345	0.0324	0.0305	0.0286
	4	0.0874	0.0836	0.0799	0.0764	0.0729	0.0696	0.0663	0.0632	0.0602	0.0573
	5	0.1241	0.1204	0.1167	0.1130	0.1094	0.1057	0.1021	0.0986	0.0951	0.0916
	6	0.1468	0.1445	0.1420	0.1394	0.1367	0.1339	0.1311	0.1282	0.1252	0.1221
	7	0.1489	0.1486	0.1481	0.1474	0.1465	0.1454	0.1442	0.1428	0.1413	0.1396
	8	0.1321	0.1337	0.1351	0.1363	0.1373	0.1381	0.1388	0.1392	0.1395	0.1396
	9	0.1042	0.1070	0.1096	0.1121	0.1144	0.1167	0.1187	0.1207	0.1224	0.1241
	10	0.0740	0.0770	0.0800	0.0829	0.0858	0.0887	0.0914	0.0941	0.0967	0.0993
	11	0.0478	0.0504	0.0531	0.0558	0.0585	0.0613	0.0640	0.0667	0.0695	0.0722
	12	0.0283	0.0303	0.0323	0.0344	0.0366	0.0388	0.0411	0.0434	0.0457	0.0481
	13	0.0154	0.0168	0.0181	0.0196	0.0211	0.0227	0.0243	0.0260	0.0278	0.0296
	14	0.0078	0.0086	0.0095	0.0104	0.0113	0.0123	0.0134	0.0145	0.0157	0.0169
	15	0.0037	0.0041	0.0046	0.0051	0.0057	0.0062	0.0069	0.0075	0.0083	0.0090
	16	0.0016	0.0019	0.0021	0.0024	0.0026	0.0030	0.0033	0.0037	0.0041	0.0045
	17	0.0007	0.0008	0.0009	0.0010	0.0012	0.0013	0.0015	0.0017	0.0019	0.0021
	18	0.0003	0.0003	0.0004	0.0004	0.0005	0.0006	0.0006	0.0007	0.0008	0.0009
	19	0.0001	0.0001	0.0001	0.0002	0.0002	0.0002	0.0003	0.0003	0.0003	0.0004

	λ	8.1	8.2	8.3	8.4	8.5	8.6	8.7	8.8	8.9	9
x	0	0.0003	0.0003	0.0002	0.0002	0.0002	0.0002	0.0002	0.0002	0.0001	0.0001
	1	0.0025	0.0023	0.0021	0.0019	0.0017	0.0016	0.0014	0.0013	0.0012	0.0011
	2	0.0100	0.0092	0.0086	0.0079	0.0074	0.0068	0.0063	0.0058	0.0054	0.0050
	3	0.0269	0.0252	0.0237	0.0222	0.0208	0.0195	0.0183	0.0171	0.0160	0.0150
	4	0.0544	0.0517	0.0491	0.0466	0.0443	0.0420	0.0398	0.0377	0.0357	0.0337
	5	0.0882	0.0849	0.0816	0.0784	0.0752	0.0722	0.0692	0.0663	0.0635	0.0607
	6	0.1191	0.1160	0.1128	0.1097	0.1066	0.1034	0.1003	0.0972	0.0941	0.0911
	7	0.1378	0.1358	0.1338	0.1317	0.1294	0.1271	0.1247	0.1222	0.1197	0.1171
	8	0.1395	0.1392	0.1388	0.1382	0.1375	0.1366	0.1356	0.1344	0.1332	0.1318
	9	0.1256	0.1269	0.1280	0.1290	0.1299	0.1306	0.1311	0.1315	0.1317	0.1318
	10	0.1017	0.1040	0.1063	0.1084	0.1104	0.1123	0.1140	0.1157	0.1172	0.1186

TABLE 6 (continued) Poisson Probability Distribution $P(x) = \dfrac{e^{-\lambda}\lambda^x}{x!}$

λ	8.1	8.2	8.3	8.4	8.5	8.6	8.7	8.8	8.9	9
11	0.0749	0.0776	0.0802	0.0828	0.0853	0.0878	0.0902	0.0925	0.0948	0.0970
12	0.0505	0.0530	0.0555	0.0579	0.0604	0.0629	0.0654	0.0679	0.0703	0.0728
13	0.0315	0.0334	0.0354	0.0374	0.0395	0.0416	0.0438	0.0459	0.0481	0.0504
14	0.0182	0.0196	0.0210	0.0225	0.0240	0.0256	0.0272	0.0289	0.0306	0.0324
15	0.0098	0.0107	0.0116	0.0126	0.0136	0.0147	0.0158	0.0169	0.0182	0.0194
16	0.0050	0.0055	0.0060	0.0066	0.0072	0.0079	0.0086	0.0093	0.0101	0.0109
17	0.0024	0.0026	0.0029	0.0033	0.0036	0.0040	0.0044	0.0048	0.0053	0.0058
18	0.0011	0.0012	0.0014	0.0015	0.0017	0.0019	0.0021	0.0024	0.0026	0.0029
19	0.0005	0.0005	0.0006	0.0007	0.0008	0.0009	0.0010	0.0011	0.0012	0.0014
20	0.0002	0.0002	0.0002	0.0003	0.0003	0.0004	0.0004	0.0005	0.0005	0.0006

	λ	9.1	9.2	9.3	9.4	9.5	9.6	9.7	9.8	9.9	10
x	0	0.0001	0.0001	0.0001	0.0001	0.0001	0.0001	0.0001	0.0001	0.0001	0.0000
	1	0.0010	0.0009	0.0009	0.0008	0.0007	0.0007	0.0006	0.0005	0.0005	0.0005
	2	0.0046	0.0043	0.0040	0.0037	0.0034	0.0031	0.0029	0.0027	0.0025	0.0023
	3	0.0140	0.0131	0.0123	0.0115	0.0107	0.0100	0.0093	0.0087	0.0081	0.0076
	4	0.0319	0.0302	0.0285	0.0269	0.0254	0.0240	0.0226	0.0213	0.0201	0.0189
	5	0.0581	0.0555	0.0530	0.0506	0.0483	0.0460	0.0439	0.0418	0.0398	0.0378
	6	0.0881	0.0851	0.0822	0.0793	0.0764	0.0736	0.0709	0.0682	0.0656	0.0631
	7	0.1145	0.1118	0.1091	0.1064	0.1037	0.1010	0.0982	0.0955	0.0928	0.0901
	8	0.1302	0.1286	0.1269	0.1251	0.1232	0.1212	0.1191	0.1170	0.1148	0.1126
	9	0.1317	0.1315	0.1311	0.1306	0.1300	0.1293	0.1284	0.1274	0.1263	0.1251
	10	0.1198	0.1210	0.1219	0.1228	0.1235	0.1241	0.1245	0.1249	0.1250	0.1251
	11	0.0991	0.1012	0.1031	0.1049	0.1067	0.1083	0.1098	0.1112	0.1125	0.1137
	12	0.0752	0.0776	0.0799	0.0822	0.0844	0.0866	0.0888	0.0908	0.0928	0.0948
	13	0.0526	0.0549	0.0572	0.0594	0.0617	0.0640	0.0662	0.0685	0.0707	0.0729
	14	0.0342	0.0361	0.0380	0.0399	0.0419	0.0439	0.0459	0.0479	0.0500	0.0521
	15	0.0208	0.0221	0.0235	0.0250	0.0265	0.0281	0.0297	0.0313	0.0330	0.0347
	16	0.0118	0.0127	0.0137	0.0147	0.0157	0.0168	0.0180	0.0192	0.0204	0.0217
	17	0.0063	0.0069	0.0075	0.0081	0.0088	0.0095	0.0103	0.0111	0.0119	0.0128
	18	0.0032	0.0035	0.0039	0.0042	0.0046	0.0051	0.0055	0.0060	0.0065	0.0071
	19	0.0015	0.0017	0.0019	0.0021	0.0023	0.0026	0.0028	0.0031	0.0034	0.0037
	20	0.0007	0.0008	0.0009	0.0010	0.0011	0.0012	0.0014	0.0015	0.0017	0.0019
	21	0.0003	0.0003	0.0004	0.0004	0.0005	0.0006	0.0006	0.0007	0.0008	0.0009
	22	0.0001	0.0001	0.0002	0.0002	0.0002	0.0002	0.0003	0.0003	0.0004	0.0004

TABLE 7 Critical Values of the Studentised q-Range (0.01 Level)

dfe	Number of Means																		
	2	3	4	5	6	7	8	9	10	11	12	13	14	15	16	17	18	19	20
2	14.0346	19.0189	22.2935	24.7166	26.628	28.1991	29.5282	30.677	31.6866	32.5855	33.3946	34.1294	34.8018	35.4212	35.9948	36.5286	37.0277	37.4959	37.9368
3	8.2603	10.6157	12.1695	13.3241	14.2403	14.9972	15.6401	16.1978	16.6894	17.1283	17.5241	17.8844	18.2146	18.5192	18.8017	19.065	19.3113	19.5427	19.7608
4	6.5113	8.1181	9.1729	9.9579	10.5823	11.0992	11.5394	11.9253	12.2639	12.5667	12.8403	13.0897	13.3186	13.5299	13.7262	13.9093	14.0808	14.242	14.394
5	5.7024	6.9757	7.8059	8.4215	8.9131	9.3208	9.6686	9.9713	10.239	10.4787	10.6955	10.8932	11.0749	11.2428	11.3988	11.5445	11.6809	11.8093	11.9305
6	5.2427	6.3312	7.0333	7.556	7.9737	8.3179	8.6113	8.8693	9.0966	9.3003	9.4847	9.653	9.8077	9.9508	10.0838	10.208	10.3245	10.4342	10.5377
7	4.9483	5.9193	6.543	7.0061	7.373	7.6784	7.9403	8.1672	8.368	8.5478	8.7107	8.8593	8.9959	9.1242	9.2423	9.3526	9.456	9.5534	9.6454
8	4.7445	5.6353	6.2039	6.6251	6.96	7.2378	7.4748	7.6813	7.8642	8.0281	8.1766	8.3121	8.4368	8.5522	8.6595	8.7597	8.8538	8.9424	9.026
9	4.5955	5.4279	5.9567	6.3473	6.6576	6.9148	7.1344	7.3257	7.4951	7.647	7.7846	7.9103	8.026	8.133	8.2326	8.3257	8.4131	8.4953	8.573
10	4.4818	5.27	5.7686	6.1361	6.4276	6.6691	6.8751	7.0546	7.2136	7.3562	7.4854	7.6034	7.712	7.8126	7.9062	7.9936	8.0757	8.153	8.2261
11	4.3922	5.1459	5.6207	5.9701	6.2474	6.4759	6.6713	6.8415	6.9922	7.1274	7.2498	7.3617	7.4647	7.56	7.6487	7.7317	7.8095	7.8829	7.9522
12	4.3197	5.0459	5.5016	5.8363	6.1011	6.3205	6.5069	6.6696	6.8136	6.9427	7.0597	7.1665	7.2649	7.3559	7.4407	7.5199	7.5943	7.6644	7.7306
13	4.2607	4.9635	5.4036	5.7266	5.9812	6.1919	6.3715	6.5283	6.6664	6.7905	6.903	7.0057	7.1002	7.1877	7.2691	7.3453	7.4168	7.4841	7.5478
14	4.2099	4.8945	5.3215	5.634	5.8808	6.0847	6.2583	6.4095	6.5428	6.6638	6.7716	6.8708	6.9621	7.0466	7.1252	7.1988	7.2678	7.3329	7.3943
15	4.1673	4.8359	5.2518	5.5558	5.7956	5.9936	6.1621	6.3087	6.4384	6.5547	6.6596	6.7568	6.8447	6.9266	7.0028	7.0741	7.1411	7.2041	7.2637
16	4.1306	4.7855	5.1919	5.4885	5.7223	5.9152	6.0793	6.2221	6.3483	6.4615	6.5639	6.6575	6.7431	6.8236	6.8975	6.9668	7.0319	7.0932	7.1512
17	4.0987	4.7417	5.1398	5.43	5.6586	5.8471	6.0074	6.1468	6.27	6.3804	6.4804	6.5717	6.6557	6.7334	6.8058	6.8734	6.9373	6.9974	7.0533
18	4.0707	4.7032	5.0941	5.3787	5.6027	5.7873	5.9443	6.0807	6.2013	6.3093	6.4071	6.4964	6.5785	6.6546	6.7253	6.7914	6.8535	6.912	6.9673
19	4.0459	4.6693	5.0537	5.3334	5.5534	5.7345	5.8885	6.0223	6.1405	6.2464	6.3423	6.4298	6.5103	6.5848	6.6541	6.7189	6.7797	6.837	6.8911
20	4.0237	4.639	5.0178	5.2931	5.5094	5.6875	5.8388	5.9702	6.0864	6.1904	6.2845	6.3704	6.4494	6.5226	6.5906	6.6542	6.7139	6.7701	6.8232
21	4.0042	4.6119	4.9856	5.2569	5.47	5.6453	5.7943	5.9236	6.0379	6.1402	6.2327	6.3172	6.3949	6.4668	6.5337	6.5962	6.6549	6.7101	6.7623
22	3.9864	4.5874	4.9565	5.2243	5.4345	5.6074	5.7541	5.8816	5.9941	6.0949	6.186	6.2692	6.3457	6.4165	6.4823	6.5439	6.6016	6.656	6.7074

TABLE 7 (continued) Critical Values of the Studentised q-Range (0.01 Level)

dfe	2	3	4	5	6	7	8	9	10	11	12	13	14	15	16	17	18	19	20
									Number of Means										
23	3.9703	4.5653	4.9302	5.1948	5.4023	5.5729	5.7178	5.8435	5.9545	6.0538	6.1437	6.2257	6.3011	6.3709	6.4358	6.4964	6.5533	6.607	6.6576
24	3.9557	4.5452	4.9063	5.1679	5.373	5.5416	5.6847	5.8088	5.9184	6.0165	6.1052	6.1861	6.2605	6.3294	6.3934	6.4532	6.5094	6.5623	6.6122
25	3.9424	4.5268	4.8844	5.1433	5.3463	5.513	5.6544	5.7771	5.8854	5.9823	6.07	6.1499	6.2234	6.2914	6.3546	6.4137	6.4692	6.5214	6.5707
26	3.9302	4.5099	4.865	5.1215	5.3223	5.4873	5.6266	5.748	5.8552	5.951	6.0376	6.1167	6.1893	6.2565	6.319	6.3774	6.4322	6.4838	6.5326
27	3.9189	4.4944	4.8466	5.1008	5.2998	5.4632	5.6017	5.7218	5.8273	5.9221	6.0079	6.0861	6.158	6.2244	6.2863	6.344	6.3982	6.4493	6.4975
28	3.9078	4.48	4.8296	5.0817	5.279	5.4409	5.5782	5.6972	5.8021	5.896	5.9803	6.0578	6.1289	6.1948	6.256	6.3131	6.3668	6.4173	6.465
29	3.8981	4.4668	4.8138	5.064	5.2597	5.4203	5.5564	5.6743	5.7784	5.8714	5.9555	6.0322	6.1026	6.1672	6.2279	6.2845	6.3376	6.3876	6.4349
30	3.8891	4.4545	4.7992	5.0476	5.2418	5.4012	5.5361	5.6531	5.7563	5.8485	5.9318	6.0079	6.0777	6.1423	6.2023	6.2584	6.3105	6.3601	6.4069
31	3.8807	4.443	4.7856	5.0323	5.2252	5.3833	5.5172	5.6333	5.7357	5.8272	5.9098	5.9852	6.0545	6.1185	6.1781	6.2337	6.2859	6.335	6.3814
32	3.8728	4.4323	4.7729	5.018	5.2096	5.3667	5.4996	5.6149	5.7164	5.8072	5.8893	5.9641	6.0328	6.0964	6.1554	6.2106	6.2623	6.3111	6.3571
33	3.8654	4.4223	4.761	5.0047	5.195	5.3511	5.4831	5.5976	5.6984	5.7886	5.8701	5.9443	6.0125	6.0756	6.1342	6.189	6.2403	6.2886	6.3343
34	3.8585	4.4129	4.7498	4.9921	5.1814	5.3364	5.4677	5.5814	5.6816	5.7711	5.852	5.9258	5.9935	6.0561	6.1143	6.1687	6.2197	6.2676	6.313
35	3.852	4.4041	4.7393	4.9804	5.1685	5.3227	5.4532	5.5662	5.6657	5.7547	5.8351	5.9083	5.9756	6.0378	6.0956	6.1496	6.2002	6.2479	6.2929
36	3.8459	4.3958	4.7294	4.9693	5.1565	5.3098	5.4395	5.5518	5.6508	5.7392	5.8191	5.8919	5.9588	6.0206	6.078	6.1317	6.182	6.2293	6.274
37	3.8402	4.388	4.7201	4.9588	5.1451	5.2976	5.4266	5.5383	5.6367	5.7247	5.8041	5.8764	5.9429	6.0043	6.0614	6.1147	6.1647	6.2117	6.2562
38	3.8347	4.3806	4.7113	4.949	5.1343	5.2861	5.4144	5.5255	5.6234	5.7109	5.7898	5.8618	5.9279	5.989	6.0457	6.0987	6.1484	6.1952	6.2393
39	3.8296	4.3737	4.703	4.9396	5.1241	5.2752	5.4029	5.5135	5.6109	5.6978	5.7764	5.848	5.9137	5.9744	6.0309	6.0836	6.133	6.1795	6.2234
40	3.8247	4.3671	4.6951	4.9308	5.1145	5.2649	5.392	5.502	5.5989	5.6855	5.7636	5.8348	5.9002	5.9606	6.0168	6.0692	6.1183	6.1646	6.2083
41	3.8201	4.3608	4.6877	4.9224	5.1053	5.2551	5.3816	5.4911	5.5876	5.6738	5.7515	5.8224	5.8875	5.9476	6.0034	6.0556	6.1045	6.1505	6.1939
42	3.8156	4.3549	4.6805	4.9144	5.0966	5.2457	5.3718	5.4808	5.5769	5.6626	5.74	5.8106	5.8753	5.9351	5.9907	6.0426	6.0913	6.1371	6.1803
43	3.8115	4.3493	4.6738	4.9068	5.0884	5.2369	5.3624	5.471	5.5666	5.652	5.7291	5.7993	5.8638	5.9233	5.9787	6.0303	6.0787	6.1243	6.1673
44	3.8075	4.3439	4.6673	4.8996	5.0805	5.2285	5.3535	5.4617	5.5569	5.6419	5.7187	5.7886	5.8528	5.9121	5.9671	6.0186	6.0668	6.1121	6.155

TABLE 7 (continued) Critical Values of the Studentised *q*-Range (0.01 Level)

dfe	\multicolumn{19}{c}{Number of Means}
	2	3	4	5	6	7	8	9	10	11	12	13	14	15	16	17	18	19	20
45	3.8037	4.3388	4.6612	4.8927	5.073	5.2204	5.345	5.4527	5.5476	5.6323	5.7087	5.7784	5.8423	5.9013	5.9562	6.0074	6.0554	6.1005	6.1432
46	3.8	4.3339	4.6553	4.8861	5.0658	5.2127	5.3369	5.4442	5.5387	5.6231	5.6992	5.7686	5.8323	5.8911	5.9457	5.9967	6.0445	6.0895	6.1319
47	3.7965	4.3293	4.6497	4.8798	5.059	5.2054	5.3291	5.4361	5.5303	5.6143	5.6902	5.7593	5.8227	5.8813	5.9357	5.9865	6.0341	6.0789	6.1212
48	3.7932	4.3248	4.6444	4.8738	5.0524	5.1984	5.3217	5.4283	5.5222	5.6059	5.6815	5.7503	5.8135	5.8719	5.9261	5.9767	6.0241	6.0687	6.1109
49	3.79	4.32	4.6392	4.8681	5.0461	5.1917	5.3146	5.4209	5.5144	5.5979	5.6732	5.7418	5.8048	5.8629	5.9169	5.9673	6.0146	6.059	6.101
50	3.787	4.3159	4.6343	4.8625	5.0401	5.1852	5.3078	5.4137	5.507	5.5902	5.6652	5.7336	5.7964	5.8543	5.9081	5.9584	6.0054	6.0497	6.0916
51	3.7841	4.3119	4.6296	4.8572	5.0343	5.179	5.3012	5.4069	5.4998	5.5828	5.6576	5.7257	5.7883	5.846	5.8997	5.9498	5.9967	6.0408	6.0825
52	3.7812	4.308	4.6251	4.8522	5.0288	5.1731	5.2949	5.4003	5.493	5.5757	5.6503	5.7182	5.7805	5.8381	5.8916	5.9415	5.9883	6.0323	6.0738
53	3.7785	4.3044	4.6207	4.8473	5.0235	5.1674	5.2889	5.394	5.4864	5.5688	5.6432	5.711	5.7731	5.8305	5.8838	5.9335	5.9802	6.024	6.0654
54	3.7759	4.3008	4.6165	4.8426	5.0183	5.1619	5.2831	5.3879	5.48	5.5623	5.6361	5.704	5.7659	5.8232	5.8763	5.9259	5.9724	6.0161	6.0574
55	3.7734	4.2974	4.612	4.838	5.0134	5.1566	5.2775	5.382	5.4739	5.5559	5.6299	5.6973	5.7591	5.8161	5.8691	5.9186	5.9649	6.0085	6.0496
56	3.771	4.2942	4.6082	4.8337	5.0087	5.1516	5.2722	5.3764	5.4681	5.5499	5.6236	5.6908	5.7524	5.8093	5.8622	5.9115	5.9577	6.0011	6.0422
57	3.7687	4.291	4.6045	4.8295	5.0041	5.1467	5.267	5.371	5.4624	5.544	5.6176	5.6846	5.746	5.8028	5.8555	5.9047	5.9507	5.9941	6.035
58	3.7665	4.288	4.6009	4.8255	4.9997	5.142	5.262	5.3657	5.457	5.5383	5.6118	5.6786	5.7399	5.7965	5.849	5.8981	5.944	5.9872	6.028
59	3.7643	4.285	4.5975	4.8216	4.9954	5.1374	5.2572	5.3607	5.4517	5.5329	5.6061	5.6728	5.7339	5.7904	5.8428	5.8917	5.9376	5.9807	6.0214
60	3.7622	4.2822	4.5942	4.8178	4.9913	5.133	5.2525	5.3558	5.4466	5.5276	5.6007	5.6672	5.7282	5.7845	5.8368	5.8856	5.9313	5.9743	6.0149
61	3.7602	4.2795	4.591	4.8141	4.9874	5.1287	5.248	5.3511	5.4417	5.5225	5.5954	5.6618	5.7226	5.7788	5.831	5.8797	5.9253	5.9682	6.0086
62	3.7583	4.2768	4.5879	4.8106	4.9835	5.1246	5.2437	5.3465	5.437	5.5176	5.5903	5.6565	5.7173	5.7733	5.8254	5.8739	5.9194	5.9622	6.0026
63	3.7564	4.2743	4.5849	4.8072	4.9798	5.1207	5.2395	5.3421	5.4324	5.5129	5.5854	5.6515	5.7121	5.768	5.8199	5.8684	5.9138	5.9565	5.9968
64	3.7546	4.2718	4.582	4.8039	4.9762	5.1168	5.2354	5.3379	5.4279	5.5083	5.5807	5.6466	5.7071	5.7629	5.8147	5.863	5.9083	5.9509	5.9911
65	3.7528	4.2694	4.5789	4.8007	4.9727	5.1131	5.2315	5.3337	5.4236	5.5038	5.5761	5.6419	5.7022	5.7579	5.8096	5.8578	5.903	5.9455	5.9856
66	3.7511	4.267	4.5767	4.7976	4.9694	5.1095	5.2277	5.3297	5.4195	5.4995	5.5716	5.6373	5.6975	5.7531	5.8047	5.8528	5.8979	5.9403	5.9803

TABLE 7 (continued) Critical Values of the Studentised q-Range (0.01 Level)

dfe	2	3	4	5	6	7	8	9	10	11	12	13	14	15	16	17	18	19	20
									Number of Means										
67	3.7494	4.2648	4.5739	4.7946	4.9661	5.106	5.224	5.3258	5.4154	5.4953	5.5673	5.6328	5.6929	5.7484	5.7999	5.8479	5.8929	5.9353	5.9752
68	3.7478	4.2626	4.5713	4.7917	4.9629	5.1026	5.2204	5.3221	5.4115	5.4912	5.5631	5.6285	5.6885	5.7438	5.7952	5.8432	5.8881	5.9304	5.9702
69	3.7463	4.2605	4.5689	4.7889	4.9599	5.0993	5.2169	5.3184	5.4077	5.4873	5.559	5.6243	5.6842	5.7394	5.7907	5.8386	5.8834	5.9256	5.9654
70	3.7447	4.2584	4.5665	4.7862	4.9569	5.0961	5.2135	5.3149	5.404	5.4835	5.5551	5.6202	5.68	5.7352	5.7864	5.8341	5.8789	5.921	5.9607
71	3.7433	4.2564	4.5642	4.7835	4.954	5.093	5.2102	5.3115	5.4004	5.4797	5.5512	5.6163	5.676	5.731	5.7821	5.8298	5.8745	5.9165	5.9561
72	3.7418	4.2545	4.5619	4.7809	4.9512	5.09	5.2071	5.3081	5.3969	5.4761	5.5475	5.6125	5.672	5.727	5.778	5.8256	5.8702	5.9121	5.9517
73	3.7405	4.2526	4.5597	4.7784	4.9484	5.0871	5.204	5.3049	5.3936	5.4726	5.5439	5.6087	5.6682	5.7231	5.774	5.8215	5.866	5.9079	5.9474
74	3.7391	4.2508	4.5576	4.776	4.9458	5.0842	5.201	5.3017	5.3903	5.4692	5.5404	5.6051	5.6645	5.7193	5.7701	5.8176	5.862	5.9038	5.9432
75	3.7378	4.249	4.5555	4.7736	4.9432	5.0815	5.198	5.2986	5.3871	5.4659	5.5369	5.6016	5.6609	5.7156	5.7663	5.8137	5.8581	5.8998	5.9391
76	3.7365	4.2472	4.553	4.7713	4.9407	5.0788	5.1952	5.2957	5.384	5.4627	5.5336	5.5982	5.6573	5.712	5.7627	5.8099	5.8542	5.8959	5.9352
77	3.7353	4.2456	4.551	4.7691	4.9382	5.0762	5.1924	5.2928	5.3809	5.4595	5.5304	5.5948	5.6539	5.7085	5.7591	5.8063	5.8505	5.8921	5.9313
78	3.7341	4.2439	4.5491	4.7669	4.9359	5.0736	5.1897	5.2899	5.378	5.4565	5.5272	5.5916	5.6506	5.705	5.7556	5.8027	5.8469	5.8884	5.9276
79	3.7329	4.2423	4.5472	4.7648	4.9335	5.0711	5.1871	5.2872	5.3751	5.4535	5.5241	5.5884	5.6473	5.7017	5.7522	5.7992	5.8433	5.8848	5.9239
80	3.7317	4.2407	4.5453	4.7627	4.9313	5.0687	5.1845	5.2845	5.3723	5.4506	5.5211	5.5853	5.6442	5.6985	5.7489	5.7959	5.8399	5.8813	5.9203
81	3.7306	4.2392	4.5435	4.7602	4.9291	5.0663	5.182	5.2819	5.3696	5.4478	5.5182	5.5823	5.6411	5.6953	5.7456	5.7926	5.8365	5.8779	5.9169
82	3.7295	4.2377	4.5418	4.7583	4.9269	5.064	5.1796	5.2793	5.3669	5.445	5.5154	5.5794	5.6381	5.6922	5.7425	5.7894	5.8333	5.8745	5.9135
83	3.7284	4.2363	4.5401	4.7564	4.9248	5.0618	5.1772	5.2768	5.3643	5.4423	5.5126	5.5765	5.6351	5.6892	5.7394	5.7862	5.8301	5.8713	5.9102
84	3.7274	4.2349	4.5384	4.7545	4.9228	5.0596	5.1749	5.2744	5.3618	5.4397	5.5099	5.5737	5.6323	5.6863	5.7364	5.7832	5.8269	5.8681	5.9069
85	3.7264	4.2335	4.5368	4.7527	4.9208	5.0575	5.1726	5.272	5.3593	5.4371	5.5072	5.571	5.6295	5.6834	5.7335	5.7802	5.8239	5.865	5.9038
86	3.7254	4.2322	4.5352	4.751	4.9188	5.0554	5.1704	5.2697	5.3569	5.4346	5.5047	5.5684	5.6268	5.6806	5.7306	5.7773	5.8209	5.862	5.9007
87	3.7244	4.2308	4.5336	4.7493	4.9169	5.0533	5.1683	5.2674	5.3546	5.4322	5.5021	5.5658	5.6241	5.6779	5.7278	5.7744	5.818	5.859	5.8977
88	3.7235	4.2296	4.5321	4.7476	4.9151	5.0514	5.1662	5.2652	5.3523	5.4298	5.4997	5.5632	5.6215	5.6752	5.7251	5.7716	5.8152	5.8562	5.8948
89	3.7226	4.2283	4.5306	4.746	4.9133	5.0494	5.1641	5.2631	5.35	5.4275	5.4973	5.5608	5.6189	5.6726	5.7225	5.7689	5.8124	5.8533	5.8919

TABLE 7 (continued) Critical Values of the Studentised *q*-Range (0.01 Level)

dfe	Number of Means																		
	2	3	4	5	6	7	8	9	10	11	12	13	14	15	16	17	18	19	20
90	3.7217	4.2271	4.5292	4.7444	4.9115	5.0475	5.1621	5.261	5.3478	5.4252	5.4949	5.5583	5.6165	5.6701	5.7199	5.7663	5.8097	5.8506	5.8891
91	3.7208	4.2259	4.5277	4.7428	4.9097	5.0457	5.1601	5.2589	5.3457	5.423	5.4926	5.556	5.614	5.6676	5.7173	5.7637	5.8071	5.8479	5.8864
92	3.7199	4.2247	4.5263	4.7413	4.908	5.0438	5.1582	5.2569	5.3436	5.4208	5.4904	5.5537	5.6117	5.6652	5.7148	5.7611	5.8045	5.8453	5.8837
93	3.7191	4.2236	4.525	4.7398	4.9064	5.0421	5.1563	5.2549	5.3415	5.4187	5.4882	5.5514	5.6093	5.6628	5.7124	5.7587	5.802	5.8427	5.8811
94	3.7183	4.2224	4.5237	4.7382	4.9048	5.0403	5.1545	5.253	5.3395	5.4166	5.486	5.5492	5.6071	5.6605	5.71	5.7562	5.7995	5.8402	5.8785
95	3.7174	4.2213	4.5224	4.7371	4.9032	5.0386	5.1527	5.2511	5.3375	5.4145	5.4839	5.547	5.6048	5.6582	5.7077	5.7539	5.7971	5.8377	5.876
96	3.7167	4.2203	4.5211	4.7355	4.9016	5.037	5.1509	5.2493	5.3356	5.4125	5.4819	5.5449	5.6027	5.656	5.7054	5.7515	5.7947	5.8353	5.8736
97	3.7159	4.2192	4.5198	4.7342	4.9001	5.0353	5.1492	5.2474	5.3337	5.4106	5.4798	5.5428	5.6005	5.6538	5.7032	5.7493	5.7924	5.8329	5.8712
98	3.7151	4.2182	4.5186	4.7328	4.8986	5.0337	5.1475	5.2457	5.3319	5.4087	5.4779	5.5408	5.5984	5.6516	5.701	5.747	5.7901	5.8306	5.8688
99	3.7144	4.2172	4.5174	4.7315	4.8971	5.0322	5.1459	5.2439	5.3301	5.4068	5.4759	5.5388	5.5964	5.6496	5.6989	5.7448	5.7879	5.8284	5.8665
100	3.7137	4.2162	4.5163	4.7303	4.8957	5.0306	5.1443	5.2422	5.3283	5.405	5.474	5.5368	5.5944	5.6475	5.6968	5.7427	5.7857	5.8261	5.8643
101	3.7129	4.2152	4.5151	4.729	4.8943	5.0291	5.1427	5.2406	5.3266	5.4032	5.4722	5.5349	5.5924	5.6455	5.6947	5.7406	5.7836	5.824	5.8621
102	3.7122	4.2143	4.514	4.7278	4.8929	5.0277	5.1411	5.239	5.3249	5.4014	5.4704	5.5331	5.5905	5.6435	5.6927	5.7386	5.7815	5.8218	5.8599
103	3.7116	4.2134	4.5129	4.7266	4.8916	5.0262	5.1396	5.2374	5.3232	5.3997	5.4686	5.5312	5.5886	5.6416	5.6907	5.7365	5.7794	5.8198	5.8578
104	3.7109	4.2124	4.5118	4.7254	4.8903	5.0248	5.1381	5.2358	5.3216	5.398	5.4668	5.5294	5.5868	5.6397	5.6888	5.7346	5.7774	5.8177	5.8557
105	3.7102	4.2115	4.5108	4.7242	4.889	5.0234	5.1366	5.2343	5.32	5.3963	5.4651	5.5277	5.585	5.6378	5.6869	5.7326	5.7754	5.8157	5.8537
106	3.7096	4.2107	4.5097	4.7231	4.8877	5.0221	5.1352	5.2327	5.3184	5.3947	5.4634	5.5259	5.5832	5.636	5.685	5.7307	5.7735	5.8137	5.8517
107	3.709	4.2098	4.5087	4.722	4.8865	5.0207	5.1338	5.2313	5.3169	5.3931	5.4618	5.5242	5.5815	5.6342	5.6832	5.7289	5.7716	5.8118	5.8497
108	3.7083	4.209	4.5077	4.7209	4.8853	5.0194	5.1324	5.2298	5.3154	5.3915	5.4602	5.5226	5.5797	5.6325	5.6814	5.727	5.7698	5.8099	5.8478
109	3.7077	4.2081	4.5067	4.7194	4.8841	5.0181	5.131	5.2284	5.3139	5.39	5.4586	5.5209	5.5781	5.6308	5.6797	5.7252	5.7679	5.808	5.8459
110	3.7071	4.2073	4.5058	4.7183	4.8824	5.0169	5.1297	5.227	5.3124	5.3885	5.457	5.5193	5.5764	5.6291	5.6779	5.7235	5.7661	5.8062	5.844
111	3.7065	4.2065	4.5048	4.7172	4.8813	5.0157	5.1284	5.2256	5.311	5.387	5.4555	5.5178	5.5748	5.6274	5.6762	5.7218	5.7644	5.8044	5.8422

TABLE 7 (continued) Critical Values of the Studentised *q*-Range (0.01 Level)

dfe	2	3	4	5	6	7	8	9	Number of Means 10	11	12	13	14	15	16	17	18	19	20
112	3.706	4.2057	4.5039	4.7162	4.8802	5.0144	5.1271	5.2243	5.3096	5.3856	5.454	5.5162	5.5732	5.6258	5.6746	5.7201	5.7626	5.8027	5.8404
113	3.7054	4.205	4.503	4.7152	4.8791	5.0132	5.1259	5.223	5.3082	5.3841	5.4525	5.5147	5.5717	5.6242	5.673	5.7184	5.7609	5.8009	5.8387
114	3.7048	4.2042	4.5021	4.7142	4.878	5.0121	5.1246	5.2217	5.3069	5.3827	5.4511	5.5132	5.5701	5.6226	5.6714	5.7168	5.7593	5.7992	5.8369
115	3.7043	4.2035	4.5012	4.7132	4.877	5.0109	5.1234	5.2204	5.3055	5.3814	5.4496	5.5117	5.5686	5.6211	5.6698	5.7152	5.7576	5.7976	5.8352
116	3.7038	4.2028	4.5003	4.7122	4.876	5.0098	5.1222	5.2191	5.3042	5.38	5.4482	5.5103	5.5671	5.6196	5.6682	5.7136	5.756	5.7959	5.8336
117	3.7032	4.202	4.4995	4.7113	4.875	5.0087	5.121	5.2179	5.3029	5.3787	5.4469	5.5089	5.5657	5.6181	5.6667	5.712	5.7545	5.7943	5.8319
118	3.7027	4.2013	4.4987	4.7103	4.874	5.0076	5.1199	5.2167	5.3017	5.3774	5.4455	5.5075	5.5643	5.6166	5.6652	5.7105	5.7529	5.7928	5.8303
119	3.7022	4.2006	4.4978	4.7094	4.873	5.0065	5.1187	5.2155	5.3004	5.3761	5.4442	5.5061	5.5629	5.6152	5.6637	5.709	5.7514	5.7912	5.8288
120	3.7017	4.2	4.497	4.7085	4.872	5.0055	5.1176	5.2143	5.2992	5.3748	5.4429	5.5048	5.5615	5.6138	5.6623	5.7075	5.7499	5.7897	5.8272
240	3.672	4.16	4.45	4.655	4.814	4.943	5.052	5.145	5.227	5.3	5.366	5.426	5.48	5.53	5.577	5.621	5.661	5.699	5.735
∞	3.643	4.12	4.403	4.603	4.757	4.882	4.987	5.078	5.157	5.227	5.29	5.348	5.4	5.448	5.493	5.535	5.574	5.611	5.645

TABLE 7 (continued) Critical Values of the Studentised *q*-Range (0.05 Level)

dfe	Number of Means																		
	2	3	4	5	6	7	8	9	10	11	12	13	14	15	16	17	18	19	20
2	6.0849	8.3308	9.798	10.881	11.734	12.4345	13.0266	13.5381	13.9875	14.3874	14.7473	15.0757	15.3748	15.6503	15.9054	16.1427	16.3646	16.5728	16.7688
3	4.5007	5.9096	6.8245	7.5016	8.037	8.478	8.8521	9.1766	9.462	9.7166	9.946	10.1547	10.3459	10.5222	10.6856	10.8378	10.9803	11.114	11.24
4	3.9265	5.0403	5.7571	6.287	6.7065	7.0528	7.3465	7.6015	7.8264	8.0271	8.2083	8.3732	8.5244	8.664	8.7934	8.9141	9.0271	9.1332	9.2333
5	3.6354	4.6017	5.2185	5.6731	6.0329	6.3299	6.5823	6.8014	6.9947	7.1674	7.3237	7.4653	7.5956	7.7163	7.828	7.9322	8.0298	8.1215	8.208
6	3.4605	4.339	4.8956	5.3049	5.6285	5.8953	6.1222	6.3192	6.4931	6.6485	6.789	6.9169	7.0344	7.1428	7.2436	7.3375	7.4256	7.5086	7.5866
7	3.3439	4.1648	4.6812	5.0601	5.3591	5.6058	5.8154	5.9975	6.1581	6.3018	6.4314	6.5497	6.6583	6.7586	6.8518	6.9387	7.0202	7.0968	7.1691
8	3.2612	4.041	4.5288	4.8858	5.1672	5.3991	5.5962	5.7673	5.9183	6.0534	6.1754	6.2867	6.3000	6.4032	6.5708	6.6527	6.7293	6.8015	6.8695
9	3.1991	3.9485	4.4149	4.7554	5.0235	5.2444	5.4319	5.5947	5.7384	5.8669	5.983	6.0888	6.186	6.2758	6.3592	6.4371	6.5101	6.5787	6.6435
10	3.1511	3.8768	4.3266	4.6543	4.912	5.1242	5.3042	5.4605	5.5984	5.7217	5.8331	5.9346	6.0279	6.1141	6.1941	6.2689	6.3389	6.4048	6.467
11	3.1127	3.8195	4.2561	4.5736	4.8229	5.0281	5.2021	5.3531	5.4863	5.6054	5.7129	5.8111	5.9012	5.9844	6.0617	6.1339	6.2015	6.2652	6.3252
12	3.0813	3.7728	4.1985	4.5076	4.7477	4.9469	5.1159	5.2625	5.3946	5.5102	5.6146	5.7098	5.7973	5.8781	5.9532	6.0231	6.0888	6.1506	6.2089
13	3.0553	3.7341	4.1509	4.4529	4.6897	4.8841	5.049	5.192	5.3181	5.4308	5.5326	5.6253	5.7105	5.7892	5.8623	5.9305	5.9945	6.0547	6.1116
14	3.0332	3.7014	4.1105	4.4066	4.6385	4.829	4.9903	5.13	5.2533	5.3635	5.463	5.5537	5.637	5.7139	5.7854	5.8521	5.9146	5.9735	6.029
15	3.0143	3.6734	4.076	4.367	4.5947	4.7816	4.9399	5.077	5.1979	5.3059	5.4033	5.4922	5.5738	5.6492	5.7193	5.7847	5.8459	5.9036	5.958
16	2.998	3.6491	4.0461	4.3327	4.5568	4.7406	4.8962	5.031	5.1498	5.2559	5.3517	5.439	5.5191	5.5931	5.6619	5.7261	5.7862	5.8429	5.8963
17	2.9837	3.628	4.02	4.3027	4.5237	4.7048	4.858	4.9907	5.1077	5.2121	5.3064	5.3923	5.4712	5.544	5.6117	5.6748	5.7339	5.7896	5.8421
18	2.9712	3.6093	3.997	4.2763	4.4944	4.6731	4.8243	4.9552	5.0705	5.1735	5.2664	5.3511	5.4288	5.5006	5.5672	5.6295	5.6878	5.7426	5.7944
19	2.96	3.5927	3.9766	4.2528	4.4685	4.645	4.7944	4.9236	5.0375	5.1391	5.2308	5.3144	5.3911	5.4619	5.5277	5.5891	5.6466	5.7007	5.7518
20	2.95	3.5779	3.9583	4.2319	4.4452	4.6199	4.7676	4.8954	5.0079	5.1083	5.199	5.2815	5.3573	5.4273	5.4923	5.5529	5.6097	5.6632	5.7136

TABLE 7 (continued) Critical Values of the Studentised *q*-Range (0.05 Level)

dfe	Number of Means																		
	2	3	4	5	6	7	8	9	10	11	12	13	14	15	16	17	18	19	20
21	2.941	3.5646	3.9419	4.213	4.4244	4.5973	4.7435	4.8699	4.9813	5.0806	5.1703	5.252	5.3269	5.3961	5.4603	5.5203	5.5765	5.6293	5.6792
22	2.9329	3.5526	3.927	4.1959	4.4055	4.5769	4.7217	4.8469	4.9572	5.0556	5.1443	5.2252	5.2993	5.3678	5.4314	5.4908	5.5464	5.5987	5.648
23	2.9255	3.5417	3.9136	4.1805	4.3883	4.5583	4.7019	4.826	4.9353	5.0328	5.1207	5.2008	5.2743	5.3421	5.4051	5.4639	5.5189	5.5707	5.6196
24	2.9188	3.5317	3.9013	4.1663	4.3727	4.5413	4.6838	4.8069	4.9153	5.0119	5.0991	5.1785	5.2514	5.3186	5.381	5.4393	5.4939	5.5452	5.5936
25	2.9126	3.5226	3.89	4.1534	4.3583	4.5258	4.6672	4.7894	4.8969	4.9928	5.0793	5.1581	5.2303	5.297	5.359	5.4167	5.4709	5.5218	5.5698
26	2.907	3.5142	3.8796	4.1415	4.3451	4.5115	4.6519	4.7733	4.88	4.9753	5.0611	5.1393	5.211	5.2772	5.3387	5.396	5.4497	5.5002	5.5478
27	2.9017	3.5064	3.8701	4.1305	4.3329	4.4983	4.6378	4.7584	4.8645	4.959	5.0443	5.122	5.1931	5.2589	5.3199	5.3768	5.4301	5.4802	5.5275
28	2.8969	3.4992	3.8612	4.1203	4.3217	4.4861	4.6248	4.7446	4.85	4.944	5.0287	5.1059	5.1766	5.2419	5.3025	5.359	5.412	5.4618	5.5087
29	2.8924	3.4926	3.853	4.1109	4.3112	4.4747	4.6127	4.7319	4.8366	4.93	5.0143	5.0909	5.1612	5.2261	5.2863	5.3425	5.3951	5.4446	5.4913
30	2.8882	3.4865	3.8454	4.1021	4.3015	4.4642	4.6014	4.7199	4.8241	4.917	5.0008	5.077	5.1469	5.2114	5.2713	5.3271	5.3794	5.4286	5.475
31	2.8843	3.4806	3.8383	4.0939	4.2924	4.4543	4.5909	4.7088	4.8125	4.9049	4.9882	5.064	5.1335	5.1977	5.2572	5.3127	5.3647	5.4136	5.4597
32	2.8807	3.4752	3.8316	4.0862	4.2839	4.4451	4.5811	4.6984	4.8016	4.8936	4.9765	5.0519	5.121	5.1848	5.244	5.2993	5.351	5.3996	5.4455
33	2.8773	3.4702	3.8254	4.079	4.2759	4.4365	4.5718	4.6887	4.7914	4.8829	4.9654	5.0405	5.1093	5.1728	5.2317	5.2866	5.3381	5.3865	5.4321
34	2.874	3.4654	3.8195	4.0723	4.2684	4.4284	4.5632	4.6795	4.7818	4.8729	4.955	5.0298	5.0982	5.1614	5.2201	5.2748	5.326	5.3741	5.4196
35	2.871	3.461	3.814	4.066	4.2614	4.4207	4.555	4.6709	4.7728	4.8635	4.9453	5.0197	5.0879	5.1508	5.2091	5.2636	5.3146	5.3625	5.4077
36	2.8682	3.4568	3.8088	4.06	4.2548	4.4136	4.5473	4.6628	4.7642	4.8546	4.9361	5.0102	5.0781	5.1407	5.1988	5.253	5.3038	5.3515	5.3965
37	2.8655	3.4528	3.8039	4.0543	4.2485	4.4068	4.5401	4.6551	4.7562	4.8462	4.9274	5.0012	5.0688	5.1312	5.1891	5.2431	5.2936	5.3412	5.386
38	2.863	3.449	3.7993	4.049	4.2426	4.4003	4.5332	4.6479	4.7486	4.8383	4.9191	4.9927	5.06	5.1222	5.1799	5.2337	5.284	5.3313	5.376
39	2.8605	3.4455	3.7949	4.0439	4.237	4.3942	4.5267	4.641	4.7414	4.8308	4.9113	4.9846	5.0517	5.1137	5.1711	5.2247	5.2749	5.322	5.3665
40	2.8583	3.4421	3.7907	4.0391	4.2317	4.3885	4.5205	4.6345	4.7345	4.8237	4.9039	4.977	5.0439	5.1056	5.1629	5.2162	5.2662	5.3132	5.3575
41	2.8561	3.4389	3.7867	4.0346	4.2266	4.383	4.5147	4.6283	4.728	4.8169	4.8969	4.9697	5.0364	5.0979	5.155	5.2082	5.258	5.3048	5.349
42	2.854	3.4358	3.783	4.0302	4.2218	4.3778	4.5091	4.6224	4.7218	4.8104	4.8902	4.9628	5.0293	5.0906	5.1475	5.2005	5.2502	5.2968	5.3408
43	2.8521	3.4329	3.7794	4.0261	4.2172	4.3728	4.5038	4.6168	4.716	4.8043	4.8839	4.9562	5.0225	5.0836	5.1403	5.1932	5.2427	5.2892	5.3331
44	2.8502	3.4302	3.776	4.0222	4.2128	4.3681	4.4987	4.6114	4.7103	4.7984	4.8778	4.9499	5.016	5.077	5.1335	5.1862	5.2356	5.282	5.3257

TABLE 7 (continued) Critical Values of the Studentised *q*-Range (0.05 Level)

dfe	Number of Means																		
	2	3	4	5	6	7	8	9	10	11	12	13	14	15	16	17	18	19	20
45	2.8484	3.4275	3.7727	4.0184	4.2087	4.3635	4.4939	4.6063	4.705	4.7928	4.872	4.9439	5.0098	5.0706	5.127	5.1796	5.2288	5.275	5.3186
46	2.8467	3.425	3.7696	4.0148	4.2047	4.3592	4.4893	4.6014	4.6998	4.7875	4.8664	4.9382	5.0039	5.0646	5.1208	5.1732	5.2223	5.2684	5.3119
47	2.8451	3.4226	3.7666	4.0114	4.2009	4.3551	4.4849	4.5967	4.6949	4.7824	4.8611	4.9327	4.9983	5.0587	5.1148	5.1671	5.2161	5.2621	5.3054
48	2.8435	3.4203	3.7637	4.0081	4.1972	4.3511	4.4806	4.5923	4.6903	4.7775	4.856	4.9275	4.9929	5.0532	5.1091	5.1613	5.2101	5.256	5.2992
49	2.842	3.418	3.761	4.005	4.1938	4.3474	4.4766	4.588	4.6858	4.7728	4.8512	4.9224	4.9877	5.0479	5.1037	5.1557	5.2044	5.2502	5.2933
50	2.8406	3.4159	3.7584	4.002	4.1904	4.3437	4.4727	4.5839	4.6814	4.7683	4.8465	4.9176	4.9827	5.0427	5.0984	5.1503	5.1989	5.2446	5.2876
51	2.8392	3.4139	3.7559	3.9991	4.1872	4.3402	4.469	4.5799	4.6773	4.764	4.842	4.913	4.9779	5.0378	5.0934	5.1452	5.1937	5.2392	5.2822
52	2.8379	3.4119	3.7535	3.9963	4.1841	4.3369	4.4654	4.5761	4.6733	4.7598	4.8377	4.9085	4.9733	5.0331	5.0886	5.1402	5.1886	5.234	5.2769
53	2.8366	3.41	3.751	3.9936	4.1811	4.3337	4.4619	4.5725	4.6695	4.752	4.8336	4.9042	4.9689	5.0286	5.0839	5.1355	5.1837	5.2291	5.267
54	2.8354	3.4082	3.7489	3.991	4.1783	4.3305	4.4586	4.569	4.6658	4.752	4.8296	4.9001	4.9647	5.0242	5.0794	5.1309	5.1791	5.2243	5.267
55	2.8342	3.4065	3.7468	3.9885	4.1755	4.3276	4.4554	4.5656	4.6623	4.7483	4.8257	4.8961	4.9606	5.02	5.0751	5.1265	5.1745	5.2197	5.2623
56	2.8331	3.4048	3.7448	3.9862	4.1729	4.3247	4.4524	4.5623	4.6589	4.7447	4.822	4.8923	4.9566	5.016	5.071	5.1222	5.1702	5.2153	5.2578
57	2.832	3.4032	3.7427	3.9839	4.1703	4.3219	4.4494	4.5592	4.6556	4.7413	4.8185	4.8886	4.9528	5.0121	5.067	5.1181	5.166	5.211	5.2534
58	2.8309	3.4016	3.7408	3.9816	4.1678	4.3192	4.4465	4.5562	4.6524	4.738	4.815	4.885	4.9492	5.0083	5.0631	5.1142	5.162	5.2069	5.2492
59	2.8299	3.4001	3.7389	3.9795	4.1655	4.3166	4.4438	4.5533	4.6493	4.7348	4.8117	4.8816	4.9456	5.0046	5.0594	5.1103	5.1581	5.2029	5.2452
60	2.8289	3.3987	3.7371	3.9774	4.1632	4.3142	4.4411	4.5504	4.6463	4.7317	4.8085	4.8783	4.9422	5.0011	5.0557	5.1066	5.1543	5.199	5.2412
61	2.828	3.3973	3.7354	3.9754	4.1609	4.3117	4.4385	4.5477	4.6435	4.7287	4.8054	4.8751	4.9389	4.9977	5.0523	5.1031	5.1506	5.1953	5.2374
62	2.8271	3.3959	3.7337	3.9735	4.1588	4.3094	4.436	4.5451	4.6407	4.7258	4.8024	4.872	4.9357	4.9944	5.0489	5.0996	5.1471	5.1917	5.2338
63	2.8262	3.3946	3.732	3.9716	4.1567	4.3071	4.4336	4.5425	4.638	4.723	4.7995	4.869	4.9326	4.9912	5.0456	5.0963	5.1437	5.1882	5.2302
64	2.8253	3.3933	3.7305	3.9698	4.1547	4.305	4.4313	4.54	4.6354	4.7203	4.7967	4.8661	4.9296	4.9881	5.0424	5.093	5.1404	5.1848	5.2268
65	2.8245	3.3921	3.7289	3.968	4.1527	4.3028	4.429	4.5376	4.6329	4.7177	4.7939	4.8632	4.9267	4.9852	5.0394	5.0899	5.1372	5.1816	5.2234
66	2.8237	3.3909	3.7275	3.9663	4.1509	4.3008	4.4268	4.5353	4.6305	4.7151	4.7913	4.8605	4.9239	4.9823	5.0364	5.0868	5.1341	5.1784	5.2202

TABLE 7 (continued) Critical Values of the Studentised *q*-Range (0.05 Level)

dfe	Number of Means																		
	2	3	4	5	6	7	8	9	10	11	12	13	14	15	16	17	18	19	20
67	2.8229	3.3897	3.726	3.9647	4.149	4.2988	4.4247	4.533	4.6281	4.7126	4.7887	4.8578	4.9211	4.9794	5.0335	5.0839	5.131	5.1753	5.2171
68	2.8221	3.3886	3.7246	3.9631	4.1472	4.2969	4.4226	4.5309	4.6258	4.7102	4.7862	4.8553	4.9185	4.9767	5.0307	5.081	5.1281	5.1723	5.214
69	2.8214	3.3875	3.7233	3.9615	4.1455	4.295	4.4206	4.5287	4.6236	4.7079	4.7838	4.8528	4.9159	4.9741	5.028	5.0783	5.1253	5.1694	5.2111
70	2.8207	3.3864	3.722	3.96	4.1438	4.2932	4.4186	4.5267	4.6214	4.7057	4.7815	4.8503	4.9134	4.9715	5.0254	5.0756	5.1225	5.1666	5.2082
71	2.82	3.3854	3.7207	3.9585	4.1422	4.2914	4.4168	4.5247	4.6193	4.7035	4.7792	4.848	4.911	4.969	5.0228	5.0729	5.1198	5.1639	5.2054
72	2.8193	3.3844	3.7195	3.9571	4.1406	4.2897	4.4149	4.5227	4.6173	4.7013	4.777	4.8457	4.9086	4.9666	5.0203	5.0704	5.1172	5.1612	5.2027
73	2.8186	3.3834	3.7183	3.9557	4.1391	4.288	4.4131	4.5208	4.6153	4.6993	4.7748	4.8435	4.9063	4.9642	5.0179	5.0679	5.1147	5.1586	5.2001
74	2.818	3.3825	3.7171	3.9544	4.1376	4.2864	4.4114	4.519	4.6133	4.6972	4.7727	4.8413	4.9041	4.9619	5.0155	5.0655	5.1122	5.1561	5.1975
75	2.8174	3.3816	3.716	3.9531	4.1361	4.2848	4.4097	4.5172	4.6115	4.6953	4.7707	4.8392	4.9019	4.9597	5.0132	5.0631	5.1098	5.1537	5.195
76	2.8167	3.3807	3.7149	3.9518	4.1347	4.2833	4.4081	4.5155	4.6096	4.6934	4.7687	4.8371	4.8998	4.9575	5.011	5.0609	5.1075	5.1513	5.1926
77	2.8161	3.3798	3.7138	3.9506	4.1333	4.2818	4.4064	4.5138	4.6078	4.6915	4.7668	4.8351	4.8977	4.9554	5.0088	5.0586	5.1052	5.149	5.1902
78	2.8155	3.3789	3.7127	3.9494	4.132	4.2803	4.4049	4.5121	4.6061	4.6897	4.7649	4.8332	4.8957	4.9533	5.0067	5.0565	5.103	5.1467	5.1879
79	2.8149	3.3781	3.7117	3.9482	4.1307	4.2789	4.4034	4.5105	4.6044	4.6879	4.7631	4.8313	4.8938	4.9513	5.0047	5.0544	5.1008	5.1445	5.1857
80	2.8144	3.3773	3.7107	3.947	4.1294	4.2775	4.4019	4.5089	4.6028	4.6862	4.7613	4.8295	4.89	4.9494	5.0027	5.0523	5.0987	5.1424	5.1835
81	2.8138	3.3765	3.7097	3.9459	4.1282	4.2761	4.4004	4.5074	4.6012	4.6845	4.7595	4.8277	4.89	4.9474	5.0007	5.0503	5.0967	5.1403	5.1813
82	2.8133	3.3758	3.7088	3.9448	4.127	4.2748	4.399	4.5059	4.5996	4.6829	4.7578	4.8259	4.8882	4.9456	4.9988	5.0483	5.0947	5.1382	5.1793
83	2.8128	3.375	3.7079	3.9437	4.1258	4.2735	4.3977	4.5045	4.5981	4.6813	4.7562	4.8242	4.8864	4.9438	4.9969	5.0464	5.0927	5.1362	5.1772
84	2.8123	3.3743	3.707	3.9427	4.1246	4.2723	4.3963	4.503	4.5966	4.6798	4.7546	4.8225	4.8847	4.942	4.9951	5.0446	5.0908	5.1343	5.1753
85	2.8118	3.3736	3.7061	3.9417	4.1235	4.2711	4.395	4.5016	4.5951	4.6782	4.753	4.8209	4.883	4.9403	4.9933	5.0427	5.089	5.1324	5.1733
86	2.8114	3.3729	3.7052	3.9407	4.1224	4.2699	4.3937	4.5003	4.5937	4.6767	4.7515	4.8193	4.8814	4.9386	4.9916	5.041	5.0872	5.1305	5.1714
87	2.8109	3.3722	3.7044	3.9397	4.1213	4.2687	4.3925	4.499	4.5923	4.6753	4.7499	4.8177	4.8798	4.9369	4.9899	5.0392	5.0854	5.1287	5.1696
88	2.8105	3.3715	3.7036	3.9388	4.1203	4.2676	4.3913	4.4977	4.591	4.6739	4.7485	4.8162	4.8782	4.9353	4.9882	5.0375	5.0836	5.127	5.1678

TABLE 7 (continued) Critical Values of the Studentised q-Range (0.05 Level)

| dfe | \multicolumn{19}{c}{Number of Means} |
---	2	3	4	5	6	7	8	9	10	11	12	13	14	15	16	17	18	19	20
89	2.81	3.3709	3.7028	3.9378	4.1192	4.2664	4.3901	4.4964	4.5896	4.6725	4.747	4.8147	4.8767	4.9337	4.9866	5.0359	5.0819	5.1252	5.166
90	2.8096	3.3702	3.702	3.9369	4.1182	4.2654	4.3889	4.4952	4.5883	4.6711	4.7456	4.8133	4.8752	4.9322	4.985	5.0342	5.0803	5.1235	5.1643
91	2.8092	3.3696	3.7012	3.9361	4.1173	4.2643	4.3878	4.494	4.5871	4.6698	4.7443	4.8118	4.8737	4.9307	4.9835	5.0327	5.0787	5.1219	5.1626
92	2.8088	3.369	3.7005	3.9352	4.1163	4.2633	4.3866	4.4928	4.5858	4.6685	4.7429	4.8104	4.8722	4.9292	4.982	5.0311	5.0771	5.1203	5.161
93	2.8083	3.3684	3.6997	3.9344	4.1154	4.2622	4.3855	4.4916	4.5846	4.6673	4.7416	4.8091	4.8708	4.9277	4.9805	5.0296	5.0755	5.1187	5.1593
94	2.808	3.3678	3.699	3.9336	4.1144	4.2612	4.3845	4.4905	4.5834	4.666	4.7403	4.8077	4.8695	4.9263	4.979	5.0281	5.074	5.1171	5.1578
95	2.8076	3.3673	3.6983	3.9327	4.1135	4.2603	4.3834	4.4894	4.5823	4.6648	4.739	4.8064	4.8681	4.925	4.9776	5.0267	5.0725	5.1156	5.1562
96	2.8072	3.3667	3.6976	3.9319	4.1127	4.2593	4.3824	4.4883	4.5811	4.6636	4.7378	4.8052	4.8668	4.9236	4.9762	5.0252	5.0711	5.1141	5.1547
97	2.8068	3.3662	3.6969	3.9312	4.1118	4.2584	4.3814	4.4873	4.58	4.6625	4.7366	4.8039	4.8655	4.9223	4.9749	5.0238	5.0697	5.1127	5.1532
98	2.8065	3.3656	3.6963	3.9304	4.111	4.2574	4.3804	4.4862	4.5789	4.6613	4.7354	4.8027	4.8643	4.921	4.9735	5.0225	5.0683	5.1113	5.1518
99	2.8061	3.3651	3.6956	3.9297	4.1101	4.2566	4.3795	4.4852	4.5778	4.6602	4.7343	4.8015	4.863	4.9197	4.9722	5.0211	5.0669	5.1099	5.1503
100	2.8058	3.3646	3.695	3.9289	4.1093	4.2557	4.3785	4.4842	4.5768	4.6591	4.7331	4.8003	4.8618	4.9185	4.9709	5.0198	5.0656	5.1085	5.149
101	2.8054	3.3641	3.6944	3.9282	4.1085	4.2548	4.3776	4.4832	4.5758	4.658	4.732	4.7992	4.8606	4.9172	4.9697	5.0185	5.0642	5.1072	5.1476
102	2.8051	3.3636	3.6938	3.9275	4.1077	4.254	4.3767	4.4823	4.5748	4.657	4.7309	4.798	4.8595	4.916	4.9685	5.0173	5.063	5.1058	5.1462
103	2.8048	3.3631	3.6932	3.9268	4.107	4.2531	4.3758	4.4813	4.5738	4.656	4.7299	4.7969	4.8583	4.9149	4.9673	5.0161	5.0617	5.1045	5.1449
104	2.8044	3.3627	3.6926	3.9262	4.1062	4.2523	4.3749	4.4804	4.5728	4.6549	4.7288	4.7958	4.8572	4.9137	4.9661	5.0148	5.0605	5.1033	5.1436
105	2.8041	3.3622	3.692	3.9255	4.1055	4.2515	4.3741	4.4795	4.5719	4.654	4.7278	4.7948	4.8561	4.9126	4.9649	5.0137	5.0592	5.102	5.1424
106	2.8038	3.3617	3.6915	3.9249	4.1048	4.2507	4.3733	4.4786	4.5709	4.653	4.7268	4.7937	4.855	4.9115	4.9638	5.0125	5.0581	5.1008	5.1411
107	2.8035	3.3613	3.6909	3.9242	4.1041	4.25	4.3724	4.4778	4.57	4.652	4.7258	4.7927	4.854	4.9104	4.9627	5.0113	5.0569	5.0996	5.1399
108	2.8032	3.3609	3.6904	3.9236	4.1034	4.2492	4.3716	4.4769	4.5691	4.6511	4.7248	4.7917	4.8529	4.9093	4.9616	5.0102	5.0557	5.0985	5.1387
109	2.8029	3.3604	3.6898	3.923	4.1027	4.2485	4.3708	4.4761	4.5682	4.6502	4.7238	4.7907	4.8519	4.9083	4.9605	5.0091	5.0546	5.0973	5.1376
110	2.8026	3.36	3.6893	3.9224	4.102	4.2478	4.3701	4.4752	4.5674	4.6493	4.7229	4.7898	4.8509	4.9072	4.9594	5.008	5.0535	5.0962	5.1364

TABLE 7 (continued) Critical Values of the Studentised q-Range (0.05 Level)

dfe	Number of Means																		
	2	3	4	5	6	7	8	9	10	11	12	13	14	15	16	17	18	19	20
111	2.8024	3.3596	3.6888	3.9218	4.1014	4.2471	4.3693	4.4744	4.5665	4.6484	4.722	4.7888	4.8499	4.9062	4.9584	5.007	5.0524	5.0951	5.1353
112	2.8021	3.3592	3.6883	3.9212	4.1007	4.2464	4.3686	4.4736	4.5657	4.6475	4.7211	4.7879	4.849	4.9052	4.9574	5.0059	5.0514	5.094	5.1342
113	2.8018	3.3588	3.6878	3.9206	4.1001	4.2457	4.3678	4.4729	4.5649	4.6467	4.7202	4.7869	4.848	4.9043	4.9564	5.0049	5.0503	5.0929	5.1331
114	2.8015	3.3584	3.6873	3.9201	4.0995	4.245	4.3671	4.4721	4.5641	4.6458	4.7193	4.786	4.8471	4.9033	4.9554	5.0039	5.0493	5.0919	5.132
115	2.8013	3.358	3.6869	3.9195	4.0989	4.2443	4.3664	4.4713	4.5633	4.645	4.7185	4.7852	4.8462	4.9024	4.9544	5.0029	5.0483	5.0909	5.131
116	2.801	3.3576	3.6864	3.919	4.0983	4.2437	4.3657	4.4706	4.5625	4.6442	4.7176	4.7843	4.8453	4.9015	4.9535	5.002	5.0473	5.0898	5.1299
117	2.8008	3.3573	3.6859	3.9185	4.0977	4.243	4.365	4.4699	4.5618	4.6434	4.7168	4.7834	4.8444	4.9005	4.9526	5.001	5.0463	5.0888	5.1289
118	2.8005	3.3569	3.6855	3.918	4.0971	4.2424	4.3643	4.4692	4.561	4.6426	4.716	4.7826	4.8435	4.8997	4.9516	5.0001	5.0453	5.0879	5.1279
119	2.8003	3.3565	3.685	3.9174	4.0965	4.2418	4.3637	4.4685	4.5603	4.6419	4.7152	4.7818	4.8427	4.8988	4.9507	4.9991	5.0444	5.0869	5.1269
120	2.8	3.3562	3.6846	3.9169	4.096	4.2412	4.363	4.4678	4.5596	4.6411	4.7144	4.781	4.8418	4.8979	4.9499	4.9982	5.0435	5.086	5.126
240	2.786	3.335	3.659	3.887	4.063	4.205	4.324	4.427	4.517	4.596	4.668	4.733	4.792	4.847	4.897	4.944	4.988	5.03	5.069
∞	2.772	3.314	3.633	3.858	4.03	4.17	4.286	4.387	4.474	4.552	4.622	4.685	4.743	4.796	4.845	4.891	4.934	4.974	5.012

APPENDIX 2: SUMMARY FLOWCHART OF DESCRIPTIVE STATISTICS

FOR CATEGORICAL (QUALITATIVE) VARIABLES ONLY

Single Categorical Variable — (e.g. Economic Sector)

Purpose	To **profile** the response categories
Summary Table	Categorical Frequency Table (One-Way Pivot Table)
Visual Display	Bar Chart or a Pie Chart
Descriptive Measure	Identify a Modal category
Application	Pareto analysis

Two Categorical Variables — (e.g. Job Status and Qualification)

Purpose	To **explore the relationship** between two sets of categorical responses
Summary Table	Cross-Tabulation Table (Two-way Pivot Table)
Visual Display	Multiple Bar Chart or a Component (Stacked) Bar Chart
Descriptive Measure	Identify a Modal category (based on joint frequencies)

Test for independence of association: Is $P(A|B) = P(A)$? (Is Conditional Probability = Marginal Probability?)
e.g. Gender vs Product Usage (Heavy, Moderate, Light)

FOR NUMERICAL (QUANTITATIVE) VARIABLES ONLY

Single Numeric Variable — (e.g. Weight of Product)

Purpose	To **show the distribution (pattern)** of data values (profiling)
Summary Table	Numerical Frequency Distribution
Visual Display	Histogram
Cumulative Table	Cumulative Frequency Distribution
Visual Display	Ogive (Cumulative Frequency Graph)
Numeric Measures	Central and Non-Central Location

        Mean (Arithmetic Average); Median (50th Percentile); Mode

        Quartiles (Lower Quartile; Upper Quartile)

Spread / Dispersion

        Range; Variance; Standard Deviation

        Interquartile Range

        Coefficient of Variation

	Shape	Uni-Modal Shapes	
		Coefficient of Skewness	Sk_p
		Symmetrical	$Sk_p = 0$
		Positively Skewed	$Sk_p > 0$
		Negatively Skewed	$Sk_p < 0$
Visual Display of Numeric Measures		Box plot	
Additional Issues	Outliers	One / more values below $Q_1 - 1.5$ (IQR)	
		One / more values above $Q_3 + 1.5$ (IQR)	
		|z-stat| > 3 where $z = \frac{(x - \mu)}{\sigma}$	
	Bi-modal / Multi-modal Distributions		
		Indicate non-homogeneous samples	
		Segment data into homogeneous sub-samples	

Two Numeric Variables — (e.g. Advertising and Sales Volume)

Purpose	To **examine** the relationship between pairs of data values	
Visual Display	Scatter plot	
Descripitve Measure	Correlation Coefficient (Linearity)	r or ρ
	Coefficient of Determination	R^2

Single Numeric Variable and one/more Categorical Variables

(e.g. Equity returns by Sector (Mining, Services, Retail) and Market Capitalisation (small cap, med cap, large cap)

Purpose	To **examine** categoric variable influences on a numeric variable
Summary Table	Segmentation Table splits the numerical sample into sub-samples (one-way/two-way pivot tables)
Visual Display	Single or Multiple Bar chart showing mean levels of a numeric variable per sub-sample (categories)

APPENDIX 3: SUMMARY FLOWCHART OF HYPOTHESES TESTS

HYPOTHESES TESTS – NULL and ALTERNATIVE HYPOTHESES and REGIONS OF REJECTION

TEST DIRECTION

LEFT TAILED

	Means		Proportions	
	One Population	Two Populations	One Population	Two Populations
Hypotheses	$H_0: \mu \geq k$ $H_1: \mu < k$	$H_0: \mu_1 - \mu_2 \geq 0$ $H_1: \mu_1 - \mu_2 < 0$	$H_0: \pi \geq k$ $H_1: \pi < k$	$H_0: \pi_1 - \pi_2 \geq 0$ $H_1: \pi_1 - \pi_2 < 0$
Rejection Region	$< -z\text{-crit}$ or $< -t\text{-crit}$	$< -z\text{-crit}$ or $< -t\text{-crit}$	$< -z\text{-crit}$	$< -z\text{-crit}$

TWO TAILED

	Means		Means	Proportions		Proportions
	One Population	Two Populations	Two / more Populations	One Population	Two Populations	Multiple Populations
Hypotheses	$H_0: \mu = k$ $H_1: \mu \neq k$	$H_0: \mu_1 - \mu_2 = 0$ $H_1: \mu_1 - \mu_2 \neq 0$	$H_0: \mu_1 = \mu_2 = \mu_3 = ...= \mu_k$ $H_1:$ At least one μ_i differs	$H_0: \pi = k$ $H_1: \pi \neq k$	$H_0: \pi_1 - \pi_2 = 0$ $H_1: \pi_1 - \pi_2 \neq 0$	$H_0: \pi_1 = \pi_2 = \pi_3 = ... = \pi_k$ $H_1:$ At least one π_i differs
Rejection Region	$< -z\text{-crit}$ or $> +z\text{-crit}$ or $< -t\text{-crit}$ or $> +t\text{-crit}$	$< -z\text{-crit}$ or $> +z\text{-crit}$ or $< -t\text{-crit}$ or $> +t\text{-crit}$	$F\text{-stat} > F\text{-crit}$	$< -z\text{-crit}$ or $> +z\text{-crit}$	$< -z\text{-crit}$ or $> +z\text{-crit}$	see 'Test for independence of association'

Analysis of Variance   Test for Independence of Association

RIGHT TAILED

	Means		Proportions		Test for Independence of Association
	One Population	Two Populations	One Population	Two Populations	
Hypotheses	$H_0: \mu \leq k$ $H_1: \mu > k$	$H_0: \mu_1 - \mu_2 \leq 0$ $H_1: \mu_1 - \mu_2 > 0$	$H_0: \pi \leq k$ $H_1: \pi > k$	$H_0: \pi_1 - \pi_2 \leq 0$ $H_1: \pi_1 - \pi_2 > 0$	$H_0:$ No association (independence) $H_1:$ An association exists (dependency)
Rejection Region	$> +z\text{-crit}$ or $> +t\text{-crit}$	$> +z\text{-crit}$ or $> +t\text{-crit}$	$> +z\text{-crit}$	$> +z\text{-crit}$	$\chi^2\text{-stat} > \chi^2\text{-crit}$

CHART 3 (a) Hypothesis Testing for Means

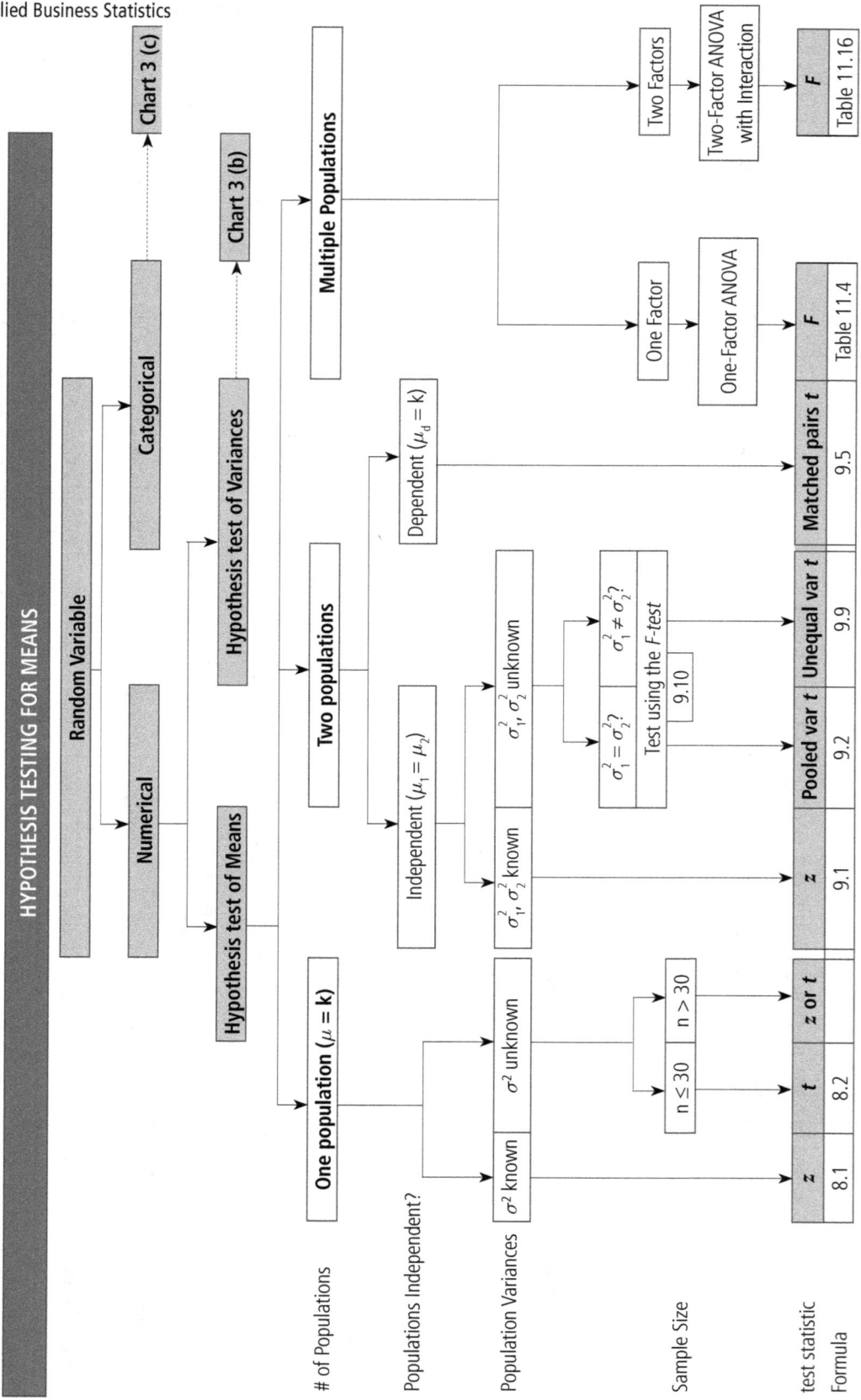

HYPOTHESIS TESTING FOR MEANS

Random Variable

- **Numerical**
  - **Hypothesis test of Means** → Chart 3 (b)
  - **Hypothesis test of Variances** → Chart 3 (b)
- **Categorical** → Chart 3 (c)

# of Populations

- **One population ($\mu = k$)**
- **Two populations**
- **Multiple Populations**

Populations Independent?

- One population:
  - σ^2 known
  - σ^2 unknown
    - $n \leq 30$
    - $n > 30$
- Two populations:
  - Independent ($\mu_1 = \mu_2$)
    - σ_1^2, σ_2^2 known
    - σ_1^2, σ_2^2 unknown
      - $\sigma_1^2 = \sigma_2^2$? Test using the F-test (9.10)
      - $\sigma_1^2 \neq \sigma_2^2$? Test using the F-test (9.10)
  - Dependent ($\mu_d = k$)

Multiple Populations:
  - One Factor → One-Factor ANOVA
  - Two Factors → Two-Factor ANOVA with Interaction

test statistic / Formula

Branch	test statistic	Formula
One population, σ^2 known	z	8.1
One population, σ^2 unknown, $n \leq 30$	t	8.2
One population, σ^2 unknown, $n > 30$	z or t	
Two populations, independent, σ_1^2, σ_2^2 known	z	9.1
$\sigma_1^2 = \sigma_2^2$	Pooled var t	9.2
$\sigma_1^2 \neq \sigma_2^2$	Unequal var t	9.9
Dependent	Matched pairs t	9.5
One-Factor ANOVA	F	Table 11.4
Two-Factor ANOVA with Interaction	F	Table 11.16

CHART 3 (b) Hypothesis Testing for Variances

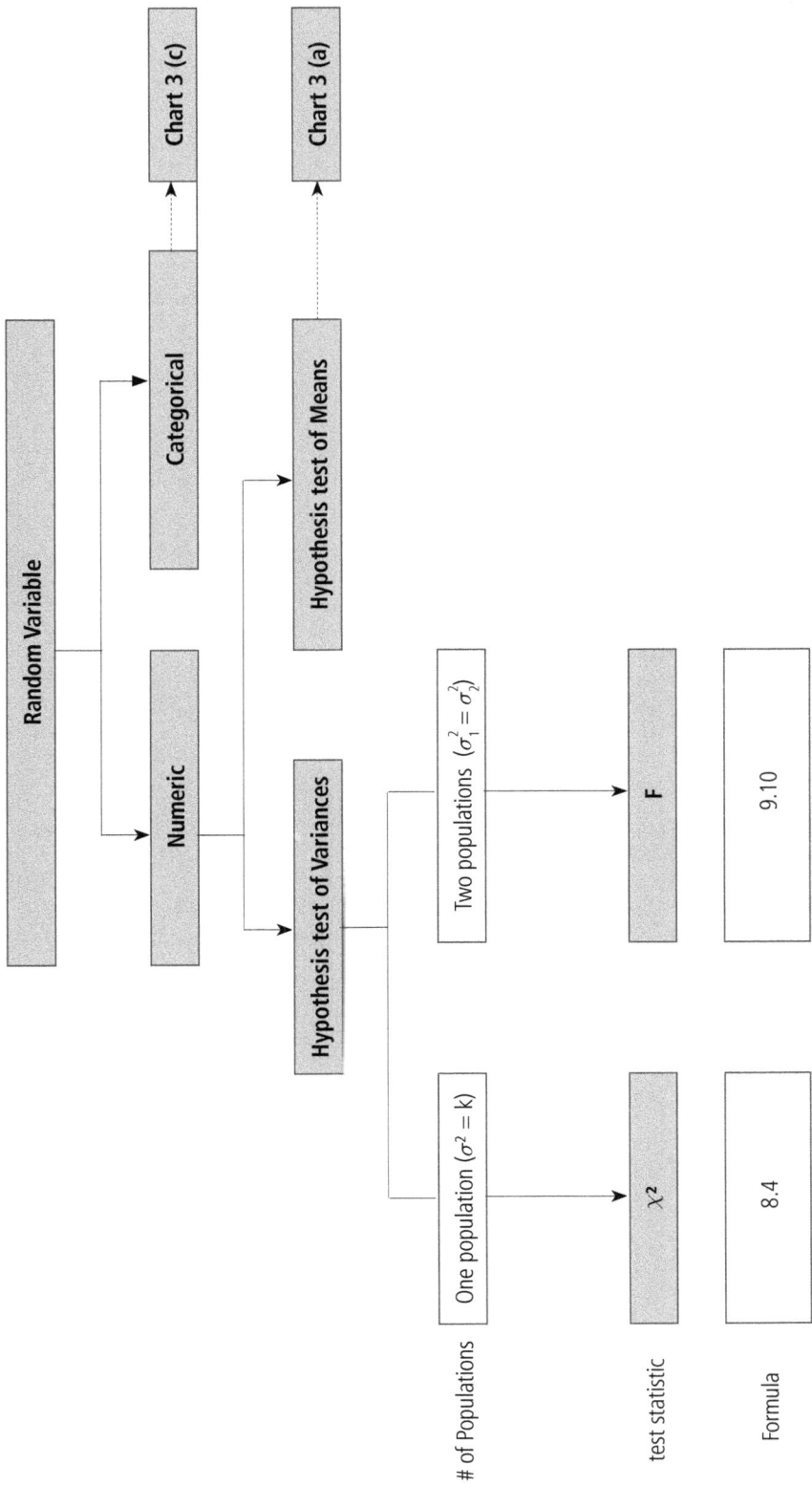

HYPOTHESIS TESTING FOR VARIANCES

Random Variable

Categorical → Chart 3 (c)

Numeric

Hypothesis test of Means ⤏ Chart 3 (a)

Hypothesis test of Variances

One population ($\sigma^2 = k$)

Two populations ($\sigma_1^2 = \sigma_2^2$)

# of Populations

test statistic

χ^2

F

Formula

8.4

9.10

CHART 3 (c) Hypothesis Testing for Proportions

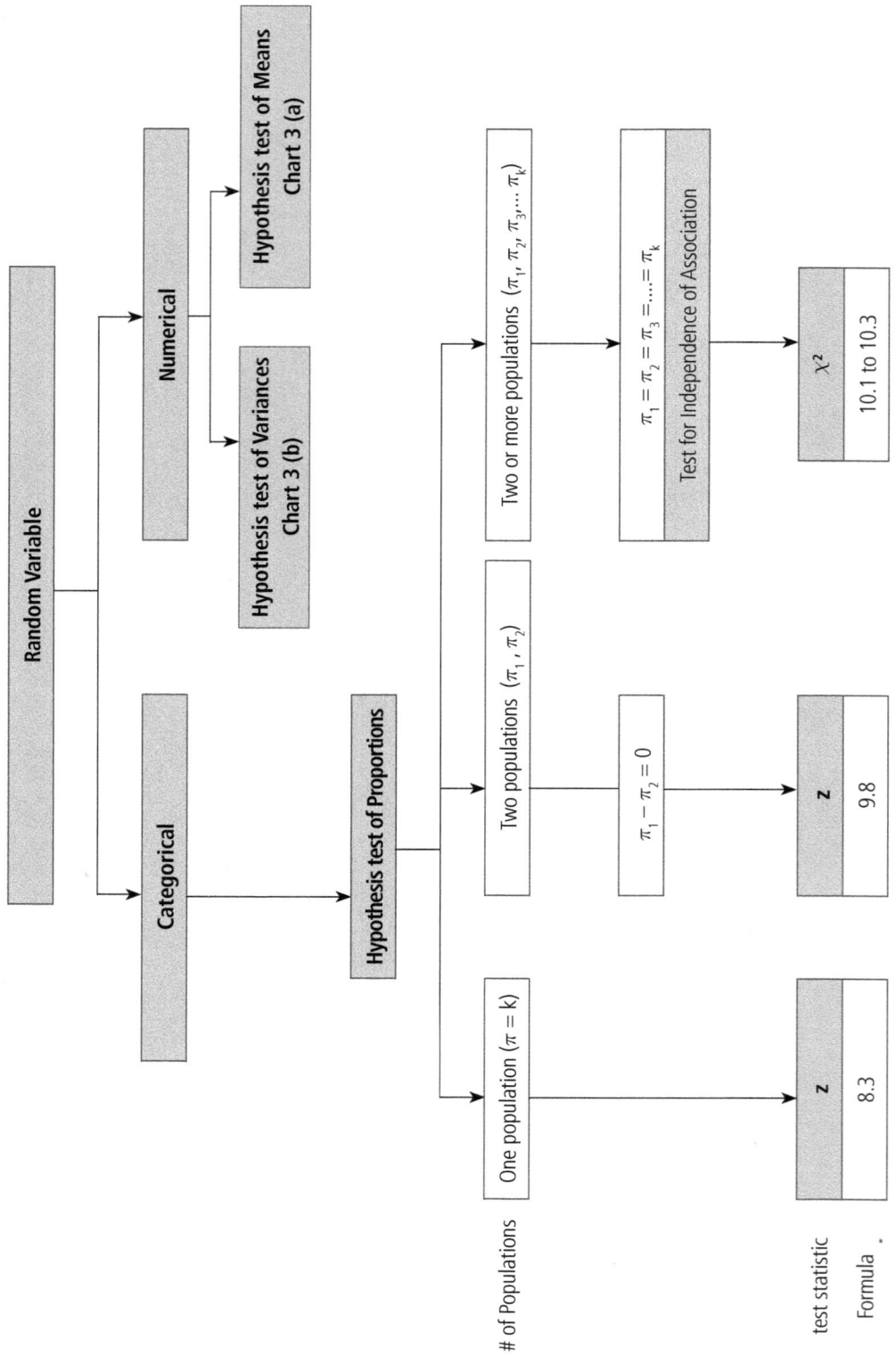

HYPOTHESIS TESTING FOR PROPORTIONS

Random Variable

Categorical — **Numerical**

Numerical:
- Hypothesis test of Variances Chart 3 (b)
- Hypothesis test of Means Chart 3 (a)

Categorical:
- **Hypothesis test of Proportions**

# of Populations:
- One population ($\pi = k$)
- Two populations (π_1, π_2) $\pi_1 - \pi_2 = 0$
- Two or more populations (π_1, π_2, π_3,... π_k) $\pi_1 = \pi_2 = \pi_3 = ... = \pi_k$ Test for Independence of Association

test statistic:
- **z** (One population)
- **z** (Two populations)
- χ^2 (Two or more populations)

Formula:
- 8.3 (One population)
- 9.8 (Two populations)
- 10.1 to 10.3 (Two or more populations)

APPENDIX 4: LIST OF KEY FORMULAE

MEASURES OF CENTRAL LOCATION

Arithmetic mean *Ungrouped data*

$$\bar{x} = \frac{\sum_{i=1}^{n} x_i}{n}$$ 3.1

Grouped data

$$\bar{x} = \frac{\sum_{i=1}^{m} f_i x_i}{n}$$

Mode *Grouped data*

$$M_o = O_{mo} + \frac{c(f_m - f_{m-1})}{2f_m - f_{m-1} - f_{m+1}}$$ 3.3

Median *Grouped data*

$$M_e = O_{me} + \frac{c\left[\frac{n}{2} - f(<)\right]}{f_{me}}$$ 3.2

Lower quartile *Grouped data*

$$Q_1 = O_{Q1} + \frac{c\left(\frac{n}{4} - f(<)\right)}{f_{Q1}}$$ 3.7

Upper quartile *Grouped data*

$$Q_3 = O_{Q3} + \frac{c\left(\frac{3n}{4} - f(<)\right)}{f_{Q3}}$$ 3.8

Geometric mean *Ungrouped data*

$$GM = \sqrt[n]{x_1 \cdot x_2 \cdot x_3 \ldots x_n}$$ 3.4

Weighted arithmetic mean *Grouped data*

$$\text{weighted } \bar{x} = \frac{\sum f_i x_i}{\sum f_i}$$ 3.5

MEASURES OF DISPERSION AND SKEWNESS

Range Range = Maximum value – Minimum value

$$= x_{max} - x_{min} \qquad\qquad 3.9$$

Variance *Mathematical – ungrouped data*

$$s^2 = \frac{\Sigma(x_i - \bar{x})^2}{(n-1)} \qquad\qquad 3.10$$

Computational – ungrouped data

$$s^2 = \frac{\Sigma x_i^2 - n\bar{x}^2}{(n-1)} \qquad\qquad 3.11$$

Standard deviation $$s = \sqrt{\frac{\Sigma(x_i - \bar{x})^2}{n-1}} \qquad\qquad 3.12$$

Coefficient of variation $$CV = \frac{s}{\bar{x}} \times 100\% \qquad\qquad 3.13$$

Pearson's coefficient of skewness $$Sk_p = \frac{n\Sigma(x_i - \bar{x})^3}{(n-1)(n-2)s^3} \qquad\qquad 3.14$$

$$Sk_p = \frac{3 \,(\text{Mean} - \text{Median})}{\text{Standard deviation}} \qquad (\text{approximation}) \qquad 3.15$$

PROBABILITY CONCEPTS

Probability $$P(A) = \frac{r}{n} \qquad\qquad 4.1$$

Conditional probability $$P(A\,|\,B) = \frac{P(A \cap B)}{P(B)} \qquad\qquad 4.2$$

Addition rule *Non-mutually exclusive events*
$$P(A \cup B) = P(A) + P(B) - P(A \cap B) \qquad\qquad 4.3$$

Mutually exclusive events
$$P(A \cup B) = P(A) + P(B) \qquad\qquad 4.4$$

Multiplication rule *Statistically dependent events*
$$P(A \cap B) = P(A \mid B) \times P(B) \qquad \text{4.5}$$

Statistically independent events
$$P(A \cap B) = P(A) \times P(B) \qquad \text{4.6}$$

Independence test $P(A \mid B) = P(A)$ 　　　　　　　　4.7

Bayes' Theorem $P(A \mid B) = \dfrac{P(A \text{ and } B)}{P(B)}$ 　　　　4.8

$n! = n$ factorial $n \times (n-1) \times (n-2) \times (n-3) \times \ldots \times 3 \times 2 \times 1$ 　　4.9

Permutations $_nP_r = \dfrac{n!}{(n-r)!}$ 　　　　　　　4.11

Combinations $_nC_r = \dfrac{n!}{r!\,(n-r)!}$ 　　　　　　4.12

PROBABILITY DISTRIBUTIONS

Binomial distribution $P(x) = {_nC_x}\, p^x (1-p)^{(n-x)}$ 　　　for $x = 0, 1, 2, 3, \ldots n$ 　5.1

Binomial descriptive measures
Mean 　　　　　　　$\mu = np$
Standard deviation 　$\sigma = \sqrt{np(1-p)}$ 　　　5.2

Poisson distribution $P(x) = \dfrac{e^{-\lambda}\lambda^x}{x!}$ 　　for $x = 0, 1, 2, 3 \ldots$ 　5.3

Poisson descriptive measures
Mean 　　　　　　　$\mu = \lambda$
Standard deviation 　$\sigma = \sqrt{\lambda}$ 　　　5.4

Standard normal probability $z = \dfrac{x - \mu}{\sigma}$ 　　　　　　5.6

CONFIDENCE INTERVALS

Single mean *n large; variance known*
$$\bar{x} - z\frac{\sigma}{\sqrt{n}} \le \mu \le \bar{x} + z\frac{\sigma}{\sqrt{n}} \qquad \text{7.2}$$
(lower limit) 　　　(upper limit)

n small; variance unknown

$$\bar{x} - t_{(n-1)}\frac{s}{\sqrt{n}} \le \mu \le \bar{x} + t_{(n-1)}\frac{s}{\sqrt{n}} \qquad \text{7.3}$$

(lower limit)   (upper limit)

Single proportion $p - z\sqrt{\frac{p(1-p)}{n}} \le \pi \le p + z\sqrt{\frac{p(1-p)}{n}} \qquad \text{7.5}$

(lower limit)   (upper limit)

Sample Size $n = \frac{z^2\sigma^2}{e^2} \qquad \text{7.6}$
– *mean*

Sample Size $n = z^2\frac{p(1-p)}{e^2} \qquad \text{7.7}$
– *proportions*

HYPOTHESES TESTS

Single mean   *Variance known*

$$z\text{-stat} = \frac{\bar{x} - \mu}{\frac{\sigma}{\sqrt{n}}} \qquad \text{8.1}$$

Variance unknown; n small

$$t\text{-stat} = \frac{\bar{x} - \mu}{\frac{s}{\sqrt{n}}} \qquad \text{8.2}$$

Single proportion $z\text{-stat} = \frac{p - \pi}{\sqrt{\frac{\pi(1-\pi)}{n}}} \qquad \text{8.3}$

Single variance $\chi^2 = \frac{(n-1)s^2}{\sigma_0^2} \qquad \text{8.4}$

Difference between two means   *Variances known*

$$z\text{-stat} = \frac{(\bar{x}_1 - \bar{x}_2) - (\mu_1 - \mu_2)}{\sqrt{\frac{\sigma_1^2}{n_1} + \frac{\sigma_2^2}{n_2}}} \qquad \text{9.1}$$

Pooled-variances t-test

$$t\text{-stat} = \frac{(\bar{x}_1 - \bar{x}_2) - (\mu_1 - \mu_2)}{\sqrt{s_p^2\left(\frac{1}{n_1} + \frac{1}{n_2}\right)}}$$

where $s_p^2 = \frac{(n_1-1)s_1^2 + (n_2-1)s_2^2}{n_1 + n_2 - 2}$ 9.2

Unequal-variances t-test

$$t\text{-stat} = \frac{(\bar{x}_1 - \bar{x}_2) - (\mu_1 - \mu_2)}{\sqrt{\frac{s_1^2}{n_1} + \frac{s_2^2}{n_2}}}$$

with $df = \dfrac{\left(\dfrac{s_1^2}{n_1} + \dfrac{s_2^2}{n_2}\right)^2}{\dfrac{\left(\dfrac{s_1^2}{n_1}\right)^2}{(n_1 - 1)} + \dfrac{\left(\dfrac{s_2^2}{n_2}\right)^2}{(n_2 - 1)}}$ **9.9**

Paired *t*-test $t\text{-stat} = \dfrac{\bar{x}_d - \mu_d}{\frac{s_d}{\sqrt{n}}}$ **9.5**

where $\mu_d = (\mu_1 - \mu_2)$

and $s_d = \sqrt{\dfrac{\Sigma(x_d - \bar{x}_d)^2}{n - 1}}$

Differences between two proportions $z\text{-stat} = \dfrac{(p_1 - p_2) - (\pi_1 - \pi_2)}{\sqrt{\hat{\pi}(1 - \hat{\pi})\left(\frac{1}{n_1} + \frac{1}{n_2}\right)}}$

where $\hat{\pi} = \dfrac{x_1 + x_2}{n_1 + n_2}$ $p_1 = \dfrac{x_1}{n_1}$ $p_2 = \dfrac{x_2}{n_2}$ **9.8**

Equality of variances $F\text{-stat} = \dfrac{\text{sample variance}_1}{\text{sample variance}_2} = \dfrac{s_1^2}{s_2^2}$ **9.10**

Chi-Square $\chi^2\text{-stat} = \Sigma\dfrac{(f_o - f_e)^2}{f_e}$ with $df = (r - 1)(c - 1)$ **10.1**

ANALYSIS OF VARIANCE – ONE FACTOR

Overall mean $\bar{\bar{x}} = \dfrac{\Sigma\Sigma x_{ij}}{n}$ **11.2**

SSTotal $= \sum_i \sum_j (x_{ij} - \bar{\bar{x}})^2$ **11.3**

SST $= \sum_j^k n_j(\bar{x}_j - \bar{\bar{x}})^2$ **11.4**

SSE $= \sum_j \sum_i (x_{ij} - \bar{x}_j)^2$ **11.5**

$$\text{Tukey's } \textbf{\textit{t-stat}} \quad = \frac{(\bar{x}_i - \bar{x}_j)}{\sqrt{\text{MSE}(\frac{1}{n_i} + \frac{1}{n_j})}} \qquad \text{11.11}$$

$$\text{Tukey's } \textbf{\textit{t-crit}} \quad = \frac{q(\alpha, k, (n-k))}{\sqrt{2}} \qquad \text{11.12}$$

ANALYSIS OF VARIANCE – TWO FACTOR

$$\textbf{SSTotal} \quad = \sum_{a}\sum_{b}\sum_{k} (x_{ijk} - \bar{\bar{x}})^2 \qquad \text{11.13}$$

$$\textbf{SSA} \quad = bk \sum_{j}^{a} (\bar{x}_j[A] - \bar{\bar{x}})^2 \qquad \text{11.14}$$

$$\textbf{SSB} \quad = ak \sum_{i}^{b} (\bar{x}_i[B] - \bar{\bar{x}})^2 \qquad \text{11.15}$$

$$\textbf{SS(AB)} \quad = \text{SSTotal} - \text{SSA} - \text{SSB} - \text{SSE} \qquad \text{11.16}$$

$$\textbf{SSE} \quad = \sum^{a}\sum^{b}\sum^{k} (x_{ijk} - \bar{x}_{ij}[AB])^2 \qquad \text{11.17}$$

REGRESSION AND CORRELATION

$$\textbf{Equation} \quad \hat{y} = b_0 + b_1 x \qquad \text{12.1}$$

$$\textbf{Coefficients} \quad b_1 = \frac{n\sum xy - \sum x\sum y}{n\sum x^2 - (\sum x)^2} \qquad \text{12.2}$$

$$b_0 = \frac{\sum y - b_1 \sum x}{n} \qquad \text{12.3}$$

$$\textbf{Confidence interval estimate for y} \quad \hat{y}_0 \pm t\text{-crit} \times \text{s.e.} \qquad \text{12.4}$$

$$\text{s.e.} = \sqrt{\text{MSE}\left(\frac{1}{n} + \frac{(x_0 - \bar{x})^2}{\sum(x_i - \bar{x})^2}\right)} \qquad \text{12.5}$$

$$\text{MSE} = \frac{\sum e_i^2}{(n - p - 1)} \qquad \text{12.6}$$

Pearson's correlation coefficient	$r = \dfrac{n\Sigma xy - \Sigma x \Sigma y}{\sqrt{[n\Sigma x^2 - (\Sigma x)^2] \times [n\Sigma y^2 - (\Sigma y)^2]}}$	12.7

$$t\text{-stat} = r\sqrt{\dfrac{(n-2)}{1-r^2}} \qquad\qquad 12.11$$

$$\hat{y} = b_0 + b_1 x_1 + b_2 x_2 + b_3 x_3 + \ldots\ldots\ldots + b_p x_p \qquad 13.1$$

$$R^2 = \dfrac{\text{SS(Regression)}}{\text{SS(Total)}} \qquad 13.2$$

$$S_e = \sqrt{\dfrac{\Sigma(y_i - \hat{y}_i)^2}{n-p-1}} \qquad 13.3$$

$$F\text{-stat} = \dfrac{\text{Variation Explained by Regression}}{\text{Unexplained Variation}} = \dfrac{\text{MS Regression}}{\text{MS Error}} \qquad 13.4$$

$$t\text{-stat} = \dfrac{(b_i - \beta_{i'})}{S_{b_i}} \qquad 13.5$$

$$b_i - (t\text{-crit}) \times std\ error\ (b_i)) \le \beta_i \le b_i + (t\text{-crit}) \times std\ error\ (b_i)) \qquad 13.6$$

$$\hat{y} \pm t\left(\tfrac{\alpha}{2}, n-p-1\right)\left(\dfrac{\text{standard error}}{\sqrt{n}}\right) \qquad 13.7$$

INDEX NUMBERS

Price relative	Price relative $= \dfrac{p_1}{p_0} \times 100\%$	14.2

Laspeyres price index	*Weighted aggregates method* Laspeyres price index $= \dfrac{\Sigma(p_1 \times q_0)}{\Sigma(p_0 \times q_0)} \times 100\%$	14.5

Laspeyres price index	*Weighted average of relatives method* Laspeyres price index $= \dfrac{\Sigma\left[\left(\frac{p_1}{p_0}\right) \times 100 \times (p_0 \times q_0)\right]}{\Sigma(p_0 \times q_0)}$	14.9

Paasche price index	*Weighted aggregates method*	
	$= \dfrac{\Sigma(p_1 \times q_1)}{\Sigma(p_0 \times q_1)} \times 100\%$	**14.8**
Paasche price index	*Weighted average of relatives method*	
	$= \dfrac{\Sigma\left[\left(\frac{p_1}{p_0}\right) \times 100 \times (p_0 \times q_1)\right]}{\Sigma(p_0 \times q_1)}$	**14.10**
Quantity relative	Quantity relative $= \dfrac{q_1}{q_0} \times 100\%$	**14.11**
Laspeyres quantity index	*Weighted aggregates method*	
	Laspeyres quantity index $= \dfrac{\Sigma(p_0 \times q_1)}{\Sigma(p_0 \times q_0)} \times 100\%$	**14.12**
Laspeyres quantity index	*Weighted average of relatives method*	
	Laspeyres quantity index $= \dfrac{\Sigma\left[\left(\frac{q_1}{q_0}\right) \times 100 \times (p_0 \times q_0)\right]}{\Sigma(p_0 \times q_0)}$	**14.14**
Paasche quantity index	*Weighted aggregates method*	
	$= \dfrac{\Sigma(p_1 \times q_1)}{\Sigma(p_1 \times q_0)} \times 100\%$	**14.13**
Paasche quantity index	*Weighted average of relatives method*	
	$= \dfrac{\Sigma\left[\left(\frac{q_1}{q_0}\right) \times 100 \times (p_1 \times q_0)\right]}{\Sigma(p_1 \times q_0)}$	**14.15**
Link relatives	*Price*	
	$= \dfrac{p_i}{p_{i-1}} \times 100\%$	**14.17**
	Quantity	
	$= \dfrac{q_i}{q_{i-1}} \times 100\%$	**14.18**

Composite

$$= \frac{\text{Basket value}_i}{\text{Basket value}_{i-1}} \times 100\%$$ 14.19

or $\quad = \dfrac{\text{Composite index}_i}{\text{Composite index}_{i-1}} \times 100\%$

TIME SERIES ANALYSIS

Regression trend coefficients $b_1 = \dfrac{n\Sigma xy - \Sigma x \Sigma y}{n\Sigma x^2 - (\Sigma x)^2}$ 12.2

$b_0 = \dfrac{\Sigma y - b_1 \Sigma x}{n}$ where $x = 1, 2, 3, 4 \dots n$ 12.3

De-seasonalised y $= \dfrac{\text{Actual } y}{\text{Seasonal index}} \times 100$ 15.5

APPENDIX 5: LIST OF USEFUL EXCEL (2016) STATISTICAL FUNCTIONS

Descriptive Statistics

AVERAGE	—	average of a set of data values
VAR.S	—	sample variance
STDEV.S	—	sample standard deviation
MIN	—	minimum data value
MEDIAN	—	median (middle value)
MAX	—	maximum data value
GEOMEAN	—	geometric mean
SKEW	—	skewness coefficient
QUARTILE.EXC	—	Quartiles for a set of data values (lower and upper)
CORREL	—	Correlation coefficient between two numeric data sets

Discrete Probability distributions

BINOM.DIST	—	Binomial probabilities (marginal and cumulative)
POISSON.DIST	—	Poisson probabilities (marginal and cumulative)

Inferential Statistics

The following functions compute the **margin of error** for a confidence interval for a mean

CONFIDENCE.NORM — uses the population standard deviation as σ is assumed to be known
CONFIDENCE.T — uses the sample standard deviation since σ is assumed unknown

The following functions compute the **critical values** of a *test statistic* (e.g. *t-crit*, *F-crit*, etc.)

T.INV	—	*-t-crit* (lower-tailed test)
T.INV.2T	—	$\pm$*t-crit* (two-tailed test)
NORM.INV	—	*x-limit* associated with a given cumulative probability
NORM.S.INV	—	*z-limit* associated with a given cumulative probability
F.INV	—	*F-crit* (lower-tailed test)
F.INV.RT	—	*F-crit* (upper-tailed test)
CHISQ.INV	—	X^2-crit (lower-tailed test)
CHISQ.INV.RT	—	X^2-crit (upper-tailed test)

The following functions compute the **probabilities** for a given distribution
They are used to find **p-values** of a hypothesis test.

T.DIST	—	*p*-value for a lower-tailed *t-test*
T.DIST.2T	—	*p*-value for a two-tailed *t-test*
T.DIST.RT	—	*p*-value for an upper-tailed *t-test*
NORM.DIST	—	left area under normal curve up to an *x*-limit
NORM.S.DIST	—	left area under normal curve up to a *z*-limit
F.DIST	—	*p*-value for a lower-tailed *F-test*
F.DIST.RT	—	*p*-value for an upper-tailed *F-test*
CHISQ.DIST	—	*p*-value for a lower-tailed X^2-*test*
CHISQ.DIST.RT	—	*p*-value for an upper-tailed X^2-*test*

www.ingramcontent.com/pod-product-compliance
Lightning Source LLC
Chambersburg PA
CBHW061737210326
41599CB00034B/6713